D1807241

INTRODUCTION TO MARKETING

OTHER BOOKS IN THE GREGG / McGRAW-HILL MARKETING SERIES

INTRODUCTION TO MARKETING

RICHARD L. LYNCH
Professor and Program Leader
Marketing Education
Virginia Polytechnic Institute
and State University, Blacksburg

HERBERT L. ROSS
Professor and Chairman
Department of Marketing
School of Business
Indiana State University, Terre Haute

RALPH D. WRAY
Professor of Marketing &
Distributive Education
College of Business
Illinois State University, Normal

GREGG DIVISION
McGRAW-HILL BOOK COMPANY

New York   Hamburg   Panama
Atlanta   Johannesburg   Paris
Dallas   Lisbon   San Juan
St. Louis   London   São Paulo
San Francisco   Madrid   Singapore
Auckland   Mexico   Sydney
Bogotá   Montreal   Tokyo
Guatemala   New Delhi   Toronto

Sponsoring Editor Mary McGarry
Editing Supervisor Lucy Ferriss
Design Supervisor/Cover Designer Judith Yourman
Production Supervisor S. Steven Canaris

Text Designer Delgado Design
Photo Editor Mary Ann Drury

Library of Congress Cataloging in Publication Data

Lynch, Richard L.
    Introduction to marketing.
    Includes index.
    1. Marketing. I. Wray, Ralph D. II. Ross,
Herbert L., (date). III. Title.
HF5415.L936 1983   658.8   83-16259
ISBN 0-07-039191-2

1 2 3 4 5 6 7 8 9 0   DOCDOC   8 9 1 0 9 8 7 6 5 4

ISBN 0-07-039191-2

PREFACE

*I*ntroduction to Marketing is a dynamic new marketing textbook that has been designed specifically for introductory marketing students at the collegiate level. Throughout, the text presents fundamental marketing concepts with sufficient depth and detail to ensure student comprehension. At the same time, the eighteen chapters are filled with real-world examples and structured experiences that guide students in applying these concepts to the operations of actual small and large businesses, service industries, and nonprofit organizations.

Introduction to Marketing was developed after extensive marketing research had determined both the current and future needs of college marketing students and instructors. This research showed the need for a textbook and supporting materials that bridge the gap between the highly theoretical texts typically used in college and university classes at the junior, senior, or graduate levels and the highly vocationalized texts typically used in short-term vocational educational programs. As a result, *Introduction to Marketing* has been specifically designed for introductory marketing students. Such students are most often enrolled in college-level or adult classes in community and junior colleges, private business schools, vocational and technical centers, or in lower divisions (freshman or sophomore years) of four-year colleges and universities.

ORGANIZATION OF THE TEXT

Introduction to Marketing features eight units, each highlighting an important aspect of modern marketing. Unit One provides students with an introduction and overview of marketing as it exists in the world *today*. At the end of the text, Unit Eight provides students with information on managing the marketing mix, including considerations of marketing for *tomorrow*. In between, Units Two through Seven provide the theory and application of the marketing mix. Unit Two deals with identifying and segmenting markets as well as with using marketing information systems and research; Unit Three is concerned with **P**roduct/Service marketing; Unit Four with **P**lace marketing; and Unit Five with **P**rice marketing; and Unit Six with **P**romotion marketing. Because of the important role played by **P**eople in marketing occupations, Unit Seven deals with employing, developing, and supervising marketing employees.

REALISTIC CONTEXT

Throughout *Introduction to Marketing,* numerous real-life examples are provided to illustrate theories and concepts being presented. These examples show how marketing is being used in profit-oriented businesses; by politicians, athletes, and other celebrities; by nonprofit organizations and social service agencies; by entrepreneurs; by businesses involved with international marketing; and by the many firms whose marketable product is, in fact, a service. Special attention has been given to showing how marketing is used and can be used by small, service-oriented businesses and by nonprofit organizations. Tables, charts, graphs, photos, cartoons, and business forms are used to illustrate and reinforce the concepts presented.

Congruent with current learning research, *Introduction to Marketing* provides ample opportunity for students to reinforce what they are studying, to apply it in real-life or hypothetical situations, and to synthesize and evaluate concepts in a real-world context. End-of-chapter and end-of-unit materials enable students to develop their abilities to make decisions, solve problems, and reach defensible judgments.

Each chapter concludes with a key points summary, a listing of terms and concepts to study, and discussion questions. At the end of each unit, applications and cases from small and large businesses, service organizations, nonprofit associations, and entrepreneurs are provided for student analysis.

SUPPORTING MATERIALS

Three supporting products have been developed for use by students and instructors:

- *Casebook for Introduction to Marketing,* by Robert J. Welsh, Richard L. Lynch, Herbert L. Ross, and Ralph D. Wray
- Marketing Peanut Butter—A Microcomputer Simulation, by Chad T. Lewis, Phil C. Lewis, and Conrad Boyle
- *Instructor's Manual and Key for Introduction to Marketing,* prepared by the seven authors involved with the complete *Introduction to Marketing* program.

The Casebook

The *Casebook for Introduction to Marketing* includes 16 cases (two per unit), ten readings taken from business journals and newspapers, and eight projects selected to further develop students' skills in applying important marketing principles and concepts in real-life situations. Over 300 review questions have also been provided to help students master important marketing principles and to help them prepare for examinations.

Microcomputer Simulation

In *Marketing Peanut Butter—A Microcomputer Simulation,* students—as marketing employees—must arrive at team decisions pertaining to each of the 4 **P**'s of marketing: product/service, price, place, and promotion. They must also make deci-

sions about personnel, e.g., the type and number of sales people to employ, their territories, etc. The simulation reinforces the idea that the marketing mix is just that—a "mix"—and that success in the marketplace requires strategic integration of the elements of the mix.

Instructor's Manual

The complete *Introduction to Marketing* program also includes comprehensive materials available for use by the marketing instructor. The *Instructor's Manual and Key* includes eight major features:

- An introduction highlighting the rationale, features, and major benefits of the program
- Suggestions for using the materials, including how to use the case method, how to use the materials in adult education classes, and a sequence of instruction appropriate for various quarter and semester options
- A bibliography/reference section useful for instructors who wish to order library or classroom supplemental materials
- Chapter-by-chapter and unit-by-unit teaching aids including unit overviews, chapter objectives, chapter teaching suggestions, key to end-of-chapter terms and discussion questions, and key to end-of-unit applications/cases
- Key to *Casebook for Introduction to Marketing*
- Transparency masters
- A test bank of objective examination questions
- Instructor's manual for *Marketing Peanut Butter—A Microcomputer Simulation*

AUTHORS' STATEMENT

Comments, suggestions, and possible additional cases and illustrative examples are most welcome from users of *Introduction to Marketing.* It is our desire to provide quality materials specifically designed for college marketing students and instructors and to improve the techniques of marketing among those involved. Your suggestions will be sincerely appreciated.

ACKNOWLEDGMENTS

Special recognition is given to two people who were important to the conceptualization of this text and its supporting materials: Dr. Melvin J. Unger and Dr. Gail Trapnell. Dr. Unger's dissertation from New York University, "The Development of an Instructional Model for a Basic Marketing Course, Using Jerome S. Bruner's Theory of Instruction as the Framework," was used as the primary basis for structuring the text outline. Dr. Trapnell assisted in further developing the outline and supporting materials.

We also wish to thank the many reviewers of *Introduction to Marketing* for their generous advice and counsel:

- Rick Giudicessi, Instructor, Industrial Management and Marketing, Des Moines Area Community College, Des Moines, Iowa
- Douglas Kornemann, Instructor, Marketing, Milwaukee Area Technical College, Milwaukee, Wisconsin
- Carl LaCava, Professor, Marketing/Management, Business Administration Department, Dyke College, Cleveland, Ohio
- Chad Lewis, Instructor, Business and Marketing, Everett Community College, Everett, Washington
- Kathy Mon, Instructor, Merchandising and General Business, Brooks College, Long Beach, California
- Patricia Mink Rath, Instructor, International Academy of Merchandising & Design, Ltd., Chicago, Illinois
- Elizabeth Strenkowski, Director, Retail Division, Bradford School, Pittsburgh, Pennsylvania
- Melvin J. Unger, Marketing, Baruch College, New York, New York
- Robert J. Welsh, Instructor, Business and Marketing, Greenfield Community College, Greenfield, Massachusetts

Finally, appreciation is extended to Ginny Lynch, Norma Ross, and Martha Wray. Their support and assistance greatly facilitated the writing of this text.

Richard Lynch
Herbert L. Ross
Ralph D. Wray

PICTURE CREDITS

Our thanks to the following for the photographs and illustrations that appear in this book:

American Demographics, Inc.: 68. Avon Products, Inc.: 130. The Bettmann Archive, Inc.: 217, 412. Black Enterprise Magazine: 72. Brooks Brothers: 195. Carol Wright Hispanic/Hanson, Nigro & Wulfhorst, Inc.: 82. Carson, Pirie, Scott & Co., Chicago: 427. Case Communications, Inc.: 100, 103. Champion International Corp.: 182. Chase Manhattan Bank: 352, 435. Clothes Quarters: 317, 319. Da-Lite Screen Co., Inc.: 487. The Daily Pantagraph: 396. The Dartnell Corp.: 477. Donnelley Marketing: 435. Eastman Kodak Co.: 435. Elrick & Lavidge, Inc.: 110. Federal Express Corp.: 141. Ford Motor Company: 197. Frank B. Hall & Co.: 237. General Foods Corp. Beverage Div., Sugar-Free Kool-Aid ® brand soft drink mix: 58. Jane Hamilton-Merritt: 9, 24, 222, 347, 358, 374, 463, 467. Haworth, Inc.: 84. Herman's (Div. of W. R. Grace & Co.): 312. Hickey-Freeman Co., Inc.: 527. Holiday Inn: 429. Hub City Terminals Inc.: 261. IBC, Inc.: 259. Iroquois Grocery Products: 302. Kay Reese & Assoc., Todd Weinstein: 3, 39, 198, 207. King Features Syndicate, Mort Walker: 446. Kimberly-Clark Corp.: 518. Kroger Co.: 320. Lillian Vernon Corp.: 404. McNaught Syndicate, Inc.: 35. Macy's Herald Square: 432. Major Market Radio: 405. Manning, Gerald, and Barry L. Reece, *Selling Today: A Personal Approach,* © 1980 W. C. Brown Publishers, Dubuque, Iowa: 38. National Marine Mfrs. Assn.: 420. The NDP Group/Kolker, Talley, Hermann, Inc.: 114. The New Yorker Magazine Inc., © 1983 Leo Cullum: 12; © 1982 Charles Addams: 91, 472; © 1982 Donald Reilly: 239. Neiman-Marcus: 63. Nussbaum Trucking Inc.: 258. J. C. Penney Co. Inc.: 285. Perrier: 28. Photo Researchers, Inc., Peter Aitken: 172; Robert Isaacs: 3; Tom McHugh: 33; Catherine Ursullo: 3. Port Authority of NY and NJ: 251. Republic Airlines: 281. Restaurant Assn.: 150. Riteway Laundry/Staley Stuart: 145. Safeway Stores, Inc.: 525. *Sales & Marketing Management,* Oct. 26, 1981, p. 40: 70. San Diego Zoo: 407. Singer Co.: 78. "Small Business in America," © 1981 National Federation of Independent Business Research and Education Foundation: 46. Spiegel Catalog: 175. State of New York/Dept. of Commerce: 431. Steinway & Sons: 390–391. Mark Stracke: 15, 203, 219, 309, 342, 360, 365, 376, 419. Sunshine Line: 149. Taurus Photos, Eric Kroll: 3; Joan Menshenfreund: 43. Texaco: 351. Time Inc., Enrico Ferorelli, LIFE Magazine: 156. The Times Mail, Bedford, Ind.: 385. Toys "R" Us: 228. Valley National Bank of Arizona: 118. Visual Merchandising & Store Design Magazine: 428. Waldenbooks: 219. The Wall Street Journal/Cartoon Features Syndicate: 315. Welch Foods: 197. Zenith Radio Corp.: 197.

TABLE OF CONTENTS

ix

INTRODUCTION TO MARKETING

UNIT 1

INTRODUCTION

CHAPTER 1

AN OVERVIEW OF MARKETING

Sarah Carter delivers papers for the Waterloo *Courier,* a newspaper with a wide circulation in northeastern Iowa. One day, Sarah decided to see whether she could increase the number of subscriptions on her route. She wrote and duplicated 110 copies of a one-page flier, attached a stamped, return-addressed envelope, and placed them under the doors of all the residents of a 110-unit apartment complex in her hometown. In the flier, she encouraged nonsubscribers to simply check an appropriate box indicating that they would like to receive the *Courier* and then place the flier in the stamped, return-addressed envelope and put it in the mailbox. Sarah received 78 returns, thereby increasing her weekly sales by over $150.

* * * * * * * * * * * * * * * * * * * *

John Gomez is the manager of the jewelry department at Woolworth's in Grosse Pointe, Michigan. Just before Father's Day, he doubled his inventory of Timex watches, placed two half-page ads for the watches in the local newspaper, hired a student to help him sell merchandise during evening hours, and set up three top-of-the-counter displays of Timex watches. All but six of the watches were sold, nearly doubling the previous year's sales for the jewelry department for the month of June.

* * * * * * * * * * * * * * * * * * * *

As part of her job, Mary Ellen Borski recently analyzed data from 1,578 returns of a carefully designed study of business people who fly on commercial jetliners at least 4 days each month. On the basis of this study, Mary Ellen recommended that plane manufacturers design and produce a jet which would permit customers to bring more luggage on the plane with them and allow for more space in the seats. She also recommended that, if possible, planes be designed with quieter engines.

* * * * * * * * * * * * * * * * * * * *

The common thread in the work performed by Sarah, John, and Mary Ellen is that they are all engaged in marketing. In fact, an analysis of labor market statistics shows that over one-third of the American labor force is employed in some aspect of marketing. Marketing is one of the most popular elective courses, and students who major in marketing often constitute the largest enrollment area in community colleges and private business schools.

WHY STUDY MARKETING?

Marketing is an important part of the American economic system. In fact, any country in which the people enjoy a reasonably comfortable standard of living relies heavily on marketing to bring products and services to the population. But especially in the United States, marketing has beer given much credit for bringing a comparatively high standard of living to a large number of people in a relatively short period of time.

Importance to the Economy

The old adage that nothing happens until someone sells something may be an exaggeration, but marketing is extremely important to the economic

Figure 1-1. Marketers at work—a vital part of the American economic system—help bring an increased standard of living for members of our society.

TABLE 1-1
SOME IMPORTANT REASONS FOR STUDYING MARKETING

Marketing

- Stimulates economic growth.
- Informs customers about products and services.
- Provides useful skills.
- Provides job opportunities.

growth and well-being of society. In the U.S. economic system, most businesses are formed with a primary goal of making a profit. After all the expenses of operating a business are paid—such as raw materials, cost of merchandise that is resold, labor, rent, utilities, equipment, supplies, taxes, and so on—the remaining amount, known as **profit,** is the owner's to do with as he or she pleases. The opposite is loss. A **loss** is incurred when the expenses of the business are greater than the sales. In order to make a profit, businesses must offer products or services that are needed and wanted by customers or consumers. There must be a demand for the products or services being offered for sale. This is where marketing plays such a vital role.

Marketing identifies the needs and desires of consumers for products and services, provides information for new and improved products and services, informs customers and consumers about the many diverse products and services available, determines appropriate prices, and places the products and services where they are needed and wanted. These marketing activities should result in an increased standard of living for members of society and, if done successfully, result in a profit for the owners of businesses that offer the products and services for sale.

Students of marketing and marketing practitioners are constantly looking for ways to improve their techniques. Is there a better or less costly way

to market this product or that service? Can the bugs be worked out of this product so that it is more satisfactory to our customers? Can shopping be made more convenient for this group of people? Can our services be expanded to reach more people?

To understand the American economy, it is necessary to have an understanding of marketing and its important role in a reasonably free, private enterprise system. Perhaps this is why nearly all schools and colleges, including high schools, community colleges, vocational schools, private business and trade schools, and 4-year colleges and universities, offer courses and programs in marketing.

Importance to Consumers

Marketing has assumed such an important role that it now consumes a large share of the purchasing dollar for all products and services consumed in this country. Economists and business people estimate that the cost of marketing is about 50 percent or more of the consumer's dollar. With the recent growth in service industries (for example, amusement parks, hotels and motels, transportation, and recreation), it is expected that the cost of marketing as a percentage of the consumer dollar will continue to increase. Thus, a large share of the consumer's dollar will continue to pay for marketing activities. It is therefore important that all of us as consumers and business people have an understanding of marketing and its role in our lives.

Marketing does affect our lives greatly. It is all around us. Stores urge us to buy their unique products. Banks offer a myriad of services from which to choose. Airlines offer to fly us higher, faster, and more comfortably. Even churches suggest that we attend more often and that we be sure to hug our kids today. The products, the services, the advertising messages, and even the consumer surveys to which we are asked to respond are a part of marketing. The newspapers and magazines we read, messages in our mailboxes, and TV and radio programs all expose us to marketing, sometimes to as many as 1,800 messages a day. Even our personalities, education, and skills are said to need marketing by way of employment résumés and interviews. Because marketing is such an important aspect of the economy and because it affects people so greatly as consumers, it is important that everyone have a reasonably good understanding of its role in the economy and its benefits.

Skills in Marketing

Perhaps one of the best reasons for studying marketing is the acquisition of skills that are useful in many occupations. Marketing is a rather complex system of business activities, including, for example, market research, product and service planning, purchasing raw materials and products for resale, transporting, storing, sales promotion, personal selling, advertising, display, financing, public relations, and management. But the academic discipline of marketing also draws heavily on communications theory, mathematics, and behavioral sciences such as psychology and sociology. As will be seen throughout this text, marketing draws on many academic fields and integrates numerous skills to bring satisfying products and services to the consumer. Anyone who studies marketing seriously and acquires marketing skills will find employers from many occupational areas in search of that knowledge and those skills.

Because of the rapid development of technology in this country, counselors often recommend that students learn a variety of job skills. Upon graduation from school or completion of a training program, it is often suggested that students be prepared to transfer specific skills into several occupations. The unique technology, processes, and skills that are identified with marketing are now recognized as being important in a wide array of occupations. The basic approaches one learns in marketing automobiles or detergents can also be used to market colleges, celebrities and politicians, family planning, health care, social programs, conservation, and minority rights. Also, the human relations and communications skills associated with analyzing customer needs and wants and then satisfying them with appropriate products and services are recognized as being important in many occupations, *not just* those specifically identified as marketing.

Career Opportunities

Marketing is one of the fastest growing occupational areas in this country. According to data extracted from government publications such as the *Occupational Outlook Handbook,* it is estimated that over one-third of this country's labor force is employed in a marketing occupation or in employment requiring marketing skills.

The opportunities in marketing are virtually unlimited. The newspaper carrier, the grocery store cashier, the travel agent, the bank branch manager, the sales representative, the purchasing agent, the account executive, the hotel clerk, the owner or manager of a small business, the stockbroker, and many of the top executives at Xerox are all marketers.

It is interesting that there are several paths by which one can enter employment in marketing. Many people begin their careers in such marketing positions as cashier, salesperson, inventory clerk, teller, restaurant worker, reservationist, and stock clerk. They may then advance through on-the-job training into supervision and management.

Many top corporate managers began as sales representatives. Many owners of businesses began as stock clerks. Many branch managers of restaurants had their first jobs behind a fast-food counter.

Many people begin employment in marketing after completing postsecondary, college-level education. They may enter the field through such positions as sales representative, assistant buyer, first-line supervisor, department manager, account executive, assistant manager, or any of a number of other titles that are used to identify marketing positions.

Because of its extensiveness and diversity, marketing also offers many possibilities for part-

RISING THROUGH THE RANKS AT K-MART

At K-Mart Corp., the world's second largest retailer, you can still rise from stock clerk to chairman of the board without a college degree. That is how Bernard M. Fauber made it to the top of the discount department store chain.

He began as a stock clerk, fresh out of high school, in a Lynchburg, Virginia, S. S. Kresge Co. variety store (K-Mart's parent). He never attended college, but worked his way up through the ranks of store management and then into the corporate hierarchy. Early in 1980, he was named to K-Mart's premier post of chairperson and chief executive officer.

The path from stockroom to boardroom is a common one at K-Mart. Of the company's top seven officers, only two are college graduates, and all have come up through the stores. Fully 40 percent of all K-Mart managers skipped college and entered the company as store clerks. The company maintains a policy of promoting from within. Hourly store employees who are so inclined have a better shot at assistant store manager and management trainee positions, the primary points of entry into management, than graduates applying from outside K-Mart.

Adapted from Charles W. Stevens, "Stockboy to Chairman," *Wall Street Journal,* December 22, 1980, p. 18. Reprinted by permission. © Dow Jones & Co. Inc. All rights reserved.

time employment for people who choose not to work an 8 to 5 day, for those who like to work at home, and for those who are interested in job sharing. The retailing industry especially offers unlimited opportunities for part-timers. In fact, retailing and many service industries could not function without part-time help. Many marketing industries, such as transportation, hospitality, and retailing, operate continuously and thus provide opportunities for those who prefer to work in the evening or late at night. There are also many marketing positions that enable one to work out of the home. Examples include sales rep, advertising artist, telephone solicitor, real estate agent, travel or tour director, financial planner, and marketing research analyst. An increase in two people's sharing one job has been seen in recent years in marketing occupations. For example, a husband and wife team may share one job as client reps in an advertising agency. Each contributes approximately 20 hours per week to the job.

MARKETING DEFINED

What does the word *marketing* mean? When asked this question, most of the general public will respond that it is advertising or selling or public relations. Few will respond that marketing has anything to do with consumer analysis, marketing research, product development, buying and pricing, distribution, or mutual exchange—but it does. To further cloud the issue, authors of marketing textbooks and managers of marketing departments often define the term differently.

There are different definitions in the literature and some confusion in practice, and perhaps there always will be. Some consider marketing to be a very business-oriented activity and discuss it only in business terms. Thus, the field includes people involved with selling, advertising, and physically distributing products. Others see marketing in a much broader context. To them, nearly everyone is engaged in marketing. The job applicant markets her credentials to a prospective employer, the teacher markets his knowledge to students, and volunteer organizations market their services to prospective clients.

Historical Overview

There is probably no single clear, concise definition of marketing that is accepted universally. Actually, the term is evolutionary in nature; that is, the term *marketing* and the activities associated with it have changed and probably will continue to change over time. Before presenting the definition of marketing to be used in this text, let us take a look at the term as it has evolved historically.

In Table 1-2, five definitions are presented that are used frequently by people involved with

marketing. The earlier definitions tend to describe marketing in strictly economic terms. Thus, according to the first definition in Table 1-2, marketing is considered as one of the three functions of a country's economic system. These functions consist of production (including manufacturing), marketing (also referred to as distribution), and consumption. Marketing is the economic function which delivers the products that are manufactured or produced to society, resulting in an appropriate standard of living. This definition implies that there is a direct and positive correlation between a country's standard of living and its marketing system: the better the system, the better the standard of living. In this definition, the term *distribution* often was used synonymously with marketing.

The American Marketing Association definition (the second definition in Table 1-2) reinforced the economic use of the term but added the concept that marketing consists of business activities. This association defined marketing as the "performance of business activities that direct the flow of goods and services from producer to consumer or user." In further descriptions of business activities, selling, promoting, transporting, buying, pricing, grading, financing, risk taking, and market research often are cited as examples.

TABLE 1-2
DEFINITIONS OF MARKETING

Developed by	Definition
Mazur	The delivery of a standard of living to society (1947)
American Marketing Association	Performance of business activities that direct the flow of goods and services from producer to consumer or user (1960)
Unknown	Getting the right goods to the right people at the right place at the right time and at the right price (Reprinted from Kotler)
Stanton	Total system of interacting business activities designed to plan, price, promote, and distribute want-satisfying goods and services to present and potential customers (1971)
Kotler	Human activity directed at satisfying needs and wants through exchange processes (1980)

Another widely used definition of marketing was associated with merchandising. Thus, retailers often considered it their role to get the right goods and services to the right people at the right place at the right time and at the right price.

Later definitions, such as the fourth one in Table 1-2, added the concept of customer satisfaction. In 1971, Stanton defined marketing as a "total system of interacting business activities designed to plan, price, promote, and distribute want-satisfying goods and services to present and potential customers." Again, the emphasis was on business activities and the distribution of goods and services. However, Stanton added two important concepts: system and want-satisfying goods and services. Marketing was viewed as a system, with interacting and interdependent parts or items functioning as a unified whole. The elements of that system (planning, pricing, promotion, and distribution) are interrelated, interactive, and interdependent. For example, pricing policies cannot be established without also considering promotion. Stanton also added the want-satisfying concept. This was very important because the customer's needs and wants became a fundamental part of marketing. This concept was exemplified in such familiar marketing slogans as "The customer is king," "Give the lady what she wants," and "Your needs are our concern." It also meant that it was the customer (or society) who was to determine the products or services to be produced and marketed, not the producers or manufacturers.

In the 1970s, the concept of exchange was added to the definition of marketing by many authorities. Exchange involves two (or more) parties who voluntarily agree to enter into a trading relationship. The trade may consist of the exchange of a product or service for money, a product for a product, a product for a service, or a service for a service. The essential point is that the exchange is mutually satisfactory and involves something of value being traded. It is interesting to note that such an apparently subtle change in the definition actually broadened the concept of marketing considerably. Previous definitions had focused on the producer or manufacturer doing the marketing. But when the concept of exchange was added, it was recognized that buyers or customers often engage in marketing. They shop around and compare the products and services available, and they may negotiate for a better deal. Thus, an industrial buyer who purchases raw materials for use in manufacturing actively solicits prices, samples, and contract terms from a multitude of producers.

The Term *Marketing* as it Is Used Today

Today, **marketing** is considered to be a coordinated system of business activities designed to provide products and services that satisfy the needs and wants of customers through exchange processes. Let us take a look at each part of this definition as it is depicted in Figure 1-2a. Throughout this text, further development and illustration of each of these aspects will be presented.

Coordinated System or Marketing Mix. As defined earlier, a **system** is described as interacting and interdependent parts or items functioning as a unified whole. So it is with marketing. When one speaks of marketing, one is speaking of a comprehensive and coordinated system. There are many parts within any system, and there are many parts to marketing. We often label and study each part separately.

For example, any company has at least four major aspects of marketing which must be considered: products and services to offer, the prices at which they should be sold, the manner in which they will be delivered to the customer, and the way in which they will be promoted. These four main parts of marketing are often referred to aggregately as the **marketing mix.** They are often called the four **P**'s of marketing: **P**roduct, **P**rice, **P**lace, and **P**romotion.

To illustrate the marketing mix, let us look at a restaurant which might be opened in any small

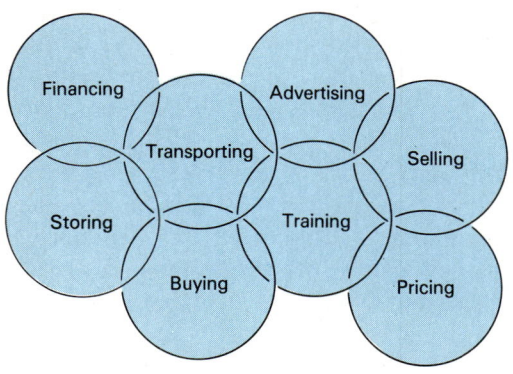

Figure 1-2a. Marketing is a coordinated system of business activities; the four major aspects of this system are known as the marketing mix, which relies primarily on the performance of *people*.

town in midwestern America. As the owner of that restaurant, you must make decisions about at least four things relevant to marketing.

- What product should you offer? Should you specialize in steaks, seafood, or fast food? Should you include a cocktail lounge? Should you have a salad bar?

- What prices should you charge in anticipation of a reasonable profit? Should you include credit card service? Accept personalized checks?

- How should you distribute your food? Take-out? Full or partial service? Over the counter?

- What promotional techniques should you consider? Radio or TV advertising? Newspapers? Billboards?

There is another **P** that must be carefully considered by marketers—**P**eople. All parts of the marketing mix are operated and managed by people. Thus, the people or personnel aspect of a business is also an important consideration of marketers. Referring to our example of the restaurant in the midwest, some questions related to personnel might include these.

- How many employees should you hire? What should their qualifications be?

- What tasks should they perform? What is a fair salary or wage?

It is the four aspects of the marketing mix and the people who perform the jobs associated with each aspect that must be coordinated carefully. You cannot make a decision regarding one aspect or ingredient of the mix without affecting another. You cannot make decisions about the product or service without also considering price or distribution. Even though you may discuss and decide about each aspect separately, all must be coordinated for effective marketing of your restaurant.

Business Activities. Marketing consists of many business activities. In large businesses, specialists are employed who often perform only one activity. In smaller businesses, such as the restaurant described in the previous section, one or two people may perform all the business activities. The owner or manager may have to buy the meat, vegetables, seafood, and other items for cooking and resale. He or she may have to determine the complete inventory, plan the menu, stock the freezers and shelves, write advertisements, wait on tables, collect payments from customers, make home deliveries, and hire and train employees. In large companies, similar business activities are performed by highly trained specialists. An entire department will be devoted to product planning, another department or division will be responsible for advertising, one will deal with inventory control, and still another will be involved with sales.

Products and Services. Stated in its simplest form, a product is something that is viewed as being capable of satisfying a need or want. In business terms, a product is viewed as the complete package or value a company has to offer customers that satisfies their needs. It includes physical products and services and related benefits.

The main or core product that a business has to offer may be a typewriter. This is the tangible item that is being offered to satisfy the customer's needs. But presumably, the customer's needs go beyond physically owning a typewriter. The customer has a need for related services, perhaps in financing the purchase of the typewriter or seeing to needed repairs. Another customer may want consultation regarding the typewriter. This customer may want to enroll in a class sponsored by the company on how to use all the new and innovative features of the typewriter. The point is that the product must be capable of satisfying the need or wants of customers. Those needs and wants include not only the physical item but related services, ideas, and personal assistance.

Sometimes there is confusion over the term *product* and the term *service*. Most companies use the definition of product that was just given. Their

Figure 1-2b. Marketing provides products and services (above) that satisfy needs and wants (top right) through exchange processes (bottom right).

product usually consists of a tangible item with related services such as credit, gift wrapping, delivery, and layaway. It is this combination of tangible product and related services that the company sees as capable of satisfying the needs and wants of its current and prospective customers.

A major and relatively recent development in this country has been the incredible growth of service industries. A service is defined as "any activity or benefit that one party can offer to another that is essentially intangible and does not result in the ownership of anything. Its production may or may not be tied to a physical product."[1] A service industry is therefore one that primarily offers as its product, an activity or benefit that is intangible and does not result in the ownership of anything.

The United States is the world leader in service industries. It is estimated that more than 65 percent of the labor force in this country is engaged in providing services. Services are provided by government workers such as police officers, fire fighters, post office clerks, public schoolteachers, and state office employees. Services are also provided by those in the nonprofit private sector, such as employees in hospitals, museums, charities, churches, private schools, and private colleges. But the largest employment in service occupations is seen in profit-oriented and marketing-oriented businesses: airlines, banks, hotels and motels, consulting firms, restaurants, real estate agencies, insurance companies, beauty salons, amusements, caterers, and so on. And that listing continues to expand and increase.

For a fee, there are now companies that will balance your budget, baby-sit your philodendron, wake you up in the morning, drive you to work, or find you a new home, job, car, wife, clairvoyant, cat feeder, or gypsy violinist. Or perhaps you want to rent a garden tractor? A few cattle? Some original paintings?
. . . If it is business services you need, other companies will plan your conventions and

sales meetings, design your products, handle your data processing, or supply temporary secretaries or even executives.[2]

Marketing has certainly been a key factor in the growth of the highly competitive, profit-oriented service industries in this country. As Americans gain more time for leisure and as products become increasingly complex and in need of servicing, the number of service industries will continue to grow. Marketing continues to discover increasing needs and wants for more services to accompany tangible products and for more services that are in effect products.

Needs and Wants. Marketing strives to satisfy the needs and wants of customers. A **need** is a state of deprivation felt by a person. A **want** is an expression of that need. Everyone has needs and wants. Some will change or intensify throughout various stages of one's life. Others will remain the same.

Often needs are categorized as physiological, such as needs for food, clothing, and shelter. Other needs may be social, such as the need for

"I was at my sister's today. They have two pots."

Figure 1-3. Wants are culturally derived!

affection, for group support, for prestige, or for being "one of the gang." Or needs may be psychological, such as the need for freedom, independence, or self-accomplishment. Whatever the need, if it is not satisfied, we are unhappy. We then want the object (product or service) that will satisfy that need.

Wants are culturally derived and vary among individuals. That is, they are shaped largely by the society in which we live or by those with whom we associate. (See Figure 1-3 on page 12.) For example, an American college student probably will want a pizza or a cheeseburger and French fries to meet his or her need for food, while a middle-aged marketing executive probably will want a salad, steak, and baked potato to fill the same need. Even more extreme, a truly hungry person in a very poor country will satisfy his or her need with any food available.

As a society becomes more complex and developed, the wants of its members expand considerably. Marketing tries to determine those wants and then, through its business activities, offer products and services to satisfy them.

Exchange.
The fact that people have needs and wants and that there are products and services which are capable of satisfying these needs and wants is a necessary part of the definition of marketing, although it is not completely adequate by itself. **Exchange** is the final part of the marketing definition. It is defined as the act of obtaining a desired product or service by offering something in return. Exchange involves two or more parties voluntarily agreeing to enter into a trading relationship. Usually, an exchange consists of trading a product or service for money.

Macro- and Micro-Marketing

Perhaps some of the confusion over the definition of marketing occurs because we do not clearly distinguish a macro from a micro approach. **Macro-marketing** refers to a society's economic system which directs the flow of products and

services from those who produce or manufacture them to those who ultimately consume them. As in the AMA definition of marketing shown in Table 1-2, macro-marketing in most economic systems is concerned with providing consumers with products and services that satisfy their needs and wants. However, the emphasis is not on the activities that individual organizations or individual consumers perform. Rather, in macro-marketing the emphasis is on how the entire system performs, taking into account the interrelated aspects of all producers and consumers. The focus in a macro definition is on distribution. In effect, macro-marketing responds to the classic economic question, How are the goods and services of a society distributed to its people? Related questions include: Who distributes them? When? To whom are they distributed? How these decisions are made varies from nation to nation, but macro-marketing objectives are basically similar: to create products and services and make them available when and where they are needed in order to improve the country's standard of living. Those who study macro-marketing place emphasis on the entire economic system, not on the individual organization or firm.

Micro-marketing, on the other hand, focuses on the organization or the individual firm. This perspective is perhaps more compatible with the definition of marketing that is used in this textbook. Micro-marketing usually begins with a thorough study of the firm's actual and prospective customers, especially their needs and wants. From there, products and services are developed to satisfy those needs and wants. These products and services are then priced, promoted, and placed where they can be sold. Finally, an exchange takes place. The product or service is sold in a mutually rewarding exchange. It satisfies the customer's need or want and, hopefully, the firm adds to its profits.

The extent to which micro-marketing is important in an economy depends, of course, on the economic structure. Economic systems today generally are classified as traditional, planned, and market or free enterprise.

TABLE 1-3
MACRO- VERSUS MICRO-MARKETING

Type	Focus	Question to Be Answered
Macro-Marketing	Study of marketing within a country's or a society's economic system.	How are the products and services of a society best distributed to its people?
Micro-Marketing	Study of marketing within a single firm or organization.	How do we best meet the needs and wants of our customers for products and services at a profit?

Traditional. A **traditional economic system** is one that is not industrialized. Factories, shopping centers, transportation systems, and warehouses are rare in a traditional economy. Answers to such economic questions as what to produce, how to produce it, and how to distribute that which is produced are based on tradition, social custom, and religion. The products that are produced usually are distributed according to birth order, sex, age, or some other characteristic that is not based on hard work or productivity. A traditional economic system has been associated historically with primitive, agricultural societies. Today, there are still a few traditional economic systems in some less developed countries in Africa and some primitive societies in Australia. Needless to say, there is little micro-marketing as we understand it in primitive or traditional economic systems.

Planned. In a **planned economic system,** government planners decide what and how much to produce, how to produce it, and to whom it is to be distributed. These government planners, often referred to as the central planning committee, develop an overall economic plan for the country. This plan may or may not take into account the needs and wants of the people in its economic decisions. The plan is aimed at accomplishing overall economic goals as defined by those in power.

There are two major planned economic systems in the world today: socialism and communism. Generally speaking, **socialism** advocates collective ownership of most of the major production and distribution systems of the society. Thus, large factories, farms, transportation systems (airlines, railroads, and highways), and utility systems are usually government-owned and operated. In socialist societies, the government operates these businesses to serve the people, not to make a profit. The purpose is to distribute products and services as equitably as possible. In most socialist economies, there is some private ownership of business and industry. Many small farms, factories, stores, restaurants, and service industries are privately owned and operated. However, in most socialist countries, nearly all industries associated with finance and banking, fuel and power, transportation (railroads and airlines), communications, steel, health care, land use, and natural resources (mining, forestry, and coal and oil production) are government-owned and operated. Examples of socialist countries include Great Britain, Denmark, Sweden, and Jamaica.

Communism is an economic theory which advocates elimination of *all* private property. In a pure communist system, all goods are owned in common (by the government) and are available to all as needed. Major economic decisions are made by the central planning committee. Production and distribution systems are owned, planned, and operated by the state. Men and women are assigned to work where the government determines they are needed or are qualified to work. Examples of countries with a communist economic system include China, the Soviet Union, and East Germany.

In an economic sense, the major difference between communism and socialism is one of degree. Socialism allows for and encourages some private ownership of business and industry, and therefore, some micro-marketing is evident. Small businesses maintain a sales staff, engage in market research, and advertise their products and services, all in anticipation of earning a profit.

In a pure communist system, there is little evidence of micro-marketing. Manufacturers have very little choice concerning product planning. They produce the quantity and quality of goods and services that are dictated by the government. Prices are also set by the government and often are quite rigid and not responsive to supply and demand. Consumers have some choice in product selection, but there often is little diversity in products and services. Business activities such as selling, advertising, and marketing research receive little emphasis and sometimes are nonexistent.

In a planned economy, macro-marketing is the concern of the government. The fundamental marketing question for the country is what to produce and how to distribute the products that are produced to people who need them. Answers to these economic questions are supplied by the government. In a pure planned economy, there is little or no need for micro-marketing.

Market or Free Enterprise. A very simplistic description of a market-directed or **free enterprise economic system** is that it is one in which the individual decisions of many producers and consumers make up the macro-level decisions for the whole economy. A pure market-directed economy would be completely free of government planning and control. People would make their own decisions about which products and services to produce, sell, and buy. Based on

these millions of decisions and the resulting competition among producers, buyers, and sellers, the system would decide what and how much to produce, how to produce it, and how to distribute it.

In a free economy, consumers make production decisions by buying or not buying the goods produced. They "vote" in the marketplace, and their vote is primarily determined by want and price. If they want a product or service and feel that the price is fair, they will buy it. If they feel that a particular product or service is priced too high or is useless or unattractive or simply does not satisfy their needs and wants, they will not buy it. Production of that product is then stopped or reduced since the company obviously cannot make a profit on it. Likewise, if products or services satisfy customers and customers are eager to buy more of them, the price goes up and profits often increase. Then more producers enter the market for these products or services, more are produced, and the price is forced down because of increased competition.

Consumers in a free enterprise economic system have freedom of choice in selecting among products and services, provided, of course, that they can afford to pay. They are not forced to buy products or services that they do not want, except perhaps public services provided through their taxes (for example, education, fire and police protection, aid for the needy, national defense, and mass transportation). People have free choice in finding employment that is satisfactory for them. Producers too are free to engage in whatever activities they wish so long as they obey the laws. A producer's goal is to receive sufficient dollar "votes" from consumers to earn a profit. Related goals are often to increase the size of the business, increase sales, enjoy a better standard of living, and do better than the competition. But in a free enterprise system, profit, growth, and even business survival are not guaranteed.

It is rare, of course, for any one system to be purely traditional, planned, or market-directed. In communist countries, there is now evidence that marketing research firms and several advertising agencies have been established to inform people

Figure 1-4. Free enterprise encourages competition among most businesses, especially restaurants.

of available products and services. Most countries with a planned economic system allow some private ownership of property. Certainly, no economy is truly "free." The myriad government rules and regulations regarding products and services, business operations, and ethics—nearly all necessary and designed to protect consumers and employees—certainly attest to something other than a free economy.

It is in the United States that the market-directed or free enterprise system is the most highly developed. Canada, Australia, and some countries in Europe also have market-directed economic systems. In the United States, most products or services offered for customer use have several producers. Companies analyze the needs and wants of current and prospective customers daily. The goal, of course, is to earn a profit by satisfying the needs and wants of consumers by

offering appropriate products and services. It is in the United States that micro-marketing has truly been developed. Thus, through a comprehensive and coordinated system of business activities, each U.S. company seeks to provide products and services to satisfy the needs and wants of its customers. If the company is successful in doing this, a satisfactory exchange takes place. The customer has a product or service to satisfy his or her needs and wants, while the business has gained a sale. It is hoped that the accumulated sales enable the business to earn a profit.

MARKETING CONCEPT

Hazel Bennet has just figured the profit for the past year from her business as owner and manager of a cleaning service. Hazel discovered that she had tripled her profits from last year. That year, too, had been a good one. It was the year when she quit her job as a maid at the Holiday Inn to start her own cleaning business.

What inspired her? Hazel realized that skills such as hers were increasingly in demand in the medium-size college town where she lives. She noticed that more and more of the college teachers, bank workers, retail employees, and executives were women. An article in the newspaper revealed that nearly 70 percent of women over 21 years of age were employed full time and that the majority of them were also wives and mothers. Furthermore, nearly 30 percent of women employed full time were classified as junior or senior executives.

Hazel contacted the local employment commission. There, she interviewed three persons who specialize in helping others locate employment. In discussing with them the needs of working women, she learned that housekeeping was a major concern of women when deciding to combine full-time employment with homemaking. Generally, these women want assistance with heavy cleaning, specifically, washing windows, scrubbing floors, waxing floors, vacuuming carpets, laundry, and "getting at least the top layer of dust" off the furniture.

Using this knowledge as a base, Hazel quit her job, hired three people to work with her, and set about meeting the housekeeping needs of her prospective clients. In Figure 1-5, three of Hazel's advertisements are shown. One was placed in the lifestyle section of the local newspaper and another in the business section; the flier was left at the employment office.

In a very basic way, Hazel's story illustrates a fairly recent philosophy of business known as the **marketing concept.** This concept simply means that a business aims all its efforts at satisfying its customers while making a profit. The concept calls for company management and employees to

think a certain way. In scheduling business activities—whether for long-range planning done at the top executive level or operational duties done at the employee level—the twin goals of customer satisfaction and profit should be kept in mind at all times. All company activities— research, production, finance, and sales—are devoted to finding out what the customers want and then creating the products and services to satisfy those wants. The theory holds that if the firm's activities are coordinated to meet the needs and wants of its customers, a profit will result.

Customer Orientation

In Hazel's case, the primary reason for the profitability of her business was attention to the needs and wants of prospective customers. She spotted a

Figure 1-5. Advertisements illustrating the marketing concept as used by a small business.

market, researched the specific needs of the market, and then set about producing a product (in this case a service) to satisfy those needs.

Give the customers what they want. In this day and age of television commercials telling us, "Have it your way," "You are the boss," and "We did it because you told us to," this principle seems rather obvious. But is it really practiced?

Historically, firms often have demonstrated far more interest in production or sales than in meeting customers' needs. Often, the primary focus was on getting the product produced. Resources and personnel were assigned to get the product out. Emphasis was placed on the manufacturing process, warehousing, distribution systems, and other aspects of production and distribution. In other companies, the focus was strictly on sales. The marketing philosophy was to find customers for products that were already manufactured and then persuade them to buy what a particular company had available. The "more is better" philosophy—increase your sales or else—was primary. A selling concept focuses on the seller. It is the seller's needs that are paramount. "Increase sales by 10 percent," "Sell 25 percent more to every customer," and "Increase volume by making eight more contacts a month" are typical sales slogans.

The marketing concept is different. It begins with an analysis of the company's prospective and actual customers and their needs and wants. Implementing the concept implies offering a coordinated set of products and services to meet those needs and wants. Finally, profits are achieved through customer satisfaction. The marketing concept is contrasted with the production and sales concepts in Table 1-4 on page 18.

To be truly customer-oriented, a company must expend considerable effort to determine customer needs and wants. One of the key business activities of the company is to research customer opinion, study potential markets, and feed this information to the product designers or the buyers of the product for resale. A salesperson in a department store listens carefully to what the customer is saying and then makes every effort to locate the appropriate product or informs the buyer that an appropriate product cannot be found. Mary Ellen Borski in the story on page 2 formally surveyed airline passengers to determine what services are wanted by frequent travelers. This information was passed on to airline management and airplane manufacturers to assist them in making product and service decisions in order to serve their customers better. A waitress in a restaurant recommends desserts to be offered based on the requests of her customers. These examples illustrate the marketing concept at a very basic level.

Coordinated Activities

A second principle related to the marketing concept is that all activities must be coordinated organizationally. This means that personnel in finance, sales, marketing research, advertising, production, and inventory control must all be committed to the marketing concept and must be aware of its philosophy. This is necessary so that the twin goals of customer satisfaction and profit can be achieved. Attention is focused on marketing—not just selling or production—and major decisions are made with the marketing concept in mind.

This philosophy must be supported by managerial and operational employees alike. Activities throughout the company should be coordinated to operationalize the marketing concept philosophy. Imagine what would happen if the activities were not coordinated.

Don Rozek is a sales representative for Marion Clothing Company, a small wholesaler of men's and boys' wear. His clients are primarily managers of men's clothing stores or men's and boys' wear sections in department stores. One of his clients is Shamus' Clothing Store in Arlington Heights, a suburb in Chicago. Don promised the manager of the store a large shipment of sweaters to meet the anticipated need for them at Christmastime. In phoning the order

TABLE 1-4
CONTRASTING PRODUCTION, SALES, AND MARKETING CONCEPTS

Area of Company Emphasis	Production Orientation	Sales Orientation	Marketing Orientation
Basic philosophy	Focus on production; sell what you can make	Focus on sales; more is better	Focus on customers; make what you can sell
Product	Emphasis on product features and construction	Emphasis on getting more sales for the product	Emphasis on developing a product based on customers' needs and wants
View of customers	Get more products manufactured for them	Get them to buy more	Find products and services to meet customers' needs and wants
Market research	Get customer reaction to product	Figure out how to increase sales	Determine customers' needs and wants
Profit	Emphasis on how to make and market products profitably	Increased sales lead to increased profits	Determine customers' needs and wants and then manufacture and deliver products profitably to meet them
Sales force	Inform customers of product	Sell more products; most important unit in the company	Help customers buy if product meets their needs; coordinate with other units in company
Promotion	Emphasize how product is made	Emphasize product features and improvement over competition	Emphasize benefits of product to meet customers' needs and wants
Storage and transportation	Extension of product; minimize costs	Extension of sales; we'll get it to you	Provided as a customer service
Internal organization	Focus on manufacturing, assembly, and warehousing	Focus on advertising, direct sales, and promotion	Focus on integrating and coordinating all business activities
Inventory	Based on production requirements	Needed to meet orders	Determined by customers' orders and needs

back to the Marion Clothing Company, Don was informed that there probably would not be sufficient inventory to complete the order for sweaters. Several of the styles depicted in the wholesaler's catalog would probably not be available, and contracts with the manufacturer had fallen through. Actually, Marion Clothing had decided that there probably would be a better market for blazers and sport coats, and so the product manager had increased his orders for these items. Don was therefore encouraged to return to Shamus and go for a substitute order. There was also some question about the terms of the contract. It seemed that the accounting department at Marion Clothing was not certain of the amount of discount that could be offered on a single-item order of this size.

Obviously, there are two problems (and probably considerably more) with the Marion Clothing Company. The company is not particularly customer-oriented, and its business activities are not well coordinated.

Credit in most companies for implementing the marketing concept philosophy can be given to top management or to the owner of the firm. Most marketing executives agree that it is top management that sets the climate, provides for the organizational structure and leadership, and provides for the training of personnel in techniques in line with the marketing concept.

Profitable Sales

The third component of the marketing concept is that profits, not just sales, should be the goal of the company. If a firm cannot make a profit, the question of whether it is satisfying customer wants is immaterial since it will not be in business for long. But profits over the long run do not always come with increased sales. In fact, some products and services may have high sales but contribute little to the profit made by a company. A well-promoted product that does not really meet the needs of the customers may sell quite well in the short range but can result in company failure in the future.

The marketing concept regards the long range as more important than the short range. In fact, some say that a product should never show a profit for the first 2 years. Often, short-term profits are sacrificed in order to work more toward long-term financial stability. The long-range survival, growth, and well-being of the business, as measured by meeting the needs and wants of its customers at a profit, are considered—not just the short-range profits.

The Marketing Concept in Use

An interesting activity for students of marketing is to examine companies at the local level to determine their business philosophy. Are they primarily production-, sales-, or marketing-oriented? How well is that philosophy shared among the people in that business? Cynics often have a field day citing rude, uninformed, and unaccommodating sales people "selling" merchandise or services at local retail stores, banks, gas stations, and restaurants. On the other hand, it is truly a pleasant experience to encounter a salesperson genuinely interested in finding merchandise to satisfy the customer's wants.

How many companies put the marketing concept into practice? It is difficult to determine. Many companies say they are truly customer-oriented. Often management expounds the marketing concept. Many advertising slogans certainly indicate a marketing concept: "Satisfaction Guaranteed or Your Money Back" (Sears), "You're the Boss" (United Airlines), and "We Do It All for You" (McDonald's). But what really happens when the salesperson works with the customer may typify anything but the use of the marketing concept.

The story of Peoples Drug on page 20 illustrates a successful use of the marketing concept.

VALUE OF MARKETING

It is easy to be critical of marketing. Critics often express their disdain through statements such as,

PUTTING THE MARKETING CONCEPT INTO PRACTICE AT PEOPLES DRUG

Peoples Drug is a 375-store operation in nine eastern states. As late as 1976, its stores were badly run down, poorly merchandised, and ineffectively arranged. Little thought was given to meeting the needs of its neighborhood patrons. In fact, in one posh urban outlet (the Watergate complex in Washington, D.C.), the first display to greet customers featured 50-pound bags of fertilizer!

In 1976, control of the chain was acquired by Lane Drug Store. The operating philosophy of Lane was to develop Peoples Drug Stores into neighborhood-oriented convenience health-care and food centers. This philosophy of meeting the health and food needs of its neighbors resulted in the following merchandising changes.

1. All outlets provide convenience food items: milk, bread, frozen dinners, ice cream, and beverages.
2. Some offer check-cashing machines; all offer a neighborhood check-cashing service.
3. Paraprofessional and home health-care products and services are provided. Some stores offer coin-operated blood pressure machines. Others have added discount optical centers; health equipment such as wheelchairs, canes, and crutches; computerized pharmacy prescriptions (enabling a shopper to refill a prescription at any one of its branches); and assistance in how to use these products and services.
4. Slow-moving items typically purchased elsewhere were dropped (air conditioners and fertilizer). Other convenience store, high-profit items were added (greeting cards, auto supplies, and household supplies).
5. Layout was improved in line with modern self-service merchandising techniques, and electronic cash registers were installed. Both innovations enabled customers to be served faster and resulted in tighter control of inventory.

The results at Peoples? Sales grew in 3 years to $140 a square foot compared with an industry average of $90. Profits increased 21 percent in a year. Those revenues catapulted Peoples to the tenth largest drugstore chain in the late 1970s.

This story was developed by the author and is based on information obtained from *Business Week*, January 22, 1979, pp. 64-65.

"Products would be a lot less expensive if we didn't have to pay for all of that advertising," "Those salespeople will do anything to make a sale," "All those ads just encourage people to buy stuff they can't afford and don't need," and "Companies just change their products a little bit each year to get you to keep on buying something new."

It is especially easy to be critical of marketing if a business ignores the marketing concept completely. All people are exposed to a variety of ads urging them to buy deodorants to cover up whatever odor happens to be bothering them at the moment. Certainly everyone has had experiences with overzealous and perhaps unethical salespeople who try to persuade customers to buy items they don't want and can't use. Sometimes people get confused and annoyed at having to examine so many different sizes of their favorite laundry detergent before finding the one that just suits their purpose.

On the plus side, marketing, perhaps better than any other single economic activity in this country, has enabled most Americans to enjoy a comfortable standard of living. It is primarily responsible for helping to determine what will be produced and the need for new technology and then distributing the results of that production and technology to the public. Marketing has provided an important information system linking producers and consumers. It has provided a mechanism for collecting information on the needs and wants of consumers and then providing those data to manufacturers and producers. A good example is the marketing of word processing equipment. Market research studies consistently determined that managers needed a better way to process the huge volume of paperwork needed for the operation of their businesses. Soon engineers developed computerized equipment and systems which could process purchase orders, prepare invoices, record sales, compute payroll, write

checks, and perform other paper processing activities in seconds. Once the technology and equipment were developed, marketers distributed the word processors by way of direct sales, advertising, trade shows, educational activities, and so on, to prospective customers.

The aggregate result of all the business activities identified with marketing has been an almost overwhelming number of products and services to satisfy the diverse needs and wants of the American consumer. Let us take a deeper look at how marketing contributes to the economic welfare of a country and its people.

Improves the Quality of Life

As discussed previously, macro-marketing refers to that part of a society's economic system which directs the flow of products and services from those who produce them to those who need and want them: the consumers. Macro-marketing considers a society's marketing activities rather than those of an individual firm.

In many less developed countries, a marketing system as we might understand it is virtually nonexistent. Most people produce their own products and then consume them. As the society continues to grow, however, a person or household's special talents are recognized. For example, one person may be very good at carpentry, one at baking bread, and one at growing vegetables. Soon an exchange process takes place: "I'll trade you my bread or several loaves of it for the table and chair you've just built. Chances are, I can bake the bread better and faster than you can, and I know you can build the tables and chairs better than I." Now several households begin to produce surplus products beyond their immediate needs, resulting in more exchange of products and services and more total products with less effort. As I produce more and more, I no longer have time to engage in exchange activity. I therefore turn my products over to one person or to a store that agrees to handle all further exchange activities. Thus a modern marketing system begins.

TABLE 1-5
THE VALUE OF MARKETING

Marketing

- Improves the quality of life.
- Distributes technology to the people.
- Creates form, place, time, and possession utility.
- Provides choices among products and services.

This basic description of exchange exists in the modern world, and the exchange system is especially advanced in the United States. As the head of a family, I no longer have to manufacture or produce all the products needed and wanted by members of my family. Instead, I can specialize. I can develop my own specialty and then exchange the results of that specialty with those who have developed theirs. Of course, many exchanges are undertaken before I finally use the money I earned from my job to buy that steak, fishing pole, or sailboat or enjoy that cruise. But the result is that theoretically, depending on what I can afford, I can enjoy more products and services and have more time in which to enjoy them.

Recently, some interesting studies have been done on less developed countries, especially those in which a great many people are impoverished. The studies seem to indicate that the quality of life in those countries could be improved by overhauling the macro-marketing system. In all underdeveloped countries, there is a very inefficient and ineffective marketing system. The food that is produced is not distributed to the masses in urban areas who are in desperate need of it. Consequently, what does reach the urban area is extremely expensive. In some countries, as much as two-thirds of an individual's income must go to buy food. The high prices of food further reduce the demand for food crops because people simply do not have the money to buy the food that is produced. There is little or no money to spend on nonfood products. As a result, farmers are reluctant to increase food production, manufacturers of nonfood items do not increase production, and the entire economic system fails to grow.

Studies seem to indicate that one answer to this complex problem is to reorganize the marketing systems in underdeveloped countries so that they become similar to the system that has been proved successful in the United States. The reorganized system basically calls for a buildup of agricultural products. Middlemen would then be organized throughout the country, and channels of distribution would be established so that products would be available in the areas where they were needed by the people. Marketing middlemen would then be trained to adopt innovative and modern methods such as refrigeration, packaging, use of multiproduct retail outlets, volume selling at low margins, and so forth. Instead of a production revolution, some specialists are now recommending a marketing revolution as the major way to improve the quality and standard of living in many underdeveloped countries.

Distributes Technology to the People

In early definitions, marketing was depicted as something between production and consumption. Marketing began as soon as production was completed. It is now recognized that marketing activities occur before production. For example, nearly all companies engage in some marketing research activities before they mass-produce a product. Although our definitions today are more broadly based, it is still important to remember that marketing does fulfill the distribution function in this economy.

As the definition on page 8 indicated, marketing includes a system of business activities. In Chapter 2, we shall further describe these activities as they relate to the type of work done by people who are employed in marketing occupations. At this point, just let your imagination go as you read a description of how marketing performs our economy's distribution function.

In Iowa, Duane Baskerville has just finished harvesting several hundred acres of sweet corn. He has contacted the manager of a local cannery, who has agreed to buy the corn and process it for resale. A local trucking firm then hauls the sweet corn to the cannery. At the cannery, the corn is processed, graded, and labeled. Mr. Harrington, manager of the local cannery, has sold this processed corn to Libby's, a wholesaler specializing in buying vegetables and selling them to supermarkets. Libby's picks up the several truckloads of canned corn and transports them to its warehouse in

Bangor, Maine. The corn is stored at Libby's until an order is received for corn from Kroger several months later. The corn is then shipped and stored at the Kroger warehouse, awaiting delivery to one of the many Kroger food stores in the area. Finally, the corn is transported to your local store, stocked on the shelf, bought by you, and finally enjoyed in the comfort and privacy of your home in Bangor during the Christmas holidays.

Sound a bit simple? Perhaps, but it is true. What has been depicted here is the traditional marketing definition of getting the right merchandise, at the right place, at the right time, to the right people, at the right price. In the above story, it is assumed that you are the right person. You wanted to buy the right product, in this case, a can of corn. You wanted to buy it at the right place—where you live, not from a farmer in Iowa. You wanted it at the right time (the holiday, not during the summer when it was first harvested) and at the right price. Presumably the price was right, despite the fact that the product had been harvested several months ago, processed, graded, transported three times, stored in three different places, probably promoted by at least three different firms, advertised by Kroger in the local paper, displayed on Kroger's shelves, and so on. Think about the number of people involved in the process. The point is that marketing enabled a Maine resident to enjoy the benefits of summer-grown corn from Iowa during the December holidays in New England.

But it is not only you who enjoy the benefits of modern marketing technology. It is also the millions of other people in this country. Marketing has contributed a great deal to bringing the benefits of technology to the masses. The latest studies show that 98 percent of Americans enjoy entertainment in the home through television. Calculators have been reduced in price so that most families can have them, shopping centers are easily accessible for most people, and even amusement centers have sprung up to take care of people's excess cash and leisure time. Of course,

the products had to be produced and the services had to be created. But marketing must be given tremendous credit, along with production, for disseminating the millions of products and services available.

Adds Value to a Product

Marketing adds value to a product or a service. It puts the product or service in a place where you can buy it and at a time when you want it. Through exchange processes, it puts the product in your possession. Economists refer to this added value as **utility,** which is defined as the power to satisfy human needs and wants. There are four types of utility, and marketing plays an important role in creating all four: form, place, time, and possession.

Form Utility. This is created by making products available in the right form. It is often said that manufacturing provides form utility, which means that products are manufactured according to consumer specifications. However, it is marketing, through its research into the needs and wants of consumers, that determines consumer specifications. For example, marketing activities determined a want for 10-speed bicycles, smaller automobiles, and home computers which would have software compatible with that found in offices. Actually, marketing and manufacturing together provide form utility.

Place Utility. This is provided when products or services are available in the right place. Through a seemingly complex system of transportation, refrigeration, and storage intermingled with warehousing, wholesaling, and retailing, marketing provides products and services at the places needed and wanted by customers. Thus, beef grown in Wyoming can be eaten by residents of Hawaii. Hawaiians can reciprocate by sharing their pineapples with people in Wyoming.

Time Utility. This is provided when products and services are available at the time when

Figure 1-6. Marketing adds *value* to a product, enabling it to satisfy consumer needs and wants. Here, a camera exhibits form, place, time, and possession utilities.

they are needed. People want candles at holiday times, a flight at a time when they need to go somewhere, and special presents for special occasions. Marketers create time utility as they adjust inventories and employees to assure that products or services are available in the right location and at the time when they are needed.

Possession Utility. This refers to the transactions necessary to ensure that transfer of ownership and the legal use of the product or service are provided. Marketers arrange for credit, cash exchange, installment buying, contracts, and other means to ensure possession.

In effect, marketing makes products and services more usable, attractive, convenient, comfortable, and accessible for the consumer by providing form, place, time, and possession utility.

Most products and services as manufactured or initially created would be fairly useless without marketing. It is difficult to imagine what the Iowa farmer would do with all that corn were it not for marketing. Can you picture what people would do with manufactured products if they were never marketed? Think of a factory full of snow tires in Detroit, but the tires are needed to cope with a 3-week blizzard in Kansas. Imagine that it is the rainy season in Oregon, but the umbrellas are still at the plant in Arkansas. Marketing adds value to products and services, but in so doing, it provides utility for the consumer. This added value does cost money—an average of about 50 percent or more of the price of the product or service.

Provides Product Choice

There is yet another valuable contribution that marketing makes to the economy. In a free market system, decisions are made by the consumer on the basis of his or her likes and dislikes for products and services. The demand is relatively greater for products and services for which the likes are most intense. Conversely, demand is considerably less for products and services which are very expensive or have little usefulness for most con-

sumers. Those who make and market products are rewarded in proportion to their ability to determine the needs and wants of prospective customers and supply products and services that satisfy them.

The significant factor is that both the buyer and the seller are free agents. The consumer is free to choose any product or service that is wanted, provided, of course, that it can be paid for. The producer is free to make any product he or she desires, provided, of course, that it is legal. The same holds true for people in marketing. They really are free to offer any product or service they desire. The producer who can supply the product with the greatest utility to consumers should gain the largest share of the total market. That is why it is so important that producers be informed of what customers need and want.

In general, the marketing system seeks to maximize choices. It provides a great variety of products and services with differing brand names, styles, prices, sizes, and quality to enable consumers to satisfy their individual wants precisely. We may not be pleased with all the products and services on the market, but we are free, at least relatively, to choose to buy or not to buy. If we keep looking, chances are that we will find just the right product or service to meet that special need or want.

KEY POINTS SUMMARY

- Marketing is a large and important part of the American economic system. The many skills one acquires from a study of marketing have applications in numerous career fields.

- The definition of marketing being used in this textbook is: "a coordinated system of business activities designed to provide products and services that satisfy the needs and wants of customers through exchange processes."

- There are four major components of marketing or decisions that must be made by a company's management regarding marketing. Known collectively as the marketing mix, the components can best be remembered through the four P's: **P**roduct, **P**lace, **P**rice, and **P**romotion. A fifth P—**P**eople—is also important to the marketing mix, since all aspects of marketing are operated and managed by people.

● Successful companies practice a business philosophy known as the marketing concept: satisfying the needs and wants of customers while making a profit.

● Marketing, perhaps more than any other single economic activity, has contributed to the relatively high standard of living enjoyed by Americans. It is primarily responsible for bringing the results of technology to the public by way of diverse products and services. It has made and continues to make products and services more usable, attractive, convenient, comfortable, and accessible to consumers.

KEY TERMS AND CONCEPTS

communism
exchange
form utility
loss
macro-marketing
market-directed or free
  enterprise system
marketing
marketing concept
marketing mix
micro-marketing
need

place utility
planned economic
  system
possession utility
profit
socialism
time utility
traditional economic
  system
utility
want

DISCUSSION QUESTIONS

1. Discuss ways in which people can benefit from a study of marketing. Identify specific occupations in which marketing skills are needed.

2. In your own words, define marketing. Then describe the term as it is used in both a macro and micro approach.

3. Describe marketing as you think it might exist in the Soviet Union, Poland, or East Germany. Then describe marketing as you think it might exist in the United Kingdom, Sweden, or Denmark. Finally, contrast marketing in these countries with marketing as you know it in the United States or Canada.

4. Identify firms in your community that seem to practice the marketing concept. What specific activities do they undertake to satisfy customers while apparently making a profit? Contrast the marketing concept with the production and sales concepts.

5. Respond to the following statements, which criticize marketing.

"Products and services would be a lot less expensive if we didn't have to pay for all that advertising."

"Marketing encourages people to buy products they don't need at prices they can't afford."

"Marketing is really nothing but high-pressured sales."

NOTES

1. Philip Kotler, *Principles of Marketing*, Second Edition, Prentice-Hall, Englewood Cliffs, N.J., 1983, p. 592.
2. "Services Grow While the Quality Shrinks," *Business Week*, October 30, 1971, p. 1.

CHAPTER 2
MARKETING TODAY

Perrier, a bottled, naturally carbonated spring water from southern France, was virtually unheard of in the United States until the late 1970s. By the early 1980s, sales were approaching $100 million yearly and the little green bottles were appearing on supermarket shelves, in some vending machines, in convenience stores, and as an alcohol alternative in cocktail lounges.

Why was Perrier so successful in crashing the fiercely competitive American soft drink market? Great Waters of France, Inc., the American subsidiary of Source Perrier, was successful because it practiced effective strategies based on sound marketing principles. First, the company engaged in market research. Data showed that the American consuming public was growing older, was more interested in good health and physical fitness, and was looking for an alternative to alcoholic and carbonated beverages.

Next, the company studied and analyzed the product. Perrier is naturally carbonated and is bottled from a spring in France. According to Bruce Nevins, president of Great Waters, the smaller bubbles in naturally carbonated water give the consumer a less bloated feeling. Rather than attempt a complete mass marketing of the product, Great Waters decided to target the segment of the population that is interested in natural products and health foods. The product was packaged in a variety of ways to meet the researched needs of prospective customers. Thus, the original 23-ounce bottle was modified to include packaging of a tri-pack of 11-ounce bottles and six- and four-packs of 6½-ounce bottles. Today the "chubby green-tinted" bottle is recognized by most Americans. See Figure 2-1 on page 28.

Before the late 1970s, Perrier was distributed in this country primarily in out-of-the-way gourmet shops specializing in high-priced imports. But to reach the large American market interested in health and natural products, Nevins placed the product primarily in supermarkets. Within 3 years, food stores (convenience stores and supermarkets) accounted for approximately 70 percent of the sales for Perrier, gourmet shops had about 5 percent, and the remaining sales were spread among restaurants, vending machines, and cocktail lounges.

Price was another important component in the marketing strategy of Perrier. Great Waters cut the price approximately one-half from its original "gourmet import" image but still kept it above that

Figure 2-1. One promotion strategy for Perrier included packaging the product to meet the various needs of customers.

of most soft drinks. This enabled the product to be promoted as a "cut above" soft drinks and made it possible to aim it exclusively at adults.

The promotion strategies consisted of a well-orchestrated mix of magazine and television advertising, testimonials, informative brochures, and sales promotion. Print advertising stressed that Perrier has "no calories" and "no chemical preservatives, flavorings, or additives of any type" and that it is a "miracle of natural carbonation." Orson Welles, an actor chosen because of his authoritative voice, told TV audiences in hushed tones that Perrier bubbles up from deep beneath the earth. Sales promotion devices given to distributors and consumers included a free case for a certain number purchased, cents-off coupons redeemable at food stores, free tasting, and "take-one" brochures attached to point-of-purchase displays. In addition, Great Waters sponsored mar-

athons for runners in New York City, Washington, D.C., and Falmouth, Massachusetts.

These marathons stressed a "run for your health" theme that tied into the growing physical fitness movement and appealed to Perrier's natural product and health food market segment.

The ultimate of marketing success—sustained sales and reasonable profit—has yet to be determined for Perrier. But it looks good. Great Waters adhered to effective marketing techniques. It utilized the results of marketing research to position the product. It focused carefully on the four aspects of the marketing mix: product, place, price, and promotion. It met the needs of a selected group of American consumers who wanted an alternative to alcoholic beverages and soft drinks with sugar, caffeine, and artificial additives.

Critics and competitors say that the success of Perrier will not last, that it is just a fad. Time and continued use of effective marketing strategies will tell. But as Perrier's Nevins stated: "I don't think our [current] popularity is any more a fad than health is. People are going to get smarter, not dumber."[1]

In this chapter, we shall take a look at where marketing takes place and what marketers and marketing managers do to make their companies successful. We shall also examine briefly the ownership of marketing-oriented businesses and some unique aspects and opportunities in entrepreneurship. The purpose of this chapter is to introduce you to marketing as it exists today and to the work of marketers and marketing managers. The concepts and marketing strategies introduced here will be developed further throughout the text.

WHERE DOES MARKETING TAKE PLACE?

Most people think marketing is something practiced only by the big corporations like Proctor & Gamble, Volkswagen, and Pepsi-Cola. They forget that Joe's Barbershop, Alfie's Fish House, and

Sara's Bakery also must engage in marketing if they are to be successful. Nonprofit agencies and services too are now using marketing techniques. Groups as diverse as the Textile Workers of America (labor union), the Church of the Latter Day Saints (religion), and the American Cancer Society have all launched marketing campaigns to promote their ideas and causes. In this chapter, we shall briefly examine marketing in profit-oriented American businesses, how it is used by nonprofit organizations, and its expansion into international arenas.

Profit Sector

The primary focus in this book is on marketing in the profit-oriented business sector. Most of the marketing strategies discussed will be primarily appropriate to profit-oriented businesses. That is, we shall study the effective marketing techniques that are used by the 90 million people employed in 15 million businesses in this country. Marketing is big business, and big businesses survive because of marketing. Businesses are of three general types: production-oriented, distribution-oriented, and service-oriented. A fourth type of business, actually a special type of service business, is the marketing of people. Examples of each of these four types of businesses are shown in Table 2-1.

Production-Oriented Businesses.
The first type, **production-oriented businesses,** includes industries such as farming, fishing, mining, and manufacturing. Firms in this group are *primarily* organized and managed for the purpose of producing a product or products. Stated another way, production-oriented businesses create form utility. Most of these firms also are concerned with marketing. Their success depends on their ability to sell the products they produce at prices that exceed their costs. In fact, the biggest problem for farmers often is marketing, especially getting their products through the channel, that is, getting the products from where they are produced to where they can be sold to the customers

TABLE 2-1 PROFIT-ORIENTED BUSINESSES CLASSIFIED

Business Orientation	Examples
Production	Manufacturing Farming Fishing Mining
Distribution	Retailing Wholesaling Agencies
Services	Finance and Banking Recreation and Tourism Personal Care Business Services
People	Celebrities Politicians Entertainers Professional Athletes

who need them. Nobody would be familiar with the products of manufacturing firms such as IBM, Kodak, or Coca-Cola if not for their huge advertising budgets and extensive marketing activities. Thus, a significant part of the labor force in production-oriented companies deals specifically with marketing.

Distribution-Oriented Businesses.
This second major category of business includes middlemen, or those in the channel where products flow from the producer to the ultimate consumer. Middlemen are engaged in distributing or moving the products from the place where they are produced to their point of consumption. Middlemen create time, place, and possession utility. They also help create form utility by keeping production-oriented businesses informed as to customers' wants and needs. **Distribution-oriented**

CAN DENTISTRY BE MARKETED LIKE CANDY?

Will toothsome American teens of the future cruise the parking lot of their local McTooth or Dental King, ordering molar exams and a side order of floss? Will shoppers be bombarded with messages to save 25 percent on impacted wisdom teeth while the flashing blue light is on? Will coupons for discounts on dentures be offered "so long as the supply lasts"?

The marketing of dentistry may never reach that level, but the growing alliance between retail stores and dentistry could forever change the way dentistry is viewed. Retailers such as Sears and Montgomery Ward have been renting floor space to dental operations since 1978. As the climate for these arrangements improves, others such as K-Mart are beginning to get involved in the relatively new field of dental marketing.

Several factors have attracted marketers to the delivery of dental care. Curt Gundmundson, president of Retail Dental Centers in Minneapolis, cites a surplus of dentists as being the major factor in retailers' ability to offer dental services in competition with the more traditional dental care delivery systems.

Restrictions on the advertising of health care have also been relaxed. According to Gundmundson, "Dentistry can be marketed like anything else." His service contracts with the retailer for space in a store, sublets that space to a dentist, and then provides the kind of marketing acumen dentists lack. "Everything about it is like a private practice, except we do the advertising and provide the dentists with business systems. . . . It's a franchise, just like Burger King or McDonald's."

In his dental care business, Gundmundson markets to the surveyed needs and wants of customers. Outlets are open from 9 A.M. to 9 P.M. in response to customers' needs for evening hours. Professional image is promoted. Ads for the service emphasize traditional care at lower prices and more convenient times. Prices are somewhat lower than in more traditional dentists' offices. Gundmundson hopes to attract some of the 62 percent of prospective customers surveyed who indicated they had not visited a dentist in at least 2 years. Relatively lower prices should also attract the "average-income" customer who typically shops at self-service department stores.

It is expected that there will be increased marketing of dental services in the years ahead. According to a company spokesperson at Ward's, dental centers are compatible with other department store services such as optical, hearing aids, and beauty shops. "It's an extension of other health care services we offer, and it helps keep customers coming back to our stores."

Adapted from *Marketing News*, published by the American Marketing Association, May 29, 1981, p. 5.

businesses buy from one source and market to another. Some take actual title to the products (wholesalers and retailers), while others (agents) perform all the business operations but do not actually take title. Agents charge a commission or a set fee for performing a service. Perhaps the most visible marketing institution is the retailer, or the person who makes it possible for customers to purchase thousands of personal and home-use items. A retail sale represents the culmination of a process which may have had its beginning thousands of miles away and may have passed through hundreds of hands and several owners before the product ended up on the consumer's table. All these middlemen, whether they be found in wholesaling, agencies, or retailing, are considered marketers.

Service-Oriented Businesses.

The third major category of businesses are those classified as **service-oriented.** As discussed in Chapter 1, a service industry is primarily engaged in offering as its product an activity or benefit that is intangible and does not result in the ownership of anything. Familiar service-oriented businesses include hotels and motels, banks, insurance agencies, repair shops, dry cleaners, amusement parks, hair care salons, funeral homes, real estate agencies, pet kennels, credit unions, bowling alleys, restaurants, brokerage houses, theaters, and airlines. There are also service-oriented businesses that facilitate the work of production- and distribution-oriented firms. In fact, these companies are in business for the purpose of providing services for other businesses. Examples include advertising agencies, consulting firms, executive employment agencies, and centralized buying offices. There are other profit-oriented service businesses that are also increasingly marketing their services and will probably do even more marketing in the future. Thus, lawyers, physicians, dentists, and home care nurses are now applying marketing techniques in the operation of their service-oriented businesses. All these industries are heavily into marketing, and a great percentage of their yearly budgets is devoted to marketing activities.

People-Oriented Marketing.

A fairly recent application of marketing strategies has been associated with the marketing of people: celebrities, athletes, and politicians. Thus, college athletes now hire a business company or agent to get the best financial and fringe benefit package from a professional team. Agents carefully research the needs of the pro team and then develop and execute a plan to market the athlete to that team. For years politicians have made extensive use of marketing activities to promote themselves and their ideas to the public. Millions of dollars have been poured into market research, commercials, brochures, and direct-mail campaigns in hopes of getting a candidate elected to political office.

Nonprofit Sector

Business activities usually thought of as marketing are increasingly being used by nonbusiness and nonprofit organizations. Recently ideas, social causes, and social services have been heavily marketed. Some ideas and social issues that have been the subject of recent marketing campaigns are depicted in Table 2-2 on page 32.

The term generally used to describe the use of marketing techniques in nonbusiness or nonprofit areas is social marketing. Other commonly used terms include idea marketing and concept marketing. **Social marketing** has been defined as the "design, implementation, and control of programs seeking to increase the acceptability of a social idea, cause, or practice in a targeted group(s)." [2] According to this definition, social marketing would describe activities designed to encourage people to attend church regularly, stop smoking, control the size of their families, support the local fine arts center, contribute to UNICEF, participate in an immunization program, stop the construction of nuclear reactors, use seat belts, support the symphony, join the Army, and so forth.

Social marketing calls for much more than public advertising or promotion. Anyone who wishes to influence others—whether to get their

TABLE 2-2
EXAMPLES OF CURRENT IDEAS AND
SOCIAL ISSUES THAT HAVE BEEN MARKETED

55 mph speed limit	Drug abuse control	Marriage	Recycling wastes
911 emergency number	Energy conservation	Mass transportation	Religion
Abortion rights	Equal opportunity	Mental health	Right to life
Affirmative action	Equal rights amendment	Military recruiting	Safety
Alcoholism control	Euthanasia	Museums	Save the Whales
Blood donations	Fair housing	Nature conservation	Scouting
Blue laws	Family planning	Nuclear energy	Seat belt use
Cancer research	Fire prevention	Nudism	Solar energy
Car pooling	Fluoridation	Nutrition	Suicide hot line
Child abuse prevention	Foster parenthood	Obesity prevention	Tax reform
Child adoption	Free enterprise	Outdoor living	Trade associations
Consumer cooperatives	Freedom of the press	Peace	United Negro Colleges
Continuing education	Gay rights	Peace Corps	United Way
Crime prevention	Gun control	Pet responsibility	Urban planning
Draft registration	Health maintenance	Physical fitness	Vegetarianism
Drinking age	Literacy	Pollution control	Veterans' rights
	Litter prevention	Population control	Voter registration
	Mainstreaming	Prayers in schools	Wife abuse prevention
	March of Dimes	Prison reform	Women's rights
		Productivity in industry	

votes, promote a cause, or stop a certain behavior—should follow *all* tried and tested marketing procedures. The marketing principles associated with product or service marketing also should be applied to idea or social marketing. Thus, marketing research should be used extensively, the target audience should be analyzed carefully, cost-effective techniques should be employed, and the marketing mix—product, price, place, and promotion—should be planned and managed carefully.

This text deals primarily with marketing principles as they are applied to products and services in the profit-oriented business sector. However, examples will be provided periodically relating the application of marketing to social causes, ideas, and people. It is recognized that increasing use is being made of marketing techniques for such purposes and that social marketing is an effective way to promote action that serves the best interests of people: exercise, better human relationships, education, conservation, better health habits, and participation in cultural activities.

International Sector

Marketing techniques are practiced not only in the United States but in the rest of the world as well. Sales and profits in foreign markets represent a significant part of the marketing structure of numerous U.S.-based firms. Standard Oil of California, Gulf, Mobil, Coca-Cola, Otis Elevator, Dow Chemical, ITT, Pfizer, and Hoover all have more than 50 percent of their sales and 50 percent of their profits from foreign markets.

Conversely, we now have Kawasaki (Japan) building motorcycles in Lincoln, Nebraska. Massey-Ferguson (Canada) builds tractors in Canton, Ohio. Volvo (Sweden) and Volkswagenwerk (Germany) build and assemble automobiles in Chesapeake, Virginia and New Stanton, Pennsylvania. Michelin (France) makes radial tires in Greenville, South Carolina. Of course, Perrier is bottled in France. Other foreign firms have "Americanized" their names while doing business in this country. Familiar companies such as Baskin-Robbins Ice Cream, Lipton Tea, Saks Fifth Avenue, Shell Oil, Bantam Books, Lever Brothers, and Capitol Records are all owned by foreign corporations.

Multinational corporations are defined as corporations "that have a direct investment in several countries and operate their facilities on the basis of the alternatives available anywhere in the world."[3] Multinationals have been a force that has spread modern marketing practices throughout the world. Basically, marketing fundamentals are the same whether they are practiced in Rural Retreat, West Virginia or Paris, France. But the extent to which they are practiced and the specific strategies that are utilized may vary from country to country. The use of marketing strategies depends on many factors: the wealth of a country, customs, technology, supply of products, governmental structure, and so on. It is especially interesting to note that even in communist countries (the Soviet Union, East Germany, Poland, and Hungary) where marketing has traditionally been shunned, marketing techniques are now being introduced. In the Soviet Union, for example, there are several hundred state-operated advertising agencies and marketing research firms.

All countries trade to some extent. We live in an interdependent world. But in terms of absolute dollars, the United States is the largest exporter and importer of goods in the world today. Approximately 30,000 American-based firms, small and large, export more than $83 billion in manufactured goods and $24 billion in agricultural products in a given year. Usually, American exports account for 17 to 20 percent of the world's total

Figure 2-2. Multinational corporations may employ familiar marketing strategies in foreign markets.

exports. Exports account for only a small fraction—approximately 6 percent—of the total goods available for sale in the United States.[4] Countries like Great Britain, Belgium, Germany, and New Zealand have to sell more than half the products they manufacture beyond their borders to maintain a reasonable level of employment and pay for imported goods. International marketing is a fact of life to most firms in those countries.

The world market is huge and expanding, especially in less developed countries that are in need of American products and technology. Economic indicators seem to be saying that foreign markets will be increasingly attractive to U.S. firms in the years ahead. Of course, this country too has proved an attractive market for foreign investors. Americans have responded quite well to Japanese radios and televisions (Sony and Panasonic), foreign motorcycles and cars (Datsun, Honda, Volkswagen, and Volvo), Italian clothing (Gucci shoes and Fendi furs), foreign electric razors (Norelco), foreign food products (Brazilian coffee), and foreign oil. The future for increased use of modern marketing techniques in foreign countries and for foreign firms marketing their products and services in this country is exceptionally bright. Already there is considerable evidence that the U.S. consumer does not know and probably does not care which products are imported and which are exported and to where. International marketing probably will be a fact of life in the United States by the year 2000, as it now is in so many other countries.

WHAT DO MARKETERS DO?

Employment opportunities in this country have changed rapidly from those found primarily in production-oriented businesses to those found in distribution- and service-oriented firms. Studies on employment indicate that about 65 percent of the American labor force was engaged in providing a service or was employed in retail and wholesale trade in the early 1980s. Employment trend analysis indicates that as much as 90 percent of the American labor force will be employed in service, retail, and wholesale jobs by the turn of the century. Much of that employment will be in business activities identified with marketing and management. Other employment will be in data processing, clerical work, public service, and government work.

The work of marketers can be classified in several different ways. Of course, determining if a specific job task really involves marketing is often subject to varying interpretation. Most business studies and the literature describe certain business activities as being related distinctly to marketing. Generally they include activities associated with the following.

- Marketing research
- Product mix
- Pricing mix
- Promotion mix
- Place mix or physical distribution
- Finance
- Risk taking
- Working with people

Marketing Research

Marketing research consists of systematically gathering, sorting, analyzing, evaluating, and disseminating information for use by company decision makers. The information must be accurate, timely, and relevant to the needs of the firm and its customers.

To be successful, all companies must gather and evaluate market information. Managers and employees of large and small businesses alike must make many decisions every day. The following is a typical example of several questions that must be answered by an assistant manager of a pizza-deli in just one hour of one day.

- How much flour should we order to get through next week's promotion?
- Which specials should we put on the menu?
- What kind of ad are we planning to run in the newspaper?
- Which one of those job applicants are we planning to hire to help the cook?
- Which brands of beer and how much of each should we stock for the big weekend?
- Do you think we'll have much family business?
- How should we set up the dining room?
- How much cash will we need for the night shift?
- Do you think there's any way we can get more customers from the college crowd?

Good marketing research can help managers and decision makers answer these questions.

There are many ways to gather information and many ways to evaluate it. Some people are employed full time to gather and provide information that is made available to many companies and individuals. They may work for a marketing research firm where they telephone or interview prospective customers in person about products or services. For example, employees of the Market Research Corporation of America analyze notes written by homemakers about certain products.

They then prepare weekly reports about new products, prices, sizes, and so on. This analysis is then sold to retailers and manufacturers. Some people work for firms that analyze advertisements, including newspaper, radio, and TV media mixes, and provide their analyses to companies willing to pay a fee. There currently are over 350 marketing research companies operating in the United States. Some gather continuous consumer and trade information which they sell in standardized report forms on a fee-subscription basis to all clients. Others are involved in custom research. Such firms work with a company to design a particular study and prepare an appropriate report based on that company's unique needs.

Some companies establish their own marketing research departments. In fact, the American Marketing Association has reported that 60 percent of companies responding to a survey indicated that they have formal marketing research departments.[5] Some employees in these departments may be in highly specialized positions such as survey expert, statistician, report editor, research designer, or instrument developer. Other firms have only one or two people who perform all of these functions and more.

Most small companies do not have a separate marketing research department or people employed full time to gather and evaluate marketing information. Marketing research and the resulting decisions become a part of the job of many employees whose responsibilities include other tasks. Managers and employees usually then do one or more of the following.

- Use comparison shoppers who analyze competitive products and services
- Read publications such as the *Wall Street Journal, Business Week,* or *Women's Wear Daily*
- Attend conferences, exhibitions, or trade shows
- Communicate with or perhaps even formally survey customers, vendors, employees, sales people, and others regarding products and services

- Hire a clipping service to gather information reports on new products, trends, technology, services, or lifestyles
- Make notes after each customer contact regarding that customer's preferred products or services and then share those notes with company decision makers

Product Mix

The product or service being offered by the company is the critical and first element to be dealt with in the marketing mix. Do we have the right products and services to meet the needs and wants of our customers? Are they packaged correctly? Are there additional services we should offer? Should this product be modified in any way? How many product lines should be offered? Answers to

HEATHCLIFF

"IF YOU DON'T LIKE IT, JUST SEND US A NASTY LETTER!"

Figure 2-3. The product must meet the needs and wants of the customer.

these and many other questions are needed as a part of product-service decisions.

Major activities associated with the product element of the marketing mix include product planning and development, buying, standardization and grading, and packaging.

People employed in product planning and development are primarily concerned with identifying, creating, or modifying products or services to meet the needs and wants of consumers. Working with marketing researchers, people employed in product planning may be involved with activities such as engineering, product testing, or inventing.

Buyers search for, evaluate, and then buy products and services for use in manufacturing, company operation, or resale to the public. People employed in buying jobs are usually referred to as buyers, stewards, purchasing agents, or bursars.

Standardization and grading are also business activities that are associated with the product element of the marketing mix. These activities involve establishing basic measures or limits to which products or services must consistently conform. A standard is a basic quality that a product or service must have if it is to be designated as having met established characteristics. Grading is the act of determining whether the standard has been met and then labeling the appropriate product or service. Meats, textiles, farm products, jewelry, animal products, and wines are examples of products that are standardized and graded. Services are also often subject to a grading process. Most people are familiar with the one- to four-star system used by experts to rate restaurants, hotels, and even soap operas.

Another business activity associated with getting the right products to consumers is packaging. Products must be packaged to meet the esthetic, size, quantity, style, and other "product" needs of the consumer. Packaging is also important to the physical distribution aspect of the marketing mix. Goods must be shipped so that they are not damaged, destroyed, or lost. They must be packaged appropriately so that they do not freeze, thaw, melt, spill, tear, burn, mix with other substances, or disintegrate.

Pricing Mix

Business activities that are associated with identifying initial and subsequent prices for products and services are referred to as pricing. So many factors affect the prices of products and services that it often is difficult to come up with the exact price that will satisfy the customer and yet allow the company to make a profit. The accuracy with which the firm prices its products or services is a very important factor in sales and profits for the company.

Pricing activities are handled in a variety of ways in different companies. In small companies, the prices usually are determined by the manager or owner following some guideline provided by the wholesaler or manufacturer. Or the manager may set the price on the basis of what she or he thinks the local market will bear. Then too, competitive products or services often influence pricing decisions.

Some companies, especially those classified as large, have a separate pricing department where specialists work on pricing strategies and economic analyses, develop discount and markup tactics, check out competitive prices, determine allowances, and do all sorts of analyses to determine the price to charge for products or services. In addition to the research and management decisions that are made regarding a company's prices, other business activities include checking invoices; marking the price on merchandise; determining markups and markdowns according to company policy; computing discounts and allowances; computing total charges for products, services, and taxes; and performing other recordkeeping and administrative support tasks.

Promotion Mix

Promotion, or the communication of information between buyers and sellers, is often considered

TABLE 2-3
DEFINITIONS OF SELECTED PROMOTIONAL METHODS

Term	Definition
Advertising	Any paid form of nonpersonal presentation of ideas, goods, or services by an identified sponsor
Personal selling	Oral presentation in a conversation with one or more prospective purchasers for the purpose of making sales
Public relations*	Creation of a favorable impression for a product, service, organization, or person to earn public understanding and acceptance
Publicity	Nonpersonal stimulation of demand for a product, service, or business unit by planting commercially significant news about it in a published medium or obtaining favorable presentation of it on radio, television, or stage that is not paid for by the sponsor
Sales promotion	Those marketing activities, other than personal selling, advertising, and publicity, which stimulate consumer purchasing and dealer effectiveness such as display, shows and exhibitions, demonstrations, and various nonrecurrent selling efforts not in the ordinary routine

Source: *Marketing Definitions: A Glossary of Marketing Terms,* American Marketing Association, Chicago, 1960.
* Definition not provided by AMA.

the heart of the marketing mix. From a marketing standpoint, the job of people employed in promotion is to inform prospective customers that the company has the right product or service available in the right place and at the right price. If the marketing concept has been followed or used, that product or service has been developed because the company listened well to the buying public and is now offering products and services based on customers' needs and wants. Therefore, the message to be communicated is intended to inform customers just how this product or that service meets their needs and wants.

There are many methods to communicate this information to prospective and actual customers. Some business people use all of them; some use a few or only one. Most promotional methods can be classified as follows: personal selling, advertising, public relations, and other sales promotion. The definitions being used for classifications of promotion are presented in Table 2-3.

Personal Selling. For years, marketing was associated with selling in the minds of many people. In fact, the first marketing textbooks dealt almost exclusively with selling activities. Today, selling is generally considered only one of the many business activities associated with marketing, but one that is extremely important.

The responsibilities of sales people vary considerably. Some may perform very specific, narrow tasks such as locating products for customers or bagging customer purchases. Others perform many tasks and have a wide range of responsibilities. A large percentage earn the minimum wage, and others are among the highest paid people in marketing. Some have earned doctoral degrees in a highly technical field; others do not hold a high school diploma. More than 40 percent of sales people work in retailing; others are found in services and wholesaling. Probably the highest-paid are found in manufacturing. And many entrepreneurs (self-employed persons) are their

CONSULTATIVE APPROACH TO SELLING

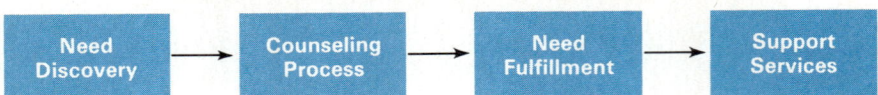

Figure 2-4. Most successful sales people use the *consultative approach* to marketing.

own sales people. Among the many titles used in the field are sales consultant, account executive, sales representative, broker, agent, customer-service representative, sales clerk, sales associate, sales assistant, sales engineer, manufacturer's representative, telephone solicitor, and salesperson.

Most sales people who are successful today adhere to the consultative approach to selling, as depicted in Figure 2-4. They first try to determine the customer's needs or wants. They interview the customer, asking questions to determine the exact need for the product. Good sales people listen carefully and then provide consultative assistance to the customer. They recommend appropriate products or services and discuss how these meet the customer's needs or wants. Their sales demonstrations, presentations, or dialogs are designed to explain fully to the customer the various features of the product or service and how these meet his or her needs or wants. Finally, to the contemporary salesperson, follow-up or support services are important. For example, instruction on how to use and care for the product is provided, delivery is made on time, contractual agreements are explained thoroughly, promises are kept, and in many instances, the customer is contacted at a later time to ensure satisfaction with the product or service.

Advertising. Advertising enables a business or organization to communicate with large segments of the population regarding its products, services, or ideas. In one form or another, it is used by virtually every business and most nonprofit public and private organizations in this country. Everyone is familiar with the television commercials of Proctor & Gamble, General Motors, General Foods, McDonald's, Pepsi, Bristol-Myers, and Anheuser-Busch. But it is the local newspaper

that is used by millions of small-town retailers and entrepreneurs to advertise their products and services. In fact, approximately 30 percent of the money spent on advertising in this country goes to purchase space in newspapers. Other media used to advertise products and services are, in order of expenditure, television, direct mail, radio, magazines, trade publications, and outdoor space (billboards, window signs, and taxi and bus signs).

Some people in advertising work strictly in one medium, for example, newspapers. They may design ad layouts, write copy, sketch illustrations, and follow through to the advertisement's publication in the newspapers. Some may work in the advertising department for a firm, for example, a department store, where they may create newspaper and magazine ads and print point-of-purchase signs. Other people in advertising may work almost exclusively at one job, perhaps as an illustrator or a copywriter. This is especially true for people employed in advertising agencies. Their activities, however, must be coordinated with those of other creative specialists to ensure well-designed, coherent advertising messages and materials. A small businessperson, perhaps with the aid of an advertising media sales representative, may do a few or all of the following.

- Decide which products or services to advertise
- Select the media
- Sketch out the ad (with artwork, illustrations, and copy)
- Write copy
- Create a commercial (radio or TV)
- Write a direct-mail letter
- Print signs or use a sign-printing machine

- Coordinate advertising with other promotional activities
- Work with people from various media, following ads through to publication

Public Relations. People in public relations try to create a favorable impression for a firm, product, service, or organization. They attempt to get publicity, or nonpaid space printed in all media that are read, viewed, or heard by a company's customers or prospective customers. Publicity is often referred to humorously as free advertising. The public relations person sees it as "news."

What should be publicized? Almost anything. Publicity is used to inform and communicate information about new products, services, brands, people, places, ideas, organizations, institutions, and countries. People employed in public relations deal with the government, the media, consumer groups, stockholders, suppliers, employees, dealers, and perhaps most important, the community. Newspapers, radio, TV, and all the other media are used for publicity purposes. TV panel shows, spot interviews on the radio, exhibits at shopping centers, citizen-on-the-street interviews, and press releases are just a few publicity techniques.

Today's public relations practitioners perform a variety of functions. Probably the most common task is the development of press releases: placing newsworthy information in the various media about employees, firms, products, ideas, or services. In large companies, specialists may be employed full time to develop product publicity that informs the public about product research and development. Many businesses and institutions organize public relations departments or employ a full-time public relations staff. In addition to writing press releases, the staff may also prepare or edit corporate communication materials such as stockholder reports, the company's position on relevant social issues, and responses to customer or public complaints. Sometimes they prepare exhibits, write and give speeches, plan meetings or conventions, and participate in community projects. Some companies employ lobbyists, who are people who deal with legislators and government officials to defeat unwanted legislation or regulations and promote those which are wanted. Often public relations specialists provide advice to company management on changes in society and the community and how such changes should affect company directions and communications.

The public or nonprofit private sector and celebrities and politicians probably make the best use of publicity and public relations experts. Colleges and universities, associations, celebrities, politicians, hospitals, governmental agencies, the military, and groups that support social or special-interest causes obtain tremendous amounts of nonpaid editorial and feature space.

Figure 2-5. Public relations helps get news media attention for new products such as microwave ovens.

For people interested in public relations careers, both profit-oriented businesses and government and nonprofit organizations can provide attractive employment opportunities.

Sales Promotion. Sales promotion consists of business activities that serve as a bridge between the selling effort, advertising, and public relations. Sales promotion people may be involved with such diverse activities as constructing displays, staffing exhibits at trade shows, displaying projects in a specially constructed booth at a business convention, selling or servicing trading stamp accounts, or administering any type of a special promotional activity (sweepstakes, contests, or rebates).

Many people employed in sales promotion work for companies where they are part of the marketing department. Some are highly trained specialists who work for a sales promotion firm (similar to an advertising agency). The sales promotion firm may contract with a business or industry to handle all of its nonadvertising promotion. Sales promotion promises to be a growth area in marketing as companies continue to look for better ways to promote their products and services.

Place Mix: Physical Distribution

A group of varying business activities are associated with getting products or offering services at the right place. Physical distribution includes the business activities involved in transporting and storing tangible products from the point of origin to the point of use or consumption. Physical distribution accounts for the largest part of each dollar that consumers spend, almost 25 cents on the average. It accounts for approximately 50 percent or more of the total cost of marketing. Estimates also indicate that physical distribution activities account for approximately 20 percent of gross national product.[6] Clearly, this is an expensive but important part of the U.S. economic structure. Physical distribution adds to consumers' satisfaction and improves their standard of living by ensuring that the right products are available

when consumers want them, at the right place, and at the right time.

Physical distribution is composed of five major elements: order processing, packaging and materials handling, transportation, storage, and inventory control. Table 2-4 gives a brief synopsis of these elements of physical distribution.

Finance

Financing is a term that is used to identify business activities that provide the necessary cash and credit to manufacture, transport, store, promote, sell, and buy products and services. Those employed in finance seek to answer questions such as these.

- Where can we get the cash to pay for this shipment?
- Where can we get the best interest rate on the money we must borrow to meet our expense obligations?
- What credit terms can we afford to give our clients?
- What system should be set up to ensure timely payment from those who owe us money?
- What are the cost-benefit expectations of various promotional media? Of various transportation modes? Of in-house advice versus the use of outside consultants? Of paying sales reps a commission versus straight salary?

The financial management and operational aspects of a business generally are not the specific responsibility of people in the marketing department. Most companies have a separate department which tends to financial affairs. However, the financing function is so closely interwoven with marketing that it is almost imperative that all people employed in marketing have some knowledge of and skills in financing. Furthermore, it is equally essential that people employed full time in financing have skills in marketing. Financial institutions such as banks, insurance companies, credit unions, savings and loan associations, and

TABLE 2-4
ELEMENTS OF PHYSICAL DISTRIBUTION

Major Elements	Description of Typical Job Tasks
Order processing	Keep track of necessary paper or use the computer to ensure that orders are being filled in an efficient and timely manner
	Complete business forms such as purchase orders, invoices, freight tickets, contracts, sales tickets, and credit slips
	Keep accurate and up-to-date records
Packaging and materials handling	Assemble products in warehouses or storerooms for packing and shipping
	Use equipment such as conveyer belts, motor scooters, forklift trucks, special containers, and computer-driven robots to move products
	Load products onto trucks, trains, planes, boats, or cars or into pipelines
Transportation	Transport products by one of several transportation modes: rail, water, truck, pipeline, and air
	Transport people by bus, taxi, plane, ship, rail, and limousine
	Assist with transportation of products or people in jobs such as flight attendant, dispatcher, reservationist, travel agent, rent-a-car salesperson, steward, and truck driver
Storage	Store products in warehouse, stockroom, or distribution center until they are transported to where they are needed
	Arrange products appropriately (on shelves, in containers, or in refrigerators or freezers) so that they can be moved rapidly
Inventory control	Maintain supply of products to balance demand for products
	Keep careful records of products available for sale and those which are sold
	Use recordkeeping systems, computers, and intuition as aids in reordering and buying products for resale

investment firms are heavily engaged in marketing their services to consumers and other businesses.

Risk Taking

Another part of the work of marketers is referred to as risk taking, which simply means bearing the uncertainties that are a part of marketing. A company or a department within a company can never be absolutely certain that customers will want to buy its products or services. Despite the use of good marketing research and information techniques, including careful analysis of customer wants and needs, some products and services simply fail in the marketplace. Furthermore, products can be damaged, stolen, destroyed, rendered obsolete, or lost. Services may be inappropriate, too extravagant or cheap, or too complicated or difficult for all but exceptionally well trained individuals to provide.

Risk taking involves trying to reduce calamities and anticipating possible losses and preventing them. Owners and managers purchase insurance to protect against losses from fire, theft, flood, shoplifting, vandalism, and accidents. They try to offer products and services that are truly needed and wanted by customers. They train their sales people and others who are directly involved with customers to listen attentively to statements about products and services. They anticipate changes in general economic conditions and try to control them, at least within the community or industry that they serve. In sum, owners and managers do all they can to manage their businesses effectively and thereby minimize risk.

Calvin Klein and Gloria Vanderbilt are both jean designers whose products were widely purchased by the teen and preteen set in the early 1980s. These jeans were considered a high-fashion item, and manufacturers knew that their popularity might not last. Market information studies show that parents are willing to purchase high-fashion items for their youngsters during reasonably good economic times. However, let general economic activity decline by as much as 1 percent, and one can anticipate that the sales of high-fashion items will decline about 15 percent. To compensate for this possible decline in economic activity, the manufacturers of Vanderbilt and Klein jeans charged approximately 25 to 30 percent more for a pair of jeans than more conservative, mass-producing manufacturers. Of course, an additional risk was also incurred. Prospective customers could have refused to pay the amount demanded for the jeans, instead preferring to buy less expensive ones produced specifically and labeled for K-Mart, Penney's, or Wards. In this instance, however, designer jeans did prove highly successful. Parents were willing to spend the extra cash for a Klein or Vanderbilt label.

Work With People

A description of the business activities identified with marketing would be incomplete without a brief discussion of the role marketers play in working for and with people. Marketing is a people occupation. There are very few jobs in marketing that require little or no contact with other humans. Perhaps a few people work only in order processing and storage or in standardization and grading, but the vast majority of people employed in marketing are in constant communication with customers, dealers, suppliers, and coworkers. Even those in the highly creative end of advertising or marketing research still must have a knowledge of people, for it is people—their needs, wants, motives, feelings, and coping styles—with whom the advertisers are trying to communicate and whom the marketing researchers are trying to study.

People are a marketing firm's greatest asset. They can make or break the company. It is the salesperson on the floor in Kinney's Shoes, the agent at World Travel discussing a trip with a prospective traveler, the cashier at Kroger's, the attendant at the Phillips 66 service station, and the receptionist at the Toshiba Manufacturing Company who provide the initial impression of the firm or store. They are the ones who communicate face to face, or "sell" to the public. Why then are so many of them apparently ill trained or poor at working with the public? Why do so many appear indifferent, uncaring, or bored? Why do so many consumers seem to mistrust sales people or tend not to believe their claims for products or services? Marketing research studies increasingly conclude that the number one complaint customers have about department and other stores is the poor or indifferent service they receive.

What is the answer? Unfortunately, there is no simple one. But in industries with a poor reputation for customer service, and especially in retailing, more attention probably should be given to hiring, training, and developing a well-qualified sales force and personnel and marketing staffs who are truly interested in working with and serv-

Figure 2-6. Ideally, a salesperson helps to serve the public, counseling the customer on his or her prospective purchase.

ing the public. The marketing concept must be practiced throughout the firm.

Marketers at all occupational levels, entry through top management, need to give attention to people skills. Training is needed in communication skills (especially listening), psychology, human relations, equity, supervisory techniques, creative conflict handling, and motivation. More attention also must be given by supervisors and managers to the recruitment, interviewing, and selection of employees and to employee training, motivation, and evaluation.

The authors of this text consider personnel to be basic to the success of marketing. Unit 7 is concerned with the people phase of marketing. After all, since people are a company's greatest asset (and they are usually its greatest expense), surely a study of people as a component of the marketing mix is imperative.

WHAT DO MARKETING MANAGERS DO?

Managers are found in every organization, and there are many managers in marketing. In fact, some say that about one out of every seven people employed in marketing is in management or performs management duties. Everyone is familiar with managers. They have many different titles: manager, assistant manager, chairperson (or chairman or chairwoman), dean, president, supervisor, executive director, superintendent, head, line supervisor, commissioner, and officer. Sometimes people who manage are called boss, whip, head honcho, or an equally imaginative title.

But it is not the title that is important in management; it is the tasks. **Management** is generally defined as the activities undertaken by one or more people to coordinate the activities of other people in order to achieve results. Note that in this definition, the focus of management is on the coordination of activities to be completed by people. Managers get their work done through people. The primary purpose of all managerial work is the accomplishment of results through the activities of other people. This description leads to four important duties or functions of management.

1. Managers Plan. They must plan to get results. Managers set up an overall plan for the business or a plan for a specific section (department) or activity (for example, promotion) of the business.

2. Managers Organize. They establish structure within the company or department and establish formal authority and responsibility within and among the various departments or work units. Managers implement processes and procedures to accomplish the objectives and strategies delineated in the plan.

3. Managers Direct. They issue assignments, instructions, and directions to accomplish the objectives and strategies delineated in the plan. Directing also means building an effective work force. Other directing activities include influencing, motivating, and leading people.

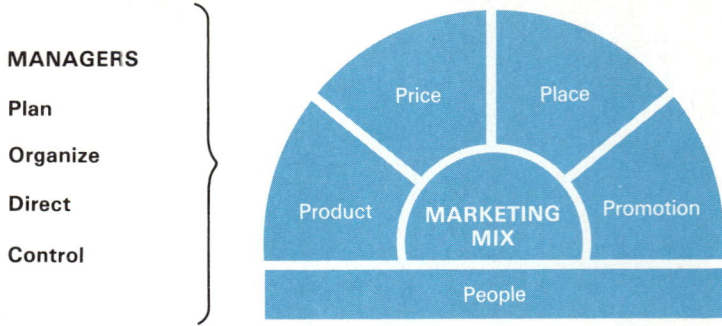

MANAGING THE MARKETING MIX

MANAGERS

Plan

Organize

Direct

Control

Price

Place

Product

MARKETING MIX

Promotion

People

Figure 2-7. Marketing managers plan, organize, direct, and control the marketing mix and business activities to achieve positive results.

4. Managers Control. They monitor progress. They evaluate processes and people. They control costs. They analyze the company's or department's operations and financial statements in line with the plan. They see that mistakes are corrected.

What is it that marketing managers plan, organize, direct, and control? Essentially, it is the marketing mix and business activities which were described previously. Thus, managers plan, organize, direct, and exercise control over product, place, promotion, price, and personnel as well as all the business activities associated with each of these aspects of marketing. This concept is illustrated in Figure 2-7 and will be developed further throughout this text.

WHAT DO MARKETING ENTREPRENEURS DO?

The all-American dream: Own your own business. Be your own boss. Work for yourself. Keep the money you make. Avoid the manager who is so good at saying yes to his or her supervisors and no to you. Make your own mistakes and live with them. Make the right decisions and profit from them.

It has probably been the dream of most people at one time or another to own and operate their own business, and many people are doing just that. They are referred to as **entrepreneurs,** which is taken from French terms meaning "to enter" and "to take." An entrepreneur organizes and manages a business "undertaking," assuming the risks for the sake of profit. The entrepreneur marshals people and resources to create, develop, and implement a business. Entrepreneurs almost always manage the business, and they assume certain risks in anticipation of earning a profit.

In Table 2-5, a partial list of tasks or jobs that are performed by entrepreneurs is presented. Of course, the entrepreneur may employ someone or contract with another business or person to perform many of these tasks. But in very small or new businesses, these tasks are performed by the entrepreneur. Note the large number of jobs that relate to marketing. You might consider using this as a checklist to analyze your potential for owning or operating a business. How many of these tasks can you perform or are you interested in learning to do? In addition to possessing the ability to perform these tasks, it is said that entrepreneurs must also be highly motivated toward business success, be goal-oriented, be independent, and be willing to devote the required time and energy to managing and operating the business.

There are two major ways to become an entrepreneur: start your own small business or obtain a franchise.

Small Businesses

Data from the U.S. government indicate that more than 1,000 new businesses are started *each day* in the United States. Of the 15 million businesses operating in this country, 14 million are classified as small, meaning that they are "independently owned and operated and not dominant in the field of operations."[7] One out of eight people is self-employed, and 70 percent of all employees in this country work for small businesses.[8]

As shown in Figure 2-8 on page 46, the vast majority of these businesses are distribution- or service-oriented. They are owned and managed by people of all ages, although the majority of the entrepreneurs were between the ages of 25 and 40 when they started their own businesses. (See Figure 2-9 on page 46.)

Unfortunately, nearly 50 percent of these small businesses fail within 5 years; another 30 percent fail within 10. According to Dun and Bradstreet, a New York business and economics publishing company, the following are eight conditions—in decreasing order of overall importance—that result in business failure.

1. Inadequate sales
2. Competitive weakness
3. Problems collecting amounts owed to the business
4. Heavy operating expenses
5. Problems maintaining control of inventory
6. Poor location
7. Excessive fixed assets
8. Other problems indicating poor managerial judgment[9]

The overall problem associated with business failure inherent in this list is incompetent management. Successful entrepreneurs are good managers, and they are good at marketing. They identify and offer products or services that meet the needs and wants of their customers. They successfully coordinate the business activities identified with marketing. They understand finance and know how to obtain, utilize, and manage the firm's financial resources. In short, they implement the marketing concept and apply effective techniques in financing, marketing, and managing the products and services offered by the business.

Economic trends in this country strongly support the continued establishment and growth of small businesses, especially in retail and service-oriented industries. Many of these businesses will be managed and operated out of the home. This is often referred to as **cottage industry** employment. Whether the business is in one's home or in a shopping mall, industrial park, or free-standing

TABLE 2-5
JOB TASKS OF THE ENTREPRENEUR

Entrepreneur's Job Task Checklist

Financier	Showperson
Insurance Manager	Billing Clerk
Shipper	Stock Clerk
Advertising Copywriter	Warehouser
Engineer	Sign Painter
Public Relations Agent	Electrician
Designer	Salesperson
Architect	Editor
Display Artisan	Supervisor
Personnel Manager	Manager
Wage Clerk	Tax Expert
Accountant	Analyst
File Clerk	Economist
Trainer	Inventor
Recordkeeper	Travel Clerk
Mechanic	Writer
Secretary	Police Officer
Researcher	Custodian

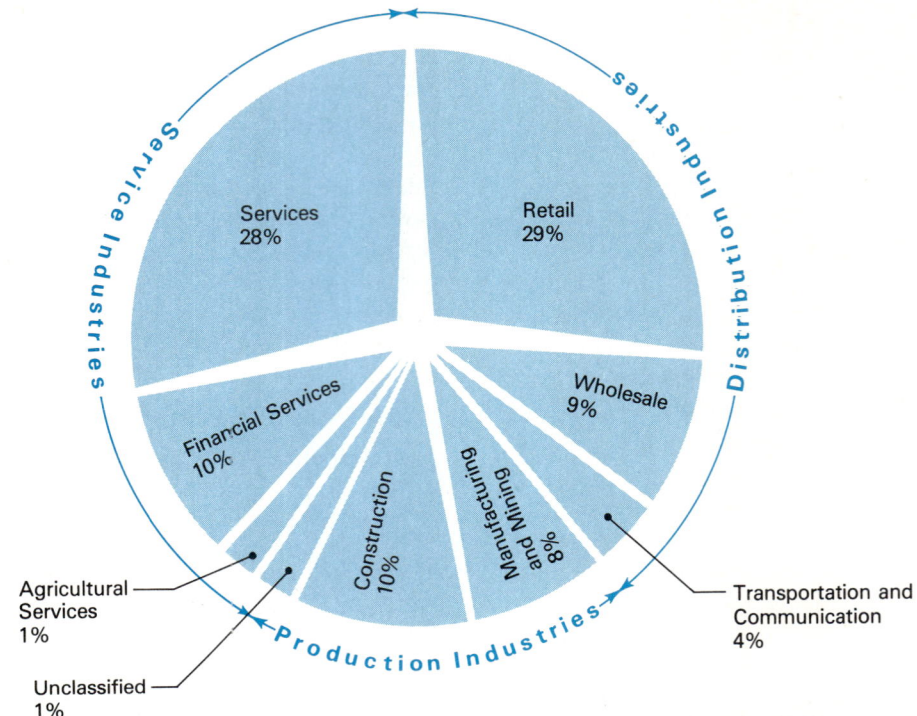

Figure 2-8. This chart shows the breakdown of small businesses by industry.

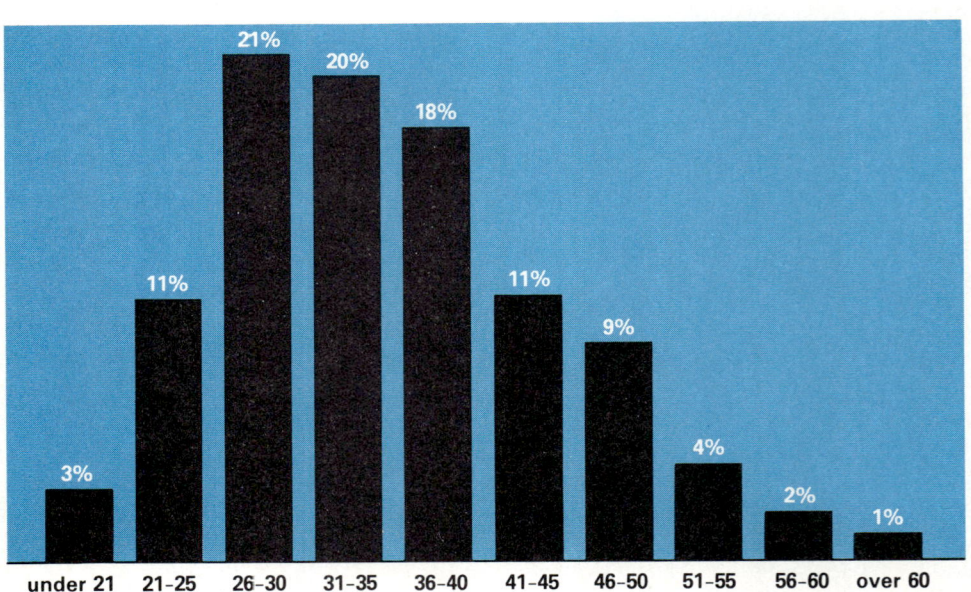

Figure 2-9. This chart breaks down the age groups in which people start small businesses.

location, the number of new small businesses is expected to double or even triple every 5 years. Government loans and other visible assistance are increasingly becoming available to the small businessperson, indicating that our government sees small business ownership and free enterprise as going hand in hand. There are tremendous opportunities for small business entrepreneurship for a person skilled in management and marketing who is willing to assume the risks inherent in the venture.

Franchising

A second form of entrepreneurship is through **franchising,** a form of licensing in which the owner of a product or a service sells the rights to distribute or market those elements which are identified in the license. Typically, the franchisor (the one who owns the product or service) retains control over the marketing strategies. For the franchisor, franchising is a way of expanding a business rapidly with limited investment, and it simplifies the sometimes arduous task of finding good managers. For the franchisee (the one who distributes or markets the product or service), it is a way to own a business quickly, for a known dollar investment, and with a very good chance of success.

Franchises range on a continuum from those which include just a few services to those in which all elements of the business—physical plant, marketing, accounting systems, training programs, operations, and even the uniforms worn by employees—are controlled by the franchisor. At one end of the continuum, a franchise may include just use of the company name and a few additional services. Ace Hardware and Certified Grocery are two examples. Car dealerships are typically in the middle of the continuum. Thus, General Motors, Ford, and Chrysler distribute their products through franchises but allow local dealers some freedom in marketing and operations. A third type of franchising that has grown rapidly in popularity in recent years involves franchising nearly all elements of a business. The most

familiar are those identified with the fast-food industry: McDonald's, Kentucky Fried Chicken, Arby's, Wendy's, Roy Rogers, Dairy Queen, Pizza Inn, and countless others found on any main street of a medium-size city in this country.

But "burgers" and "bigness" are not characteristics of franchising. Here are a few other examples.

- Over 1,000 franchised hair salons are now operating in this country. Fantastic Sam's, a Memphis-based firm, has a network of 178 shops coast to coast. Minneapolis-based The Barbers Hairstyling for Men and Women has 120 salons, of which 75 are franchised. Or you can buy into John Amico's Hair Performance Salon for $60,000 to $125,000. For this franchise fee, you will receive training in Amico's "angles and elevations of architecture" style of haircutting plus assistance with site selection, building design and construction, marketing, promotion, and management training.

- Century 21 Real Estate affiliates now number over 7,500, a growth in just 8 years from 17 independently owned and operated offices in Orange County, California.

- Eastern Onion is the singing telegram brainchild of Mary and Jim Flatt. The company began in Las Vegas and now boasts 34 offices around the country. You can own a franchise for $15,000 to $50,000 depending on location. The license includes songs, costumes, acts, advice on finding performers, recordkeeping procedures, and advertising plans.

- Eric Young of Santa Rosa, California, is currently marketing franchises for his Pet Prevent-a-Care, Inc., business. Among other services, Pet Prevent offers pet vaccinations from a mobile trailer in high-traffic and populated areas.

- Talented at repair work? Electronics? Tronics 2000 of Bloomington, Indiana, is now franchising electronic repair shops. For $10,000 in a populated area of at least 600,000, a franchisee can get assistance with marketing and training.

PROSPECTIVE BURGER KING FRANCHISES FACE WHOPPING COMPETITION

Every year about 1,000 people apply to Burger King for a franchise. Only a tenth are successful. In this rigorous competition, knowledge of or even interest in food counts for little. The candidates could as well be prospective Midas Muffler dealers. What Burger King is mainly looking for is people who have management ability, enthusiasm, willingness to follow instructions to the letter, and $110,000 in liquid assets. Typically, Burger King provides the land and building, while the franchisee finances signs, lights, broilers, computer-regulated French fry fryers, and other fittings. The franchisee's total outlay averages $179,000 a store.

Successful applicants spend a week working in an existing restaurant to see if they like the business, then 6 weeks of basic training at a regional center, and finally 9 days at Burger King University (BKU) in Miami, where they are tutored in everything from labor relations to the proper spacing of hamburger patties on a broiler—one quarter of an inch apart.

Franchisees recently graduating from BKU include Richard Connolly, 34, a former Long Island 7-Up distributor who will be opening a Burger King in Elkin, West Virginia; Ronald Broatch, a 39-year old high school counselor from northern California, and his wife Annette, who will start one in Bellingham, Washington; and Stephen Olson, the 23-year old son of a Colorado franchisee. Olson and his partners have taken over a failed franchise in Vail.

They are likely to earn a handsome return. A well-managed store with sales of $717,000 a year, the current average for Burger Kings, should provide the franchisee with a pretax income of $70,000. A franchisee who performs well with one store often gets to put up another nearby and then maybe a few more, until he or she bumps up against the 1-hour-radius limit that is one of Burger King's new restrictions on store operators. Franchisees can still dream, as long as their dreams are regular size, not Whoppers.

Source: Lee Smith, "What It Takes to Start a Store," *Fortune*, June 16, 1980, p. 96. © 1980 Time Inc. All Rights Reserved.

Franchising has become a major force in the U.S. economy. Almost one-third of all retail sales in the United States in a recent year were franchise sales. Franchise businesses employ over 4 million people in nearly a half-million establishments.[10] Chances for success in franchising are significantly better than if you start your own business from ground zero. According to data from the U.S. Chamber of Commerce, 8 out of 10 franchisees succeed. However, before entering into a franchise arrangement, ask the following.

- Has the business been profitable?
- Is it adaptable to my community?

- Does the franchisor have a good reputation?
- Is the franchisor well organized?
- Are there good financial controls?
- Does the franchisor have a good credit rating?
- Are the cash requirements and other investments realistic?
- What are my annual financial obligations to the franchisor?
- What services do I get for my franchise fees?

These questions refer specifically to franchising. Many other considerations relative to starting any business also apply to franchising.

In many respects, and especially for aspiring entrepreneurs, franchising has become the American way of doing business. It is an excellent way for a person to break into business with some of the risks being assumed by someone else. However, the success of any franchise, or for that matter any entrepreneur, will depend heavily on his or her finding a compatible and reputable franchisor and then effectively applying marketing fundamentals and strategies.

KEY POINTS SUMMARY

- Marketing activities take place in many environments and institutions, including production-, distribution-, and service-oriented businesses. Nonprofit organizations and celebrities also use marketing techniques. Increasingly, American products and services are being marketed abroad and foreign products are being marketed in this country.
- Approximately one-third of the American labor force is employed in some aspect of marketing. Increasing numbers of employees will be needed in marketing occupations in the years ahead.
- Marketing employees work in marketing research or in business activities identified with the four aspects of the marketing mix: product, pricing, promotion, and place. Others are employed in such marketing-related activities as finance, risk taking, and personnel management.
- Marketing managers plan, organize, direct, and control the marketing mix. That is, they manage the business activities associated with product, place, price, promotion, and related activities.
- Entrepreneurship—organizing and managing a business and assuming the risks for the sake of profit—represents another opportunity to utilize one's talent and skills in marketing. Nearly 14 million small businesses currently are operating in this country. The vast majority are distribution- or service-oriented industries.

KEY TERMS AND CONCEPTS

cottage industry
distribution-oriented
  businesses
entrepreneurs
franchising
management
multinational
  corporations
production-oriented
  businesses
service-oriented
  businesses
social marketing

DISCUSSION QUESTIONS

1. Discuss the various environments in which marketing is taking place in your community. Identify typical production-, distribution-, and service-oriented businesses. Provide examples of organizations that are making effective or ineffective use of social marketing. Are there firms that are marketing their products or services abroad? Are there foreign-based firms marketing products or services in your community?

2. Using as a basis a small business in your community—a travel agency, restaurant, gas station, bank, or clothing store—describe the marketing and management tasks that people do in that business. What and how many marketing activities does each person perform? What education or training experiences does each person need to perform those tasks?

3. Discuss the role of marketing management in a small business or for a manager or assistant manager of a department in a large business. If possible, interview such a person and see how he or she views the management role. Approximately how much of the manager's overall time is devoted to planning? Organizing? Directing? Controlling? What other tasks must the person perform?

4. What do you see as the major advantages of franchising as opposed to starting your own business from ground zero? The disadvantages? If possible, identify a franchised business in your community. Respond to as many of the questions on pages 48 and 49 as you can that apply to that business.

NOTES

1. Adapted from Nancy Giges, "Perrier Hopes to Bubble Its Way into American Goblets," *Advertising Age,* July 25, 1977, pp. 1, 61; Roger B. May, "French Bottler Tries to Replace US Pop with Natural Fizz," *Wall Street Journal,* April 12, 1978, pp. 1, 44; and "Perrier: The Astonishing Success of an Appeal to Affluent Adults," *Business Week,* January 22, 1979, pp. 64–65.
2. Philip Kotler, *Principles of Marketing,* Second Edition, Prentice-Hall, Englewood Cliffs, N.J., 1983, p. 602.
3. E. Jerome McCarthy, *Basic Marketing,* Richard D. Irwin, Homewood, Ill., 1978, p. 590.
4. Marianne McGowan, "Small Ohio Businesses Urged to Boost Exports," *Columbus Dispatch,* September 23, 1981, p. B7.
5. William J. Stanton, *Fundamentals of Marketing,* 5th ed., McGraw-Hill, New York, 1978, p. 46.
6. Louis E. Boone and David L. Kurtz, *Contemporary Marketing,* 3d ed., Dryden Press, Hinsdale, Ill., 1980, pp. 257–258.
7. U.S. Small Business Administration Annual Reports, Department of Commerce, Washington, D.C., 1974–1979.
8. *Entrepreneurship in Vocational Education,* National Center for Research in Vocational Education, Columbus, Ohio, 1982.
9. As reported in Kenneth R. Van Voorhis, *Entrepreneurship and Small Business Management,* Allyn and Bacon, Boston, 1980.
10. Neesa Sweet, "The Fine Art of Franchising," *Sky,* published by Delta Airlines, 1981.

APPLICATIONS/CASES

APPLICATION 1: CROWD CAPS

"Entrepreneurs are the answer to the American economic problem," claims Brett Johnson, Harvard junior and president of Crowd Caps Co., which in its second year took in over six figures in gross sales. Brett decided to start his own business and do his own marketing because he feels big corporations lack entrepreneurial creativity, mobility, and enthusiasm. "A small independently owned organization has advantages because management is closer to the grass roots," he says.

As a college freshman, Johnson embarked on his business venture. He sold lightweight painter's caps with a silk-screened red H on the front at the Harvard-Yale football game. The first year's sales were modest, but Brett had great visions for the future of his company: "Every day I would wake up with a new idea for marketing my product."

Johnson believed that he possessed a more exciting alternative to the traditional printed T-shirt for business promotional items. He won contracts with Pepsi-Cola, the Army ROTC, and a Barry Manilow world tour among others to produce thousands of his "Crowd Caps" with silk-screened designs and logos. He aggressively pursued the college market with his Crowd Cap and cashed in big with school stores, clubs, and sports contracts. In the third year of operation, he grossed over half a million in sales.

But Johnson's entrepreneurialism does not end with this one business idea. He hopes to use the "very creative marketing system" which he has developed and "take a lot of great ideas that are floating around out there and make them sell."

Adapted from Brett M. Kingstone, "From Munchies to Crowd Caps: College Entrepreneurs," *Wall Street Journal*, June 1, 1981, p. 26. Reprinted by permission. © Dow Jones & Co., Inc., 1981. All rights reserved.

a. Do you agree with Johnson's first statement, "Entrepreneurs are the answer to the American economic problem"? Defend your response.

b. Do you agree with his second statement, "A small independently owned organization has more advantages because management is closer to the grass roots"? Defend your answer.

c. To what do you attribute Johnson's success? What fundamental "creative marketing system" principles did he use to market Crowd Caps to the Harvard crowd and then to business groups?

d. In your community or class, are there "any great ideas floating around" that you can now take and "make them sell"?

APPLICATION 2: MARKETING THE MOVE FOR SPOUSES

During the past 10 years, there has been a strong trend toward more women entering and remaining in the labor force. The majority of working women are married and are mothers. In fact, there are now more than 25 million two-paycheck families, and that figure is expected to increase considerably in the years ahead. Many of these women are in management and supervisory positions.

A recent survey showed that 90 percent of wives and husbands both of whom held supervisory or management positions were most concerned about job transfers and the disruptive effect such transfers might have on their family lives and careers. If transfers were necessary, these men and women thought that companies should assist spouses in employment relocation through a job-finding agency, contacts in other companies, or job counseling.

Suppose you work for an employment agency in a large city. Your primary function has been to recruit and place middle management and supervisory personnel for retail stores, discount houses, and retail service businesses such as travel agencies, finance companies, and restaurants. The management team at your firm is considering providing an additional service for its clients. They are proposing that assistance be provided for the spouses of clients to help them locate employment in the area appropriate to their education and experience. A considerable discount on fees will be offered to this second member of the family who utilizes the services of your employment agency.

You have been asked to present your reactions to this suggestion and your ideas for marketing this new service briefly to the other members of the management team.

a. How has the marketing concept been applied to identify this new service?

b. Identify the components of the marketing mix that must be considered before a decision is finalized. What additional information must be obtained or researched for each of these components before a decision is made?

c. What business activities would have to be utilized to market this new service?

d. Occasionally, one's "gut" or initial reaction to a suggestion is the best one. What is yours?

CASE 1: MARKETING A COTTAGE INDUSTRY

Suzanne and John Leski need your advice. They are a young couple with two preschool children. They met several years ago while both were employed in the advertising department of a large retail chain store. John was an illustrator working primarily on newspaper and direct-mail advertisements. Suzanne designed window and interior displays for the downtown and branch stores and supervised their installation.

Four years ago, Suzanne voluntarily left the store to become a full-time homemaker. John has continued to work in the advertising department. He was recently appointed assistant manager and given increased responsibility.

For years, both John and Suzanne have utilized their creative talents by making many products. Suzanne is especially talented at making home-use arts and crafts items such as holiday decorations, quilts, pillow cases, afghans, and wall hangings. She also makes macramé jewelry. John's specialty is painting portraits and landscapes.

Two years ago, the Leskis began seriously to consider turning their hobbies into a business. On a very small scale, they began to sell some of their products. Most sales have been due to special orders. That is, someone would phone and ask one of them to make a particular product. Last year, the Leskis grossed $7,850. Not a great amount, but with John's income at the store, it was sufficient to provide them with a comfortable living.

Now John and Suzanne are considering turning this part-time, special-order business into a full-time retail operation. Despite his promotion, John is not completely satisfied and has often wanted to spend more time painting. Suzanne would like to convert the front porch and living room of their home into this business. She feels that with both of them working "at home," they could effectively combine their parenting responsibilities with their business operations.

The following are additional facts that may be important to the situation.

• Both John and Suzanne pride themselves on quality work. All previous customers have been exceptionally pleased with their purchases. In fact, recent orders have increased significantly because of word-of-mouth advertising. It is getting difficult for John to find time to keep up with requests for paintings.

• John has had some training in business operations. He received a 2-year associate degree from a community college. His program included two courses in accounting, one in business supervision, and one in marketing. However, most of his studies were in commercial art. Suzanne has a 4-year degree with a major in psychology. She has completed a few courses in advertising.

● Suzanne has estimated that it will take approximately $60,000 in gross sales for the first year to pay for their basic living expenses plus supplies and materials, some baby-sitting help, the house payment, utilities, taxes, and other business-related expenses. Of course, additional costs will result if they decide to increase their inventory and buy products from manufacturers or wholesalers for resale. They have not really considered what it will cost for promotion, recordkeeping, and other labor expenses, equipment and furnishings, and so forth.

● It may be possible for the Leskis to receive a small business loan. Neither one is sure how to find out about funding possibilities.

● Initial inventory may be a problem. John has 14 paintings that are as yet unsold. Suzanne has approximately 200 products ranging in retail price from about $5 for many small products to 15 quilts that should bring about $100 each.

● John and Suzanne have not done any sophisticated research on their competition. They live in a metropolitan area of approximately 300,000 people. There are four large shopping centers, and each has at least one arts and crafts or hobby shop. Also, many of the department stores have such shops. Of course, none of these departments includes handmade items or original paintings. But there are some local painters, and religious and craft groups often advertise products for sale that are similar to those made by Suzanne.

a. What skills and experiences does each of them bring to this new business venture? What deficiencies?

b. Using the marketing mix as a basis—product, price, promotion, and place—draw up a list of questions that should be answered or personal and business factors that must be considered *before* the business is operated on a full-time, retail basis. What are some factors to consider regarding personnel?

c. Are there factors other than those specifically related to the marketing mix that should be considered by the Leskis?

d. What do you think? Based on your experiences and analysis of the situation, do you think John and Suzanne could retain their comfortable style of living if he were to quit his job at the store and they were to open up an arts and crafts store in their home? Any alternative suggestions?

CASE 2: FAMOLARE'S WAVY SOLE SHOE

In the stodgy U.S. shoe industry, where intervals between significant design innovations seem like stretches of geologic time, it was something of a shock in the mid-1970s when Joseph P. Famolare, Jr. (pronounced Fa-mo-*la*-ray), began marketing a shoe with a four-wave sole. It was an imaginative enough innovation, but few people thought that it would sell. Famolare himself admits that "My customers thought I was nuts." One of his major retailers called the shoe "a real turkey." When Famolare's own sales force got a look at the new line, a quarter of them quit, convinced that their commissions would dwindle to nothing.

Aside from Famolare, the president and 75-percent owner of closely held Famolare, Inc., the only people who liked the shoes were those who counted the most: the consumers. Their purchases of Famolare's shoes in 8,000 department stores and specialty shops lifted the company's sales from $15 million to nearly $100 million in just 5 years. Joe Famolare will not talk about earnings, but the company's profit margin runs substantially higher than the domestic shoe industry's average of 4.5 percent.

In designing the four-wave sole, Famolare took shrewd aim at a market of young women, whose tastes have often advanced the frontiers of accepted style. Almost immediately, they began buying his new line: the "Get There," a conventional shoe with a wavy sole, and the "Hi There," a wedge high heel with a wavy sole. Both shoes appealed simultaneously to two markets: fashion and casual. Fashion shoes, with their uncomfortable lines and angles, have been generating business for podiatrists for years, but Famolare offered an appealing shoe that was also comfortable for walking. The four waves of the thermoplastic sole and the contoured leather interior support the foot and absorb the shock of walking on hard surfaces. From the start, his new line sold best in the west and the sunbelt, where the lifestyle is casual.

Famolare maintains company offices in Manhattan, Vermont and Florence, Italy. All the shoes are manufactured in Italy and shipped to Boston or flown by plane to Hartford, where they are transported to the company's distribution headquarters in Brattleboro, Vermont.

In the early 1980s, Famolare changed some of his marketing strategy by broadening his line to attract men and women over 30. He made the wavy sole into a "classic," that is, a shoe like the loafer, the sandal, or the pump, which have such broad and basic appeal that they survive shifts in fashion.

In addition to his knack for designing new styles, Famolare is a master of promotion. Even before he introduced the "Get There," he accompanied two dozen Sardinian dancers and musicians on a 2-week tour of the United States, drawing publicity for the company during stops from Rockefeller Center to the Golden Gate Bridge. The company has sponsored hot-air balloon races, footraces, and 3-day festivals. Famolare himself once participated in a promotion stunt by roller skating atop a float in a Minneapolis parade. He even employs a clown-magician whose job is to enliven the normally somnolent shoe departments of retail stores by pulling shoes out of hats.

In all his efforts, Famolare is trying to link his shoes with the current interest in personal health and the outdoors. In its advertising, the company concentrates on walking comfort, and it has been tying its shoes into the promotion of outdoor events such as jogging and hot-air ballooning.

Famolare has also been selling the shoes under his own designer label. Nearly 100 stores are licensed to use his name. He expects the use of the designer label and the mystique that surrounds it to help distinguish Famolare shoes from those of his chain-store imitators.

A further planned strategy is to market the shoes in Japan and to put more effort into the largely untapped market in the northeast. His biggest retailers seem confident that the new styles and imaginative promotion will result in vigorous sales, and they are betting on him with large initial orders. Moreover, many retailers contend that there is a lot of vitality left in wavy soles. It may prove impossible to turn wavy soles into a classic shoe, but Famolare has demonstrated that he is an imaginative entrepreneur who, like the magician he sends around to stores, can always pull a new shoe out of his hat. "They'll be wearing my shoe in corporate offices in Manhattan," he insists, "and once I have them they won't leave me."

Adapted from Stephen Solomon, "A Ride to Golconda in a Wavy Shoe Sole," *Fortune*, July 30, 1979, pp. 104–106.

a. Describe how Famolare used the marketing concept first in the original design of the wavy sole shoes and then later in its modifications.

b. Describe Famolare's strategies for product, place, and promotion. Do you have additional suggestions for him regarding these three aspects of the marketing mix?

c. Why do you suppose Famolare has the shoes manufactured in Italy? What challenges will he face if he decides to market shoes in Japan? In the American northeast?

UNIT 2

THE MARKET

CHAPTER 3

IDENTIFYING AND SEGMENTING MARKETS

A local automobile dealer has just planned a training session for sales people to work on techniques for selling cars to women. The female editor of a magazine for women has been invited to talk to the automobile dealers in a large city about how to treat women customers. Regional dealer sales meetings for one manufacturer are designed to help the dealers market to women. Another company is holding car clinics for women as a customer service. What is happening? The automobile industry has recognized women as an important consumer target market. Marketers are influenced by facts like these.

1. Women annually spend an estimated $30 billion for new cars.

2. Women buy or have a major influence on at least half of all car purchases.

3. Women account for 39 percent of new car purchases annually.

4. In 1980, 55 percent of the buyers of Buick Regals were women.

5. A *Woman's Day* survey showed that 85 percent of new car purchases involve women.

6. The number of women car buyers doubled between 1967 and 1977.

7. In 1981, the Ford Motor Company predicted that 55 percent of Ford EXP buyers would be women.[1]

Obviously, the automobile industry realizes that women have identifiable needs and wants in cars. Although no specific car is branded as a "woman's" car, the marketer can identify women's preferences and characteristics as a market and develop special strategies to appeal to them. The automobile industry is working hard to identify and reach the women's market.

MARKET IDENTIFICATION

The marketing concept states that a business seeks to determine the needs and wants of target markets and to satisfy customers in those markets while meeting the profit goals of the firm. Every marketer must give a lot of thought to the implications of this basically simple idea. Marketers are successful only if they satisfy customers at a profit. Customers are people: individuals, groups, and organizations. People are the key element in market identification. When specific groups of people are identified by their many and varied characteristics, these market groups may be combined into market segments. The marketer is then challenged to select a strategy or strategies that will be effective in satisfying a target market. The whole process of market identification begins with answering the question, What is a market?

What Is a Market?

A market always includes people, but these people must have certain qualifications to be thought of as a market for products or services. They must have needs and wants that are not satisfied, and they must have the purchasing power to buy the products and services that satisfy them. For example, a consumer who wants a high-priced sports car but has no money does not constitute a complete market. The missing part of this market is the consumer's ability to pay for the car. The purchasing power is not there. Therefore, a very practical definition of a **market** includes people with the purchasing power and the willingness to buy specific products and services.

A market may include one person or a large group of people who have similar needs and wants or who buy together. For example, several people who want to jog for fun and for health reasons would create a market for athletic shoes designed for jogging. A family of five might decide together to purchase a television set. People in businesses or other types of organizations also are part of a market. A school system that buys chairs for classrooms is part of a market that would include all school systems as potential buyers of certain types of chairs. Marketers are always interested in how many people are available to become part of a market.

Purchasing power means that people have the money to spend to get what they want. In the case of organizations, purchasing power is used by a person who has the authority to spend the organization's money. This idea could apply as well to a family in which the parents have authorized the children to spend a certain amount of family money on clothing.

The most challenging part of identifying a market is often the determination of people's willingness to buy. People and organizations have wants and needs that relate to specific products and services. The marketer must try to find out what people want. If the marketer can determine what people would like to have, specific products or services can be marketed to those people. The marketer must study the characteristics of people by trying to determine which people make up a market, where they are located, and what influences their behavior. Classifying people by types of markets is a step toward meeting this challenge.

Basic Types of Markets

Marketers design products and services to meet the demands of many different types of markets. Identification of the type of market directly influences the marketing strategies that may be used to reach that market. For example, a marketer could choose to try to sell to all the people in the United States or to all organizations of a certain type. Good marketing practice requires the early identification of two basic types of markets commonly called the consumer market and the industrial market.

The Consumer Market. All people are consumers and are part of the consumer market. The **consumer market** is made up of people who buy products and services for personal use and satisfaction. The idea of personal use includes products and services consumed by a family, household, or other consumer group. The important criterion in determining which type of market one is dealing with is the consumer's reason for the purchase. For example, a person who purchases a calculator to use at home for personal recordkeeping is part of the consumer market for calculators. In this situation, the calculator is a **consumer product** because it was purchased by the consumer for personal use. If that same calculator were purchased by a businessperson for use in an insurance office, it would be used in the industrial market and would require a somewhat different marketing strategy.

The consumer market is the largest market in terms of number of members. Although some marketers may try to appeal to all consumers, no

Figure 3-1. No single brand satisfies the entire market. Sugar-free drink mixes appeal to a particular segment.

as some schools, religious and charity groups, and social societies should be included in this market if they meet social needs and not primarily the personal needs of their members. Other industrial market members include manufacturers, contractors, mining firms, utilities, government agencies, wholesalers, retailers, and financial institutions.

The industrial market is an important potential market. However, as with the consumer market, the marketer needs to determine carefully the reasons for the purchase of a product or service. In fact, industrial market buyers are specialists in buying procedures. Their salaries and jobs often depend on purchase contracts that eventually produce a profit. This market is not only a tough competitive market, it is also larger in sales volume than the consumer market because most products are bought and sold in several industrial markets before being sold as consumer products.

single brand of product satisfies the entire market. The consumer market has so many different characteristics and influences that marketers usually attempt to reach only parts of it. To get a feel for the complexity of this market, consider the differences in consumers' ages, occupations, size of families, personalities, lifestyles, attitudes, and social groups. These characteristics of the consumer market will be discussed later in this chapter.

The Industrial Market. The insurance business that purchased a calculator for use in its office provides a good example of a member of the industrial market. The organizations in this market do not buy products for personal use. They use products and services in several ways to make a profit or, in the case of nonprofit organizations, to meet the social needs of people. The **industrial market** is made up of businesses and organizations that use products and services to run a business, to resell or to produce other products and services. The members of the industrial markets are sometimes called intermediate customers. The major members of the industrial market are producers, trade industries, governments, and nonprofit organizations. Nonprofit organizations such

MARKET SEGMENTATION

Market segmentation is an important step toward successful marketing. **Market segmentation** is the process of dividing the total market into smaller parts which include customers with similar characteristics. Each identified segment is made up of people who are more similar in behavior, lifestyles, and goals than the overall market is. For example, all consumers seek some form of recreation. This idea places all consumers in a total market, but consumers relax and have fun in many different ways. If we identified a group with similar interests, we might find a group that wants to have fun in an active, physical way. There are still many alternatives for the consumer, but we could zero in on those who like snow skiing. We then would have a smaller group with an identifiable common interest. However, if we were planning to market skiing equipment products, we would have to seek even more specific characteristics of skiers. The large number of different types of skis and equipment accessories provides evidence of the different possible segments. The marketer is faced with many decisions concerning the criteria for selecting a good segment and the

SKI RESORTS TARGET NEW MARKETS

Ski resort owners face a difficult marketing task. They must shake off the image of skiing as a sport for the young and wealthy. These upscale consumers are becoming an increasingly smaller percentage of ski resort customers. Competition is getting tougher, and resorts must increase their marketing efforts to attract new skiers in new target markets.

Aspen Ski Company in Colorado is now trying to change its image from a trendy, high-priced resort by promoting lower price and using appeals to short-stay, cost-conscious skiers. Skiers from Denver are being offered a 30 percent discount on lodging, skiing, and air fare if they book on Tuesday for the following weekend.

Vail Associates Inc. is going after the middle-aged market, some of which has dropped out of skiing. Vail hopes to appeal to skiing's senior citizens—the over-40 market—by stressing value and emphasizing safety.

Keystone Resort in Colorado also hopes to tap the older market. It sent word to its ad agency that models should have a few gray hairs. Keystone is grooming its slopes to appeal to an older crowd by smoothing the moguls (bumps) on the ski runs. Free lifetime passes are given to skiers who are over 70.

Waterville Valley in New Hampshire is enticing young families to ski by introducing a nursery program for very young skiers. In Colorado, Steamboat and Telluride resorts let children under 12 ski free when accompanied by an adult. Other resorts are designing beginners' runs that are located closer to main runs so that families can stay closer together.

Ski resorts are good examples of service marketers who are affected by geographic location, snow conditions, and the number of skiers in the market. These marketers are taking a serious look at new target markets and market segmentation.

Based on information obtained from "Restyling Skiing's Trendy Image," *Business Week*, November 29, 1982, pp. 107–108.

bases for segmentation. Read the story above that tells how ski resorts, which are service marketers, have targeted new markets.

Criteria for Market Segmentation

Marketers can use four criteria for selecting market segments. The marketer should have answers to one or more of these questions.

- Is the segment measurable?
- Is it large enough?
- Is it reachable?
- Is it responsive?

Potential segments can then be rated on the basis of these questions. The best segment would produce positive answers to all four questions.

MEASURING THE LAWN-CARE MARKET SEGMENT IN YOUR COMMUNITY

The number of consumers in a market who have lawns to care for may be quite measurable. The problem may be to determine what percentage of these consumers have a lifestyle and value system that motivate them to keep their lawns free from weeds. Although it is not easy, the marketer must arrive at some useful measure of a potentially profitable segment. Read the list of demographic and psychographic measures in the "what if?" questions below.

What if you want to start a lawn-care service business in your community? You will need both demographic data and psychographic data to identify target markets.

Demographics

What is the size of the population?

What is the consumer purchasing power?

How many consumer residence lawns?

What is the community's economic condition?

How many business lawns?

What is the climate and the growing season?

Psychographics

Do the consumers want attractive lawns?

Can they learn new lifestyle behavior?

Are they interested in outdoor living?

Do they want to improve and change?

Are they proud of their homes?

Do they have a good self-image?

Will they respond to a new service?

Will business people set a good social example?

Measurable. Some important bases for segmentation are easily identified and measured. If you wanted to market a product to women over 60 years of age who live in a certain geographic territory, you could determine the number of consumers in this group through published economic and statistical data. Population figures, income groups, size and number of families, occupations, and educational levels are examples of measurable characteristics. People's personalities, lifestyles, and self-concepts may have to be analyzed, and these factors are very difficult to measure.

Large Enough. A segment must have enough numbers of potential customers to be able to generate a profitable sales volume. However, this numerical goal is always looked at in the context of the type of product involved. If you were marketing $42,000 automobiles, you would need fewer buyers in your segment than if you were marketing $6,000 automobiles. You would have to sell seven lower-priced automobiles to equal the sales revenue of one expensive automobile. Another factor is competition and possible market share. You would consider the market size and growth potential before deciding to locate a new motel at an intersection where four motels are located. The critical size factor is the number of customers you can pull to your product or service.

Reachable. The most reachable segment for a specific marketer would be made up of consumers who are not buying from the marketing channels this marketer uses. A marketer of food products may already sell through supermarkets. A different food product aimed at a different segment could be displayed near existing products. Promotional efforts could be sent through existing media. Any identifiable segment is potentially reachable, but marketers must be able to answer two questions: How can we communicate with this segment? and How much will it cost? Of course, the decision involves the final test: profitability.

Responsive. This criterion really relates to one element of the definition of a market: Are the people in the segment willing to buy? Can the marketer develop a marketable product or service and a marketing program that have a perceived advantage over other products or services? The challenge to the marketer is to learn what consumers need and want but are not able to buy and then design a product or service to bridge that difference. Consumers are responsive when their needs and wants are satisfied. Serious joggers have been very responsive to athletic shoes designed for the special needs of jogging.

Bases for Market Segmentation

After one studies the criteria for market segmentation, t becomes apparent that identifying effective market segments can be difficult. Marketing practice includes the relatively simple methods of trial and error, intuition, and copying what other marketers do. These methods may produce very good segments, but they often are ineffective. Markets are complex and constantly changing. Marketers need to use the best methods available to identify segments. Although no single method is best or always works in all situations, four bases of segmentation are commonly used: demographic, geographic, psychographic, and behavioral. Table 3-1 shows some bases for segmentation of a product market.

Demographic Segmentation. When **demographics** is used for segmentation, the market is divided into groups on the basis of variables

TABLE 3-1
THE CONSUMER MARKET—BASES FOR SEGMENTATION

Demographic	Geographic	Psychographic	Behavioral
Population numbers	Cities	Lifestyles	*Individual Influences*
	Counties	Activities	Motives
Age	States	Interests	Attitudes
Sex	Regions	Opinions	Learning
Family	Nations	Personality	Perceptions
Households	Subdivisions	Self-concept	
Income	Rural areas	Psychological	*Group Influences*
Education	SMSAs*	influences	Cultural values
Location	SCSAs*		Social stratas
	Movement		Reference groups
			Family units

*See page 71 for definitions of these terms.

such as population, age, sex, households, families, income, occupation, and education. These are the most commonly used variables for identifying segments. They are easy to quantify and relatively easy to find. They are used to determine the size and features of segments even when other bases, such as lifestyle, are used. In fact, demographic factors often need the support of other factors to determine a good segment. For example, a high income alone would not identify people in the market for expensive yachts if their interests were not related to boating. Income is important as an indication of purchasing power, which is a necessary element of a market. In spite of their limitations, demographic variables are useful and must be applied effectively by every marketer. Demographic characteristics of the consumer market are discussed in detail later in this chapter.

Geographic Segmentation.
This is probably the most obvious form of market segmentation. Where consumers live strongly affects needs, wants, and behavioral patterns. Subdivisions, cities, counties, states, regions, and nations become the bases for geographic segmentation. Products are often related to geographic regions where either snow or sunshine is present most of the year. Products designed for the consumers in a specific city, such as shirts that say I ♥ N.Y., are good examples. Magazines are printed with special copies for certain geographic regions; marketers' advertisements are included to appeal to that region. Clothing preferences are influenced by the western outdoors region or by the eastern urban region. Obviously, geographic location factors suggest consumers with similar characteristics, but further analysis may be necessary to identify subsegments with specific interests and lifestyles.

Psychographic Segmentation.
Marketers are increasingly interested in developing a psychographic profile of a market segment. **Psychographics** includes such factors as lifestyle, personality, self-concept, and other psychological influences on consumer behavior. This method suggests that people within one demographic or geographic group will display many different psychographic characteristics. For example, lifestyle research determines people's activities, interests, and opinions (AIOs). The lifestyle profile of a jogger might reveal the activity of running 6 miles every day, an interest in being outdoors, and an opinion that running leads to a healthy mind and body. Joggers make up an excellent market for special clothing and running shoes. When these AIO measures are used, lifestyle profiles are developed which identify the similar characteristics of lifestyle groups. Sports, hobbies, travel, fashion, home, family, and community are some examples. Although difficult to measure, psychographic variables are useful and important to marketers. They will be analyzed in depth later in this chapter.

Behavioral Segmentation.
In this method of segmentation, consumers are grouped according to their responses to product or service features and the benefits desired. Another commonly used factor is the rate of use of a product or service by customers. For example, heavy users of a brand may have measurable characteristics that are different from those of light users or nonusers. A marketer could segment on the basis of the heavy users of a brand and continue to promote product features that appeal to them effectively. Identification of the characteristics of the nonusers might reveal why they do not like the brand and reveal the features of a slightly different brand that might be appealing.

Many marketers feel that behavioral segmentation through the use of desired benefits is the most effective method of segmentation. It obviously fits the basic marketing concept. You can see how effective the method might be by considering the benefits that are desired in a toothpaste. You probably think of such benefits as decay prevention, good taste, and teeth whitening. Thus, it is no surprise that the leading toothpaste brands have product features that provide those specific desired benefits.

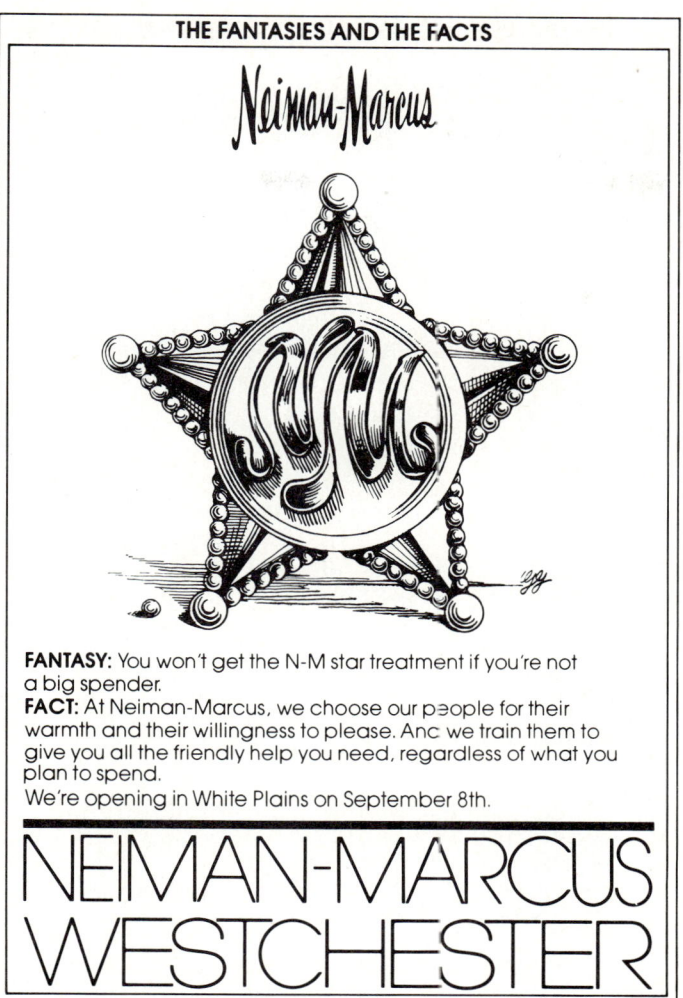

Figure 3-2. Psychographic and behavioral characteristics may include thriftiness and a positive reaction to friendly service.

Identifying Target Markets

Every marketer begins a business with the goal of trying to serve customers in better or different ways than other marketers. Successful marketers know that they must understand the characteristics of their potential market. They must aim the marketing mix at specific customer groups to have the opportunity to make a profit. Therefore, identifying and selecting target markets are very important tasks for all marketers.

Marketing strategies that are aimed at *everybody* in a total market are seldom if ever successful. Think of some of the best selling product brands. You probably thought of such brands as Coca-Cola, Pepsi-Cola, Crest, and Kleenex. Not one of these brands satisfies all the customers in any market because each total market is made up of several and often hundreds of small market segments.

Target marketing is a technique in which the seller identifies the different customer segments

REACHING TARGETS, COMMUNICATING VALUE ARE CHALLENGES TO MARKETERS

Reaching target markets effectively and making consumers see the practical value of new technologies are two of the biggest challenges facing marketers, according to Stuart D. Watson, consultant to and former chairman of Heublein Inc., Farmington, Conn.

"Until consumers are convinced that a product or service adds value to their lives, it isn't going to sell," he said in a convocation address at DePauw University, Greencastle, Ind. "Finding true value and demonstrating it convincingly are the jobs of the skillful marketer."

If the value is to be communicated, Watson said, the marketer must know how to reach the right audience and what to say to that audience. That requires marketing research on changing public attitudes which are reflected in changing lifestyles and consumer buying intentions.

"The needs and wants of the consumer, to be addressed in the marketing message, and the choice of media are two of the principal factors in determining marketing communication," he said. "They are decisive in target marketing, which is the hottest development in marketing today, and it's being driven by changes in the marketplace, changes in demographics and economics.

"There is no communication if no one is getting the message. Communication doesn't begin with the speaker, it begins with the receiver."

Zeroing in on the right target has become more important as the discretionary dollars of U.S. consumers have dwindled. More products than ever before are competing for those dollars, and there are more avenues than ever before available to impart information about those products to consumers.

Adapted from *Marketing News*, American Marketing Association, December 10, 1982, p. 10.

and selects one or more as specific targets. A marketing mix is then designed to appeal to each of these segments. The benefit to the customers in each segment is products and services that better satisfy their needs and wants. The benefit to the marketers is more total sales and profits from satisfying selected segments than there would be if the attempt were made to satisfy the total market.

Target marketing is a very important technique for marketers of any size to master. Read the above article in which a marketing consultant gives many good reasons why reaching target markets is so important. Increased costs of business operations, more educated customers, intense competition, and computer-supported information processing are some of the important reasons why marketers are using target marketing today. Possibly the best reason is that target marketing fits the marketing concept so well: to satisfy customers and to make a fair profit.

Target Marketing Strategies

Marketers' strategies involve many different marketing offerings, such as brands, models, prices, and unique features, in relation to the size of the market. At one extreme, the marketer offers essentially one product or one service for all the customers in a total market. At the other extreme, the marketer offers a lot of product or service variations to a relatively small segment of the market. Between these extremes, many possible variations of product and service combinations exist. All these possibilities present opportunities for target marketing because marketers can aim at specific and clearly defined target markets. Marketers classify target marketing strategies as undifferentiated, differentiated, and concentrated. These strategies are illustrated in Figure 3-3 on page 66. Each strategy is useful in some situations, but no one strategy is best in all situations.

Undifferentiated Marketing.
Marketers who use the strategy of **undifferentiated marketing** do not market to different segments. The undifferentiated technique involves the use of one product and one marketing approach that will appeal to the largest number of people in the market. The marketer tries to hit the average needs of these people. This strategy seems to work best with items that have a few basic features, such as gasoline, paper towels, coffee, cola beverages, and household cleaners. Generally, the customer perceives very little difference between competing brands. The differences may consist of only promoted but not obvious features, including packaging, brand names, and advertising. The marketer believes that customers do not expect a product to be perfectly matched to their needs. These customers seem willing to accept a product that is close enough to be useful.

One of the most important advantages of undifferentiated marketing is the potentially lower cost of production. Efficiency resulting from mass production may keep costs down. Another benefit results from fewer design changes. The lowest priced disposable Bic and Papermate ballpoint pens provide good examples. Promotional campaigns may be cost efficient as well because one basic idea is often used for the total market. Media discounts may be available because of large and repetitive market usage. The most serious potential disadvantage for the marketer using the undifferentiated strategy relates to competition. If the marketer is very successful, competitors will move in to share the success. If the marketer is not filling needs closely enough, competitors will arrive in the market to close the gap between what people want and what they are getting.

Differentiated Marketing.
A strategy that increasing numbers of marketers are using is called **differentiated marketing.** With this strategy, the marketer identifies several different segments in the market and supplies different products and programs for each segment. The marketer attempts to provide products to better match the needs and wants of specific types of customers. For example, consumers have hundreds of varieties of shampoos to choose from. Even one marketer's brand will offer several choices depending on the consumer's type of hair and preferences. Cameras and automobiles are other good examples.

The obvious goal of a differentiated strategy is to create more sales than would result from an undifferentiated strategy. This is often the result because most customers are more satisfied with specific products. Customer loyalty to a specific brand may be higher, and better repeat purchases may be the advantageous result for the marketer. A better share of the market may be achieved for the total of all brands in a product category. As in most marketing situations, a better strategy for improved sales results also increases the cost of doing business. Differentiated marketing usually increases production, inventory, promotion, and administrative costs because the marketer is working with more brands. However, increased costs are not a serious disadvantage if increased sales revenues produce increased profits.

Concentrated Marketing. The strategy of aiming at one market segment in an attempt to market the best possible product and service mix is known as **concentrated marketing.** The goal is a strong market share in a very specific segment. The type of segment can vary a lot. The appeal may be high price, status, economy, power, or many other possibilities. For example, Timex appealed initially to consumers who wanted a low-priced, dependable watch; Accutron continues to appeal to a higher-priced, status market; Hewlett-Packard markets only higher-priced, high-quality calculators; and Gerber has concentrated on marketing products for babies.

The principal advantage of concentrated marketing is the outstanding reputation a marketer may achieve as a specialist for a certain market. This advantage can lead to higher profits and a good return on investment. The primary disadvantage is the risk of the customers in one segment changing their demands and turning away from the product. Basically, this is a risk accepted by most marketers, and it often leads to diversifying into several markets with other products.

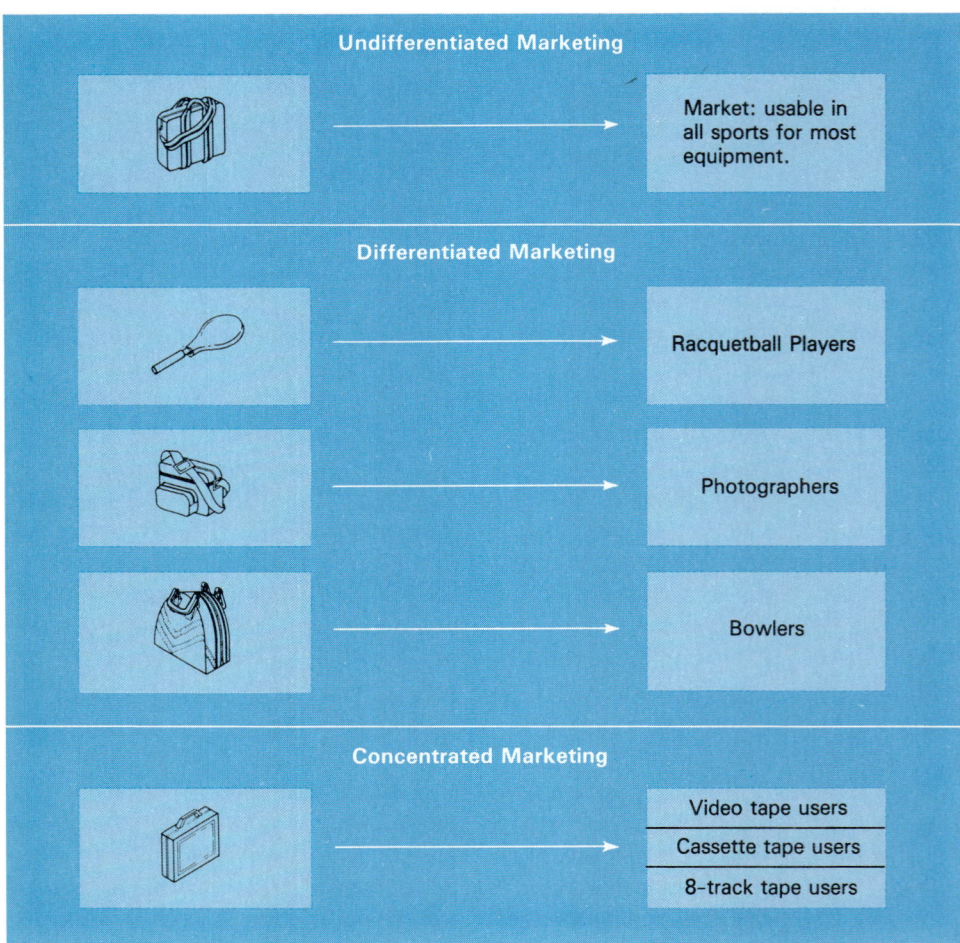

Figure 3-3. Target marketing strategies. Products such as suitcases, special racquet covers, camera cases, bowling bags, and tape carriers require different marketing strategies.

A MARKET FOR A PAN WITH A HOLE IN ITS MIDDLE

H. David Dalquist is the founder of the Minneapolis-based company that makes Nordic Ware cookware. Along the way, he managed to create a $35 million company and boost the fortunes of a local food-processing giant on the strength of an unassuming little aluminum pan with a hole in the middle.

Dalquist and his brother were setting up a small aluminum castings business near Minneapolis. Several women from Hadassah, a Jewish women's service organization, asked Mr. Dalquist if he could include among his line something they called a "bund" pan ("bund" meaning something on the order of "fellowship"), which was used to make an old world-style cake. The pan Mr. Dalquist subsequently renamed the Bundt pan was vaguely similar to an angel food cake pan, only bigger and with fluted, curved sides.

On the face of it the Bundt pan did not seem like a real breakthrough product, and indeed sales were not spectacular for the first 10 years or so. Enter the mass media. Within a 1-year period, around 1961 or so, *McCall's, Good Housekeeping,* and *Better Homes & Gardens* devoted major spreads to the uses of the Bundt pan, which offered the single advantage of eliminating a lot of the work that a layer cake required. Sales mushroomed.

A few years later Pillsbury Co. and Land O' Lakes began offering the Bundt pan as a premium, and in 1969 Pillsbury decided to make a special line of mixes intended for use with the pan. Pan and mix were displayed side by side in stores.

"They thought they would have reasonable success but they were totally unprepared for what happened," Dalquist says. "The demand was something like 6 to 10 times higher than their fondest expectations." Pillsbury discovered that the pan and mix, sold together, outsold the mix sold alone by 3 to 1.

Adapted from Ed Zotti, "Ideas Brew in Inventors' Kitchens," *Advertising Age,* July 12, 1982, p. M-10.

THE CONSUMER MARKET

Consumer markets are dynamic, by which we mean they are energetic, forceful, and always changing. Our discussions on markets, target marketing, and market segmentation have emphasized the critical importance of the marketer's constant analysis of markets. Now we shall look at the consumer characteristics that are used in demographic segmentation. Next we shall examine some consumer characteristics that are involved in psychographic segmentation. Then we shall explore consumer behavior by using a problem-solving model that focuses on individual and group influences on consumer behavior. Marketers should be able to describe a market and understand consumer behavior. These are essential abilities leading to the satisfaction of consumers in the marketplace. The above story about the development of a market for the Bundt pan provides a good example of a marketer's response to the demands of consumers.

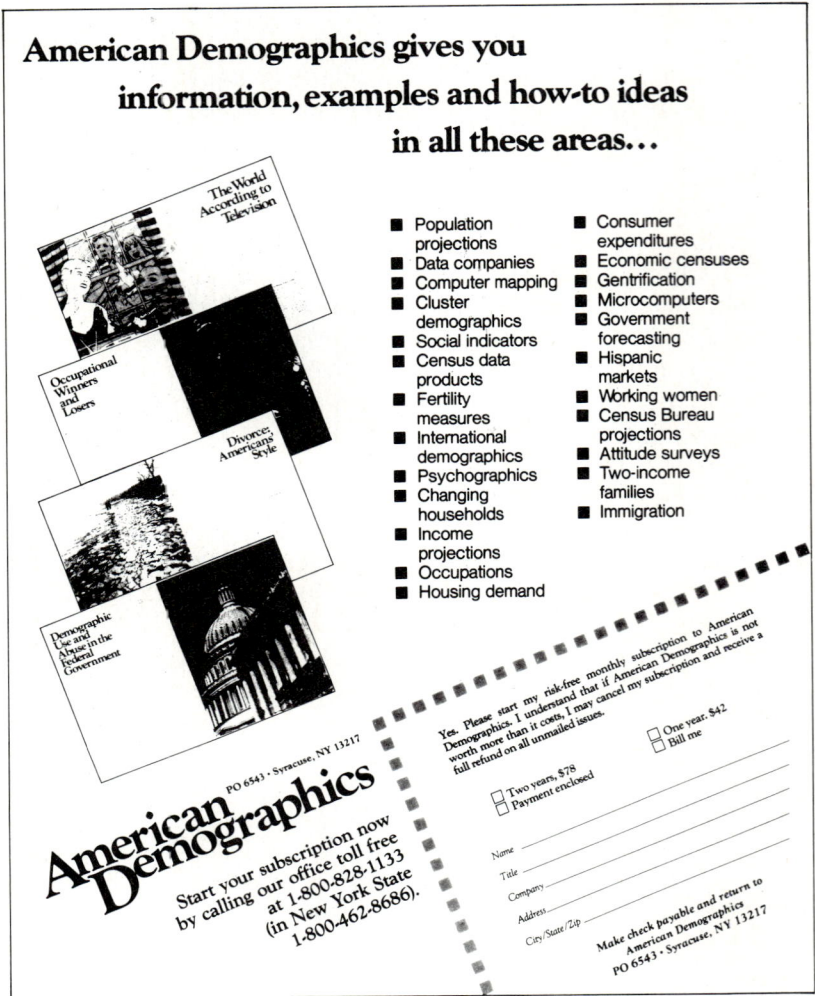

Figure 3-4. *American Demographics* **is a good source for demographic data and marketing ideas.**

Demographic Characteristics of Consumers

Marketers watch the numbers and trends in demographics in an attempt to analyze and predict changes in their markets. Demographic characteristics of consumers in general in the United States are important, and these national trends are also relevant to regional and local markets. Sometimes national changes predict what will be occurring in certain smaller markets. A starting point for all marketers is to understand the use of national and large-area demographic measures. Marketers should then learn to study and measure the demographics within their identified markets. We shall look now at the eight most commonly used demographic variables: population, age, sex, family, households, income, education, and geographic location. (See Figure 3-4, which shows demographic topics as discussed in the valuable publication *American Demographics*. Notice such topics as population projections, income projections, changing households, and occupations.

Population. Marketers are interested in population numbers and trends. The number of people in a market suggests how many will be demanding products and services. For the marketer, a steadily increasing population would be ideal. The population of the United States is over 220 million and is predicted to reach 245 million by 1990. Marketers like a high birthrate because babies mean new consumers and new business. Actually, the rate of population growth has been decreasing because of a lower birthrate. Several factors have contributed to the declining birthrate: fewer marriages, increased acceptance of birth control, and the changing role of women in society. Some analysts predict continued population growth in the United States because of increased immigration and a decline in the death rate. If the rate of population growth decreases in a specific market, marketers can no longer rely on significantly increasing numbers to cause higher sales and profits. If this happens, effective market segmentation and target marketing become even more critical.

Age. Marketers are interested in the number of people in various age groups and the changing trends in the age mix. Because there are now fewer young people and more older people, the average age of the U.S. consumer is going to rise for several years. There will be a significant decrease in the number of people through 19 years of age and a very large increase in the 35 to 54 age group and the 65 and over group. The increase in middle-aged adults is a good factor for marketers. This is the age of high income and big spending. The increase in older people suggests increases in the marketing of health-care services, medicines, special housing, and new types of recreational opportunities. Because of some similarities of behavior, the segmentation of the consumer market by age groups is practical for many products.

Sex. Marketing either to women or to men is a common segmentation strategy. However, some consumer behavior patterns are changing. The principal cause for this phenomenon has been the changing role of women. In fact, we shall notice this effect in the family, household, and income variables as well. The young woman of today will work longer, marry later, and begin having children later. She will continue to be independent and make her own purchasing decisions. When married, she will make decisions with equal authority with her husband. As indicated in the story that opened this chapter, the automobile industry is an excellent example of marketers who are appealing to women as a market segment. For example, several models of the Ford Mustang are designed to meet the preferences of women owners and drivers.

Family. A **family** is a group of two or more related persons. The family is the most important consumer group for the marketer. All the activities and stages of family development create markets and demand for products and services. Marriage, children, home purchases, vacations, moves, and many other family activities present new product demand situations for marketers. Obviously, marketers are extremely concerned about trends and changes in family formation and structure. The trend in the United States is toward fewer children per family unit. The causes for this phenomenon relate to several demographic variables but include later marriage, higher divorce rate, planned parenthood, and more working wives. The result is not necessarily fewer sales, but the nature of the market is changing. Actually, smaller families with two incomes may mean increased markets for luxury products. Higher-quality products and status items should sell better. Vacation services and leisure products should appeal to the new type of family. The most obvious positive effect may be on housing types and home furnishings.

Households. A **household** is a person or persons, related or unrelated, occupying the same housing unit. A person living alone is a household, and a family is considered a household. The number of households in the United States is increasing faster than the total population. This

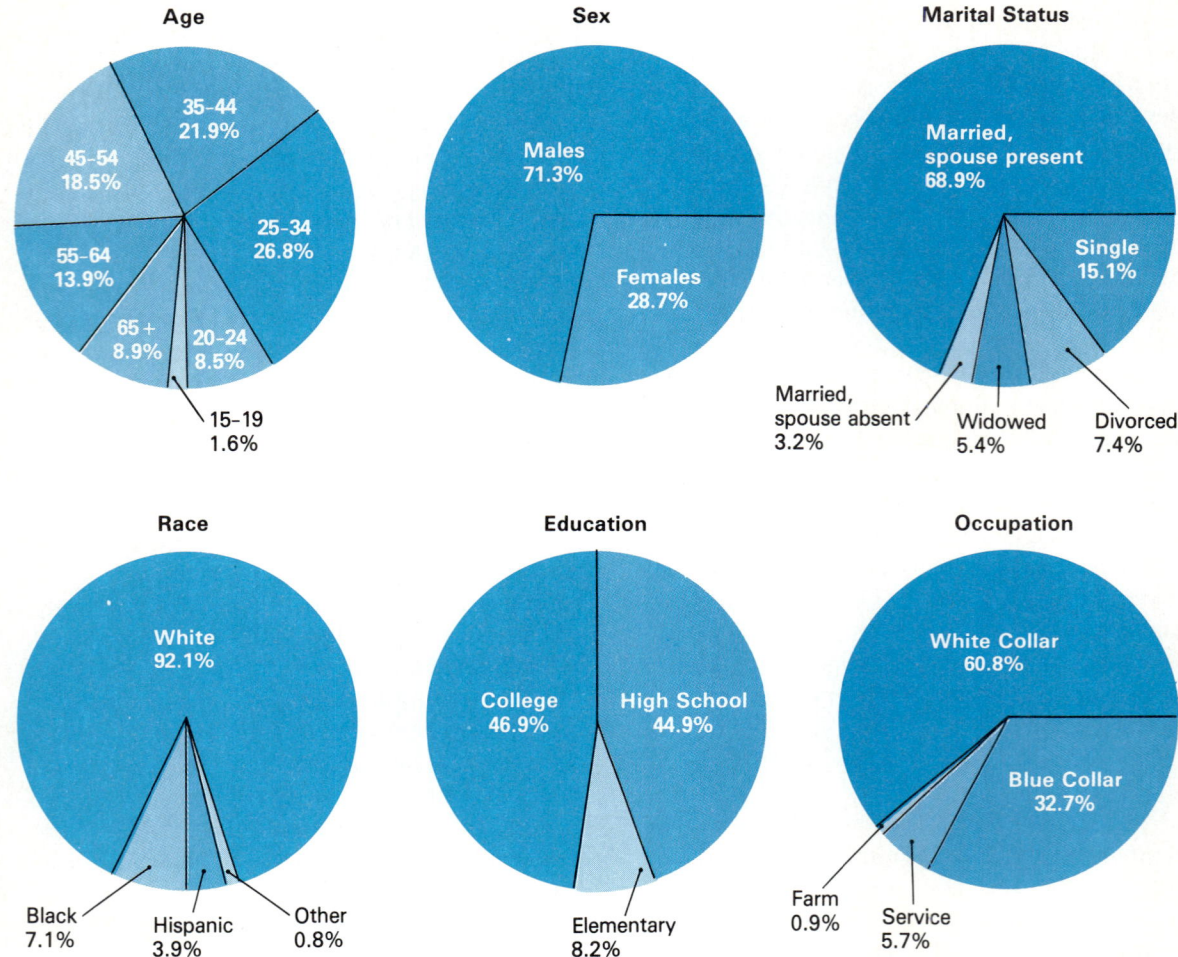

Figure 3-5. Demographics—income. How the consumer income pie is split by age, sex, marital status, race, education, and occupation.

relative increase is significant for marketers. Demand is increasing for certain products, such as home appliances, automobiles, housing units, home furnishings, and utilities. Household measures reveal differences between family and non-family households. Marketers are interested in the needs of the SSWD group, which refers to single, separated, widowed, and divorced consumer households. Such households tend to buy food in smaller quantities, buy less expensive and smaller appliances, and buy different types of furniture and furnishings. Some household groups, such as

college students and young workers living together, need to be studied for their behavior as a consuming unit. Apparently, the increasing number of households and the corresponding one-person household are market characteristics that will be important for a long time.

Income. Because people with purchasing power are good potential buyers, income is a common basis for segmenting markets. Marketers often aim their products at specific income levels: high, middle, and low. The trend in the United

States is toward higher income for the average household, with an increase in middle- and higher-income groups and a decrease in the number of low-income consumers. The middle-income market is a growing and significant one for marketers. Marketers can respond by upgrading the quality of products, offering additional services, and offering more luxury items. In spite of inflationary pressures, the consumer's **real income** (the total purchasing power of income) has been increasing. This means more discretionary purchasing power for the typical household. **Discretionary purchases** (sports cars, fashion clothing, recreation, and vacations) are purchases a consumer can make after paying for necessities. Marketers need to study consumer spending patterns as well as the distribution of income. The important trend for marketers to recognize is the effect on behavior when more money is available after necessities are purchased. Figure 3-5 shows income percentages for demographic groups.

Education. Marketers now are interacting with increasingly better-educated consumers. In general, these better-educated consumers want higher-quality products and services. Consumers not only are staying in educational programs longer (more high school and college graduates), they also are learning more through television, radio, newspapers, magazines, and books. The implications of these trends for marketers are many. Better-educated consumers will recognize value in relation to price. They will understand communication better, and so advertising will have to be accurate and informative. Exaggerated claims will be less effective. Products will have to be marketed to meet consumers' expectations. Study the ad from *Black Enterprise* magazine in Figure 3-6 on page 72. Notice the use of several demographic data percentages, especially educational factors. In this ad, the marketer has presented a demographic profile of customers.

Geographic Location. Geographic location may be a basis for segmentation by itself, but it is useful as a demographic measure as well. Marketers realize that a population is not evenly distributed throughout a market and that consumer behavior is affected by where a consumer lives. These ideas were presented in the earlier section on geographic segmentation in this chapter. The additional ideas that are important relate to the geographic movement of population. For example, approximately 12 to 15 percent of Americans move each year. Each move creates new market demands and consumer decisions that have to be made in a short time. New marketers have to be found by the consumers for household goods, food, services, and clothing. Consumer movement tends to reflect changing lifestyles and values. For several years in the United States, consumers have been moving from colder climates to warmer areas, from rural to urban areas, and from the central city to the suburbs. More recently, there has been some movement back to the central city with its improved recreational and cultural opportunities. Some movement to rural areas and small towns is in evidence, and this suggests consumer interest in more natural and simpler lifestyles.

Many sources of data are available to help marketers stay current on consumer location trends. One source is the "Survey of Buying Power" published annually by *Sales & Marketing Management* magazine, which groups population and purchasing power data by metropolitan areas. The U.S. Bureau of the Census is another excellent source of consumer location data grouped into Standard Metropolitan Statistical Areas (SMSAs). An **SMSA** consists of an integrated economic and social unit containing one city of at least 50,000 people or two cities with a combined population of at least 50,000. There are 305 SMSAs which account for approximately 75 percent of the U.S. population. The consumer move to metropolitan areas is recognized by the U.S. Bureau of the Census, which identifies 15 super-cities as Standard Consolidated Statistical Areas (SCSAs). Each **SCSA** contains one SMSA with a population of 1 million or more and one or more adjoining SMSAs. More than one-third of the U.S. population resides in these 15 SCSAs. Additional sources of demographic data are presented in Chapter 4.

Figure 3-6. Magazine ads recognize the importance of meeting the expectations of better-educated consumers.

Psychographic Characteristics of Consumers

One of the newest trends in the analysis of consumer markets is the use of psychographic characteristics. These characteristics include measures of lifestyle, personality, and self-concept. Demographics is very useful in studying consumers, but it does not reveal anything substantial about interests, likes and dislikes, and personality traits. Psychographic characteristics are more difficult to obtain and measure, but today's marketers are finding them worth the effort for understanding and marketing to the consumer. To understand the use of psychographics by a service marketer, read the article about cable TV subscribers on the opposite page. These consumers' interests and opinions will influence the marketer's service offering.

Lifestyle. Consumers' **lifestyles** include things they do, things they are interested in, and their values and concerns about living. Lifestyle research, which is also called psychographic

PSYCHOGRAPHICS ON CABLE TV SERVICE SUBSCRIBERS: WHAT DO THEY WANT?

Cable TV subscribers want news, music, and safety services, according to a series of marketing research reports prepared by the ELRA Group, East Lansing, Michigan.

The findings are based on more than 9,000 telephone interviews in 23 new cable markets nationwide. The interviews were part of the firm's CableMark surveys, conducted for cable operators who want to assess community needs.

National and international news was a stated interest of 80 percent of those interviewed, 72 percent said they were interested in a channel featuring contemporary music, and 81 percent wanted a fire and burglar alarm system. Another 75 percent desired a "medical alert service."

Other service offerings, and the relative interest in them, were as follows.

- Local weather reports, 68%;
- Cultural programming, 62%;
- Las Vegas club acts, 61%;
- Black entertainers channel, 54%;
- Children's programs, 53%;
- Women's programs, 52%;
- Sports channel, 46%;
- Stock market prices, 46%;
- Religious programs, 34%;
- Spanish-language movies, 25%; and
- Shopping channel, 17%.

"The high degree of interest in contemporary music is especially interesting," remarked Robert LaRose, ELRA's research director. "Recently announced programming efforts in this area may only be scratching the surface of a huge potential market.

"There seems to be a great appetite for news. On the other hand, sports do not appear to be a big draw for new subscribers."

A variety of local programming opportunities also exist, according to the CableMark surveys. High interest was expressed in receiving courses for credit (65 percent) and in viewing public access programs (63 percent).

Other local programming opportunities include cablecasting proceedings of state legislatures (57 percent) and current job opening listings (54 percent).

Pay television services apparently have an eager market, according to a recent study in Southern California. Potential subscribers wanted to subscribe to an average of four pay services, with some households wanting as many as nine pay services.

The most popular pay services are viewdata, pay movies, pay-per-view movies, sports, and Broadway plays.

Adapted from *Marketing News*, American Marketing Association, Nov. 27, 1981, p. 12.

research, involves measures of activities, interests, and opinions (AIOs). Consumers are given hundreds of AIO statements and are asked to respond by selecting alternatives that run from "definitely agree" to "definitely disagree." Here are some examples.

I enjoy participating in sports.
People should attend church every week.
Foreign-built cars are better than U.S. cars.
Smoking should be prevented by law.
Riding a motorcycle is exciting.
Television commercials are very helpful to consumers.
In general, people are becoming less moral.
A fun evening is reading a book.
Shopping with friends is better than shopping alone.
The best programs on television are sports broadcasts.
There is too much sex and violence on television.

Based on the answers to hundreds of statements like these, patterns of consumer lifestyles can be determined. Consumers can be grouped into lifestyle types, and different marketing appeals can be made to each type. Individual consumers do not have identical lifestyles, but those who have similar lifestyles can be grouped into target segments. See Table 3-2 for examples. Characteristics of each of these consumer types can be studied. Then a marketing strategy for a specific product can be planned to appeal to one or more of the types. For example, the appeal to the family man for marketing a camera could be to use it to take pictures of the members of his family. Food product appeals to single people and to parents might have to be quite different because of their different interests and activities. Marketers can use these general lifestyle studies as guides to identifying their customer groups.

Personality. Marketers generally have been successful at using personality traits to develop product appeals that interest specific consumers. Personality is believed to affect a consumer's buying behavior. For example, would a Pontiac Trans-Am and a Chevrolet Chevette appeal to different personalities? Do different clothing styles appeal to different consumer personalities? Personality is difficult to define in a practical way, but it relates to marketers' products and services. It may be described as an internal

TABLE 3-2
LIFESTYLE DIMENSIONS

Activities	Interests	Opinions	Demographics
Work	Family	Themselves	Age
Hobbies	Home	Social issues	Education
Social events	Job	Politics	Income
Vacation	Community	Business	Occupation
Entertainment	Recreation	Economics	Family size
Club membership	Fashion	Education	Dwelling
Community	Food	Products	Geography
Shopping	Media	Future	City size
Sports	Achievements	Culture	Stage in life cycle

Source: Joseph T. Plummer, "The Concept and Application of Life-Style Segmentation," *Journal of Marketing*, January 1974, pp. 33–37.

system that influences a person's thoughts and behavior. We believe that personality causes one to respond with a certain amount of consistency to similar situations. Each person develops a unique pattern of traits that influence responses.

One technique frequently used by marketers to evaluate consumers' personalities is called the trait-factor approach. The consumer is observed as having a specific set of unique traits. A personality profile of a consumer can be derived from measures of such traits as shy-venturesome, relaxed-tense, joiner-independent, humble-assertive, reserved-outgoing, and practical-imaginative. There are many readily available lists of descriptive terms that are used to identify personality traits. A consumer's personality or a group's average personality may be determined by a combination of traits. One advantage of this approach is the ease with which traits can be quantified. Promotion appeals can be made to consumers who are friendly, aggressive, orderly, achievers, exhibitionists, or compliant. The image of a brand may reflect consumers' personalities. A sports car may have an aggressive image and appeal, a soft drink may suggest friendly relationships, and a household cleanser may seem tough and hardworking.

Another useful approach to personality study is referred to as psychoanalytic because it is based on an explanation of personality developed by Sigmund Freud. Freud theorized that three components make up a personality: the id, the ego, and the superego. In each person, each of these components plays a specific role in the personality and is in conflict with the other components for control of the personality. The id seeks instant satisfaction of biological instincts. It is appropriately associated with the pleasure principle because it seeks to relieve any tensions in the person quickly. The ego is the mediating part of personality. It is associated with the reality principle. It seeks to balance and control the demands of the id in relation to the long-term needs of the person. The ego relates to the things learned from experience. The third part is the superego, or the perfection principle. The superego consists of the moral and judgmental aspects of a personality. It is the conscience factor and the seeker of ideal goals. The ego works at resolving conflicts between the two personality extremes of the id and the superego. Freud's personality theory is used by marketers but is not as measurable or objective as the trait theory. Freud's theory can be related to marketing appeals that stress these ideas: have fun now, be the best you can be, buy yourself the best—you're worth it, take a vacation and escape, select a product that is durable and economical, and live life to the fullest.

Self-concept. The buying behavior of consumers often reflects the way they see themselves. The goal for marketers is to try to match a product closely with the self-concept of a consumer. Consumers' possessions and activities suggest something they want to say about themselves. In fact, much of the people's behavior is based on a goal of maintaining or improving a positive image. The most important type of self-concept may be the consumer's self-image. This is a realistic appraisal of how consumers see themselves. Some products appeal to self-image because they are practical: The clothing is right for a body type, or a cosmetic is pure and natural. The ideal self is the concept of what the consumer would like to be. The consumer may set goals to improve the ideal-self concept. For example, the ideal self would suggest books that improve skills, cosmetics that reach for more sex appeal, or clothing that is above the average in fashion. Consumers are also concerned about how others see them. This is sometimes called the other's self-concept. If this is the dominant concept, consumers purchase products that they think their friends want them to have. The selection of a socially visible product such as clothing and jewelry would be influenced by this concept.

The psychographic characteristics of lifestyle, personality, and self-concept are useful and valuable to marketers but do not explain all consumer behavior. Therefore, demographic and psychographic characteristics must be used together in various combinations in certain markets to try to understand consumers.

TABLE 3-3
AN EASY AND USEFUL CONSUMER BEHAVIOR MODEL

Steps	Consumer's Action
1. Problem recognition	My car is making a weird noise. I want to drive a dependable car.
2. Search	I could look up automobile service in the Yellow Pages. I remember two garages I have used before. I have noticed an independent service marketer on Main Street. I call my friends for recommendations.
3. Alternative evaluation	I do not want to go to new repair service companies. I did not like the service at the two garages I used before. The service marketer on Main Street looks clean and would be convenient. One of my friends highly recommends the one on Main Street.
4. Choice	I called the Main Street automobile service. They can check my car tomorrow morning.
5. Outcomes	I am satisfied with the service. The mechanics were skilled. My car runs great, and the price was fair. The customer area was clean. I will return to this marketer.

CONSUMER BEHAVIOR

Consider the following situation. You are a marketer, and a consumer makes these comments to you. "I am a potential customer of yours. Why should I buy from you? How will I benefit from a business transaction with you? I have a lot of choices in the marketplace; what is so different about your product? I do not have to buy from you. You cannot force me to buy from you." These appear to be unusually tough statements, but they are not. Consumers are independent decision makers. They see problems and try to solve them. They set goals and try to accomplish them. They want satisfaction.

Consumer behavior refers to the acts of individuals and groups in the problem-solving process of obtaining and using products and services for personal satisfaction. Consumer behavior is influenced by many personal or internal factors such as motivation, attitudes, learning abilities, and perception. The behavior of consumers is influenced also by group factors such as culture, social strata, reference groups, and family interactions.

Marketers need to understand what influences consumer behavior. They need to analyze how consumers behave and why they behave as they do. Marketers who understand consumer behavior make better marketing decisions.

Consumers as Problem Solvers

A problem for a consumer is the recognition that needs and wants are not satisfied or that a goal has not been accomplished. For example, you have a consumer problem when you remember that a friend's birthday is tomorrow. You want to please your friend, but you do not have a gift. You have a consumer problem when you learn that you are out of your favorite soft drink. You have a consumer problem when you realize that a product you have used for a long time is no longer available or is no longer satisfactory.

Consumers use a decision-making process when they solve these problems. Their behavioral goals are purposeful, and they have reasons for what they do to accomplish those goals. After a purchase is made, the consumer may learn that a better solution was available. But at the time a product was selected, it seemed to be the best solution. Remember the tough-talking consumer who cannot be forced to buy? Consumers want the freedom to choose. They want facts and advice from marketers, but they will decide how to use these factors to solve their problems.

Consumer decision making follows specific steps in consistent sequence. The decision-making process is a model of consumer behavior. The model includes five steps: problem recognition, search, alternative evaluation, choice, and outcomes. See Table 3-3 for an example.

Problem Recognition. Problem recognition is the first step, and the decision-making process cannot begin without it. It is defined as the perceived and significant difference between what a consumer wants and what that consumer has. A young woman may recognize a problem because she wants a pair of shoes like the ones her friend has. She has many pairs of shoes, but the significant difference is the new style. Part of her motivation (a frequent cause of problem recognition) is the desire to have things in common with her friends. Consumers often recognize problems because their needs and wants change even though the present product is still working. Many electronic digital watches have been purchased by consumers who owned traditional watches that kept good time. Of course, problem recognition occurs when consumers' wants stay the same while their solutions change. The most frequent

situation involves simply using up a product—toothpaste, for example. When your toothpaste is gone, you simply realize that you need to replace it with the same brand. Another common situation occurs when you realize that your present solution is not satisfactory. You still want a toothpaste that prevents decay, but you doubt that your present brand is doing this well.

Search. The second step involves the consumer's efforts to find ways to solve the recognized problem. The consumer first goes through an internal search process. This is a mental check which may lead to a purchase without any external search. For example, the consumer who is out of toothpaste may simply think about the desired benefits and confirm that the present brand is good. The search is complete in the consumer's mind, and the brand will be purchased at the first convenient opportunity. This is an efficient, routine way to search for solutions to problems: to continue to use the same product brand. Marketers like these loyal customers, and marketing strategies are designed to remind customers and to make these brands readily available. However, external search occurs when consumers decide to look for other brands or types of products as new solutions to problems. This situation leads consumers to visit stores, read ads, study TV commercials, talk with sales people, and ask friends for advice. External search is used when the consumer perceives the problem to be more serious, very complex, more expensive, a higher risk, or more important than the average situation.

Alternative Evaluation. The third step involves the study and comparison of different ways to solve the recognized problem. The external search usually leads to several ways to reach the consumer's goal of choosing a satisfactory product or service. Each alternative will have advantages and disadvantages. Often one product has unique features that are desirable while another product has equally desirable but different features. Consumers attempt to solve this problem by comparing product features with the benefits desired in a specific product. These benefits are usually specifications and criteria wanted. Consider these examples. A consumer wants a car that gets 30 miles to a gallon, a shampoo must be fragrant and mild, a coffee must be free of caffeine, and a fabric must be soft but durable. Some criteria are less measurable than others. For example, the strength of flavors in foods is a very subjective criterion and is affected by the perception of the individual consumer. Marketers help consumers evaluate alternatives by giving facts and specific product data, providing samples, giving demonstrations, and allowing trial-use periods.

Choice. If the consumer matches the desired benefits with one product, the fourth step is reached. This is the decision that one brand has the best potential to solve the problem. Many factors influence the purchase selection: the nature of the contract, method of payment, packaging and delivery, warranty, service contract, and many other point-of-purchase activities. Marketers can influence consumer choice by making these activities as attractive and efficient as possible. The choice of a specific brand may be influenced by the consumer's perception of the services provided by the store. Choice is the result of evaluating alternatives and comparing the product and service features of the best alternative with the benefits expected.

Outcomes. The fifth step in the process occurs after the purchase. Every purchase results in some measure of satisfaction or dissatisfaction. As consumers begin using the items purchased, they continue to evaluate the products and services. Satisfaction results if the purchased items live up to the consumer's expectations. This is a form of reward to the consumer for purchasing a brand from a marketer. Satisfied consumers usually will return to the same marketer to buy the same brand. Marketers receive benefits from satisfying consumers, including loyalty to the company and repeat purchase behavior.

Dissatisfaction is the outcome when a consumer's expectations are not confirmed. If this happens, consumers may return to the marketer to seek an exchange or a refund. This may give the

marketer the opportunity to satisfy a customer eventually and can be a good situation in the long run. The worst result occurs when the customer is dissatisfied with a purchase and decides never to buy from that marketer again. There are certain situations in which potential dissatisfaction is very high.

1. The purchase decision is psychologically significant.

2. Several alternative products and services have desirable but unique features.

3. The product or service will have to be used for a long time.

4. The product or service is relatively expensive for the consumer.

5. The product or service is complex, and information about it can be easily misunderstood.

6. The consumer's personality indicates a person who is often difficult to please.

You can think of many more situations that relate to specific types of products or services. For example, parents are extremely sensitive to purchase situations involving their children's safety.

Figure 3-7. Postpurchase marketing: a free sewing lesson.

The implications for marketers from a study of consumers' postpurchase outcomes are important. Consumers have so many alternatives for solving problems that the marketer may not have many opportunities to satisfy them. Marketers should continue to contact their customers during the outcomes stage. Sales people can call to check on the use of a product and offer to help. Some companies have a series of free lessons following purchase of such products as sewing machines, microwave ovens, and photographic equipment. Continuing to advertise and to send literature are important marketing actions during this postpurchase period. Customers may be placed on a mailing list for new catalogs and idea magazines for owners.

Marketers can often avoid dissatisfaction by providing accurate and useful information during the search and alternative evaluation stages. This may help the customer form realistic expectations of what the benefits of the product will be.

Individual Influences on Consumer Behavior

The problem-solving behavior of consumers is influenced by individual factors that are psychological and internal. Marketers should seek information that helps answer these questions: What motivates my customers? What are their attitudes toward my marketing mix? How do they learn? What affects their perception of products and services?

What Motivates Customers? Inner forces that help people reach their goals are referred to as **motives.** They help people become excited about doing something, and they direct people's behavior toward doing it. When consumers are motivated, they have wants and needs that are not satisfied. When these needs are satisfied, the consumer is no longer motivated in relation to that specific need, but a higher-level need may take over. Many consumer needs derive from physical situations. When we are hungry, thirsty, too hot or cold, tired, in pain, or uncomfortable, we are motivated to solve the problem. Some of the most motivating needs come from psychological and social situations. If people want to be liked, feel secure, be loved, be respected, achieve a goal, or influence others, they are motivated to behave in such a way that these problems are solved. The goal of marketers is to show their products and services in the best possible relationship to the motives of consumers.

What Are Customers' Attitudes?

Attitudes are learned tendencies to respond in a favorable or unfavorable way toward an idea or an object. Attitudes help consumers adjust to different situations by associating a previously learned attitude with the new object. For example, a consumer may have a favorable attitude toward a new product because a well-liked friend says it is a good product. Attitudes provide direction to consumer behavior, and this results in satisfaction. Consumers use their attitudes to help them solve problems. If a consumer has had a rewarding experience with a store or product, a favorable attitude will cause that consumer to expect the same level of satisfaction the next time. If this behavior continues, the consumer becomes a loyal customer and probably influences friends with this positive attitude. Consumers with strong attitudes do not change them easily. Strong attitudes, either favorable or unfavorable, develop in relation to things that are very important to the individual. For example, a young woman may believe that her social life depends on her being well dressed. She would have strong, positive attitudes toward high-quality, fashionable clothes. Consumers who believe strongly in economy and efficiency would have favorable attitudes toward products that are durable and save money. Consumer attitudes are one of the most accurate predictors of future purchase behavior. Marketers must try to maintain favorable attitudes toward their products or try to change unfavorable attitudes.

How Do Customers Learn?

Learning is a change in a behavior or thinking process resulting from experience. Marketers are interested in how consumers learn because marketing strat-

TABLE 3-4
SEPTEMBER TOP ADS IN AWARENESS BY INDUSTRY (% of responses)

Airlines

1. United   15.2
2. Eastern   12.4
3. American   6.5

Breakfast Foods

1. Kellogg's   7.8
2. Cheerios   4.5
3. Wheaties   3.1

Cameras and Equipment

1. Kodak   28.4
2. Canon   13.4
3. Polaroid   5.4

Cars and Trucks

1. Ford   14.0
2. Toyota   11.0
3. Chevrolet   10.5

Coffee and Tea

1. *Maxwell House* 15.7
2. Folger's   12.1
3. Sanka   11.8

Cosmetics and Fragrances

1. Maybelline   3.8
2. Avon   3.7
3. Estee Lauder   3.0

Fast-Food Restaurants

1. McDonald's   45.6
2. Burger King   8.4
3. Wendy's   4.4

Gum and Candy

1. Wrigley   8.3
2. Doublemint   5.6
3. Trident   4.8

Home Electronics

1. Atari   19.4
2. Intellivision   4.1
3. Sony   3.3

Laundry Products

1. Tide   18.3
2. Cheer   4.9
3. Solo   3.4

Medicine and Drugs

1. Tylenol   19.8
2. Anacin   8.8
3. Bayer   6.8

Packaged, Canned, Frozen Foods

1. Birds Eye   5.9
2. Stouffer's   4.3
3. Green Giant   3.1

Paper Products

1. Bounty   12.1
2. Charmin   10.8
3. Scott's   8.4

Soap and Shampoo

1. Prell   5.6
2. Ivory   5.2
3. Head & Shoulders 4.4

Pet Food

1. *Kibbles 'n Bits* 7.1
2. Alpo   6.5
3. Purina   5.7

Soft Drinks

1. *Pepsi-Cola*   27.8
2. Coca-Cola   24.3
3. 7UP   7.0

Question (asked of 1,260 adults): Of all the ads for (category) you've read, seen, or heard in the last month, which ad first comes to mind? Italicized brands indicate new category leaders this month.

Source: SRI Research Center Inc., Lincoln, Neb., as published in *Advertising Age*, October 25, 1982, p. 68.

These are the leading brand names for these categories of products and services. Consumers remember these names. Why would you want your product, service, or company name to rank this high in your market?

egies should help consumers remember brand names, services, store locations, good prices, and special promotions. Table 3-4 shows a regular study reported in *Advertising Age* that measures how well consumers have learned the brand names of products and services.

Marketers use stimuli to influence consumer behavior. A *stimulus* is something that reaches our senses, such as a sound, a light, an odor, a flavor, or an object touched. People often learn what a stimulus means through repetition or close association. Our responses show that we have learned, and they become habits or automatic behaviors. For example, people learn to sing certain advertising jingles without trying. People learn brand names because they see them many times every day.

People learn some things because their behavior is reinforced or punished. *Reinforcement* means that people are rewarded for doing something; they get a compliment or a tangible reward for performing well. The marketer rewards consumers with good products and services if the consumers respond to a promotional campaign. Punishment causes people to learn because their acts result in pain or loss of a good thing. Consumers are punished if they travel 10 miles to a store and discover that the product is not as advertised or is not available. The consumer is punished for responding and learns not to go to that store. This process involves the person in a choice between ways of doing things that cause reward or punishment, resulting in learning.

Consumers learn about marketers' products and services because of relationships and meanings of actions. People learn because they set goals, perform activities to reach those goals, and gain insight from what they accomplish. Learning something complex (driving a car, operating a computer, or decorating a room) may be the goal that is set. People are rewarded for reaching the goal, and they learn what they must do to reach that goal. Learning by setting goals is related to the problem-solving model of consumer behavior that was discussed earlier in this chapter. Very important and complex consumer decisions involve learning by setting goals and solving problems.

Consumers' learning behavior should be studied by marketers and applied in marketing strategies. The first time a consumer encounters a new, complex product (a stereo system or a home computer), learning will be relevant to the interaction between consumer and marketer. After several product brands are studied, the consumer will employ learning techniques for comparisons and choice. A marketing stimulus (advertisement, brand name, price, or service) will affect learning and behavior in relation to brands purchased frequently on a routine, habitual basis.

What Affects Customers' Perceptions? **Perception** is the process in which incoming stimuli are organized, interpreted, and given meaning. You have had the experience of hearing a sound but not knowing what it is. You continue to listen, hear it again, and decide what it is. You then determine that it is something you should respond to or disregard. All perception is selective since people cannot focus or concentrate on all the stimuli around them at one time. The challenge to the marketer is to use stimuli that hold a consumer's attention and result in accurate perception. Consumers' perceptions are affected by needs, motives, values, interests, attitudes, and memory. For example, if a consumer is a stereo enthusiast, every printed advertisement and television or radio commercial will be perceived readily. The consumer will attend to these stimuli and probably learn brands and product information easily. On the other hand, if people are not interested in a certain activity, they will not be as aware of stimuli or will reject them. One important type of perception is the ability to perceive differences between stimuli. Marketers would like to help consumers perceive the differences between their brands and competing brands.

Group Influences on Consumer Behavior

Consumers are social people. They interact with others, join organizations, share values, and set standards for groups. Much of the behavior of consumers is influenced by what they think other consumers want them to do. Consumers often make purchases to satisfy another consumer. Marketers need to analyze cultural values, social strata, reference groups, and the family unit as group influences on consumer behavior.

Cultural Values. **Culture** refers to a set of learned values, attitudes, and forms of behavior shared by people and transmitted through generations. Culture influences behavior. The Carol Wright Hispanic ad shown in Figure 3-8 is a good example. Notice the Hispanic preference for frozen yogurt, which suggests a cultural influence. Consumers behave in certain ways because they have learned from their parents and grandparents. Most cultural values are learned through family, church, and school. Other institutions, such as youth groups, clubs, sports teams, and political groups, may influence some people significantly. Cultural norms suggest that a majority of people accept certain values or perform certain activities. Marketers should know what the trends in cultural values are in their markets. Trends in American cultural values include being youthful, conserving time and enjoying leisure time, using natural resources carefully, being democratic and providing equal rights, being natural, seeking a simpler life, being healthy and active, and doing meaningful work.

Social Strata. **Social strata** are divisions of people with similar values, lifestyles, interests, and behavior. These divisions are commonly called social classes and represent the largest grouping of consumers for marketing appeals. Marketers do not judge one stratum or class as better than another but rather as appropriate or inappropriate for their products. If a group of consumers of any size has similar characteristics, it is a potential market segment and target market. The most commonly used system of classifying social strata identifies upper, middle, and lower groups and then divides each of these into an upper and lower subgroup. The average American (hardworking, home-loving, law-abiding, and patriotic) is in the lower-middle and upper-lower strata of this system. These consumers represent the

Hispanics enjoy 31% more frozen yogurt* than non-Hispanics.

What's more, Hispanics are more loyal brand users than non-Hispanics.

Which is why you should consider the Hispanic marketplace when you're trying to build a brand or increase its share. And the way to do it is with the Carol Wright Hispanic co-op mailing to 2.1 million households.

For only $20 per thousand, it offers a unique, entry-level medium. Get the facts by calling (212) 889-1543, s'il vous plait.

*Source: Simmons Market Research Bureau
A Study of Media & Markets

Figure 3-8. Advertising can focus on cultural influences on behavior.

norm of our society, and marketers respond with mass-marketing techniques that appeal to them. Large supermarkets, mass merchandisers such as K-Mart and Sears, products such as Coca-Cola and Pepsi-Cola, and nationwide chain stores are good examples of marketing to the middle majority. The consumers in higher social strata are better educated, have higher incomes, have more professional occupations, and are more status-minded. The consumers in lower strata generally are poorly educated, do not plan ahead, are less motivated to improve, and tend to live for present satisfactions. Social strata are meaningful to large marketers, but smaller consumer groupings are needed for most marketers.

Reference Groups. A **reference group** consists of several people who have similar values and interests, interact frequently, and influence each other. Most people join groups for identification, information, status, and rewards. Once they have joined the group, they modify their behavior to conform to the norms of the group. Members of a group tend to behave in similar ways. They buy similar clothing, food, jewelry, cars, and many other products. Some reference groups are made up of a few close friends who spend time together frequently but informally. Other reference groups may be structured, with dues, membership rules, meetings, and required activities. Reference groups of all sizes are excellent target markets. If a marketer can appeal to one important member or several members who are close to the group norm, other members will buy from that marketer.

Family Units. The family is one of the marketer's favorite reference groups. The family was presented earlier in this chapter as a demographic characteristic of the consumer market. Let us now look at the family as a social group. The members of a family are typically very close in values, have many common goals, and communicate frequently. They choose and consume many products together: cars, home furnishings, food, vacations, and insurance, for example. Marketers are increasingly marketing to the family as a single decision-making, consuming unit. The trend in the United States is for father, mother, and children to make most of their consumer buying decisions together.

THE INDUSTRIAL MARKET

In the first part of this chapter, an industrial market was defined as the businesses and organizations that use products and services to run a business, resell them, or produce other products and ser-

vices. Several types of industrial market members were mentioned, but here we shall discuss the characteristics of three major types of industrial markets: producer, reseller, and government. The specific characteristics and buying behavior of industrial customers have to be considered. Their business positions involve them in professional buying procedures, and they represent a challenging market to identify and sell to.

Major Types of Industrial Markets

A marketer of any size may have the opportunity to sell to an industrial business or organization. Such markets must be classified by the function and purpose of the organization. The classification system is important because marketing strategies must be varied to make an appeal to the industrial use of the products and services involved. For example, a manufacturer of plastic toys needs a steady supply of chemicals to use in the processing of plastic parts. If you were a marketer of these chemicals, you would need to stress quality, price, and reliable service. You would have to maintain a specified quality and specific delivery dates over time to keep this manufacturer as a customer. If you sold chemicals to a drug company for consumer consumption, quality control might be even more important. Chemicals sold for use in industrial cleaning compounds may be sold by stressing quantity discounts. When one is marketing to producers, resellers, or governments, the use of the product and the buyer's specifications are very important.

The Producer Market. The **producer market** is made up of organizations that use products and services to produce other products and services. Examples of industries in this market include manufacturing, agriculture, mining, construction, transportation, public utilities, communication, finance, insurance, real estate, and service organizations. The classification of industrial products used by these industries is presented in Chapter 5. These producers buy products to use to make other products or to use in the operation of the business. In either situation, the purpose of

Figure 3-9. Business serving business: An interior decorator calls on a firm to suggest ways of improving the business environment.

buying products is to use them to increase sales and make a profit.

The Reseller Market. The **reseller market** includes organizations that buy products to resell at a profit. They buy products and services for the purpose of conducting their business operations as well. The reseller market is made up of wholesaling firms and retailing firms. Resellers are challenged to maintain an assortment of products and services that will satisfy their customers. Marketers who successfully sell to resellers typically help them analyze their customer markets and provide the products to serve them. Large companies such as IBM and NCR sell electronic cash register systems to retailers to help them serve customers more accurately and faster. Smaller companies also may sell products and services to retailers. Interior decoration, carpeting, cleaning service, alarm systems, business forms, and dis-

play counters represent just a fraction of the types needed. A typical reseller buys products, supplies, and services from hundreds of local marketers. Resellers are often called middlemen or intermediaries, and they are discussed in Chapter 7.

The Government Market. The **government market** is made up of federal, state, and local government units that buy products and services to meet the needs of the citizens in each unit. The government market is the largest in the United States, accounting for over 20 percent of the gross national product. Governments buy an incredible array of products and services ranging from extremely complex scientific products for the space program to pieces of chalk for a school classroom. Almost every marketer has a product or service that a government unit may consider buying. Also, as government services to people expand, the potential marketing opportunities continue to grow. Marketers must be careful to learn what government agencies and buyers want. Government buyers are not motivated to make a profit. They buy to meet specifications at the lowest cost, knowing that they are subject to constant review by the public. Marketing to government can involve much paperwork and complex procedures, but the payoff in sales can be very rewarding.

Characteristics of Industrial Customers

Earlier in this chapter, many details of the consumer market and characteristics that influence marketing strategies were examined. Marketers who want to sell to industrial customers must know their characteristics. It is helpful to realize that industrial customers are like consumers in many ways, but the differences are significant. Let us look at some of the differences.

Industrial customers are purchasing specialists. Their buyers are trained professionals who want specific product information and technical data. The marketer who sells to industrial markets must have sales representatives who know their products and the business system they serve. For example, a representative of an industrial power tool company must know the technical capabilities of each tool, its proper use, and its cost factors.

Several executives are often involved in the purchase decision for an industrial product. A single industrial purchase may affect several phases of a business and may involve huge amounts of money. Paper products and business forms are used in every phase of large and small industrial firms. A paper salesperson usually will call on several levels of management and office personnel before a sale is made. These facts suggest that the sales presentation will be more complex than it is in the average consumer situation and must be prepared very thoroughly and accurately.

The industrial marketer usually sells to fewer buyers, but each buyer usually is involved in a larger transaction volume than individual consumers. A company may depend on sales made to only a few industrial customers rather than to thousands or millions of consumers. There are some obvious economic advantages to selling bigger contracts less often, but each presentation is extremely important, and the pressures are greater on the industrial marketer than on the average consumer salesperson. A university might award a contract to a local drapery marketer to decorate 800 dormitory windows. If you had made this sales presentation to the university's purchasing department, you would have to be well prepared, and the pressure would be great.

Industrial customers often are concentrated geographically. This concentration may help make marketing more efficient and reduce selling costs as compared with marketing to consumers who are scattered throughout the country or a large region. The industrial marketer may find several key customers located in one large urban area or in one state. For example, even small to medium-size cities with populations of 100,000 to 500,000 have many industrial marketers needing such products as mailing systems, microcomputers, and cleaning supplies. Manufacturers, finan-

cial firms, wholesalers, and retailers of similar types often are clustered in just a few locations in a metropolitan area.

The industrial market is influenced by a demand for products and services which is derived from the demand for consumer goods. If consumers buy fewer automobiles, the demand for steel from manufacturers will decrease. Marketers of industrial products must watch the sales of relevant consumer products in order to anticipate changes in demand for their industrial products.

Industrial Buyer Behavior

Industrial buyers generally are described as more rational than consumers. This is not always true, but it is true that selling to industrial customers requires that specific objectives be satisfied. These objectives are determined by the needs of various functions in the organization, and they must be satisfied to give the firm an opportunity to make a profit or meet social needs. Purchase criteria usually are specified more precisely by the industrial buyer than by the consumer.

The industrial buyer is very much concerned about price, but always in relation to value. The quality of products at a given price is the most important factor in most industrial purchases. The quality of industrial products directly affects the quality of the products and services sold by the industrial firm.

Successful marketing to industrial buyers means that reliable technical assistance is provided through a positive relationship between the buyer and the seller. The industrial buyer will return to the marketer who provides products and services that perform the way they are supposed to. Useful advice on marketing strategy often is given in addition to technical product information, and contract agreements are fulfilled on time. The industrial buyer's job and future income may depend on these types of relationships.

The behavior of industrial buyers is influenced by the type of buying situation. Industrial buying situations often are classified in three types: straight rebuy, modified rebuy, and new task.[2]

The straight rebuy is a routine reorder situation involving products purchased repeatedly without any changes. The buyer chooses from standard lists of products and often buys from habit from the same suppliers. Typing paper and pencils for an office usually are purchased this way. Suppliers need to provide efficient service and maintain consistent product quality. Automatic reordering systems are commonly used in straight rebuy situations.

The modified rebuy situation occurs when different products are purchased or similar products are purchased from different suppliers. Something is modified in the buying situation from previous purchases, such as product specifications, buying terms, or prices. A retail furniture store's purchase of special carts, small trucks, and other equipment for moving furniture would be done this way. The marketer would suggest new models and new methods since the last purchase by this retailer. This buying behavior requires special attention from sellers who want to keep a good relationship or acquire new buyers.

The new-task situation means that a company is buying a product for the first time. This is the most complex situation, and it is the most challenging to both the buyer and the seller. Examples would include a new stereo sound system for a restaurant, a new computer for an insurance company, or a new conveyor system for a wholesaler's stockroom. Industrial marketers need to make their best selling efforts here, hoping to develop long-term buying-selling relationships.[3]

The industrial market is so big, complex, and varied that it may appear too competitive to enter as a small marketer. The variety of organizations in the three major types suggests a challenging market to reach. Manufacturers range through such product areas as chemicals, electronics, fuel, information processing, metals, telecommunications, and rubber. The names of big industrial marketers are scary when one thinks of competing with them: Dow Chemical, RCA, Exxon, IBM, NCR, Reynolds Metals, U.S. Steel, AT&T, GTE, and Goodyear. Actually, a smaller firm may have some marketing advantages over large marketers. A smaller firm may market computing devices that larger computer manufacturers do not care to handle, or it may be able to give specialized service to industrial marketers who have been overlooked or neglected by the major firms. This small-firm strategy is called *market niching* and depends on specialization.[4] The industrial market is always open to a small marketer who has special skills, knowledge, products, and services.

KEY POINTS SUMMARY

- A market includes people as individuals, groups, or organizations with the purchasing power and the willingness to buy specific products and services.

- A consumer market is made up of people who buy products and services for personal use and satisfaction. The industrial market is made up of businesses and organizations that use products and services to run a business, to resell them, or to produce other products and services.

- Target marketing is a marketing technique in which the seller identifies different customer segments and selects one or more as a specific target. A marketing mix is then designed to appeal to each of these segments.

- Market segmentation is the process of dividing the total market into smaller parts which include customers with similar characteristics. Bases commonly used for segmentation include demographics, geographic factors, psychographics, and behavioral variables.

- Marketers need to learn the demographics of customers within their identified markets. Demographic variables include population, age, sex, family, households, income, education, and geographic location.

- A study of psychographic characteristics gives marketers additional valuable insight into consumers' lifestyles, personalities, and self-concepts. Demographic and psychographic characteristics are used together to develop a better understanding of consumer markets.

- Marketers who understand consumer behavior make better marketing decisions. Consumers use a decision-making process to solve problems and seek satisfaction with products and services.

- The problem-solving behavior of consumers is influenced by individual factors such as motives, attitudes, learning, and perception and by group factors such as culture, social strata, reference groups, and family.

- The three major types of industrial markets are producer, reseller, and government. These markets are further classified by the function and purpose of industrial organization.

- Industrial buyers are like consumers in many ways, but the differences are significant. Industrial buyers are purchasing specialists, are concentrated geographically, are involved in larger-volume transactions, and are more consistently rational and technical in their decision making.

KEY TERMS AND CONCEPTS

attitudes
concentrated
  marketing
consumer behavior
consumer market
consumer product
culture
demographics
differentiated
  marketing
discretionary
  purchases
family
government market
household
industrial market
learning

lifestyles
market
market segmentation
motives
perception
producer market
psychographics
real income
reference group
reseller market
SCSA
SMSA
social strata
target marketing
undifferentiated
  marketing

DISCUSSION QUESTIONS

1. Each of the following products could be either a consumer or an industrial product: a calculator, a bar of soap, and a stereo system. Explain the use that would identify each product with the consumer market or the industrial market.

2. No single brand is purchased by all consumers, and no single marketing strategy is best in all situations. Do you agree or disagree with this statement? What are your reasons?

3. Assume that you are the manager of a fast-food restaurant such as McDonald's or Burger King. Describe several psychographic characteristics that your customers might have that cause them to like your products and services.

4. Discuss the influences on consumer behavior in each of the five steps of the decision-making model during the purchase of a camera.

5. Discuss the group influences on consumer behavior in relation to clothing products.

6. Why is selling to the average industrial customer a different challenge from selling to the average consumer customer? Explain the differences.

NOTES

1. Julie Candler, "A Long Drive for Recognition," *Advertising Age,* June 22, 1981, p. S-24–26.
2. Patrick J. Robinson, Charles W. Faris, and Yoram Wind, *Industrial Buying and Creative Marketing,* Allyn & Bacon, Boston, 1967, pp. 12–14.
3. For extensive and excellent information on industrial buying behavior, see Frederick E. Webster, Jr., and Yoram Wind, *Organizational Buying Behavior,* Prentice-Hall, Englewood Cliffs, N.J., 1972.
4. For a useful discussion of this idea and several ways to specialize, see Philip Kotler, *Marketing Management: Analysis, Planning, and Control,* Prentice-Hall, Englewood Cliffs, N.J., 1980, pp. 285–287.

CHAPTER 4
MARKETING INFORMATION SYSTEMS AND RESEARCH

Information is knowledge derived from study, experience, or instruction. Information plays an important part in helping people control their lives. You receive some information about your own life in routine ways. The gas gauge on your car is registering empty. As a result, you put gas in the tank before trying to drive any distance. Your checkbook shows a balance of $100, and so you decide to delay writing a check for $150 to buy a new jacket. You discover that you are out of milk, so you go to the store and buy more.

Other information comes regularly from outside sources. The newspaper advertises a sale on the type of camp stove you want, and so you go to the store and buy it. Your neighbor tells you that the tomato plants you want are available at the garden supply store, and so you go to buy them. On a television talk show, a home economist demonstrates a technique for removing grease stains from a carpet, and so you follow the recommended procedure on your own carpet.

Still other information must be obtained by doing research in a systematic, organized manner. You want to buy a new videocassette recording (VCR) system. You gather information by reading consumer magazines and catalogs, visiting stores

and talking with sales people, and talking with friends who have VCR systems. As a result of this research, you decide which VCR to buy.

The information gathered from internal sources (the gas tank and checkbook), external sources (newspapers, TV, radio, and friends), and systematic research helps people solve problems and make decisions. Information is such an important part of everyday existence that people would have a very hard time managing without it. Imagine driving a car without a gas gauge or speedometer. Think of working with a checkbook that has no check register in which to record checks written and to calculate the current balance.

In this chapter, you will learn that information also plays a vital part in the operation of any marketing business. Information is gathered from internal sources, external sources, marketing research, and market modeling (such as asking what would happen if . . .).

MARKETING INFORMATION

Marketing information is the key to solving marketing problems and making marketing decisions. How do marketing problems and marketing decisions differ? Actually, they are very closely related. Problem solving deals with searching for various alternatives or for an appropriate answer to a particular difficulty. Decision making stops the problem-solving process by making a commitment to one specific alternative. But both problem solving and decision making may lead to additional problems and the need for further decisions. Read on page 90 how the Nestle Company solved a marketing problem through the effective use of marketing information. How did they decide that Taster's Choice coffee could be the romantic link?

Information for Decision Making

In solving marketing problems and making marketing decisions, information is the key to success. In the process of reintroducing Taster's Choice coffee, we can assume that information was used in the form of sales reports to determine the need to increase sales of Taster's Choice. External information was gathered in the form of reports on the competition, Maxim. Scientific experiments were conducted to gather information on improved freeze-drying methods, and information was gathered on the cost of a better grade of coffee bean. Consumer surveys were conducted to gather information on consumer preferences. Nestle then used all this information to come to the ultimate decision about how to reintroduce Taster's Choice coffee.

The actual decision-making process can be broken down into eight basic steps, and information is needed to complete each step successfully.

1. Identify the Problem to be Solved. If the problem was "How can we reverse the declining sales volume?", information on sales figures would be needed. This information would come from inside the company. If the problem was the assessment of a new business opportunity, information on the proposed product or service, the target market, and the competition would be needed. This information would have to be gathered from outside sources.

2. Get All the Facts. All available information about the problem should be gathered. How long has the product or service been on the market? Is the quality constant? What competing products or services are available? What techniques are being used?

3. Identify the Decision-Making Rules. What are the decision-making limits? How much money is in the budget to implement the decision? What alternatives will be overruled by management? How soon must the decision be made?

4. Identify Alternatives. Within the bounds of the decision-making rules, all logical alternatives should be identified.

5. Evaluate Alternatives. Pertinent information should be gathered for all the alternatives so that the feasibility of each one can be considered.

6. Select an Alternative. The most feasible alternative should be chosen on the basis of the information gathered.

7. Make a Decision. The final decision should be based on a further investigation of the feasibility of implementing the best alternative.

8. Implement and Follow Up. Implement the decision and evaluate the results of your choice. If the decision is not producing the desired results, take corrective action.

Marketing Information Yesterday and Today

Many years ago, formal systems and techniques for gathering marketing information played a much less important role in decision making. When producers sold their products locally, they had frequent contact with customers and received direct feedback on the effectiveness of their products. The early products and services were simpler and were brought more directly to customers. The typical customer choice was easier and less demanding because of fewer products and services in each market. Marketers were able to make valid decisions on the basis of first-hand knowledge of customer likes and dislikes.

NESTLE'S TASTER'S CHOICE: THE ROMANTIC LINK

The Nestle Company tackled a problem-solving situation that yielded both a decision and additional subproblems. Throughout the problem-solving process, valuable marketing information was gathered from various sources.

The Nestle Company wanted to increase sales of its Taster's Choice freeze-dried coffee. To solve this problem, they decided to improve both the quality of the coffee beans and the freeze-drying process. This decision created a subproblem: How should the company reintroduce the improved coffee? For years both Nestle and General Foods, with its Maxim, have stressed the engineering marvels of soluble beverage crystals known as freeze-dried coffee. The target market has been the over-35 confirmed coffee drinker. This process evokes images of coffee taken at its absolute peak of flavor and frozen into a solid block. In the next split second, all the moisture is evaporated from the block, leaving tiny crystals that are poised to explode into flavor once heat and water are reapplied.

To solve the problem of how to reintroduce the new, improved Taster's Choice, Nestle gathered information by conducting a survey of coffee drinkers. The company asked consumers to recall their favorite cup of coffee. Very frequently, coffee drinkers recalled a cup of coffee shared with a loved one, with the experience almost always being a memorable one.

The consumers carried over their good feelings about a particular moment into a good feeling about the cup of coffee that went along with that experience. As a result of their research, Nestle decided to relaunch Taster's Choice by trying to link good coffee with some of the finer moments in life. Nestle's coffee group vice president, William Savel, refers to this approach as "romantic linkage." They also decided to target their advertising to a younger group of consumers who have not accepted coffee drinking as fully as the 40- to 60-year old group. Savel believes that "You have to mature into a taste for good coffee."

The decision to use romantic linkage and appeal to a younger consumer created another problem: developing the actual advertising spots for television. The company decided to commission the staff of Leo Burnett and Company of Chicago to create two 60-second and three 30-second television spots that reflect the romantic atmosphere Nestle desired. The ads feature the tender moments between a man and a woman and appeal to the moment when only a cup of coffee will do.

Rewritten from "Will Romance Perk Up Nestle Sales?" Westchester Rockland Newspapers, April 25, 1982, p. B-1. Original article by Doug Williams.

Small marketers continue to benefit from this type of direct interaction with customers.

Today the marketing process is generally more complex. The producers of products are farther removed from the people who buy them, and this distance creates an information gap. To create further marketing problems, the consumer is increasingly more sophisticated about likes and dislikes. In the 1950s the average consumer may have selected a package of hotdogs, a bag of potato chips, and a bottle of a soft drink because the children enjoyed the taste of the particular brands chosen. Today a significant number of consumers are more likely to select only hotdogs that contain no nitrites, only potato chips without preservatives, only vegetables with no salt added, and only soft drinks that contain no caffeine.

Earlier consumers were also used to receiving bits of misleading and exaggerated information as a normal part of advertising. They were told that breakfast cereal was "shot from guns" and that bread would help build "strong bodies in 12 ways." Now more truthful information is presented to customers through advertising (with some emotional and exciting claims added). For example, the packages on most products present complete information about the ingredients used to manufacture those products.

The Scope of Marketing Information

From the preceding discussion, it may look as if marketing information affects virtually every aspect of marketing, and it does. Accurate and timely information is the key to both long-range and short-term goal setting. It reduces risk by supplementing and reinforcing a manager's judgment. It may be said that it is a way of validating intuition, and it is the only valid way in which customer attitudes can be monitored. Managers at the Nestle Company may have had a hunch that a more romantic and emotional advertising campaign would appeal to customers in the early 1980s, but they used marketing information to substantiate that feeling, thus reducing the risk. In many instances, information is used as a means of

"Would you say Attila is doing an excellent job, a good job, a fair job, or a poor job?"

Figure 4-1. Accurate and timely information on customer likes and dislikes can benefit a marketer.

gaining support for a favored alternative solution to a problem or even as a means of defending a decision that has already been made.

Accurate use of marketing information is the only efficient way of monitoring the success or failure of a company's marketing efforts. Detailed information can pinpoint both problem areas and possible growth areas and can point the way to solving the problems and realizing growth.

Marketing information also plays an important part in the advertising and promotion of a product or service. Accurate information enhances the credibility of both the company and the product. In many instances, as in the data used on food package labels, the use of accurate marketing information is a legal requirement.

THE MARKETING INFORMATION SYSTEM

Imagine for a moment that you have been asked to gather all the pertinent marketing information for the past week for a company the size of Exxon, IBM, or General Electric and to place it in a pile. Your accumulated collection would include accounting reports, operating statements, sales records, cost information, records of specific accounts, competitive product information, promotional information, information about economic conditions, current information from marketing models, and current marketing research. The finished stack of marketing information for the week might easily reach the roof of a high-rise office building. Of course, a huge pile of marketing information that has not been sorted or classified is of no use to the marketers who must employ this information in their decision making. In almost every organization, the problem associated with marketing information is not a lack of information but an overabundance. Unfortunately, such information is almost useless if it is spread around the company in an unorganized fashion. Pertinent information that is spread among six or seven different offices, dozens of computer tapes and memory disks, and a number of different individuals within the company cannot possibly serve as a valuable resource for problem solving and decision making. Marketing information must be centralized, organized, and available to the people who need to use it.

What Is a Marketing Information System?

In virtually all successful companies, the problem of unusable marketing information is being solved by the introduction of marketing information systems. Business firms use the term **management information system** (MIS) to refer to the overall system that supports decision making in the firm. Marketers use the term **marketing information system** (MKIS) to identify the system that supports decision making in marketing. A marketing information system is an organized set of procedures designed to gather, sort, analyze, evaluate, and distribute the information used for making marketing decisions.

In many ways, the MKIS is the nerve center of a company, and it can be compared with a thermostat in a house. The thermostat is set at a certain level and monitors the temperature of the surrounding air. If there is a deviation in air temperature, the thermostat calls for more heat or more cooling. The MKIS is "set" for a certain level of profit and monitors the company's performance in the marketplace. If there is a deviation from the goal, the MKIS signals the need for action to correct the problem. However, unlike the thermostat, the MKIS does not always institute corrective action automatically. It is the marketer who decides on corrective action.

Although organized methods using simple techniques of gathering and storing marketing information have always been used, almost all MKIS systems are now computerized. Smaller firms that cannot afford large full-scale computers are now making use of less expensive microcomputers or buying research data from marketing research firms and general data sources.

Each marketing information system is tailor-made to fit the needs of the individual business using it. An important part of the process of designing an MKIS should be the questioning of potential users of the system. A list of useful questions is shown below.

1.   What types of decisions are you usually required to make?

2.   What information must you have to make these decisions?

3.   How detailed should this information be?

4.   How frequently must you receive this information?

5.   What is the source of this information?

6.   What additional information would you like to have?

7.   What information do you usually supply to others?

8.   How detailed is this information?

9.   How frequently do you supply this information?

10.   What specific changes would you like to see in the current procedures for receiving and supplying information?[1]

The objective of developing an MKIS should not be to create the most elaborate possible system. Instead, it should be to develop a system that meets the needs of the people who will use it and that fits within the firm's budget.

What Are the Components of a Marketing Information System?

With the advent of more computer use, marketing information systems have become increasingly sophisticated. Today's MKIS often is made up of four different sources of information: internal information, external information, marketing models, and marketing research, as shown in Table 4-1.

Internal Information. The internal information that flows into the marketing information system can be separated into four broad categories: operating information, sales analysis information, inventory control information, and information from marketing personnel. Operating information comes from an analysis of the firm's production, sales, and financial records. The most helpful source of operating information is the operating statement, or profit and loss statement. Sales information comes directly from the firm's sales records. Inventory control information is created at the time (or point) of sale. The fourth category of internal information is information received from marketing personnel. This source often is overlooked by marketers.

External Information. External marketing information sometimes is referred to as marketing intelligence. In some ways the gathering of this information can be compared with the gathering of military intelligence. External information should include data about markets, competitors, products, services, advertising and promotion, and economic conditions. Read the excellent ideas on how to gather market information in the article on page 94. This advice was presented to opticians, who are professional service marketers. Notice the practical ideas for gathering data for the small marketer's MKIS.

Marketing Models. This relatively new aspect of MKIS utilizes the computer or microcomputer and enables the marketer to determine what would happen if . . . . Marketing models are

TABLE 4-1
COMPONENTS OF THE MARKETING INFORMATION SYSTEM (MKIS)

Internal Information	External Information	Marketing Models	Marketing Research
Operating information	Market data	Anticipate	Collects specific data
Sales analysis information	Competitive information	effects of	Analyzes these data
Inventory control information	Product information	changes in:	Makes specific suggestions
Information from company personnel	Advertising/promotion	Product	gestions
	Economic conditions	Price	
		Place	
		Promotion	
		Personnel	
		Predict results of actions	

PRACTICAL MARKET INFORMATION IDEAS FOR OPTICIANS—LEARN YOUR MARKET

The greatest tool any marketer can have is the most accurate and complete information possible. Who are you selling to? Where do they come from? What sort of surroundings would they prefer when purchasing their lenses and frames and in filling their other optical needs? Most of this demographic information is obtainable from such sources as your local Chamber of Commerce, City Hall, the U.S. Department of Commerce, the U.S. Bureau of the Census, and *Sales and Marketing Management* magazine.

Information to look for should include the size of the town, city, or metropolitan area in which you are located and the ease of travel within the area. You want specific figures, not a general "feeling." Data you gather should answer questions such as the rate of growth of your business compared to the growth of your area. Is your business growing at least as fast as the population increase? What are the patterns of social movement?

Additional information, including metropolitan travel patterns and foot traffic count in neighborhood shopping areas, is available from the city planner's office, traffic department, or similar governmental units in most cities. These data enable you to determine if your location takes advantage of local population and travel patterns in terms of its accessibility and convenience and what the characteristics are of the foot traffic which passes your office daily. Get an inexpensive counter and have an assistant make periodic checks of the people count at your location and at other locations you may be thinking of. Are you in the mainstream? If not, should a move be considered?

The Yellow Pages and professional associations' membership lists can indicate how many other dispensers are working within your general area, including other opticians, optometrists, dispensing ophthalmologists, and other groups dealing in optical products. If you are in an area of high concentration of dispensers relative to the population count, you should be doing everything possible to attract the attention of customers so they will think of you when buying their glasses.

Census data will indicate what sort of people make up the population in the area in which you do your business. Are they older, younger? Has the character of your area been changing in the past few years? More retired people? More college students? This information, available from your local library, will provide clues to probable lifestyle and taste in eyeglasses. One possibility is to keep a record of your new walk-in customers for a month or so and determine their general characteristics.

Have some friends ask around to find out what others are saying about your operation. Is your selection as varied and as carefully chosen as those of your competitors? Are your prices high or low for your area? How is your reputation doing?

Adapted from *Marketing Techniques for Ophthalmic Dispensers: A Manual for Opticians,* American Optical Corporation, prepared by Management Directions Inc., Cambridge, Mass., 1977, pp. 7–8.

used primarily to pretest new product acceptance, evaluate the effects of various price structures, and analyze the effects of alternative advertising media. Models are discussed later in this chapter.

Marketing Research. Marketing research is an important part of the MKIS. When the other components of the MKIS zero in on a problem area that must be solved or a project that should be explored more fully, marketing research is employed to collect specific data, analyze the data, and form a basis to make specific problem- or project-related suggestions. Table 4-2 shows the percentage of American companies doing several leading types of sales and market research. You can see from these percentages that marketers use several types of research activities extensively.

Marketing research is used by all marketers (small, large, service, consumer product, or industrial product types). Some marketers consider marketing research as a way to solve problems that are discovered in the MKIS. In some cases, marketing research may identify a problem and solve it for decision making by marketing management in the MKIS. In either case and whether the process is simple or complex, both marketing research and a marketing information system are needed by marketers.

INTERNAL INFORMATION

Internal information in the form of operating statements, sales analysis reports, inventory control information, and reports from marketing personnel help marketers evaluate a firm's present level of performance. They can then compare this current information with both expected performance and previous performance and predict future success or failure. This information then becomes the basis for decision making.

Operating Information

The operating statement, or profit and loss statement, is a financial summary of the results of operating a company over a specified period of time. It is usually prepared for a month, quarter of a year, or year, but if necessary, it can be prepared weekly. The operating statement is also used as

---

TABLE 4-2
MARKET RESEARCH ACTIVITIES OF AMERICAN COMPANIES

Type of Sales and Market Research	Percent of Companies Involved
A. Measurement of market potentials	93
B. Market share analysis	92
C. Determination of market characteristics	93
D. Sales analysis	89
E. Establishment of sales quotas, territories	75
F. Distribution channel studies	69
G. Test markets, store audits	54
H. Consumer panel operations	50
I. Sales compensation studies	60
J. Promotional studies of premiums, coupons, sampling, deals, and so on	52

Adapted from Dik Warren Twedt, *1978 Survey of Marketing Research,* American Marketing Association, Chicago, 1978, p. 41. Reprinted by permission.

the basis of many computerized marketing models that will be described in a later section of this chapter.

The operating statement shows whether the firm has operated at a profit or a loss. A scaled-down version of a typical operating statement is shown here. Let us examine how this simplified statement is put together and what each component means as a source of internal information.

Gross sales less returns and allowances
   = net sales
Net sales less cost of goods sold
   = gross margin
Gross margin less expenses
   = net profit or loss

Gross sales is the total amount charged to all customers during a time period. Both returns and allowances are subtracted from gross sales to arrive at net sales. A return is the money that has been refunded, or credited, to a customer when products are returned. An allowance is a price reduction that is given to a customer who is not satisfied with the products purchased but decides to keep them. Net sales is the total dollar amount the company actually receives for the sale of products or services.

Next, the cost of goods sold is subtracted from the net sales figure to obtain the gross margin. The cost of goods sold is the amount the company pays to obtain the goods that have been sold. If the company manufactures the goods, this is the cost of raw materials, labor, and overhead to manufacture the goods.

The gross margin, or gross profit, is the amount of profit before the expenses of running the business and paying the sales staff. Expenses such as advertising, sales salaries, commissions, administrative salaries, warehousing, delivery, and rent are subtracted from the gross margin to equal net profit, or the money actually earned by the company before taxes. If expenses are larger than gross margin, a net loss is recorded.

The operating statement provides marketers with several tools for evaluating the operations of

TABLE 4-3
A.B.C. COMPANY OPERATING STATEMENT FOR THE YEAR ENDING DECEMBER 31, 19—

		Percent
Gross Sales	$945,000	105
Returns and Allowances	45,000	05
Net Sales	900,000	100
Cost of Goods Sold	495,000	55
Gross Margin	405,000	45
Expenses	315,000	35
Net Profit The *Bottom* Line	90,000	10

a business in comparison with this year's goals and with performance in past years. These tools are called operating ratios, and each is a percentage figure that can be used for evaluation.

Table 4-3 shows an operating statement with dollar figures and percentage figures. Net sales is equal to 100 percent, and each of the other items is expressed as a percentage, or ratio, of net sales.

In our example, the gross margin ratio is 45 percent. This means that gross margin is 45 percent of net sales. If the gross margin ratio is too low, a marketer may decide to find a less expensive supplier of goods, reevaluate the selection of merchandise so that a higher price can be charged, or pay suppliers more promptly in order to receive greater cash discounts.

The sales returns and allowances ratio is 5 percent in the example. If this ratio is higher than in previous years, it may indicate that the quality of the product has declined or that the sales staff is using high-pressure techniques in selling.

In our example, the expense ratio is 35 percent and the net profit ratio is 10 percent. Net profit is the all-important bottom line that is often referred to by business managers. Because net profit depends on a combination of gross and net sales, gross margin, and expenses, marketers sometimes have difficulty pinpointing the problem when the net profit ratio is too low. One immediate way to raise this ratio is by lowering expenses and ultimately the expense ratio. But this solution is not always as easy as it sounds. Lowered expenses can also result in lowered profits because when budgets are cut, advertising may be less effective and fewer sales people may be available to call on customers.

Fortunately, computerized marketing models allow marketers to ask "what if" questions about their operating statements and receive feedback without actually making the contemplated changes.

Analysis of Information Reports

The marketer who examines the sales figures in the operating statement is given very little infor-mation about the sales of the company. To better understand sales, inventory, and personnel infor-mation, marketers often examine sales-related reports, some of which may be prepared by a computer. Reports based on sales and inventory information are discussed below.

Sales by Region or Territory. The sales of each region or territory can be compared with those of every other territory. This comparison can include average salary in each territory, average expenses, total sales costs (salary plus expenses), and total sales in each territory. It also can include sales cost ratios for each territory (total sales cost divided by total sales). This comparison gives the marketer a means of pinpointing territories where there is an unusually high sales cost ratio so that the cause of the problem can be investigated fur-ther. A sales quota refers to the level of sales expected from a region, territory, salesperson, or product.

HEALTH AND RACQUET CLUB
NEW MEMBERSHIPS--AUGUST
QUOTA/ACTUAL/PERFORMANCE RATIO

TYPE OF MEMBERSHIP	DOWNTOWN			WESTERN VALLEY		
	Q	A	%	Q	A	%
PLAN A	40	35	-12.5	15	16	+06
PLAN B	25	38	+52	10	10	--
PLAN C	25	13	-48	10	8	-20
FAMILY	20	25	+25	30	52	+73
SENIOR	20	30	+50	25	27	+08
TOTAL	130	141	+08.5	90	113	+25.5

Figure 4-2. Computers can generate sales quotas for a region, territory, salesperson, or product. Here, quotas are compared for two locations of a health club.

The actual sales are compared with the sales quota, and then a ratio of performance to quota can be calculated. It is relatively easy for marketers to spot problem areas when these ratios are used. If a salesperson (or product or region or territory) is performing at only 60 percent of quota, the marketer should investigate this problem area further. On the other hand, if a product is selling at 120 percent of quota, the marketer should make an effort to take full advantage of the demand for this hot item.

Inventory Control Information. A large portion of a marketer's investment is tied up in maintaining inventory to meet the needs of the customer. The point-of-sale (POS) terminal system is a computerized system that allows marketers to update inventory information automatically at the point of sale, which is the cash register. The system calls for either indexing a special set of numbers into the cash register along with the price or running a special wand over specially coded labels on the merchandise.

In 1981, the National Retail Merchants Association (NRMA) and Touche Ross & Co., a New York accounting firm, conducted an extensive survey on the uses of POS equipment. A 35-page survey was sent to 524 retail companies with a total of 56,592 stores. Small, medium, and large chains from five industry segments—specialty, department, discount, variety, and full-line—were included in the study. The results clearly showed that retailers who installed POS equipment primarily to improve their merchandising and operating information and decisions met their expectations in almost every case.

The two major benefits of POS equipment, according to respondents to the NRMA survey, are these.

● POS provides them with more accurate, more useful, and faster information.
● POS provides them with the ability to operate with reduced inventory levels and markdowns while increasing inventory turns and gross margins. [2]

In other words, by getting more accurate marketing information quickly, these stores are able to save money by keeping less of it tied up in inventory and by taking fewer markdowns. They are also able to increase their stock-turn rates. The inventory-turn rate (or stock-turn rate) is the number of times the average inventory is sold each year. A faster inventory-turn rate helps ensure that the store's merchandise will be sold while it is still in demand. It also permits the store to keep a smaller inventory on hand and allows it to realize a profit on the inventory investment earlier than it did in the past. These POS improvements are reflected on the gross margin line of the operating statement.

Electronic cash registers, microcomputers, and other data recording equipment are coming down in price and are becoming more feasible alternatives for small marketers. In fact, automated reordering systems tied to suppliers' computerized systems are increasingly common. The National Retail Merchants Association publishes a book entitled *POS Trends in the 80's* for small and large, chain and independent retailers. This is one of the trends in MKIS, with the computer as the catalyst.

Reports from Marketing Personnel. Marketers sometimes overlook the importance of using their own marketing personnel as a source of marketing information. Sales people in the field have an excellent opportunity to get first-hand information from customers about product likes and dislikes. Sales people also have an opportunity to gather valuable information about competing products and services and about changes in the marketplace.

Unfortunately, much of the information gathered by sales people is never passed on to marketing decision makers. If there is no formal information-reporting system or an inefficient one, important information may disappear, be delayed, or be distorted as it is passed from person to person.

Companies that design a marketing information system to include prompt, accurate input from marketing personnel find that they benefit from this important source of information. The input may be in the form of frequent and detailed call reports, face-to-face conferences whenever possible, regularly scheduled conference calls, or any other system that would take advantage of the fact that marketing personnel have daily contact with customers.

EXTERNAL INFORMATION

- Who are the purchasers of our products and services?
- What are their income levels?
- What do they like and dislike?
- What products or services compete head on with ours?
- What is our market share?
- Which media should we use for advertising?
- Is the economy positively or negatively affecting the sales of our products and services?

These are just a few of the hundreds of questions marketers seek to answer as they gather external marketing information, or intelligence.

Systematic Gathering of Information

Systematic gathering, storing, and retrieval of external marketing information is essential if the information is to be of use in decision making. For marketers in small businesses who want to compile their own data collections, research consultant Lee Adler suggests that after analyzing their sales figures, they should begin **"desk research."**[3] This term refers to the collection, synthesis, and orderly distillation of all available material on a particular industry. Sources include trade magazines, trade associations, professional societies, government agencies, special-purpose libraries, and research houses.

Much of this desk research can be done by mail or phone. Then the information must be analyzed into topical areas. A routine must be established for keeping the data collection up to date. Adler says that "This fund of knowledge serves as a basic source when specific problems arise. It is the source to which you turn first before you start any other inquiries." Adler indicates that it is also relatively easy to undertake a systematic study of the competition. "This may be done by assembling competitive sales and technical literature, analyzing your sales people's call reports, systematically debriefing them in person, clipping and filing competitive advertising, visiting booths of competitors at trade shows, and carefully listening to your customers—especially to their complaints."

Many larger companies either keep their own computerized data collection as a part of the MKIS, or use the services of a new industry that has grown up around on-line **databases,** which are huge banks of information that is being processed, stored, and delivered electronically. On-line data are controlled directly by or in direct communication with a computer.

In his *Fortune* magazine article "Everything You Always Wanted to Know May Soon Be On-Line," Walter Kiechel III explains that databases have solved some important research problems: the legwork of research, the tedious job of digging in the stacks, and the nightmare of finding that a key source is misplaced or out on loan.[4]

The new on-line libraries "can drop what you want literally in your lap." A retailer planning to open a new store at, say, 608 Oak Street in Scarsdale need only get on-line access to the SITE II database (produced by CACI Inc.) and tap in the appropriate ZIP Code. The retailer gets an immediate printout of the demographics of the surrounding neighborhoods: population, home values, family income and educational level, even the number of cars and major appliances in each household. A manufacturer of dry dog food can query SOLO (produced by a Time Inc. subsidiary) to find out almost instantaneously how the product market share is holding up.

Types of Information Needed

Information on markets, competitors, products, promotion, and economic conditions is part of the

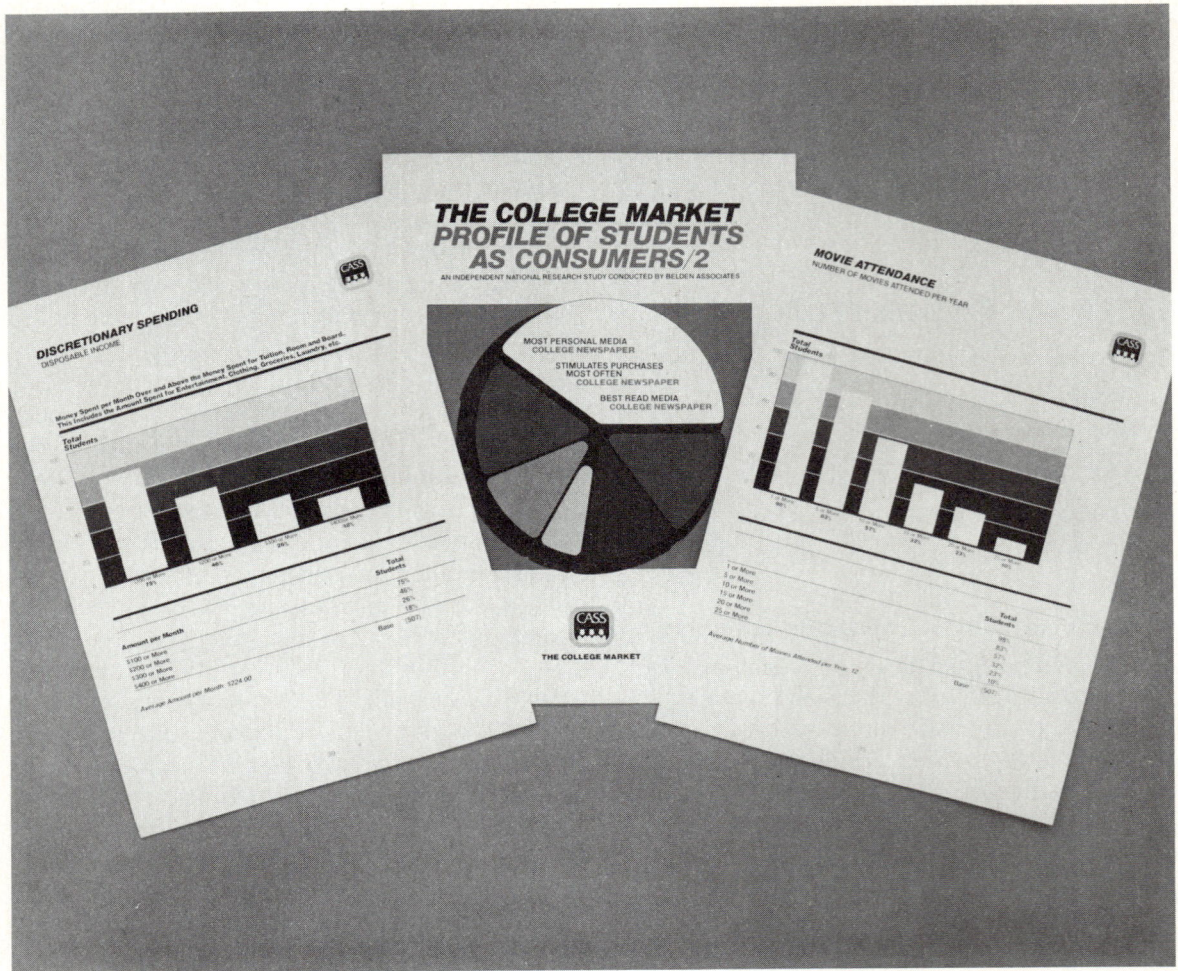

Figure 4-3. Profiles of college students' behavior patterns help determine the college market potential.

external information marketers need to help with their decision making.

Market Potential. Marketers need information about the largest number of units of a product or service that can possibly be sold in a given geographic area during a given time period. If the potential is high, they probably will decide to invest more money in advertising and sales than they will if the potential is low. An estimate of the market potential will help marketers determine the actual sales estimate for the particular product or service in question. If competition is strong and the product or service is new, marketers can expect to capture only a small market share the first year in a particular locality.

For existing products and services, marketers want to know who the loyal purchasers are. These are people who repeatedly buy the product or service. The goal of marketing decisions should be to keep the loyal purchasers satisfied, and the job of satisfying them will be easier if marketers know some basic facts about their purchasers. What are the income levels of the purchasers of our products and services? What do they like and dislike? Why do they buy the product instead of a competing product? How can we make the product even better suited to their needs and wants?

A leading manufacturer of panty hose hired a marketing research firm to determine what customers thought of their products. The manufacturer was surprised to learn that many women felt that the panty hose must have been designed by men who were unfamiliar with the female anatomy because the products fit poorly and were uncomfortable to wear. The customers who were interviewed had specific suggestions to improve both the comfort and the fit, and those suggestions were passed on to the manufacturer, who redesigned the product.

Competitors. Marketers want to keep an eye on the competition at all times. It is important to know what new competitive products are being developed and what improvements are being made in existing products and services. As soon as these facts are determined, marketers can take steps to meet or beat the competition.

It is also helpful for marketers to determine what market share each competitor holds. If a leading competitor is beginning to lose some of its hold on the market, it would be to the advantage of marketers to determine why this is happening. If the shift in customer loyalty has not affected a company's share of the market, it may be possible to take advantage of the disenchantment of the competitor's former customers by promoting the fact that your product or service can give these people what they have been looking for.

Marketers use a number of different techniques for gathering outside information about competitors. They read competitors' annual reports, visit trade shows, monitor both advertising and news items in newspapers and trade magazines, and systematically poll sales people on their observations of the competitors. Some large companies, including Westinghouse, Citicorp, and Sperry Rand, have staff members who are primarily responsible for the monitoring of competitors.

Promotion. Marketers must gather as much information as they can on the relative effectiveness of various advertising media (TV, radio, newspapers, magazines, and so forth) and on the relative effectiveness of various types of advertisements and advertising strategies. Two research studies on the effectiveness of advertising are described in this chapter. This type of research information often is presented in trade journals and can be gathered by the marketer who must make important decisions about how to spend advertising dollars effectively.

Economic Conditions. Federal, state, and local government publications, trade magazines, and newspapers are a few of the many sources that marketers can use to keep abreast of current economic conditions. Gross national product and disposable income are two important indicators that help marketers with both long-range and short-term goal setting. Marketers who are able to respond to a need on the part of the consumers to conserve, or cut back, when the economy indicates will be at an advantage. Examples of products that meet the needs of consumers in a conservation-minded economy are cars with high gas mileage, shower heads that conserve water, and improved forms of insulation that conserve heat.

By reading business papers such as the *Wall Street Journal*, marketers can become aware of some of the additional effects that tough economic conditions have on marketing. "People want a very strong feeling of pleasure when they buy things," says Leo J. Shapiro, who heads a market research firm in Chicago. "If you think about how bad things are economically, you want to treat yourself well." He goes on to explain that during a recession, people enjoy buying things for which the first cost is also the last. They do not want to go into debt. As a result of this desire for luxury at a one-time cost, items such as clothing, toys, candy, and entertainment items sell very well. [5]

MARKETING MODELS

This third important component of a marketing information system is the use of marketing models. A **model** is a set of interrelated variables that are set up to represent a real system, process, or outcome. By using marketing models, marketers can ask such questions as, What would happen if I raised my advertising expenditures 15 percent and at the same time raised my prices 5 percent?

"Whether we know it or not, we're all 'modelers,'" explains J. Reginald Rhodes of Burke Marketing Services in Cincinnati. "The busy brand manager who forgoes a sit-down lunch for a carry-out sandwich most likely has 'modeled' the waiting time at his favorite lunch spot, and it came up 'buzz, click, whirr, 20 minute wait.'" Rhodes explains that we all "model" our lives, from choosing what line to stand in to thinking about business decisions. Rhodes defines models as the "organizing structures that we use to sort out pieces of information so that they fit together reasonably and help us make sense out of what is going on."[6]

The models that are most valuable to marketers are predictive models, which grow or evolve from experience. They allow the user to reduce risk by relying on the model to predict what will happen as a result of a given action. Predictive models are developed by consistently applying the same measures to marketing actions so that one can begin to understand, evaluate, and predict the marketplace results of those actions.

When predictive models are programmed into a computer, they provide marketers with instant feedback to their "what if" questions. Frequently developed models include advertising budget models, pricing models, site selection models, and models to identify optimum product features. After a series of modeling experiments, Anheuser-Busch was able to understand better how advertising affected their sales. As a result, they were able to cut their advertising expenditures from $14.8 million to $10 million a year. Contrary to what they thought before the experiments, sales and profits continued to rise and the

cost of advertising for each barrel dropped by half.[7]

A small marketer uses predictive models in many ways. Internal records may reveal that a previous advertising campaign that increased costs 10 percent resulted in a 20 percent increase in sales. The marketer's model would be as follows. If I increase advertising 10 percent, sales will increase 20 percent. This will give the marketer a way to predict how much merchandise to have on hand and how many sales people to have on duty. Of course, many variables such as weather, competition, and consumers' attitudes may affect the outcome, but the marketer has a model as a basis for making decisions.

MARKETING RESEARCH

Marketing research is a very important component of the marketing information system. While the purpose of the entire MKIS is to perpetuate a consistent flow of meaningful information that will help marketers solve problems and make decisions, marketing research concentrates on finding solutions to specific problems that have been identified by a company.

Marketing research is an objective system designed to collect, analyze, and report information and findings relevant to a specific problem or situation facing a company. Marketing research may be employed to solve such problems as these.

- How can we realize better sales from our exterior house paint?

- What services do prospective customers want from cable TV?

- How can advertising for cable TV be made interesting enough so that viewers *want* to watch it?

- What should dry cleaners do differently to increase sales volume?

- What effect do temporary price reductions, display alternatives, and newspaper advertisements have on products such as fruit juice and laundry detergent?

Figure 4-4. Marketing research can find solutions to a specific problem or situation.

Every marketer, large or small, needs an understanding of marketing research techniques. If your firm is large enough to have its own marketing research department or even a few marketing research staff members, you will be better prepared to work with these specialists if you understand the basic marketing research process. Your understanding will help you work together to plan research studies that are within your budget, assure that you are collecting the right information for your needs, and interpret the results correctly. If you are in a small firm, you will be involved in using marketing research techniques yourself to solve problems and make important decisions.

Figure 4-5 shows some marketing research techniques offered for a fee by a marketing research firm. The letter was mailed to relatively small marketers to promote the services of this research company. The list of research studies shows some practical techniques that small marketers can use to help make better marketing decisions.

THE RESEARCH PROCESS

No two marketing research studies are exactly alike, and the process that is presented here is not meant to be a set of steps that *must* be followed in all research. In some studies, two of the steps may be combined. In other studies, the decision may be made to halt the study after the preliminary investigation of the problem is made.

The general process for performing a marketing research study is presented in Table 4-4 on page 105. Each of the six steps in the process will be discussed in detail in the sections that follow.

WABASH VALLEY MARKETING RESEARCH

1605 South Third Street
Terre Haute, Indiana 47801

May 26, 19--

Janet B. Adams
Video Boutique
218 Brookside Plaza
Bloomington, IN 47000

Dear Ms. Adams:

We conduct marketing research studies for your business that give you the data you need to make better marketing decisions. We have collected relevant secondary data for the business and consumer populations in Indiana and central Illinois. We collect primary data specifically designed to solve your marketing problems. We have had great success with specific, short-term research studies for smaller companies. Our staff consists of well-trained professional researchers and interviewers.

Here is a list of some of the many types of research studies we conduct.

TV day-after recall	Attitudinal studies
Readership studies	Mail surveys
TV ratings	Customer counts
Radio ratings	Comparison shopping
Ad tests	Focus groups
Copy testing	Shopper's checks
Product testing	Panel discussions
Consumer audits	Telephone interviewing
Store audits	Public opinion polls
Store distribution checks	Psychographic studies
Package and design studies	Depth interviewing
Image studies	

Wabash Valley Marketing Research is a member of the Wabash Valley Marketing Association, Terre Haute Chamber of Commerce, Better Business Bureau, Market Research Trade Association, and American Marketing Association.

Let's talk about your marketing needs. You will find that we offer reasonable, competitive rates.

For additional information call me at (812) 259-1718.

Sincerely,

Julie C. Grim

Julie C. Grim
Research Director

bas

Figure 4-5. Independent firms can perform a number of marketing research activities for small or large companies.

TABLE 4-4
MARKETING RESEARCH

Steps in the Marketing Research Process

1. Formulate the problem.
2. Gather preliminary information.
3. Conduct preliminary investigation.
4. Plan and conduct formal investigation.
   a. Determine information needs.
   b. Determine information sources.
   c. Determine methods for gathering primary data.
   d. Design forms on which to gather data.
   e. Design the sample.
   f. Collect data.
5. Process and analyze data.
6. Prepare written report.

Step One: Formulate the Problem

Probably the most difficult task in the research process is formulating the research problem. Many marketers have only a vague notion of what they want to investigate when they prepare to begin research. This vague notion may be a statement such as, "What should we do about selling the new product?" or "Is our advertising effective?" or "How can we stop declining sales?" Although these statements sound like problems, they are actually symptoms of the real problems. To pin down the real problem, the researchers and marketers execute step two of the research process.

Step Two: Gather Preliminary Information

During this step, researchers talk with people within the company to try to gain some insight into the problem. They also study the internal information that was discussed earlier in this chapter. For the problem "What should we do about selling the new product?" researchers and marketers would discuss the key features of the product with man-

agement and product management. They would study the original plans for manufacturing the product and compare the planned product with the finished product. They might obtain copies of the operating statement for the suggested product so that they could determine the promotion budget that is available. The precise research problem might be phrased, "How can the $80,000 promotion budget for the new product best be spent to reach the target market?"

The problem "Is our advertising effective?" might be phrased, "Do customers recall television ads the day after they are shown?" The problem "How can we stop declining sales?" might be phrased, "Why are the sales of product X declining in territory A?"

This stage of the research process is often referred to as the exploratory stage. During the **exploratory stage,** preliminary research is conducted to develop a clear definition of the research problem. After the problem has been clarified, the conclusive stage can begin. During the **conclusive stage,** structured data collection and analysis are aimed at the solution of a specific problem. In our research process, the conclusive stage of research begins with step four. At this time, the collection of data is both time-consuming and expensive, and so it is extremely important that all research that is done be of help in solving the specific problem.

Step Three: Conduct Preliminary Investigation

In some ways this overlaps step two. Once researchers have gotten an idea of the real problem by talking with people within the company, they talk about the problem informally with people outside the company. These resources may include customers, competitors, advertising agency representatives, wholesalers, consultants, and retailers.

One method for talking informally with resources during this step in the research process is the focus group. A **focus group** is a group of consumers who meet a marketer's target specifications and are brought together to discuss marketing strategies and their needs and wants as consumers. The group usually consists of 8 to 12 people who gather in a comfortable setting. A moderator guides the discussion, starting with general conversation and getting more specific as the session progresses. Marketing executives might be behind a one-way mirror in the next room or might receive tapes (video or audio) of the sessions.

In her *New York Times* article "Consumer Panels Give Their Views—Focus Group Use Growing," Sandra Salmans explains that "focus groups have grown increasingly common in recent years because they are relatively fast and cheap. While a comprehensive survey may cost $25,000, a single focus group may range from $1,200 to $2,000. . . . The main users of focus groups are packaged-goods companies, and the usual members are average consumers. General Mills, for example, which brings out six major new products and perhaps 20 extensions of product lines each year, conducts at least one focus group every day, somewhere in the nation."[8]

Two new products that were "born" in focus groups are Pepsi Light (after consumers said they added lemon to diet soda to kill the unpleasant aftertaste) and Kissing Barbie (after a group of little girls confessed to making Barbie "kiss" Ken).

If they are used properly in the preliminary investigation step of the research process, focus groups can give companies numerous ideas about questions to ask during the formal research process. They can be used also as a part of the formal research process itself.

As a result of their preliminary investigations, researchers find sometimes that a formal investigation is not necessary. This happens most often when the company decides against pursuing a new project because the results of the preliminary investigation have produced enough conclusive information to assure the company that the project is not a feasible one.

Step Four: Plan and Conduct Formal Investigation

This is by far the most time-consuming and expensive step in the research process. It is also the most complex, because it consists of six substeps.

1. Determine information needs.
2. Determine information sources.
3. Determine methods for gathering primary data.
4. Design data gathering forms.
5. Design the sample.
6. Collect the data.

Determine Information Needs. When the decision has been made to go ahead with the formal investigation, this first step is necessary in order to plan a logical course of action. What exactly are you going to look for as you seek to solve your problem? If the problem is to determine how to convert nonusers of brand X to users of brand X, you would want to collect information such as the following.

- What is the brand that is bought by most non-users of brand X?
- How does brand X differ from the leading competitor?
- What are the major advantages to consumers who choose to buy brand X?
- Why do nonusers choose not to purchase brand X?
- What are the differences in characteristics between users and nonusers of brand X?

Determine Information Sources. After you decide what information you must collect, you should decide where and how to get that information. There are two major sources for research information: primary data and secondary data. **Primary data** are data gathered specifically for the research project you are now working on. **Secondary data** are data that have been collected for some other purpose. The major advantage to using secondary data is that the data already exist and are relatively inexpensive to gather. Another advantage is that it takes much less time to gather secondary data than primary data. Often researchers rush into gathering primary data when plenty of acceptable secondary data could just as well be used. The library is one of the first places to look for secondary data in the form of government publications, regularly published periodicals, books, monographs, and commercial data. Table 4-5 contains a listing of selected sources for government information, and Table 4-6 contains a list of selected sources for nongovernment secondary data.

These sources of secondary data and all others should be evaluated according to a set of simple criteria before they are accepted for use.

- **Is the source reliable?** It is important to determine whether information was collected in an acceptable manner and reported honestly.

- **Does the source provide information that meets our needs?** Irrelevant information is of little use, even if it is easy and inexpensive to obtain.

- **Is the source current?** Reports that are outdated may provide information that is now inaccurate for your purpose.

- **Is the source accurate?** Unfortunately, some

TABLE 4-5
SELECTED SOURCES OF GOVERNMENT INFORMATION

A. Publications	B. Agencies
American Statistical Index (Congressional Information Service), annual with monthly updates	Bureau of Census
Annual Survey of Manufacturers (Department of Commerce), annual	Bureau of Labor Statistics
Business Statistics (Office of Business Economics), biennial	Congressional Information Service
Catalog of U.S. Census Publications (Bureau of Census), quarterly	Consumer Product Safety Commission
Census of Manufacturers (Bureau of Census), every five years ending in 2 and 7	Department of Commerce
Census of Population (Bureau of Census), every ten years ending in 0	Department of Labor
Census of Retail Trade, Wholesale Trade, and Selected Service Industries (Bureau of Census), every five years ending in 2 and 7	Environmental Protection Agency
Census of Transportation (Bureau of Census), every five years ending in 2 and 7	Federal Reserve System
County and City Data Book (Department of Commerce), several times each decade	Federal Trade Commission
Federal Reserve Bulletin (Federal Reserve System), monthly	Food and Drug Administration
Monthly Labor Review (Bureau of Labor Statistics), monthly	National Center for Educational Statistics
Monthly Urban Review (Bureau of Labor Statistics), monthly	National Center for Health Statistics
Statistical Abstract of the United States (Department of Commerce), annual	National Technical Information Service
Survey of Current Business (Office of Business Economics), monthly	Office of Business Economics
Vital Statistics Report (Health, Education, and Welfare), monthly	Small Business Administration
	Statistical Reporting Service, Department of Agriculture
	United States Postal Service

TABLE 4-6
SELECTED SOURCES OF NONGOVERNMENT SECONDARY DATA*

A. Periodicals

		B. Commercial data:†
Advertising Age, weekly	*Journal of Marketing,* quarterly	The following commercial research houses sell information to subscribers.
Business Horizons, bimonthly	*Journal of Marketing Research,* quarterly	A. C. Nielsen
Business Week, weekly	*Journal of Retailing,* quarterly	Arbitron
California Management Review, quarterly	*Journal of Small Business Management,* quarterly	Audit Bureau of Circulation
Chain of Store Age, monthly	*MSU Business Topics,* quarterly	Audits and Surveys
Columbia Journal of World Business, quarterly	*Nielsen Researcher,* bimonthly	Dun and Bradstreet
Editor & Publisher's Market Guide, annual	*Progressive Grocer,* monthly	IMS (pharmaceutical data)
Fortune, semimonthly	*Rand McNally Commercial Atlas and Marketing Guide,* annual	Market Research Corporation of America
Graphic Guide to Consumer Markets, annual	*Sales and Marketing Management,* monthly (annual survey of buying power)	National Family Opinion
Harvard Business Review, bimonthly	*Stores,* monthly	National Purchase Diary Panel
Journal of the Academy of Marketing Science, quarterly	*University of Michigan Business Review,* quarterly	R. L. Polk (mailing lists, automobile data)
Journal of Advertising, bimonthly		Selling Area-Marketing, Inc. (SAMI)
Journal of Advertising Research, quarterly		Simmons (readership)
Journal of Business, quarterly		Standard Rate and Data Service
Journal of Consumer Research, quarterly		Starch (readership)

* This table is a representative listing. Many other sources can be found in any business library.
† For excellent coverage of commercial data sources, see Donald R. Lehmann, *Market Research and Analysis,* Richard D. Irwin, Homewood, Ill., 1979, pp. 208-245.

Reprinted with permission of Macmillan Publishing Co. from *Marketing* by Joel R. Evans and Barry Berman, © 1982 by Macmillan Publishing Co., pp. 63-64.

secondary sources are not very careful in collecting and reporting data. You should be able to evaluate the methods used by the secondary source.

Determine Methods for Gathering Primary Data.
If enough secondary data are not available, and if the project warrants the expense and time necessary for further research, the mar-

keter will want to work with the research staff to determine methods for gathering primary data. There are three basic methods that can be used to gather such project-related data: survey, observation, and experimentation.

The Survey Method. A **survey** is a method of gathering data by asking questions of a specific number of people (a **sample**) who have been selected from a larger group. A survey is a good way to find out what the opinions of customers are. Unfortunately, surveys can be expensive and time-consuming. Also, the researcher has to work hard to get accurate and meaningful data from respondents.

There are three basic methods of surveying respondents: by mail, by telephone, and in person. Each method has its advantages and disadvantages.

Surveying by Mail. A mail survey is an economical method of surveying, provided that there is an adequate return rate. The survey involves developing a **questionnaire** (a form containing questions) and mailing it to selected participants. These people are asked to return the completed form by mail.

The mail survey is free from interviewer bias because it is completed by the respondent and often is returned anonymously. However, there are several disadvantages to mail surveys. It is often difficult to obtain a good mailing list for a broad-scale survey. (The selection of respondents and sampling will be discussed in a later section of this chapter.) Another difficulty results from the fact that returns may not be usable or reliable, especially when important data are not supplied by the respondent. Still another limitation is the fact that there is no opportunity for the researcher to explain unclear questions or ask additional questions to clarify responses.

Surveying by Telephone. Telephone interviewing can seek responses to questions requiring quick, short answers and to questions requiring respondents' opinions and ideas. The telephone interviewer can ask follow-up questions that probe for additional ideas. For example, the questioner may ask, What do you like about the service at Bill's Cleaners? This question could be used in a local telephone survey.

Telephone interviews have the advantage of being more flexible than mail surveys because interviewers can ask questions that encourage respondents to answer. If a local survey is conducted, the expense of postage and travel is

avoided and responses are obtained very quickly. The cost of long-distance calls may be a disadvantage for surveys covering large geographic areas. However, larger surveys make increasing use of a central interviewing facility for placing calls, using the Wide Area Telephone Service (WATS). Big geographic areas can be surveyed at costs lower than those for personal interviewing. The telephone sample is limited to respondents with telephones that are listed. Also, it is easy to refuse to participate in the survey simply by hanging up the telephone.

In spite of these relatively minor disadvantages to telephone surveying, researchers continue to use this method. One survey was completed in East Lansing, Michigan, by a communications and media research organization called the ELRA Group. This organization conducted a survey to gather information that addressed the question, What services do prospective customers want from cable TV and what effect will this have on advertising and marketing possibilities?[9] This research is discussed on page 73.

For their survey, the ELRA Group completed more than 9,000 telephone interviews with randomly selected respondents in 23 markets in 11 states across the United States. The markets represented most of the major cable franchises or franchise areas that will be coming "on line" in the next 3 years. Over 47 percent of those interviewed indicated that they were very interested or somewhat interested in an in-home shopping channel that would show them merchandise that could be delivered to their homes or be held for pickup later. The items that these respondents were most interested in buying from home were food products, apparel, and household products.

Surveying in Person. The third method of surveying is the personal interview. Although this method is both expensive and time-consuming, it has the advantage of being the most flexible method. Trained interviewers talk face-to-face with respondents. If a respondent does not understand a question, it can be rephrased more clearly. Also, interviewers can observe respondents as

Figure 4-6. Ad for a market researcher shows interview techniques for primary data gathering in a variety of situations.

well as hear them. One inherent disadvantage to this method, however, is the fact that the interviewer may interject personal biases into the interview situation.

To gather information that addressed the question, How can dry cleaners retain customers and increase volume? Dr. Ernest Dichter combined the personal interview approach with the use of focus groups, structured questionnaires, and psychodrama (role playing on the part of the respondents). In his survey of 20 dry cleaners and 350 customers for the International Fabric Care Institute, Dr. Dichter found that people have an emotional attachment to their clothes and are reluctant to have them cleaned too often because some of their own personality may be cleaned out of the clothes. He also found that people are somewhat threatened by dry cleaners and that these merchants should pay more attention to human relations. Respondents volunteered the valuable suggestion that if customers could "subscribe" to the dry cleaning service for a flat fee each month, they probably would use the service more often.[10]

Another research study that used this method is interesting in that it reflects on the validity of a number of other studies. The purpose of this study was to determine whether overstatement of readership exists when a "recent-reading" technique is employed to measure the audience. The problem of overstatement occurs in studies that ask consumers to list the magazines they read regularly.

People frequently indicate that they read more magazines than they actually do. The recent-reading technique asks consumers what magazines they have read recently.

For this study, a deck of 160 cards was prepared, with each card containing the logo from one magazine. However, among the 160 cards were 22 containing fictitious logos for magazines that either did not exist or were no longer being published. It is not possible that the consumers surveyed could have read any of these 22 magazines.

A total of 510 personal interviews were conducted for the study: 264 men and 246 women. Each participant was handed the complete stack of cards. First they were asked to divide the cards into three piles. One pile was for magazines that the respondent had definitely read in the last 6 months. The second pile was for magazines they were not sure about. And the third pile was for magazines that they definitely had not read.

The interviewer then asked, for each of the magazines in the yes pile, how many out of four issues the respondent usually read. This same question was asked for the maybe pile.

Then the interviewer asked an additional readership question. Respondents were asked again to divide the cards into three piles. This time the yes, maybe, and no piles were for magazines that they had read in the last 2 weeks.

The study showed that many of the fictitious magazines and defunct magazines had a number of loyal readers. The results of the study were projected to a universe of 153 million adults to show the magnitude of the overstatement problem in trying to determine valid readership figures. For example, of the defunct or fictitious weekly publications, *Popular Sports* had the most "readers" (2,780,000, or 2 percent) followed by *News-events* (2,340,000, or 1.6 percent) and *Women's Weekly* (1,290,000, or 0.08 percent).[11]

The study concluded that the recent-reading technique did lead to overstatement on readership. For our purposes, this study indicates that marketing research findings should be used as one of the important tools in the decision making process but that the marketer must reserve judgment about using the numbers shown in any study of this type without considering the possibility of overstatement. Numbers are essential to research studies, but their meaning must be interpreted very carefully.

The Observation Method. The second basic method that can be used to gather project-related data is observation. Using this method, the researchers simply observe behavior. This involves watching and recording the events they see. As opposed to the survey method, researchers avoid direct contact with people being observed. In fact, people should not even know that they are being observed. One use for the observation method might be to determine whether customers are attracted by a particular type of store display. Another might be to see how long customers have to wait before they are able to order in a restaurant.

Observation does not always have to be done by the researcher. Mechanical observation devices such as cameras and recorders can be used. Observation has the advantage of being a relatively simple method to employ. The respondent does not have to agree in order to cooperate. However, observations are subject to the biases of the observer and cannot indicate why respondents act as they do.

The Experimental Method. The third basic method that can be used to gather project-related data is experimentation. When researchers use experimentation, they try to establish a cause-and-effect relationship by controlling one variable and trying to produce a desired effect in another variable. This method is used frequently in test marketing a new product. If the company is unsure which of two marketing strategies to use, it tries each one in a different test market.

An article published in *Advertising Age* reported the results of a study that compared the effectiveness of two different types of TV advertisements: emotional and rational. From 39 com-

PIGGLY WIGGLY EXPERIMENTS

In this example, experimental research addressed the task of assessing the impact of short-term supermarket strategy variables. The experiment was conducted in one store of the Piggly Wiggly supermarket chain that was chosen for its loyal and varied clientele. Two of the products tested were Camay soap (bath size) and Piggly Wiggly frozen pie shells (two in a package). The experiment sought to determine the effect that temporary price reductions, display alternatives, and newspaper advertising had on unit sales of these products. Competing brands and alternative sizes for the experimental products were ordered, stocked, and shelved by the experimenters and were kept at regular price and usual display throughout the experiment. The experimenters then varied the price, advertising, and display space for these items in a scientific and controlled manner.

The experimenters found that the highest sales level (143 units) for Camay soap occurred when the product was advertised at a low price and treated to an in-store display. The next highest sales level was only 88 units and occurred with no advertising, a low price, and a special display. "The impact of special display as well as its effect in combination with price reveals that in-store promotion is perhaps the most powerful short-term strategy alternative available to supermarket management."

For Piggly Wiggly pie shells, "sales in units increased steadily as price changed from regular (26 units) to reduced (33 units) and then to cost (44 units)." "As display level changed from regular shelf space to expanded shelf space and then to special display, sales in units increased from 20 to 26 and then jumped to 57—again demonstrating the power of in-store promotion. Moreover, special display is significantly different from both regular and expanded display."

Based on information obtained from David B. Montgomery, *Marketing Information and Decision Systems: Coming of Age In the '70s,* Marketing Science Institute, Cambridge, Mass., August 1973, pp. 29–30.

mercials for regularly advertised products, 6 were chosen for use in the study: 3 rational and 3 emotional. The rational commercials were for Off, Lestoil, and Super Shade by Coppertone. The emotional commercials were for Fritos, Ramada Inns, and Dial Soap.

Four hundred women in the Grand Rapids, Michigan, area participated in the study. Each was shown a control commercial and three of the six test commercials in her own home on cable TV.

The day after the commercials were shown, half the participants were asked to recall the brand names of the products they had seen advertised in the commercials. The other half were shown the commercials for a second time. But this time the brand identity was masked from both the audio and the video. For the rational commercials, those participants who were asked to recognize the masked commercials scored 19 percent higher than the ones who were asked to recall those commercials. But for the emotional commercials, the participants scored a surprising 68 percent higher on recognition than they did on recalling the same commercials. On the basis of this experimental research, researchers suggested that advertisers should take another look at the possible use of emotional advertising.[12] Read on the opposite page how Piggly Wiggly used experimental research.

The advantage of using the experimental method is that actual cause and effect relationships can be identified in a scientific manner in order to help the marketer with future decisions.

The major problem with conducting controlled experiments is the difficulty of controlling the variables.

Some additional popular marketing research methods are identified in Table 4-7 as defined by *Sales and Marketing Management*. The first research method defined is the very popular technique of using consumer diary panels. The article on page 115 describes the panel method as used by three marketing research companies. The NPD advertisement on page 114 will help you understand this marketing research service and how marketers can benefit from the results.

TABLE 4-7
POPULAR MARKETING RESEARCH METHODS

Diary Panel A group of consumers who have agreed to keep a written record, or diary, of their purchases. The diary usually includes such information as date of purchase, brand bought, size, number of items, price of each item, whether or not a special offer was involved, and how the consumer found out about the offer. Sometimes consumers are also asked to record the Universal Product Code for the items.

Focus Group A group of 8–12 consumers who meet a marketer's specifications in terms of usage of a particular product category. The group is brought together, with a moderator, to discuss products, promotions, advertising, and other marketing strategies.

Retail Audit A measurement among retail outlets that can monitor total sales by brand and also inventory, price, distribution, point-of-purchase materials, and shelf-space allocation.

Scanner An electronic checkout system for supermarkets that reads the Universal Product Code on merchandise and records the item, its price, and the time of purchase. The data are stored in the supermarket's computer and are reported weekly to store management and to research purchasers.

Scanner Panel A group of consumers who have agreed to present a plastic identification card to the supermarket checker each time they shop. The card permits the recording of the supermarket's scanner data for each consumer on the panel.

Warehouse Audit A measure of merchandise shipments, by brand and size, from warehouses to food stores or drugstores.

Source: *Sales and Marketing Management,* March 16, 1981, p. 52.

Figure 4-7. Research using consumer diary panels helps to answer questions about consumer behavior and to predict future trends.

Design Data Gathering Forms. As you have already learned, the data gathering form for research is called a questionnaire. Designing a good questionnaire is one of the researcher's most difficult tasks.

In designing the questionnaire, only necessary questions should be included, and all questions should be easy to answer. Questions must be phrased in such a way that the respondent knows specifically what is being asked. Avoid confusing lead-ins such as "on the whole." Organize the questionnaire so that you ask easy-to-answer questions first and leave the harder ones for later. Position classification questions (age, sex, and occupation) and identification questions (name and address) last. If a respondent chooses not to answer classification or identification questions, some of the questionnaire data may still be used.

CONSUMER RESEARCH USING DIARY PANELS

The invitation in the pink business-size envelope seemed designed just for me. If I faithfully recorded my purchases in certain categories for a year, I would earn points that would qualify me for a prize.

Being much in need of one of those prizes, a toaster, and being naturally inclined to want to argue and justify—even grocery purchases—I sped the questionnaire back. Despite my zeal, I lie dead somewhere in a computer bank—no more pink envelopes.

Soliciting demographically balanced consumers to cooperate in such ventures is a business that is rapidly growing more sophisticated in measuring techniques and in specialized offerings to the client. A plethora of companies offer a variety of services, all designed to assure the client that their techniques can predict the consumer's behavior.

It is also a field that electronics bids fair to revolutionize within the decade, although the traditional companies in the field insist that there will always be a need for the old-fashioned diary filled out carefully by consumers who are given incentives to do so.

Thus, despite the advent of scanners, diary panel test marketing continues in the traditional ways. Three large companies dominate the national scene. NPD (the National Panel Diary) has two ongoing national panels of 6,500 families each that report monthly some 40 to 50 categories of purchases. MRCA's (Market Research Corp. of America) National Consumer Panel reports food, beverages, personal care items, and textile and clothing purchases from 7,500 households on a weekly reporting basis.

NFO (National Family Opinion) has a pool of over 220,000 out of which it is operating 3 or 4 major diary operations—not all the data pool is operating at one time.

All told, an estimated 100 national panels are now in operation that a client might want to plug into. Local panels are widely available as well. NPD alone has 42,000 panelists in over 50 local test markets. Another couple of dozen companies offer custom research (as do the large companies) either for the client who has a specialized need that no existing panel is addressing or for someone who wants to pull focus groups out of a panel for other research.

The process is pretty much the same across the board. A blanket mailing is sent out which yields a rough 10 percent return (perhaps more if there has been prescreening offered by some custom companies). Respondents are then weeded out to obtain a stratified quota sample, then demographically projected either nationally to the total U.S. population or locally to reflect demographic consideration. NPD estimates that 8 percent of people contacted respond, and that out of 1,000 initially recruited, 280 will stay in place for 12 months. All panels are updated periodically to maintain numbers as well as to monitor demographic variables such as state and family head education.

Adapted from Carol Poston, "Dear Diary Panel," *Advertising Age*, February 9, 1981, pp. S-10–S-11.

The design of the questionnaire is also important. It should be laid out so that it is easy to read and complete. Look at the format of the questionnaire shown in Figure 4-8. Would you be able to complete it easily? Notice the simple marking technique and the coding for tabulation.

Before the questionnaire is used, it must be pretested. This means that people similar to the ones who will be the actual respondents should be asked to complete the questionnaire so that hidden problems can be identified and eliminated.

Design the Sample.

Because it usually is not possible to survey every person who could possibly help solve a particular research problem, a small number of those people, or a sample, is chosen at random (each person has an equal chance to be in the sample) from all the people who could possibly help (called the **universe** or population).

It is important that the sample be large enough to actually represent the population or universe. As one example of sampling, if 45 percent of the population in a particular community is over the age of 65, then 45 percent of the participants in the sample should also be over 65 to keep the sample in proportion to the population. Three sampling techniques that are often used in marketing research are the simple random sample, the stratified random sample, and the area, or cluster, sample.

Simple Random Sample.

For this sample, researchers begin with a list of the members of the population and simply choose members in a random fashion. This might be compared with pulling names out of a hat, assuming that all the members of the population were equally represented within the hat full of names.

Stratified Random Sample.

For a stratified random sample, the population is divided into subgroups. Then each subgroup is treated like a simple random sample. This type of sample is used when the researcher wants to make sure that members of each of the subgroups are included in the sample.

Area (Cluster) Sample.

For the area, or cluster, sample, a random sample is taken of a smaller area. For example, for a random sample of Cleveland, Ohio, residents, it would be possible to list all the blocks in the city and then select a random sample of clusters of blocks. From that sample, every house or every other house in the cluster could be the target of the survey.

Collect the Data.

It is necessary to train the field-workers who will actually collect the data for a research study. When interviewing and observation are important parts of the research process, poorly motivated or poorly trained field-workers can cause the quality of the research project to drop significantly. If researchers supervise their field-workers as closely as possible and impress on them the value of their work, the results should be good.

If data collection depends on the mailing of a questionnaire, a carefully written cover letter should be prepared to accompany it. This letter should explain the purpose of the study and encourage recipients to return the questionnaire. Usually a postage-paid return envelope is enclosed for the recipient's use, and sometimes incentives are used. An incentive is a gift to encourage participation in a research study. The incentive might be bookplates or a bookmark which is enclosed with the questionnaire when it is sent out. The cover letter might say that this small gift is to thank the recipient in advance for taking time to complete the questionnaire. Alternatively, the incentive might be promised to the recipient after the completed questionnaire has been returned. In this case a book or a merchandise certificate might be used.

Step Five: Process and Analyze Data

Before data can be used, the data must be summarized, processed, categorized, tabulated, and interpreted. This step includes counting numbers and putting them together in usable categories. Interpreting is the establishment of meaning for these numbers or words and symbols. If you managed a video-games business, you could process

DEPARTMENT STORE CUSTOMER RESEARCH

INSTRUCTIONS:

Mark X in the appropriate boxes. Please disregard the small numbers: they are for machine tabulation only. The questions can be answered most easily by the member of the household who does *most* of the shopping.

	1. Do you have a charge account at these stores?		2. Have you made a purchase in these stores during the last year?		3. Have you shopped these stores in the last 30 days? (Even if you did not make a purchase.)		4. In which of these stores did you shop on your MOST RECENT TRIP? (Even if you did not make a purchase.)
	YES	NO	YES	NO	YES	NO	
Carson Pirie Scott & Co.	C7 ☐ 1	☐ 2	C16 ☐ 1	☐ 2	C25 ☐ 1	☐ 2	C34 ☐ 1
Sears, Roebuck and Co.	C8 ☐ 1	☐ 2	C17 ☐ 1	☐ 2	C26 ☐ 1	☐ 2	C35 ☐ 1
K-Mart	C9 ☐ 1	☐ 2	C18 ☐ 1	☐ 2	C27 ☐ 1	☐ 2	C36 ☐ 1
Robeson's	C10 ☐ 1	☐ 2	C19 ☐ 1	☐ 2	C28 ☐ 1	☐ 2	C37 ☐ 1
Montgomery Ward & Co.	C11 ☐ 1	☐ 2	C20 ☐ 1	☐ 2	C29 ☐ 1	☐ 2	C38 ☐ 1
Goldblatt Bros.	C12 ☐ 1	☐ 2	C21 ☐ 1	☐ 2	C30 ☐ 1	☐ 2	C39 ☐ 1
W. Lewis & Co.	C13 ☐ 1	☐ 2	C22 ☐ 1	☐ 2	C31 ☐ 1	☐ 2	C40 ☐ 1
J.C. Penney Co.	C14 ☐ 1	☐ 2	C23 ☐ 1	☐ 2	C32 ☐ 1	☐ 2	C41 ☐ 1
Zayre	C15 ☐ 1	☐ 2	C24 ☐ 1	☐ 2	C33 ☐ 1	☐ 2	C42 ☐ 1

5. On which day of the week did your most recent shopping trip occur? (Mark only one.)

C43

Monday	Tuesday	Wednesday	Thursday	Friday	Saturday	Sunday
☐ 1	☐ 2	☐ 3	☐ 4	☐ 5	☐ 6	☐ 7

6. How many family members participated in your most recent shopping trip? (Mark only one.)

C44 1☐ 1 2☐ 2 3☐ 3 4☐ 4 5☐ 5 6☐ 6 7☐ 7 8☐ 8 9 or more ☐ 9

11. How many family members are presently living in your household? (Exclude any boarders.)

C73 1☐ 1 2☐ 2 3☐ 3 4☐ 4 5☐ 5 6☐ 6 7☐ 7 8☐ 8 9 or more ☐ 9

12. What is the age of the head of your household?

C74

| 24 or under ☐ 1 | 35–44 ☐ 3 | 55–64 ☐ 5 |
| 25–34 ☐ 2 | 45–54 ☐ 4 | 65 or over ☐ 6 |

13. Are there children living in your household?

C75 No ☐ 1 Yes ☐ 2 How many in each age group?

	9 years old or less (Mark only one) C76	10–19 years old (Mark only one) C77	20 years old or older (Mark only one) C78
0	☐ 0	☐ 0	☐ 0
1	☐ 1	☐ 1	☐ 1
2	☐ 2	☐ 2	☐ 2
3	☐ 3	☐ 3	☐ 3
4	☐ 4	☐ 4	☐ 4
5 or more	☐ 5	☐ 5	☐ 5

Figure 4-8. This illustration shows selected questions from a recent consumer questionnaire.

the data in a simple research project by tabulating the numbers gathered during a specific time. Categories could be established for men, women, over 20 years of age, and under 20. The data could be interpreted by relating them to how long each group played games and how much money was spent. Advertising decisions might result, or price-reduction coupons might be given to frequent customers.

This is one step where many researchers fall down in their responsibilities. Raw data that have not been analyzed are of little use to the marketer or researcher. If the questionnaire has been made up entirely of objective questions, this step can be done with the help of the computer. Processing the data can be an exciting part of the research process.

However, if the questionnaire also contains open-ended questions on which respondents can express their own opinions, the processing and analyzing procedure becomes much more difficult. Open-ended questions are useful in gathering ideas from customers, but it is often very difficult to categorize, or group, statements about

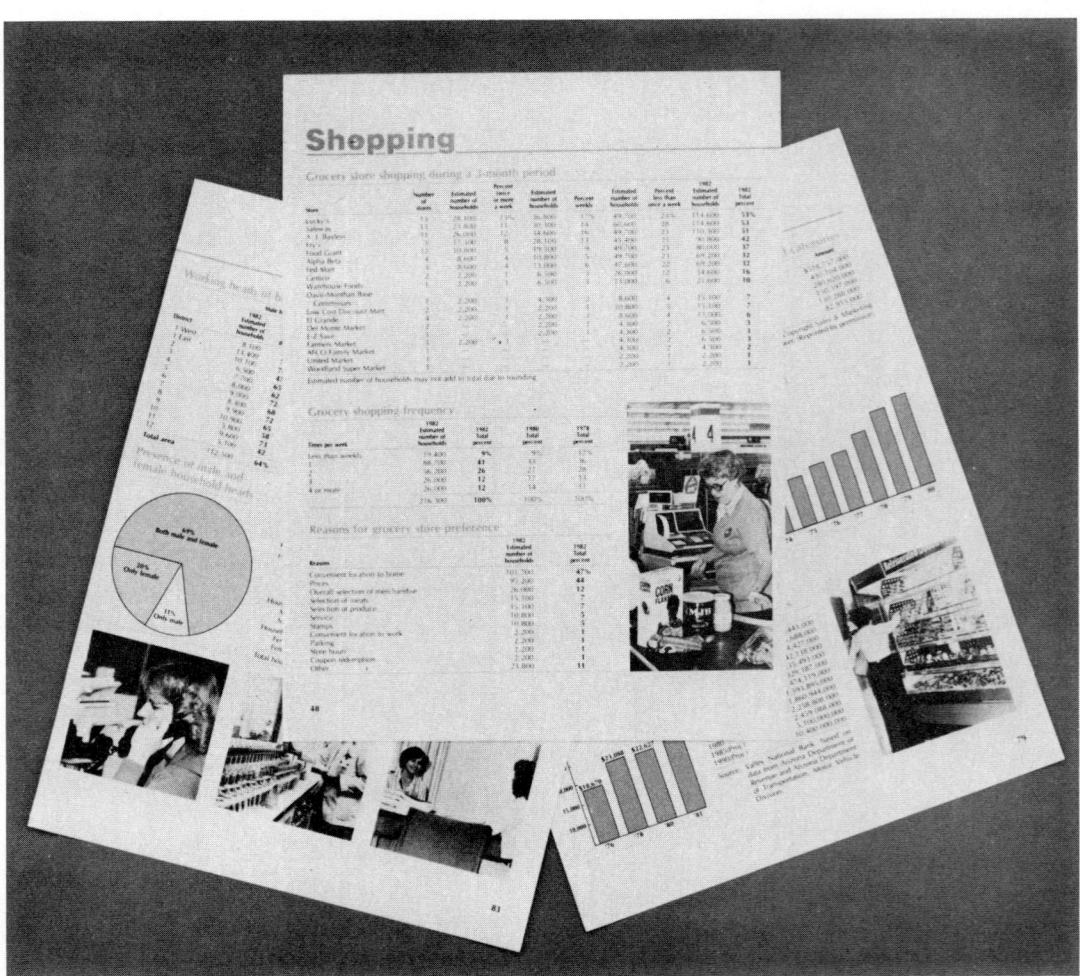

Figure 4-9. Charts, graphs, and tables reduce the results of market research to a clear and objective presentation as in this material from a firm in Tucson, Arizona.

product and service likes and dislikes. Often the results of these open-ended questions are simply listed verbatim, and marketing decisions are made after studying the most serious or common ideas.

After objective questions have been processed and analyzed, the results often are presented in the form of charts, graphs, and tables that make the results easier to understand and apply to the research problem.

Step Six: Prepare Written Report

The last step in the research process is writing the report. Researchers should make sure that the report is clearly written and easy to understand. It should be focused on the problem that was researched, and it should include a summary, conclusions, and recommendations. The purpose of the written report is not to produce something that can be admired as a work of art. Instead, it is meant to be a tool that is used by the marketer in problem solving and decision making. Research reports for large marketing firms are almost always prepared in written form, often with an oral report to management by the research team. Small marketers may perform simple but effective marketing research and make decisions without preparing a formal written report. The research output should be used to make decisions. This is the practical application.

RESEARCH APPLICATIONS FOR SMALL MARKETERS

Marketing research and information systems are used extensively by large marketers. Large sales volume and research budgets support the use of research and data gathering for decision making. However, as indicated throughout this chapter, small marketers have to use marketing research and some form of MKIS in their businesses. The steps and techniques described in this chapter may be used. The size of the study, the amount of data gathered, the time used, and the dollars spent all have to be scaled down to be practical for the small marketer. Let us look at some examples of research applications used by small marketers.

A small retail marketer of handcrafted items used observation research techniques to help make decisions on types of toys to sell. The marketer donated toys to a preschool-age day care center for the opportunity to observe children playing with different types of sample toys. For example, the marketer watched the children's reaction to handcrafted wood trucks, cars, and wagons. Which models did they reach for? Continue to play with? Operate easily? Break quickly? Simple notes were taken, and tabulations were made easily. The practical research resulted in better decisions on which types of toys children of this age would like and parents would buy.

A small restaurant located near a university competed with McDonald's and Wendy's. This marketer's research goal was to learn how he could appeal to the university students and increase patronage and sales volume. A short questionnaire was prepared which asked respondents to evaluate the three restaurants. College students were hired to distribute the questionnaires in the dormitories and then collect the completed questionnaires. The results were alarming but very informative. The marketer's restaurant was ranked first by only 4.4 percent of the student respondents. Only 42 percent of the respondents were even aware of his recent advertising. However, quality of food and service were ranked very high by respondents who had eaten there in the last month. As a result of this research, the small marketer increased his sales volume significantly by improving his promotional campaign to university students on the basis of the results of this relatively inexpensive research study.

A laundry and dry cleaning service marketer evaluated two sources of advertising by using a simple research technique. She was located in a market that was served by two newspapers, a weekly and a daily. She had determined that she could afford to run only two ads a week. Should she run one ad in each newspaper or two ads at different times in one newspaper only? She knew the costs of an ad in each newspaper and the readership numbers for the market. She did not know which newspaper would generate more customers per ad dollar. The research study was simple. She ran a coupon ad in both newspapers at the same time. Each newspaper coupon was coded for identification. She could then tabulate the number and percentage of coupons redeemed for service from each newspaper. The result was a better understanding of which newspaper generated more customers for her type of business. Although she continued to advertise in both newspapers regularly, the research results helped her decide to spend two-thirds of her advertising dollars in the weekly newspaper.

Here are some additional examples of research studies that were performed by several small marketers. A small food store marketer invited several women customers to talk with him in a focus-group arrangement to learn what they liked and disliked about his store. He made several improvements in his products and services and paid his customers with steaks. The owner-manager of a small sports clothing store for women used a customer panel of women tennis players to help her select new lines of tennis clothing. Her research involved measuring responses from different age groups and from different city markets. A small department store combined data from internal sales records and an external survey of customers' demographic data. The results showed that the store's most loyal customers had a higher average number of children than the general population in this market. The children's clothing department was enlarged, and sales volume increased significantly.

Small marketers use marketing research and information systems. The data numbers may be hundreds rather than thousands or millions. The data may be gathered on very simple forms rather than on expensive printed forms. The data may be processed on calculators rather than computers. The interpretation may be arrived at by one or a few decision makers rather than several large research and management teams. But the results often will be just as exciting and important to the decision maker.

- Marketing information is the key to solving marketing problems and making successful marketing decisions.

- Information is needed to successfully complete each of the following decision-making steps: identify the problem, get all the facts, identify the decision-making rules, identify alternatives, evaluate alternatives, select an alternative, make a decision, implement the decision, and follow up.

- A marketing information system (MKIS) is an organized set of procedures designed to gather, sort, analyze, evaluate, and distribute the information needed to make marketing decisions. Almost all MKISs are computerized.

- A marketing information system is made up of four major sources of information: internal information, external information, marketing models, and marketing research.

- Internal information in the form of operating statements, sales analysis reports, inventory control information, and reports from marketing personnel help marketers evaluate a firm's level of performance.

- Information on markets, competitors, products, promotion, and economic conditions is part of the external information needed to help marketers with decision making.

- A model is a set of interrelated variables that are set up to represent a real system, process, or outcome. Marketers can use marketing models to try to predict what would happen in real markets if they changed price, promotion, product, or location variables.

- Marketing research is an objective system designed to collect, analyze, and report information and findings relevant to a specific problem or situation facing a company.

- Marketers use two major sources for research information: primary data, which are gathered specifically for the research project that is currently being worked on, and secondary data that were collected for some other purpose.

- Three methods used to gather primary data are survey, observation, and experimentation.

- The output of a marketing research study should be a written report which presents data, analyzes the data, and makes suggestions for the solution to the problem. The overall purpose of marketing research is to help the marketer make better marketing decisions.

KEY TERMS AND CONCEPTS

conclusive stage
databases
desk research
exploratory stage
focus group
management information system (MIS)
marketing information system (MKIS)
marketing research

model
primary data
questionnaire
sample
secondary data
survey
universe

DISCUSSION QUESTIONS

1. Explain the major differences between a marketing information system and marketing research.

2. Marketing personnel are an excellent source of internal information. Assume that you own and manage a retail clothing store. What types of information should you get from your personnel to help you make marketing decisions?

3. For additional information for your retail clothing store, you may need to seek external sources. Describe some types of information you would expect to obtain from these sources.

4. Why do marketers often need both secondary data and primary data to solve problems?

5. Using the three basic methods of gathering primary data (survey, observation, and experimentation), describe how you might use each method to solve a problem in a clothing store.

NOTES

1. Adapted from Philip Kotler, "A Design for the Firm's Marketing Nerve Center," *Business Horizons,* Fall 1966, p. 70.
2. "New NRMA Study Documents POS Benefits," *Stores* magazine, March 1982, pp. 14–16.
3. Lee Adler, "Marketing Research: Being Your Own Marketing Researcher Is Not as Difficult as It Sounds," *Sales and Marketing Management,* November 16, 1981, pp. 133–134.
4. Walter Kiechel III, "Everything You Always Wanted to Know May Soon Be On-Line," *Fortune,* May 5, 1980, pp. 226–237.
5. John Curley, "Games, Other Luxuries Sell Well as Slump Slows Sales of Durables," *Wall Street Journal,* May 6, 1982, p. 31.
6. J. Reginald Rhodes, "Modeling Discomforts," *Advertising Age,* October 26, 1981, pp. S16–S17.
7. David B. Montgomery, *Marketing Information and Decision Systems: Coming of Age in the '70s,* Marketing Science Institute, Cambridge, Mass., August 1973, pp. 29–30.
8. Sandra Salmans, "Consumer Panels Give Their Views—Focus Group Use Growing," *New York Times,* April 5, 1982, pp. D1–D2.
9. Don E. Schultz, "Consumer Poll Plugs into Cable," *Advertising Age,* October 26, 1981, pp. S30–S31.
10. Interview with Dr. Ernest Dichter, Ernest Dichter Associates, 1982.
11. Clark Schiller, "Remembered, but Never Read," *Advertising Age,* October 26, 1981, pp. S14–S15.
12. David Berger, "A Retrospective FCB Recall Study," *Advertising Age,* October 26, 1981, pp. S36–S38.

APPLICATIONS/CASES

APPLICATION 3: SEGMENTING A MARKET BY AGE

In an attempt to discover various marketing opportunities, many businesses divide the population into segments. One way to do this is to consider the population as segmented by age. For this project, you will be asked to consider the life cycle of a human from birth to death, given some information and assumptions about each step in the life cycle. You also will be asked to indicate some products and services that would be appropriate for each segment.

Note that segments and assumptions vary from one individual to another and were somewhat arbitrarily established for the purpose of providing an example here.

a. List concrete examples of products and services that are suited to and should be targeted at each particular age segment.

b. As the population ages, how should businesses change their marketing strategies?

APPLICATION 4: MARKETING A PRODUCT THAT FITS TO A TEE

One of the outgrowths of the economic difficulties of the 1980s has been an increased emphasis on market segmentation. In an effort to target their advertising dollars more precisely and identify people who are likely to buy or use their products and services more accurately, businesses at the manufacturing and retail levels have been attempting to divide their markets and sell to them.

To illustrate this at the manufacturing level, consider golf balls. One is the same as another. They are all white and round and have funny little dimples. Until recently, this was undeniably the case. All golf balls are still round, but the similarity stops there. Some are designed to be hit high in the air and others low. Some are designed to be hit farther than others, and some are supposed to go in a more straight line. They are not even all white.

Age segment	Name	Characteristics
0–4	infants/babies	Completely dependent on parents
5–12	children	Begin school, growing up
13–18	adolescents	At school, may work part-time
19–30	singles or young marrieds	Begin full-time employment, begin to establish household
31–45	parents	Appliances wear out, income rises, children arrive and are supported
46–65	empty nesters	Increased leisure time, increased income, savings, investments
66 and over	senior citizens	Retirement, eventual death

In the summer of 1981, Wilson Sporting Goods introduced an orange golf ball into the market. Most of their competition laughed, for golf is a game of tradition, and golfers are noted for conservatism. However, the new product was surprisingly popular. Many other manufacturers of golfing equipment began producing and marketing colored golf balls, some orange, some yellow, and in one case, pink. Soon, over 40 million colored golf balls a year were being sold by Wilson and its competitors.

a. You are the owner of a sporting goods store that sells golf equipment. How would you identify three different market segments for colored golf balls?

b. How are manufacturers of golf balls differentiating their product in other ways? How does this relate to market segmentation?

CASE 3: WHAT GOES UPHILL MUST COME DOWN

Skiing began as a means of transportation in the snowy climates of northern Europe about 5,000 years ago. It first was put to many practical uses, such as hunting, herding animals, and moving between places. Then it was adapted to the military and used during the winter months by the armies of several nations. This skiing closely resembled what is referred to today as Nordic, or cross-country, skiing.

Alpine, or downhill, skiing evolved as the skiing techniques suitable to the relatively flat terrain of the Scandinavian countries were modified to work in the Austrian Alps. Different equipment and skills were required to work on the steep slopes, and the ability to turn fairly quickly was developed. Soon skiing began to be used in competition as people vied to see who could turn most quickly and who could get from the top of a mountain to the bottom fastest. It was an arduous adventure, since the only way to get to the top of the mountain before racing down was to climb.

Times have changed. Today skiing is a sport (actually two: downhill and cross-country) that provides recreation for over 14 million people in the United States. An important part of our economy, it provides employment for a large number of people in the many ski areas and retail stores catering to the skier. In addition, countless others are employed in manufacturing and supplying the accessories necessary for the sport, feeding the skiers, and transporting them to the slopes. Annually, an estimated amount in excess of $3.5 billion is spent on skiing in this country, making it a major industry.

Skiing seems to be a sport dominated by the young. About half of all adult skiers are under 30, and only about 6 percent are over 55. Those who ski are twice as likely to be employed in professional or managerial occupations as their nonskiing counterparts and have a median household income of $22,376. Incidentally, downhill skiers earn more than cross-country, a median income of $22,874 as opposed to $21,463.

Skiers are willing to travel. Many live and work in the metropolitan areas of the east and west coasts. Consequently, over 60 percent travel up to 250 miles one way to indulge in the sport. When doing this, they generally use their own cars. For those traveling to the ski resorts in the Rockies, air travel is popular, a fact that certainly contributes to Denver's Stapleton Airport being one of the busiest in the nation.

Skiers have other interests in life. Over half of them garden, ride bicycles, hike, and camp, and over 40 percent play tennis and sail. They participate in these activities far more often than the rest of the population.

With over 8,300 ski shops, more than 700 ski areas, and hundreds of manufacturers of skis, boots, poles, clothing, and accessories, competition for the skier's dollar is keen. Thus marketing plays an important role in the success of these business operations. Using the information in Chapters 3 and 4, answer the following questions.

Based on author interview and information obtained from Jeff Palmer, "White Paper on Skiing," *Ski Industries America,* McLean, Virginia, March 1982.

a. Why would it be helpful to know trends in the age of the population?

b. What trend relative to age is mentioned in your text? How would this be helpful to you as the owner of a ski area?

c. Why would it be helpful to segment downhill from cross-country skiers?

d. What use is information on other interests of skiers? How would the publisher of a ski magazine use this information? How would the owner of a ski shop use it?

e. What target market strategies would you suggest for a ski resort in the Rocky Mountains? Why?

CASE 4: WHO WILL BUY AN ELECTRIC CAR?

Usually the proclamation that "we're number one" carries status and is used by successful companies. In the case of U.S. Electricar Corp., the number one manufacturer of electric cars in the United States, the status may be present, but the success is uncertain. The problem is that the size of the market for electric cars has not yet been determined.

U.S. Electricar has been in business about 7 years, manufacturing and selling battery-powered electric cars named the Lectric Leopard. These cars are basically Fiats or Renaults that have been modified by removing the gasoline engine and replacing it with a battery-powered one. The modification also includes a pack of 16 batteries in the trunk. The Lectric Leopards sell for a price that varies from $9,000 to $13,000 depending on the model. The cars run for about 50 miles before the batteries run down, and then an 8-hour recharge is necessary.

Currently, the company is producing about 250 cars annually and generating well over $1 million in sales. There has been only one profitable quarter in the 7 years in which they have been doing business, but the company hopes for dramatic improvement. They recently reached a 10-year agreement with Fiat for the purchase of cars without engines and accessories.

Although U.S. Electricar is number one in sales, another company, General Motors, is doing research on electric cars and the market for them. At this time, GM has set aside $35 million for research and development of an electric car. According to a spokesperson, they do not plan to introduce it into the market until 1986 at the earliest and probably not until 1990. As to the market for electric cars, a GM public relations manager states, "I don't think anybody really knows what the market is." In reference to U.S. Electricar's sales, he continues, "You can sell 50 a month of almost anything in this country."

In considering the market for their products, most auto manufacturers try to obtain some information about their customers and their motives for buying. Typical information would include data about the age, sex, and marital status of new car buyers. In addition, data concerning income, educational level, and socioeconomic status would be helpful. Motives for buying could include economy, durability, price, status, luxury, appearance, road handling, and riding comfort.

U.S. Electricar would like to expand. Its chairperson is talking of increasing production to 20,000 to 30,000 Lectric Leopards annually in the near future. Although production of this many is feasible, two questions need to be answered: What is the market for electric cars? and How large is it?

Based on information obtained from "Electric Corp. Faces Uphill Climb in Unknown Market," *New England Business*, May 18, 1981, pp. 24–26.

a. What will be a possible effect if the company increases its production dramatically without pursuing these two questions?

b. How would the company go about defining the market for the Lectric Leopard?

c. To answer these questions, does the company need internal or external information? What types?

UNIT 3

PRODUCT/ SERVICE

CHAPTER 5

MARKETING PRODUCTS AND SERVICES

A tennis racket is a relatively simple product. Even if you have never played tennis, you probably have seen and held a racket. If you are a tennis player, you have selected and purchased a racket from among many on the market. Maybe you have purchased and used several. In any case, you may be surprised at the complexity of this apparently simple product.

To understand how complicated the marketing of one type of product can be, let us play a consumer question game about tennis rackets. You are going to buy a new racket. How many brands can you choose from? How many different models are available? What choices do you have in terms of materials? What range of prices can you expect? What features are available? What are some benefits you might expect from the use of these rackets?

There are more than 30 major brand names of good-quality rackets for sale in the United States. This number excludes many rackets sold in variety and discount stores as toys or for the very casual player. Each company brand offers several models, and the total comes to at least 188. Rackets can be grouped according to construction materials used: wood, wood composite, metal, metal composite, and graphite. You probably would pay at least $50 for a good racket, and you could pay as much as $500 for an unstrung racket. Rackets may be selected to meet your personal requirements by varying the weight, balance, head size, grip size, flexibility, and type of strings in addition to the brand name, model, material, and price. We could use hundreds of words to describe the benefits you should receive from the use of certain rackets. Rackets are described with words like these: power, control, flexible, responsive, maneuverable, firm, sensitive, stable, lightweight, comfortable, large sweet spot, reduces bad shots, smooth, durable, reduces vibration. That must be more than most people would want to know about tennis rackets, and we used only some of all the variables involved in either consuming or marketing rackets.[1]

If an apparently simple product like this involves so many factors, how do we identify and market products and services? Maybe a tennis racket is more than just a racket. Maybe a racket is a better product because the consumer buys a service (tennis lessons) from a tennis professional. Maybe a consumer buys a racket to please friends, have fun, or achieve status. What should marketers consider when planning to market products and services?

WHAT IS A PRODUCT?

Most consumers say that a product is something to buy. Marketers often respond by saying that a product is what they sell. Both answers are correct, but a product is much more. One may buy a product that is wood, metal, or plastic, but these are physical features only. What is being purchased is actually the total utility of a product. (See the ballpoint pen example below.) The satisfaction derived from the product will result from the buyer's perception of the combination of physical features and services related to the product. Marketers must think of these potential satisfactions sought by consumers when they plan products. Planning a product or service is a complex and challenging task for the marketer. Developing the product or service concept is the important first step. Let us look at the definition of the marketer's product concept which leads to the development of a product-service mix that satisfies customers.

An Example of Total Product Concept

Consumer Product
A quality ballpoint pen.

Consumer's Basic Need
To make visible lines on paper.

Physical Features
Metal, plastic, and ink; moving, mechanical parts; clean, neat appearance.

Service Features
Guaranteed forever.
Free repairs when needed.
Free replacement if not repairable.

Psychological Features
A status symbol, admired by friends.
A secure feeling, a pen forever.
A "friend," reliable and always there when needed.
Helps relieve tension; senses of touch and sight.

Total Product
A bundle of utilities.
Satisfaction for the price.
Product meets expectation.

Product Concept

One can look at the product concept by referring back to tennis rackets. Why does a consumer want to purchase it? What clues are there in this product example that suggest the concerns marketers should have in developing a product concept? A product is purchased for more reasons than its physical features. Every product is a set of problem-solving benefits; this is the basic concept of the total product. Marketers develop a product concept by first determining what people really want in the product. Marketers have to market these basic benefits. The features of the product then are developed to satisfy the benefits that are desired by the customer. The features include the tangible object, brand name, package, quality, and styling. Related services complete the total product. These include services such as warranty, repair, user instructions, delivery, and follow-up training and advice. If these ideas are combined, we arrive at a product concept that has three levels: basic benefits, physical features, and related services. Look again at the ballpoint pen example.

We have now put together the ideas needed to define a product. A **product** is a combination of benefits, physical features, and services designed to satisfy the needs of a market. Remember that a market includes people with the purchasing power and the willingness to buy specific products and services. Marketers must keep in mind that the actual meaning of a product is the perception of the total product by the consumer or industrial buyer. Take another look at behavioral influences as presented in Chapter 3. Effective marketers are able to match their product concepts to the needs of specific market segments.

Product Mix

A large retail store may offer 14,000 or more products for sale to its customers. K-Mart, Safeway, and Sears are good examples of such marketers. Other marketers may sell only a few different types of products. For example, some service stations may sell only three grades of gasoline and a

A GENERAL ELECTRIC PRODUCT MIX FOR A CONSUMER'S DAY

BRING YOUR DAY TO LIFE.

GET OFF TO A RUNNING START. GE can really save you time in the morning. And money, too. The rebates listed on the last page [of this brochure] bring you good deals on a selection of good things.

> GE Brew Starter Coffeemaker
> Cassette Clock Radio
> GE Stereo Escape Cassette and Headphone

DO YOUR HOMEWORK IN CLASS. Now you can spend more time out of the house, studying, working, or doing whatever you want. Just let GE work for you at home, automatically (and economically, thanks to our new rebate offers).

> Potscrubber Dishwasher
> Countertop Microwave Oven
> Washer/Dryer

GO FROM FAST FOOD TO QUICK CUISINE. GE has cooked up some great deals on appliances that can help make a good meal good and fast.

> GE "Food Saver" Refrigerator
> Grill/Griddle Range
> GE Meal Fixer

ENTERTAIN THE TROOPS AFTER SCHOOL. If the weather forces you to scout around for indoor fun, you will be prepared with GE.

> GE Widescreen 4000 TV
> Heat Pump/Air Conditioner
> TV Band Radio

SOFTEN THE LIGHTS AND BRIGHTEN AN EVENING. GE sets the stage for family night with soft lights plus bright new ideas in home entertainment.

> VHS Video Cassette Recorder
> Performance Sound II TV
> Toast-R-Oven Toaster
> GE Lighting Products

MAKING A MAGIC MOMENT ON A MOMENT'S NOTICE. When you are having the time of your life, do not waste a moment of it. Let GE help.

> Home 'N Go Stereo
> Out of Sight 1400 Retractable Cord Dryer

WE BRING GOOD THINGS TO LIFE. GENERAL ELECTRIC

few types of oil. Regardless of the size of the marketing firm, every marketer must plan the product assortment or mix carefully. A **product mix** is the combination of all product items and product lines that a specific marketer offers for sale. (See General Electric's application of this concept in the example on the opposite page.)

A product mix is developed by putting together a number of product lines. A **product line** is a group of closely related products. A group of products may be considered related for several reasons. Products may be included in a line because they have a similar function. For example, a line may include a variety of video games. That line would be made up of a number of product items. A **product item** is a separate unit that can be identified by a different brand name, number, price, size, color, or one of many other attributes. Examples of product items in a line of video games might include such brand names as Atari Space Invaders, Colecovision Zaxxon, and Mattel Intellivision Star Strike. Additional items would be dozens of game cartridges, storage modules, remote controls, and add-on equipment items. As new products are developed, the marketer expands a product mix by adding new lines and new items. Of course, the size of the mix is affected by the number of lines and items that are dropped or reduced. We shall discuss the development of new products later in this chapter.

When marketing a product mix, marketers need to consider its width, depth, and consistency. **Product width** is the number of different lines offered to customers. **Product depth** is the number of items or brands in the total mix. Depth also can refer to the number of items in a line. With good depth in a mix, customers have many brands, colors, sizes, prices, and styles to select in matching their needs. A selected part of Avon's product mix and depth are illustrated in Figure 5-1 on page 130. **Product consistency** is the relationship of product lines and items in terms of final-use benefits to the customer. Customers perceive good consistency if a complete matching outfit of clothing can be purchased in one store. A consistent product mix in a hardware store furnishes

customers with all the tools and materials to do a specific repair job. Imagine buying a camera and then discovering that the marketer does not sell matching lens, flash units, or film. That would be a product mix without consistency.

Decisions in relation to these three dimensions of the product mix are very important to the marketer. Department stores and mass merchandisers attempt to satisfy all three dimensions and attract all types of consumers. Certain departments, however, may have better depth than others in the same store. A store may be known for depth in its appliance department but may be very shallow in its photography department. Consumers may see the photography department as a place to buy a few types of cameras or film at reasonable prices. A camera store usually offers a narrower product mix than the total department store's mix, but it will offer far greater depth and often better consistency between its product lines.

Product mix decisions for manufacturers involve the same dimensions. Large manufacturers such as General Electric and Proctor & Gamble typically market hundreds of thousands of items in a very wide and deep product mix. They strive to maintain consistency as well. General Electric's product mix goal (see the example on page 128) could be to offer every possible electric appliance a consumer needs in the kitchen. Other large manufacturers may choose to market a narrow mix or just one line with great depth. Examples of the narrow mix approach include Michelin (radial tires), Midas (mufflers, shock absorbers, and brakes), and Electrolux (vacuum cleaners). Many relatively small marketers make a substantial profit by narrowing their mix and being very thorough and consistent. This is a strategy that can be used to compete against marketers with wide mixes.

Product-Service Mix

The marketer's total product offering includes varying proportions of tangible products and intangible services. The **product-service mix** is a combination of products and services offered to a

WIDTH AND DEPTH OF SELECTED AVON PRODUCTS

Perfumed Soap	Shampoo	Hand Cream	Toothpaste
Toccara	New Vitality	Rich Moisture	Twice Bright
Odyssey	Naturally Gentle	Vita-Moist	
Foxfire	Keep Clear	Care Deeply	
Candid	Clean & Lively	Fresh Takes	
Timeless	Body Bonus	Silicone Glove	
Tasha	Henna Rich		
Ariane	Hi-Light		
Unspoken	Salon System		
Emprise			
Tempo			
Moonwind			
Charisma			
Field Flowers			
Hawaiian White Ginger			
Honeysuckle			
Roses, Roses			
Wild Jasmine			

Product Mix Width (horizontal axis); *Product Line Depth* (vertical axis)

Figure 5-1. These selected products show the width of Avon's product mix and the differences in depth among product lines. Avon's total mix includes more than 1,300 cosmetic, jewelry, household, and personal accessory lines. Product lines include makeup, bath products, skin care, soaps, candles, hair care, women's jewelry, men's jewelry, and deodorants. The consistency in Avon's product mix is excellent: a popular fragrance is usually available in ten different products.

specific market, and it ranges from an offering of *product only* to an offering of *service only*. There are four types of product-service combinations that marketers must consider.

1.   Entirely Tangible Product. This is basically a tangible product with no specific services attached to it. The customer usually buys it without salesperson assistance and can use it without advice or special instructions. Examples include pencils, candy bars, toothpaste, and combs.

2.   Tangible Product With Important Services. This type of product requires accompanying services and is more valuable to a customer with the services. The category usually involves products that are somewhat complex in use, and are usually purchased with salesperson assistance. Examples include stereo equipment, cameras, kitchen

appliances, automobiles, and power tools. The category includes products that are accompanied by warranties, service contracts, user's training sessions, and installation service and advice, and are usually sold with a demonstration. Although the customer buys the basic product for its value, the difference in related services between brands or marketers may be the decisive purchase factor.

3.   Major Service With Accompanying Products. The basic item purchased here is a service, but the total product includes some tangible products. A person who goes to a hairstylist may be impressed with the skills of the service marketer but will be influenced as well by the quality of products used to perform the service. A house painter has to use quality paints and supplies. Related products may influence the selection of an airline, plumber, or interior decorator.

MARKETING PROFESSIONAL ATHLETES

An important service marketing field has developed in sports marketing, especially in the marketing of professional athletes. Superstar athletes may make more than $1 million annually. They need help in negotiating contracts and investing their money. Talented young athletes need help in breaking into the sports world with good financial contracts.

W. F. Sports Enterprises is a firm that provides marketing services to represent and market athletes. Walt Frazier and Irwin Weiner combine their talents to head this New York-based firm. Frazier is a former NBA all-star who spent most of his playing career with the New York Knickerbockers. Weiner is an attorney who controls the company's finances and investments. Frazier capitalizes on his sports star reputation to contact and attract college players with professional potential. Most of W. F. Sports's clients sign with the company immediately after leaving college.

Professional athletes provide a highly marketable service. Their contracts and financial affairs are increasingly complex and involve huge sums of money. Leading examples are Larry Bird of the Boston Celtics, who has a multimillion dollar contract, and Magic Johnson of the Los Angeles Lakers, with a contract for 26 years. The top client for W. F. Sports is Julius "Dr. J" Erving of the Philadelphia 76ers, who earns more than $1 million annually. These superstars need the services of firms like W. F. Sports. Such young men typically are transformed suddenly from low-income college students to millionaires. But they know that potential injuries and inevitable aging will cause a relatively brief athletic career. The value of the service-marketing abilities of W. F. Sports is apparent.

The company negotiates contracts and manages the financial affairs of 30 to 40 professional athletes. Its staff includes accountants, lawyers, secretaries, and marketing and public relations personnel. The firm helps set up investment funds, insurance benefits, tax-deferred annuities, and contracts for personal appearances, endorsements, and franchises. W. F. Sports receives a 5 percent commission on contracts and 20 percent on promotional activities. The firm is an excellent example of the marketing of an intangible service: the abilities of athletes who perform for millions of sports fans.

Adapted from Harold R. Merahn, "Walt Frazier Shoots for the Stars," *Marketing Communications*, November 1981, pp. 34–35.

4. **Entirely Service.** In this category there may be some tangible representation of the service, but the consumer is purchasing the benefit of an intangible service. An insurance contract may be represented by words printed on paper, but the service is potential protection from financial loss. Other examples include a movie, a spectator sports event, and advice from an attorney or a psychologist. See the story above on marketing professional athletes.

Many more steps could be positioned in this scale from product only to service only. However, the important consideration for marketers is the identification of product and service benefits and combinations of these benefits that will satisfy customers. The following sections of this chapter will continue to explore the characteristics of products and services that are important to marketers.

PRODUCT CLASSIFICATIONS

Let us now look at some ways in which classification of products is helpful to marketers. Different marketing strategies are needed to market products with different classifications. Advertising, pricing, and selling techniques are affected by the nature of the product. Undifferentiated, differentiated, and concentrated marketing strategies as presented in Chapter 3 are dependent on the useful classification of products. For example, paper towels, which are a relatively simple product, might be marketed best by using an undifferentiated strategy. A more complex product such as high-fidelity stereo systems might be marketed best by using a differentiated strategy. This example shows that a product can be classified as simple or complex. There are many other useful ways to classify products: large or small, low-priced or high-priced, necessities or luxuries, and tangible or intangible. As a consumer or marketer, one can think of several other possible classifications.

Each of these classifications can be related to specific marketing strategies. Let us take one important system as an example: durable and nondurable products. Durable products can be used many times over a relatively long time period. Examples include furniture, clothing, appliances, jewelry, tools, and automobiles. Consumers expect a durable product to have a long life. Personal selling is a strategy that usually is required to market durables. The price of a durable product is often high enough to cause the consumer to shop and compare. Guarantees, installation, delivery, and credit plans often are used to help market durable products. Of course, there is usually a long interval between purchases of similar durable products. This means that consumers need to study new features and current information each time they make a purchase. Nondurable products usually are consumed in a short time. For example, many food products are consumed in one use. Many nondurable products last through just a few uses: soap, insecticide, medicines, and cosmetics. Many of these products are purchased frequently, and specific brands or types are purchased repeatedly. Marketers try to have these products available in as many types of stores as possible. Advertising is used heavily. Customers often make selections on the basis of advertising and displays and without salesperson help.

The most important product classification system is the identification of products as used by the consumer market or the industrial market, as was discussed in Chapter 3. We shall give a lot of attention to the characteristics of consumer products and industrial products. The same product may be classified in either category. The position depends entirely on the purchaser's intended use of the product. The calculator example in Chapter 3 was used to illustrate a product intended for personal use by a consumer or for use in an office for business purposes. Let us look at what marketers need to know about the characteristics and types of consumer products and industrial products.

Consumer Products

A **consumer product** is an item that is purchased by a consumer for personal use and satisfaction. The use of the product is the determining factor that makes it a consumer product. A truck may be used to transport home and lawn care items such as firewood and mowers; a stereo system is used to enjoy pleasing sounds and improve the home environment; golf shoes may help a consumer make better shots; and pancake syrup is purchased for eating pleasure at home. These are simple examples that have important implications for marketers of consumer products. In every situation, the consumer's perception of potential satisfaction is the target of the product's features. This idea is consistent with our previous discussions of consumer behavior and market segmentation.

There are several consumer behavior characteristics that are particularly important to the marketers of consumer products. Consumers are problem solvers. When they recognize a problem, they want to find a product that will solve it satisfactorily, quickly, and as efficiently as possible. Consumers usually buy products in small quantities. They seldom build big inventories of one product, although marketers effectively encourage large-quantity purchasing at times with pricing strategies. As a general trend in the United States, consumers shop in small groups of family and friends. Personal advice from members of these groups and from experts in a product category is often very influential. Although mail and telephone orders are common ways of buying consumer products, most consumers select products by touching them, looking at them, and using them in demonstration or during trial periods. Mass merchandisers and self-service marketers

are well aware of these behaviors. In-home marketers (Tupperware, Avon, Amway, and Shaklee) are experts at using these behaviors to sell consumer products.

Several consumer characteristics that actually influence the marketing and classification of consumer products have been presented. One of the most important classification systems is based on how consumers shop for products. The classification of consumer products offers many implications for marketing strategies.

Classifying Consumer Products

A very useful classification system identifies consumer products as convenience, shopping, specialty, and unsought products. See Figure 5-2a for an illustration of this system. Convenience and shopping products are differentiated by the degree of shopping effort the consumer is willing to use. Specialty and unsought products are differentiated by the degree of preference a consumer has established for a product. You will understand these types of products very quickly if you picture

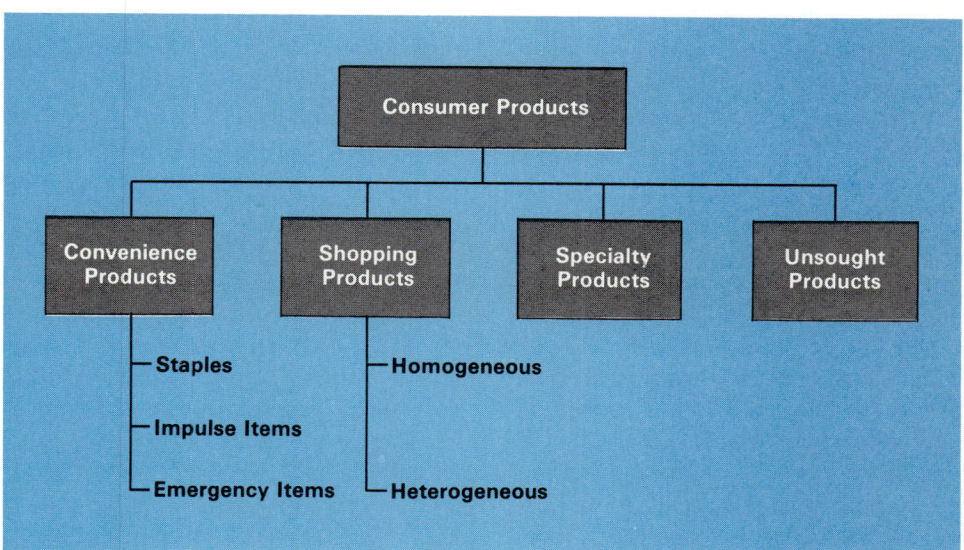

Figure 5-2a. The four classes of consumer products. Convenience products are purchased regularly; shopping products require more effort; specialty products have some unique feature; and unsought products are unknown to the consumer.

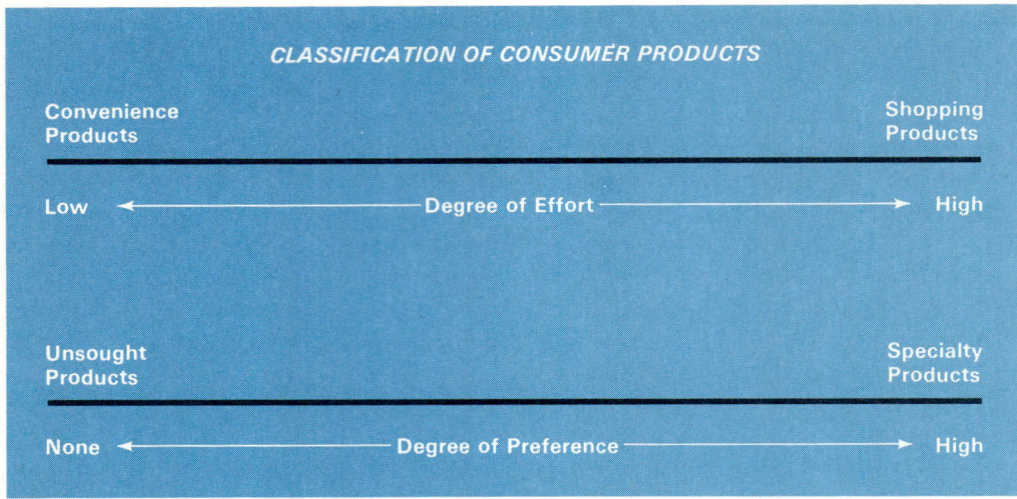

Figure 5-2b. Degrees of effort and preference range widely among classes of products.

convenience and shopping products at each end of a line of low or high shopping effort. Now picture specialty and unsought products at each end of a line of preferred to unknown products. Figure 5-2*b* will help you see the positioning of these types.

Convenience Products.
Convenience products (some business people call them convenience goods) are purchased by consumers regularly with a minimum of time and effort. They are relatively inexpensive and are bought frequently. They are purchased routinely with very little comparison or shopping effort in each buying situation. Candy bars, bread, soft drinks, gasoline, and bath soap are convenience products for most consumers most of the time. The determination of a product as a convenience product is based entirely on the consumer's perception. The product is one that the consumer knows something about, has probably purchased before, wants to be able to find easily, and can purchase at a fair price with maximum convenience. The implications for marketing strategy are obvious. Marketers display these products in prominent, easy-access locations in as many retail outlets as possible. Retailers typically position these prod-

ucts in main aisles, at ends of counters, and around checkout counters. Supermarkets, drugstores, and mass-merchandise discount stores offer many examples of effective marketing techniques for convenience products.

Marketers further subdivide convenience products into three types: staples, impulse, and emergency. **Staples** are products purchased on a routine basis with little decision making involved at the time of purchase. Staples are items such as bread and milk that show up on food lists every week. Consumers develop habits of buying certain brands or buying from certain stores without much evaluation. Big changes in price often will cause a consumer to purchase another brand, but the different brand must be very convenient to locate and buy. Even though there usually is very little difference between brands of staple products, consumers simplify the buying effort by planning to buy only preferred brands.

Impulse items are convenience products that are purchased without planning or searching effort. If you were marketing impulse items, you might place them in vending machines located where people could see them. Candy bars are a typical impulse item. Consumers purchase them when they think they need them and when the purchase is convenient. After the need is satisfied, the consumer will not react on impulse to that particular product for some time. The products placed around checkout counters are typical impulse items.

Emergency items are convenience products that are purchased when a need is urgent. Obviously, emergency purchases are not planned. The consumer is surprised by a situation and rather suddenly needs a product to solve a problem. Snow shovels, tire repairs, medical supplies, repair tools, and even food products are examples of emergency products. The marketer should have a satisfactory product conveniently available at a reasonable price. An alert fraternity sold a large number of low-priced plastic rain ponchos at a football game when an unexpected rainstorm occurred. Even these consumers sitting in the rain watching their favorite football team would not have purchased $30 raincoats.

Shopping Products.
Shopping products include items that are purchased after a lot of searching effort and comparison of product features. Consumers will spend time and effort shopping for different brands and with different marketers, comparing quality, styles, prices, durability, and many other features. Furniture, appliances, fashion clothing, automobiles, and stereo equipment are shopping products for most consumers. These products tend to be more durable, more expensive, and more socially visible than most convenience products. Consumers shop for these products by displaying a variety of behaviors. Consumers typically will go to several stores, look at several brands, ask questions of sales people, talk with friends and family, study promotional materials, and read articles in magazines. The marketing of shopping products should include informative advertising that is very helpful to the consumer. Sales people need to know their products and be able to communicate their knowledge to customers. Prices and product features must be effective in conveying utility benefits and product values. Manufacturers direct their advertising to consumers and provide promo-

tional materials and service programs for dealers who sell shopping products.

Marketing strategies are more effective if shopping products are divided into two types: homogeneous and heterogeneous. While these two words may seem intimidating, they have simple meanings and very practical applications. **Homogeneous shopping products** are seen by consumers as very similar in quality. People have to shop for these products very carefully to find differences that justify purchasing one rather than another. Different brands of small appliances, radios, record players, and hair dryers may be very similar in apparent quality and performance. If the consumer perceives very little difference in homogeneous products, price and related services may be the shopping differences. In fact, price is often the critical difference for this type of shopping product.

Heterogeneous shopping products are perceived as having different features between brands. The consumer sees differences in appearance, functions, quality, and many other features. For example, one television brand may have a remote control unit while another brand does not. Price will be relevant to the decision, but the remote feature may be the decisive factor if that is what the consumer wants. The quality and features may be more important to the customer than small but reasonable price differences. Other products that are frequently heterogeneous for consumers include automobiles, clothing, furniture, large appliances, and stereo equipment.

Remember that *homogeneous* means "similar" and *heterogeneous* means "different." In both cases, the consumer does a lot of shopping. With homogeneous products, the marketer often emphasizes similarities between competing brands and then markets price or promotional differences. With heterogeneous products, the marketer emphasizes apparent and actual differences between competing products.

Specialty Products.
Specialty products are perceived as unique in some way and are highly preferred by some consumers. Customers

are very loyal to specialty products and will go to extremes to acquire them. The consumer has made a decision to purchase these products repeatedly without making comparative shopping efforts each time. As the name indicates, specialty products are special in that they provide the benefits desired by certain consumers. Expensive sports cars, high-fashion clothing, health foods, custom-made objects, and artwork are examples of these types of products. Such products are usually expensive and are usually priced higher than most other products. Many of these products are first searched for as shopping products by most consumers and become specialty products for certain customers who like the products very much. The result is a number of very loyal customers who do not compare products but will invest time and effort to get to the specialty product. After discovering a certain bakery, a customer may drive many miles to obtain a special type of cake which may cost 3 times the price of a cake from a local supermarket. Marketers of specialty products have to work hard to maintain their special status position and match the special desires of their customers.

Unsought Products. While specialty products are well known and preferred, at the other end of this classification line are products that are not known by the consumer. **Unsought products** are those which consumers know nothing about or do not care to know about. In many cases, consumers know of these products but do not believe that the products would solve any of their consumer problems. Life insurance, fire and burglar alarms, encyclopedias, and water softeners are good examples. New products fit this classification because consumers have not seen them or been introduced to them. The challenge to the marketer is to move unsought products to another classification, preferably that of a specialty product. By definition, unsought products suggest an exceptional marketing effort. Life insurance is an example. A typical young consumer may not give any thought to protecting a financial future. The insurance salesperson may have to make several presentations before the consumer

understands and decides to buy. If the consumer remains satisfied with the product and the agent's service, the life insurance company and the salesperson may become part of the specialty product and service for this customer. The successful marketing of typically unsought products and services may be one of the major contributions of marketing to the improved standard of living of many consumers.

Marketing Consumer Products

A specific product may fit into more than one consumer product classification. The classification depends on the shopping habits and perception of the individual consumer. Let us use shampoo brands as an example. Prell and Head & Shoulders are two best-selling brands that a consumer may buy because they are convenient. These brands are available almost everywhere shampoos are sold. They are relatively inexpensive and are not changed frequently through content or package design. These are some of several brands a consumer may choose with very little shopping effort. After a lot of searching and comparing, a consumer may select a shampoo by Gillette called For Oily Hair Only. The choice may be made after the consumer has read the labels on several shampoos recommended for oily hair. After shopping for and using this brand, the consumer may decide to purchase it repeatedly. For Oily Hair Only would then become a specialty product for this consumer because it is perceived as special in providing a desired benefit. Redken is a shampoo brand that is a good example of an unsought product. Redken is sold only in beauty salons by professional hairdressers. The consumer may know nothing about the brand until being introduced to it by the professional salesperson. If the consumer is satisfied after using Redken, the brand may become a specialty product for this consumer. Any brand of shampoo can be marketed for each product classification, depending on the consumer's situation and perception of the brand.

One can learn a lot about product classifications by watching the strategies of marketers in their advertising and promotions. Marketing strategies are influenced significantly by product classifications and the related consumer behavior characteristics.

Industrial Products

An **industrial product** is an item used by an industrial marketer to resell, to run a business or organization, or to produce other products or services. The major types of industrial marketers are producers, trade industries, governments, and nonprofit organizations. Examples and characteristics of these marketers were presented in Chapter 3. The industrial market is an enormous, complex, and important market. The organizations in this market use products and services in several ways to make a profit or meet social needs. The businesses and organizations in the industrial market range from very small companies to some of the largest firms in the world.

A small company builds ceiling fans for homes and uses Westinghouse motors. These motors are industrial products. Goodwill Industries buys varnish to refinish old furniture. A retail store buys mannequins for displaying clothing. A pharmacy buys a van to use to make deliveries of prescriptions to customers. The owner of a small craft shop buys silk fabric to make artificial flowers for special occasions. A financial analyst buys a microcomputer to help analyze customer problems. An ice cream parlor buys a detergent to clean the floor. In each case, the item purchased is an industrial product. It is purchased to be sold at a profit, used to produce products and services, or help satisfy customers.

Classifying Industrial Products

The quantity, diversity, and complexity of industrial products is difficult to imagine. There are hundreds of thousands of types of industrial products, a much greater variety than exists for consumer products. An automobile is a consumer product made from many industrial products. A paper clip is an example of a simple industrial product a company may purchase, while the same company may purchase an industrial building costing millions of dollars. Consumer products are classified on the basis of the shopping habits of consumers. Industrial products are classified according to how purchasers use the products in the business or organization.

Marketers of industrial products need to understand the use classification system. The industrial buyer is usually very certain of the use of a product. Purchase criteria are specified precisely. Price and the quality of products are important because they directly affect the quality of products and services produced. Technical product information is extremely important to industrial buyers because they are purchasing specialists. The classification of industrial products by use is a very practical system that is used by all industrial marketers.

The classification system includes four major groupings of industrial products: materials and parts which become a part of the finished product, installations and equipment which are used to make the product, supplies and services which are used in the operation of the business, and resale products which are purchased to sell to industrial customers with little or no change in the products. The characteristics of these product groups are listed in Table 5-1 on page 138.

Materials and Parts. **Materials** are products that are used in the finished product after additional processing. For example, copper may be made into a wire which becomes part of an electric motor. Materials may be farm products, natural products, or manufactured materials. Examples of farm products include vegetables, fruits, livestock, cotton, wheat, corn, and many animal products. Examples of natural products include iron ore, fish, wood, crude petroleum, and many minerals. Manufactured materials are farm and natural products that have been processed to some extent. For example, iron ore is made into iron, and wheat is made into flour. The manufactured materials, iron and flour, will be processed further and used in finished products, such as a bicycle or a loaf of bread.

Parts are products that are used in a finished product without further change or processing.

TABLE 5-1
CLASSIFYING INDUSTRIAL PRODUCTS

Group 1	**Materials**	used in the finished product
		processed further
		farm products, natural products, and manufactured materials
		examples are fruits, vegetables, corn, fish, wood, iron ore, and steel
	Parts	used in the finished product
		no additional processing
		often called components or fabricated parts
		examples are zippers, tires, motors, and light bulbs
Group 2	**Installations**	major items of long life; not part of finished product
		affect scale of operation
		often called capital assets
		examples are heavy machinery, trucks, computers, and buildings
	Equipment	used in the making of other products
		do not affect scale of operation
		do not become part of finished product
		examples are typewriters, forklift trucks, and cash registers
Group 3	**Supplies**	used in the regular operation of the business
		do not become part of the finished product
		regular expense items of low unit value
		examples are office paper, cleaning compounds, pencils, and paints
	Services	intangible products used in the operation of a firm
		expense items that do not become part of the finished product
		often called business services
		examples are cleaning, repairing, consulting, and decorating
Group 4	**Resale products**	purchased to be sold to industrial customers
		form is not changed or is changed slightly
		changes are in packaging, combining, and arranging
		time, place, and possession utilities are added

Parts often are called component parts or fabricated parts. A part is a complete product which becomes a part of a bigger and more complex product. For example, a battery becomes part of a watch or an electronic game. The battery has no real value until it becomes part of another product. Motors, tires, zippers, speakers, and light bulbs are examples of products that are used as parts. Many industrial marketers buy component or fabricated parts and assemble them to make finished products. A small shop may sell floral arrangements made from fabricated flowers purchased from another industrial marketer that makes the artificial flowers from fabric.

Installations and Equipment. Installations are products that are expensive, major items that have a long life and affect the scale of operation of the business. Examples include business buildings, trucks for a delivery firm, computers for a data processing company, and heavy machinery for an aluminum plant. These often are referred to as capital assets for the marketer. The term *scale of operations* refers to the fact that the amount of business is related to the number or capacity of installation products owned. For example, one would expect a delivery firm with 20 trucks to be able to accept more orders than a firm with 5 trucks. Installations represent relatively large dollar investments for each unit and often are made to the specifications of the buyer. Personal selling and continued service are important. If you were purchasing a large computer for your data processing business, you would want a lot of personal and technical advice during the selection process. The computer installation is a big investment. It will last a long time, provide new programs that keep it technically current, and affect the amount of business you can handle.

Equipment represents accessory products that are used in the making of other products but do not influence the scale of operations. Accessory equipment (this term is used frequently for this category) includes portable tools, typewriters, calculators, cash registers, forklift trucks, and price-marking machines. See Figure 5-3 for an IBM advertisement for a small business computer, which is an industrial product. Like installations, accessory equipment items do not become part of the finished product. Accessory equipment is generally less expensive and has a shorter life than installations. Equipment items are capital assets that can be depreciated. For example, a calculator may be depreciated in 5 years by using

Figure 5-3. This advertisement for business equipment stresses its ability to satisfy the industrial buyer's purchase criteria.

a specific percentage of the cost as a tax deduction each year. If purchased in large quantities, these items may be bought directly from the manufacturer. However, most accessory equipment items are purchased through middlemen because the orders are frequent and small.

Supplies and Services.
Supplies are products that are used in the regular operation of a business and do not become part of the finished product. Supplies are regular expense items that support the use of equipment, installations, and materials. They are purchased in a manner similar to the way in which consumers purchase convenience products. They are purchased with a minimum of effort, using a straight rebuy technique such as an automatic reorder system. Supplies have a relatively low unit value when compared with other industrial products. When marketers have determined that a supply item has acceptable quality, low price becomes the important variable. Examples are cleaning compounds, office paper, oils, pencils, paints, nails, and paper clips. Many marketers refer to supplies as MRO items: maintenance, repair, and operating supplies.

Services are intangible products that are purchased by industrial marketers to support the operation of the firm. They often are called business services, and they include business advisory services and maintenance and repair services. Like supplies, services are expense items and do not become part of a finished product. Examples include general cleaning, consulting, legal advice, repairing installations and equipment, design ideas, engineering, and decorating. These services are purchased from other businesses and outside agencies. A manufacturer and marketer of small electronic games might hire an advertising agency to develop a promotional campaign. The manufacturer would use this business service because the agency has a very good reputation, because the agency personnel are reliable, and because their work results in increased sales.

Resale Products.
Resale products are purchased by industrial marketers to be sold to other industrial customers at a profit. The form of resale products is not changed or is changed only slightly. For example, wholesalers and retailers buy appliances, clothing, packaged foods, cameras, and radios to sell just as they were produced. These products may be identical to products sold to consumers. However, they are industrial resale products if they are purchased for resale to other industrial customers, organizations, government units, and institutions. A camera may be sold to a professional photographer, appliances and packaged foods may be sold to a school system, and a radio may be sold to a business for its office. The slight changes may involve different packaging, combinations, and number arrangements. Marketers may buy products in large quantities and package them in smaller quantities. Candy, nuts and bolts, garden seeds, and many food products are examples. Industrial marketers buy resale products with the needs of industrial and organizational customers in mind. The form utility of the product is already there. The marketer adds time, place, and possession utilities.

Marketing Industrial Products

Industrial marketing strategies use the same basic marketing principles that are used for consumer products. All the aspects of the marketing mix are involved, but the needs of industrial and organizational customers result in special emphasis on certain parts of the mix. The most important goal of the industrial marketer is to help industrial customers buy products and services that will contribute to a profit-making situation. For example, marketers of business computers stress that the cost of a computer will be saved through better business decisions. A chart may show features of one computer that gives the buyer more for the money than competitive products. The IBM advertisement in Figure 5-3 stresses the product's capability, capacity, ease of use, value, and dependable service. Industrial and organizational buyers place great emphasis on price-value relationships, continuous supply, and reliable service.

To illustrate the marketing of industrial products, assume that you own and manage a firm that markets business forms. You sell to schools, churches, professional organizations, service businesses, retailers, and small manufacturers. You buy standard business forms from large printing companies that advertise in various trade journals. You design custom forms and have them printed by local firms. Personal selling and technical service for your customers are very important parts of your marketing mix. Your sales people are actually consultants to your customers. They seek profitable sales by helping your industrial and organizational customers improve their business operations. Your products range from standard forms that customers reorder automatically to custom-designed special-order forms for unique customer problems. Part of the value of your prod-

ucts is delivery when the customers want them. Your prices are competitive but not the lowest in the market. Your customers accept slightly higher prices because of your service and reliability.

SERVICES

Earlier in this chapter, the concept of a product-service mix which ranges from a product-only offering to a service-only offering was discussed. The goal in this section is to identify services by characteristics and types and to discuss special considerations in the marketing of services. A **service mix** is all the types of service offered by one marketer. See Figure 5-4 for an example of one

Figure 5-4. Priority 1 mail, picked up from the customer and collected at a branch station for overnight delivery, is part of the Federal Express service mix.

service in the Federal Express service mix. A **service** is an intangible activity that results in customer satisfaction but not in the ownership of a tangible product. Examples include seeing a movie, getting advice from a doctor, traveling in an airplane, or having a sitter for a dog. Tangible products were used to show the movie, but the viewers do not own them. If popcorn is purchased at the movie theater, this is a separate transaction involving a tangible product. The emphasis here is on the marketing of separate and identifiable services.

TABLE 5-2
IMPLICATIONS FOR SERVICE RETAILING IN SEVERAL AREAS

Services (as compared with goods)	Changes Needed for Services Retailing
a. Measuring Performance	
Capital expenditures vary widely for different services.	Return on net worth may not be the most important measurement of the value of a service to the retailer.
Little or no inventories are required to offer services.	Turnover, markdown controls, and other goods-related controls are not appropriate.
Higher labor costs.	Profit after labor costs replaces the gross margin of goods retailing.
Some services support the sale of goods.	Supporting services should be evaluated differently from services that are sold.
Cost accounting is more important.	Job-specific records will be required to assess the profitability of each sale of a service.
b. Store Organization	
More specialized supervision.	Separate management for service areas will be required.
More specific search for service employees.	Nontraditional sources for identification of employees should be used.
Lower employee turnover.	Frequent salary and performance reviews should be carried out.
Higher pay for skilled craftspeople than for merchandising personnel.	Pay levels will need to be adjusted upward over periods of longevity for service employees.
c. Production	
More involvement in manufacturing of the service.	Production skills will need to be obtained by supervisors.
More emphasis on quality control.	Supervisors must be able to assess the quality of a service performed for a customer.

The marketing of services presents a special challenge to businesses. Marketing traditionally has been aimed at the selling of tangible products with supporting services. Although marketers were aware of pure services, they did not think that any different marketing strategies were needed. Today marketing of services is increasingly important and is receiving more attention from marketers. As an example of this trend, study Table 5-2, which shows the interest retail marketers have in service marketing. Observe that services are compared with goods

Services (as compared with goods)	Changes Needed for Services Retailing
More need to monitor consumer satisfaction.	Need for research with prior customers to measure their satisfaction with the service.
More need to refine scheduling of employees.	Maximizing the service employees' time requires matching consumer demand to ability to produce the service.
Quality must be consistent among all outlets.	Standards for consistency of the service must be established and continually evaluated. Central training may be required for craftworkers in multiple branch operations.

d. *Pricing*

Services vary in cost, thus pricing is more difficult.	Prices may be quoted within a range instead of an exact figure before the purchase.
More difficulty in price competition or promotion based upon price.	Services should be promoted on the basis of criteria relative to price.

e. *Promotion*

Value is more difficult for consumers to determine.	Consumers need to be convinced of value through personal selling.
Difficult to display within store.	Signs or a service center are required to notify customers of services availability.
Visual presentation is more important.	Photographs of before-and-after may be possible with some services.
	Testimonials may be possible with other services.
Cross-selling with goods is important.	A quota or bonus, for goods salespersons who suggest services, will lead to increased service selling.
More difficult to advertise in catalogs.	Conditions for the sale and performance of the service must be specified.

Adapted from J. Patrick Kelly and William R. George, "Strategic Management Issues for the Retailing of Services," *Journal of Retailing*, Vol. 58, No. 2, Summer 1982, pp. 40–42.

(products) and that needed managerial changes are described for the retailing of services. As another example, the American Marketing Association held its first conference devoted entirely to the marketing of services in February 1981.[2] Many marketers refer to services as a growing market. Most estimates place the proportion of consumer income spent on services at 50 percent and increasing.

There are many reasons for the increased growth of services, and they are all important to marketers. Consumers are living faster and more complex lives. They hire more service specialists such as financial advisors, employment consultants, attorneys, accountants, and psychologists. Consumers' incomes are increasing. They can afford to buy services which they either do not want to or cannot perform for themselves. New products created by a faster-paced technology cause new service demands. Consider the service potential on just these electronic products: computers, stereos, televisions, calculators, appliances, and communication systems. Consumers' lifestyles are changing. They travel more, have more leisure time, are more involved in active sports, and want to be healthier. In general, consumers are becoming more interested in self-improvement. They want to learn, create, improve, and grow. The number of services and their importance to consumers are indications of the growing importance of services.

A marketer must study consumer demand for services and the relevant demand for industrial or business services. There is a high probability that you are or will be involved in the marketing of services. Services are important because marketing is becoming more competitive and complex. Management often must rely on business service experts to provide advice in such areas as promotion, taxation, accounting, personnel relations, research, building and interior design, and finance. Business service firms often are able to perform a specialized function better and at lower cost than a company's own staff. Services in relation to data processing and computer technologies are examples.

Characteristics of Services

Services are marketable, needed, varied, and complex. Despite their variety, they share distinctive characteristics that marketers use as a basis for specific marketing programs. Keep in mind that services are performances, actions, and efforts that satisfy customers. This idea underlies the classification of services as intangible, perishable, variable, and inseparable.

Services Are Intangible. Customers are not able to check out services before they buy them by using their senses of taste, smell, touch, sight, and hearing. This makes it more difficult for consumers and businesses to choose services. You do not know that you are satisfied with a movie until you see it, after the purchase has been made and the service has been performed. The actual service cannot be displayed in a business firm or demonstrated entirely. Marketers of services have a particular challenge to help the customer visualize the potential benefits of the service. In marketing a vacation trip, a travel agent can help customers see themselves relaxing in a far-off place. Brochures, movies, and meetings with former happy vacationers help customers see the benefits. Personal selling is very important in the marketing of a service. The reputation of the service marketer and word-of-mouth communication from satisfied customers are extremely important. Advertising can personalize the service by using believable facts and evidence of reliability.

Services Are Perishable. Services have value only at the time when they are performed, and they cannot be stored for use at a later time. An empty seat on a bus or at a concert, a plumber with no work for several hours, and a motel with empty rooms are examples of service values that have perished. One will not buy a seat on a bus for a time and trip that have expired. One may buy a recording of a concert, but that is a different product. The problem for service marketers is to match service supply to changing demand. How many seats for a concert? How big a bus for a certain trip? How many workers for specific times? Service marketers use several techniques to try to match supply and demand. Lower prices at low-demand times may keep services in action. Computerized reservation systems for lodging firms, transportation marketers, and professional organizations help in planning. Part-time employees can serve during peak demand. Service marketers must plan, promote, and price effectively to avoid economic loss. Tangible products held in inventory may eventually sell. Service value and profit are lost forever if they are not performed during a specific time period.

Services Are Variable. Many conditions make it very difficult to standardize services. People do not perform the same way time after time. Different marketers will not perform the same type of service in exactly the same way or with the same quality of output. A favorite hairstylist does not style a customer's hair equally well every time. A professional basketball team is not at its peak each time it plays. However, the best service marketers do perform better more often. Customers return to such marketers and tell others about their good service. Because service depends to a great extent on the personnel involved, training programs and high standards are important. Airlines, hotels, motels, and banks are examples of service marketers that try to provide consistently friendly, courteous, and efficient service. These marketers are so competitive that friendly service from one of them as perceived by a customer may be the only marketing advantage. See Figure 5-5.

Services Are Inseparable. A service is inseparable from the person who performs it. A customer who wants a specific person to perform a service usually will not accept another serviceperson. Because of this characteristic, service marketers can build a clientele of customers who return to them repeatedly for service. A problem may develop when the marketer cannot handle all potential customers personally. This can limit the scale of business operation and limit sales and profit. For example, one serviceperson can repair

Figure 5-5. Riteway Cleaner, a small marketer in greater New York City, develops its business by stressing quality service.

only so many television sets in a single day's work. Several strategies can be used to overcome this limitation. If you were marketing a television repair service, you could train service personnel thoroughly and supervise their work very carefully. The customers would need to be assured that you check the workers and approve each service output. Every service job has the two important factors of time and quality. A service worker can be more productive if quality can be maintained or improved while work time is decreased. As a service marketer, you want to provide very good equipment, supplies, and working conditions to help increase productivity.

Types of Services

Thousands of different types of services are purchased by consumer and industrial users. They are not classified as neatly as tangible products, but marketers do use some groupings that relate to the ways in which services are marketed. People-based services are performed by professionals, skilled laborers, and unskilled laborers, with equipment used as support systems. Examples include medical doctors, automobile mechanics, hairstylists, janitors, business consultants, and tax accountants. Equipment-based services are performed with extensive use of machines, electronics, and power devices. Examples include vending machines, movie theaters, dry cleaning, airlines, data processing, and security systems. Different types of labor are needed to operate, install, and maintain the service equipment.

Many services have to be performed with the customer present. Dental, medical, and beauty care services are examples. Other services are performed with direct input from the customer. These include tax, accounting, investment, legal, rental, communication, recreation, and educational services. Still other services are performed on tangible property owned by the customer. Repair, cleaning, maintenance, decoration, and improvement services are examples. In all cases, services are performed on something of value to the customer. A service transaction is a very personal relationship between buyer and seller.

As is true with tangible products, services are purchased for personal use by consumers or for business use by industrial marketers. The following list shows consumer services as classified by the U.S. Department of Commerce.

1. Housing (includes rentals of hotels, motels, apartments, houses, and farms)

2. Household operations (includes the purchase of utilities, house repairs, repair of equipment, and household cleaning)

3. Personal business (includes legal, financial, accounting, and advertising services)

4. Recreation (includes rental and repairs of recreational equipment, food service, entertainment activities, and clubs and organizations)

5. Personal care (includes laundry, dry cleaning, and beauty care service)

6. Medical care (includes medical, dental, and nursing services; hospitalization; eye care; and health care)

7. Transportation (includes automobile repair, insurance, car leasing, and passenger service)

8. Insurance and financial (includes personal and property insurance, tax service, and investment advice)

9. Private education (includes learning personal skills such as driving, sewing, crafts, art, and keyboarding)

10. Communications (include telephone systems, telegraph systems, broadcasting companies, and special business communication systems)

Industrial firms (profit-seeking businesses, government units, and nonprofit organizations) buy many of the same services that consumers buy. Transportation, insurance, and communication services can be considered either consumer or industrial services, depending on their use. Industrial firms also purchase specialized services such as the selected industrial services in this list.

Accounting, auditing, and recordkeeping
Architectural services
Building maintenance
Cleaning (building, linen, and uniforms)
Communication
Computer services
Consulting
Detective agencies and other protective services
Display services
Educational services
Employment
Engineering services
Financial services
Insurance
Leasing services
Legal services
Marketing research services
Medical
Promotional services
Repair
Stenographic services

A SERVICE MARKETER SUCCESS STORY: START SMALL AND GROW BY BEING FLEXIBLE AND MEETING DEMAND

Jeff Stoops got started in the trucking business when he realized that truckers were making $10,000 a year more than he was as a junior high school teacher. Ten years later, Stoops Express operates 137 trucks, and the firm's 34-year-old president and sole owner predicts that his company will bring in $15 million this year.

Hidden behind cornfields at the junction of I-69 and State Road 67 near the tiny town of Daleville, Indiana, Stoops Express does not look like a transcontinental transportation company. But Jeff Stoops did not set out to build a trucking empire. As a student at Ball State University, Stoops first drove trucks in the summer for a grain elevator in Emporia, Indiana. He graduated in 1969 and got a job teaching social studies and coaching football and basketball at a small junior high school but he kept driving during summer vacations.

"In 1971, I looked around and saw truck drivers making $18,000 a year while teachers were making $8,100," Stoops recalls. His father, Buick and Pontiac dealer in Elwood, helped Stoops finance the purchase of a tractor-trailer, which he leased to other trucking firms. By 1975, Stoops had a fleet of 12 trucks that were hauling material for the auto and steel industries.

That was the year when the automobile recession hit the midwest's economy, idling half of Stoops's rigs. Ask Stoops about the recession and he just smiles. "That was the best thing that ever happened to us," he says. "If it weren't for the auto recession, we'd still be hauling steel around the midwest, which means not doing much business."

Stoops had the inspiration to buy refrigerated trailers and to establish a series of routes to California, shipping manufactured parts and retail goods for Fortune 500 companies and backhauling fresh fruits and vegetables to supermarket chains in the midwest. "That recession taught me a lesson," he says. "One thing that moves all the time is food."

Stoops Express was founded in 1976, when Stoops decided to quit leasing out his trucks. He applied for and received the Interstate Commerce Commission licenses needed to operate on his own. He went to the ICC with the backing of his major midwest-based customers, who, he says, "feel more comfortable dealing with a midwestern trucker." He repays their support by providing financial statements "to prove that we're not trying to hit home runs off of them."

He is also working to protect his company from the eventual slump he expects in long-haul trucking. Because of fuel costs and deregulation, he believes that truckers will have to give up routes of 1,000 miles or more to railroads, whose "piggyback" services offer greater efficiency and flexibility. "But I'm not going to sit back and let the railroads take away my business," says Stoops. He's established a promising short route to Chicago where many trains pick up trailers to piggyback to California.

Adapted from INC./December 1981, p. 46.

Testing laboratories
Transportation (see the story on page 147)
Utilities (gas, water, and electricity)

Service marketers may develop different marketing programs for services sold to consumers or to industrial users. The previous discussion about applying a marketing mix to target markets is appropriate for the marketing of services.

Marketing Strategies for Services

Some specific strategies were presented in the discussion of characteristics of services. Let us look now at some strategies that are particularly important in the marketing of all services. The basic principles of marketing apply to services. A service is planned, priced, promoted, and placed in a market. Service marketers of any size need to apply the basic marketing concept effectively. However, six strategies are essential to the marketing of services.

Plan Services to Satisfy Specific Needs and Wants. Service planners need to plan to satisfy an adequate number of customers with similar needs in a market segment. But the service is finally performed to meet the specific needs of one customer. The service offering must be flexible. The selection of the exact service arrangement for each customer or client usually is accomplished with a lot of communication at the time the service is performed. For example, you might plan a lawn-care service for a market in your community. You would study the general needs of lawn owners based on climate, soil conditions, and types of vegetation. However, the serviceperson would adapt the quantity and types of chemicals needed for each customer's lawn. A good service marketer of lawn care could meet any customer's specific demands.

Use Tangible Symbols. To help customers understand an intangible service, service businesses often use tangible symbols. Brand names are good symbols for this strategy. Avis, Hertz,

United Parcel Service, Federal Express, Holiday Inns, and Best Western are well-known examples of brand names used to stand for services. Certain colors and advertising logos often are used as related symbols. For example, Chem Lawn uses bright green to suggest the results of using their service. Even a small service marketer should use tangible symbols to communicate to customers the nature of available services. A plumbing business might be named Home-Care Plumbing to convey the idea of careful plumbing services for the home as differentiated from plumbers for big business. Service personnel often wear uniforms to symbolize a service, such as a blazer with a logo on the pocket worn by an insurance agent. The environment in which the service is offered is another tangible symbol. Service customers often judge a service by the cleanliness of the mechanic, the truck, the waiting room, or an entire building. These tangible symbols are evidence of the nature of the service. In this function, they are very similar to the packaging of a product. The customer's perception of the intangible service may be influenced positively by these tangible symbols.

Stress Benefits. A service is purchased without knowing the outcome. The challenge to the service marketer is helping the customer picture the resulting benefits. This is closely related to what the customer needs and wants. A customer wants a weed-free lawn, an attractive hairstyle, pipes that do not leak, a well-groomed dog, or an exciting vacation trip. Personal selling often is extremely important in this strategy. Of course, advertising is used to stress ideas and mental pictures of benefits. Positive word-of-mouth advertising from satisfied customers is very important for the service marketer, and many service customers select a service marketer on this basis only. Again, this is an application of the marketing concept. A service should provide perceivable benefits for customers. Tennis lessons should help a person play better, weight control classes should result in a better body, and sewing classes should help a person make better clothes.

Educate Personnel to Communicate and Market the Services. A good service marketer is a teacher. Customers need to be taught how to use a product, enjoy a service, or prevent frequent problems from misuse or misunderstanding. For example, a serviceperson who repairs a washing machine should not only repair it correctly but also teach the customer how to use the machine in ways that prolong its useful life. Service personnel need to understand how their appearance, attitudes, and behavior influence the value of the service. If the serviceperson is dirty and impolite, the total service may be perceived as negative even though the mechanical problem has been corrected. Service purchase and usage are complex procedures and often involve stress situations for the customer. Service personnel must be taught how to communicate with customers, through both words and actions, to contribute to customer satisfaction and enhance future sales.

Price Services Sensibly. By using information on cost, demand, and competition, service marketers can arrive at fair prices. Many service marketers add a set percentage to known costs to arrive at a selling price. A shoe repair service may establish price by charging for the cost of materials plus 80 percent added on for labor. A minimum labor charge such as $10 or $20 an hour may be set, with additional charges based on materials used and time spent on the job. Like product marketers, service marketers always must consider competitors' prices for similar services in a market. If a marketer offers the same service at a lower price or a better service for the same price, these competitive efforts should be rewarded by more sales. However, the service marketer must put together a total service mix that is perceived by the customer as better and of more value than the services of competitors.

Services also are priced on the basis of demand factors. Quantity discounts and cash discounts may be used in pricing services. Handball court time may be less for an hour if the customer buys 1 hour a week for a whole year. For many spectator events, one pays more for a seat closer to

Figure 5-6. Marketing services: A discount on skate rentals encourages use of the Rockefeller Center Rink.

the participants. Service marketers may benefit from pricing service units at different rates. For example, motels charge a different rate for rooms with more beds, a better view, or easy access to the pool. Of course, the overall goal of pricing is to satisfy customers and make a profit. If the price is too high, customers will go to competitors or try to perform the service themselves. For example, many consumers attempt home repairs and auto repairs when they feel that the prices of services are too high. The best pricing strategy for the service marketer is to set price according to the perceived value customers place on the benefits.

Personalize the Services. A marketer should turn the personal nature of services into a competitive advantage. Service transactions are very personal and depend on a close relationship between the buyer and the seller. The service marketer is at the same time the producer, manager, and salesperson for a service. The customer

Figure 5-7. In marketing services, advertising should stress ideas and mental pictures of benefits.

often is involved directly in the performance of the service. Customers who are satisfied with the personal quality of service are more likely to return to the marketer and tell others. This strategy is the foundation of all service strategies. The quality of personal service perceived as better by the customer is a competitive advantage.

Marketing Services

The marketing of services for personal use and for business use will continue to be a challenge to marketers. The challenge involves the effective application of marketing principles to the unique needs and characteristics of service markets. The demand for services will continue to increase, and marketing opportunities and positions will increase as well. Services will continue to relate to the marketing of tangible products. New markets for services often develop with new product markets. For example, the incredible volume of sales of personal and business computers has created a related service market. The new market involves the training needed to use the computer. Of course, the manufacturers and marketers of hardware and software provide services with these

products, but millions of computer users need some form of computer instruction. The answer to this need is the marketing of a service: training in the use of computers by independent training companies (service marketers). This is a good example of the marketing of a service that will be important by itself and will encourage the purchase and use of computers, which are the tangible product. Although the marketing of services and the marketing of products are different in many ways, they have similarities in the use of basic marketing principles and in the application of the marketing concept of satisfying customers.

KEY POINTS SUMMARY

- A product is a combination of benefits, physical features, and services designed to satisfy the needs of a market.

- A product mix is the combination of all product items and product lines that a specific marketer offers for sale. A mix is measured by its width, depth, and consistency.

- The marketer's total product offering is a product-service mix that includes varying proportions of tangible products and intangible services.

- Different marketing strategies are needed to market products with different classifications. The most important product classification system is the identification of products as they are used by the consumer market or the industrial market.

- A very useful classification system identifies consumer products as convenience, shopping, specialty, or unsought products.

- Convenience and shopping products are differentiated by the degree of shopping effort the consumer is willing to use. Specialty and unsought products are differentiated by the degree of preference a consumer has established for a product.

- A specific product can fit into more than one consumer product classification. The placement depends on the shopping habits and perception of the consumer.

- An industrial product is an item used by an industrial marketer to resell, to run a business or organization, or to produce other products or services.

- Industrial products are classified on the basis of how purchasers use the products in their businesses or organizations. The classification system identifies the products as materials, parts, installations, equipment, supplies, services, or resale products.

- The marketing of services is increasingly important and is receiving more attention from marketers. A service is an activity that results in customer satisfaction but not in the ownership of a tangible product.

- Services have distinctive characteristics that marketers use to develop specific marketing programs. They are intangible, perishable, variable, and inseparable.

- A service marketer's strategy is to perform service activities in ways that are perceived as better by customers. Service transactions are very personal and depend on a close relationship between the buyer and the seller.

KEY TERMS AND CONCEPTS

consumer product	installations
convenience products	materials
emergency items	parts
equipment	product
heterogeneous shopping products	product consistency
	product depth
homogeneous shopping products	product item
	product line
impulse items	product mix
industrial product	product width

product-service mix
resale products
service
service mix
shopping products

specialty products
staples
supplies
unsought products

DISCUSSION QUESTIONS

1. Explain several product mix strategies a small marketer might use to compete against large marketers such as K-Mart, Safeway, or Sears.

2. Using only one tangible consumer product, explain a consumer purchase situation in which your product is a convenience, shopping, specialty, and unsought product.

3. Assume that you own and manage a retail business that sells consumer products that could be convenience, shopping, specialty, or unsought. Describe your type of business and explain the marketing strategies you use to appeal to consumers for each product category.

4. Why is the industrial product classification system based on how purchasers *use* the products? What influence does this system have on strategies to market industrial products?

5. The marketing of services is different from the marketing of tangible products. Do you agree or disagree with this statement? Explain your position.

NOTES

1. Jody Thum, "The 1982 Buyer's Guide to Tennis Racquets," *Tennis*, 1981, pp. 68–74.
2. For many informative articles about this conference on the marketing services, see James H. Donnelly and William R. George, *Marketing of Services*, American Marketing Association Proceedings Series, American Marketing Association, Chicago, 1981.

CHAPTER
6
PRODUCT DEVELOPMENT
AND MANAGEMENT

A paper towel is a very common, simple product. What could be new about another brand of paper towel? What could a marketer do to introduce a new paper towel? In 1981, Scott Paper Company introduced a new paper towel with the brand name Job Squad. It was described as a different type of disposal towel that could be used to do *all* the jobs around the house, like a squad of workers. Scott introduced Job Squad as the first Supertowel. One sample towel was enclosed in a colorful package and mailed to consumers. The consumer was encouraged to feel the paper towel, read what people said about it, and use it. Then the consumer was told to take the enclosed 20 cent coupon to the store and buy a roll of Job Squad. Brand-name promotions, samples, and coupons are good techniques for introducing a new brand. Together these techniques led to a successful launch of Job Squad paper towels.

Paper once was a new product. Later, the paper towel was a new product. Now there are variations of paper towels that marketers call new products. Very few products that marketers call new are entirely new inventions, but the task of developing and marketing them is risky, challeng-

ing, and important. Almost every marketer has to do a good job of developing and selling new products.

This chapter looks at the marketing of new products. As the paper towel example illustrates, there are several degrees of "new" in product introduction. A new product may be successful because it is new, but marketers need to know why so many new products fail and what is needed for new product success. We shall look at the steps in the development of new products from the idea stage to the introduction of the product on the market.

Just as all living things go through an aging process, products go through life cycle stages. Marketers use product life cycle analysis to help them plan marketing strategies. Next we shall discuss influences on the rate of adoption of new products into markets. What are the characteristics of customers who buy early and of those who buy later? What characteristics of products affect the rate of purchase? The last section of this chapter provides an introduction to marketing strategies involving branding, packaging, and labeling.

MARKETING NEW PRODUCTS

Marketers need to market new products with some regularity. Customers demand change: new models, styles, colors, and ways of solving problems. All successful product brands and items eventually must be modified, improved, or replaced. Every marketer, large or small, must maintain a flow of new products. Thus, a plan for developing or finding new products is essential.

Newness is difficult to define in products. A company may design, manufacture, and sell a product that is different from other products on the market. A retail marketer may sell a product for the first time to customers. In these examples, a new product is developed by the manufacturer and purchased for resale by the retailer. Some products are marketed as new when there may be only a slight change in some part of the marketing mix. For example, a toothpaste may be new because it has a new flavor and form—Colgate Winterfresh Gel. At the other extreme, a product may be the result of truly innovative technology. Examples include television, the transistor, and the electronic computer. Thousands of products that are actually variations of an original innovation are introduced by marketers as new products. A simple, practical definition of a **new product** is any item that a marketer offers to customers for the first time.

From the marketer's point of view, any product is new if it is new to the company and requires different marketing mix strategies. From the customer's point of view, a product is new if it is seen for the first time or perceived as different from other products. If these two conditions meet in one marketing transaction, the product is probably a truly innovative new product. The microwave oven is a good example. Its technology was innovative, and the consumer had to learn new ways of cooking. Today the microwave oven is not considered a new product on the market. However, a consumer who has never used or owned one would perceive it as a new product. The salesperson should present it as the exciting, new product it actually is for this consumer. New models, new technological improvements, new features, and new brands keep marketers and consumers excited about new products.

Marketers may develop new products by using each aspect of the marketing mix: product, promotion, place, price, and information about people. Product changes include form, features, models, and innovations. There are many examples: ballpoint pens, color televisions, instant coffee, digital quartz watches, synthetic fabrics, and electronic calculators.

Customers can see the physical changes and can understand the change in product performance and function. Promotion may create an image of newness. Advertisements may call attention to slight changes that are important to the customer. Technological changes in a car's engine that result in more miles to a gallon must be communicated effectively. The customer will not see some improvements in quality and must be told about them. Changes in package design create new products. The packaging of deodorants is a good example, with sprays, sticks, roll-ons, liquids, and creams in different containers. Beverages placed in different containers such as glass bottles, plastic bottles, flip-top cans, and different-sized containers are actually new products. Ocean Spray is marketing juice drinks in an aseptic package called a Paper Bottle. See page 181 for a related story. The same content in a new package is regarded as a new product. Marketers consider products as new when they are placed in different distribution outlets. L'Eggs Pantyhose are sold in supermarkets, Timex watches are sold in many types of businesses other than jewelry stores, and Avon products are sold only in consumers' homes. A change in price may create a new product by making the product available to different customers. Some consumers will not buy clothing that is too low in price, and some will not buy if the price is too high. In the final analysis, a product is what people perceive it to be. If a consumer thinks a product is new and different, it is a new product. Consumers see newness in many subjective factors, such as color, style, service, environment, and appearance.

INSTANT COFFEE: WHEN WAS IT A NEW PRODUCT?

Read this story by the marketer who introduced the new product. Guess when instant coffee was a new product.

We started 3 years ago, my associates and I, with a new product, a crystallized coffee put out under the brand name of G. Washington Prepared Coffee. We organized the G. Washington Coffee Refining Company to take over a small going business and develop the distribution of what we have described as a prepared, refined, or crystallized coffee.

We have dodged the use of the words *extract* or *essence* as a description of the product because of the undesirable associations those words have. Besides, the product is not strictly an extract. It is the result of a refining process, just as sugar is the result of a refining of sugar cane or sugar beet. The best part of the coffee is there, powdered, for handy packaging in tins.

We laid out three lines of development. First, we arranged a tryout at Atlantic City that summer of 19_____. Second, we put a small advertisement in the *Saturday Evening Post* in the hope of getting a line on the attitude of the public in all sections toward a prepared coffee. Third, we planned to get distribution and educate the retail grocers and others through territorial agents. We were feeling our way.

We had one strong talking point: convenience. G. Washington Coffee is made in an instant, in the cup. The powdered or crystallized coffee is dropped in and dissolves in an instant when hot or cold water is poured over it.

Our sales people handled the proposition in this way. One of them would call on a dealer with a case containing two vacuum bottles, a can of sugar, and a can of G. Washington Prepared Coffee. One vacuum bottle contained hot water. The other bottle contained cream.

The New Product Challenge

A marketer must have a steady flow of new products, but these products are challenging to develop and difficult to market. Let us look first at some reasons why new product development may be such a challenge. Then we shall look at the kinds of marketing organizational environments that can produce new products.

New products cost a lot to develop. Of course, they are worth the cost if they sell and make a profit. A large manufacturer may spend millions of dollars on the development of a single consumer product. Estimates indicate that Polaroid spent $600 million developing the SX-70 camera. Economic conditions, more sophisticated technology, costly capital equipment, and increasing interest rates are just a few of the reasons for generally increasing costs. Even small marketers with smaller budgets have relatively high cost problems with new products. For example, even a retailer who selects a new product for

The salesperson introduced himself and then made a cup of instant coffee on the spot by putting a spoonful of the crystallized coffee into a cup and dissolving it instantly with the hot water. This was served to the grocer, with or without cream and sugar. Our sales people were calling on the leading grocers. A great majority of the latter were impressed by the demonstration and stocked goods.

We had great hopes in regard to our sampling. We spent $25,000 trying out a campaign in New England, but so far as getting any tangible results, it was a flat failure. I am disposed to think, however, that the failure was due to the fact that our samples were too small, whether for the purpose of making an impression or for securing a fair test. The sample contained only enough for four cups, that is to say, less than four teaspoonfuls. It certainly was too small to start a habit or break the old one.

We have been criticized for making use of the name G. Washington and the well-known Washington signature. The Washington for whom our coffee is named is not the immortal George Washington, of the English branch, who has won a right to the use of his own name. This George Washington is the inventor of a kerosene vapor lamp which is on the market today. He worked 14 years on this coffee-refining process. We kept the brand name, but we subsequently changed the name to instant coffee.

Four months after our start we had secured a foothold in what is generally acknowledged to be one of the most difficult markets in the world and were selling the equivalent of 42,500 cups of coffee every morning. Now, after 3 years, our sales have reached the equal of about 1 million cups a day.

The date of the introduction of instant coffee as a new product? 1910.
Adapted from Printer's Ink, October 2, 1913, p. 3.

resale has costs of buying, financing, stocking, displaying, promoting, and selling. For these reasons, marketers need a good system for selecting new products that will have a high probability of success. Some marketers may limit expenses for new products by modifying existing brands and imitating new products developed by other marketers.

Competition is always challenging for marketers. New products may be needed to try to catch up to the competition or to try to get ahead.

In the fiercely competitive marketing world, a successful new product soon is joined by many competitive brands. Marketing schedules are speeded up, and decisions often are made with a minimum of facts and under conditions of time stress. In general, products are on the market a shorter time, and marketers have less time for product planning.

Consumers want new products but are increasingly difficult to satisfy. The analysis of consumer behavior is challenging in itself. When

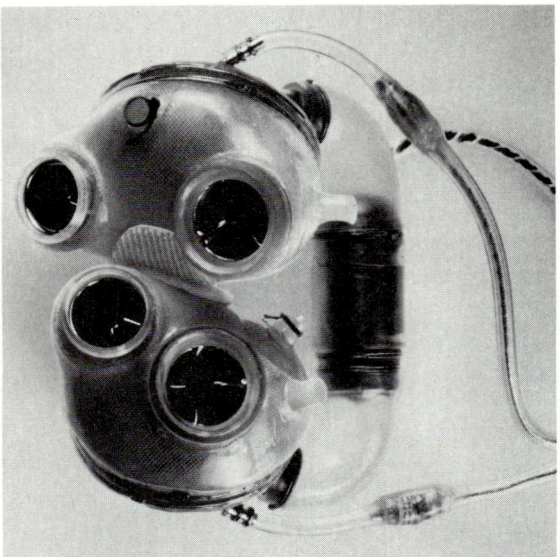

Figure 6-1. New, sophisticated products, such as the Jarvek artificial heart, must comply with strict government standards.

one adds the matching of new products to consumer wants, marketers have a tough assignment. If economic conditions of inflation and higher prices are added, consumers may be even less receptive to new products. The challenge is even greater to marketers when consumers are less willing to take risks. Marketers must consider as well the large number of product choices available to the consumer.

A major problem with many product types is the task of satisfying government standards for the protection of the consumer and the environment. Food products, toys, medicines, automobiles, and industrial equipment are examples. Marketers may have the technology and materials to develop a new product, but governmental and social constraints may be prohibitive. Major issues in this area have involved artificial sweeteners, automobile safety equipment, and nutritional elements in foods. Marketers want to satisfy society's needs and must meet government standards.

Not many new products satisfy all or even most consumers. Marketers usually need to aim their new product ideas at smaller market segments. This is both a problem and a solution for marketers. The problem is that the marketer may need more new product ideas or variations to meet more target markets. The solution may result from a better matching of an idea with a smaller, identifiable market that has more specific characteristics.

Organizing for New Product Development

Marketers of all sizes must develop an organizational environment that can introduce new products with a high probability of success. The most common ways that companies organize for new product development are described here.

1. Product Manager. Product managers are marketing managers for a single product, product line, or brand. In department stores, they may be called merchandise managers. They usually handle the marketing strategies for existing products and help in developing new products. They take over the management of new products at the introductory stage.

2. New Product Committees. The committee plan is very common. A committee may be formed from top management in areas such as manufacturing, accounting, research, finance, engineering, and marketing. Such committees usually review and approve new product ideas which are then turned over to regular product management for further development.

3. New Product Departments. Large companies may have the resources to form a full-time department responsible for developing new products. The department is made up of new product development specialists. If the company can support this plan, it is superior to the committee plan. This department would take new products from the idea stage to the stage of full-scale introduction on the market.

4. Venture Teams. A venture team is a special group of experts from various departments in the company. They are increasingly popular in large industrial firms in the United States. The venture team is put together to bring a specific product to market. The members work together on a full-time basis until the task is accomplished. They often are separated from the rest of the company and report to top management. Venture teams tend to be used for very important new product developments.

These organizational structures are common in many marketing firms, especially in medium to large companies. The smaller the firm, the more difficult it is to free managers from day-to-day operations to develop new products. Personnel usually are assigned to work on new product development only on a part-time basis. This is a major challenge to the management of the small marketing firm. If specific personnel cannot be assigned to new product development full time, blocks of time must be designated for performing this function. Management must create an environment that rewards new ideas, perhaps a type of new product venture team concept with shorter time commitments. Several hours a week can be set aside for creative and innovative thinking. In very small firms, this is a simple technique for getting management away from the regular operations to think about new products. Small marketers often do new product planning when they meet with suppliers' representatives, study catalogs, observe the competition, meet with sales people, and talk with customers.

New Product Risk. Every marketer introduces new products hoping for success but assuming a considerable risk of failure. Marketers are aware of many reasons why new product marketing is risky. A marketer can lose millions of dollars on a new product, and spending large amounts of money on a product does not guarantee its success. The marketing of Ford's Edsel is a classic example. Read the story on pages 158-159.

Marketers continue to be concerned about the failure rate of new products. Studies report failure rates ranging from 20 to 80 percent.[1] Marketers often refer to the 80 percent failure rate, but more recent research studies indicate that a lower percentage may be more realistic. A study by The Conference Board published in the February 8, 1980, issue of *Marketing News* found that 33 percent of products introduced in 1975–1980 were classified as failures by the firms that marketed them. These percentages are for products that were newly launched into markets. Another measure was reported in a classic study in 1968, revealing that of 58 product ideas, only 1 becomes a successful new product.[2] The A. C. Nielsen Company did studies of the success ratios of products for several years and found a success rate of 47 percent in 1971 and 35.5 percent in 1977.[3] Note the decreasing success percentage, which means an increasing failure rate according to the definition of success used in this study. The test of success was whether the product was introduced nationally after being test marketed. The manufacturer's judgment was used to determine the product's success or failure.

Based on the number of studies, the number of published articles, and the frequency of conference discussions on new product failures, marketers are alarmed at the failure rate. Marketers often point to the product failures of well-known companies as examples of what can happen. Many of these companies are familiar ones. Do you remember their products that failed?

- Dupont's Corfam (leather substitute)
- Colgate's Cue Toothpaste
- Campbell's Red Kettle Soups
- IBM DiscoVision (videodiscs)
- Scott Paper's Babyscott Diapers
- Gillette's Nine Flags Men's Cologne
- Bristol-Myers's Resolve Analgesic

Of course, these same companies have had many product successes. However, the question marketers must keep asking and answering is, Why do new products fail?

There are many reasons why new products fail. One of the most frequent and important reasons is that the product does not have a unique

PROFILE OF A FAMOUS NEW PRODUCT FAILURE

The Ford Motor Company's Edsel automobile was probably marketing's most costly new product failure. Marketers can learn a lot from analysis of why an apparently well-planned, well-researched, and heavily promoted product failed. Small marketers may gain some satisfaction from knowing that big marketers with large resources also make mistakes.

The Edsel was introduced into the medium-price market in 1957. The car was planned, researched, and developed over a period of 10 years. About $50 million was spent on promotion before the introduction of the car. Ford had spent about $250 million on development costs. The product ultimately became an approximately $350 million loss.

The idea for the car was very good. Because not enough Ford owners were trading up to the higher-priced Mercury, the company needed more brands in the medium-price line. Economic projections predicted that more consumers would trade up to higher-priced cars in the 1960s. Extensive marketing research was conducted. Consumer image studies and personality portraits revealed that Ford should develop a car with status appeal for young executives and professionals. Thousands of names were researched and tested, but the family name of Edsel finally was selected.

The car was designed for distinctive styling. Ford had the advantage of being able to create a new car from scratch. A unique vertical front grill was developed which was intended to give the Edsel a classic look. Other product features included a push-button transmission, luxury appointments, and a high-performance 345 horsepower engine.

A separate dealer organization was set up to distribute the Edsel. The brand was expected to sell so well that dealers who were Edsel specialists were not allowed to sell any other Ford cars. Dealers were carefully selected and strategically placed throughout the country. The advertising campaign was a quiet, sophisticated one that avoided the use of the word *new* because this would have suggested a common product introduction.

advantage over other products in the market. The marketer may try to promote a difference, but consumers may not see the product advantage. Sometimes the product is a favorite of management and is pushed along even though objective marketing facts suggest negative results. The timing of the product's introduction may be wrong, such as a car that gets low miles to a gallon when consumers want economy. A product will fail if it is not designed well and does not perform correctly. Other reasons include excessive production costs, poorly executed marketing mix strategies, and uncontrollable economic, competitive, and societal conditions.

Extreme efforts kept the Edsel's appearance a secret. The intent was to build up consumer curiosity and interest, but this limited the testing of advertising ideas in test markets. The entire promotional campaign had to hit all over the country at the same time.

Ford expected to sell 200,000 Edsels a year. Over 6,500 orders were taken the first day dealers showed the car, but only 34,481 were sold in the entire year of 1958. Production was discontinued in November 1959, and the final number of Edsels sold was 109,466.

What caused this product failure? Some of the factors were uncontrollable by Ford Motor Company. An economic recession began in 1957, and the sales of medium-price cars of all makes declined. Also, a trend began about this time from bigger cars to less-powerful economy cars. The automobile industry in general was being criticized in books and in the press as merchants of wasteful power. The poor timing of the introduction of the powerful, luxurious Edsel was a big step toward failure.

Ford's marketing actions also contributed to the failure. Market research was well done, but it was done several years before the product was introduced. The market was different when the product arrived. Many people made fun of the style, especially the horse-collar shape of the vertical front grill. The worst product error was lack of quality control. The first Edsels had many mechanical problems, and the car soon developed a negative reputation that was difficult to overcome. Finally, consumers just did not see the Edsel as the unique, distinctive car that Ford was trying to market.

A poor brand name usually does not cause product failure, but most marketers feel that the Edsel name was not helpful. Fortunately for Ford Motor Company, the Mustang was introduced a few years later and became a highly successful product and brand name.

Adapted from Robert F. Hartley, *Marketing Mistakes,* Grid Publishing, Columbus, Ohio, 1981, pp. 115–127.

New Product Success. If marketers become too concerned about the risk of new product failure, they may lose their market share positions through being too conservative. This chapter began with a discussion about the importance of a steady flow of new products. As a consumer, you can appreciate how exciting the discovery of a new product can be. Read about the new product success of Tostitos on page 160. $165,000,000 in annual sales can be very exciting for the marketer!

The Conference Board study that revealed a 33 percent failure rate for new products should be restated to emphasize the 67 percent success rate

TOSTITOS: A NEW PRODUCT SUCCESS STORY

Frito-Lay has been very successful in the corn chip snack-food business since Fritos were introduced in 1932. Fritos have continued with a good share of the market in a solid maturity stage. Doritos, the triangular corn chip, was introduced in 1965. It had reached more than $100 million in annual sales by the early 1970s, achieving consistent increases in sales volume and market share since its introduction, but it entered a maturity stage in 1974 with sales flattening out for several years.

With the leveling sales trend of Doritos, Frito-Lay began looking for ways to increase the sales of Doritos or for new product ideas. Market research of consumer attitudes toward Doritos suggested that the product's nacho cheese flavor had good potential. But many consumers considered Doritos to be too heavy, thick, and crunchy. Trends toward lighter-tasting foods in general and the increasing popularity of Mexican foods were important factors in Frito-Lay's decision to avoid big changes in Doritos. Instead, they planned to develop a new corn chip product with a Mexican ethnic theme. It took Frito-Lay 6 months to take the new concept from the initial stages to development of positioning, packaging, advertising, and merchandising programs. The brand name Tostitos came from a variation on *tostados* and a continuation of the Frito-Lay *os* ending: Fritos, Doritos, and now Tostitos. Tostitos were made in round chips to simulate authentic Mexican tortillas and to differentiate the product from the triangular-shaped Doritos.

Tostitos were first test marketed in 1977 in Houston and Phoenix. The sales volume in these two markets was so much higher than expected that the tests were extended to two non-Mexican markets, Minneapolis and Omaha. Results showed a product with excellent potential.

A $10 million advertising campaign was used, aimed mostly at network television, to introduce the product. Retailers who knew the solid Fritos and Doritos products readily accepted and stocked Tostitos. The entire marketing mix was well planned and well executed. The result was an outstanding introductory sales volume in 1980 of $140 million. The product jumped almost immediately into a growth stage with $165 million in sales in 1981.

When a new product such as Tostitos is introduced to a product mix including other successful corn chip products, the new product often takes significant amounts of sales from the mature products. Marketers call this cannibalization. The happy result for Frito-Lay was very little cannibalization. Doritos actually increased in sales by 20 percent in 1981. The Tostitos round tortilla chip with the authentic Mexican style is a great example of successful new product introduction.

Adapted from Tom Bayer and B. G. Yovovich, "Snacking on Success," *Advertising Age,* March 15, 1982, p. M-10. Reprinted with permission. © Crain Communications, Inc.

for new products. In the September 18, 1981, issue of *Marketing News,* Edward M. Tauber, a professor of marketing at the University of Southern California, stressed the idea that U.S. marketing researchers should end their preoccupation with the reasons why new products fail and begin focusing on why products succeed. He encouraged marketers to accept the challenge of predicting new product performance by understanding why new products succeed.

A report published in *Sales and Marketing Management* indicated that marketers are not improving their success ratios with new products but are continuing to improve their abilities to develop new products. A survey of 700 corporations by Booz, Allen & Hamilton revealed that in the 1976–1981 period, 65 percent of new product introductions met company criteria for success. A survey covering 1963–1968 reported a 67 percent ratio.

Despite that lack of progress, marketers expect new products to contribute 33 percent of total profits in the 1981–1986 period, a sharp rise over the 22 percent share achieved in 1976–1981. Part of the improvement will stem from stepped-up introductions, with the typical company planning to launch 10 new products in the next 5 years versus 5 in the last 5 years. Marketers with successful new product track records are distinguished by certain characteristics, says John M. Harris, senior vice president. "They use a formal new product process that does a better job screening ideas, identify the strategic roles to be played by new products, devote more management attention and financial resources to the early stages, and learn from their experiences."[4]

The message here is that marketers know the value of new product introductions and try to use good strategies to increase their probability of success.

What can successful new products do for a company? The obvious answer is that they can increase sales and profits. New products can be used to diversify product offerings and expand product lines. This outcome will help a company produce sales in different seasons since when sales are down in some product lines, they will be up in the in-season lines. Retail marketers seek new products to keep customers returning to them for exciting new ways to improve their lifestyles. Manufacturers develop new products to keep middlemen active in their distribution system. Overall, new products enhance a marketer's image as a modern, innovative, quality firm that is changing with the times and will be perceived as a dependable business for a long time.

Successful marketers learn from product failures and seek new product success with better strategies. A good example is Ford Motor Company's introduction of the Mustang after the death of the Edsel.

Developing New Products

Marketers should think of the development of new products as a process, a sequence of steps leading to the introduction of the new product in a market. See Figure 6-2 on page 162 for a picture of these steps. The first step is the generation of ideas from many sources. The second step is the screening of those ideas for their quality and potential value to the company. The third step is analysis of the idea by using sales, cost, and profit estimates. The fourth step is the manufacture of a limited number of physical products. The fifth step is selling the product in test markets to get customer reactions. The sixth step is the introduction of the product in one or more markets with a complete marketing program.

As you read about each step in the process, keep in mind that the steps are applied in many different ways. Some large manufacturers have an extremely formal procedure that generates thousands of new product ideas and ends with the introduction of several new products. Manufacturers tend to use all the steps in the process, but they do not always use every step. For example, a product may be rushed to the market without test marketing just to try to beat the competition.

STEPS FOR DEVELOPING NEW PRODUCTS

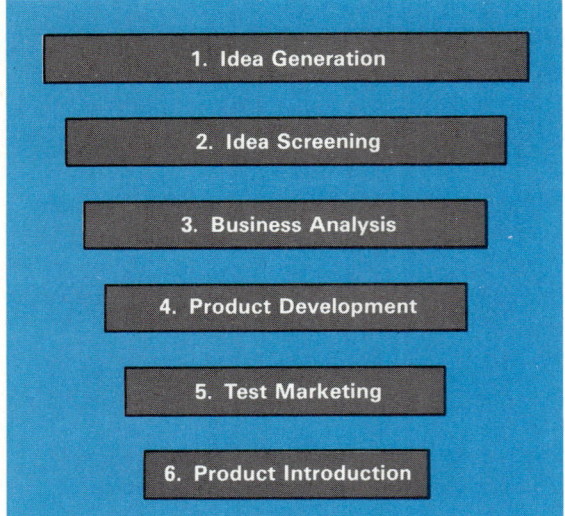

1. Idea Generation

2. Idea Screening

3. Business Analysis

4. Product Development

5. Test Marketing

6. Product Introduction

Figure 6-2. Developing new products. This wedge shape indicates that many ideas are needed to progress through the steps that lead to a successful new product.

Retailers and wholesalers may use all six steps, although the product development step may involve product acquisition rather than production. Small marketers of all types apply these steps, but often in an informal and intuitive way.

This story of one small service marketer's use of the new product development steps will illustrate the practical application of the process. A hairstylist in a small shop listened to one of his customers for a new product idea. The customer said that she dropped coins in a small box to save money for her next trip to the stylist. The stylist then decided to try to design a bank for his customers. After coming up with a few ideas and sketches, he took them to a plastic-molding firm. The eventual result was an attractive plastic bank shaped like a flowing hair design with a comb through it, very similar to the hairstylist's shop logo. He named it the Beauty Bank. At first, he gave the banks to regular customers and recorded the cost as advertising. A wholesale supplier liked the idea and wanted to sell them to other retail

shops. More banks were produced, and the result was a sales volume large enough to make a profit on the product.

Of course, this story omits many details of actions, time, effort, and decisions. Actually, each step in the process is like a hurdle that the product must get over to reach the next step. Stop or go decisions are made at each step.

Idea Generation. The **idea generation** stage goes from the beginning of a product through the originating and collecting of product ideas. New product development starts with an idea, and ideas come from many sources. Large companies use a program for planned idea generation. New product managers, committees, and departments may be organized to generate ideas. Many ideas originate in less formal ways. Customers are excellent sources of new product ideas. Marketers should listen to customers to identify the benefits they want. This is the marketing concept at work: Determine consumers' needs, wants, problems, and behaviors and then satisfy them.

Marketers use many external sources to generate product ideas. They watch competitors' products to learn which ones are attracting customers. A similar product with some variation may become a new product. Ideas can come from trade associations, marketing research firms, consultants, advertising agencies, and marketing publications. Of course, some of these sources are costly to use, and others are available to all marketers, such as publications and trade associations.

Many new product ideas originate from technology and research within the firm. The rapid development of electronic products is a good example. Scientific research in laboratories and special departments can generate many ideas. In fact, any employee in a firm may generate product ideas. Employees may be encouraged with incentive programs and suggestion systems to create ideas. Sales people are often the best employee group for ideas since they interact with customers and with management. Sales people are in the best position to relate the firm's products and resources to the problems of the product users.

Many new ideas are needed to end up with one usable idea. Management needs to create an environment conducive to idea development. Ideas should be appropriate to the type of business, but at this stage, all new ideas should be welcomed and considered. The only ideas rejected at this point are those which are obviously not related to the business objectives and are not feasible to develop. The next stage is the evaluation of the quality of all the ideas that the firm could turn into products.

Idea Screening.

Most of the ideas generated in the first stage should reach the **idea screening** stage, where ideas not compatible with company objectives are eliminated. Now the company begins to get tough and to drop bad ideas as quickly as possible. The product is still essentially an idea. The firm has not made a major investment in it yet.

Several techniques are used to try to keep the good ideas and drop the bad ones. Some firms require the product manager (committee, team, or department) to write up the product ideas as a broader concept. This concept statement would include a description of the product idea and its future benefits for the firm. The general feasibility of its design and manufacture or development by the company should be presented. The matching of the product to existing or potential target markets must be considered.

Key people in the firm should be sought for opinions about product ideas during this stage. Quick and inexpensive fact-gathering methods are needed. Production, design, finance, and marketing personnel may give estimates of the value of a product idea relative to each function of the business. At this point, some firms may use a rating form with rating scales, objective questions, and check lists to help make a drop-or-keep decision. A rating device may help rank the product ideas that will move on to the next stage. The two types of errors management tries to avoid are keeping a product idea that will fail and rejecting a product idea that would have been a success.

Business Analysis.

During the **business analysis** stage, the product idea is examined from an objective business perspective. Future sales, costs, and profits will be estimated as well as possible. The sales history of similar products in the firm will be checked, and a prediction will be made. The firm will check secondary data sources to try to determine financial data for all products of this type on the market. It will estimate minimum sales and maximum sales. Given these ranges, cost and profit figures can be estimated. The firm needs to estimate potential market demand for a short time and for a long time. It will play several what-if games in relation to investment, costs, demand, sales, markets, competition, and profitability.

This stage, like the previous two, is still a matter of on-paper concept testing. A lot of time and effort may be involved up to this point. But if the firm goes beyond this point with the product idea, the costs increase at a rapid rate. This is a critical point in the new product development sequence. Marketing management should not have any major doubts about a product as an addition to the product mix. No product can be a certain success in the future, but the idea should have good market potential at this stage.

Product Development.

If the decision is made to go ahead, the product idea must be developed into a technically feasible product. In the **product development** stage, physical products are constructed, usually on a limited-production basis, so that laboratory tests and consumer reaction can be studied. The responsibility for product development is turned over to engineering and production. Pilot models in small quantities are manufactured. In our simple product example about the Beauty Bank, several versions of the plastic model were molded by hand. When the manufacturer determined that the product could be made to the specifications of the designer, several models were constructed to see whether they would be sturdy enough for use by consumers. For example, they were tested for durability in the plant with coins and pressure tests. Several consumers who were friends of the hairstylist-designer were asked to study the models in a small version of a consumer-reaction panel.

Large companies producing more complex products submit their products to more sophisticated and extensive tests. These are production and laboratory tests to determine the performance of products against specifications in the product design. Fabrics are tested for color fading; appliances are tested for function and safety; watches and calculators are tested for accuracy under various conditions. Panels of potential consumers are brought in to try the models in typical use situations. In limited numbers, consumers may be given samples of the product to use in the home or in other actual use situations away from the laboratory. Tests should be conducted over a long enough period and under conditions as normal as possible in order to reflect actual use patterns. Strengths and weaknesses of the product design should be learned. Modifications may be made in further production to capitalize on the strengths and avoid the weaknesses.

Evaluation must be extremely tough at this stage because the next two stages, test marketing and full-scale production, commit the firm to major investments.

Test Marketing. **Test marketing** involves offering the new product in a sampling of markets to customers in normal buying conditions. The object is to test the product and its marketing program in actual markets in which consumers do not know that they are being tested. Consumer reaction can be measured in terms of sales volume, repeat purchases, and problems or complaints. Retailers and wholesalers can react to marketing strategies in relation to the new product. The overall purpose of test marketing is to get feedback on all the elements of the product's marketing mix.

The manufacturer of consumer products may test market a new food product in the supermarkets of a few cities. See Table 6-1 for a list of the most commonly used cities for test marketing in the United States. If market reaction to the product is good, the product may be introduced as quickly as possible throughout the national market. A national restaurant chain such as McDonald's or Wendy's may test market a new sandwich in a few stores in several different types of geographic markets. Frito-Lay's Tostitos were tested first in Houston and Phoenix and later in Minneapolis and Omaha. A retailer who owns nine stores may test a new product in only one.

Test marketing may be used to get the problems and defects out of the product before full-scale introduction. The test stage may help the marketer learn successful strategies for advertising, distributing, and selling. Sometimes adjustments in techniques that are learned in testing may allow the marketer to reduce the risk and the costs of introduction. If the test is a success, the results may be used as a demonstration for other dealers to encourage them to market the new product.

Not all marketers test market, and not all products need to be tested. Marketers may skip this stage of product development for the following reasons.

1. Test market costs are high compared to the average costs of product introduction and normal risk of failure. Test marketing is expensive. The marketer may obtain product information that indicates a high probability of product success without testing.

2. Test marketing delays the introduction of the product to a full-scale market. If the delay is too long, market conditions may change. A test market delay may be even more dangerous if it gives the competition sufficient time to get their products into the market.

3. Test market cities may not predict national results. Consumer behavior, marketing strategies, and scale of operation may not transfer effectively to national or even regional markets.

4. Test marketing does not guarantee successful product information. Some marketers feel that the time and effort put into testing in sample markets would be spent better in actual product information.

TABLE 6-1
THE NATION'S MOST POPULAR TEST MARKETS*

1. Albany–Schenectady–Troy
2. Albuquerque
3. Amarillo
4. Atlanta
5. Boston
6. Buffalo
7. Charleston, WV
8. Charlotte
9. Chicago
10. Cincinnati
11. Cleveland
12. Columbus, OH
13. Dallas–Fort Worth
14. Dayton
15. Denver
16. Des Moines
17. Erie, PA
18. Fort Wayne
19. Fresno
20. Green Bay, WI
21. Houston
22. Indianapolis
23. Jacksonville, FL
24. Kansas City, MO
25. Lexington, KY
26. Lubbock, TX
27. Memphis
28. Miami
29. Milwaukee
30. Minneapolis–St. Paul
31. Nashville
32. Oklahoma City
33. Omaha
34. Orlando–Daytona Beach
35. Peoria
36. Phoenix
37. Pittsburgh
38. Portland, ME
39. Portland, OR
40. Providence
41. Quad cities: Rock Island & Moline, IL Davenport & Bettendorf, IA
42. Rochester, NY
43. Sacramento–Stockton
44. San Francisco
45. St. Louis
46. San Antonio
47. San Diego
48. Seattle–Tacoma
49. South Bend
50. Spokane
51. Syracuse
52. Tampa–St. Petersburg
53. Tucson
54. Tulsa
55. Wichita

*In alphabetical order, not listed by rank.

Adapted from *Sales & Marketing Management*, March 15, 1982, p. 72. Based on *S&MM's* studies.

The challenge to the marketer is to do the testing as efficiently as possible and to obtain useful data for decision making. Computer simulations of product introductions provide one alternative to test marketing. Regardless of the amount of test marketing performed or the alternatives used, most marketers use this stage to adjust their marketing mix strategies before product introduction.

Product Introduction. The product introduction stage is reached when the marketer places the new product on the market and a complete marketing program is in effect. This stage is also known as **commercialization.** The marketer now is involved in full-scale production and marketing of the product to target markets. The product may be introduced in regional markets first, such as the midwest, east coast, or west coast. Products often are introduced in large-city markets and then in medium-size and smaller markets. Products may be aimed at market segments identified by demographic or psychographic characteristics or both. Some marketing firms may aim a new product at the complete national consumer market. In practice, marketers refer to this introduction as a **national rollout.** In fact, marketers say that they have rolled a product when they introduce a new product to any market or move a product from a smaller to a larger market.

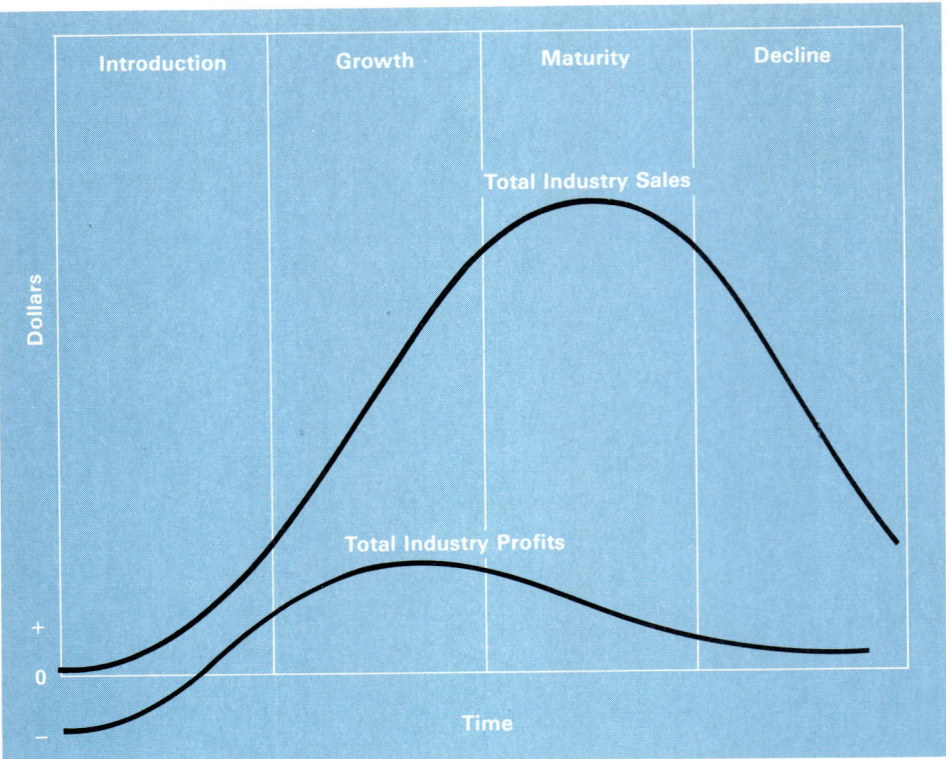

Figure 6-3. Product life cycle. This chart shows the traditional stages—introduction, growth, maturity, and decline—through which a product passes.

The product introduction stage is actually the beginning of the product life cycle. This is an exciting point in product management for any marketer. Let us look now at the strategies involved in the product life cycle.

PRODUCT LIFE CYCLE

After the introduction of a new product, marketers hope to keep it alive for a long time. The marketer's goal is to develop a product that generates sales and produces a satisfactory profit during its life on the market. The stages that a product passes through from introduction to removal from the market are called a **product life cycle.** The product life cycle (PLC) is most commonly thought of as the progression of a product through four stages: introduction, growth, maturity, and

decline. If the product fails to provide a satisfactory return after a long period of rapidly declining sales, it is dropped, and marketing efforts are applied to new or successful products.

Figure 6-3 illustrates an average pattern of sales and profits during the life of a product. The vertical axis (dimension) of the chart measures the sales and profits in dollars. The horizontal axis measures time. Study the chart as you consider the basic characteristics of each stage of the PLC.

1. Introduction is a period of beginning sales that usually increase slowly without generating profits.

2. Growth is a period of rapid sales increase and high unit profits.

3. Maturity is a period of a decreasing rate of sales increase and eventually a level amount of

sales. Total profits peak early in this period and then start to decline.

4. Decline is a period when sales and profits decrease at a rapid rate.

The product life cycle is not the same for all products. Some products may reach a growth stage quickly, peak in sales, and decline very rapidly. For example, a toy product introduced for Christmas may go through its entire PLC from October to January. Some products, such as Kleenex facial tissues, may stay in a maturity stage for many years. Durable products such as color television sets may remain in each stage for a great many years. The PLC pattern in Figure 6-3 is called a traditional sales curve. Note that the sales curve shows the amount of sales in relation to time. The determination of the PLC stage for a product is the rate or direction of sales. A product in the introduction stage is selling at a slowly increasing rate. When the rate of sales increase is much faster, the product enters the growth stage. A marketer would know this by comparing sales volume figures or by recording sales volume on a PLC chart. When the rate of sales growth slows noticeably or the sales volume levels off and starts to decrease slowly, the product is in the maturity stage. When sales decline at a rapid rate, the marketer knows that the product is in the decline stage.

Not all marketers make charts to show PLC stages for products, but all marketers use some measures and their judgment to estimate PLC stages. Even the small marketer benefits from analysis of sales, profits, competitors, customers, and strategies through applying the concept of the product life cycle.

Using the Product Life Cycle

Marketers have many reasons for using the product life cycle as a decision-making concept. One of the most important is the need for the marketer's new products to become profitable as quickly as possible. As was discussed earlier in this chapter, the development of new products is expensive and risky. Once a product has been introduced to the market, the marketer's goal is to move it to the growth stage as quickly as possible. Another important reason for effective PLC use is the general trend toward shorter life cycles. This trend places more pressure on the marketer to make good product management decisions. A shorter life cycle may be caused by the following situations.

- **Technical Change.** If technical change in a specific industry occurs at a faster rate, certain products will have a shorter life cycle. Industries affected by electronic technology are causing shorter life cycles in calculators, audiovisual equipment, and computers. Improved models are preferred by customers and often make previous models obsolete.

- **Competitive Entry.** If it is relatively easy for competitors to market products similar to yours, these products will tend to have a shorter life cycle. New models will need to be developed sooner to meet the competition. In some cases, a change in promotion or distribution may meet competition. In one classic marketing example, there were 52 competing electric toothbrushes on the market within 2 years after General Electric entered the consumer market with one. Of course, protective patents and high costs of production slow the life cycle of some products.

- **Market Acceptance.** If consumers like a product idea and accept it quickly, the product will reach the maturity stage sooner than usual for that type of product. Whether it stays in the maturity stage for a long time depends on consumer preferences and continued support. In general, today's consumers are accepting new ideas faster than the consumers of several years ago. Consumers want change (remember the discussion of consumer behavior in Chapter 3), and this leads to shorter life cycles. Rapid change in clothing fashions, fads, and high-technology products are obvious. Even staple items such as paper towels are changed by modification of size, design, color, package, and sometimes function.

● **Effective Communication.** Faster and more effective communication may shorten a product life cycle. Communication with markets through media causes a product to reach the growth stage faster and move to the maturity stage if the product is good. If the product is no good and promotion through media encourages consumers to try it early, the product may have a short life cycle because it will mature soon and die quickly. Internal communication through the use of computers is providing data faster and allowing quicker decisions. Marketers may have the ability to react faster to market situations. A shorter life cycle may result if product changes are made faster. Of course, the same data can be used to help extend the life of a product.

When to Use the PLC. Marketers use PLC analysis to help them plan strategies for marketing products in each stage. Each of the four stages (introduction, growth, maturity, and decline) may require specific applications of the marketing mix in the form of strategy techniques. For example, certain types of promotion may be more effective during introduction than during maturity. A lower price may be used during introduction, and a higher price may result in increased sales during the growth stage. Marketers can use the PLC to compare the marketing of similar products. If a company introduced a new breakfast cereal 2 years ago, it can follow a new cereal's sales progress and PLC pattern today. Marketers use the PLC to help time the introduction of new products in relation to current products. If you introduce a new flavor or model of a product in your brand name while another one of your products is in the growth stage, you may steal sales from it and cause it to mature too early. Also, marketers use the PLC to help extend the life of a successful product or decide when to drop an unsuccessful one. Thus, the fundamental purpose of the product life cycle is to manage the product. When marketers talk about managing the PLC, they actually mean that they are using measures of sales, profits, time, rate, customers, and competition to help make decisions about product marketing.

Limitations to the PLC. The product life cycle is a useful concept for marketers, but there are problems and limitations in its use. The PLC can be used to predict general patterns of sales for a product, but predicting when the next PLC stage will appear is very difficult. Also, the prediction of how long a stage will last is difficult. The use of the PLC may show that a maturity stage has been reached because sales have leveled, but market conditions may lead to an increase in sales and a new growth period. Marketers should be careful to use the PLC to compare similar types of products. A marketer should not make decisions about products with a long life cycle (tools) by using products with a short life cycle (garden seeds). Some critics of the PLC concept suggest that the greatest problem with its use occurs when a product's sales decline. Marketers may determine that the product is in a decline stage in the PLC and make decisions which cause sales to continue to decline and the product to fail.[5]

Product Life Cycle Stages

Most marketers use the PLC as a guide for strategic marketing actions. We shall look now at marketing actions that usually are effective during each stage of the PLC. A marketer would use these actions as beginning points for planning a strategy for a specific product in a specific market situation. Some marketing actions are taken to try to change the direction of the PLC. For example, assume that you are marketing a dog food. Sales have started to slow, and you determine that you are about to enter the maturity stage. You may decide to try to stay in the growth stage by using a new promotional campaign. If you had decided to accept the entrance of your dog food into the maturity stage, you probably would not have put as much additional money into promotion. As we examine marketing strategies for each stage of the PLC, keep these two general approaches in mind: Accept the pattern of the PLC, or attempt to change the pattern.

Another challenge the marketer faces in practical use of the PLC is the selection of the product level for analysis and application. The PLC con-

TABLE 6-2
EXAMPLES OF PRODUCT LIFE CYCLE STRATEGIES

Introduction Stage	Growth Stage	Maturity Stage	Decline Stage
1. Give free samples of the new product.	1. Make product available in more outlets.	1. Increase marketing efforts at point-of-sale.	1. Market only to brand-loyal market segments.
2. Blitz the market with advertising.	2. Add new sizes, new packages, and new styles.	2. Introduce lower-priced models of an established brand.	2. Make slight design changes at minimum cost.
3. Display the new product with a product that is selling well.	3. Advertise to induce repeat purchases.	3. Offer more services with the product.	3. Reduce promotion costs.
4. Offer the new product at a price lower than competition.	4. Promote to stress brand name.	4. Offer temporary price reductions.	4. Reduce number of product models to best sellers.
5. Offer free trial-usage periods.	5. Widen advertising to reach new market segments.	5. Create more attractive and useful packages.	5. Sell only to channel outlets with best performance records.
6. Introduce quality products at a price above competition.	6. Reduce prices to reach new markets.	6. Use all channels and more outlets.	6. Maintain low price to produce a satisfactory profit.
7. Offer price-off coupons on the next purchase.	7. Introduce new models and new features.	7. Design exclusive or innovative features.	7. Reduce all marketing efforts and marketing costs.
8. Give products to influential users.	8. Encourage buyers to use product in more ways and more frequently.	8. Change advertising messages for different segments.	
9. Offer special inducements to distributors: price allowance, cooperative advertising, special displays, exclusive distribution.	9. Offer special sales aids to present dealers.	9. Improve quality of some models and raise prices.	
	10. Expand distribution system to more outlets.	10. Stress brand name.	

cept may be applied to a product class (calculators), product form (printing calculators), product line (calculators and accessories), brand (Texas Instruments calculators), or individual product (Texas Instruments TI-55). A PLC analysis can be done on any of these levels. Marketers must select the level that is appropriate for their businesses and products. See Table 6-2 for examples of PLC strategies.

Introduction Stage. The **introduction stage** is the beginning of sales of a new product to customers in one or more markets. Sales volume begins at zero and usually increases very slowly. There are no profits at first, and they remain low. If the product involves a very new or different idea, market acceptance is slower. Products that are relatively expensive or complex also cause a longer (slower) introductory period. New products that are modifications or slightly changed models tend to be accepted faster. Microwave ovens were introduced slowly because early models were expensive, appeared complex, and required new ways of cooking. Automatic coffee makers such as the Mr. Coffee brand had a short introductory period because they were not very expensive and were easy to use.

The overall goal of the marketer is to use marketing strategies that increase sales as quickly as possible. The marketer would like a very short introductory stage because this always means rapidly increasing sales. The product needs a lot of promotion during this stage. Promotion expenses often are higher during this stage of the PLC than in any other. Potential customers are not aware of the new product. The goal of promotion is to build awareness which leads to interest and preference for the product. Marketers of new products for consumers promote heavily through such media as newspapers, magazines, radio, and television. Packaged food products typically are promoted this way. At the same time, products must be sold and move through the channels of wholesalers and retailers to be ready for customers at the right time. Sales people must be prepared to sell the new product. Marketers of industrial products usually introduce new products by sending sales representatives to call on business customers.

Prices of new products during the introductory stage may be high or low. A marketer who introduces a product with high prices believes that early purchasers of the new product will pay the price to be among the first to own it. This strategy suggests that the price can be lowered when demand decreases. The initial high price is used to cover developmental and promotional costs. A low price is used when marketers want to sell a large volume of the new product as quickly as possible. Low price may establish a good market share position and discourage competitors. Many practical pricing strategies that can be applied to the stages of the PLC are discussed in Chapters 10 and 11.

Marketers use many techniques to encourage customers to try a new product. A 1 ounce sample of new shampoo may be attached to a regular brand. The consumer may send in a coupon and receive a free sample of Excedrin. A television set (unlikely to be a free sample) may be tried for 3 days in the customer's home at no charge. New products may be returned for a full refund in 1 week with no questions asked. Industrial marketers encourage other marketers to buy their products by using price reductions, sample products, trial periods, and rebates.

The principles of new product introduction are the same for any marketer. The specific techniques must be appropriate for the product, marketer, and potential customers. A large marketer may spend millions of dollars to promote the introduction of a new product throughout the nation. A small retailer may spend hundreds of dollars to advertise a new brand for sale in a city market. Both cases represent applications of the PLC introductory stage.

Growth Stage. In the **growth stage,** sales increase at a faster rate than during any other stage. The time, cost, and effort used to market the product are beginning to pay off. The company is beginning to make a profit on each item sold, and total profits increase because of greater sales volume. Costs for distribution and promotion for each unit are decreasing because they are spread over a larger volume of products. For example, an advertisement that costs $100 might have sold 100 items during the introduction stage, but it sells 1,000 items during the growth stage. During the growth stage, the customers who tried the product buy more and tell their friends to buy. Word-of-mouth advertising is beginning to work.

Because one or more products are growing and successful in a given market, new competitors will enter the market. This action tends to expand the market with new variations of the basic product. More retailers and different types of retailers begin to stock the products. Competition begins to get tough. Market share and loyal customers are more difficult to keep. In spite of this competition, marketers are able to maintain price levels because of overall increasing demand. Even though there are more marketers and types of products, the product continues to attract more buyers.

The goal of the marketer is to keep the growth stage working as long as possible. These are the ideal marketing conditions: increasing sales, decreasing unit costs, increasing profits, and an increasing number of customers. However, a company cannot sit back and enjoy this position. It will not last unless marketing strategies are applied effectively. If you are a retailer, this is the time to find products of this type with improved quality and new features. The marketer will want to stress good brands, good services, and good location. You have been advertising to make customers aware of new products. Now you want to advertise to remind and encourage customers to come back to you. You may want to lower prices a little to appeal to another level of shoppers. As you expand your product offerings, you probably will offer a wider range of prices to appeal to several types of customers. During this time, industrial marketers are performing similar marketing strategies and searching for new market segments. They are seeking new distribution channels—more wholesalers and retailers to use and sell their products.

Improved product quality, new models, new features, new styles, repeat customers, new customers, new market segments, new channels, maintained prices, and effective promotion are all characteristics of the growth stage. The growth usually does not continue for a long time because markets get saturated, customers' demands change, or competitors divide and share the market. The smart marketer knows that this eventually happens and works to hold on to a good share of the market.

Maturity Stage. During the **maturity stage,** the rate of sales increase begins to slow down and the sales volume levels off. Look at Figure 6-3 again. When the sales volume line changes from a sharp angle upward to a flat line, sales are not increasing as fast and the product is in the maturity stage. Some marketers call this the peak sales, or saturation, period. The product has reached a point at which customers are buying about as much of it as they need and want. The maturity stage usually constitutes the longest period. Campbell's soups, McDonald's hamburgers, and Coca-Cola are examples of products that have been in a maturity stage for a long time and show no signs of declining.

For many reasons, the maturity stage presents a major challenge to marketers. Competition is strong. There are many competitors in the market, and competitive marketing strategies are increasing. Because of marketers' efforts to satisfy customers, competing products have similar features. More money is spent promoting small differences between products. Because of increasing promotion and distribution costs, profits begin to decrease. Many marketing strategies are duplicated quickly by several competitors.

This intense competition results from an inviting market when several marketers are enjoying a growth period with a product. Many companies jump into the production and marketing of the product and cause an eventual surplus on the market. The surplus leads to price reductions as one technique to try to increase or maintain sales. Lower-priced models of the product are introduced rapidly. Small electronic calculators and digital watches are two products that illustrate this situation. Eventually, the majority of marketers drop out of the market. Only a few may remain with a market share large enough to maintain a satisfactory profit. The calculator market is a good example, with Hewlett-Packard, Texas Instruments, Canon, Sharp, and Casio among a few brands that appear to be holding the biggest market shares.

It is during the maturity stage that the real marketing strategy battle takes place. The best marketers survive, and the inefficient and weak get out of the market. To stay alive, the marketer must be very effective with the elements of the marketing mix. Products may be improved, prices may be lowered, promotion may be increased and improved, and distribution systems may be changed. A common strategy during the maturity stage is to find new markets for a firm's products. The firm must look for segments that have not tried its product. The classic example is Johnson's Baby Shampoo being promoted to adults as a mild shampoo for everyone. Another strategy encourages present customers to use the product in more ways and more frequently. Detergents are promoted for use in the kitchen, bathroom, and garage. As a consumer, you can recall the many ways marketers have encouraged you to use cat litter, spray disinfectant, and skin lotion.

One of the most important techniques during the maturity stage is to change the product. Adding and improving product features can stretch the life of a product. New models, flavors, styles, or sizes may initiate a new period of growth or at least help a marketer maintain a share of the market. New features may make a product more attractive by improving speed (kitchen mixers and hair dryers), adding functions (calculators and cameras), improving durability (work gloves and power tools), and changing styles (clothing and furniture). These examples provide only a small sample of the many ways in which marketers attempt to find a competitive advantage which will increase sales and maintain a satisfactory profit.

Decline Stage. During the **decline stage,** sales decrease at a rapid rate. In some cases, the decline may be slow but steady over a long time period. Black and white television sets, AM radios, and 45 rpm records are examples of products that are declining slowly but may continue selling for a long time. In other cases, the decline is very fast, as with product failures (the Ford Edsel and Colgate's Cue toothpaste), fashion and fad clothing, unsuccessful technology (quadraphonic stereo), and humorous gimmicks (pet rocks). Some products, such as hula hoops, have very

Figure 6-4. A woodburning stove is one example of a product that was once in decline but has benefited from increased demand due to increased energy costs.

short life cycles with fast decline stages and then return to the market in a few years for another short PLC. Clothing styles and colors do this. Some products have a long, slow decline stage and level off to a small but steady share of the market. Fountain pens, manual typewriters, straight razors, CB radios, and wood-burning stoves are examples. These types of products may continue to be in limited demand for decades. Economic, environmental, and societal conditions may cause a wave of increased demand. The use of wood-burning stoves during periods of energy conservation is a good example.

The decline stage is the time for the marketer to reduce costs and begin to reduce the number of models offered. The total promotion effort often is reduced, but promotion to selected markets may be continued as long as a profit can be made. Some products in this stage cost very little to produce, and some customers will continue to use a product without any new advertising. For example, many older people continue to use certain brands of liniments and salves that are no longer promoted. Prices are reduced slightly or maintained at a level which provides a small but adequate unit profit.

Sales decline for many reasons. New products with distinct advantages take sales away from other products. Customers try some new products, do not like them, and do not buy them again. Competitive companies may flood the market with too many similar products. Marketers often refer to these as "me-too" products. Changes in consumer preferences and lifestyles make some products obsolete. Many products die because they are poorly designed, produced, and marketed.

Product Elimination Strategies

During the discussion of the product life cycle, you probably noticed that the strategies tend to emphasize adding new products and features and extending the life of a product. Typical techniques include finding new users, discovering new uses, encouraging increased frequency of use, and generally appealing to brand-loyal customers. New models incorporating small or significant changes may extend the life of a product. Changes in packaging, brand names, distribution channels, promotional campaigns, and price are all marketing mix strategies that seek to stretch specific stages and the entire PLC.

Marketers should try to make a profit from products for as long as possible, but every marketer faces the problem of knowing when to drop a product or line. Marketers tend to neglect the technique of product elimination. Weak products often are allowed to continue in the marketer's product mix for too long. If these products are producing almost no sales and no profits, the decision to eliminate is easy. The difficulty lies with products in the advanced decline stage, especially when they are declining very slowly. The costs often are hidden. For the retail marketer, the weak product is taking up valuable shelf and

storage space. Inventory costs build up, and sales people's efforts are wasted in displays or price changes. Advertising monies may be lost. Customers may get a negative perception of the store if out-of-date or unpopular products are stocked. Industrial marketers may lose money on expensive production runs, sales representatives' time, and dealers' confidence in the firm. The biggest potential cost is the loss of business caused by delaying the introduction of profitable new products while giving attention to weak products.

There are good reasons for carrying products in stock even though they do not produce enough sales volume to earn a profit. Some products need to be carried to complete a line of products. An appliance department may not make a profit from its inventory of ice crushers, but its advertised policy is to sell every type of kitchen appliance. A certain hardware store is expected to stock a variety of nails even though several types and sizes do not sell often.

Many marketers carry weak products and lines too long because keeping them in stock is easier than dropping them. Marketers should know some of the warning signals which indicate that a product is in trouble. Declining sales volume is an easy cue to follow. A decreasing market share may indicate that a product is not selling as well as similar products and competitive products. Current sales are low compared with past sales records or predicted sales. Prices must be lowered constantly to maintain sales. Large increases in promotion do not produce related increases in sales. Sales people and customers complain about problems with the products. Increasing or disproportionate amounts of management time are needed for the product. Costs are increasing as a percentage of sales. Competitive products appear to be selling better. Alternative products offer better potential sales volume and other marketing advantages.

Large marketing firms may use product review committees and computer-based decision-making models to make product elimination decisions. Marketers of any size can use a check list of factors or a list of questions based on these warning signals to make decisions on dropping products. The overall goal of the marketer is to maintain a product mix that includes mature products and a steady flow of new growth products that satisfy customers at a profit.[6]

PRODUCT ACCEPTANCE IN THE MARKET

Marketers can foster the acceptance of new products and product modifications by studying the ideas found in adoption and diffusion processes. **Adoption** is the decision of a consumer to buy and use a new product over a period of time. **Diffusion** is the pattern and rate of acceptance of new products by consumers. Adoption is concerned with the characteristics of consumers that influence them to buy products either soon after they are introduced or much later. The diffusion process is influenced by the rate of adoption and the characteristics of products that affect the speed of the adoption process. The basic goal of the marketer is to implement marketing strategies that speed the diffusion process.

Characteristics of Adopters

Adopters are consumers who buy and continue to use a new product. Consumers are different in their reactions to new products. Some like to try new products right away, while others react slowly with a wait-and-see attitude. Some of the consumers who adopt later are influenced by those who adopt quickly. New ideas are communicated from consumer to consumer in ways that affect the rate of the diffusion process. Marketers need to learn the characteristics of different types of adopters and learn how to reach them with marketing strategies. A practical classification of adopters identifies them as early, middle, or late adopters.

Early Adopters. **Early adopters** are the first consumers to accept a new product. They are innovators. They are generally very social people and communicate easily. They are open-minded, venturesome, and willing to accept risks. They enjoy the role of leadership and often influence others to purchase a product after they have pur-

chased it. Marketers want to identify and sell to early adopters in a market. These are the consumers who will be the first to buy a new car model, wear a new clothing style, or try a new food product. They enjoy telling others about their experience. If a marketer can get the early adopters to buy a new product, the product will move more quickly into a growth stage in the PLC. Early adopters can be reached with advertising that stresses differences, change, uniqueness, and innovation. Marketers have discovered that early adopters tend to relate to products that fit their lifestyles. For example, the consumer who adopts a new fashion in clothing may not be an early adopter of a new type of kitchen appliance. Nieman-Marcus, Bloomingdales, and I. Magnin are examples of retailers who successfully market to early adopters.

Middle Adopters. **Middle adopters** are the consumers in the mass market who buy and continue to use a product. These consumers are in the large group of average consumers and represent the norm of society. The mass market is considered to be 65 to 70 percent of the population. This group includes such a wide range of consumers that some marketers break it down into faster and slower middle adopters. In practical application, this entire group has some common characteristics. They tend to watch the early adopters and buy the product when the price is lower. Also, they tend to watch each other and buy when the majority of people are using a product. They respond to mass-media advertising. They tend to be typical Americans who want to do what is socially right and popular. They respond to change, but not as quickly as the early group. Sears, K-Mart, and J. C. Penney are examples of retailers that successfully market many of their products and their store image to the middle adopters.

Late Adopters. **Late adopters** are the last consumers to purchase a product. They seldom adopt a product until it is well into the maturity stage. They are suspicious of innovations and new ways of doing things. They tend to be very strong in cultural, ethnic, and family traditions. Late

Figure 6-5. Advertising in the widely-distributed Spiegel catalog stresses innovation for early adopters; product popularity for middle adopters; and classic durability for late adopters.

adopters tend to be older and at the lower ends of social and economic strata. They are extremely conservative and seek lower prices. Marketers should stress dependable and low-priced products to this group. These people like to hear that a product is good because it has been built the same way for a long time. They have less confidence in their ability to identify new features that improve product function. Extreme changes or rapid changes in products often frighten these consumers. Marketers need to use techniques that help these consumers reduce the risk in the purchase.

G. C. Murphy and F. W. Woolworth variety stores are examples of retailers that often market to late adopters.

Product Characteristics Affecting Acceptance

The acceptance of a new product is affected by the characteristics of the product. Some of these characteristics speed up the adoption process, and some slow it. Of course, marketers want to design products with features that help speed adoption.

Five general characteristics are considered important influences on the rate of adoption and eventual level of acceptance: relative advantage, compatibility, simplicity, divisibility, and communicability. Many additional and more specific characteristics may be important factors also, such as cost, perceived newness, novelty, and demonstrability.

Relative Advantage. Most marketers feel that this is the most important single characteristic that increases the rate of adoption. A new product appeals to early adopters if they perceive features in it that make it better than other products. One can see many examples in consumer products and promotion: a calculator that plays music, a watch with a special alarm, a battery that lasts longer, a microwave oven that cooks faster, or a brand name that attracts more attention. The easier the advantage is to perceive, the quicker it will be accepted. The Polaroid camera that produced a picture in minutes is a good example of a product with an easily perceived relative advantage.

Compatibility. A new product will be accepted faster if it is compatible with the existing values of the consumer. The product should fit the lifestyle and past experiences of the consumer. Consumers who believe in being physically healthy probably will perceive new running shoes as being compatible with their values. Microcomputers are compatible with people's desire for making personal data processing as efficient as possible. Automobiles or furnaces that waste fuel would not be compatible with energy-conscious people. In general, a product that fits easily into a consumer's way of doing things will be adopted earlier.

Simplicity. The easier a product is to understand and use, the faster the rate of adoption. Promotion of a new product is usually very effective if it helps a consumer readily understand how easy the product is to use. Cameras have point-and-shoot simplicity, a kitchen appliance requires the consumer simply to push a button, and a sewing machine performs fancy stitching electronically. Products often have simple operations because of high-technology production. Marketing must help the consumer see simplicity in use and avoid fear of product complexity. Microwave ovens have not saturated the consumer market, partly because they require different and apparently complex ways of cooking. Personal computers will be adopted faster if consumers realize that they can be used without an understanding of the technology built into them.

Divisibility. If a product can be divided into smaller parts so that the consumer can try it before final purchase, adoption will be faster. Most products can be tried in some way. Marketers must be certain that the consumer understands how to try the product. A good technique is to give samples of the product, as in the promotion of food, cosmetics, and medical items. Durable products may be demonstrated or used on a limited basis, as in the selling of bicycles, power tools, and appliances. Marketing techniques that reduce the risk of purchase are helpful, such as liberal return privileges, clearly stated warranties, and reliable guarantees.

Communicability. If consumers can talk about a new product easily and want to do so, it will diffuse faster. Products that are visible in social situations are communicated easily. A consumer who wears a new suit may be complimented and will tell where it was purchased. Products that are used with friends fall into this category. Tennis rackets and golf clubs will be compared and discussed readily. Products that help consumers do common things easier and better will be talked about. Activities involved in home care, furniture, clothing, recreation, eating, and transportation suggest many products with features that can be communicated easily.

The general product characteristics are supported by several factors that may lead to faster adoption. Products that cost less tend to be adopted faster. Products that can be demonstrated easily and clearly do diffuse faster (calculators). Products that provide an immediate reward to the consumer tend to be adopted faster (food products). A product that is perceived as clever or novel may be purchased quickly while it is new (Rubik's cube). In general, any adoption process is faster if the consumer perceives the product or feature as genuinely new and not just because the marketer puts the word *new* on the package or uses it in promotion.

PRODUCT IDENTIFICATION STRATEGIES

Imagine that you are talking with a friend about some old products you like and some new products you saw recently. You probably will use brand names to help describe the products. If someone mentioned a shirt or blouse with an alligator on it, would you think of the names Izod and Lacoste? If we played a word association game, would your answer to *soft drink* be Coca-Cola and to *toothpaste* be Crest? If your answer was not these two best-sellers, would you answer with the brands you use regularly? Have you ever purchased a product because you liked the package and did not really know much about the contents? Those are the ways consumers identify, talk about, choose between, and remember different products. Branding and packaging are important strategies that help customers accomplish these search and purchase behaviors.

Branding Strategies

Branding is the strategy of using a name, design, symbol, or combination of these elements to identify the products and services of a marketer. The overall purpose is to develop a brand that effec-

Figure 6-6. Brand names help consumers to readily identify products, services, and organizations.

tively differentiates a product from the products of competitors. The following terms relate to branding.

1. A **brand name** is that part of the brand which can be spoken. Any product asked for by name is a good example, such as Aim, Folgers, Cheerios, Right Guard, and Timex.

2. A **brand mark** is a symbol, design, letters, or special colors that you associate with a specific brand. Examples include the walking fingers of the Yellow Pages, Chrysler's five-pointed star, and John Deere's leaping deer symbol.

3. A **trademark** is a brand name or brand mark that has been given legal protection. Marketers use a ™ after the brand to tell competition that it is theirs. This means that the company has applied for registration of its brand with the U.S. Patent Office. When the brand is approved by this office, the company receives a registered trademark and puts an ® beside the brand.

A brand is a valuable part of the total product and must be protected by the marketer. Even though a trademark is registered, the marketer is responsible for protecting it. For example, Coca-Cola and Coke are well-known registered brand names. The Coca-Cola Company has a full-time staff that works to prevent illegal use of the names. Some brand names are so well known that consumers tend to use them as common names for all the products in a group. Kleenex, Xerox, Thermos, and Kodak are examples. These marketers must advertise the differences in their products to keep their trademarks from becoming public property. Former trademarks that were lost to common public use are cellophane, kerosene, cola, aspirin, and linoleum. The challenge to the marketer of a brand name such as Kleenex is to capitalize on its popularity but market it in a way that will induce consumers to demand Kleenex facial tissues when they use the name.

Importance of Branding. Can you imagine shopping for products in stores like K-Mart, Sears, and Safeway without using brand names?

The importance of branding is obvious. People use the brand name for identification and communication. Customers can develop a loyalty to a brand and buy it repeatedly over time. Customers can use brand names to shop and buy more efficiently. Brands are used by customers to reduce risk. The brand is of consistent quality or it is not purchased again. The brand name actually becomes the product in the customer's perception. The customer wears an Izod, drives a Mustang, runs in Adidas, and drinks Dr. Pepper. The customer does not need more words to identify the product.

Through the use of brands, marketers can build an image. A new product with a brand name can be positioned in a market in which its distinctive characteristics appeal to specific targets. As a marketer, can you imagine trying to advertise specific products without using brand names? A marketer can build on the loyalty to a brand by adding new models and expanding a line. For example, a line of Canon cameras is designated as AV-1, AE-1, AL-1, and A-1. Each model has special features, but each has the brand image of a Canon. General Motors does not let the consumer forget that a Chevrolet is a GM product. Branding helps consumers compare products when they want to. However, branding often helps the marketer when the customer is so loyal to a brand that no price comparisons are made. Bayer aspirin maintains a price higher than that of less well-known brands because Bayer customers have a strong preference for the brand and are satisfied with the product.

Brand Classification. One classification system designates brands as family or individual. A **family brand** involves the use of the same brand name on all products or an entire line. Campbell Soups, General Electric, and Del Monte are examples. Actually, family branding is a strategy that gives the marketer positive benefits from loyal customers. The marketer must maintain consistent quality throughout the line. A customer who dislikes a General Electric washer may not buy a GE stove. This is the risk the marketer takes to get the potential family-brand benefit that a customer who likes one GE product will like all GE products. An **individual brand** is the use of a separate brand name for each product in the mix. Consumers ask for Crest toothpaste without using the company name, Proctor & Gamble. Individual brands can result in better product identification for marketing. Also, negative customer attitudes may not transfer to other products in the company. Some marketers effectively use both individual-brand and family-brand strategies. General Motors builds on its family reputation but stresses individual brand identification in Chevrolet, Pontiac, and other brands.

Another classification system is based on who owns the brand: the manufacturer or the middleman. A **manufacturer's brand** is used on products owned and sponsored by a manufacturer whose primary function is production. Marketers often refer to these brands as national brands, but this does not necessarily mean that they are distributed nationally. **Middlemen's brands** are owned and controlled by retailers and wholesalers. These brands often are referred to as private brands or dealers' brands. Most of the products in the United States are manufacturers' brands. They are often respected brands, heavily advertised and consistent in quality wherever sold. Middlemen create their own brand names for several reasons: to benefit from customer brand loyalty, control costs and increase profit margin, and increase sales and profit. Large retailers such as Sears and J. C. Penney market many private brands. For example, Sears successfully markets its well-known private brands for batteries (Diehard), tools (Craftsman), appliances (Kenmore), and many other products. J. C. Penney is developing some effective brand names such as The Fox for shirts, Plain Pockets for jeans, and MCS Series for stereo components.

A recent addition to branding is the no-brand technique called generic products. **Generic products** are unbranded, are packaged in plain designs, and are lower-priced than other brands. Generics are increasingly popular in food supermarkets. Table 6-3 shows market share percentages for the top 25 types of generic products in supermarkets. A. C. Nielsen research studies on generics indicate that the market share range is

TABLE 6-3
TOP 25 GENERIC PRODUCT CATEGORIES BASED ON UNIT SALES

Top 5 (market share range 6.8–9.6%)

1. Canned salad fruits
2. Garbage bags
3. Preserves
4. Jelly
5. Cream substitutes

Second 5 (market share range 6.0–6.7%)

1. Diet salad dressing—Dry
2. Canned spaghetti sauce
3. Aluminum foil
4. Chocolate syrup
5. Canned mushrooms

Third 5 (market share range 4.8–5.8%)

1. Baking soda
2. Shortening
3. Cat litter
4. Canned applesauce
5. Liquid detergents

Fourth 5 (market share range 4.3–4.8%)

1. Powdered breakfast drinks
2. Iced tea mixes
3. Lemon/Lime juice
4. Liquid bleach
5. Potatoes, dehydrated

Fifth 5 (market share range 3.7–4.3%)

1. Grape juice
2. Canned cling peaches
3. Apple juice
4. Noodles and dumplings, dry
5. Canned green beans

Source: J. L. Parks, *Generics In Supermarkets: Myth or Magic?*, A Special Report from A. C. Nielsen Company, 1981, Winter/Spring 1980–81.

between 4 and 10 percent. Prices of generic products are generally 15 percent below private labels and 30 percent or more below the average price of all brands.[7] Customer reaction to generic products has been interesting. Customers buy generics without knowing who the manufacturer is. If a problem develops, they complain to the retailer. This action tends to place the generic product close to a private brand in the perception of the customer. Generics are popular with consumers who are very price-conscious and perceive the quality as satisfactory. Apparently, for most consumers, generics do not provide the psychological satisfaction and consistent quality that are found in branded products.

What Makes a Good Brand Name? In general, a good brand name simply helps customers identify a product and adds value to the product. Therefore, a successful brand name is a good brand name. Some are good because they are short; others are effective because they are long and descriptive. Here are some criteria that seem to fit successful brand names.

- They are easy for consumers to say and remember.
- They relate to the values or features of the product.
- They are distinctive, unusual, and interesting.
- They appeal to the type of consumer to whom the product is targeted.

Just like the new product idea, the new brand-name idea should be developed with the satisfaction of customers as the primary goal.

Packaging Strategies

Packaging is the design and production of the physical container for a product. A package is the physical container that becomes a part of the total utility of the product. The package may be the important difference between two products. The consumer may not be able to differentiate between two perfumes but will choose the one in the more attractive package. As perceived by this consumer, the package makes the significant difference. In many purchase situations, the consumer buys the package, not the contents.

Packaging serves several purposes as a marketing mix strategy. One is the function of protecting and holding the product. Obviously, it keeps food from being crushed, liquids from evaporating, fragile materials from being broken, and so on. The package is also an important part of the promotion function. The package is attractive, colorful, artistic, and identifiable in a crowd of other packages. The package usually provides the shopper's first view of the product. With the high proportion of self-service and the emphasis on display in retailing, the package is often the salesperson.

The health and safety of people has always been a major concern of marketers and manufacturers of all products, especially food, drugs, cosmetics, and household products. Pharmaceutical manufacturers have packaged medicinal drugs in containers that small children cannot open. Dangerous chemicals for household use are sealed in packages that resist accidental spilling and are plainly labeled as dangerous or poisonous. Warning labels on packages help customers avoid injury through misuse of the product.

In 1982, the importance of safe packaging became a very serious issue. Several people died from cyanide poisoning of Extra-Strength Tylenol capsules through criminal tampering with packages. Several other food and drug products were tampered with, resulting in injury to consumers in many locations throughout the United States. The criminal tampering apparently occurred after the products were placed on display in retail stores. Drug, food, and many other consumer product companies rushed to devise better packaging that was more resistant to tampering. For example, Johnson & Johnson introduced a new Tylenol package that was tamper-resistant with three safety seals. The outer box had glue-sealed flaps, an inner foil was sealed over the container opening, and the container cap was covered tightly

WHY A PAPER BOTTLE?

Ocean Spray's Paper Bottle is an aseptic package made of several layers of flexible paper and polyethylene, with a foil lining. It looks somewhat like a single-serving cereal box. Such packages are already in use in Europe and the far east. The package and the juice are sterilized separately, and then the package is filled. Bacteria cannot grow in the airtight package. Hence the name aseptic. The contents are shelf stable for at least 6 months.

Ocean Spray president Hal Thorkilsen says the company decided to try aseptic packaging because its conventional glass and metal packages have become expensive. "We've always been premium priced," he says, "and we thought we were likely to price ourselves out of the market" because of rising package costs. By using aseptic packaging, Thorkilsen says, the manufacturer gets 50 percent more cases of product in a highway trailer, and the retailer realizes a better than 35 percent improvement in the use of shelf space.

Thus he estimates that the 250 ml (8.5 ounce) single-serving size now available will save the consumer about 10 percent of the retail cost of juices in other types of packaging (approximate retail price is $1.15 for a three-pack). The 1 liter package of ready-to-serve juice and the 250 ml package of shelf-stable liquid concentrate, both scheduled for later introduction, should save the consumer 20 to 25 percent and 25 to 30 percent, respectively, assuming, of course, that retailers pass their savings on to consumers.

Adapted from Rayna Skolnik, "Scanners Juice Up Ocean Spray's Test", *Sales and Marketing Management*, March 15, 1982, p. 80. Reprinted by permission. © 1983.

with a shrink-plastic neck seal. In addition, a bright yellow warning label told the customer not to use the contents if any of the safety seals were broken. A government-industry task force on tamper-resistant packaging set up by the Food and Drug Administration began preparing to recommend federal regulations for over-the-counter drugs. However, the most impressive actions were taken by the marketers and manufacturers who were rushing voluntarily to package their consumer products in containers with more than one antitampering device.

Some packages are functional as a second-use product. The package may be a plastic box for storing other items, it may be a glass bottle that becomes a vase, or it may be a refillable bottle that can be used several times.

The package must be convenient to use. To the consumer, this means easy and safe to use, open, reseal, handle, and store. Read the story above about Ocean Spray's new Paper Bottle, which is an aseptic package. A new way to open or dispense product contents can increase sales without any other change in the product.

Marketing middlemen want packages that serve all these functions and can be processed effectively in their businesses. They want packages that make attractive displays and stack easily

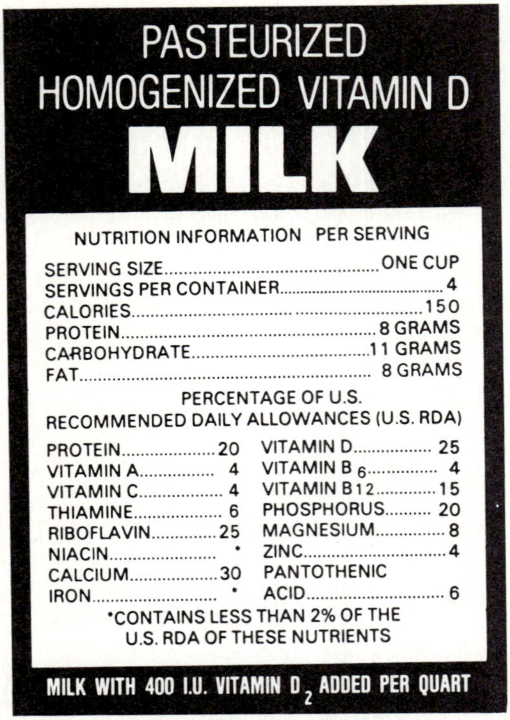

PASTEURIZED HOMOGENIZED VITAMIN D
MILK

NUTRITION INFORMATION PER SERVING	
SERVING SIZE	ONE CUP
SERVINGS PER CONTAINER	4
CALORIES	150
PROTEIN	8 GRAMS
CARBOHYDRATE	11 GRAMS
FAT	8 GRAMS

PERCENTAGE OF U.S. RECOMMENDED DAILY ALLOWANCES (U.S. RDA)

PROTEIN	20	VITAMIN D	25
VITAMIN A	4	VITAMIN B6	4
VITAMIN C	4	VITAMIN B12	15
THIAMINE	6	PHOSPHORUS	20
RIBOFLAVIN	25	MAGNESIUM	8
NIACIN	*	ZINC	4
CALCIUM	30	PANTOTHENIC	
IRON	*	ACID	6

*CONTAINS LESS THAN 2% OF THE U.S. RDA OF THESE NUTRIENTS

MILK WITH 400 I.U. VITAMIN D_2 ADDED PER QUART

Figure 6-7. Nutritional labels, while not required in packaging, are valuable to customers and have been added voluntarily by manufacturers, especially for products whose high nutritional contents make the purchase more appealing.

on shelves. They want packages that do not break open or spill out the contents and make costly messes. They want packages that contribute to a shelf life long enough for the product to be purchased by customers.

Packaging serves one of its most important functions as an identification strategy. It provides a place to put the product label. A label is a display of information about the product and the marketer. The label gives the customer information about the care, use, and preparation of the product. Labels explain the important characteristics and potential benefits of the product. The label may include the Universal Product Code scanning lines which are being used increasingly in checkout operations, inventory control, and marketing

research. Nutritional labels have been added voluntarily to products by marketers as a valuable service to consumers. See Figure 6-7 for an example.

The value of packaging and branding strategies as a part of the marketing mix is difficult to measure but obviously is extremely important. Packaging and branding are such vital and visible parts of the product that success or failure often is determined by customer reaction to these two strategies.

KEY POINTS SUMMARY

- Every marketer must maintain a steady flow of new products by using a plan for developing or finding new products.

- For the marketer, a product is new if it is new to the company and requires a different marketing mix strategy. For the consumer, it is new when it is seen for the first time or is perceived as different from other products.

- Every marketer introduces new products hoping for success but assuming considerable risk of failure. New product failure rates range from 20 to 80 percent but may average around 33 percent.

- Marketers should study product failure but emphasize the characteristics of successful new products that enhance a marketer's image as a modern, innovative, quality firm.

- New products are developed by following a sequence of steps: idea generation, idea screening, business analysis, product development, test marketing, and product introduction.

- The product life cycle (PLC) is the progression of a product through four stages: introduction, growth, maturity, and decline. Each stage involves strategy decisions influenced by sales, profits, and time.

- Marketers use the PLC to accomplish their overall product goal of introducing new products that increase sales and reach a profit position as quickly as possible.

- Marketers like to stay in the growth stage as long as possible because it includes increasing sales, decreasing unit costs, increasing profits, and increasing numbers of customers.

- Sales volume levels off in the maturity stage. Competition is very strong, and marketers try to improve products, lower prices, and promote more efficiently.

- The decline stage is one of rapidly decreasing sales. Marketers try to reduce the costs of marketing the product and keep it profitable as long as possible.

- Products that diffuse faster have a perceivable relative advantage, are compatible with consumers' values, are simple to use, can be tried easily, and have features that can be communicated easily.

- Branding and packaging are important marketing strategies that help customers identify, talk about, choose between, and remember different products.

KEY TERMS AND CONCEPTS

adoption	idea screening
branding	individual brand
brand mark	introduction stage
brand name	late adopters
business analysis	manufacturer's brand
commerciali-	maturity stage
zation	middle adopters
decline stage	middlemen's brands
diffusion	national rollout
early adopters	new product
family brand	product development
generic products	product life cycle
growth stage	test marketing
idea generation	trademark

DISCUSSION QUESTIONS

1. Newness is difficult to define in product introduction. Explain what can be new about a product from the marketer's point of view and the consumer's point of view.

2. You own and manage a marketing firm. You have called a meeting of your marketing managers. Give them some reasons why your company accepts the challenge of new product development.

3. You want to encourage the generation of ideas for new products in your firm. Develop a plan for creating an environment which encourages new ideas.

4. Why does a marketer like to keep a product in the growth period of its product life cycle for as long as possible?

5. Although the PLC is a useful concept for marketers, why is it sometimes difficult to use for decision making?

6. If one of your products has entered the decline stage, what marketing strategies would you use to keep it profitable for as long as possible?

7. Choose an actual consumer product and assume that you are going to introduce it to a new market. Describe the product's characteristics that you think will speed its adoption.

NOTES

1. C. Merle Crawford, "Marketing Research and the New Product Failure Rate," *Journal of Marketing,* vol. 41, April 1977, p. 51.
2. *Management of New Products,* Booz, Allen and Hamilton, Management Consultants, Chicago, 1968, p. 9.
3. Marketing Research Group, "New Product Success Ratios 1977," *Nielsen Researcher,* no. 1, 1979, p. 5.
4. Adapted from *Sales and Marketing Management,* March 15, 1982, p. 108.

5. For an important article that provides a critical review of the PLC concept, see Nariman K. Dhalla and Sonia Yuspeh, "Forget the Product Life Cycle Concept," *Harvard Business Review,* vol. 54, January–February 1976, pp. 102–112.

6. For an in-depth treatment of product management and product life cycle strategies, see Yoram J. Wind, *Product Policy: Concepts, Methods, and Strategy,* Addison-Wesley, Reading, Mass., 1982.

7. J. L. Parks, *Generics in Supermarkets: Myth or Magic?,* A. C. Nielsen Company, Northbrook, Illinois, 1981.

APPLICATIONS/CASES

APPLICATION 5: KINDER CARE LEARNING CENTERS INC.— MARKETING A SERVICE

Kinder Care is the service brand name for a national chain of child-care centers. The idea was originated in 1968 by Perry Mendel, a real estate developer who wanted to use the same techniques of standardization that had worked for motels and fast-food chains. He was convinced that the trend toward mothers working outside the home would continue. He saw a growing demand for centers where children could be cared for during the day while both parents work. The company name, Kinder Care Learning Centers, describes the underlying idea of the service.

Kinder Care is aimed at the middle-class family that needs two paychecks and cannot pay premium prices for day care. Each center is an attractive environment designed for children. Classrooms are airy and open with 35 square feet of space per child. A play area includes jungle-gyms, swing sets, and small swimming pools. Kinder Care stresses learning. This tends to overcome the guilt feeling parents may have when leaving their children to go to work. The children are served a nutritional hot breakfast, lunch, and snacks. The centers accept children as young as 3 months and as old as 12 years. An added after-school program for older children increased total revenues by 20 percent. A summer camp program was started in 1972 to maintain enrollment during the nonschool season.

Kinder Care Learning Centers are very successful, and the company's revenues and market share position are increasing.

a. Explain why Kinder Care is a good example of a service marketer.

b. What marketing strategies for selling a service have contributed to Kinder Care's success?

APPLICATION 6: KINDER CARE'S INDUSTRIAL SERVICE

In 1981, Kinder Care Learning Centers Inc. added an industrial service to its service mix. A separate marketing program was developed and named Kindustry. Corporations can offer Kindustry, an employer-based child-care program, as a job benefit for employees. Employer and parent may share the costs in various proportions. Some employers pay all the costs.

The idea appeals to corporations because it often keeps valuable employees from quitting work to raise a family. It also provides a solution to the problem of what working couples can do with school-age children before and after school. A Kinder Care staff member picks up the child and takes him or her to school. After school, the staff member delivers the child to the nearest Kinder Care Learning Center. Here the child is entertained and taught until a parent arrives on the way home.

Source: John Halbrooks, "Kinder-Care's Standard Formula for Success," *INC.*, October 1981, pp. 84-85.

a. Why was this new industrial service a successful extension of the Kinder Care consumer service?

b. What marketing strategies would you recommend to Kinder Care for further growth as a service marketer?

CASE 5: CONSUMER CALCULATORS —A MATURE MARKET

Calculator manufacturers and marketers are trying to develop niches for their products in the consumer market. Almost everyone owns an electronic pocket calculator. The market is nearly saturated. At the high-priced end of the market, companies such as Hewlett-Packard and Texas Instruments are trying to extend their markets by developing programmable calculators and hand-held computers. For example, Hewlett-Packard has developed a calculator with complementary products: cassette memories and battery-operated printers. The new system is like a personal, portable computer. After the customer buys the basic calculator, many accessory products will be needed. Thus, new markets are opened up.

At the lower-priced end of the market, which includes the majority of consumers, calculator manufacturers are fighting to produce and market calculators that will meet the demands of consumers. Such leading producers as Casio, Sharp, and Canon are searching for ways to sell to consumers who already have one or more calculators that perform many functions.

a. What marketing strategies can the calculator companies use to extend this maturing market or develop new growth markets?

b. Describe some new types of calculator products that these companies have marketed to keep product life cycles alive.

CASE 6: NEW PRODUCT INTRODUCTION—KODAK DISC PHOTOGRAPHY

In 1982, the Eastman Kodak Company introduced a new line of cameras with the brand name KODAK Disc Cameras. The new camera products were designed to use another new product, KODACOLOR HR Disc Film. The new shape and format of the film and cameras introduced a new system that Eastman Kodak Company called disc photography. In a message to photo retailers, Walter A. Fallon, chairman and chief executive officer, made the following comments.

For picture-takers, this brand-new world was brought on by a massive investment in research, product development and manufacturing technology. The investment was made following extensive market research undertaken by Kodak—research designed to establish as specifically as possible what consumers want from photography.

This was the first major product change in Kodak cameras since the introduction of the KODAK INSTAMATIC Camera series in 1963. The INSTAMATIC Cameras introduced 126 and 110 film in drop-in cartridges and were popular in the 1960s and 1970s.

One of the truly innovative features of this new photography system is the disc film format. The new KODACOLOR HR Disc Film is a thin circular disc 2½ inches in diameter. The film is high-speed, sharp, and fine-grain, producing 15 bright color pictures from each disc. The film is enclosed in a light-tight case that opens and closes automatically inside the camera. The compact shape of the small flat disc allows easy carrying, and the film can be inserted in the camera only in the correct way.

Three models of the new camera were introduced at the same time in 1982: the KODAK Disc 4000, 6000, and 8000 Cameras. The KODAK Disc Cameras were said to offer consumers decision-free photography. Just aim and push one button. The features included automatic built-in electronic flash, motorized film advance, solid-state electronic control, and a full 5 year warranty. Eastman Kodak stressed that the cameras were designed to make it easy for people to take pictures under difficult conditions without making adjustments on the camera. The disc film format made the slim, lightweight design of the camera possible: easy to carry, easy to use, and easy to load. Consumer research has revealed that people like the thin vertical design better than the thin horizontal format of the 110 cameras. The KODAK Disc 8000 Camera includes an electronic self-timer and a built-in digital quartz alarm clock.

Kodak showed great concern for film finishers; companies that develop and print pictures. Consumers who bought the new cameras and film needed to have their film processed conveniently, and Kodak was ready with new equipment systems. In addition, the disc film provided some new features and advantages for finishers. Each disc has a computer bar code that automatically numbers each order. The disc film format eliminates the splicing of rolls of film. The magnetic core of the disc film provides reorder and reprint information for automatic printing. Finishers needed to be sold on these advantages because the new processing required a large capital investment.

The promotion of the KODAK Disc Cameras to consumers began on May 23, 1982, with advertising in the most popular TV shows, magazines, and newspapers. Kodak's goal was to reach nearly every consumer many times by the end of the year. The initial advertising message stressed the excitement and newness of disc photography. One of the principal themes was that Kodak was offering a new way of taking pictures. Later advertising emphasized specific camera features and the many advantages of these brand-new cameras. The cameras were promoted for their go-anywhere portability and aim-and-shoot simplicity in all consumer and family lifestyle situations.

Kodak offered free point-of-purchase materials to retailers. Signs, banners, mobiles, and camera displays were available to dealers before the consumer advertising began. Television, newspaper, and radio advertising packages were available for local promotion. Kodak stressed that people never had so many reasons to buy a new Kodak camera from the dealer.

a. Analyze the brand-name strategies for these new Kodak products.

b. Describe the characteristics of early adopter consumers that these products appeal to.

c. What are the product characteristics of these cameras and film that will speed up the diffusion process?

d. Evaluate the techniques used by Kodak to introduce the product to finishers and retailers.

e. How did Kodak make effective use of PLC introductory stage strategies?

CASE 7: DEVELOPING A NEW PRODUCT—THE SONY WALKMAN

The Sony Walkman was a creative new product idea that combined the quality of audio high fidelity and portability. Before the invention of the Walkman, consumers could not have both sound quality and easy portability. With the Walkman, consumers can jog, roller-skate, ride bicycles, or do almost anything while listening to their favorite music in high-fidelity stereo. The Walkman is the best-selling pocket-size, lightweight, compact stereo cassette player with featherweight headphones.

The Sony Walkman has been an incredible marketing success. It was introduced in 1979, and its sales doubled each of the first 3 years. By 1982, stereo cassette players named Walkman I, II, and III had been marketed. Two additional models offered FM radio and recording capabilities.

How was the product idea generated? In 1978, an organizational change in Sony's audio division resulted in the end of the production of radiocassette recorders and tape recorders. The tape recorder division was forced to develop new ways to generate business and profits. The staff got together for discussions day and night for a week. The best idea generated was to make a portable stereo recorder.

The first machine was a combination of a business dictating machine and a pair of heavy headphones. The sound was good, but the machine was big and clumsy. The Sony research laboratory was experimenting with new lightweight headphones at this time. The two ideas were combined, and the Walkman product idea was on its way. Akio Morita, Sony's chairman, heard about the prototype and became very excited about the idea when he saw it demonstrated. Engineers incorporated several ideas for product features and completed the final design and specifications just 5 months after the tape recorder division lost its radiocassette business.

Morita formed a new product team by gathering 10 people from different Sony divisions: production, product planning, design, advertising, sales, and export. They were charged with deciding on all the strategies for the Walkman. Morita appointed himself product manager. The goal of the team was to launch the Walkman within 6 months.

At meetings, the team discussed specifications of the new model. The production schedule was drawn, and a decision was made on the quantity to be produced. Cost structure and pricing also were decided. There were heated discussions about what to name the product. Various promotional ideas were formulated. Package designs were presented. Presale consumer tests were conducted. All the conceivable activities surrounding the Walkman business were discussed thoroughly in this group.

An early idea for the name was Hot-Line, but the sales force did not think it would appeal to the general public. Another early idea was Stereo Walkie, but Toshiba had already registered the name Walky. A suggestion was made to combine *walk* with *man* and name the product Walkman. The name had great support, but there was concern about the name because it was not a proper English word. At one time, Sony had four different names for the same product: Walkman in Japan and Asia, Sound-About in the United States, Stowaway in the United Kingdom, and Freestyle in Sweden. Separate logotypes and package designs were made for each of these names. Large amounts of advertising money were used to promote different names in different markets.

Morita decided that all these efforts were wasteful and wanted to unify the product under one name, Walkman. He successfully convinced all the overseas subsidiaries about the adoption of the worldwide name. Sony then started to sell the same Walkman product around the world. The result is a worldwide marketing success story.

Adapted from Shu Ueyama, "The Selling of 'Walkman'," *Advertising Age*, March 22, 1982, pp. M-2, M-3, M-37. Reprinted with permission. © 1982 by Crain Communications Inc.

a. Analyze the brand-name Walkman as a product identification strategy.

b. Assume that you are developing a product to compete with the Sony Walkman. Create some brand names and tell why each is a good branding strategy.

c. The Walkman was developed in a very short time by Sony. Why was this new product development successful?

d. Why did consumers adopt the Sony Walkman at such a fast rate?

e. When the Walkman reaches a maturity stage in the PLC, what strategies will Sony need to use to maintain sales volume?

UNIT 4

PLACE

CHAPTER
7
CHANNELS OF DISTRIBUTION

The Brooklyn manufacturer of Tale Lord jeans has been in business since 1929, first as a manufacturer of overalls and later as a producer of jeans. But like many small businesses, Tale Lord Manufacturing Company reached a point at which sales and profits declined drastically. The owner, whose father had founded the company, started thinking about retirement.

His 31-year old son borrowed $450,000, bought the business, renamed it Revolver Jeans Ltd., and retained the Tale Lord trademark. He ordered a Japanese-made computerized embroidery machine. While most back pockets of designer jeans sport the maker's logo and distinctive stitching, Tale Lord designed pockets showing full scenes such as a motorcyclist riding through the mountains or a tiger walking under palm trees. The embroidery machine was placed quickly into service, and the company obtained copyrights on 60 pocket designs.

In the past, Tale Lord Manufacturing Company had limited its distribution of products mostly to the New York metropolitan area. The new owner, however, decided to expand the distribution area. When such a decision is reached, a number of other questions are posed.

- Should we employ our own sales force to sell to retail outlets?
- Should we offer franchises to retail outlets?
- Should we seek wholesalers who in turn will sell to retailers?
- Should we display our products at trade shows and in merchandise marts?
- Which promotion techniques will prove effective in making our products more salable?

Answers to these questions must be reached when a manufacturer such as Revolver Jeans Ltd. determines how to get its products to markets and subsequently sell them. A number of marketing institutions may be involved, and their inclusion is determined by the target customers, the product, the producer's status and objectives, and the middlemen's status and objectives.

Revolver Jeans Ltd. chose to dispatch sample-laden sales representatives to the Philadelphia and Baltimore areas and farther afield to New England, California, and Florida. They stirred up interest in Tale Lord jeans at the National Association of Men's Sportswear buyers' meeting. As a result, test orders started flowing in from the

Marine Corp's Camp Lejeune post exchange in North Carolina, J. C. Penney Company stores on the west coast, and the Gap Stores.[1]

Small manufacturers and producers as well as large corporate firms grapple with decisions about getting their products into the marketplace. There is more to this task than meets the eye. Factors to be considered by the manufacturer or producer in directing the flow of products and services to the consumer or industrial user will be examined in this unit. Retailers, wholesalers, and service outlets also grapple with place decisions. In some cases, retailers, wholesalers, or service vendors may be powerful enough to influence the path that a product or service will travel. In this unit, we shall also look at how business people consider better and less costly ways of getting goods and services from the producer to the consumer.

CHANNELS OF DISTRIBUTION DEFINED

A **channel of distribution,** which sometimes is referred to as a **trade channel,** consists of middlemen, sometimes called intermediaries, who buy, sell, or are involved in the process of moving products or services to the buyer. Stated another way, the channel refers to the course taken by the product or service on its journey to the ultimate user. As products move through the channel, title and possession may change. The following concepts are important.

1. A trade channel does not include firms such as railroads and banks which render a marketing service but play no major role in negotiating purchases and sales.

2. Sometimes one must distinguish between the title to goods and the channel for the physical movement of goods. Frequently these routes are partially different. A contractor may order a large load of sand and gravel from a local building supply house. The product is shipped directly from the sand and gravel producer to the contrac-

tor to minimize freight and handling costs. The channel for the title and for its invoice, however, would be producer to building supply house to contractor.

3. The channel for a product extends only to the last person who buys it and makes no further significant change in its form. When the form is altered and another product emerges, a new channel is started. When lumber is milled and made into furniture, two separate channels are involved. The channel for the lumber may be lumber mill to broker to furniture manufacturer. The channel for the finished lumber may be furniture manufacturer to retail furniture store to consumer.[2]

Products and services which pass through distribution channels may be classified into different groups. From the standpoint of producers and manufacturers, the total market divides first into two large segments—the consumer market and the industrial market—which were discussed in Chapter 3.

Channels for Consumer Products and Services

A marketer may build a better product or offer a better service than that of the competitors, but if it is not in the right place at the right time, it will not generate sales. Channels are used to place the product in the right location. Marketing personnel often find that place decisions are of the highest importance because they are harder to change than product, price, or promotion decisions. It is difficult to change place decisions after agreements and leases have been signed with retailers and wholesalers.

Business organizations or individuals (wholesalers, retailers, agents, and brokers) specializing in carrying out the transfer of title between the manufacturer or producer and the customer are called **middlemen.** In a few cases, the middlemen may not accept title to the products. Instead, they may simply facilitate the sale of products or services. Middlemen may also perform a number of other marketing activities.

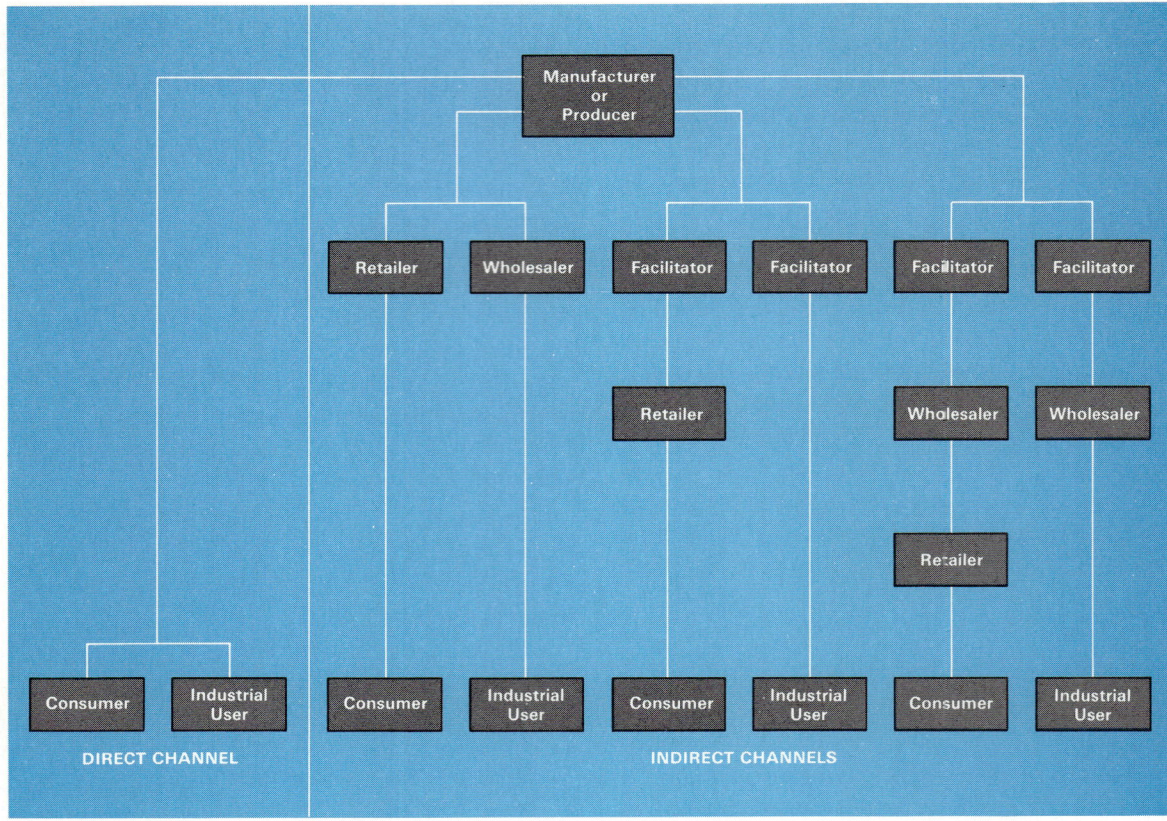

Figure 7-1. Direct and indirect channels of distribution for consumer and industrial products and services.

In a **direct distribution channel,** the manufacturer or producer sells to the ultimate consumer. A bakery produces pies and cakes and sells them directly to the consumer. A dry cleaner sells a service directly to the consumer. In each case, the flow of products or services is dependent on the sales effort of the producer. Many producers, however, cannot transact sales directly with each consumer. Therefore, the creation of a channel for indirect distribution becomes necessary. **Indirect distribution channels** require the use of middlemen in selling products and services or facilitating such sales. Figure 7-1 shows the structure of direct and indirect channels.

Manufacturer-Consumer Channel.
When direct and indirect channels were described earlier in this chapter, examples were cited to demonstrate the direct sale of products or a service to a consumer. A nursery which grows its own plants and trees may sell them directly to the public. Local pizza parlors, hairstyling salons, moving and storage firms, and many other manufacturers or producers may sell products or services directly to the consumer.

Some producers prefer to handle the entire distribution job themselves. Their motto is, "If you want the job done right, do it yourself." In any community, one can cite a number of examples of producers selling directly to consumers. The firm's location close to its target market allows it to monitor changes in customers' attitudes. As a result, the firm is able to adjust its marketing mix quickly.

CORRECTING ERRORS: CHANGING PLACE DECISIONS

The electric typewriter, which was introduced in the early 1950s, made the job of typing easier and faster. Correcting typing errors, however, was difficult. Eventually, Bette Graham, a young secretary and amateur artist, discovered that she could use paint to cover typing errors. Within 5 years, her product, Mistake Out (produced under the corporate name Mistake Out Company, later changed to Liquid Paper Corporation), was in great demand by other secretaries.

At first, Graham and her son spent weekends filling orders from her kitchen. Soon they were selling 100 bottles a month by marketing Liquid Paper to office-supply dealers. Within 10 years, Liquid Paper Corporation was producing more than 500 bottles a minute of their correction fluids for sales worldwide.

Note that as the popularity of the product increased, Graham was faced with place decisions, that is, how to get the product to the right place at the right time. Many small entrepreneurs have encountered similar experiences. When the product becomes a winner, direct channels may no longer suffice.

Adapted from "A Century of Entrepreneurs," National Federation of Independent Business Research and Education Foundation, San Mateo, Calif., 1981.

Many small producers start operations on a limited scale. As the product increases in popularity, the marketing strategy changes, and the producer may decide to make the product available to more customers, perhaps on a national scale. At that point, the producer may decide to move from a direct channel to an indirect channel. Consider the example on this page as it relates to place decision making.

Typically, one or more of five methods are used by the manufacturer or producer to sell directly to the consumer: (1) advertising, (2) sales representatives, (3) retail outlets, (4) mail order, and (5) telephone solicitation. The first method involves using local, regional, or national advertising to offer products for sale. The consumer orders the product directly from the manufacturer or producer, and no personal contact between buyer and seller is made. Producers of seeds and garden bulbs often offer their products directly to consumers.

With the second method, the producer or manufacturer employs sales reps to make contact with buyers in an attempt to sell products. A variety of products including prefabricated homes, some household products, brushes, and cosmetics are sold in this way. Classic examples of this approach are the consumer's purchase of garden produce directly from the farmer as well as manufacturers such as the Fuller Brush Company and Avon Products. In addition, a variety of services are sold by this method, including insurance, real estate, investments, and lawn care. The sales reps, who sometimes are called manufacturer's representatives or agents, may perform functions in addition to selling, such as delivery, collecting accounts, and making adjustments to ensure customer satisfaction.

IN THE BEGINNING: PEPPERIDGE FARM SOLD THROUGH MAIL ORDER

Established in 1937, Pepperidge Farms, Inc., resulted from a mother's concern for her son's health. To improve the boy's asthmatic condition, Margaret Rudkin learned how to make whole wheat bread entirely from natural ingredients. She developed a reputation throughout the community for her nutritious and delicious bread. First friends and doctors bought loaves, and soon she had a substantial mail-order business. Her husband, a stockbroker in New York City, helped the growing business by delivering orders to a food specialty store across from Grand Central Station.

With orders increasing rapidly, Mrs. Rudkin moved the bakery from her kitchen to her converted garage. The Connecticut town where she lived allowed her to run a small business from her residence because it created badly needed jobs in a time of unemployment. Today the company, owned by Campbell Soup, produces over 100 kinds of fresh and frozen goods, and its several locations employ approximately 5,200 people.

From 1937 until the present, a number of place decisions have been made. Without doubt, many of these decisions have influenced the success of Pepperidge Farm products. From direct channels, in which Mrs. Rudkin first sold products to friends and doctors and responded to mail orders, the products are now available throughout the land.

Adapted from "A Century of Entrepreneurs," National Federation of Independent Business Research and Education Foundation, San Mateo, Calif., 1981.

In some cases, manufacturers or producers own their own stores or retail outlets. For example, a bakery or a small furniture manufacturer often will sell the finished products through their own retail outlets. Usually this occurs when the product or service is sold within a local geographic area as opposed to national or sectional areas. However, there are exceptions. Carpet mills, for example, may operate local retail outlets and also sell through nonowned retail outlets in distant areas. Manufacturer-owned retail outlets or stores should not be confused with franchised outlets. It is, however, often difficult and sometimes impossible for the consumer to tell the difference. Franchising has become very important in place decisions for consumer products and ser-

vices. We shall look at franchising organizations as a channel strategy later in this chapter.

Some manufacturers or producers of consumer products may use catalogs to sell to individual consumers or to groups such as church, school, and fraternal organizations that hope to resell the products and earn money in a fundraising project. In these cases, the manufacturer is assuming the role of catalog retailer or catalog wholesaler. Beich Candy Company, for example, has flourished with a distribution channel that relies solely on sales to organizations. Jewelry, vitamins, garden seeds, and even clothing are among the products sold at retail prices by the manufacturer or wholesaler to consumers through mail orders. Tours, vacation trips, insurance, and other services are made available through the mail.

While more frequently used by a retailer or wholesaler as a method of selling, telephone solicitations are increasingly used by manufacturers or producers to sell products and services. When a chimney sweep (a producer of a service), obtains a list of homeowners and then calls each of them to offer the service, the telephone becomes an instrument for selling directly to the consumer.

Manufacturer-Retailer-Consumer Channel. The retailer is one of the most important middlemen in the distribution channel and sells most of the products and services used for personal consumption. Some manufacturers of consumer products choose to sell their products through large-scale retailers such as chain and department stores. This is especially true when the place strategy is one of **exclusive distribution,** which involves the choice of only one retailer in a limited market area. Automobile retailers provide an example of exclusive distribution, but other consumer products such as furniture and even some clothing pass through such distribution channels.

Manufacturers or producers may prefer to place their products in exclusive retail outlets for one or more of the following reasons.

1. They may be able to choose only retailers that have good credit ratings.

2. They may avoid retailers that have a reputation for making numerous returns and requesting too much service.

3. Retailers that are unable to place orders large enough to justify sales calls and service may be avoided.

4. Manufacturers may avoid retailers that for a variety of reasons are not able to do a satisfactory marketing job.

Some manufacturers or producers sell directly to retailers as a result of product attributes such as perishability, bulk, degree of standardiza-

Our "Own Make" shirts
in new stripes on broadcloth

The craftsmanship of our own people goes into the famous Brooks Brothers shirt, which we make in our own workrooms. Here, fine cotton broadcloth with stripes of considerable understatement, with the classic "Polo" button-down collar which Mr. John Brooks originated 80 years ago. Blue-wine, tan-wine, green-wine on white. Collar sizes 14½ to 17, sleeves 32 to 36. $25

Street Floor

ESTABLISHED 1818

Brooks Brothers
CLOTHING
Men's & Boys' Furnishings, Hats & Shoes
346 MADISON AVE. NEW YORK, N.Y. 10017
LIBERTY PLAZA · SCARSDALE · PARAMUS

Figure 7-2. Brooks Brothers, which distributes shirts under its own label, is part of a manufacturer-retailer-consumer chain.

tion, service requirements, and unit value. Fresh-baked products, for example, require a relatively short distribution channel because of the dangers associated with delays and repeated handling. When Trina Gaylor bakes fresh cream pies, she may make immediate deliveries to the full-service restaurants that sell her product. Products that are bulky, that is, heavy in relation to their value, such as building materials and bottled soft drinks, usually require a channel which will minimize the shipping distance and the number of handling turnovers. As a result, a regional manufacturer or producer will sell directly to retailers. Unstandardized products and services follow a similar route. When Nieman-Marcus Department Store offers its annual "ultimate" Christmas gift, the product or service is far from standard. When Sears places an order for Kenmore appliances with the Whirlpool Corporation, only the manufacturer-retailer-consumer channel will suffice. Products requiring installation and maintenance service usually are sold and maintained by dealers who have been given exclusive rights. The big three automobile manufacturers, for example, provide dealers with exclusive rights. Products of high value often are sold by the manufacturer's sales force to the retailer. Expensive watches, diamonds, home computers, and a variety of other products fall into this category.

Retailers may be able to influence the channel structure. For example, if you design and develop a new self-locking women's handbag, obtain a patent, and hope to start manufacturing operations, you are faced with place decisions. How will you get your product into the marketplace? You approach Carson Pirie and Scott, a large Chicago-based department store, to determine whether they would be willing to handle it. They agree to handle it, but only on an exclusive basis. In other words, there can be no **selective distribution,** that is, choosing other middlemen who will do a good job with the product. Nor can there be any **intensive distribution,** which refers to the sale of a product through any responsible and suitable middleman that will stock or sell it. Because you are eager to win the Carson Pirie and Scott account and believe that their marketing efforts will be exemplary, you agree to the terms. In this case, the retailer has influenced the channel design. Large retailers with **corporate chains,** that is, a group of two or more stores linked together under one management and owned by stockholders, are more likely to be in a position to

influence channel decisions than smaller retailers.[3] Small manufacturers or producers are more vulnerable to the demands of large retailers than large manufacturers. Figure 7-3 demonstrates the different types of channel distribution.

Why do retail store managers prefer to buy directly from the manufacturer? This is not the preference of all retailers. But some retailers that are able to perform the marketing activities usually associated with physical distribution believe that they can make merchandise available to consumers at a more favorable price. Did you know that most apparel is sold by manufacturers directly to retailers? Retail organizations may prefer to buy in large volume from the manufacturer when they have the financial means to make such purchases possible. They believe that they are rewarded by gaining the advantage of having the latest merchandise, obtaining lower prices, and receiving the manufacturer's sales aids, such as advertising and display materials.

Retailers operate this country's 2 million stores and often are the customers' only contact with numerous channels of distribution established for various products and services. Retail institutions will be examined in greater detail in Chapter 8.

Manufacturer-Wholesaler-Retailer-Consumer Channel.

As middlemen for consumer products passing through channels of distribution, **wholesalers** buy products from manufacturers and sell them to retailers. This channel often is considered the most common channel for consumer products. However, there are various types of wholesalers, and the activities they perform vary. The definition here applies only to wholesalers linked between manufacturers and retailers of consumer products. Later in this chapter, wholesalers of industrial products will be discussed. In Chapter 8, wholesale institutions will be examined.

Suppose a manufacturer makes golf balls. Thousands and thousands of the balls pop off the assembly line each day. If golf balls are the manufacturer's only product, there is probably a discrepancy of quantity, that is, a difference between

CONTINUUM OF POSSIBLE CHANNEL TARGET RETAILERS

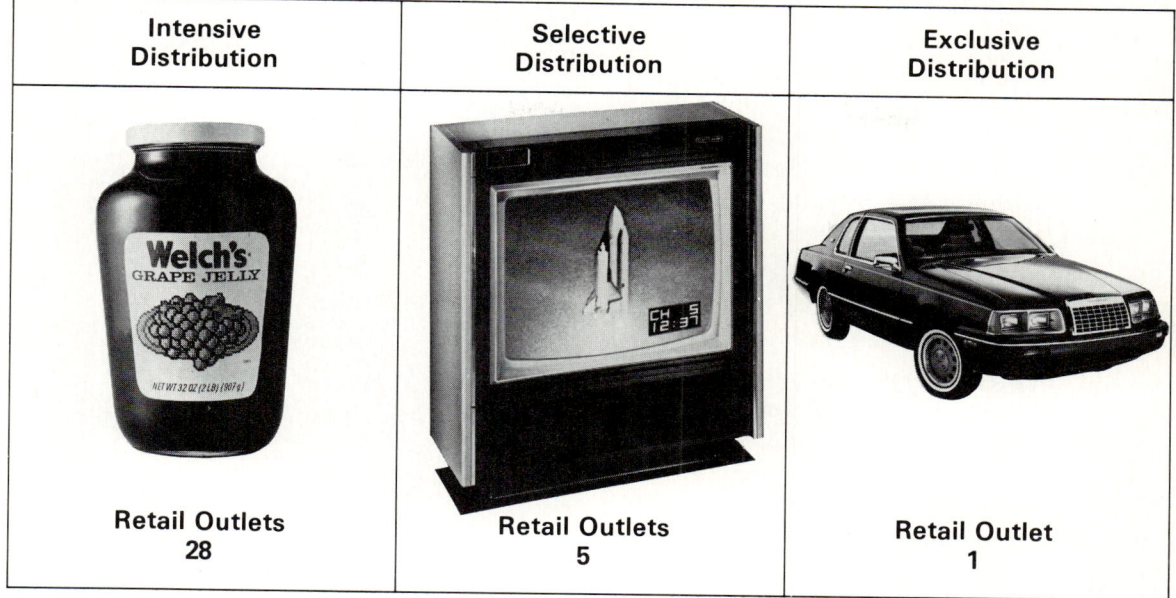

Intensive Distribution	Selective Distribution	Exclusive Distribution
Retail Outlets 28	Retail Outlets 5	Retail Outlet 1

Figure 7-3. Continuum of possible channel target retailers: U.S. city, population 45,000.

the number of balls that each retailer would like to purchase and the number that the manufacturer would like to sell. In addition, the retailer probably would be unhappy with the discrepancy of assortment, that is, only golf balls. The retailer may want to purchase from a supplier who can furnish golf tees, gloves, shoes, bags, clubs, and other related items. Otherwise, the retailer must deal with several different manufacturers. As a wholesaler, one of your tasks would be to adjust the discrepancies through regrouping activities. Through buying, you would accumulate golfing equipment from various manufacturers. You also might **break bulk,** that is, break cases of golf balls, tees, and other products into smaller units to satisfy the purchasing desires of retailers. You might sort the golf balls and repackage those with imperfections as "seconds." As you accumulated golfing equipment from various manufacturers, you would develop a line of heterogeneous products to give the retailer what was desired. Someone in the channel must assume these responsibilities. If the manufacturer is unable to serve in that capacity, chances are good that a wholesaler will.

In addition to these activities, the wholesaler often assumes responsibility for activities that are associated with the actual movement and storage of products. In other words, the wholesaler helps create both time and place utility. Such activities are referred to as physical distribution and will be explored in Chapter 9.

Why do manufacturers sometimes prefer to include wholesalers in the distribution channel? Wholesalers are an important link in many channels, buying products in large quantities from manufacturers or producers and selling smaller quantities to retailers in various geographic regions of the country or world. Reasons usually cited for the inclusion of wholesalers include the following.

1. The manufacturer may prefer to devote its attention to production and as a result seek wholesalers that are able to position the product in the marketplace at the right time and place.

2. The geographic concentration of target customers may be so widespread that the manufacturer can transact sales best with multiple wholesalers as compared with an even greater number of retailers.

3. The price of the product offered for sale may dictate the inclusion of wholesalers. Obviously, a small manufacturer cannot afford to disperse a large sales force for small, low-priced items. The typical sales call is very expensive.

4. Wholesalers have personnel in place who know their customers and their needs and wants. A new manufacturer may find it too costly to develop a well-trained sales force.

5. A successful wholesaler may add prestige to a manufacturer's product. If a new cannery planned to sell Blumberg canned goods to a retailer, the cannery might encounter problems because it is unknown and has not yet established a reputation. A reputable wholesaler, on the other hand, may have achieved status in the eyes of retailers and thus will experience greater success in introducing the new line of canned goods.

Why do retailers sometimes prefer to include wholesalers in the distribution channel? Retailers may find it advantageous to purchase from a wholesaler for one or more of the following reasons.

1. The wholesaler may be willing to sell in smaller quantities than the manufacturer.

2. The wholesaler may be in a closer location and provide faster delivery.

3. The wholesaler may be more willing to offer credit and other services.

4. It may be unnecessary for the retailer to plan stock needs far in advance, since orders can be placed as often as necessary.

5. Some small retailers may find that there are no savings in buying directly from the manufacturer.

Manufacturer-Facilitator-Wholesaler-Retailer-Consumer. A third middleman sometimes is included in distribution channels for consumer products and services. This middle-

Figure 7-4. A real estate broker may act as a selling agent for the owner of the house.

man, however, appears in different forms in various distribution channels. While wholesalers take both title to and possession of the products, the third middleman may not do either. Therefore, we have chosen to call this middleman a facilitator.

A **manufacturer's agent** is a facilitator who operates under contract with the manufacturer to sell products in an exclusive territory. A **selling agent** is a similar type of middleman. However, the selling agent usually handles the entire line of products and is not limited to restricted territories. Agents do not take title to products but are responsible for selling to wholesalers. In some cases, they bypass the wholesaler and sell to retailers. These sales facilitators, who sometimes are called brokers or manufacturer's representatives, receive compensation from the manufacturer in the form of commissions or fees. Some textile and grocery products as well as furniture and electrical goods are sold with the assistance of facilitators.

In some channels for services, the broker may represent the only middleman in a channel. In such cases, the broker usually represents the seller. Upon completion of the sale, the relationship between the broker and seller is discontinued, and it may be renewed only when selling services are needed again. Real estate, stocks, bonds, and other securities are familiar examples of such channels. Real estate brokers, often operating small, specialized firms, receive 6 or 7 percent of the selling price for the services they provide.

Place Objectives for Consumer Products and Services

It was explained in Chapter 5 that products do not fit into neat categories for classification. While the classification of consumer products is useful to marketers when they formulate place strategies, the classification system is not rigid. What may be convenience products to one consumer may be shopping products to another. To someone with a limited budget, a pair of shoes may be a shopping item. To another person, a pair of Gucci shoes may be a specialty item. Nevertheless, marketers can arrive at some place strategies based on imprecise classifications. Consider the following discussion.

- **Convenience Products.** If you are a baker of bread or a manufacturer of other products that are purchased frequently, your items need **maximum exposure.** That is, they should be placed in many outlets. Suppose you develop and produce a new contact lens cleaning solution. The product needs maximum exposure. As a result, it should be available in places where health and beauty aids are sold: drugstores, supermarkets, variety stores, and some department stores. Impulse items such as chewing gum, snack foods, and soft drinks need maximum exposure and preferred display space. Although emergency products require widespread distribution, they should be placed near the probable point of sale.

- **Shopping Products.** Homogeneous products such as branded appliances, furniture, and

sporting equipment need adequate exposure to facilitate price comparisons. Heterogeneous products such as clothing, jewelry, and home accessories should have adequate representation in major shopping districts and large shopping centers to facilitate comparisons with similar products.

- **Specialty Products.** Specialty products such as a Rolls-Royce automobile, a Christian Dior tie, Lenox china, and Rogers Brothers silverware may represent items for which some buyers are unwilling to accept a substitute. The place strategy restricts such products, often deliberately, to a few outlets. The products then are promoted through advertising in "status" magazines.

- **Unsought Products.** Unsought products and services such as gravestones, insurance, and wheelchairs may be placed in fewer, selected locations. People simply do not shop for such items until they are needed. Aggressive promotion is necessary for success.

Franchising as a Place Strategy. Franchising has become an important method for establishing middlemen in distribution channels. The franchise operation brings a corporation with a product or service, such as McDonald's hamburgers or Holiday Inn, together with an individual or group desiring to start a business. According to Rachman and Mescon, "the **franchiser** (corporation) grants the **franchisee** (the individual or group) the exclusive right to use the franchiser's name in a certain territory, usually in exchange for an initial fee plus monthly payments."[4] Both the agreement and the individual business are called a **franchise.**

Usually, the franchiser will not grant a franchise unless the franchisee has enough money to market the product or service successfully to the consumer. The franchiser, however, usually gives the owner of a franchise assistance, and training to help ensure success. McDonald's "Hamburger University" in Illinois awards a "bachelor of hamburgerology degree" to franchisees completing the training program. Such franchises may allow the corporation to place its product or service into high-volume sales locations. McDonald's now has franchise operations in student centers at Ohio State University, the University of Cincinnati, and Illinois State University.

Automobiles and fast foods are among the many products a franchised middleman buys from the manufacturer or producer and sells to the consumer. Services also are sold by franchisees, as evidenced by Holiday Inns, Century 21 Real Estate, and other firms providing a franchised service. Franchising continues to increase in importance as a place strategy. Nearly one out of every three dollars of retail sales is made by a franchise.[5]

Dual Channels. A manufacturer may choose to use dual channels as a place strategy. While the term is common in marketing terminology, it is a bit misleading. Actually, the manufac-turer may use **multiple channels,** that is, more than two distribution channels.

Some products are distributed in multiple outlets, and a single channel will not suffice. A magazine publisher may sell the product directly to consumers through mail subscriptions. The same publisher may sell magazines to a national magazine service (wholesaler), which in turn sells to small retailers. The publisher also may use the services of a manufacturer's agent to sell magazines to independent wholesalers, who subsequently sell to large-scale retailers. Figure 7-5 shows how complex these channel networks can become as manufacturers and producers struggle to reach various consumers in the most efficient and profitable manner.

There is also danger in trying to visualize definite channels for similar products or services. The manufacturer or producer may find that a

CHANNELS OF DISTRIBUTION

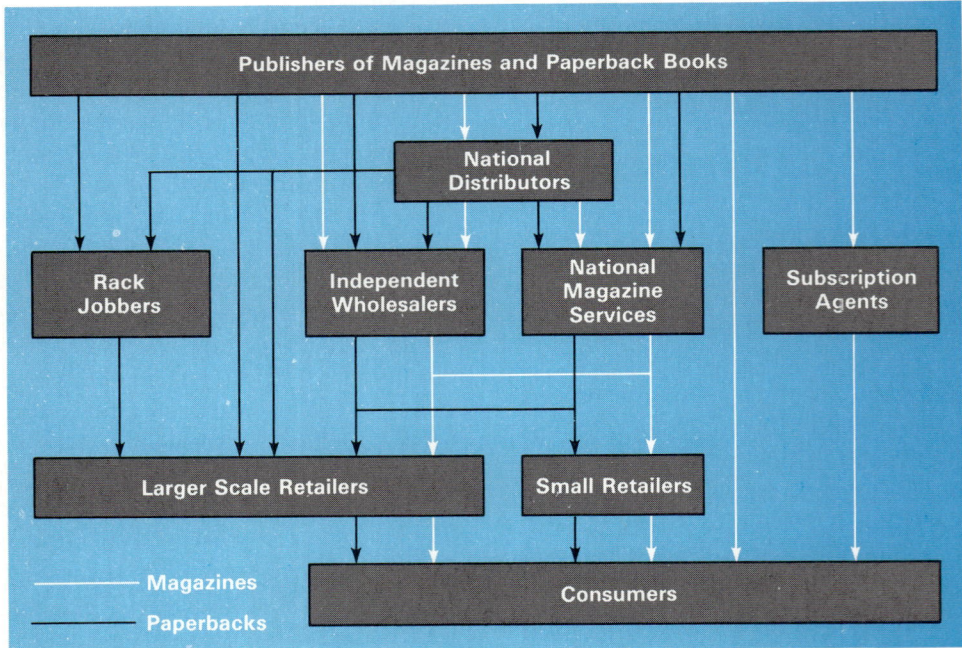

Figure 7-5. This chart shows the multiple channels of distribution for publishers of magazines and paperback books. *Adapted from Edwin H. Lewis, "Descriptions and Comparison of Channels of Distribution," Section 4, p. 5, in* Handbook of Modern Marketing, *edited by Victor P. Buell, McGraw-Hill Book Company, 1970.*

GOING TO MARKET: WILL NONCONVENTIONAL CHANNELS WORK?

Petroleum companies sell gasoline and oil in service stations, food products are marketed in supermarkets, furniture is bought in furniture stores, and prescriptions usually are filled at drugstores. Apparel and accessories are purchased in men's and women's clothing stores as well as department stores. Yet there are exceptions to these typical marketplaces, and many of these exceptions have proved quite successful.

One company that does it differently is Lance Incorporated, a snack food company in Charlotte, North Carolina. Once a small family-owned firm that produced peanut butter crackers, Lance has branched out into cookies and other crackers but has retained the mainstay of the business, peanut butter crackers. What is unusual about Lance is that it has shunned the traditional distribution channels used by cookie and cracker competitors. While firms such as Nabisco and Keebler concentrate on large distributors who handle many product lines, Lance maintains a sales force of some 1,700 people. The Lance sales force actually is made up of independent entrepreneurs who have their own trucks, maintain inventories, and sell the product.

Another significant difference between Lance and its competitors is where they sell their products. Lance snack foods are sold in gas stations, commercial offices, industrial plants, convenience stores, and soda shops—almost everywhere except supermarkets. In a recent year, the cookie and cracker business grew by an estimated 5 percent, while Lance's growth was more than double that rate. An unconventional choice of a marketing channel may yield greater profits than the conventional choice.

Adapted from "Gargling with Peanut Butter," *Forbes*, October 14, 1977, p. 114. Reprinted with permission.

channel differing from that of the competitors works best. Consider the example above.

Channels of Distribution for Industrial Products and Services

In the competitive world of sales and services, a bit of imagination may mean the difference between sluggish and brisk sales. This is especially true in the industrial market, where a few better-informed buyers usually place larger orders. Industrial marketers, regardless of size, try to become knowledgeable about distribution channels in an effort to gain a competitive advantage over competitors. Survival of the fittest does apply in the marketing of products and services.

Manufacturer-Industrial User Channel. Many manufacturers or producers of industrial products, especially smaller ones, choose to sell directly to the industrial buyer. A small firm manufacturing paper cartons to be used for shipping canned goods may sell its product directly to canneries. An industrial contractor specializing in the installation of clean air emission equipment may sell the service to a steel mill. Larger manufacturers or service suppliers also make use of the direct channel.

The direct sales route is more popular for industrial products and services than for consumer products and services for the following reasons.

1. There are relatively fewer industrial buyers as compared with the number of consumer buyers.

2. If the product is used as a component part of the final product by the buyer, large orders usually are received.

3. Often the product must be customized to fit the buyer's need. The buyer may prefer to deal directly with the manufacturer and the company's engineer to specify product design.

4. Sophisticated parts, equipment, machinery, fabricated materials, or tools may create the need for expert knowledge on the part of the seller. Buyers want to know how the product operates, what it can do, and why it fulfills their needs.

5. Buyers of industrial products make infrequent purchases. Equipment usually has a long life span. Raw materials, operating supplies, fabricated parts, and materials often are purchased through contracts which may run for a long period of time.

Can you think of examples of the direct sales route for industrial products and services? Here is one idea to get you started.

Suppose you own a glass factory. You specialize in the production of glass for cars. If you can sell your product to automobile manufacturers, there will be few buyers simply because there are few car manufacturers. Since your product will be used as a component part of the final product, orders will be large. Cars continue to roll off the assembly lines, and the manufacturers' buyers will want to ensure that sufficient component parts are on hand. Your product must fit the various models of cars being produced. Therefore, it must be

customized for the models produced. The car manufacturers' buyers possess technical knowledge about glass. You will need a sales representative who can talk about air pressure, air friction resistance, and fusing qualities. Finally, if you win the account, orders are likely to be placed infrequently, although you may have a staggered delivery schedule and continue shipping glass under one contract for a long period of time.

While it is an established fact that large quantities of industrial products are sold directly to industrial users, middlemen are important in distribution channels for industrial products. This is especially true when buyers purchase in smaller quantities. As more producers and manufacturers of industrial products locate in the sunbelt and in states offering a pro-business climate, the geographic distance between industrial producers and industrial users contributes to the need for middlemen.

Manufacturer-Industrial Distributor-Industrial User. The term **industrial distributor** is used to cover all industrial wholesalers such as oil well supply houses, mine and smelter supply firms, machinery dealers, and mill supply houses. The industrial distributor purchases products and raw materials from producers and manufacturers and subsequently sells them to industrial users. The Texas Bearing Company, for example, may purchase machine bearings from various manufacturers and resell the bearings as component parts to machinery manufacturers.

Industrial distributors usually are located in areas with a high concentration of industrial users. Often this enables the industrial distributor to serve users more effectively than the manufacturer. Industrial distributors for oil well drilling equipment, for example, are located in the regions of the country that produce oil.

Distributors perform a number of important services such as storing products or raw materials at strategic locations and making them available on short notice to the user. They may be staffed to supervise installations, and they usually maintain an inventory of repair parts. An industrial distributor specializes, with fewer lines and products than a wholesaler of consumer products. Therefore, the distributor is likely to become more familiar with each product and give it greater attention.

Manufacturer-Facilitator-Industrial User.

The assistance that an agent may provide to manufacturers and wholesalers in making sales was discussed earlier in a look at distribution channels for consumer products. Agents do not take title to industrial products or assume the ordinary risks of marketing. Instead, agents are able to devote a considerable amount of time to the sale of industrial products.

Manufacturers of industrial products may find that an agent has knowledge of the market and can be helpful in selling to the industrial user. There are many large and small firms making single products or narrow lines of products. Often the expense of keeping a company sales force is too great. Under such conditions, a competent agent middleman may offer an established sales force that knows the markets and possesses the required technical knowledge.

Figure 7-6. Industrial selling agents often know the product and the marketplace, and can be of help to the industrial user.

Suppose you develop and manufacture a new shutoff valve to be inserted into the nozzle of hoses connected to self-service gasoline pumps. The valve is an unsophisticated part, and it is inexpensive. However, it is effective and prevents an overflow of gasoline as self-service gasoline customers fill their tanks. It also stops the pump on an even money amount, such as $15.75, as opposed to $15.77. For this inexpensive part, however, you cannot afford to keep your own sales force in the field. Even if you could, gasoline retailers probably would prefer to purchase the items from someone who could offer other pump parts. As a result, you might use agents who sell replacement hoses, nozzles, and other gasoline pump equipment to service station owners. Chances are that the manufacturer of the pump hose was in a similar situation since that single product was too inexpensive for maintaining a sales force. Thus, as a result of building an assortment of products and offering a sales force that knows the market, the agent serves a valuable role for both manufacturers or producers and industrial users.

The type of agent described above is a manufacturer's agent. Such agents work for several noncompeting manufacturers and can be useful in any field where many small manufacturers need representation.

A selling agent works like a manufacturer's agent, but may handle competing lines. If other firms decide to offer shutoff valves for the nozzles of gasoline hoses, the selling agent may offer their product as well as the one you have developed. While it is common for manufacturer's agents and selling agents to sell to industrial users (manufacturers, contractors, people engaged in the service trades, and so forth), they also may sell to other wholesalers.

Facilitators who do not take title to the industrial products also assist in the buying and selling activities. Their contributions are extremely important, yet they often operate at a relatively low cost, perhaps between 2 and 6 percent of the selling price. They may occupy a place in the channel of distribution between a producer or manufacturer and an industrial user, or they may be positioned between a producer or manufacturer and a wholesaler.

Mike Keegan operates an auto auction barn. His buyers and sellers are brought together, and demand and supply interact to determine the wholesale price while autos are being inspected. Mike concentrates on keeping overhead costs low. The facilities are plain, and the rental costs are low. Mike charges a set fee or commission for the use of his facilities and service.

Auction companies are important in bringing buyers and sellers together for buying and selling transactions. Many agricultural products such as fruit, livestock, and tobacco move from producers to buyers through this facilitator.

Brokers also bring buyers and sellers together. Their service is to act as a reservoir of knowledge about what buyers need and what is available. They aid in buyer-seller negotiations and earn a commission from the party who engaged their service. Food brokers, for example, often are engaged by a cannery to find seasonal produce. They may later act as a middleman between the cannery (food processor) and the buyer (supermarket chain).

Commission merchants also facilitate buying and selling transactions. **Commission merchants** do not take title. However, they may handle the product, complete the sales transaction, and remit the selling price, minus their commission, to the seller. Commission merchants are used for a variety of products. A commission merchant, for example, may agree to sell corn or wheat to a food processor at the market price or the best price obtainable. Often, these merchants represent small producers wishing to reach buyers in a central market and finding it impractical if not impossible to maintain their own sales forces.

As international marketing has become more commonplace, facilitators are seen assisting buyers and sellers in both export and import. These agents perform in much the same manner as manufacturer's agents. Export or import commission houses differ from full-service export and import merchants. Facilitators are commonplace in international marketing because merchant wholesalers are reluctant to finance goods that pass slowly through the channel as they are moved long distances from an international exporter to an international importer. As a result, the best that many producers and manufacturers can do is to use facilitators who act as agents in assisting with the exchange of title.

Wholesalers and facilitators play an important role in moving products and assisting in the exchange of title. Therefore, a closer examination of middlemen for industrial products will be presented in Chapter 8. At this point, however, we shall consider other place strategies as they relate to channels of distribution for industrial products.

Place Objectives for Industrial Products and Services

As you learned in Chapter 5, industrial products and services may be classified into categories. While there is no automatic best place for each category of industrial products or services, some ideal place objectives may be formulated as a result of studying the various classifications.

● **Installations.** Used buildings and land rights require widespread selling efforts by someone knowledgeable about the facilities and the potential buyers and their operations. Therefore, a broker who specializes in handling industrial facilities may be valuable in bringing buyer and seller together and assisting with negotiations. New buildings, on the other hand, need to be handled by a seller with technical and design skills. The seller may choose to deal directly with the buyer. Custom-made equipment also requires highly technical skills on the part of the seller, who must visualize and design equipment and applications to meet the buyer's demand. Again, the seller probably will deal directly with the buyer. Standardized equipment such as diesel engines and lathes, on the other hand, may be distributed by industrial distributors or their middlemen who know the product and the customers.

● **Accessory Equipment.** Accessory equipment such as typewriters, forklifts, and portable drills requires widespread availability and selling efforts. In many cases, the equipment is bought and sold by industrial distributors or specialized wholesalers.

● **Raw Materials.** Raw materials include natural products such as lumber, copper, iron ore, and oil and farm products such as corn, wheat, cattle, and fruits and vegetables. While some of the products are sold directly to the industrial user, facilitators often are positioned between the producer and the industrial user. Usually natural products are more likely to be sold by producers to industrial users, while facilitators are used to reach buyers in central markets who are interested in agricultural raw materials.

● **Component Parts and Materials.** Component parts which are custom-made usually require direct negotiations between the engineering staffs of both buyer and seller to arrive at the proper specifications. Other component parts and materials that are processed to commonly accepted standards, such as automobile tires, oil filters, or air-conditioner filters, may require widespread distribution. Here, industrial distributors frequently sell the products to industrial users.

● **Supplies.** Supplies often are divided into three classifications: maintenance, repair, and operating supplies. As a result, they are often referred to by the acronym MRO. Maintenance supplies such as cleaning compounds, light bulbs, and nails require widespread distribution. Industrial distributors typically handle such items. Repair parts such as nuts and bolts also may be handled by industrial distributors. Other repair parts which are not routinely needed may be supplied through prompt deliveries by the manufacturer. Operating supplies such as paper, pencils, paper clips, and lubricating oils are made available on a widespread scale and usually are handled by industrial distributors.

● **Services.** Services such as computer repair, legal advice, and architectural design must be available to industrial users across the country. The producer often deals directly with an industrial firm. In some situations, such as computer repair, the manufacturer may train service technicians for an industrial distributor.

Cooperative Chains. Earlier, it was explained that dual channels often are developed for consumer products. The same thing happens when industrial products move through channels. More than one channel may be needed to reach industrial buyers. Sometimes the dual channel develops because of industrial buyer action as opposed to the seller's actions.

When products are bought for resale, the resellers may form a **cooperative chain.** That is, they may band together to set up their own wholesaling organization. As a result, they are able to buy in larger quantities, often at a lower price, and perform activities such as receiving, storing, bulk breaking, assembling, transporting, and so forth.

Suppose you started a building materials sales outlet in your community. Your customers are building contractors, freelance carpenters, and specialized technicians such as electricians, plumbers, and roofers as well as do-it-yourselfers. If your sales are modest, you may experience difficulty in buying directly from producers or manufacturers. If the owners of building materials outlets in nearby communities are experiencing the same difficulty, you might band together and form a cooperative chain. Together, your orders are larger, and consequently, you may buy directly from producers and manufacturers. As a result, you may bypass industrial distributors (wholesalers). However, you must be prepared to assume the tasks they ordinarily would perform.

Integration. The building materials example really represents a step toward **vertical integration,** meaning that a manufacturer or middleman assumes two or more successive links in the channel of distribution. Vertical integration may occur in channels of distribution for consumer products as well as industrial products. Florsheim Shoes, for example, serves as a manufacturer, wholesaler, and retailer. Advantages of vertical integration include the following.

1. Assurance of materials and supplies.
2. Greater buying power.
3. Better control of distribution.
4. Reduction in executive overhead expenses.

Horizontal integration also may be taking place here. **Horizontal integration** is the acquisition of firms at the same level of activity. If instead of forming a cooperative chain, the building material outlets were merged under one central ownership and management, then horizontal integration would occur. The new expanded firm would be better prepared to handle discrepancies of quantity and of assortment as a result of additional outlets.

CHANNEL DECISIONS

What is the best way to move products to consumers: through direct channels or indirect channels? Channel decisions are important and may spell the difference between average and unusual success. However, there is no right or wrong way. Channels of distribution are always on trial. Many small businesses have flourished and become large corporate firms, and others have failed miserably as a result of their decisions concerning channels of distribution. For most consumer and industrial products, there is considerable competition, and this is one of the economic forces that bring about change.

Who Determines Channels of Distribution?

While one might expect the producer or manufacturer to have complete control in choosing a channel of distribution, this may not be the case. In the distribution of most products, a **channel captain,** or channel leader, emerges. The channel captain may be a retailer, wholesaler, manufacturer, or producer. The channel captain determines the channel design and, to a considerable extent, what marketing activities other channel members will perform.

Suppose you set up a small manufacturing business and produce wind chimes. You are eager to expand production and spread your costs over more units. You approach J. C. Penney and discover that they are interested in handling the product. To win the account, however, you must produce the chimes to meet their specifications, have the chimes branded, and accept their plans for marketing the product. Because they are likely to buy in huge quantities, they are able to dictate the terms and emerge as the channel captain.

Wholesalers too may be able to specify the quality of products they handle, decide on the type of promotion, set prices within limits, and make other important decisions. The manufacturer or producer in such cases is willing to go along in order to get the wholesaler to buy and sell the products.

Kathy Berberet, a small realtor in a southwestern city, decided to obtain a franchise from Realty World. She discovered that although a franchise is an independent business, the franchiser plans advertising and sales promotion and spells out the marketing role of each party. Franchisers are the most obvious channel leaders.

Figure 7-7. Loading and unloading fruit is a part of channel distribution to the consumer.

Manufacturers producing products that are in great demand usually can assume the role of channel captain. Such firms can select middlemen, supply promotional aids, establish service policies, determine prices, and define the marketing roles of channel members in other ways.

Design Decisions. Key factors for selecting channels include the product, target customers, the producer's status and objectives, and the middlemen's status and objectives. In the earlier discussion of channel captains, the importance of the status of producers and middlemen was illustrated.

The nature of the product and the demand for the product also must be weighed in design decisions. Chewing gum, for example, is a convenience product which customers expect to buy in a variety of retail establishments and through non-store vending machines. In this case, the manufacturer has a product which calls for intensive distribution. As discussed earlier, that means maximizing the number of retail outlets used to distribute the product. Channels must be developed or chosen which will move the gum through thousands of retail outlets—supermarkets, drugstores, discount stores, variety stores, service stations, restaurants, and others—to the ultimate customer. To reach these numerous and varied outlets, a number of different wholesalers will be required. The manufacturer would find it difficult if not impossible to provide a sizable sales force to sell this inexpensive item. On the other hand, retailers would no doubt object to dealing with numerous sales reps for small, inexpensive items such as chewing gum.

Some products, such as industrial diamonds used for selected cutting tools, or Rolls-Royce automobiles, require few outlets, and the channel is designed for exclusive distribution. That is, the number of wholesale or retail outlets for the product is limited intentionally. In the case of industrial diamonds, the producer or importer may have sales representatives or use selling agents to reach industrial buyers. According to McGraw-Hill Research, an average in-person industrial sales call cost $178 in 1981.[6] Considering the fact that sales calls do not always yield sales, the producer may elect to use agents or other industrial middlemen. Products such as Rolls-Royces may require only one dealer or franchise in a large city or geographic area.

Product considerations are important influences on channel design.

1. Generally, channels of distribution are longer for convenience products because such products must be retailed in many different types of outlets. Convenience goods usually are low-priced, and a sales call is not economically feasible.

2. Shopping and specialty goods are sold in fewer outlets and usually at a higher price. Since fewer outlets are required and the price per unit is higher, greater sales effort by the manufacturer or producer is common. Hence, the channels are shorter. It is common for products such as furniture and office equipment to be sold by the manufacturer to the retailer.

3. Perishable food products such as fresh vegetables, fruits, and dairy products tend to have short channels because of the time factor. Items such as "fad" fashions are also perishable. They too move through shorter channels.

4. Usually, higher-priced products have shorter channels than lower-priced items. There are, of course, exceptions.

5. Bulky products such as coal, lumber, petroleum, and heavy equipment which are costly to load, transport, and unload tend to have shorter channels.

6. When considerable postsale technical service is required, as with complicated industrial equipment, the channel is usually shorter. In fact, it may involve only the purchaser and manufacturer.

7. Tailor-made or customized products tend to have short channels. Usually, the producer sells to the ultimate industrial user or consumer.

8. A producer of a number of related products is more likely to use a shorter channel than a producer of a single product. In the case of health foods, if only one product is produced, the cost of dealing directly with retailers becomes prohibitive. However, if the manufacturer produces a dozen products, sales to retailers rather than wholesalers may be feasible.

Conflict Versus Cooperation. It must be recognized that a channel of distribution may consist of a number of separate firms or entrepreneurs. Often these firms are small and are operated by an owner, partnership, or family unit. While the need for cooperation is obvious, sometimes the objectives of firms differ and a conflict of interest between and among channel members may exist.

Horizontal conflicts may be defined as issues arising between two marketing institutions at the same level. Two or more independently owned service stations, for example, located in the same small community and carrying the same brand of gasoline, may engage in a price war. **Intertype conflicts** result from the use of different types of retail outlets in the same marketing area. If the same brand of appliances is sold by appliance dealers, department stores, and furniture stores, the appliance dealer may express anger if there is reason to believe that department stores are receiving faster delivery. **Vertical conflicts** may occur between or among members of the same channel of distribution. When a manufacturer believes that a wholesaler is carrying an inadequate inventory to service retailers, a vertical conflict is created.

Conflicts usually are reduced in **corporate vertical systems.** In such systems, the manufacturer owns and controls the distribution outlets. In **contractual vertical systems** such as franchises or long-term contractual agreements between buyer

TABLE 7-1
THREE TYPES OF VERTICAL MARKETING SYSTEMS

Type of System	Description	Examples
Corporate	Channel is owned by a single organization	Singer Corporation; Sears; Firestone; Eagle Stores; Holiday Inn
Administered	Channel is dominated by the channel captain	Campbells; Corning Glass; O. M. Scott and Sons; Magnavox; General Electric
Contractual	Channel membership is based on contractual agreements among members	*Wholesale-Sponsored Chains* IGA; McKesson and Robbins; Western Auto *Retail Cooperatives* Associated Grocers *Franchises* McDonald's; Coca-Cola bottlers; Century 21 Real Estate; Midas Mufflers; Ramada Inn

and seller, conflicts may arise if the franchiser or franchisee or the buyer or seller believes that the other party is failing to abide by the terms of the contractual agreement. In **administered vertical marketing systems,** in which the manufacturer is strong enough to get voluntary cooperation from middlemen, conflicts are not prevalent. Samsonite luggage and Scott Lawn products may be so appealing that they entice wholesalers and retailers to cooperate voluntarily in matters such as levels of inventory, display space, advertising, and pricing. See Table 7-1.

Regardless of the marketing system used, coordination of efforts in moving the products along their journey to ultimate consumption is desirable. When the expectations which middlemen have of other middlemen differ, conflicts are created. The retailer may expect liberal payment terms which a wholesaler is unwilling to offer. A manufacturer may promise an exclusive territory to a wholesaler in return for the wholesaler's promise to make a "majority effort" to generate business within the area. While sales may increase, the manufacturer still is not pleased.

Such conflicts may be disruptive to the flow of products.

Cooperation of channel members becomes especially important when alternative channels are structured. Industrial firms selling to the garment industry find most of their buyers in the southwestern regions of the country and in Los Angeles. Surfing equipment buyers are concentrated along coastal areas. Because of warehousing and transportation costs, channels structured for direct sales become a more feasible alternative than they would be if buyers were spread across the country. The manufacturer may decide in some cases to open a sales branch in geographic areas where buyers are heavily concentrated and use middlemen in areas that are sparsely populated by buyers. All buyers, however, will expect to receive fair treatment whether they buy from a manufacturer's representative or a wholesaler. Thus, the wholesaler must cooperate fully to accommodate all buyers.

As a small manufacturer grows and expands output, middlemen often are needed to perform other marketing activities. (See Table 7-2 on page

210.) The manufacturer may wish to devote full attention to production. After demand for the product has been established, middlemen may be willing or even eager to handle the product. Consider the following example.

In 1964, Robert Taylor, who founded Minnetonka, Inc., started manufacturing perfumed soap and packaged it in a pump container in his basement. Three days each week were devoted to the manufacturing

TABLE 7-2
FUNCTIONS OF FULL SERVICE WHOLESALERS

Function	Rationale
Buying	Wholesalers are able to offer a wide array of products to retailers. If supermarkets, for example, bought all products directly from manufacturers and producers, the buying function would become unwieldy, time-consuming, and expensive.
Selling	A wholesaler may have an established sales force that can reach retailers effectively. The producer or manufacturer, often distantly located, may be unable to carry out the selling function efficiently.
Physical distribution	Wholesalers may receive carload shipments from manufacturers in a distant area. The wholesaler is able to store the large quantity, break it into smaller quantities, and arrange shipment to area retailers.
Financing	In some cases, wholesalers may finance the products which they purchase and resell to retailers. Usually, credit is extended by the wholesaler for a normal billing cycle of 30 days, although wholesalers sometimes provide credit for extended periods.
Assuming risks	Wholesalers assume a risk for products in their possession. Prices can plummet from fluctuations in the economy or from price wars. Perishable items are subject to spoilage, and natural disasters such as fire or flooding are always possible.
Demand creation	Often, wholesalers place advertisements in local trade journals and offer retailers sales promotional displays. Also, wholesalers may provide cooperative advertising funds to retailers. Such efforts are beneficial to both the manufacturer and the retailer.
Grading and standardizing	The wholesaler on occasion sorts and grades products purchased from producers. This is especially true with agricultural products such as oranges, eggs, lettuce, and other fresh produce items.
Research	Distance often isolates manufacturers from their customers. The wholesaler becomes a communications link and passes information from the retailer back to the manufacturer. Thus, manufacturers are able to obtain information about product sales and their customers' likes and dislikes.
Managerial assistance	Wholesalers may provide assistance to retail managers: helping them design inventory systems, suggesting improved operational techniques, or assisting in resolving problems.

process and the rest of the time to sales. Sales totaled $39,000 the first year, and he dreamed of someday achieving $1 million in sales. In 1980, profits reached $5.5 million.[7]

Needless to say, a number of middlemen are interested in the product today.

Pushing or Pulling Products and Services Through Channels

The push-pull concept is also closely related to promotion and will be discussed in greater detail in Chapter 12. Nevertheless, a producer who desires to move products to the end of the channel should consider the push-pull concept as channel decisions are reached. Middlemen, especially retailers, are not as concerned with the concept since they already control the end of the channel.

Pushing Products. Pushing products, that is, using aggressive sales promotion techniques and personal selling, is directed at middlemen. The producer tries to persuade selected middlemen to handle the line of products. In essence, the producer tries to organize a team of middlemen who will work well together in moving the product to the final customer.

Pulling Products. Pulling products through the channel occurs when the producer directs advertising and sales promotion efforts such as samples and coupons at the final customer. The idea is to build strong demand so that customers will request the product and middlemen will be forced to carry it to satisfy their customers. Middlemen usually are told about promotions beforehand so that they will be ready to assume a role in the distribution channel if the promotion is successful.

Producers often use both push and pull for the same product. This concept is discussed further in Chapter 12.

Society today is dependent on marketing channels to move the products and services needed to fill people's wants and needs to the right place at the right time. In Chapter 8, the role of middlemen (retailers and wholesalers), who serve such a vital role in distribution channels, will be examined. Physical distribution presents some challenging considerations in moving products along their journey to the ultimate consumers or industrial users. This topic will be explored in Chapter 9.

KEY POINTS SUMMARY

- Channels of distribution, which sometimes are called trade channels, include middlemen who are involved in moving products or services from the manufacturer or producer to consumers or industrial buyers.

- When manufacturers or producers sell directly to the consumer, they use one or more of five methods: advertising, sales representatives, retail outlets, mail order, and telephone solicitation.

- Middlemen exist because they can provide a service for either the buyer or the seller.

- Franchising as a place strategy is one of the fastest growing methods of marketing products and services.

- Facilitators may be positioned between a manufacturer or producer and a buyer or between a wholesaler and a buyer. They do not take title to products. Instead, they negotiate the transfer of title.

- Manufacturers of both consumer products and industrial products are faced with the need to structure channels to fit a more scattered and shifting market.

- Generally speaking, low-unit-value items travel through longer channels than high-unit-value items.

- Highly technical products as well as perishable products usually are moved through short channels.

- The lowest-cost channel is not always the best channel. Profit maximization is an important consideration in choosing channels.

- Vertical integration takes place when a manufacturer or wholesaler assumes two or more links in the channel of distribution. Horizontal integration is the merger of firms at the same level within a channel of distribution.

- In most channels, a channel captain emerges. The channel captain may be a manufacturer or a producer, a wholesaler, or a retailer. The channel captain usually is able to dictate the marketing activities that other channel members will assume.

- In a successful distribution channel, each member cooperates with others and conflicts are avoided.

KEY TERMS AND CONCEPTS

administered vertical systems
break bulk
channel captain
channel of distribution
commission merchants
contractual vertical systems
cooperative chain
corporate chain
corporate vertical systems
direct distribution channel
exclusive distribution
franchise
franchisee
franchiser

horizontal conflict
horizontal integration
indirect distribution channel
industrial distributor
intensive distribution
intertype conflict
manufacturer's agent
maximum exposure
middlemen
multiple channels
selective distribution
selling agent
trade channel
vertical conflict
vertical integration
wholesalers

DISCUSSION QUESTIONS

1. Why are multiple channels sometimes used to move a single product to buyers?

2. How does channel choice become dependent on the product? On target customers? On producer's status and objectives? On middlemen's status and objectives?

3. Under what conditions is a manufacturer or producer likely to emerge as the channel captain? A wholesaler? A retailer?

4. Under what conditions would a firm desire intensive distribution? Exclusive distribution? Selective distribution?

5. In an ideal situation, each channel member will cooperate with others. In practice, this does not always happen. Cite some examples of conflicts and indicate why they arise.

6. Why is the direct sales route chosen for some industrial products, with other middlemen being bypassed?

NOTES

1. Adapted from Gail Bronson, "How Old-Line Jeans Producer Fashioned Survival Strategy," *Wall Street Journal*, May 4, 1981, p. 29. Reprinted by permission of the *Wall Street Journal*. All Rights Reserved. © Dow Jones and Company, Inc.
2. William J. Stanton, *Fundamentals of Marketing*, 6th ed., McGraw-Hill, New York, 1981, p. 284.
3. Warren G. Meyer, Peter G. Haines, and E. Edward Harris, *Retailing Principles and Practices*, 7th ed., McGraw-Hill, New York, 1982, p. 17.
4. David J. Rachman and Michael E. Mescon, *Business Today*, 2d ed., Random House, New York, 1979, p. 41.
5. U.S. Bureau of the Census, *Statistical Abstract of the United States*, Government Printing Office, Washington, D.C., 1977, pp. 831–837.
6. *Laboratory of Advertising Performance Report*, McGraw-Hill Research, No. 8013.6, New York.
7. Associated Press, "Manufacturer Has Fresh Idea," *The Pantagraph*, Bloomington, Ill., June 21, 1981, p. E-3.

CHAPTER

8

MIDDLEMEN:
RETAILERS AND WHOLESALERS

"**E**veryone is after the working woman's paycheck," says Kay Rand Lloyd, editor of *Working Woman* magazine. This has led to what department stores call **"creative merchandising"**: offering the customers a wide array of products to fulfill their wants and needs, along with services that include fashion advice, investment and career counseling, and even evening college courses—all on the store's premises.

If you cannot keep women interested in merchandise, you need something to tie into their lives, something to bring customers into a store and increase sales. Ford Motor Company parked new cars at three Filene's department stores in the Boston area. A woman race car driver was present to explain auto maintenance, and a woman banker gave advice on how to finance a car purchase. Two models strolled about wearing the latest in casual weekend fashions from White Stag.

Manufacturers sponsor national and sometimes local advertising to entice customers, while retailers and wholesalers not only try to make their products available at the right place but also are concerned about bringing the product or service and the customers together. In essence, they are creating both place and time utilities, that is, having the products or services in the right place and at the time when the customer wants to make a purchase. After attending a seminar at Kaufmann's, a stylish Pittsburgh department store that is a division of May Department Stores Company, Karen Hrapczak bought $140 of clothes she "just happened to see on the way out." In this case Kaufmann's served as the right place and, because of the seminar, brought the customer and merchandise together at the right time.

Dayton's, an upscale Minneapolis department store that is a division of Dayton-Hudson Corporation, has a wardrobe planning service that originally was designed for women executives. After 1,900 women became steady clients, the service was offered to men. Within 6 months, about 500 men had signed up for the advice.

"Anytime we do anything in the form of a how-to clinic, we get instant business," says a Pittsburgh department store executive. Mrs. Lloyd, the *Working Woman* magazine editor, says she is amazed by the number of women who spend their after-work hours at department store seminars. A lecture she gave at Kaufmann's on career advancement was attended by about 500 women. "I was overwhelmed," Mrs. Lloyd said. Working women "are so thirsty" for recognition, information, and an opportunity to be with other such women that "by gum, they come."[1]

After reading these paragraphs, one might get the impression that department stores are resorting to gimmicks as promotional devices instead of concentrating on place strategies. But note that in each example, the department store was offering a product or service at the right place and at the right time. Middlemen earn a profit by performing marketing activities that offer locations for products and services that customers want.

Middlemen play an important role in creating place, time, and possession utilities. Retailers represent the front line of business. That is, they are the only contact that millions of consumers have with the countless channels of distribution that make up this country's supply system. There are about 2 million retailers in the United States today. Approximately 383,000 wholesalers and facilitators, on the other hand, perform services required in the exchange of title and possession of products as goods move to manufacturers, producers, fabricators, processors, other wholesalers, service-oriented business firms, and retailers. With the exception of the industrial user, they may never meet the consumers of the products they handle. First, we shall consider retail institutions and the roles assumed in place strategy, and then we shall discuss wholesale institutions.

RETAILERS

Over 80 percent of all retail firms are classified as small-scale businesses. They each employ fewer than 20 people and do less than $500,000 in business annually.[2] Retail institutions are often small and specialized. However, they are characterized by other factors. Retailing is easy to enter. In contrast to manufacturing, the financial and legal requirements for opening a retail business are few. Small restaurants, produce shops, sewing and yarn centers, health food stores, service stations, and similar retail outlets may require rela-

TABLE 8-1
RETAILERS CLASSIFIED BY SIZE

Paid Employees	Percentage of Retail Stores	Percentage of Retail Sales
0–3	65	15
4–7	16	13
8–19	12	20
20 or more	7	52

Source: *Statistical Abstract of the United States*, 102d Ed., 1981, pp. 816–817. Note that some of the businesses with fewer than 20 employees do more than $500,000 in business annually.

tively small financial outlays. The statement that there is no room for the small independent is not true in the field of retailing.

Many successful small-scale retailers have expanded their businesses and grown into large-scale retail operations. J. C. Penney, for example, which today is considered a large mass merchandiser with over 2,000 outlets, was founded as a single store in Kemmerer, Wyoming, in 1902. Some large-scale retailers operate their business in a single location. Others, however, have hundreds of stores in the United States and other countries. Retailers also become involved in international marketing.

Retailing consists primarily of buying a satisfying assortment of products for some consumer market segments, making these products available at a reasonable price, and persuading the customers that the products will satisfy them.[3] Retailing focuses on the final consumer, not focusing on industrial users. They are served by other middlemen.

Types of Retailers by Organization

Retailers can be classified by type of ownership, such as chain stores, independents, voluntary chains, and franchises.

Chain Stores. A **chain store** consists of a group of stores that are centrally owned and managed and sell similar products. According to the U.S. Bureau of the Census, a chain organization is a group of 12 or more stores. The largest retailers in this country are chain stores, including such firms as Sears, Wards, K-Mart, J. C. Penney, and Woolworth's. The chains use the centralized buying concept and consequently are able to buy in huge quantities from the manufacturer or producer. Thus, wholesalers often are deleted from the channel of distribution. In some cases, the chain may contract with a manufacturer to produce products to be sold under a private brand name. Sears, for example, buys appliances from the Whirlpool Corporation to be sold under the Sears exclusive brand name of Kenmore. Chain stores are able to reduce the cost of operating in a number of ways. Advertising and promotion costs may be spread among more than one store.

Independent Stores. **Independent stores** are singularly operated by a proprietor, partnership, or corporation. An independent retailer may be guided by the old maxim that goods well bought are half sold. Because they are not confined to centralized buying, they may react to customer buying trends and fads more quickly than chain stores. As a result, an independent retailer has an opportunity to make the right products available at the right time.

Voluntary Chains. Independent retailers may band together in cooperative chains. Cooperative chains were discussed in Chapter 7, where it was explained that a group of retailers may band together to set up their own wholesaling organization. In doing so, they become strong enough to buy directly from the manufacturer. A **voluntary chain** is initiated and sponsored by a wholesaler to assure that retail outlets exist for the products which the wholesaler handles. The independent Grocers Association (IGA), Allied Federated Stores, and True Value Hardware Stores are examples of voluntary chains. The wholesaler will assist each independent retailer, which in turn will buy all or most of its merchandise from the wholesaler. This enables the wholesaler to buy larger quantities from producers or manufacturers at competitive prices. The retailer benefits from the competitive prices and from expert assistance such as suggestions on store layout, inventory systems, display methods, advertising, and other operational concerns.

Franchises. The franchised retailer, which was discussed in Chapter 7 as a channel place strategy, has the advantage of national advertising, cooperative buying, and other benefits which the independent retailer lacks. Rexall Drug Stores and Midas Muffler Shops are among retail outlets formed and operated under the emblems of larger companies. The largest growth in franchises, however, has occurred in service businesses. Most service businesses, many of which are not classified as retail firms, are necessary for the typical consumer. The franchised firms may supply workers to clean a home, dry-clean clothing, groom a lawn, plan a vacation trip, supply a rented auto, board a pet while the owner is away, make a motel room available, serve meals, and provide a host of other services.

Types of Retailers by Merchandise

Retail institutions can be divided into various categories based on the merchandise handled. The chief types of retail stores are general stores, mass merchandisers, department stores, specialty stores, variety stores, supermarkets, discount or low-margin stores, mail-order firms, and nonstore retailers.

General Stores. General stores carry a number of lines of merchandise without any significant degree of departmental organization. Such stores, which typically are located in smaller communities, handle lines of merchandise broad enough to take care of many if not most of the community's needs. Groceries and related com-

TABLE 8-2
KINDS AND NUMBERS OF FRANCHISED BUSINESSES

Kind of Franchised Business	Number of Establishments
Auto and truck dealers	32,000
Restaurants (all types)	68,600
Gasoline service stations	152,000
Retailing (nonfood)	39,500
Auto and truck rental services	8,000
Automotive products and services*	47,000
Employment services	5,200
Tax preparation services	9,600
Accounting, credit collection, and general business services	3,200
Camp grounds	1,000
Construction, home improvement, maintenance, and cleaning	16,600
Convenience stores	16,500
Educational products and services	3,600
Equipment rental services	2,000
Food retailing	16,300
Hotels and motels	5,900
Laundry and dry-cleaning services	2,900
Recreation, entertainment, and travel	4,900
Soft drink bottlers	1,800
Miscellaneous	4,200

*Includes some establishments with significant sales of nonautomotive products such as household appliances, garden supplies, and so on.

Source: *Statistical Abstract of the United States,* 102d ed., 1981, p. 819.

modities, dry goods and notions, apparel and shoes, hardware, home furnishings, farm supplies, and gasoline and oil usually are included in the inventory.

In 1929, the U.S. Bureau of the Census reported that 104,089 general stores existed in the United States. In some regions of the country today, it is impossible to find a general store. The decline of general stores may be attributed to a number of factors, including the farm-to-city movement, the improvement of roads and means of transportation, and the rising importance of fashion merchandise. While general stores are insignificant in numbers and sales volume, they represent a type of retailing that was important in the past.

Mass Merchandisers. Sears, Roebuck and Company; K-Mart; J. C. Penney Company, Incorporated; F. W. Woolworth Company; and Montgomery Ward and Company are among the nation's largest retailers. They have grown so large and offer such a variety of merchandise that they are classified as mass merchandisers.[4] **Mass merchandisers** sell a number of lines of products—apparel and accessories, household linens and dry goods, small wares, and in some cases, furniture, home furnishings, hardware, and appliances—all under one roof.

Some mass merchandisers provide a place for a variety of services. In 1979, Montgomery Ward and Company opened "Law Store" booths in two of its San Diego outlets and started considering others for additional stores.[5] Mass merchandisers also have started looking at smaller cities and towns as places to offer their products. Companies such as Sears and K-Mart are emphasizing smaller markets for their new store programs and are developing small-store prototypes to serve such areas. Sears began developing its "K30" and "K40" small stores several years ago. The little stores, with 30,000 to 40,000 square feet, do not carry furniture or carpets and nonessential lines such as toys or garden supplies. They also do not have much warehouse space. Instead, they

Figure 8-1. The old-fashioned general store carried merchandise for most of the community's needs.

depend on frequent deliveries. K-Mart also began dabbling in small markets in 1974, when it opened its first 40,000 square foot store (compared with big-city stores ranging up to 94,000 square feet). So far, only 30 percent of K-Mart's stores are in nonmetropolitan areas, but in the next few years, about half of its new stores will go into smaller markets. [6]

Place decisions are important even for the country's largest retailers. Their strategy is to make services as well as products available in the places where they are needed and wanted. Mass merchandisers also try to reach markets in small as well as large communities. Scaled-down versions of stores that carry products in great demand are necessary, however, if the mass merchandiser is to operate a profitable enterprise in a smaller market.

Department Stores. A **department store** is defined by the U.S. Bureau of the Census as an establishment that normally employs 25 or more people and is engaged in selling general lines of merchandise in each of the following three categories.

- Furniture, home furnishings, appliances, and radio and TV sets
- General line of apparel and accessories for the entire family
- Household linens and dry goods (*dry goods* is a term used to identify piece goods and sewing notions)

The concept of a department store is essentially that of a large store offering a vast variety of merchandise and organized on a departmental basis. While some department stores operate as independents, it is estimated that 80 percent of stores with annual sales exceeding $1 million are organized and operated as chains. Such large department stores are able to employ professional buyers who visit merchandise marts and attend trade shows to buy directly from the manufacturer.

Department stores serve as a dominant middleman for a number of reasons.

1. They sell not only apparel but other products ranging from linen to fine china, and they are equipped to serve the needs of most consumers.
2. They offer a variety of services to consumers, including credit, extended shopping hours, delivery, wrapping service, the right to return merchandise, and, often, free parking.
3. In addition to products, they often offer services for sale such as eye examinations, income tax preparation, hair care, banking, insurance, and travel.
4. They usually are situated in key shopping areas, both downtown locations and suburban shopping centers.
5. Department stores are fashion leaders in many cities. They are the first retailer to carry assortments of the newest styles and models.

Department stores continue to respond to a changing environment, bringing new and diverse marketing tactics into practice in order to cope with the problems of modern retailing. The installation of electronic point-of-sale (POS) equipment has streamlined a variety of functions such as verifying charge accounts or approving the acceptance of personal checks, keeping a perpetual count of merchandise inventory, changing prices, producing sales reports quickly, and adding returned merchandise back into the inventory. The use of optical character recognition (OCR) wands and slots enables stores to have faster checkouts with greater accuracy.

In the past, store-issued credit cards were a factor in creating store loyalty. When credit cards were issued by Maison Blanc, a department store in New Orleans, the holder could use the card only at that store. Today, as more banks issue credit cards, which often are referred to as plastic money, department stores throughout New Orleans or any other city will accept the bank-issued cards. As a result, the advantage that one store might have held over another because shoppers possessed a store credit card is being lost.

Some department stores continue to expand the lines of the products and services they sell. Car rentals, interior decorating services, and pharmacy departments are not unusual in large stores. While product lines are blurring—that is, many stores carry identical merchandise—some stores place an emphasis on merchandise that is unavailable in other outlets, and some stores are adding imported products and private-label fashion designs.

Department stores today are characterized by formal recruiting and training programs to satisfy the need for professional managers. College and community college graduates often are sought for positions in top and middle management. However, some stores still follow the practice of bringing management personnel up through the ranks. In these stores, the aspirant for a managerial position starts on the selling floor, moves into a department manager position, and subsequently moves up the career ladder.

Another change prevalent in today's marketing environment is the increasing use of nontraditional advertising media. Cable, network, and local TV commercials are supplementing newspaper advertising. Catalogs, which once were distributed biannually, are being replaced with more frequent mailings that have an appearance similar to magazines. They are characterized by high-quality photography and carefully designed and edited layouts, and they are produced on glossier paper.

Specialty Stores. According to the U.S. Bureau of the Census, a **specialty store** is one that carries a limited line of related products, such as a jewelry store, a shoe store, or a sporting goods

Figure 8-2. Specialty stores carry limited lines of products in order to attain an excellent assortment in their selected type of merchandise.

store. Specialty products, which were defined in Chapter 5, should not be confused with specialty shops. The term *specialty* implies a limited variety of products when it is used to identify specialty stores, while the term *specialty products* refers to items that the shopper will make a special effort to obtain. Some specialty stores do offer specialty products such as Christian Dior shirts. Others, such as Singer Sewing Machine Stores, offer shopping products.

The specialty store may be large or small, although the majority of these middlemen operate small establishments. The store may be owned by a proprietor, partnership, or corporation. It may be a small independent boutique, or it may be one of a chain of stores such as Casual Corner. Specialty stores sometimes are referred to as **limited-line stores** because they carry a relatively complete assortment of a single line of products or some related lines of merchandise.

Suppose that you enter a store called the County Seat. You find numerous pairs of jeans, but you cannot expect to buy hair spray, a watch, or other unrelated items. To fulfill your wants and needs in one location, you would probably choose a department store, a mass merchandise store, or a discount store.

Because specialty stores limit the lines of merchandise stocked, they usually have an excellent assortment and have particular appeal in the apparel field, featuring the latest fashions.

When specialty stores are organized as a chain, they have highly capable buyers who select merchandise that will satisfy customer. When purchasing for a chain, the buyer is able to place orders for large quantities. This creates special appeal for the inclusion of specialty stores as middlemen in selected channels of distribution. Examples of specialty chains include Brooks Fashion Stores, The Gap Shoes, The Men, and Waldenbooks.

Variety Stores. A **variety store** carries a wide range of merchandise in a limited number of low or relatively low price lines. Some variety stores are independent organizations, but most are units of chain organizations. Once known as 5 and 10 cent stores, variety stores such as Ben Franklin, Kresge, and Woolworth's served as important middlemen in central business districts. After the advent of scrambled merchandising, Kresge closed their 5 and 10s and opened K-Mart junior department stores.

A few years ago, variety stores were important links in distribution channels. Today, however, some people believe that variety stores may be reaching the brink of extinction. It should be noted that a number of small-scale variety stores, both independents and small chains, are flourishing. Discount Den, Danners Big 3-D Stores, Murphys, and McCrory are examples. Today's variety stores are still characterized by low-priced items and cash and carry sales. Many variety stores are approaching some department stores in terms of the assortment of merchandise carried. Managers are striving to develop a more sharply defined image which emphasizes the differences of convenience and service between variety stores and rival discount operations.

Supermarkets. A **supermarket** is a large departmentalized food store carrying a wide variety of fresh, frozen, and packaged foods as well as many related items. The first supermarkets appeared in the 1930s, but their phenomenal growth did not occur until after World War II. Because of the low markup on food products, early supermarkets found it difficult to generate sufficient profit to satisfy owners and at the same time retain earnings for expansion. As a result, such stores began to stock more nonfood convenience products. Such items, which also are found in drugstores and some variety stores, carry a greater gross margin. This practice of stocking and selling nontraditional product lines is known as **scrambled merchandising.**

An early pioneer in scrambled merchandising, Fred Meyer, sold food and other merchandise in Oregon. Meyer's philosophy evolved from supplying products to satisfy human basic needs. According to Meyer, "There are three basic things humans have needed since they were civilized. They must have food, clothing, and a place to live."[7] The Meyer food and merchandise chain supplies food, clothing, and a variety of other products. It also has established a savings and loan business, installing mini-savings and loan branches in more than 20 of its stores. Thus, Meyer has satisfied the need for a place to live by providing mortgage money for homes.

As more women join the work force and additional meals are eaten outside the home, supermarkets have begun to add delicatessens. Often the shoppers are provided with eat-in deli sections within stores, or prepared food items may be taken home.

Other developments which have affected supermarkets are the emergence of discount supermarkets, combination supermarkets, and convenience stores. The **discount supermarket,** or "box store," is designed to cut operating costs. Instead of shelving products, customers select cans of food, detergents, and similar items from the cartons in which they were shipped. The customers also carry their purchases from the store to their automobiles. Only a minimum amount of service is provided. As a result, the store is able to offer more competitive prices.

The **combination supermarkets,** or "superstores," resemble the hypermarket, a large discount store that originated in France. Such stores go beyond the concept of scrambled merchandising. Among the many products offered are food items, apparel, household wares, hardware,

GROCER CREATES SUPER SUPERMARKET

Things to pick up at the supermarket: a dozen eggs, a loaf of bread and a life insurance policy.

Kroger Co., the nation's second-largest supermarket chain after Safeway Stores Inc., opened its first Kroger Financial Center inside an Ohio supermarket last week, offering shoppers the opportunity to make financial investments at the same time that they bring home the bacon.

"Shoppers today are busy people. Our consumer research shows that one-stop-shopping is increasing in importance to customers in the 1980s," said Lyle Everingham, Kroger's chairman, in an earlier announcement of the joint venture with Capitol Holding Corp.

Kroger, based in Cincinnati, announced that in addition to the new 300-square-foot office inside its Grove City store, it soon will be offering mutual fund investments and insurance policies at several other Columbus, Ohio-area stores in the partnership with the Louisville, Ky., insurance concern.

Everingham said the new in-store financial centers are an outgrowth of trends in the American economy. "Our experience with offering as many as a dozen service specialty departments in our modern superstores and combination stores bears out that this is what shoppers want. Financial services represent a logical extension of the one-stop-shopping concept," he said.

But many supermarkets offer small brokerage services inside stores, such as check cashing or providing space for electronic teller machines from local financial institutions; and other retailers have already entered the investment field.

Capital, a $3.8 billion insurance holding firm with seven affiliates, mostly in southeastern states, will manage the new Kroger centers, providing automobile, homeowners, renters and condominium insurance policies as well as three kinds of life insurance.

In addition, Capital has contracted with the Vanguard Group of Investment Cos. of Valley Forge, Pa., to offer two money-market mutual funds with check-writing privileges, three mutual funds investing in bonds and two others investing in common stock. The office is expected to also offer membership in an automobile club, credit-card protection and a property registration and inventory service.

Adapted from Associated Press, "Grocer Creates Super Supermarket," *The Pantagraph*, Bloomington, IL, September 19, 1982, p. E5.

Figure 8-3. Discount supermarkets ("box stores") cut operating costs by stacking items in the cartons in which they were shipped.

leisure-time products, and a variety of services such as dry cleaning, shoe repair, and minor auto repairs.

While not really supermarkets, **convenience stores** such as 7-Eleven, Minit Markets, and U-Tote'M are conveniently located, carry a limited assortment of fast-moving food items, and are open for long hours. Sometimes they offer self-service gasoline islands. Their prices usually are higher than those of conventional food stores, but customers are willing to pay for the convenience. One benefit of such stores is that customers believe they can get in and out much quicker than in larger supermarkets.

Discount Stores. *Discount Merchandiser,* a trade magazine for the discount industry, defines a **discount store** as a departmentalized retail establishment using many self-service techniques to sell hard goods, health and beauty aids, apparel and other soft goods, and other general merchandise. Operating at an unusually low profit margin, a discount store may be an independent, a chain, or a department within a store. Service Merchandise, Hills Department Stores, Wal-Mart, Zayre Corporation, and Kuhn's Big K Stores are examples.

Discount stores achieve low-price appeal through high-volume sales and the curtailment of plush interior fixtures and some customer services such as delivery.

Initially, discounters sold brand-name appliances and durable goods. Inexpensive, non-branded items such as children's wearing apparel and men's shirts, often imported from Japan, Taiwan, and Hong Kong, were added later.

Today, many discount stores carry both nationally advertised brands and private brands.

FACTORY DISCOUNT OUTLETS VERSUS FULL-PRICE RETAILERS

The manufacturer's or factory discount store differs from an independent or chain-owned discount store in that the manufacturer owns the outlet. Manufacturer-owned stores lead to other problems. Consider the following example.

Louis Bedrin feels betrayed. "It hurts us," he says. "It's not fair."

For 23 years, Mr. Bedrin's Jack and Jill shop in Memphis carried Health-Tex children's clothing. Then Health-Tex, a Chesebrough-Pond's unit, opened a factory outlet in a Memphis mall, selling its own goods at prices that left Mr. Bedrin out of the running. A T-shirt he had been selling for $6.50 went for $3.99. Trousers he offered for $9.50 were priced at $4.99. "I got fed up," Mr. Bedrin says. "I dropped the line."

Everybody likes a bargain, and the developers of shopping centers are clustering factory outlet stores and other "off-price" discounters in malls. These stores appeal to inflation-ravaged consumers by offering prices 20 to 60 percent below those found in department stores. But the trend is certain to strain relations between manufacturers and full-price retailers. From fewer than a dozen in 1979, the number of no-frills, off-price centers had risen to more than 45 by midsummer 1981. Another 100, mostly in the south and the east, were on the drawing boards. The number of deep-discount outlets also has increased steadily from an estimated 350 in 1972 to more than 7,000 in 1981 according to the *Save on Shopping Directory*, a consumer guide.

"It's a very, very dangerous trend from the independent store's point of view," says Nathaniel Mendelson, president of Youth Fashion Guild, a New York clothes-buying office. "Major retail stores are a big part of our business, and we wouldn't like to lose any of them," says John David Franklin, director of retail operations for the Ship N' Shore apparel unit of General Mills. "But I don't think there is a manufacturer who has opened a factory outlet and not lost some regular retail business." Manufacturers are under steady pressure from shopping center developers to open factory outlets. Fearing that they might dilute the worth of its name, Ship N' Shore will allow its 19 outlets to dwindle to about 10 to avoid association with low-priced products.

Some companies do not seem to be worried about the problems. In El Paso, Viola Sportswear, Incorporated, a licensee of Sasson, the jeans maker, will half own a new development. William Carter Company, a children's clothing maker based in Massachusetts, does not worry about having 50 factory outlets while department stores are charging full price for its goods. "We don't feel they dilute our image," says a company representative.

The most common characteristics of these stores include the following.

1. Assortments of merchandise are limited to popular items, colors, and sizes.

2. The store's major feature is low-priced merchandise. In some cases, the low prices result from low markup rather than low quality.

3. The self-service approach to retailing is used. With the exception of cashiers, only a limited number of employees may interact directly with customers.

4. Stores are open long hours and, where permitted by law, often on Sundays.

5. The stores are large and may contain from 50,000 to more than 200,000 square feet.

6. The buildings may appear austere. Store fixtures are usually inexpensive, and with the exception of fashion areas, the use of carpeting is rare.

7. Ample free parking usually is available.

While discount stores remain popular, such stores face stiff competition from other retail outlets that have adopted the scrambled merchandising technique. Some major discounters, such as Korvette, Woolco, and W. T. Grant, have been unsuccessful in combating both competitors and recessionary economic conditions. As a result, they have closed their stores.

Some stores that originated as discount outlets, such as K-Mart and Target, have moved into higher-traffic locations and have added personal services. With the use of advertising and other promotional tools, these stores are attempting to shed their original image and become known as quality junior department stores that feature competitive prices.

Mail-Order Firms. Press a button and the gas barbecue grill on page 200 of Sears' summer catalog comes to life on the TV screen, puffing smoke while the viewer listens to the steaks sizzle. This phenomenon of a space age catalog was made possible by a videodisk and a TV screen and was part of a limited experiment at nine Sears stores in Washington, D.C. and Cincinnati, Ohio.[8] The videodisk contained all 17,872 items in the catalog, in full color and with an accompanying commercial with sound and music. By pressing a button, the viewer could zero in on still displays of the product. If the viewer pushed another button, close-up views with details and prices appeared on the screen. If the customer decided to purchase the item, a telephone call to the store would complete the sale. Thus, new technology is enabling firms that receive and process mail orders to streamline their operations.

The first **mail-order company,** that is, a company that sells and delivers by mail, was founded in 1872 by Montgomery Ward, but the number of retail mail order firms expanded quickly. While mail orders represent an old-fashioned method of retailing, they now are more popular than ever. This popularity may be attributed to one or more of the following factors.

1. In many families, both the husband and wife work, thus reducing the amount of time they are willing to spend shopping for products.

2. High prices of gasoline make mail-order buying attractive for many customers, especially those who must travel long distances for shopping.

3. Mail-order stores may offer substantial reductions in prices because the retailer is able to locate in less expensive low-traffic areas, avoids the costs of expensive fixtures and equipment, and does not need to provide large parking lots and other customer services.

4. As the population begins to include more elderly people, shut-ins, and disabled citizens who have difficulty reaching stores and completing their shopping, shopping by mail becomes a viable alternative.

The large, familiar mail-order retailers are Sears, Montgomery Ward, and J. C. Penney, which also operates a chain of mass merchandising stores. A number of other retail middlemen,

MERCHANDISE IN PRINT: CATALOG FEVER SPREADS

Today almost every top retail merchant has at least one glossy, four color catalog a year, and several have many in what is becoming one of the fastest, most reliable methods of retail marketing. Catalogs evidently have come of age. Not only are stores that never had them suddenly revving up catalog production, many that never dreamed of doing mail-order selling are beginning to encourage orders by mail and phone.

Why have retailers suddenly been struck with catalog fever? Many merchants have recognized the fact that stores, facing an increasingly competitive market, simply do not differ that much in terms of what they are selling. For merchants searching for ways to set themselves apart in consumers' minds, catalogs provide an answer. A slick, 30 to 50 page book with snappy copy and imaginative photography can give a store a competitive edge.

A second reason is that the customer does not want to spend time in stores. In some cases, the customer may not have the time. Thus, a catalog is one way of making a sale.

As far as the future is concerned, the public definitely can expect to see more catalogs in general along with more "direct response" books, allowing customers to shop at home.

Some stores such as Garfinckel's, a fashion retailer in Washington, depend on catalog production agencies to make their merchandise come alive in pictures and words. Others, such as Saks Fifth Avenue, have created their own catalog production divisions.

Adapted from Joi Nunzio, "Selling with a Special Delivery," *Advertising Age*, November 1, 1982, p. M18.

including department stores and specialty stores, have demonstrated success with more limited lines of merchandise. L. L. Bean, with only one small outdoor recreation store in Freeport, Maine, has developed a $50 million a year mail-order operation.

Some retailers operate successful mail-order operations without stores. Speigel's once operated retail stores and sold merchandise by mail order as well. In 1976, Speigel reported $265 million in sales. By 1981 sales were up to $350 million, and the company had 4,000 fewer employees.[9] The success of "The New Speigel" hinges on a new marketing strategy that considers the need of the working woman and offers products for fashion-conscious customers.

In addition to the large mail-order firms, numerous individuals have been attracted to the mail-order business. They establish a source for merchandise, print catalogs, and mail the catalogs to prospective customers. Often such firms are established as a part-time or sideline business venture.

Nonstore Retailers. Robert Tolan recently opened Tolan's Arcade in an area which he leased at the Rivership Shopping Center. The games (pinball and electronic) represent a form of retailing a recreational service through vending machines. Econ-O-Wash and Dry Cleaning, Pritts Auto Car Wash, and the Koin Kitchen, which dispenses sandwiches, soups, desserts, coffee, and soft drinks through machines, are other small retail firms that sell products and services through machines. Newspapers, cigarettes, candy, combs, handkerchiefs, and nail clippers are among the many convenience products available in vending machines. Banking services and even insurance also may be vended. The major advantages of automatic vending machines are that they do not require sales people and are available 24 hours a day.

The Retailer's Role in the Marketing Mix

Assume that you decide to open a retail establishment. Retailers, like other marketers, must make strategic decisions concerning products, prices, places, promotions, and personnel if they are to succeed as middlemen. What kinds of decisions will you be faced with and what types of strategies will you be required to devise? Let us explore some answers to these questions.

Products. Selecting products that appeal to customers requires analytical decisions. The retailer must respond to customer needs and wants, and the selection of products for resale cannot be taken lightly. If the right product is to be made available at the right place, the retailer must evaluate products on the basis of the following questions.

1. Is the item available for my department or store?

2. Does the item have appeal for a specific customer group?

3. Will it stand up well in use?

4. Is the item clearly not a duplication of products already in stock or on order?

5. Will my customers be able and willing to buy it at the retail price that I will have to set?

6. Is it a good value at its price?

7. Will it provide a satisfactory profit margin in view of volume opportunities?

8. Is the item properly packaged?

9. Are special resources available from the supplier? Are they desirable?[10]

If affirmative answers are given to most of these questions, the product is likely to be a good choice.

Staple products, that is, items for which there is a continuing and repetitive demand, present the easiest product decisions. On the other hand, fashion goods present dangerous pitfalls as well as excellent sales opportunities. If fashions change quickly, the retailer may be looking at unsalable products. Then too, product assortment must be considered. How many items of a given size, color, style, and so on, should be stocked?

Retailers have devised a number of strategies to compile the information they need for decision making. They consult with sales representatives who are employed by wholesalers and manufacturers. These representatives show retailers what is new in the market and indicate how the products are selling in other retail establishments. The retailer may visit market centers in such cities as New York, Dallas, Chicago, and Los Angeles. There the retailer personally inspects a variety of merchandise. The retailer also may attend trade shows where the products of many suppliers are on display. Retailers study trade journals such as the *Daily Men's Record, Women's Wear Daily,* and *Modern Retailer* to discover product information. Some retailers join other stores in supporting an agency that specializes in locating the most suitable products for its member stores. Many retailers use **comparison shopping,** which refers to visiting the stores of competitors to determine which products are selling well and at what prices, styles, colors, and so on.

Prices. The retailer that makes a special effort to learn more about the spending patterns of prospective customers and subsequently establishes stock price lines that match such spending patterns is more likely to experience success. Today's retailer is faced not only with shifting levels of disposable personal income but with social changes which have an impact on the prices customers are willing to pay.

Increasingly, some communities are becoming more affluent than others. One- and two-person households now outnumber larger families. New magazines such as *Metropolitan Home* and *Your Place* are evidence of the attention devoted to affluent, unmarried people. Higher-priced restaurants, clothes, and sports cars appeal to this group of customers. On the other hand, people living and working in less affluent communities and those restricted to fixed incomes find lower-priced lines of merchandise more affordable.

Places. Store location and store layout represent place decisions for retail managers. Suppose a marketer decides to open a small, independent supermarket. How will the marketer decide where to locate the store? Will the decision be based on the vacancy of suitable premises? Nearness to the marketer's home? Familiarity with the neighborhood? Availability of a small supermarket that is offered for sale? Too often, small retailers make place decisions without considering other factors. The trading area represents a geographic region from which the store will draw customers. However, one should examine the shopping patterns of customers. A store selling convenience items may benefit from being located near customers, a store selling shopping goods may benefit from being located near similar stores to permit customers to make comparisons, and a store selling specialty goods does not need to be located near others for comparison purposes. Instead, it should be accessible to customers.

Demographics and psychographics often are used in the site selection process. To select sites for a new store, a marketer might use census data, interview developers and builders, and talk to local newspapers and community groups to learn more about prospective customers. Most merchants need to develop a profile of the customer they hope to reach. Appealing to everyone just does not work anymore. Merchants need to know age groups, educational levels, earning power, and taste preferences.

Because of the increased number of site choices and a more marketing-oriented approach, retailers are probably more aware than ever of what their primary trade area must look like. Toys "R" Us, the Rochelle, New Jersey, based retailer, requires a market of at least 250,000 people of which 25 to 28 percent must be children. The market must also be large enough to support four stores, each of which will be located on the path of a major shopping mall.[11]

In any given trading area, attention must also be focused on traffic flows. Suburban shopping malls may attract a high proportion of shopper traffic in some communities, while the central downtown area affords greater shopping traffic in other communities. As the decision concerning the location variable is pondered, attention should be given to the distance shoppers must travel, the availability of public transportation, and parking convenience.

In addition, the cost of rent cannot be overlooked. While caution should be exercised, the cost of rent does not automatically mean higher prices. A larger volume of business may offset the cost of a more expensive location. Also, stores offering delivery service may find that a low-cost, out-of-the-way location adds to operating costs.

While the retailer may create a place atmosphere that is appealing and inviting to customers through store layout, it is the customers' perceptions that determine whether the store has a warm and pleasant shopping atmosphere. Some tips for retailers include these.

- Keep the color selection simple.
- Make the color scheme suitable for the products on display. Look for clues in the color of merchandise or packages.

Figure 8-4. Shopping malls are the preferred location for retail stores like Toys "R" Us, which depends on a heavy flow of consumer traffic.

- Avoid bright colors and contrasts which disturb the customers and detract from the merchandise.
- Allow sufficient space around colorful articles to avoid clashes.

Carefully planned layout may contribute to overall place efficiency and generate sales. Strategically placed impulse items often are selected by customers. Fast-moving items placed in various locations throughout the store may generate traffic past slower-moving items. This is particularly true in supermarkets and convenience food markets. By placing bread, dairy products, beverages, and similar fast-moving products in different aisles, the store leads its customers through various aisles so that they may select additional items.

Promotions. Advertising, personal selling, sales promotion, and public relations also contribute to the success of retailers. A manufacturer or wholesaler may influence place decisions by advertising a product to the extent that consumer demand is so strong that retailers are eager to stock and sell the item. Cooperative advertising also may entice retailers to handle certain products. Cooperative advertising is created when a national advertiser, usually a manufacturer, and a retailer combine advertising efforts. In such cases, both the product and the store location are emphasized. The national advertiser and the retailer share the cost of the advertising.

Today the order is change, and retailers must adapt or perish. Change and adaptation require skill and technical know-how. However, this does not mean that only retailers and sales people with years of experience can attain success. In 1980, Richard Ross, a 19-year old, opened a retail outlet, a tiny, 150 square foot shop in Cincinnati's Union Terminal Mall that he called the Jelly Bean Factory.[12] When the news media began carrying stories about President Reagan's taste for jelly beans, the shop's business boomed. But Ross bolstered his success with a special marketing technique: miniature tin scoops with which he dished out free samples to potential customers. Nearby retailers were impressed by the fact that people would line up two and three deep in front of the Jelly Bean Factory. Thus, being well prepared, well informed, and well organized does not require years of experience.

Although they are expensive, customer services may be crucial in some retail outlets. Other retailers, such as discount outlets, may find that customers expect only minimal service. Customer services sometimes may be viewed as sales promotion and public relation tools. They may prove to be very important in place strategy. Examples of customer services include the following.

- Extending credit and accepting credit cards
- Offering product guarantees in addition to those offered by the manufacturer
- Implementing a policy of accepting returned merchandise and allowing exchanges or giving refunds
- Providing free alterations or adjustments to purchases
- Offering free delivery service
- Making gift-wrapping services available
- Maintaining accessible parking facilities

Personalized services such as advising the customers and lending installation tools also may be provided. While discount stores, supermarkets, and variety stores are not expected to provide a wide array of customer services, department stores, specialty shops, and limited-line stores may find that customer patronage is increased as a result. The costs involved in providing the services usually are viewed as operational expenses as opposed to promotional expenses. Nevertheless, such services may reflect on the image of the retailer. Each service is costly to the retailer, which must accept a lower profit margin or pass the costs on to the consumer in the form of higher prices. Ample evidence exists to demonstrate that some customers are willing to pay for added services.

Other promotional considerations will be examined in detail in Unit 6.

Personnel. Retail management training or the lack of it can be of paramount importance. Continuing education programs are routinely filled with individuals seeking to improve their competencies in retail management.

Retail managers are responsible for planning, organizing, directing, and controlling.

- Planning involves setting objectives, preparing budgets, establishing policies and procedures, and making decisions.
- Organizing involves staffing, establishing positions and duties, and training personnel.
- Directing involves delegating work activities to others and leading and motivating employees.
- Controlling involves measuring and correcting.

Operational expenses, lines of merchandise carried, promotional efforts, and customer services are some of the areas that must be monitored continually. Otherwise, managers may be faced with a sluggish firm that is no longer competitive.

Management is especially important to small entrepreneurs because of the following differences between large retailers and small retailers.

1. Large retailers usually have management in depth. Small retailers, on the other hand, rely more heavily on single-level management.

2. Individual management mistakes seldom are fatal to large retailers. A single mistake on the part of a small retailer may result in closing the store.

Personnel within the firm are responsible for making decisions, plotting strategies, and performing day-to-day marketing tasks. But large retailers do not have all the advantages. Increased size may permit specialization and efficiency only up to a certain point. Large retail operations, however, may become ponderous and slow-moving. An aggressive, small retail firm that is competently managed can make a distinct advantage out of smallness. The owner may reach a decision before the decision makers in a large establishment can be assembled. On-the-spot decisions can be made in a small establishment before a supervisor in a large firm can make an appointment with a manager. Finally, the owner of a small firm can get to know the names of customers, what they are buying, and what they are thinking.

To be successful, the small retailer must develop versatility. Suppose a small retailer's interest and knowledge is in the area of selling. The retailer spends much time pursuing sales. In the meantime, buying is neglected, goods that are received pile up, recordkeeping and cost controls are left to chance, and in general, a lot of important activities are neglected. Many small retailers must wear all these hats, and some of them do not fit any too well. The small retailer can compensate somewhat for weaknesses by carefully selecting employees who can fill the gaps. In addition, the small entrepreneur can seek consultative services from the Small Business Administration, the Service Corps of Retired Executives, and knowledgeable individuals.

WHOLESALERS

Wholesalers are not as visible to the public as retailers. Nevertheless, they are important middlemen who play a large role in transferring title to and possession of products to others who buy them either for resale or for industrial use. Perhaps you have heard someone say, "I can get it for you wholesale." What is really meant is that the person can obtain a product at a reduced price. The wholesaler does not usually sell to the ultimate consumer. You learned in Chapter 5 that consumer products handled by middlemen are viewed as industrial products when they are intended for resale to a consumer. As a result, the wholesaler is viewed in terms of handling industrial products, some of which pass through industrial product channels and others of which make their journey through consumer product channels and ultimately become consumer products.

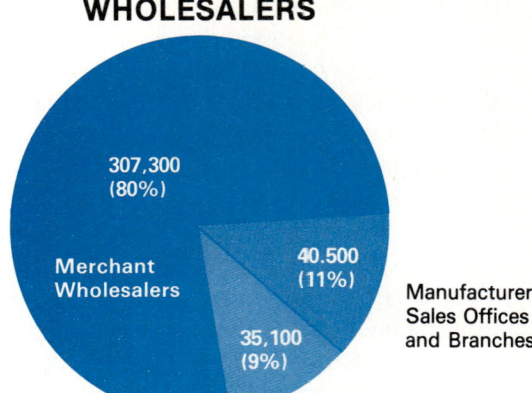

WHOLESALERS

Figure 8-5. This chart shows the type and numbers of wholesalers (rounded to nearest 100). *Source:* Statistical Abstract of the United States, *102d Edition, 1981, p. 40.*

Types of Wholesalers by Organization

Wholesalers in the United States are classified into three broad groups by the federal government: manufacturer-owned operations, merchant wholesalers, and merchandise agents and brokers. Merchandise agents and brokers were referred to as facilitators in Chapter 7 because they do not take title to the products and in many cases may not take physical possession of the products. See Figure 8-5 for a breakdown of the types and numbers of wholesalers.

Manufacturer-Owned Operations. As a general rule, manufacturers must be able to generate substantial sales for their products before it becomes profitable for them to serve as wholesalers. Keep in mind that when a manufacturer serves as a wholesaler, the manufacturer must carry out marketing activities such as selling, warehousing, transporting, financing, assuming risks, creating demand, standardizing, conducting research, and sometimes, providing managerial assistance to retailers. When manufacturers establish their own wholesaling facilities, these may be sales offices or sales branches.

Sales offices do not carry inventory and may employ only one or two sales representatives and a secretary, depending on the size of the operation. The products are shipped directly from the manufacturer to the buyer, although the sales representative may assist the buyer in assembling and servicing the product. In some cases, the manufacturer believes that the operation of a sales office is more economical than using wholesalers. Then too, the manufacturer may not be able to find desirable wholesalers to carry the products. Some wholesalers that carry competing products simply may not be interested in carrying competing brands. A sales office operation gives the manufacturer a great deal of control over how the products are sold. The sales representative may provide technical assistance to buyers and provide the manufacturer with information about the changing needs of the market.

A **sales branch** maintains inventory. As a result, quicker delivery of products to buyers may be arranged. The manufacturer, which maintains sales branches, assumes the costs associated with physical distribution (warehousing, materials handling, carrying an inventory, processing orders, assembling, shipping, and so on). Personnel employed in sales branches may provide managerial assistance to clients, conduct credit evaluations, and collect money on overdue accounts.

Merchant Wholesalers. Merchant wholesalers may be viewed as full-service wholesalers or limited-service wholesalers. **Full-service wholesalers** may handle either consumer or industrial products, and they may buy, sell, grade, store, break bulk, assemble, transport, finance, take risks, and gather market information. **Limited-service wholesalers,** on the other hand, do not engage in all these activities.

Wholesale operations, like retail establishments, may be owned by proprietors, partnerships, or corporations. Some wholesalers attempt to carry a full line of merchandise in a given field

such as hardware, groceries, or furniture, and they are referred to as "general-line wholesalers." Others may carry a limited line of items such as hosiery and are known as "specialty" or "limited-line wholesalers." These terms will be defined in greater detail when we look at types of wholesalers by operation.

Another useful classification of wholesalers is based on the territory in which they operate. **National wholesalers,** as the name implies, tend to operate on a national scale. In practice, however, they may not operate on a national scale. Instead, they may have branch houses in major cities such as New York, Chicago, and Dallas. Retail buyers may visit the branch houses, which often are located in merchandise marts or trade centers, to select merchandise and place orders. Other national wholesalers maintain their own sales forces to call on prospective buyers. Baker and Taylor Company, a national distributor of books, buys books from various publishing houses and maintains a sales force to sell to book retailers, libraries, and other middlemen. Wholesalers restricting their sales coverage to a limited number of states are known as sectional or **regional wholesalers. Local wholesalers,** such as produce wholesalers, limit their operations to a metropolitan area or an area within the confines of a radius of 75 to 150 miles of their headquarters.

Merchandise Agents and Brokers.
Agent middlemen differ from merchant wholesalers in that they do not take title to the merchandise and generally perform only a few marketing activities. Agent wholesalers operate in many different fields, but they typically concentrate on such lines as foods, grain, copper, steel, machinery, electronic supplies, and textiles. As we look at wholesalers from the point of view of their method of operations, we will examine the main types of agent middlemen, including brokers, commission houses, manufacturers' agents, selling agents, and auction companies, as well as export and import agents. Whenever a large enough group of buyers or sellers needs some

A PLACE IN THE ROCKIES FOR AN ELECTRIC SUPPLY HOUSE

Starting a distributorship from scratch sounds exciting, but few people attempt it. In 1976, however, with $10,000 in inventory and a rented shed on the edge of town, David Crum founded Crum Electric Supply Company in Casper, Wyoming. Now the company is humming with annual sales of $7 million and a staff of 32.

A degree in electrical engineering and energy development may have been factors in Crum's success. But before taking the plunge into electrical wholesaling, he took time to talk to some future customers and find out what they found missing in local service. His research showed that customers were relying on service out of Denver, at the closest. "There really wasn't anybody application-oriented, and customers needed someone like that," according to Crum.

The competing electrical supply houses looked on Crum's operation as a specialty house. Before they realized that he was selling a full line of stock, he had captured a larger percentage of the market.

Since 1976, the population of the Casper metropolitan area has increased by 10,000 (from 69,000 to 79,000). Employment in certain key areas also has advanced. Mining jobs have jumped from 4,600 to 7,200, and construction jobs have risen from 1,800 to 3,900.

special marketing service, there are always enterprising individuals who will set up a business to provide it.

Types of Wholesalers by Operation

Full-service wholesalers perform all or nearly all wholesaling service activities. These activities benfit both the producer or manufacturer and the middleman to whom the wholesaler sells. Among the possible wholesaling service activities are the following.

1. The wholesaler supplies the producer or manufacturer with a sales force. At the same time, the wholesaler forecasts customers' needs and buys accordingly.

2. Wholesalers store products, reducing the producer or manufacturer's need to carry large inventories. The warehouse expense is assumed by the wholesaler. As a result, as wholesalers purchase products, the producer or manufacturer receives payments which provide working capital.

3. The wholesaler breaks bulk and regroups into quantities more compatible with buyers' desires. In addition, the wholesaler will build assortments desired by the buyers.

4. Since the wholesaler carries an adequate inventory of products and offers the buyer prompt delivery service, the buyer may be able to reduce the size of inventory carried. This enables the buyer to use the funds that otherwise would be invested in inventory as working capital.

5. The wholesaler reduces the credit risks for producers and manufacturers. A distant manufacturer or producer selling directly may have diffi-

The growth experienced by Casper dovetailed perfectly with Crum's plans for his expanding electrical distributorship. In 1979, Crum opened a branch in Gillette, Wyoming, followed by another in Evanston, Wyoming, in 1981.

Together, the three locations put six outside sales people on the road and keep another eight busy with inside sales. The sparse population and the huge distances between cities in Wyoming impose special problems on the sales force. Crum Electric came up with a unique way of coping with the distances. Rather than making sales calls in the traditional sedan, sales people visit accounts in three-quarter ton pickup trucks. That way they can carry odds and ends to customers as well as stock transfers between branches.

Throughout the wholesaling industry, there are still niches a smart entrepreneur can fill. The ability to perceive those niches may well be the quality that distinguishes success from mediocrity.

Adapted from Mary Kuntz, "The Frontier Spirit Pays Off," *Electrical Wholesaling*, August 1982, pp. 34–36.

culty evaluating all the potential credit risks presented by various buyers. The wholesaler, on the other hand, may be more familiar with the buyers and in a better position to evaluate their credit status.

6. The wholesaler often extends credit to buyers, sometimes for several months. In essence, the wholesaler is financing the customers for a period of time. This may be one reason why customers prefer to be served by a wholesaler.

7. The wholesaler is in a position to provide information to the producer or manufacturer as well as to the buyer. Since the wholesaler is close to the buyers and is able to evaluate their reactions, passing this information along to the producers or manufacturers may reduce the need for some marketing research. At the same time, the wholesaler's sales force may be specialists in the products they sell. They may provide a buyer with price and technical information as well as suggestions on how to install and assemble products, sell products, and operate more efficiently.

8. If sales representatives are sent to buyers, the buyers are relieved of the responsibility of looking for supply sources. The buying function is simplified because the buyer needs only evaluate the various products offered.

9. Since the wholesaler owns the inventory, the wholesaler and buyer can complete a sales transaction without the assistance of other intermediaries such as an agent or broker.

The wholesaling activities described above are elements of the wholesaling functions that were presented in Table 7-2. Let us look at the full-service wholesalers who perform these activities.

Full-Service Wholesalers. Petroleum distributors want to have the capacity to serve the total product needs of service stations, garages, and owners of truck fleets. A dental supply distributor strives to maintain a complete inventory of products needed by dentists. A food service equipment distributor is interested in providing the original equipment, additional equipment that is needed later, and repair parts and service to restaurants and fast-food outlets. These middlemen are known as **general merchandise wholesalers.** That is, they carry a general assortment of products in two or more distinct lines. The petroleum distributor may offer gasoline, oil, oil filters, spark plugs, fan belts, radiator hose, and a general assortment of other products needed by service station operators.

A **general-line wholesaler** offers a broad assortment of products within a single merchandise line or, at most, limited products in closely related lines. General-line wholesalers are important middlemen for products such as drugs, hardware, and plumbing and heating equipment and supplies. A pharmaceutical distributor, for exam-

ple, may sell lotions, medicated soaps, and elastic support bands in addition to drugs.

Specialty wholesalers carry only part of a merchandise line. However, within the restricted offerings, they handle a very complete assortment. In the wholesale grocery trade, for instance, a specialty wholesaler may handle frozen pizzas. Pizzas made from a variety of ingredients and packaged in a variety of sizes would be offered. Specialty wholesalers are likely to provide strong promotional support for the products handled. A distributor of frozen pizzas, for example, may handle in-store promotions by erecting a special display and arranging for bite-sized samples to be given to prospective customers.

Full service is not necessarily related to the variety of product lines a wholesaler handles. Full service refers to the fact that the wholesaler performs all or nearly all wholesaling service activities.

You may buy wheat from farmers to resell at a later time to food processors (flour mills and cereal manufacturers). This is the only product you handle. You receive the wheat and then clean, dry, and store it. You break bulk into truckload or carload quantities, depending on the needs of the buyer. You arrange for transportation to the buyer and extend the buyer credit. You assume risks while the wheat is in your possession, since it may spoil, become infested with insects, or be subject to flood or fire loss. Perhaps the price will drop while the wheat is in your possession. You offer the buyer information about new varieties of wheat available, competitors' prices, and more efficient materials handling systems. You are a full-service merchant wholesaler, and you handle only one product.

If a marketer employs from 1 to 25 employees, the firm is considered to be a small wholesaling firm. A medium-size wholesaling organization is slightly larger, with 25 to 100 employees. Should more than 100 employees work for a mar-

Figure 8-6. A general-line candy wholesaler offers a broad assortment of merchandise that is typically sold in candy stores.

keter, the firm is considered a large wholesaling operation.[13]

While full-service wholesalers are called merchant wholesalers or industrial distributors, some of these middlemen are identified by more specific titles because of the nature of their operations. **Rack jobbers** are wholesale middlemen who sell consumer products to selected types of retailers. Hair-care salons, for example, may be furnished with an attractive display rack stocked with shampoos, rinses, sprays, brushes, and combs by a rack jobber. Cigars and tobacco, greeting cards, snack foods, paperback books, and magazines are among the products commonly sold to supermarkets and drugstores by such jobbers. With the expansion of scrambled merchandising, the importance of the rack jobber has increased. Rack jobbers are expanding into hardware, variety, and other types of retail stores and service establishments.

As a wholesale entrepreneur, the rack jobber has become an attractive middleman within selected channels of distribution for a variety of reasons. A few rack jobbers can furnish a wide variety of products to retailers. The rack jobber supplies the racks or display units to shelve the products and stocks the units with only the fastest moving merchandise. The L'Eggs units are an example of one of the most successful racks. The rack jobber usually but not always places the products into retail establishments on **consignment.** That is, the retailer is not billed until the products are sold. The merchandise is prepriced, and the retailer is responsible only for providing floor space and collecting the money for purchases at checkout stations.

Why would a retailer purchase products from a rack jobber? Here are some reasons.

1. If the products are placed in the retailer's establishment on consignment, the retailer need not tie up funds in inventory.

2. The rack jobber will service the rack. As a result, the retailer need not place orders or become involved in materials handling.

3. The rack jobber will provide a continuous and reliable source of products.

Why would a middleman choose to operate as a rack jobber? The reasons may not be as obvious, but they are valid.

1. By placing products into a retail establishment, the rack jobber moves them out of a warehouse and into an area which offers potential sales.

2. Because the rack jobber establishes records of retailers' needs quickly, buying can be adjusted to prevent over- or understocking.

3. Once the units are placed in a retail store, it is likely that the retailer will remain loyal to the rack jobber and less likely to buy from competitors. As a result, the rack jobber establishes a place to market the products.

Other full-service wholesale middlemen include agricultural grain terminals, large-scale import and export merchants, and petroleum bulk plants.

Wholesalers operating **agricultural grain terminals** who purchase grain from local elevators located throughout the grain-producing states are, as was mentioned earlier, usually identified as full-service middlemen. They in turn sell the grain to food processors such as milling companies, cereal manufacturers, distillers, exporters, and the government. By taking advantage of carload and truckload rates and differences in market prices from area to area, the terminal operator is able to make a profit. Local elevators that are operated as smaller wholesale operations are willing to purchase grain from farmers and resell to the terminal because local elevator operators often lack sufficient storage space and because prices are subject to fluctuations between the time when purchases are initially made and the time when grain is needed for processing.

The typical large-scale **import or export merchant** is classified as a full-service wholesaler. The emphasis on international trade today is increasing the importance of this middleman. As was mentioned in Chapter 7, facilitators (brokers and agents) often have been used to bring buyers and sellers together because of the reluctance of merchant wholesalers to invest in an inventory that in some cases may take several weeks to transit. Nevertheless, full-service import and export merchants are needed to bring products and buyers together. Import and export merchants may maintain branches in a number of countries. In addition to the services normally expected of full-service wholesalers, they must deal with customs, insurance, currency fluctuations, and more complex shipping arrangements.

Petroleum bulk plants may be owned by independent wholesalers or in some cases by petroleum refiners. Independent wholesalers receive, store, and ship fuel oils, diesel fuel, gasoline, and other petroleum products. Wholesalers of petroleum products may sell to service stations for resale to consumers, to commercial users such as airline terminals, or to the ultimate customer for home heating purposes. When petroleum bulk plants sell to the ultimate consumer, they assume the position of retail middleman as opposed to wholesale middleman.

Limited-Service Wholesalers.
Limited-service wholesalers perform only a few of the activities normally associated with wholesaling operations. They do, however, accept title to products sold. Thus, limited-service wholesalers buy and sell as well as perform some but not all wholesaling service activities. Included among such middlemen are truck wholesalers, cash and carry wholesalers, mail-order wholesalers, and drop shippers.

Truck wholesalers maintain warehouses stocked with fast-moving products which they sell and deliver to retailers along a predetermined route. An example involving Lance Incorporated was presented in Chapter 7. Potato chips, bakery items, fruits and vegetables, and tools for service stations and automotive repair garages are also examples of products sold by truck wholesalers. As a specialty, or limited-line, wholesaler, this

middleman can furnish fresh products, enabling the retailer to buy in smaller quantities and reduce the risk of loss. Orders are small, and the cost of operating a warehouse and trucks, which frequently must be refrigerated, is quite high.

Cash and carry wholesalers do not provide credit or make deliveries. These wholesalers are used primarily by small retailers for products that are not immediately available through wholesale merchants. A small meat market, for example, may go directly to a seafood wholesaler and purchase fresh seafood products for immediate sales.

Mail-order wholesalers may specialize in a limited number of products, including jewelry, cosmetics, specialty foods, and other items. They send colorful catalogs to retailers and to industrial and business buyers depicting the products offered. They maintain no sales representatives, and their customers usually are found in small outlying areas. Orders are received by mail or telephone, filled, and sent by the most efficient means of transportation.

Drop shippers derive their name from the fact that the products sold are delivered directly from the manufacturer to the retailer or industrial buyer. These middlemen do take title to the goods, but they do not accept actual possession. Drop shippers may sell coal, lumber, steel, and other products that often are sold in carload quantities. In such cases, it is desirable to minimize the physical handling of the product. Chemicals and other products subject to deterioration during periods of extended storage also may be sold by drop shippers.

Facilitating Middlemen.
Manufacturers' agents, selling agents, import and export agents, brokers, commission houses, and auction companies are independent middlemen that do not take title to products. Instead, they actively negotiate the transfer of title from the seller to the buyer.

Manufacturers' agents and selling agents, which were discussed in Chapter 7, operate on a contractual arrangement with the seller. By contrast, import and export agents, brokers, and commission houses may act on behalf of either the seller or the buyer. Auction companies always represent the seller.

Sellers often choose to be represented by a manufacturers' agent for the following reasons.

1. They offer an extended contractual arrangement to sell the seller's products within an exclusive territory. The seller then may choose other direct or indirect channels for other territories.

2. They represent sellers of noncompeting but related products.

3. They agree to allow the seller to retain authority with regard to prices and terms of sale.

4. In many cases, in both industrial and consumer markets, the manufacturer's agent can, because of intimate contact with the market, offer advice to the manufacturer or producer on a wide variety of matters, including styling, design, and pricing.

However, selling agents have more authority. They handle all the manufacturer or producer's output and in essence become the firm's marketing department. Some marketers are cautious about choosing selling agents because they want to avoid putting all their eggs in one basket. Because of the contractual arrangement, the manufacturer or producer may be in trouble if the selling agent does not perform well. If the manufacturer or producer can make a good choice, however, there are benefits to be gained.

1. By taking over the marketing activities, the selling agent frees the manufacturer or producer to concentrate on production.

2. Some selling agents provide financial assistance to manufacturers and producers. This practice was initiated years ago, when selling agents in some cases were financially stronger than manufacturers and producers.

3. A selling agent who is close to buyers may offer the manufacturer or producer guidance in styling, design, and pricing.

4. Sometimes the selling agent may take over some or all responsibility for sales promotion and advertising.

Selling agents are common in the marketing of both industrial and consumer products. They frequently handle textiles, industrial machinery, metals, chemicals, and canned foods.

Another group of agents engaged in assisting foreign or domestic buyers and sellers in negotiating sales are known as **import and export agents.** They should not be confused with import and export merchants since the agents do not take title to the products exchanged. Instead, they function much like a broker, and their primary responsibil-

Figure 8-7. Insurance is one example of a service frequently sold through brokers.

ity is to bring buyers and sellers together. Often they tend to specialize by product. An import agent, for example, may seek buyers for exporters of guava fruit grown in tropical countries. The buyers may be retailers, wholesalers, or food processors.

Often, **brokers** are selected to negotiate purchases or sales because they tend to specialize. That is, each broker tends to specialize in arranging transactions for a limited number of products or services, and this causes the broker to be well informed about conditions in particular markets. The broker is employed more often by the owner of goods seeking a buyer than by a buyer seeking a supply. Brokers are prevalent in the food industry, selling seasonal products. A small cannery that operates only 3 months each year may employ a broker to find buyers for the canned products. When the transaction is completed, the broker receives a commission from the buyer or seller who engaged the service.

Commission houses, which sometimes are referred to as commission merchants, are independent firms specializing in products offered in central markets. They are similar to brokers except that they actually handle goods, complete transactions, and remit the selling price (minus their commission) to the seller. Commission houses frequently are used by producers or manufacturers that are unable to accompany each shipment to the central market. The commission house accepts the products and makes them available for the buyer to inspect. While the commission house sells products at the best possible price, there is usually no problem over prices because they are determined by supply and demand at the time the products are sold.

> Tony Morgan raises beef cattle in Greeley, Colorado. When the feeder cattle are ready for market, Tony ships them to stockyards in Denver or Kansas City. He finds it impossible to accompany each shipment personally. A commission house receives the cattle at the stockyards and negotiates with meat-packing companies to sell the livestock.

Commission houses are used to handle other farm produce. In addition, it is common for small firms producing textiles to use commission houses to reach buyers in central markets without having to maintain their own sales forces.

As implied by the name, **auction companies** accept possession of but not title to sellers' products and offer the products for sale through competitive bidding. The auction method of selling leaf tobacco dates back to the time of the Civil War. Other products frequently but not always supplied by agricultural producers are sold by auction. It was mentioned in Chapter 7 that automobiles sometimes are bought and sold by middlemen at auctions. It also is common for firms to liquidate their stock, fixtures and equipment, and even land and buildings at auctions. Auction companies are able to bring about a rapid transaction, although the price is determined by competitive bidding, not by the seller. Auction companies collect from the buyers and remit the proceeds, minus their commissions, to the seller.

The Wholesaler's Role in the Marketing Mix

The wholesaler's distribution functions encompass a broad marketing area that starts at the agricultural or extraction point and moves to the manufacturer's, fabricator's, refiner's, or processor's plant. The wholesaler's services are needed again as the products leave the plants and are moved to the next buyer, for example, a manufacturer that uses the fabricated products, an institutional buyer that perhaps represents a hospital, or a retailer who will resell the products. The wholesaler operates in an environment of constant change. As a result, the wholesaler is concerned with the marketing mix—products, prices, places, and promotions—as well as the personnel needed to serve effectively as decision makers and perform the necessary activities.

Products. In the marketing field, there is an old adage that nothing happens until somebody sells something. Conversely, it must be equally true that nothing happens until somebody buys something. Planning purchases for resale involves many of the same considerations applicable to purchase planning by retailers.

If you decide to become a wholesaler, you will find that buying for resale is of major importance. Products which you handle must permit subsequent resale at prices customers are willing to pay while returning a reasonable profit on your investment. You or your purchasing agent or buyer will look at products in terms of cost, quantity, quality, service, and perhaps even more important, the opportunity for profitability.

Regardless of whether the wholesaler is classified as a general-line or a limited-line operation, there are two important purchasing considerations.

1. The quality of products handled should be the best possible for each price range. Suppliers of brand labels usually maintain quality standards, but for some private brands, wholesalers have to set up their own procedures for assuring quality.

2. Wholesalers must be concerned about service from the source of supply. The product should be available in the quantities wanted at the time desired. In addition, the wholesaler may pose the question, Will the supplier do everything possible to promote the product and obtain business from and for the wholesaler?

The number of products to buy complicates the task of the wholesaler that attempts to make products available at the right time. Computers often are used to indicate quantities of products needed to replenish inventory to optimal levels. A manufacturer or retailer, however, may run special promotions on given products, and then the wholesaler will view a dwindling supply or, worse, run completely out before a new order is received. Then too, seasonal fluctuations can mean that a wholesaler's inventory is inadequate to meet increased demand for products.

Prices. The purpose of price setting by wholesalers is to recover the cost of acquisition,

"Just ask it. 'How many burgers can the Free World eat?'"

Figure 8-8. Information about consumer demand is essential!

storage, and marketing in addition to earning a fair return on investment. However, the value and price determined by the wholesaler must approximate the value and price determinations made by the buyer. Otherwise, wholesalers will find that potential buyers refuse to purchase the products handled. Other considerations are also important to the wholesaler, such as price stabilization, market share maintenance, profit maximization, and competitive action or reaction.

Many wholesalers use a "standard" markup, that is, a percentage that is applied to each product line or to the entire inventory. Profit maximization means determining the price which will achieve the maximum profit. If the wholesaler's price is below a point at which buyers are willing to pay, profit is lost. If the price is above that point, sales are lost. Although it is difficult to determine and implement, there is a point at which profit can be maximized.

Wholesalers, like other business firms, face competition. Other wholesalers offer similar products. As a result, competition becomes a factor in price setting. Cash discounts, trade discounts, and quantity discounts also influence the actual price that the wholesaler's customers must pay. These discounts are defined and explained in Chapter 11.

TABLE 8-3
U.S. WHOLESALERS: WHERE ARE THEY LOCATED?

Geographic Regions	Number of Establishments
Northeastern states (ME, NH, VT, MA, RI, CT)	18,830
Middle Atlantic states (NY, NJ, PA)	68,682
East north-central states (OH, IN, IL, MI, WI)	67,201
West north-central states (MN, IA, MO, ND, SD NE, KS)	39,814
South Atlantic states (DE, MD, DC, VA, WV, NC, SC, GA, FL)	54,186
East south-central states (KY, TN, AL, MS)	21,844
West south-central states (AR, LA, OK, TX)	42,323
Mountain states (MT, ID, WY, CO, NM, AZ, UT, NV)	19,040
Pacific states (WA, OR, CA, AK, HI)	50,917
United States	Total 382,837

Source: *Statistical Abstract of the United States,* 102d ed., 1981, p. 821.

Places. The goal of place management for both full- and limited-service wholesalers is to maintain optimum inventories and move the products to the buyers when they are needed. Local wholesalers may operate from a single site. Rack jobbers, truck wholesalers, and cash and carry wholesalers are likely to locate in a central spot within the area which they serve. Regional and national wholesalers, however, may operate from multiple warehouses and perform service activities in more than one place. Determining the ideal location for wholesale establishments is an exceedingly complex undertaking.

Transportation is a major factor. What will it cost to move the products in? To move them out? What types of transit carriers are available? How frequently do they make trips to designated areas? This is only the beginning. The nature of the product may be a determinant in choosing a location for a wholesaler. Petroleum bulk plants, grain terminal operations, and firms that handle flammable or hazardous products may be restricted to certain locations because of stringent zoning ordinances. A wholesaler may require special power sources to operate refrigerated units or grain dryers. Like retailers, wholesalers must be concerned with the cost of renting facilities.

The wholesaler has to examine each factor and establish alternatives before reaching a decision about location. This is a common occurrence in your daily life, although you may not stop to think about how to make decisions. Suppose you have an appointment downtown this afternoon. You may walk, although it will take more time to reach your destination. You may take a cab, but you cannot count on getting one when needed and reaching your destination on time. You may drive your own automobile, but parking lots are crowded and expensive. In deciding what to do, you simply measure the advantages and disadvantages of each alternative and select the one you believe to be most advantageous. General-line and specialty wholesalers go through the same process in selecting a location.

Facilitators, that is, middlemen who do not take possession of products, are likely to work out of offices. Their offices will be located in areas where their services are needed. They frequently choose locations in central market areas.

Promotions. Like manufacturers and retailers, wholesalers find that promotional efforts are necessary. The promotions may be designed to achieve either of two objectives. The wholesaler may need to promote the firm, that is, build an image that buyers (manufacturers, retailers, industrial users, and so forth) will find desirable. The wholesaler also may use promotional efforts to move products to buyers.

Wholesalers survive in a distribution channel only so long as they can perform their activities more efficiently and effectively than a competitor. It is therefore important that the wholesaler become known as a reliable source of products, a cooperating link within the channel, and a supplier that buyers wish to deal with. Many wholesalers take the initiative in letting buyers know that they are dependable, courteous, and ethical. They may highlight these facts in ads placed in trade journals that are received by buyers. But actions speak louder than words. Word of mouth soon travels through the industry, and buyers usually recognize reputable wholesalers.

Products may be promoted in various ways. Again, ads appearing in trade journals make buyers aware of the wholesaler's line of products. Seasonal promotions often offer a large price reduction for items purchased several months in advance of the normal season. The reduction is possible because the wholesaler moves products in possession to the buyer and recovers the money invested in the products. Wholesalers also find that special deals such as two-for-one sales or give-away-with-purchase packages have appeal to retail buyers and other customers. Providing retailers with point-of-purchase displays also has proved to be an effective sales promotional device for wholesalers.

Personnel. Full- and limited-service wholesalers need talented personnel in key positions to be able to respond to and meet the challenges of the 1980s. Warehouse managers, traffic managers, purchasing agents, inventory control managers, supervisors of order pickers, sales representatives, credit and collection managers, and office managers are examples of positions of leadership which may be needed by large wholesalers.

Expanded distributorships have grown so rapidly in the past few years that skilled supervisors and managers have not been available in adequate numbers to train and supervise new employees. As a result, wholesalers and their trade associations have been speaking out about their personnel and training needs. Community colleges, private business schools, vocational-technical institutions, and universities recently have begun to respond to the problem by offering courses and programs to train people for entry into the wholesaling industry.

Nevertheless, the problem of attracting talented personnel will not dissipate in the near future. Robotic technology, mechanized storage and retrieval equipment, and computerized control systems are proliferating in large wholesale firms so rapidly that sufficient numbers of trained operating and maintenance personnel are difficult to recruit. In addition, individuals trained in product or service technology are needed by various wholesalers. The fundamentals of electricity, for example, are just as important as the principles of distribution for anyone who aspires to a career in the electrical supplies distribution industry. Some wholesalers have employed individuals trained as pharmacists to assume responsible positions in the distribution of health-care products. With over 100 product line associations serving the distribution industry in the United States, many distributors are looking for people who have knowledge of their products or services.

Since many of the country's wholesalers are small and cannot afford to offer formal training programs for new employees, how are they to fill their needs for personnel? Wholesalers should continue to emphasize the need for trained personnel. As taxpayers, they should encourage their community colleges and postsecondary vocational-technical institutions to add programs to the curriculum that will train individuals to assume the positions that need to be filled. They should be willing to serve on advisory committees set up by institutions to obtain suggestions and advice. Finally, wholesalers can assist educational institutions in training personnel for wholesale distribution positions by making internships available to students.

- Middlemen play an important role in creating place, time, and possession utilities. The nation's 2 million retail establishments and 383,000 wholesalers and facilitators serve as middlemen.

- Chain stores are centrally owned and managed and sell similar products. Independents, on the other hand, are singularly owned and operated by proprietors, partnerships, and corporations. Independents sometimes band together in a voluntary chain to set up their own wholesaling organization.

- Mass merchandisers have started looking at smaller cities and towns as places to offer their products. They also are adding services as they diversify their operations.

- Retailers are discovering that catalogs are becoming one of the fastest, most reliable methods of selling.

- Retailers are increasingly concerned about their marketing mix, that is, products, prices, places, and promotions as well as personnel who make strategic decisions and perform operational activities.

- Wholesalers are classified into three groups: manufacturer-owned operations, full-service and limited-service merchant wholesalers, and facilitators who do not take title to the products.

- Sales offices do not carry inventory, while sales branches do maintain inventories of products.

- General-merchandise wholesalers carry a general assortment of products in two or more lines. General-line wholesalers carry a broad assortment of products within a single line, while specialty wholesalers carry a very complete assortment of products but only in a partial line.

- Facilitating middlemen are manufacturers' agents, selling agents, import and export agents, brokers, commission houses, and auc-

tion companies that negotiate the transfer of title from the seller to the buyer.

- One of the problems faced by wholesalers today is attracting talented personnel with specialized skills and knowledge.

KEY TERMS AND CONCEPTS

agent middlemen
agricultural grain
   terminals
auction companies
brokers
cash and carry
   wholesalers
chain stores
combination
   supermarkets
commission houses
comparison shopping
consignment
convenience stores
creative
   merchandising
department stores
discount stores
discount supermarkets
drop shippers
full-service
   wholesalers
general-line
   wholesalers
general-merchandise
   wholesalers

import-export agents
import-export
   merchants
independent stores
limited-line stores
limited-service
   wholesalers
local wholesalers
mail-order company
mail-order wholesalers
mass merchandisers
national wholesalers
petroleum bulk plants
rack jobbers
regional wholesalers
retailing
sales branches
sales offices
scrambled
   merchandising
specialty stores
specialty wholesalers
supermarkets
truck wholesalers
variety stores
voluntary chain

DISCUSSION QUESTIONS

1. Some people believe the middlemen push prices up. Farmers, for example, sometimes make statements such as, "The middleman is responsi-

ble for high prices at the retail level." Do you agree? Explain.

2. What are the distinguishing characteristics between independent stores and chains?

3. In the story "Factory Discount Outlets versus Full-Price Retailers" on page 223, it is obvious that in some cases conflicts are created. In Chapter 7, you learned about horizontal, intertype, and vertical conflicts. Which of these types of conflicts have occurred? Why?

4. What is the difference between a general-merchandise wholesaler and a full-service wholesaler?

5. Explain the differences between a cooperative chain and a voluntary chain.

6. What selling points might a rack jobber use to encourage a retailer to stock the products offered by the rack jobber?

NOTES

1. Adapted from Barbara Toman, "Department Stores Start Adding Seminars and Services to Attract Working Women," *Wall Street Journal,* July 19, 1982, p. 17. Reprinted by permission of the *Wall Street Journal.* © Dow Jones & Company, Inc. All Rights Reserved.

2. Harland E. Samson, Wayne G. Little, and John W. Wingate, *Retail Merchandising,* 9th ed., South-Western Publishing Company, Cincinnati, 1982, p. 51.

3. Adapted from Jerome E. McCarthy and Stanley J. Shapiro, *Basic Marketing,* 2d ed., Irwin-Dorsey Limited, Georgetown, Ontario, 1979, p. 367.

4. Mary D. Troxell and Elaine Stone, *Fashion Merchandising,* 3d ed., McGraw-Hill, New York, 1981, p. 232.

5. "Where Consumers Buy Legal Advice at Retail," *Business Week,* July 2, 1979, p. 44.

6. Steve Weiner, "With Many Cities Full of Stores, Chains Open Outlets in Small Towns," *Wall Street Journal,* May 28, 1981, pp. 1–19. Reprinted by permission of the *Wall Street Journal.* © Dow Jones & Company, Inc. All Rights Reserved.

7. "Nothing Really Changes," *Forbes,* January 23, 1978, p. 68.

8. "Sears' Catalog Goes Electric," Sunday *Herald Times,* Bloomington-Bedford, Ind., May 10, 1981, p. 51.

9. Associated Press, "Speigel's Sights Are on the Elite Crowd," *The Pantagraph,* Bloomington, Ill., September 13, 1981, p. E-6.

10. Harland E. Samson, Wayne G. Little, and John W. Wingate, *Retail Merchandising,* 9th ed., South-Western Publishing Company, Cincinnati, 1982, p. 245.

11. Janet Neiman, "Retailers Should Know Their Place," *Advertising Age,* November 1, 1982, p. M22.

12. Dean Rotbart, "Starting a Business Separates the Men from the Boys," *Wall Street Journal,* August 12, 1981, p. 1. Reprinted by permission of the *Wall Street Journal.* © Dow Jones & Company, Inc. All Rights Reserved.

13. William P. Danenburg, Russell L. Moncrief, and William E. Taylor, *Introduction to Wholesale Distribution,* © 1978, pp 26–28. Reprinted by permission of Prentice-Hall, Inc., Englewood Cliffs, N.J.

CHAPTER
9
PHYSICAL DISTRIBUTION

Anheuser-Busch Incorporated has shared a common problem with other beer producers. Tests have shown that beer breaks down and becomes stale when stored at temperatures above 42 degrees. Demand for beer always increases in the summer months. Breweries, however, have been unable to produce at peak capacity during off seasons because of the temperature problem in unrefrigerated warehouses. How can beer producers build inventories during slack beer seasons for distribution during peak seasons, particularly the hot summer months?

During 1981, Anheuser-Busch produced 58 million barrels of beer. A goal was set to increase production to 80 million barrels in 4 years and increase Anheuser-Busch's 30 percent market share to 40 percent. To achieve this goal, the storage problem had to be solved. Anheuser-Busch launched a program with its distributors—about 900 across the country—to install controlled-environment warehouses in which beer is stored at 42 degrees year-round. To offset the high costs of operating cooling units, the inside walls of warehouses were lined with 12 inches of insulation.

One distribution problem, however, often leads to another. The distributors, who were small entrepreneurs acting as wholesalers for a local area, quickly discovered that beer containers sweat when the temperature is dropped to 42 degrees. The sweat, or condensation, caused damage to the cartons and created problems in physically handling the merchandise. As a result, packaging had to be improved.[1]

This is just one example of challenges encountered in the physical distribution of goods and services as attempts are made to achieve the marketing objective of delivering the right products to the right customer at the right time and at the right place and at the right price.

PHYSICAL DISTRIBUTION: A DEFINITION

The National Council of Physical Distribution Management (NCPDM) has defined **physical distribution** as follows.

A term employed to describe the broad range of activities concerned with efficient movement of finished products from the end of the assembly line to the consumer, and in some cases includes the movement of raw materials from the source of supply to the beginning of the production line. These activities include freight transportation, warehousing, materials handling, protective packaging, inventory control, warehouse site selection, order processing, market forecasting, and customer service.[2]

Physical distribution thus involves more than a manufacturer's shipping clerk checking the number of cartons loaded on a truck and waving good-bye as the truck pulls away from the loading dock. As products are chartered for their course or journey through the channel, a number of activities are essential in the development and operation of efficient flow systems.

A number of important decisions and activities must be completed before products actually can be shipped. As a marketer develops the place aspect of the marketing mix, decisions are influenced to a considerable degree by the channel captain.

Physical distribution decisions include the need to do the following.

1. Choose the locations where inventory should be stored

2. Enter into contracts with middlemen to assure storage space or establish warehouses

3. Plan a materials handling procedure

4. Design an inventory control system

5. Arrive at procedures to be followed in processing orders

6. Select methods of transportation

Obviously, effectiveness and efficiency in the process of moving products along their journey are dependent on sound decisions. Marketers' skills in making and carrying out these decisions give the goods both place and time utilities, as was discussed in Chapter 1. Such skills are needed because nearly *half* the cost of marketing is spent on physical distribution.

Choosing Storage Location

Various factors should be considered in arriving at decisions about where inventory should be stored. Economies of time and transportation costs often dictate that warehouses or distribution centers be located in areas where there is a huge demand for the product. Manufacturer-owned warehouse facilities become transfer points to serve wholesalers, manufacturers' branch outlets, and retailers. Wholesaler-owned warehouse facilities serve other retailers.

In practice, the costs of owning or renting and operating several dispersed warehouses also must be considered. Thus, marketers must try to answer the question, Should the inventory be dispersed in several warehouses in scattered locations or concentrated in fewer warehouses in more centralized locations? Obviously, for small convenience items such as candy bars, the product will pass through wholesaler-owned warehouses that are dispersed across the country. But manufacturer's replacement parts for cars, for example, will be distributed to dealers from fewer manufacturer-owned warehouses.

This leads to another question: Who chooses the locations? The channel captain, or channel leader, often is strong enough to dictate the locations. However, the nature of the product and the distribution strategy may influence the need for several decentralized locations or fewer centralized locations. Henry Field Seed and Nursery Company, located in Shenandoah, Iowa, sells products through mail orders and consequently does not need additional locations. In the opening passages of this chapter, however, it was pointed out that Anheuser-Busch requires approximately 900 wholesalers with warehouses across the country.

Information derived from research proves valuable in making a decision on the number and location of distribution centers. After gathering information about transportation methods, freight

WAREHOUSE LOCATION

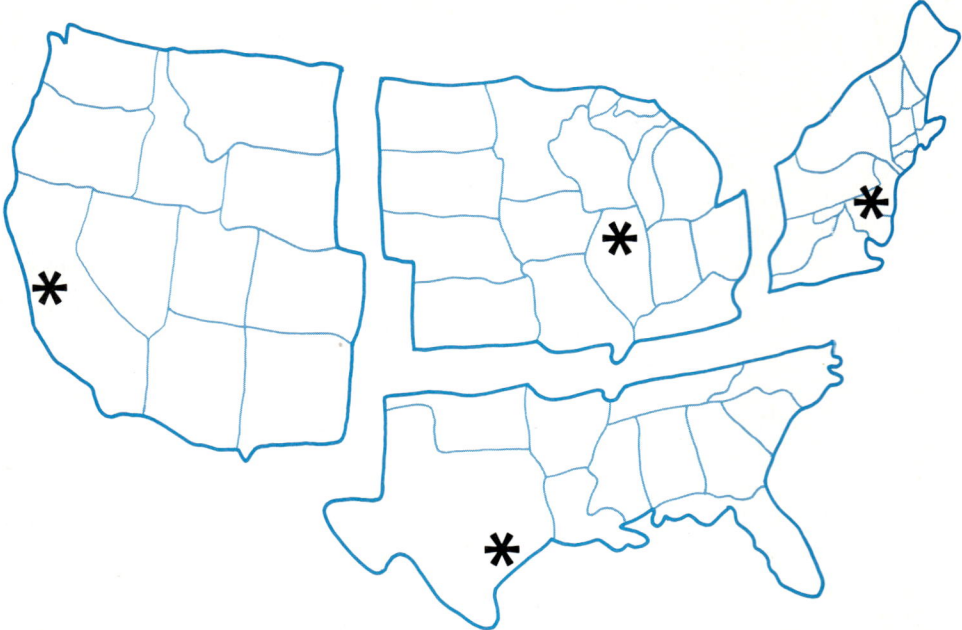

Figure 9-1. A manufacturer of smoke detectors, whose products are distributed nationally, may choose to locate warehouses in various geographical regions.

rates, transit times, warehousing costs, and customer buying patterns along with other factors, a company can simulate the operations and predict the costs of several location plans.

Distribution Centers

In recent years, many manufacturers have established one or more large distribution centers. **Distribution centers** are special warehouses designed to store products for short periods of time and speed the flow of products. These huge centers, aided by the latest techniques in computer-programmed inventory processing, automated materials handling, and an improved selection of alternative transportation modes, are able to process orders quickly. Their costs of operation often are offset by reducing the number of warehouses, eliminating out-of-stock situations, and improving the communications systems.

A few years ago, Libby, McNeill & Libby established five distribution centers to replace 214 warehouses. International Minerals and Chemical Corporation reduced annual operating costs by 35 percent after establishing 13 centers to replace 44 warehouses.[3]

The decision to use centralized distribution centers as opposed to dispersed warehouses should be weighed carefully. First, a marketer should recognize that a close relationship exists between physical distribution and sales. The speed and cost of delivery have a positive correlation with sales. If products are unavailable or if the price is too high, sales will suffer. In addition, the capital of a firm is used more effectively when inventory levels are matched closely with sales expectations. The volume of products stored and the length of time for which they are stored can lead to financial problems. Seldom-needed products that must be carried in several dispersed warehouses represent capital that could be invested in more salable products. Thus, the speed of delivery, the cost of delivery, and a coordinated inventory become important factors in decisions concerning storage locations.

WAREHOUSES

For many products, the warehouse merely serves as a protective storage facility. For other products, such as whiskey, cheese, and lumber, the warehouse serves as a holding facility in which the product can age or season. Some warehouses must be equipped with special refrigeration units to serve as a holding point for food, chemicals, and other perishable items. Other special warehouse facilities are needed for grain, which may absorb dampness while stored, for volatile bulk petroleum products, and for other bulk liquids.

Manufacturers, wholesalers, and retailers have three alternatives to examine before making a decision about warehouses.

1. They can purchase private warehouses.
2. They can lease warehouses.
3. They can use public warehouses.

After a brief description of each alternative, we shall explore the factors that should be examined before making a decision.

Private Warehouses

A **private warehouse** may be owned by a manufacturer, wholesaler, or retailer. Private warehouses owned by wholesalers or retailers are likely to be located near the place where the product will be needed. Manufacturers ship products to regional warehouses where the products are stored until orders are received.

Leased Warehouses

A **leased warehouse** operates in the same manner as a private warehouse. The lessee, or the one who leases (manufacturer, wholesaler, or retailer), obtains a storage facility in return for rental payments. In essence, a leased warehouse serves as a private warehouse. The lessee has fewer rights than an owner, however, and may not be permitted to change the premises or sublease any or all of the storage facility.

Since privately owned and leased facilities are distinguished only by rental payments, leased facilities are mentioned here only because such rental payments represent an inflexible business expense. When such a facility is owned outright, the manufacturer, wholesaler, or retailer may depreciate it as a tax-deductible item over a number of years. Rental payments represent business expenses and must be subtracted from gross margin (profit).

Public Warehouses

Public warehouses are owned by parties other than the manufacturer, wholesaler, or retailer. They receive and store products for a fee which is based on the space used, the length of time during which products are stored, and the handling or processing required.

Many public warehouses are equipped to store only general merchandise that does not require special facilities. Others, however, are designated by the U.S. Bureau of the Census as "special warehouse and storage facilities" or "special commodity warehouses." These special commodity warehouses may contain refrigerated units, grain dryers, or tanks for bulk liquids.

Bonded Warehouses

A **bonded warehouse** is not a type of warehouse like the ones described above. Instead, it may be either a private or a public warehouse which has taken out a bond to assure that certain taxes or import tariffs or fees are paid to the U.S. Treasury. Both tobacco and alcoholic beverages are stored for long periods for aging purposes. If the producer or manufacturer were forced to pay excise taxes on these products at the beginning of the storage period, a prohibitive sum of money would have to be invested for a prolonged period. When the products are stored in a bonded warehouse, a government custodian is designated to make sure that excise taxes are paid as the products are withdrawn from the warehouse and continue their journey through the various channels of distribution.

Choosing a Warehousing Option

Suppose someone asked the following question. If you managed a firm marketing track lighting, would you own or lease storage space, or use space in a public warehouse? Before you could answer the question, you would have to examine a number of other considerations.

In a privately owned or leased warehouse, the manufacturer, wholesaler, or retailer must establish a work force to physically handle the products. It is also necessary to divide bulk shipments such as carloads into smaller units before shipping the smaller units to customers. An inventory control system must be established and maintained. Procedures for processing orders must be established and followed. Selecting the best method of transportation and subsequently making transportation arrangments is no small task. Specialized labor and management personnel often are required, and public warehouses offer such services. Each firm requiring warehouse facilities must decide whether it can effectively assume such tasks or whether these services can be performed best by public warehouses.

Some manufacturers are able to pass warehousing concerns on to wholesalers and retailers. In such cases, the manufacturing firm ships products to the middleman, who maintains a warehouse. Regardless of arrangements between the manufacturer and middlemen, decisions about warehousing become an important factor in physical distribution.

In arriving at this decision, the firm should consider the quantity of products to be stored. If the quantity is large, the costs of operating a warehouse can be spread over a large number of prod-

uct units. That way, the cost may be lower than the cost of using a public warehouse. Should the quantity of items in inventory be much lower than the warehouse's capacity, however, the firm may find that the costs are prohibitive.

Public warehouses tend to provide a flexibility unavailable in privately operated warehouses. If a new product is introduced or demand for an existing product escalates, public warehouses usually can provide the additional space needed. On the other hand, if a manufacturer decided to drop a product line, the action could be taken without concern as to what would happen to warehouse expenses.

The nature of the product also should be reviewed. Some products are produced or consumed on a seasonal basis. In many parts of the country lawn furniture is purchased only during summer months. Christmas decorations and toys are another example. If production of such products continues throughout the year, the manufacturer may decide to own or lease a warehouse. When production and consumption are concentrated in a season, as with some agricultural products, public warehouses may be chosen. Also, products such as iron ore and grain frequently are shipped from northern states by waterways. During winter months, shipping may be halted as a result of frozen waterways. Customers may be compelled to exceed regular inventory requirements because of delayed deliveries. In such cases, facilities leased for the short term are desirable.

Leasing warehouse space or using public warehouses may in some cases be preferable to owning warehouses. Some states have laws which define a firm "doing business" within the state as an enterprise that owns a building of any kind within the state. As a result, a firm organized as a corporation may have to pay some form of corporate tax to a state merely because it owns a warehouse within that state.[4]

Marketers recognize that products stored in inventory represent funds that are invested. Warehouse receipts issued by public warehouses serve as evidence that designated products are in stor-

DISTRIBUTION CENTER TAKES A DOWNTURN—UNDERGROUND

As cattle graze across the range just west of Kansas City, a traffic jam is forming 150 feet below ground in a giant cave. In the 1950s, Inland established a food distribution center in caves which were created by mining in the 1890s.

Inland Storage Distribution Center, a unit of Beatrice Foods Company, contains 18 million square feet. Other firms have recognized its advantages and have rented space for their own distribution centers. Underground rents often are only half as high as those above ground. Energy bills for a warehouse are 90 percent lower underground. Construction costs are lower since the roof, the floor, and some walls come with the location.

There are other advantages. A representative of Consolidated Meat Distribution Center said: "Our competitors have to wait for months to add on to their warehouses. But if a big restaurant tells us, 'We will be needing an extra 120,000 pounds of crab legs,' we just rent some more space from Inland."

On a typical day, trucks pull out laden with food for Los Angeles, Philadelphia, Oklahoma City, Buffalo, Brooklyn, Chicago, and Jacksonville. Barrels of strawberries from Mexico are shipped to jam makers or ice cream factories. Almost 10 percent of the frozen food consumed in the United States passes through the distribution center's tunnels.

Inland also leases storage space for company files and nonfood items. The foreign-trade zone is particularly active. Manufacturers can store imported goods duty-free until they are ready to sell the items. Thus, goods such as shoes from Spain and South Korea, machinery from Europe, and wines from France are stored in the caverns.

Fifty-seven businesses now lease space. In addition to Inland, the major developer is the Great Midwest Corporation, which is growing so fast that it calls itself a "subterropolis." Every day, 3,000 people report to work through the entrance, a 16 foot high, 30 foot wide hole bored into the base of a bluff that also accommodates railroad cars and tractor-trailer rigs. Two miles of track and 6 miles of paved road weave among giant limestone pillars left as ceiling supports.

What is the future of underground locations? Other cities also are trying underground commercial development. Because of its icy winters, Montreal has built a complex of shops and theaters underground in the past decade or so. Scandinavian and other European countries are building down, too. The American Underground-Space Association, which is open to laymen as well as engineers, architects, and other professionals, says that its membership has grown 30 percent a year, to 1,500 members, since it started 5 years ago.

Adapted from Meg Cox, "Kansas City Businesses Move Underground to Stay Cool, Ease Expansion, Save on Rent," *Wall Street Journal*, June 26, 1981, p. 21. Reprinted by permission of the *Wall Street Journal*, © Dow Jones & Company, Inc. All Rights Reserved.

age. The receipts may be used as collateral to secure a loan from a bank.

Each marketer should examine warehousing options before reaching a decision. If a warehouse is needed, the choice should be based on the needs and abilities of the marketer, that is, the need to store products, divide bulk shipments, or process orders and the ability to establish a warehouse work force, maintain an inventory system, select transportation methods, and invest money in inventory. Would you decide to own, lease, or use storage space in a public warehouse for your track lighting fixtures?

Monitoring Change

For many years, observers in the field of marketing pointed out the fact that new technology and innovations were being applied to production while the physical distribution system maintained the status quo. Today, however, physical distribution is changing. Some of the changes have been brought about through product processing procedures, and others can be attributed to physical distribution operations.

In 1981, for example, Dr. William Roberts, vice president of Dairymen Incorporated, announced that milk which could be stored at room temperature for more than 3 months without losing its fresh flavor would soon be on the shelves in American supermarkets.[5] Using a new pasteurizing process, raw milk is heated to 280 degrees for a few seconds and then cooled rapidly to about 70 degrees before being placed in hermetically sealed packages that provide protection against light, air, and bacteria. As a result, the product becomes less perishable and does not require refrigerated storage units. This is an example of a processing procedure which has made an impact on physical distribution.

The Tandywine Wholesale Company, a distributor of hardware products, receives nails in kegs from the manufacturer. In past years, material handlers would open the kegs and repackage the nails in 1, 5, and 10 pound packages before resale and shipment to hardware and building materials outlets. Today, Tandywine employs robotic technology to accomplish the task, using a machine that weighs and packages the nails at a much greater rate of speed and with greater accuracy. This illustrates how changes in physical distribution comes about. Today's technology is being applied to physical distribution. Dramatic changes have been forecast for the future. The astute marketer will monitor such changes through observation, additional study, and reading current periodicals.

MATERIALS HANDLING

Materials handling is a process of assembling, packing, weighing, and moving products from a producer to a warehouse, from a warehouse to a carrier, and from one carrier to another.[6]

Physically moving products into the warehouse and removing them for shipment is an expensive process and represents a major portion of the total cost of physical distribution. A few years ago, multistory warehouses were located along railways and waterways. Human resources were required to lift and carry the products to and from the storage locations. Some of these older warehouses are still in use today. As trucks and planes became more important freight carriers, newer warehouses were constructed in less congested areas. In fact, today many distribution centers occupy spacious, sprawling one-story buildings in industrial parks. Such locations provide loading platforms that are accessible to both trucks and railroad spurs.

The modern warehouse is equipped with conveyors, forklifts, and other mechanized equipment to move products into and out of the storage facility. Such equipment has alleviated some of the need for expensive, often unionized labor. Pallets that travel along the floor as a hydrofoil boat travels on water, with a friction-free cushion of air between the pallets and the floor, also have gained popularity for moving products within warehouses. Some experiments with completely automated warehouses have been conducted.

Figure 9-2. Materials handling today includes modern equipment for large-scale physical distribution.

Copied from logistic command centers developed by the U.S. military services, automated storage and retrieval systems are dependent on computerized electronic commands. Robotic technology also has received attention as an innovative method to automate warehouses. Even with such automation, human labor still is needed to operate the computer, make decisions about storage locations, and pack assembled materials.

A small retailer or wholesaler requiring local warehouse space may be unable to afford to equip a warehouse with all the automated amenities. An appliance retailer, for example, may rely on human labor to move products received into the warehouse and subsequently to move products that have been sold to the delivery truck.

or discrepancies between what was shipped and what was received. Shipments received may be **containerized,** which means that the shipment is enclosed in containers of wood, metal, or some other material typically 8 feet high, 8 feet wide, and 20 to 40 feet long. As a cargo handling system, containerization is designed to ensure that the shipment is not opened from the time it leaves the shipper until the time it reaches its destination. While containerization makes en route transfers between different modes of transportation easier and protects the products from damage and theft, some problems remain unsolved. Containers have not been standardized, which has created problems for shippers and carriers. In addition, inspection of products en route is hampered.

Receiving

As products arrive at the warehouse, they must be unloaded and inspected to discover any damage

Storing

After products have been received and checked, they must be sorted and assigned to appropriate storage areas which are especially equipped to accommodate them. Shelving, racks, bins, or other warehouse fixtures hold the products and provide proper protection until they are needed.

Some products require special environments and must be placed in temperature-controlled or dust-free areas. Other products, such as photo film, may be sensitive to light. Even the amount of humidity in the air must be controlled for certain products.

INVENTORY CONTROL

Inventory control is a response to one basic question: How many individual product items should be kept at the warehouse? Since products stored in warehouses represent invested capital, one goal of inventory control focuses on the need to minimize this investment. At the same time, manufacturers, wholesalers, or retailers storing products pursue a goal of filling all orders. Unfilled orders often represent lost sales. The overall goal becomes somewhat conflicting as a firm seeks to minimize its investment in stored items but maximize its ability to fill incoming orders. Thus, a number of factors deserve attention as marketers struggle with decisions concerning inventory control.

Market Needs and Cost Factors

A balance between market needs and cost factors should influence the quantity of inventory. Market needs are discovered by analyzing the sales forecast, that is, the predicted sales of a firm's products. Different techniques are used for forecasting sales. One technique simply involves asking informed managers within the firm about their expectations for sales. Another technique is to gather opinions of sales representatives in the field about their predictions for sales. Buying power indexes, which are published in the *Sales & Marketing Management* magazine, along with other indicators such as economic conditions, intensity of competition, and product demand, are weighed carefully in projecting future sales. While sales forecasting is still an imprecise art,

information gathered through marketing research by business firms, trade associations, and governmental agencies has made it possible to predict national, regional, and local market demands more accurately.

There are five factors to consider in balancing market needs with cost factors.

1. **Customer Service Level.** This refers to the cost of sales lost through failure to have the right product in the right place at the right time. Costs associated with **back ordering,** that is, deferring the shipment of goods out of stock until new stock is received, also should be included in this category.

2. **Transportation Costs.** Transportation costs may be determined readily since most common carriers publish rates. However, if a private carrier is used, the transportation costs will be more difficult to compute. (See page 260 for definitions and discussions of common and private carriers.)

3. **Warehousing Costs.** Warehousing costs should not be confused with inventory carrying costs. Warehousing costs can best be calculated by determining the expenses that can be eliminated or increased by changing the number of warehouse facilities or the operational costs associated with each facility.

4. **Lot Quantity Costs.** This acquisition category includes costs of issuing and closing orders, related costs of handling orders, materials handling, scheduling, and expediting.

5. **Inventory Carrying Costs.** Included in this category are interest on the investment of products while they are stored; inventory service costs, such as insurance and inventory taxes; holding costs, which include rented or owned storage space; and risk costs, including losses from damage, deterioration, spoilage, or theft.

The marketer may use computer-assisted simulations in applying cost factors to varying inventory levels. Through such simulations, the most acceptable customer service level inventory requirements at minimized costs may be discovered. Each of the cost factors described above may be programmed into a computer. The simulation begins by inputting orders to be filled. All combinations of costs, service levels, and delivery times may be tested. Then the computer yields data that may be analyzed further for decision-making purposes. Using this technique, Hart-Wesson Foods discovered that $1 million in annual expenses could be avoided with no decline in the quality of customer services.[7]

Business Logistics

The term *logistics* means the art of calculations. The word as used in military science has to do with moving, supplying, and quartering troops. **Business logistics** denotes a total approach to the distribution system, including all the activities involved in physically moving inventory from the point of origin to the point of use or consumption. In order to minimize the cost of carrying inventory, a firm will examine not only the number of distribution centers or warehouses maintained but all its distribution policies. Given a desired customer level, a firm should examine the costs associated with maintaining multiple warehouses as compared with the costs of using faster

means of transportation such as aircraft. Inventory reductions that do not require increased transportation costs or reduced customer service levels lead to greater profits. If transportation costs are increased by an amount equal to the costs associated with smaller inventories, profits will remain the same.

Business logistics involves an examination of the tradeoffs that are necessary when establishing customer service levels and reviewing various costs of the distribution system.

Suppose a small firm in the western region of the country develops a new plastic disc on which stereo sound may be recorded. The disc is far superior to those offered by other suppliers. It will not warp, and dust will not adhere to its surface. The firm will employ its own sales force to sell the disc to recording studios, primarily in Nashville, Tennessee. The firm must make a decision about renting storage space in Nashville or shipping directly to recording studios, which are primarily in Nashville. An illustration of the firm's analysis is given in Table 9-1.

In this example, it is assumed that customer service is the same for both alternatives. In actual practice, the cost of lost sales and the costs associ-

TABLE 9-1
THE IMPORTANCE OF TRANSPORTATION, WAREHOUSING, AND INVENTORY COSTS
***Problem:* Should a public warehouse be used in Nashville, Tennessee?**

	Cost to Company	
	Using Public Warehouse	Shipping Directly to Buyer
Transportation costs		
To public warehouse from plant	$ 17,356	
From public warehouse to buyer	8,678	
To buyer from plant		$ 34,705
Warehousing costs	22,529	
Inventory carrying costs	75,707	81,450
Total costs	$124,270	$116,155

ated with back-ordering are difficult if not impossible to measure. Furthermore, it is assumed that lot quantity costs remain the same for each alternative. Thus, the business would save $8,115 by shipping directly to buyer. While this illustration may oversimplify the logistics of minimizing costs, it illustrates the importance of transportation, warehousing, and inventory carrying costs.

The Economic Order Quantity Concept

In many business firms, determination of the best inventory level is based on reliable data and good judgment. Assume that you are the purchasing manager for NewsPrint Wholesalers and must decide how large an inventory to keep in stock. You probably would ask the following questions.

1. *How important is this material? What would be the cost to your customers of having to stop production in case you cannot fill their orders?* Obviously, newsprint paper stock is very important since no paper can be published without it. In the event that you are unable to supply paper to news publishers and they must stop production, your customers will lose the revenue earned by selling papers and large sums that would have been generated from selling advertising space.

2. *What is the cost of storage and security?* Tons of paper to be stored require a large warehouse. Material handlers will need forklifts to move the paper in and out of the warehouse. Since the paper is flammable, insurance will be needed to reduce the risk on paper stored in the warehouse.

3. *Will the material deteriorate or spoil while in storage?* If the roof does not leak, there should be no problem with storage losses. However, humidity or paper-eating insects can cause a problem, as can excessive dust or dirt.

4. *Is the price of newsprint stable or subject to rises and declines?* Since paper costs have risen steadily over the past few years, the price trend seems to be upward-bound. Current economic forecasts, however, should be helpful in answering this question.

TABLE 9-2
THE IMPORTANCE OF ORDER COSTS, CARRYING COSTS, AND TOTAL COSTS

Quantity Purchased	Ordering Costs	Carrying Costs	Total Costs
12,500	$60,000	$15,000	$75,000
15,000	50,000	18,000	68,000
17,500	42,850	21,000	63,850
20,000	37,500	24,000	61,500
22,500	33,325	27,000	60,325
25,000	30,000	30,000	60,000
27,500	27,275	33,000	60,275
30,000	25,000	36,000	61,000
32,500	23,075	39,000	62,075
35,000	21,425	42,000	63,425

5. *Is there a price reduction for buying high quantities?* Nearly all paper mills give quantity discounts.

6. *How fast is this material used?* By reviewing your customer accounts, you can determine how much paper is shipped from the warehouse on a weekly or monthly basis.

The answers to these questions indicate clearly that a large inventory must be kept at all times. Data concerning the cost of storage and security, prices, discounts, and quantities bought by industrial users are used in arriving at a decision about the level of inventory. For some products, however, the decision is more difficult because the factors are more complex.

As a result, marketers have formulated the **economic order quantity** (EOQ) concept to balance ordering costs and carrying costs with the desired level of satisfying customers' orders. When inventory is obtained from outside vendors, ordering costs including expenditures for telephones, clerical assistance, purchasing agents' time, and postage are incurred. A key element of inventory carrying cost is the amount a firm must

FINDING ECONOMIC ORDER QUANTITY

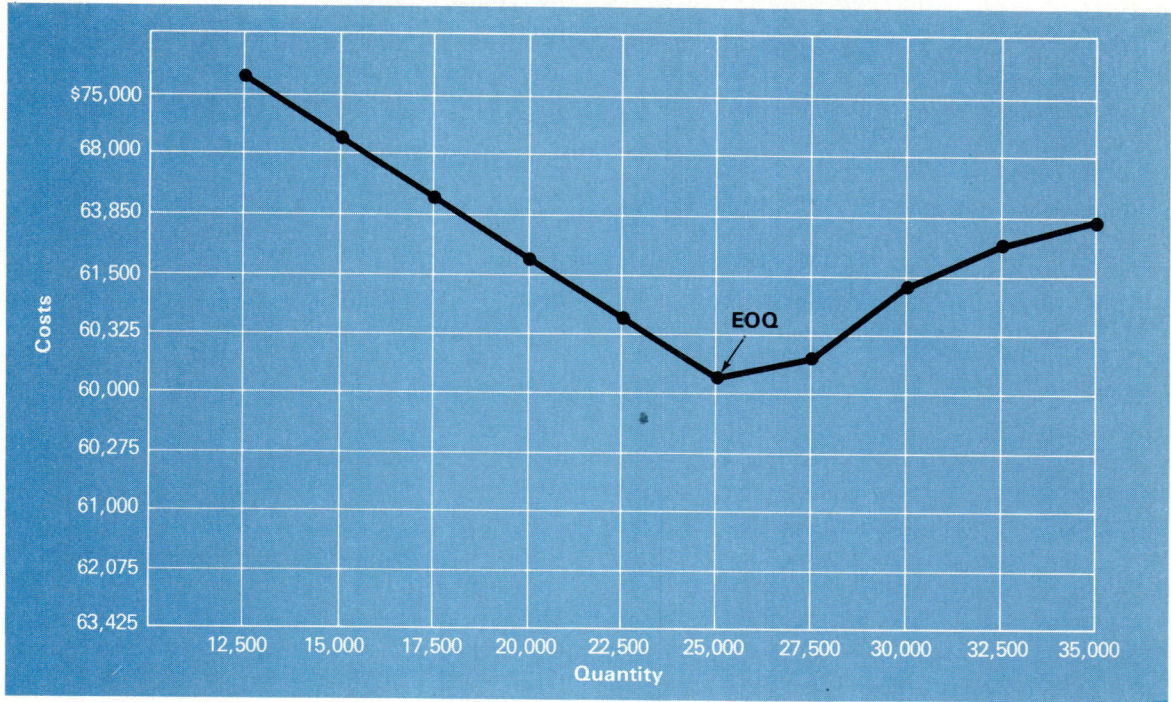

Figure 9-3. The economic order quantity is reached when total costs reach their lowest point.

pay to finance the required investment in inventory. Carrying costs also may include taxes that a state levies against the inventory as well as insurance against losses from fire, theft, or other disasters. In addition, expenses are incurred in operating a warehouse, although such expenses may vary depending on ownership or rental payments for warehouse space.

As illustrated in Table 9-2, ordering costs decrease as the order size becomes larger. However, carrying costs are greater. The EOQ is reached when the total costs reach their lowest point before starting to increase again. Thus, the data presented in Table 9-2 show the total costs decreasing to the point at which 25,000 units are ordered. This may be better understood by studying Figure 9-3.

Thus, the EOQ can be used by a firm in determining how much to order. But it fails to show the number of times an order should be placed. Referring to Table 9-2, a firm expecting to

sell 150,000 units would order 6 times (150,000/25,000 = 6). Since there will be a time lapse between the date when orders are placed and the date when units are received, the firm must anticipate the length of time needed for the order cycle and place its orders accordingly. Otherwise, the warehouse may run out of stock and be unable to fill outgoing orders.

Basic Stock Lists and Model Stock Plans

Basic stock lists are used in inventory control systems in which the product or a slightly altered product is included in the inventory year after year. The EOQ concept works well in such situations because it yields the quantity to be reordered. Some products, however, fluctuate in demand. In such cases, it may be desirable to carry a more sizable inventory than would be required ordinarily to prevent stockouts or backorders. This excess inventory is known as **safety stock.**

Other products, especially fashion clothing, may be carried for only one season. Thus, inventories of such products stored in warehouses are subject to obsolescence. As a result, the manufacturer, wholesaler, or retailer will study past sales records to determine expected sales on the basis of sizes, prices, and units sold in the past. The firm then will place into inventory what it considers to be an ideal or **model stock.**

Computer Technology

The value of the computer in physical distribution has been cited already as a tool for simulating operations and predicting the costs of various warehouse locations and for automated storage and retrieval systems. Computer technology also is being used in inventory control systems.

Records of inventory lists may be stored in computer memory banks. As items enter or leave the warehouse, the memory banks are updated to reflect the new total. When needed, accurate lists of inventory items may be produced quickly. The computer may be programmed to place orders automatically when stocked items reach the point at which stock needs to be replenished. The computer also has the capacity to track products and alert warehouse managers to increases or decreases in the flow of products leaving the warehouse.

As computer technology becomes more sophisticated and communications between computers become commonplace, the orders for basic stock may flow throughout the channel from computer to computer. The manufacturer or producer may be able to discover how many products are actually in inventory throughout the country as a result of intercomputer communications.

PROCESSING ORDERS

This is an important component of physical distribution. Prompt, accurately filled orders generate goodwill, while mistakes and tardy responses to orders create ill will and poor relationships with other middlemen or customers. The actual processing of orders includes activities which can be divided into two broad areas: the physical task of assembling and shipping the order, and the office work which accompanies the physical task.

Assembling and Shipping

For certain products, standardizing, grading, and packaging activities must be completed. **Standardization** means making sure that a product meets a certain standard. A produce wholesaler that had fresh peaches stored in a warehouse would inspect the peaches before shipping or delivering them to a supermarket to make sure they were not overripe. Failure to perform this activity might lead to the loss of the customer. **Grading** involves sorting products according to size, quality, or some other standard. Eggs are graded by size, such as jumbo, large, medium, and small. Products such as clothing, tires, paint brushes, and meats are also graded. The major types of standards used for grading include (1) basic weights and measures, (2) sizes, shapes, or dimensions, (3) chemical or technical properties, (4) quantity units for sale or handling, and (5) characteristics apparent to the human senses.

For many products, standardizing, grading, and packaging are tasks performed by the manufacturer. In some cases, however, these functions may be assumed by a middleman. Packaging is the use of containers and wrapping materials to protect, contain, identify, promote, and facilitate the use of a product. In many instances, the package is viewed as an extension of the product; it makes using the product easier. Examples include toothpaste, hair spray, paint spray, and bottles of rubber cement that contain a brush. **Physical distribution packaging** is a term that embraces all materials and devices used integrally with shipments to help them move more efficiently through the entire distribution system.[8] In this definition, cushioning materials, corrugated boxes, drums, and the like serve to contain and protect products as they journey through distribution channels.

The actual assembling of a product for reshipment from the warehouse is dictated in part by the nature of the product. Order pickers receive cop-

UNLOADING EXPENSES WITH FORKLIFTS

Forklift trucks seem to be everywhere, at manufacturing and warehousing sites across the country. They are used to haul aircraft brakes, stack pallets of new tires, move skids piled high with railroad ties, and load boxes of polyvinyl chloride onto railcars. For many firms they are indispensable. Yet they cost about $18,000 apiece. In large firms, when an aging forklift needs to be replaced, the plant or warehouse manager typically puts out a call to a distributor for a new one. Before placing an order, smaller firms are more prone to track economic data, select a supply source, and negotiate the contract.

In recent years, following the raw material shortages that cropped up after the Arab oil embargo in 1973 and the double-digit inflation that pushed up the cost of most industrial goods, large corporations such as B. F. Goodrich, General Motors, Proctor & Gamble, and General Electric have been beefing up their purchasing staffs. B. F. Goodrich, for example, no longer relies on plant or warehouse managers in towns like Bloomington, Indiana; Calvert City, Kentucky; and Port Neches, Texas, to place separate orders for forklifts from a half dozen different suppliers. Instead, the corporate purchasing staff places one order with two suppliers for the 120 or so forklifts that Goodrich needs annually. The total saving to Goodrich is about $400,000 a year.

Adapted from "Purchasing Control: A Key," © 1981 by The New York Times Company. Reprinted by permission.

ies of the purchase order and assemble the various products for the outgoing shipment. In some one-story, sprawling warehouses where the products stored are small and lightweight, the order pickers glide through the aisles on roller skates picking the needed products. In other cases, carts travel through the warehouse, and products are picked by assemblers and loaded onto the carts. Forklifts may be used to move heavy products such as appliances to an asssembling area near the shipping dock.

Units sometimes are price-marked and repackaged for shipment. Containerization again may be used to protect the products while they are being shipped. Other physical distribution packaging may be used, depending on the nature of the product. If the order in cumulative form represents less than a truckload or carload, shipping labels designating the name and address of the receiver must be affixed to each package or container.

A bill of lading—a contract issued to a shipper by the transportation agency, listing the products shipped, acknowledging their receipt, and promising delivery to the destination point—must be prepared. As a carrier accepts the order and the shipment leaves the storage facility, the warehouse has completed a cycle of receiving, storing, assembling, and reshipping activities.

Office Tasks

Office personnel are needed in warehouses to open and process incoming purchase orders and to prepare invoices to accompany outgoing orders. Management should establish policies to

STRAIGHT BILL OF LADING
ORIGINAL - NOT NEGOTIABLE
SINGLE SHIPMENT PICKUP ☐

NUSSBAUM Trucking, Inc.

SHIPPER NO.

CARRIER NO.

DATE

CONSIGNEE (TO)		SHIPPER (FROM)	
STREET		STREET	
CITY, STATE	ZIP	CITY, STATE	ZIP
ROUTE		VEHICLE NO.	

NUMBER SHIPPING UNITS	Kind of Packaging, Description of Articles, Special Marks and Exceptions	Weight (SUBJECT TO CORRECTION)	Rate	CHARGES (for Carrier use only)

Note — Where the rate is dependent on value, shippers are required to state specifically in writing the agreed or declared value of the property.
The agreed or declared value of the property is hereby specifically stated by the shipper to be not exceeding.

Subject to section 7 of the conditions if this shipment is to be delivered to the consignee without recourse on the consignor, the consignor shall sign the following statement.
The carrier shall not make delivery of this shipment without payment of freight and all other lawful charges.

TOTAL CHARGES ▶

$_____ per _____

(Signature of Consignor)

FREIGHT CHARGES:
FREIGHT PREPAID except when box at right is checked

Check boxes if charges are ☐ to be collect

"THIS IS TO CERTIFY THAT THE ABOVE NAMED ARTICLES ARE PROPERLY CLASSIFIED, DESCRIBED, PACKAGED, MARKED, AND LABELED AND ARE IN PROPER CONDITION FOR TRANSPORTATION, ACCORDING TO THE APPLICABLE REGULATIONS OF THE DEPARTMENT OF TRANSPORTATION."

RECEIVED, subject to the classifications and tariffs in effect on the date of the issue of this Bill of Lading, the property described above in apparent good order, except as noted (contents and condition of contents of packages unknown), marked, consigned, and destined as indicated above which said carrier (the word carrier being understood throughout this contract as meaning any person or corporation in possession of the property under the contract) agrees to carry to its usual place of delivery at said destination, if on its route, otherwise to deliver to another carrier on the route to said destination. It is mutually agreed as to each carrier of all or any of, said property over all or any portion of said route to destination and as to each party at any time interested in all or any of said property, that every service to be performed hereunder shall be subject to all the bill of lading terms and conditions in the governing classification on the date of shipment.
Shipper hereby certifies that he is familiar with all the bill of lading terms and conditions in the governing classification and the said terms and conditions are hereby agreed to by the shipper and accepted for himself and his assigns.

SHIPPER	CARRIER **NUSSBAUM TRUCKING, INC.**	
AUTHORIZED SIGNATURE	AUTHORIZED SIGNATURE	DATE

Figure 9-4. A bill of lading is prepared for every product shipment that leaves the warehouse.

be followed in granting credit and in collecting past-due accounts. Office personnel follow such policies in determining the credit terms that appear on invoices. Office personnel also record payments for merchandise shipped; receive, process, and pay warehousing expenditures; and prepare letters that are sent to other middlemen or customers with past-due accounts.

TRANSPORTATION

Transporting products through the channel of distribution usually is the largest single item in the overall cost of physical distribution. The transportation decision must be influenced not only by price but by a number of other marketing concerns: the nature of the product; locations of

Quality & Service Since 1933

H   485

Illinois Biscuit Company, Inc.

• 1013 West Washington •
Bloomington, IL 61701
(309) 828-9824

SOLD TO: _____   ACCT No. _____   DATE _____   TERMS _____

ADDRESS _____   CITY _____   SALESPERSON _____

STOCK #	DESCRIPTION	QTY	PRICE	AMT	STOCK #	DESCRIPTION	QTY	PRICE	AMT	STOCK #	DESCRIPTION	QTY	PRICE	AMT
0-001	Salerno Angel Cakes				13-102	RC 19OZ Assorted Cr				13-101				
0-002	Salern Animal CX 11				13-103	RC 19OZ Chocolat Cr								
0-003	Sal Animal CX 144CT				13-104	RC 19OZ Duplex Crem					Banana			
0-004	Salerno 8 oz. Butter				13-105	RC 19OZ Lemon Crem					Duplex			
0-005	Salerno 1 lb. Butter				13-106	RC 19OZ Vanilla Cr					Chocolate			
0-006	Salerno Coco. Bars				13-106A	RC 19OZ Peanut Butt					French Van			
					13-109	RC 16OZ Strawberry					Peanut Butter			
0-011	Salerno Family Pack				13-110	RC 16OZ Vanilla Cr					Lemon			
0-012	Sal Double Fudge Cr				13-111	RC 14OZ Butter Thin					Strawberry			
0-013	Sal 18 oz. Fancy Crem				13-112	RC 14OZ Choc. Thins								
0-014	Salerno Fig Bars 14				13-113	RC 14OZ Cho Chip Th								
0-015	Salern Fudge Sundae				13-114	RC 14OZ Coco. Thin					Stripe Dainty			
0-016	Salerno Ginger Snap				13-115	RC 14OZ Lemon Thins					Milko Graham			
0-017	Salerno Hippodrome										Fig Bars			
0-018	Salern Iced Oatmeal				3-072	Danish Coconut Bars					Butter Cookie			
					3-072E	Danish Del Windmill					Choc. Chip			
0-019	Sal Pnt Butter Cr				8-088	Gardetto Brdstix Ch					Windmill			
0-020	Salerno Mint Cremes				8-089	Gardetto Brdstix Gr					Coco Bars			
0-021	Salern Royal Graham				8-090	Gardetto Brdstix On					Iced Oatmeal			
0-022	Salern Royal Strip				8-091	Gardetto Brdstix Sa					Oatmeal			
0-023	Sal Vanilla Wafers				8-092	Gardetto Brdstix Se								
0-025	Salerno 2-1 Sndwch				9-093	Six Gun Chili Mix					Extenders			
0-026	Salerno Almond Cres										Chair Backs			
0-027	Salerno Choc. Chips				3-057	FFV Roman Meal Box 7					Dumps			
0-028	Salerno 1 lb. Graham				3-058	FFV Ham/Cheese Box 7								
0-029	Sal Dainty Oyster				3-059	FFV Pizza Thins Box								
0-030	Salerno 1 lb Saltine				3-060	FFV Stone Wheat Box				2-054	R.G. Oatmeal 18 oz.			
0-031	Salerno 7 oz. Saltine				3-061	FFV Wheat Snack CX7				2-055	R.G. Cookie Jar 18 oz.			
0-032	Sal Geo- Town CX 11				3-062	FFV Appetizer Thins				2-056	R.G. Chip Chip 18 oz.			
0-039	Devonshire Melba Rd				4-075	Cornnuts Regular				2-057	R.G. Macaroon 10½ oz.			
0-040	Devonshire Melba Ts				4-076	Cornnuts Bar-B-Q				2-058	Rippin' Good Fudge Fluffs			
0-041	Flavor Tree 12 Ct				5-077	Beer Nuts—12 oz. CA				2-059	Rippin' Good Picadilly			
1-042	Butterfly Crisp				5-078	Beer Nuts—Bag				2-060	R.G. Frosted Fruits			
11-096	H-A Creme Wafer Stx				6-079	#12 Cake Cone				2-061	Rippin' Good Stripes			
11-098	H-A 10 oz. Sugar Waf				6-080	#12 Color Cone Cups								
					6-081	#12 Sugar Cone					Warner's Candy			
					6-082	#24 Plain Cone Cup				14-121	Warner .79 Candy Bg			
					6-083	#48 Plain Cone Cups				14-122	Warner .89 Candy Bg			
					7-084	Pretzels				14-121	Warner .98 Candy Bg			
	Column One Total					Column Two Total					Total purchases			

Signature_____

Figure 9-5. Invoices accompany outgoing orders to state amounts due and terms of payment.

warehouses and middlemen; inventory size, with special attention devoted to order and delivery time requirements; and the ability of the carrier to deliver products to the desired destination.

In the business world today, international trade is commonplace; it creates new complexities in selecting methods of transportation. When General Motors Corporation wanted to sell Yugoslavia $12 million in locomotive and diesel engines in 1979, the eastern European country insisted that GM buy about $4 million in Yugoslavian cutting tools in exchange.[9] **Countertrade agreements,** in which one country agrees to buy from another country if reciprocal buying occurs, are becoming more frequent, and the goods must be transported physically from country to country.

Another new development in consumer behavior has created special problems for transportation managers. Today's Americans live in the age of "depletephobia," or the fear of running out of things.[10] Long lines at gasoline stations during the 1970s brought Americans face to face with the idea that supplies of oil were not infinite. Coffee, sugar, and even water are examples of other shortages that have been faced in the past. The shortage mentality that developed as a result of such shortages is well known. If a facetious remark is heard on television or radio concerning a shortage, stores are mobbed the next day with panic buyers prepared to stock up on or horde the product. A transportation manager will want to make sure that the firm's products are available in such cases. Otherwise, sales will be lost to competitors.

Transportation Classifications

The U.S. Department of Transportation (DOT) establishes national transportation policies to provide the country with fast, safe, and efficient transportation. Various commissions, agencies, or boards then regulate specific types of carriers. Transportation carriers are classified according to their operating rights. If the carrier is involved in interstate commerce, it operates under the jurisdiction of the Interstate Commerce Commission. Carriers that limit their service to a single state are regulated by that state's transportation agency. There are three classifications of carriers, and each group operates with different privileges.

Common carriers provide services to any firm for a fee. Common carriers are certified for public convenience and necessity by the federal government. In cases where interstate commerce is not involved, they are certified by the state within which the common carrier operates, but federal law requires that freight rates be published and be identical for similar types of products. In addition, the certificate specifies whether the service tendered is scheduled or nonscheduled. Common carriers usually transport all kinds of products. However, they may specialize and limit their services to a particular kind of product such as liquid petroleum products, steel, or grain.

Contract carriers are certified to transport items according to an agreement between the carrier and the shipper. The fee specified in the agreement is negotiated and may differ from agreement to agreement. Such carriers may provide transportation to a firm on a one-time basis or a continuing basis.

Private carriers are owned and operated or leased carrier equipment restricted to an individual firm. Such carriers usually are exempt from the rules of regulatory agencies. However, they must abide by state laws which grant licenses to such carriers and which may impose weight restrictions.

In actual practice, firms may choose carriers from the three classifications depending on what they perceive to be the advantages or disadvantages. A firm may, of course, elect to use a combination of carriers fitting into more than one classification. At this point, let us look at specific modes of transportation.

Railroads

While railroads have lost a great deal of traffic to other modes of transportation, they still represent an important method of transportation. Many different types of freight cars are available to shippers, including flatcars, tank cars, gondola and hopper cars, refrigerated cars, and other spe-

Figure 9-6. By loading truck trailers onto flatcars (piggyback service), shippers' agents like Hub City Terminals can offer flexible transportation.

cialized types. Piggyback and fishyback services enable railroads to provide more flexible service. **Piggyback service** occurs when truck trailers loaded with goods are placed on railroad flatcars. The trailer on flatcar (TOFC) enables shippers to load trailers with products and place them on flatcars. When the train reaches the nearest railway terminal, the piggyback trailers are attached to trailer trucks and continue their journey over the highways. The **fishyback** trailers are loaded on cargo ships or barges to continue their journey. This prevents the need to unload and reload the items being transported. "Stack-pack" and "Vert-a-Pac" freight cars are available to transport automobiles.

Rail transportation is usually less expensive than other ways of transporting products. Substantial savings may be offered to firms shipping carload quantities as compared with smaller quantities. In an attempt to remain competitive, railroads permit shippers to pool their shipments into carload lots when the receivers are located in one area.

Railroads also offer in-transit privileges. **Diversions in transit** permit the shipper to start the products in one general direction and establish or change destinations as long as the change or new destination involves forward movement of the cars. California fruit growers, for example, may start a shipment eastward and subsequently decide to direct separate carloads to Kansas City, St. Louis, Chicago, Memphis, Indianapolis, Cincinnati, and Boston. At appropriate diversion points, the cars are rerouted to the appropriate destinations. Backtracking is not permitted.

Processing in transit permits a shipper to have the products unloaded, graded, manufactured, or otherwise processed and later reloaded and shipped on to the final destination. Wheat shipped from Kansas, for example, may stop en route and be made into flour and then continue to the destination point.

While bargaining and negotiation have led to the establishment of special railway transportation rates in certain sections of the country, most products shipped by rail go under a class rate or a commodity rate. Perishable products or products of similar size, for example, are grouped into classes. In fact, thousands of products of similar size are classified in this manner. For each class, a **class rate** is established which is based upon the nature of items being shipped, weight, and distance and that rate is higher than the commodity rate. **Commodity rates** are used for bulky products such as grain, iron ore, sand, lumber, and coal. Commodity rates are established for each product moving between receiving and destination points. The majority of railroad shipments are accepted under commodity rates. For example, unit trains (large, single-commodity trains) loaded with autos and moving from Detroit to New York offer rate reductions and speedier service.

In addition to the attributes of railroad transportation already mentioned, computers give shippers instant information on the progress of freight cars carrying their products. The major disadvantage of such shipments is the inability of railroads to reach many places.

Highways

Highway transportation ranks high in meeting the needs of many manufacturers. Improved highways, better equipment for trucking and materials handling, and in some cases, a cutback in stringent state highway laws have enabled trucks to emerge as a very effective transportation medium.

Once the merchandise is loaded, it does not have to be unloaded until it reaches the receiver. Therefore, less packaging may be required. Speed is another advantage of trucks. This has enabled wholesalers and retailers to operate with smaller inventories. In some situations, as a result, the burden of storage has been shifted from retailer to wholesaler and from wholesaler to manufacturer. Indeed, long-distance delivery has become commonplace, with huge truck-trailer rigs zipping along the highway from one city to another and from coast to coast.

Trucks are also a very effective carrier for medium and short hauls. Observation of busy streets or major highways will quickly reveal numerous trucks engaged in medium- and short-distance delivery missions. Such trucks may be refrigerated to transport perishables or may pull tank trailers which hold liquid products. Other specialized trucking equipment accommodates a variety of items such as cement, telephone poles, asphalt and crushed stone, and flat bulky items that require a platform-type carrier. The major advantage of trucks is their ability to reach various geographic destinations. The major disadvantage is vulnerability to traffic tie-ups, bad weather, equipment breakdowns, and traffic accidents. Truck transportation for some products is more expensive than rail transportation.

Waterways

Originally, the pattern of industrial development in this country was determined largely by the location of inland and coastal waterways. The Great Lakes and their connecting channels with the St. Lawrence Seaway provided transportation routes for the iron ore deposits at the head of Lake Superior and the steel-producing region south and east of Lake Erie. The Mississippi River connecting the northern and southern areas of the country, with the Ohio River providing an east-west connecting route, was of extreme value in the early part of the industrial revolution. Internal waterways such as the Tennessee River also have had a significant impact on the shipment of products.

These waterways are still important today, but other modes of transportation have opened other regions of the country to industrial development. The government has been instrumental in financing improvements in water channels and installing locks to maintain maritime transportation.

Ships and barges provide the cheapest form of freight transportation for most products, but they are the slowest mode. Speed, however, may not be of major importance for some raw goods, grain, sand, and coal. With the growth of interna-tional trade, water transportation is becoming increasingly important. Air transportation, which offers the only alternative, is too expensive for many heavy or bulky products.

Another disadvantage of water transportation is that another form of transportation usually is needed to complete delivery. Ships and barges now carry loaded truck trailers so that the shipment can continue on its journey without unloading and reloading of the products. In the past, when lakes and rivers froze during winter, all shipping was halted. Today, cutter ships plow through the frozen channels, cutting away the ice and reopening the waterways. This has enabled shipping service to continue during most of the year.

Water transportation, which is regulated by the U.S. Maritime Commission, is mainly of two types: liner service and tramp service. **Liner service** provides freight transportation on assigned routes on a scheduled basis. **Tramp service** is provided on a contract basis.

Pipelines

Since pipelines usually are owned by the company using them, they are considered private carriers. In the future, however, companies may share the cost of constructing and subsequently using this transportation mode. The Alaskan pipeline, for example, was financed and built by a group of oil companies working together. Although pipelines usually are confined to the delivery of petroleum products, their construction requires a large financial outlay. Once they are in place, operational costs are low. While a pipeline usually transports a single product moving in one direction, it serves as a dependable mode of transportation that is not subject to labor problems or the weather. In addition, there is no problem with empty carriers that must be sent back to the point of origin, as is the case with other carriers.

Products move through pipelines at a slow pace, but pumping stations may be installed to increase the speed of flow. In recent years, attention has been focused on methods that will make pipeline transportation more versatile. Solids such as coal and wood pulp have been suspended in water and flushed through pipelines.

Airlines

The greatest advantage of air transportation is speed. No firm knows this better than Federal Express. Operating a private fleet of jets, Federal Express emphasizes speed with its slogan: "When it absolutely, positively has to be there overnight." For certain perishable products or items needed quickly, such as repair parts or medicine, speed may be an overriding factor in choosing a transportation medium. While air freight is costly when compared with other transportation modes, a machine breakdown which disrupts the operation of a production plant or water system, the paving of a highway, or the drilling of an oil well may create situations in which speed is of the essence. Flowers and plants grown in subtropical areas are shipped to northern areas by plane. Without air service, perishable products like these simply could not be used in certain sections of the country. The frequency of flights and their ability to reach overseas destinations are other strong selling points for air freight.

Products such as electronic and computer devices are sensitive to rough, bouncy transportation modes. To accommodate such products for transportation, United Airlines offers a Soft Touch container. The container holds up to 10,000 pounds in a volume of 497 cubic feet and includes a tie-down mechanism to ensure a stable ride for the cargo. Purolator Courier Service provides Sky Pak containers at no extra charge. Purolator promises overnight door-to-door delivery by offering a combination of air and ground transportation services. Jumbo jets, with their increased cargo space and lifting power, have tended to make air freight more feasible for a greater variety of products. Flying Tiger Airlines uses specially equipped jet freighters to guarantee delivery of heavyweight cargo of almost any kind, including cattle. As air freight becomes more common, marketers are discovering that savings in other aspects of physical distribution, such as smaller inventories, fewer warehouses, and faster delivery, tend to offset the higher transportation rates.

Airlines, however, do have some special problems. Labor difficulties such as the controllers' strike of 1981 may delay or cancel departures and arrivals. Weather may close airline terminals during extremely foggy conditions, blizzards, or ice storms. In addition, air freight equipment may need repairs which result in costly delays.

Two federal agencies regulate air transportation. The Federal Aviation Agency (FAA), a division of the U.S. Department of Transportation, is responsible for inspecting and rating civilian aircraft and crews. The Civil Aeronautics Board (CAB) is charged with handling economic questions connected with domestic airways and helps develop international air transportation.

Other Transportation Modes

The decision factors generally examined in arriving at transportation decisions thus include speed, frequency of delivery, dependability, capacity to transport bulky products, access to pickup and delivery points, and costs. In practice, the transportation decision usually is arrived at by the party paying the shipping charges. While there are numerous exceptions, the buyer frequently pays the transportation fee and indicates the preferred transportation mode on the purchase order. Terminology associated with transportation shipping charges, such as free-on-board, zone pricing, and delivery pricing, is discussed in Chapter 11.

Suppose a small drugstore in Elizabethtown, Kentucky, is running low on insulin and needs delivery quickly. A telephone call to the E. I. Lilly Company, a large pharmaceutical supplier in Indianapolis, Indiana, will speed the ordering process. Since commercial flights do not land in Elizabethtown, another speedy means of transportation is needed. A major bus line such as Greyhound will provide delivery of the parcel on the next scheduled trip. Later in the day, the pharmacist can pick up the insulin at the local bus station in Elizabethtown. Bus lines such as Greyhound and Trailways make frequent trips to

TRANSPORTATION MODES

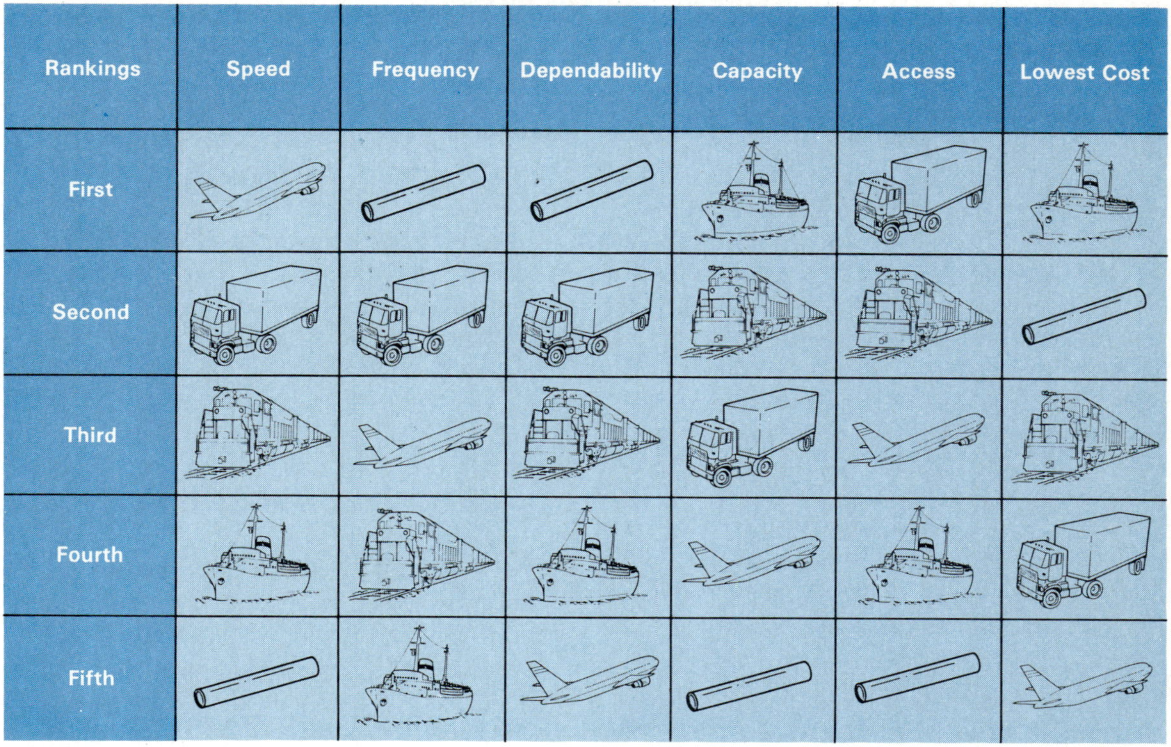

Rankings	Speed	Frequency	Dependability	Capacity	Access	Lowest Cost
First	(airplane)	(pipeline)	(pipeline)	(ship)	(truck)	(ship)
Second	(truck)	(truck)	(truck)	(rail)	(rail)	(pipeline)
Third	(rail)	(airplane)	(rail)	(truck)	(airplane)	(rail)
Fourth	(ship)	(rail)	(ship)	(airplane)	(ship)	(truck)
Fifth	(pipeline)	(ship)	(airplane)	(pipeline)	(pipeline)	(airplane)

Figure 9-7. Depending on what aspect of transportation is important, shippers may choose different transportation modes.

major cities and stop at smaller towns and cities along the route. They provide delivery service for small packages at a reasonable rate.

The U.S. Postal Service also provides a simple method for shipping small parcels. The shipper must abide by strict regulations which dictate the type and size of a package, its contents, and how it must be wrapped, tied, and labeled. Parcel post service is classified as fourth class mail, which means that it has low priority as far as processing and delivery. While the rates are low, delivery may be slow. For faster service, shippers may pay a higher fee for air parcel post, special delivery, Express Mail, or Priority Mail. Some small parcles may be sent by first class mail.

United Parcel Service (UPS) also provides delivery service for small parcels which do not exceed 50 pounds. The service is well suited for delivery of nonperishable items. UPS maintains modern terminals and provides local and long-distance delivery in all states.

Freight Forwarders

The **freight forwarder** is a specialized marketing firm designed to assist firms that ship in quantities less than a carload or truckload. The freight forwarder collects shipments from various firms and consolidates them into carload or truckload quantities. The freight forwarder earns a profit by charging a more expensive "less than carload or truckload rate" and then pays the carrier carload or truckload rates. The shipper benefits by having the freight forwarder pick up the shipment and, when it reaches its destination, arranging for delivery to the buyer.

THE COST OF PHYSICAL DISTRIBUTION

If you visit the National Zoological Park in Washington, D.C., you will find a sign near the alligator compound that contains information about that animal's habitat, life span, and eating habits. The description concludes with the following statement: "It is understandably difficult to get an exact measurement of an alligator's length." While a physical distribution system is not likely to bite off your hand, neither will it remain docile while you attempt to measure its cost. Inventories may bulge and then be reduced. Orders may pour in and require that material handlers receive overtime pay in order to handle the volume. Transportation costs may increase. When least expected, a forklift may need to be replaced. Nevertheless, each firm should review physical distribution systems continuously for efficiency, cost reduction, and profit improvement. The following pointers reveal some methods for analyzing such systems.

1. Reexamine Costs. An analytical "walk-through" of operations may turn up a number of inefficiencies or at least suggest ways in which present practices can be improved. A congested shipping dock may be a symptom of problems in the order-processing section. Opportunities for pilferage increase with the number of dock doors and congestion on the dock. Labels on cartons that are easily read prevent misrouted shipments. Other deficiencies may be discovered.

2. Check Opportunities to Consolidate Shipments. An analysis of shipping patterns may reveal instances in which a slight change in scheduling shipments offers a significant opportunity for increasing volume and gaining a better rate from a carrier. Sales reps may promise speedy delivery regardless of whether it is needed. In such cases, accumulating orders for a few days may lead to substantial savings in transportation costs. It also may be possible to persuade customers to enter their orders earlier or to order larger quantities at less frequent intervals.

3. Minimize, to the Extent Possible, the Number of Carriers. As additional carriers are used, smaller volumes may be handled by each carrier. Thus, the shipper, working with a number of carriers, begins to lose control. Carriers have less interest in small accounts and may fail to maintain service standards. This is an ever-present danger of "divvying up" traffic. In addition, bargaining for better transportation rates may be more difficult than would be the case with fewer carriers.

4. Review Sales Accounts for Profitability. The clerical costs of filling a 500 pound order are enormous in comparison to filling a 40,000 pound order. Unless customer service policies are set forth, the orders are likely to be handled in the same manner. Perhaps small, odd-shaped packages should be handled differently and shipped by other transportation modes.

5. Balance Work Loads. In some warehouses, zone picking may be a more efficient way to assemble orders. If personnel are working in crews, the owner must look for inefficiencies. Often, the larger the crew, the greater the inefficiency. Planning and balancing work loads is important in reducing costs.

6. Check Inventory Turnover. Within limits of practicality, the more times an inventory can be turned, the more it will save in investment dollars. Rapid inventory turnover also reduces the risks of product obsolescence or deterioration.

7. Avoid Irreversible Commitments. Where there is uncertainty about sales volume or storage space needed, permanent capital investments should be avoided. Public warehousing and common carriers provide shippers with maximum flexibility and minimum risk or commitment. Private warehouses and contracts with private carriers can be established later, after sales volume has demonstrated a need for them.

Physical distribution is an expensive process, often costing as much as or more than the product itself. However, great strides are being made to streamline operations, apply technology, reduce costs, and improve service levels. These strides are important as distribution systems try to deliver the product to the right place at the right time.

- Physical distribution requires decisions concerning locations where inventory is to be stored, establishment of warehouses or distribution centers, plans for a materials handling system, establishment of an inventory control system, development of procedures to be followed in processing orders, and selection of methods of transportation.

- Business firms have the option of owning or leasing private warehouses or using public warehouses. Bonded warehouses exist to assure that a bond to cover taxes or import tariffs and fees will be paid to the U.S. Treasury when products are sold.

- Firms seek to maximize their ability to fill orders while minimizing cost factors. This process requires tradeoffs between customer service levels and the cost of acquiring, maintaining, and warehousing inventory, as well as transportation.

- A balance between market needs and cost factors should influence the quantity of inventory. Five factors to consider in balancing market needs with cost factors are customer service level, transportation costs, warehousing costs, lot quantity costs, and inventory carrying costs.

- The economic order quantity concept is helpful in arriving at physical distribution decisions when the inventory is composed of basic stock. For stock subject to rapid obsolescence, such as fashion items, a model stock plan should be followed.

- Transporting products as they move through the channel of distribution usually represents the largest single item in the overall cost of physical distribution. The six decision factors used in comparing modes of transportation are speed, frequency of scheduled departures and arrivals, dependability, capacity to handle large orders or bulky items, access to receiving and delivery points, and costs.

- Transportation modes are classified into three groups: common, contract, and private carriers. Each classification offers the shipper advantages and disadvantages which must be weighed in arriving at the carrier choice.

- When deciding how large an inventory to keep in stock the purchasing manager should consider the following questions. (1) What will be the cost in case orders cannot be filled? (2) What is the cost of storage and security? (3) Will the product deteriorate or spoil while in storage? (4) Is the price subject to rises and declines? (5) Is there a price reduction for buying large quantities? and (6) How fast is the product sold or used?

back-ordering
basic stock list
bill of lading
bonded warehouse
business logistics
class rate
commodity rate
common carrier
containerized
contract carrier
countertrade
  agreement
customer service level
distribution center
diversions in transit
economic order
  quantity
fishyback service
freight forwarder
grading

inventory carrying
  costs
leased warehouse
liner service
materials handling
model stock
physical distribution
physical distribution
  packaging
piggyback service
private carrier
private warehouse
processing in transit
public warehouse
safety stock
standardization
tramp service
transportation costs
warehousing costs

1. Earlier in this chapter, the objective of physical distribution was given as follows: to deliver the right goods to the right customer at the right time and at the right place. Yet later in the chapter, it was pointed out that many firms are replacing numerous warehouses with a few distribution centers. This seems to be contradictory to the goal. Does a rationale exist to explain what seems to be a discrepancy between the goal and actual practice?

2. The traffic manager is responsible in most cases for choosing methods of transportation. The decision factors include the following.

a. Speed
b. Frequency of delivery
c. Dependability
d. Capacity to transport bulky items
e. Access to delivery and pickup points
f. Costs

Suppose you are the traffic manager making decisions for each of the following products.

(1) Flowers grown in California to be shipped to Boston

(2) Automobiles assembled in Detroit to be shipped to dealers in Dallas

(3) Coal mined in West Virginia to be shipped to Michigan

(4) Human organs from a donor bank in Alaska needed in New York

(5) Limestone produced in Indiana to be shipped to New Mexico

(6) Crude oil from Alaska to be shipped to the continental United States

Which transportation method is most likely to be chosen, and what is the dominant decision factor?

3. What is the difference between private and public warehouses? Explain.

4. Do you agree with the following statement? "If a product is unique, it requires a smaller amount of safety stock." Why or why not?

5. What is the difference between product packaging and physical distribution packaging?

6. Physical distribution adds value to products by creating time, place, and possession utilities. Explain this concept and cite examples to demonstrate the values added.

NOTES

1. Adapted from Dave Haake, "B & J Sales to Keep Cool," *The Pantagraph*, Bloomington, Ill., June 25, 1981, p. E-1.
2. Donald J. Bowersox, *Physical Distribution Management*, Macmillan, New York, 1968, p. 4.
3. William G. Stanton, *Fundamentals of Marketing*, McGraw-Hill, New York, 1975, p. 437.
4. John J. Coyle and Edward J. Bardi, *The Management of Business Logistics*, West Publishing Company, St. Paul, Minn., 1976, pp. 114–115.
5. Associated Press, "Long-Life Milk to Appear in U.S. Markets Soon," *The Pantagraph*, Bloomington, Ill., May 10, 1981, p. B-13.
6. Ralph Mason, Patricia Rath, and Herbert Ross, *Marketing Practices and Principles*, 3rd Edition, McGraw-Hill, New York, 1980, p. 283.
7. Arthur M. Geoffrion, "Better Planning with Computer Models," *Harvard Business Review*, July–August 1976, pp. 92–99.
8. Warren Blanding, *Blanding's Practical Physical Distribution*, Traffic Service Corporation, Washington, D.C., 1978, p. 4–41.
9. Associated Press, "Counter-Trade Builds in World's Commerce," *The Pantagraph*, Bloomington, Ill., June 7, 1981, p. F-7.
10. Associated Press, "Americans Fear Running Out," *The Pantagraph*, Bloomington, Ill., May 10, 1981, p. F-4.

APPLICATIONS/CASES

APPLICATION 7: AROUND-THE-CLOCK BROKERAGE SERVICES

More and more brokerage companies, including San Francisco's Charles Schwab and Company and Boston's Eastern Capital Corporation, are recognizing that investors want around-the-clock access to world markets.

Harold Ramby calls the Boston corporation at 12:09 a.m. from his home near Springfield, Ohio, to check on the closing prices of orange juice and pork belly futures.

Alexander Nicolas calls the San Francisco company at 2:46 a.m. from Seattle to check on the Hong Kong price of gold. He is so nervous about his investments that he cannot sleep.

Some call because they have no other time to trade. "I fly a helicopter 14 hours a day," says Stephen Bird, who places a call at 1:20 a.m. to check on wheat, oats, and Japanese yen futures.

Robert Adler of Staunton, Illinois, makes his second call at 3:38 a.m. to place an order for gold on the Hong Kong market.

As an observer of brokerage firm trading houses, you decide that 24 hour service is needed in Los Angeles, Denver, New Orleans, Memphis, Miami, Kansas City, Chicago, New York, and Portland. This would place the service in each of the geographic regions of the United States.

Adapted from Christopher Grisanti, "Now There Are Brokerage Firms for the Investor Who Can't Sleep," *Wall Street Journal*, August 27, 1982, p. 15. Reprinted by permission of the *Wall Street Journal*. © Dow Jones & Company, Inc. All Rights Reserved.

a. What possible place strategies might be followed to position the brokerage service in the cities identified?

b. Under what conditions would you choose one strategy over another?

APPLICATION 8: ZEVIN'S SUPERMARKET

Roberta Zevin recently established a small neighborhood supermarket. Sales have not been too brisk. While an ample number of customers visit the market, they run in and pick up a loaf of bread from shelving near the checkout counter or grab a quart of milk from the dairy case near the entrance. Mrs. Zevin believes that if her customers would move through the aisles in the store, they would select a number of impulse items as well as other tempting food items in stock. In fact, she points to a recent study by the Point-of-Purchase Advertising Institute showing that two-thirds of purchase decisions are made while the shopper is in the supermarket. Because you are studying marketing, she has asked you for some ideas concerning store layout. Prepare a list of 15 fast-moving items that are likely to attract "run in and run out" customers. Then devise a plan for strategically locating these items in order to pull traffic through the various aisles of the store.

APPLICATION 9: PREPS FOR RENT INC.

Michael Raus of Louisville, Kentucky, views himself as being a "preppy." A student studying international business at American University in Washington, Raus returned to Louisville during the summer between his freshman and sophomore years. Jobs were impossible to find, and so Raus and several of his former classmates from Country Day School in Louisville started a business they called Preps for Rent Inc. They mowed lawns, parked cars, painted houses, cleaned horse stalls, gathered hen house eggs, and tended to all other sorts of scutwork.

The business went well, and Mr. Raus started selling Preps for Rent franchises for $350 each. Franchises were sold in Dallas and on Martha's Vineyard and Nantucket. For their money, franchisees got a 12-page operations manual, including dress code. While tending gardens, preppies wear khaki Bermudas and Topsiders. Parking cars at parties, they wear Oxford shirts, blue blazers, Madras ties, khaki slacks, and brown loafers. In inclement weather, of course, Gortex ponchos and L. L. Bean hunting boots are accepted apparel.

Upon returning to school, Raus turned his Louisville operation over to his brother Gregg, a senior at Country Day. Raus then returned to school with the intention of marketing more franchises by advertising in newspapers at 12 colleges with "a tendency toward preppiness." Among them were Harvard, Yale, Princeton, Washington and Lee, and the University of Virginia.

Adapted from David P. Garino, "Here's A Way to Give Your Home That Clean-Cut Ivy League Look," *Wall Street Journal,* September 7, 1982, p. 25. Reprinted by permission of the *Wall Street Journal.* © Dow Jones & Company, Inc. All Rights Reserved.

a. What are the major disadvantages of entering into a franchise agreement with Raus for Preps for Rent?

b. Evaluate the marketing place strategy for Preps for Rent.

CASE 8: CATFISH FEVER

Background

New industries often are born in turmoil. An opportunity presents itself, and suddenly a certain product is in great demand. A vast new market opens up. Entrepreneurs rush in with visions of untold riches dancing in their heads.

These days it is the Mississippi delta that is giving birth to a new industry, and it is experiencing the usual growing pains. Catfish farming is catching on because the demand for fish in general and for catfish in particular is high.

Your Inheritance

You have just inherited 10 huge catfish ponds, each of which contains 20 acres. You journey to the Mississippi delta country, a victim of "catfish fever," hoping to become a prosperous catfish farmer. You realize, however, that you should learn more about catfish farming. After a visit with an instructor at Mississippi Delta Junior College in Moorhead, Mississippi, you discover some facts about catfish farming.

The Facts

First the bad news. Catfish farming is not a venture without risks. A catfish is a fragile animal. If the oxygen in the water falls too low, a whole pond can die within an hour. While there are ways to replace oxygen, there are no known cures for many of the mysterious diseases that plague catfish. Even if the fish survive, they must pass a rigorous taste test before they can be sold.

Now the good news. You also discover that the average American eats nearly 13 pounds of fish or other seafood a year and that the consumption seem to be increasing. Most of the increase, moreover, is for fresh or frozen fish, not canned or cured fish (like tuna). In fact, production of farm-raised catfish jumped 30 percent in 1981 over the 1980 production level.

Fish feed can easily run $1,000 a day for your ponds. But after expenses are paid, your profits may be about $400 an acre, or $80,000 annually on your 200 acres of ponds. Your catfish ponds as presently stocked are worth $625,000. In order to earn a 12 percent return on this value, your profits must equal $75,000 annually. While it may be possible to earn more than 12 percent if you sell the ponds and reinvest the money, you also recognize that through appreciation, your ponds are likely to increase in value each year.

The instructor tells you that many of the local catfish farmers sell their fish harvest to local processing plants for prices ranging from $0.55 to $0.65 a pound. The processors resell some of the fresh fish to restaurants, supermarkets, and fish markets. Some fish are dressed and frozen prior to resale, and in some cases, some of the fish are ground and the meat is mixed into fish cakes.

Your Plans

You quickly discover that lack of knowledge and experience has not deterred other people from getting into the act. Neighboring catfish farmers have backgrounds in banking, the ministry, crop dusting, and sales work. Your ponds are well stocked, and a veteran catfish farmer has agreed to provide assistance when you need it.

Since fresh catfish sell for higher prices than frozen or processed fish, you decide to set up distribution channels for fresh fish as opposed to selling to a processor. As a result, you hope to increase your profits to perhaps $500 per acre, or a total of $100,000 annually. You are aware that initially it may be costly to establish such channels. However, once the distribution channels are in place, your long-run profit picture will be brighter.

Adapted from "Catfish Fever," in *A Guide to Enterprise*, published by WGBH Educational Foundation and distributed by Public Broadcasting Service, Boston, 1981, p. 16.

a. Which type of distribution channel, direct or indirect, are you most likely to establish? Why?

b. What type of outlet, classified by products carried, is most likely to carry your product?

c. If you sell your product to a California-based chain of restaurants, which transportation method is most likely to be chosen? Rank the decision factors used in comparing transportation methods as they relate to your product.

d. What type of containers would you envision using to ship your product in a fresh, non-processed form to buyers?

e. If you sell your product to buyers outside the Mississippi delta area, what expenses are you likely to encounter that could be avoided by selling to local processors?

f. Under what conditions is a middleman likely to be able to assume the role of channel captain?

CASE 9: THE MILK AND EGG CASE

Background

Some IGA supermarkets (voluntary chains) would like to buy eggs and milk from their IGA wholesaler. This direct exchange would be a a breakaway from the traditional store-door delivery system used for many years, in which IGA supermarkets obtained eggs from egg jobbers and milk from dairies (truck wholesalers). It would not be an easy switch to make, however. Some IGA wholesalers looked into the idea of warehousing milk and eggs and then backed off when confronted with some of the obstacles that had to be overcome.

The Problem From an IGA Retailer's Perspective

"The big problem with store-door deliveries is cost," said one IGA retailer. "First, there is the high cost of transportation. It's extremely difficult for egg jobbers and small dairies to absorb these high costs and still be competitive. IGA wholesalers should be able to make eggs and milk available at a lower cost since their delivery schedules bring them to the store anyway."

IGA retailers also would like to order their milk and eggs along with their regular orders. If they receive five deliveries a week, they can get milk and eggs five times a week. Otherwise, milk and eggs are delivered only on the days when the truck wholesaler's route includes the store. If IGA wholesalers handled milk and eggs and a retailer was in urgent need of eggs, a phoned order would permit delivery the next day.

IGA retailers believe there is another benefit from purchasing eggs from their wholesaler, one that involves retailer advertising. If the wholesaler has plenty of large eggs for retailers, it is easy to advertise that fact. When different jobbers supply eggs, a broad advertising program is risky and egg prices are not consistent. Sometimes a jobber may run short of large eggs, and different jobbers often have different prices.

The Problem From an IGA Wholesaler's Perspective

IGA wholesalers have found that egg cartons are made of a hard material that will not absorb the many little shocks and bumps that occur during frequent handling. Warehousing personnel are not accustomed to such fragile items, and eggs must be handled four times: when picked up at the supplier's establishment, when unloaded at the distribution center, when loaded on a truck for delivery to stores, and when unloaded at the supermarkets.

Milk cartons also are fragile, and leakage can cause extensive damage, resulting in extra work and expense. On top of these problems, milk has one big problem that can make a wholesaler forget all the others. Milk cases must be returned to the dairy, and empty cases take up the same amount of truck space as full cases. In addition, wire and plastic milk cases seem to disappear in many retail establishments.

Your Task

J. M. Jones Company in Urbana, Illinois; Gateway Foods in LaCrosse, Wisconsin; and Fleming Foods in Joplin, Missouri, all of which are IGA wholesalers, have become intrigued with the idea of handling milk and eggs. They have engaged you as a consultant to offer some answers, ideas, and suggestions. More specifically, they would like answers to the following questions. Before responding, you may wish to interview a supermarket manager or food distributor to learn more about the distribution of eggs and milk.

Adapted from Wells Norris, "Warehousing Milk and Eggs," *IGA Grocergram,* February 1980, pp. 7–9.

a. Will IGA wholesalers be able to specify to egg suppliers changes in the cartons used, that is, cartons which utilize a softer pulp material that will cushion the contents? Or will egg suppliers present an argument that egg cartons represent product packaging and that wholesalers are responsible for physical distribution packaging?

b. What suggestions would you offer regarding the problems encountered by rough handling of eggs and milk by warehouse crews?

c. Will the costs vary for handling different size orders for retailers? Stated differently, if one retailer orders 10 cases of eggs and another orders 100 cases, will the costs involved in delivering the two orders vary?

d. Will retailers have better control over their milk and egg inventories as a result of buying from an IGA wholesaler?

e. Will the empty milk cases present a space problem on trucks?

f. How might the IGA wholesaler handle the problem of leaky milk cartons? The problem of disappearing milk cases?

UNIT 5
PRICE

CHAPTER 10
THE BASICS OF PRICE

- Purolator brings the cost of overnight package delivery down to earth.
- Get a $50 rebate direct from Uniroyal.
- Passengers aren't the only ones who profit from our low prices. (People Express)
- Express Mail introduces more for less.
- U-Haul costs you less. Here's why.
- The lowest-priced high-mileage Japanese imports—Dodge Colt and Plymouth Champ— just became the lowest priced cars in America—Bar none!

It is virtually impossible to open a newspaper or magazine or turn on the radio or television without being bombarded with information about the prices of a variety of products and services. These ads are paid for by companies whose marketers know that price is an important factor in the consumer's decision to buy. Consumers may refuse to buy a product or service if the price is not right. But what makes a price right or wrong from the consumer's point of view?

Let us play a version of the Price Is Right game to see which of the two suggested prices you might consider right for each of the following products or services.

1. A 6 ounce jar of moisturizing cream
   a. $0.59
   b. $3.50

2. A disposable ballpoint pen
   a. $0.98
   b. $9.98

3. A 1.5 ounce candy bar
   a. $0.35
   b. $1.19

4. A daily newspaper
   a. $0.40
   b. $1.00

5. A five-year old used car in good condition
   a. $300
   b. $3,000

6. A watch for a graduation gift
   a. $5
   b. $25

7. An eye examination and prescription for eyeglasses
   a. $7.50
   b. $30.00

8. A small cordless vacuum cleaner
   a. $30
   b. $60

9. A frozen 16 ounce pizza at the supermarket
   a. $3.39
   b. $9.95
10. A pair of leather shoes
   a. $10
   b. $60

Now check your answers. Although there are no real correct or incorrect answers, it is likely that at least eight of your answers will correspond with the following choices.

1. *b*, 2. *a*, 3. *a*, 4. *a*, 5. *b*, 6. *b*, 7. *b*, 8. *a*, 9. *a*, and 10. *b*

What is it that makes a price right from the consumer's point of view? The lowest price is not always the right price, as you can see from our game. Whenever you chose the higher of two prices, it was because the lower price did not seem to be enough to pay for what you were getting. Your reasoning may have gone something like this. "Even though the $5 watch looks like a fantastic deal, it probably will not run very long or keep accurate time. If I give it as a gift and it breaks in a few days, I'll be very embarassed." "A $7.50 eye exam sounds like too much of a bargain. Maybe the examiner isn't qualified to examine eyes and prescribe glasses." "The $10 leather shoes look OK, but I know they're cheap. They will probably fall apart right away. Even if they wear well, other people may be able to tell that they cost only $10."

On the other hand, whenever you chose the lower price, it was because the smaller amount seemed to be adequate for the product or service and because the larger amount seemed too high. You may have reasoned as follows. "If the pen is disposable, I will not pay any more than a dollar, no matter how well it writes." "If I am going to pay $9.95 for a pizza, it will be at a pizza parlor where it is freshly made and served hot."

The choices in this short pricing game may seem relatively easy to make, but pricing decisions from the marketer's point of view are often very complex. The marketer's pricing decision may involve a range of only a few cents for inexpensive items or many dollars for higher-priced items. The price that is charged for a product or service can be the difference between success and failure.

THE ROLE OF PRICE

Price is one of the four Ps in the marketing mix. The other Ps are product, place, and promotion. In the mix, price plays several important roles. It is a communication device, a measure of value, and a competitive technique. It also affects exchange and influences profits.

Communication Device

Prices are one way in which marketers communicate with their customers. The prices that are charged by a marketer help create the image of the marketer's business in the eyes of the customer. Have you ever walked into a restaurant and asked to look at the menu before being seated? If the restaurant does not *appear* to be elegant but the price of the average dinner is $35, the restaurant may be trying to communicate to customers that the quality of its food is excellent. As a customer, you have the choice of asking to be seated or selecting another restaurant.

Prices also can communicate a bargain image. If you are shopping for a dress or coat for a special occasion, you probably will steer clear of stores that advertise "all dresses under $15" or "all coats $12."

These examples represent two extremes in which price is used to communicate an image that the customer may not be comfortable with. However, the price range set by a particular business also can be used to create the right type of image for each customer and each buying situation.

Measure of Value

Price is frequently an indicator of value to the customer. If two similar products or services vary in price, the higher-priced one often is assumed to be better even if it is not actually of better quality. In the pricing game you just completed, you probably assumed that the $3.50 moisturizing cream was superior to the $0.59 cream, even though they may have exactly the same ingredients with the exception of the fragrance. Because the price difference is seldom this dramatic, some customers will choose to buy the "superior" product even if there are no apparent differences. Gasoline, corn oil, and aspirin are products that are relatively homogeneous, but customers frequently pay a higher price because a particular product seems to be or is perceived to be of superior quality.

Of course, there are numerous cases in which the higher-priced product is actually a superior product. The difference in price often reflects the fact that better materials and more careful manufacturing techniques have been used to create the higher-priced product. A bookcase handcrafted from solid walnut should be priced higher than a bookcase that appears to be similar but has been mass-produced from fiberboard and veneer.

It is interesting to note that many consumers will purchase products that seem to be priced too high even though they feel at the time of the purchase that they are being "ripped off." Recent research has shown that consumers feel cheated when they are asked to pay $2 a gallon for gasoline, but at the same time they may not feel cheated paying $3.50 a gallon for soft drinks. The consumer's perception of a fair price for a product or service is based on the recent historical price of that product or service. If the price for any product greatly exceeds its recent historical price, it will be seen by most consumers as an unfair price.

Gasoline was priced at around 30 cents a gallon during the 1950s and 1960s. During the 1970s, the price began to rise rapidly above what was considered the "fair" price of 30 cents. However, as time passes, most consumers adapt to the new higher price for a product or service that is very much needed or wanted. Then the higher price becomes the new fair price.[1]

In all marketing exchanges, the person who is buying the product or service measures its value in another way that does not depend solely on the price. The value of any purchase is equal to the total benefits the buyer will receive from the product minus the costs the buyer must incur in order to receive the product or service. You can measure the value of your new coat by weighing the costs (your shopping time, the price of $225, and the loss of alternative uses for your money) against the benefits (warmth, admiration of others, and self-confidence gained from looking stylish). If the costs are greater than the benefits, you probably will delay the purchase or decide on an alternative purchase that has more value to you.

Competitive Technique

There are very few products or services on the market today that are not vulnerable to price competition from other sources. Even when the products or services involved are recognized brands that represent quality, brand loyalty is seldom strong enough to insulate them from competition

Figure 10-1. Prices can communicate a bargain image.

from less expensive products and services with similar value.

The Sony Corporation has had a long-standing policy of avoiding price wars in the consumer electronics industry because it does not want to risk its quality image with messy head-to-head price competition. However, in the fall of 1982, caught by an eroding market share and a slow-down in consumer spending, Sony offered a rebate of $50 on basic Betamax videocassette recorder units. In the price war of VCRs, the consumer was the clear winner. In a period of 9 months, VCR prices dropped as much as 20 percent. One appliance retailer indicates that when price competition drives the price of large electronic purchases down to the $495 or $595 price range, this acts as a "magic trigger" for the public, and sales begin to pick up dramatically. [2]

The consumer electronics industry is by no means the only industry that has competitive price competition. Other industries that engaged in very active price competition in the early 1980s include airlines, candy manufacturers, and automobile manufacturers.

Effects on Exchange

Without the element of price there would be no marketing as we know it, because the final agreement on price prompts the actual buying and selling of a product or service: the marketing exchange or transaction. Very few consumers and even fewer businesses have enough capital resources to purchase any product or service they want without determining whether the price fits within a budget. Even if they did have an ample supply of capital, it would be decidedly poor business or personal financial management to buy without considering the effect of the price paid. When consumers are considering a large purchase such as a car, a television, or a vacation trip, they even may sit down with paper and pencil and calculate the effects of the purchase on their budgets before making the exchange of their money for the product or service. Even when consumers make small purchases, they make sure those purchases fit within an acceptable price range. You

may decide that you can spend between $2.49 and $4.99 a pound for coffee, depending on price fluctuations among the different brands you like. If the price of a brand goes above $3.49, you probably will not buy that brand. If there is no brand of coffee within your price range at a particular store, you probably will look elsewhere to find a lower-priced pound of coffee before you raise the upper limit of your range of acceptable prices or change to another product, such as tea.

Read the story on the next page about Pic 'N' Save, a retailer with an interesting approach to the use of price as a means of affecting exchange.

Influence on Profits

Price is a major factor in determining how profitable any product or service can be. Finding the right price is an important but difficult task. Profit is the amount that remains after total expenses are subtracted from sales revenue. If you manufacture plastic dolls at a total expense of $3.50 each and sell each doll for $5.00, your profit is $1.50 a doll. If you were to raise the price and sell each doll for $6.00 without increasing expenses, your profit would be $2.50 a doll. The prospect of raising prices looks very attractive in terms of individual dolls, and you might be tempted to keep raising the selling price in order to increase profits. But unfortunately for marketers, for every increase in the price of the doll, the demand for it decreases to some extent. This means that at $5.00 a doll you might sell 10,000 dolls, but at $5.50 a doll you might sell only 7,500. On the other hand, for every decrease in the price of the doll, the demand increases to some extent. Thus, if you were to decrease the price to $4.50, you might sell 12,500 dolls. The difficult task for the marketer is determining the degree of increase or decrease in demand that is caused by each decrease or increase in price. Then finding the right price becomes somewhat like a balancing act as the marketer weighs the factors of price and demand. However, the marketer always must remember that profit on a product or service will result only if sales revenues are greater than the total expenses of marketing that product or service.

PIC 'N' SAVE: BARGAINS TOO GOOD TO PASS UP

Pic 'N' Save has been described as a "78-store refuge for wayward merchandise and an orphanage for manufacturers' closeouts, overruns, has-beens, and never-wases." Pic 'N' Save has no continuing lines of merchandise. Instead, it sells whatever the buying staff has been able to find in the last few months. Behind each stack of merchandise is an interesting story.

Pic 'N' Save's success stems from the fact that its buyers concentrate on buying brand-name closeouts at 25 percent of the full retail price and selling them for 50 percent of that price. In the process, everyone comes out a winner. The manufacturer is able to bury its big mistakes by unloading them to Pic 'N' Save, the customer is able to buy name-brand products for half the retail price, and Pic 'N' Save makes a tidy profit.

If you walk into a Pic 'N' Save store, you probably will find many products with recognizable names: Jell-O, Wrigleys, Lever Brothers, and so on. These products include soup, sunglasses, soap, mouthwash, underwear, Star Wars T-shirts, and literally thousands of others. Next month you probably would find a store full of many different items of merchandise. Most items are priced under $10 because Pic 'N' Save customers usually can buy them without consulting family or friends. The atmosphere is one of "get 'em while they're hot."

In their successful retail operation, Pic 'N' Save's owners have found that price not only affects exchange, it often can cause the exchange to happen. "Pic 'N' Save whets the impulse buying urge and fattens its margins by conspicuous lack of advertising. . . . At any given moment, Pic 'N' Save's devotees have no idea what they may discover in the stores, so stopping by regularly becomes almost mandatory. In a lot of cases customers aren't going to use the item, but they remember seeing it for $5," says the store founder. "Now they see it for $2, so they buy it because it's a bargain and they can't pass it up."

Adapted from John Merwin, "Lemons to Lemonade," *Forbes*, vol. 130, no. 5, August 30, 1982, pp. 60–61.

THE MEANING OF PRICE

Now that we have examined the many roles that price plays in the marketing process, let us take a look at the definition of price and the factors that help marketers determine price. The simple number that represents the price of a product or service is actually a powerful influence in the marketing mix. However, its determination is not easy, and it is influenced by a complex variety of factors.

Definition of Price

Price is the amount of money (or the equivalent amount in product or service values) for which anything is bought, sold, or offered for sale. Price is an important concept for both the buyer and the seller. It is the value that is placed on any product or service.

Suppose you agree to drive a neighbor to work every day for several weeks in exchange for assistance in landscaping your yard. The price or value of the exchange would be an agreed on number of rides and hours of landscaping labor. Price may be based on factors that are monetary, nonmonetary, or a combination of the two. If you pay $20 for a shirt, the exchange is monetary. If you trade one service for another (driving for labor) or one product for another or if you exchange trading stamps or coupons for a new toaster, the exchange is nonmonetary. The price is both monetary and nonmonetary if you trade your used car and money for a new car.

Price Factors

The price that ultimately is paid for any product or service is a combination of a number of factors. It is influenced by the quantity and quality of the product or service purchased, the quantity of value (monetary and nonmonetary) given up, the premiums or discounts that are offered and accepted, the exchange transactions, and the type of payment.

"Price by Any Other Name Means Money Paid." Anything of commercial value has a price. Here are a number of different ways price is expressed in the marketplace.

Price is all around us. You pay *rent* for your apartment, *mortgage payments* for your house, *tuition* for your education, and a *fee* to your physician or dentist. Airline, railway, taxi, and bus companies charge you a *fare*; the local utilities call their price a *rate*; the local bank charges *interest* for the money it lends; and you pay a *maintenance charge* on your condominium. The price for driving a car on an expressway is a *toll*, the company that insures your car charges you a *premium*, and the garage that fixes your car charges you a *service charge*. The guest lecturer charges

an *honorarium* to tell you about a foreign country, and the marketer pays *dues* to belong to the American Marketing Association. You make *donations* to charities, and the clubs to which you belong may make a special *assessment* to cover unusual expenses. An attorney you use regularly may ask for a *retainer* to cover legal services. The "price" of an executive is a *salary*, the price of a salesperson may be a *commission*, and the price of a worker is a *wage*. Finally, although economists may disagree, many people feel that *income taxes* are the price citizens pay for the privilege of making money. [3]

Quantity of Product Purchased

As a general rule, if a product or service is bought in large quantities, the buyer will save money on the individual units purchased. A typical example involves the marketing of a service—printing. Assume that you need to have 50 business cards printed to use for a short period of time. You do not want to order more because your telephone number soon will be changed. Because the minimum charge for printing business cards is $20 an order, each card will cost $0.40. However, if you were to order 500 cards, the charge would be only $25, or $0.05 a card.

From the service marketer's point of view, the time-consuming and expensive part of printing business cards is setting the type, planning an attractive layout, and operating the printing press. Once the press is running, it makes little difference whether 50 cards or 500 are run because the card stock on which the business cards are printed represents a relatively inexpensive part of the total expense.

The same rule often applies to buying products that are not made to order. Assume that you are marketing portable color televisions to hotels, motels, and institutions and that your average sale is 40 TV sets at a time. If you approach a large hotel chain that is willing to order 2,000 sets, you can afford to lower the price of each set because you will have saved the many hours of marketing time it usually takes to sell that many sets. The reduced amount of paperwork alone would represent a significant reduction of expense.

Quantity of Value Given Up

In every exchange transaction, the purchaser and the seller must agree on the value that is to be given up by each of them before the exchange will take place. Simply put, this is a decision about how much of a product or service will be exchanged for how much money. In total, this decision may include many variables, such as product feature options, delivery terms, services wanted, and payment plans.

Quality of Product Provided

As has been discussed, when two products of equal quality are priced differently, consumers often assume that the higher-priced product represents better quality. However, in many other instances there is a real difference in quality between lower-priced products and services and those which are priced higher. Leather shoes generally cost more than shoes made from synthetic materials, custom-tailored clothing costs more than other ready-to-wear clothing, and the services of a professional typist usually cost more than the services of a high school student who types part time after school.

Premiums and Discounts

The price that is quoted for a product or service is sometimes more than the price that actually and eventually is paid. When sales are down, marketers often encourage customers to buy by offering special price incentives.

Consumers can benefit from price reductions on travel, appliances, cars, cameras, and many other items. Of course, the marketer benefits if sales volume increases more than expenses or if the price reduction has a promotional value, such as finding new customers. Recently, one airline offered unlimited mileage, excursions, visit USA, supercoach, supersaver, single-level, and day/night fares at the same time. Each of these special discount fares had differences in terms of restrictions, days away from home, or possible stopovers. One of the problems with this amount of discounting is the confusion it caused both travel agents and travelers.[4]

In an effort to move products and services in a sluggish market, many sellers use less confusing pricing techniques, including factory rebates, discounts, special price cuts, and trade-in offers. A typical example is a rebate of $1 for each unit of horsepower, up to a limit of $100, offered on outboard motors by the Brunswick Corporation. Other examples are cash rebates of $10 to $100 on camera lenses by Olympus, a $10 trade-in on any camera in any condition toward the purchase of a Pentax Auto 110, and matching rebates of $30 to $100 offered by Portland's Smith's Home Furnishings and General Electric for microwave ovens, refrigerators, and ranges.[5]

Exchange Transaction

The activities involved in the exchange transaction constitute a factor in the prices of many products and services. This is particularly true when the price is not finalized without some bargaining. When new car shoppers look at the prices listed on the stickers, they may have an attack of "sticker shock." But when they recover, they realize that the sticker price is a point from which bargaining can begin.

Even when the price of a particular product cannot be lowered from the sticker or listed price, sales people can add some degree of value to the product during the sale by adequately explaining the product features, carefully describing the recommended product care techniques, and instilling a sense of pride of ownership in the customer.

Type of Payment

The type of payment is such an important factor in the price of any product or service that some consumers think of purchases in terms of monthly payments instead of the total price to be paid. A

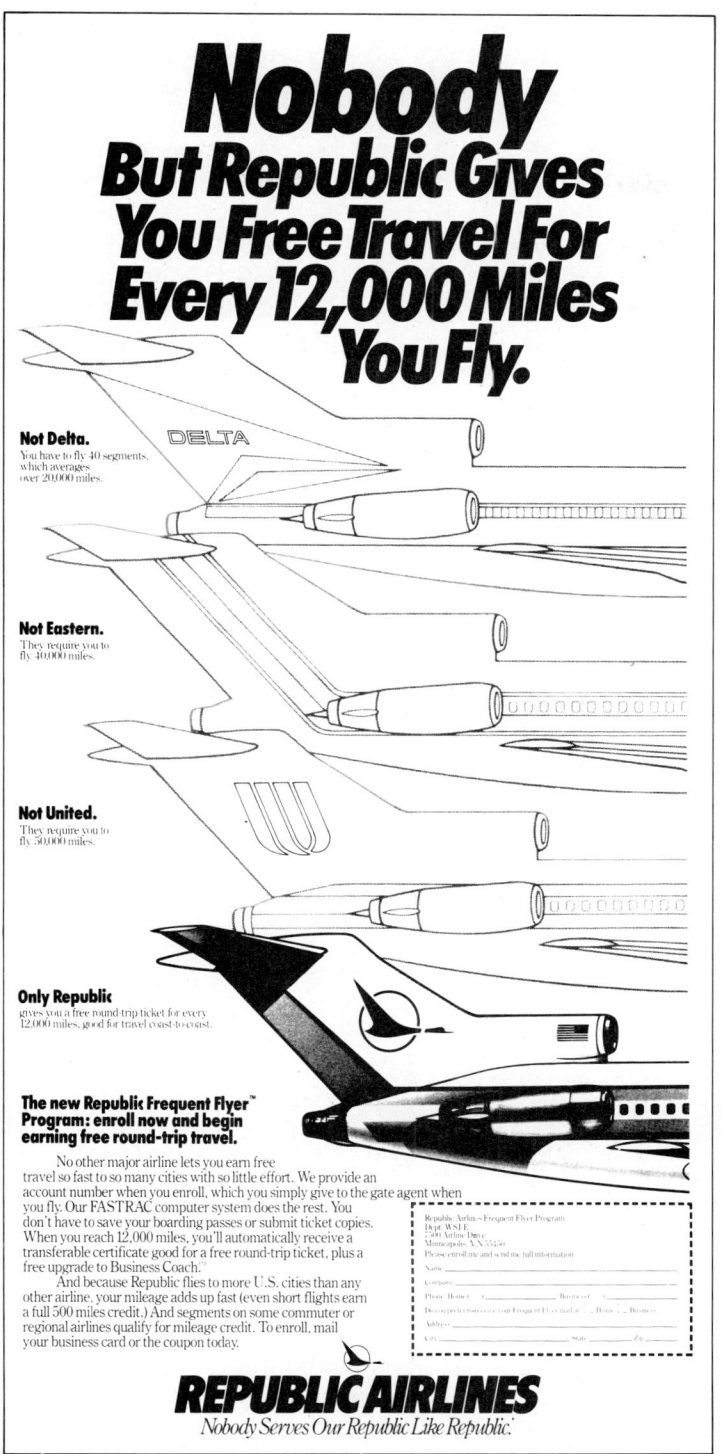

Figure 10-2. Special price incentives offered by airlines include a bonus round trip in exchange for frequent use.

consumer who can buy a stereo for $35 a month may not be concerned with the fact that the total price is $75 more than that of the competing brand and that the interest rate is adding to the cost. From the seller's point of view, it is costly to delay the receipt of payment because a great deal of cash can be tied up in large charge account balances. The seller could be using this cash to buy merchandise inventory that turns over faster. However, credit payment plans are used extensively by marketers to increase sales volume and are considered valuable in the marketing of price.

FACTORS INFLUENCING PRICING DECISIONS

Pricing is a major marketing strategy. In the mid-1960s, a survey of businesses showed pricing to be the sixth most important marketing activity out of 12 activities ranked by business executives. It was considered less important than product research and development, marketing research, sales personnel management, advertising and sales promotion planning, and customer services.

However, when business executives were surveyed again in the mid-1970s, pricing was named the most important of the 12 activities. Today even more than in the mid-1970s, because of high interest rates, a shortage of energy, high unemployment, and increasing competition from foreign suppliers, pricing is an important marketing strategy. [6]

Both internal business factors and environmental factors enter into pricing decisions. In this section, we shall discuss each of these factors briefly in order to develop a basic understanding. You will gain further knowledge for application of these factors in pricing decisions as you study the rest of this chapter and Chapter 11. This discussion will apply ideas developed in Chapter 4 on marketing research and marketing information systems. Figure 10-3 shows influences on pricing decisions.

Internal Pricing Factors

Factors inside the firm that influence pricing decisions include costs control, profit pressures, and

INFLUENCES ON PRICING DECISIONS

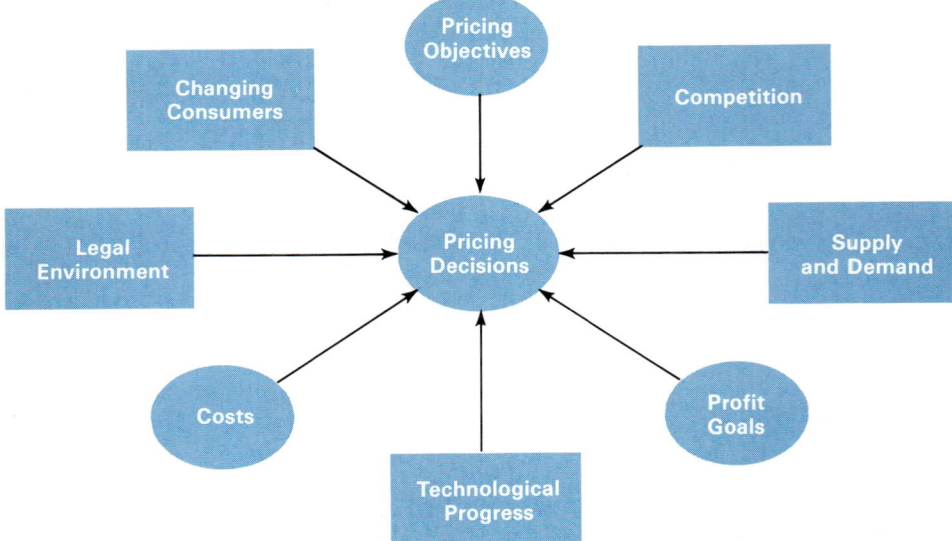

Figure 10-3. Both internal and external factors enter into decisions about price.

pricing objectives. These factors are difficult for marketers to control; they must be studied constantly, and they cause frequent changes in pricing decisions. They are interacting factors. Increasing costs may cause decreasing profits, a change in pricing objectives may cause an increase in costs, and profit pressures may cause a change in pricing objectives.

Costs Control. As inflation continues to plague the economy, the costs of manufacturing and marketing products and services will continue to rise. Controlling these costs is a constant challenge for all marketers. It is this challenge that leads marketers to search for less expensive and more efficient ways to market products and services.

Profit Pressures. In the fall of 1982, the F. W. Woolworth Company made the decision to close their Woolco Department Stores so that the parent company could try to reduce its losses and increase company profits. On a very large scale, this is the type of decision that must be made about every product or service. A small marketer may face the same type of decision on whether to continue selling a brand of toys or continue offering delivery service. If a product or service is not priced high enough or produced inexpensively enough to be profitable, few businesses can afford to continue to offer it for sale. The goal for most items is to return a satisfactory level of profit. Some products or services are used to generate customer traffic or satisfy customers in a general way and may not return a specific profit. However, they do contribute to the overall profitable nature of the marketing firm.

Pricing Objectives. Both costs control and profit pressures relate to the formulation of a firm's pricing objectives. A firm may establish the price objective of offering the lowest prices in town for its type of products. To establish this reputation in its market, the firm would have to accept lower profit margins on many products. If the goal is to price products and services so that

the firm will become the number one volume marketer in the market, the firm can expect to have higher costs in service and promotion to support that goal. Firms need to establish pricing objectives that are both realistic and measurable if they are to be of any value. For example, the firm might set a pricing objective which would specify an increase in sales volume of 10 percent over last year. This is a realistic and measurable objective. Pricing objectives must reflect the overall marketing goals of the company. Is being number one in sales volume in the market a realistic goal and does it fit the resources and image of the company?

Pricing objectives typically include such specific goals as sales maximization, profit maximization, satisfactory or fair return on investment, sales target return on investment or sales, target market share, and pricing above, equal to, or below that of the competition. We shall study these objectives in detail after looking at environmental factors.

Environmental Pricing Factors

You own and manage a service station. Can you imagine trying to operate your business successfully without knowing what prices your competitors are charging in your market area? Would a record and tape marketer make it in business without knowing what is new in the design of laser disks, the demand for new types of disks, and the prices of competitive brands? It is not possible for a marketer in any size business to make effective pricing decisions and use pricing as an important marketing strategy without being aware at all times of several critical environmental factors that affect pricing decisions. These include increased competition, rapid technological progress, changes in supply and demand, a changing legal environment, and better informed customers.

Increased Competition. "The time and money teenagers spend on Pac Man is time and money they aren't spending on their record collections. Add home taping, widespread counterfeiting, and a dearth of exciting new artists to that, and you have some big problems in the record business."[7] Experts estimate that competition from video games has cost the record business as much as $1 billion a year.

The competition that influences pricing in most businesses comes from both existing products and new products. If a firm chooses to ignore the threat of possible competition from new products, it may be in for an unpleasant surprise when profits begin to decline. Sometimes, as in the record industry, the impact of new competition is so great that an entirely new marketing approach is needed. One record industry expert suggests that record companies abandon their trend of going after blockbuster albums with multimillion dollar sales. Instead, they should aim albums at regional or social groups. Then the companies should attempt to broaden this narrow target by appealing to other regional or social groups. This type of approach was used with an album called "Private Eyes" by Daryl Hall and John Oates. The album started as a pop record but then crossed over to become the number one record among black listeners.[8]

Another interesting experiment in the record business is the renting of records by service marketers for a fraction of the retail selling price. Customers are able to rent new albums for 2 days for only $1.98 as opposed to paying the purchase price of $8 or $9. It is the hope of the marketers that consumers will want to own the rental records and will pay the difference in price between the rental and ownership prices so that they will not have to return the albums.[9]

Rapid Technological Progress. In the declining record industry, a dramatic new technological discovery called digital audio is considered the biggest innovation since stereo transformed hi-fi. The marketing of digital audio disk (DAD) players may enable record companies to entice customers into their stores. The DAD system stores music in the form of computer codes that can be reproduced with all the brilliance and clarity of a live performance. This is just one example of technological progress that may have an effect on pricing decisions for both stereo records and home video game cartridges.[10] Other product areas in which one can observe the effect of rapid technological progress on marketing are communication systems, calculators, computers, banking services, office equipment, and kitchen appliances and gadgets for the home.

Technological progress also can help firms by providing ways to cut costs and speed production. These savings can be passed on to the consumer in the form of price reductions. In the face of rising costs, these technological advances can help companies maintain current prices or slow their rate of increase. The increasingly widespread use of microcomputers helps companies simplify paperwork and enables them to benefit from the current information that has been processed by the computer, such as payroll, inventory, costs, sales, and profit records.

Changes in Supply and Demand. Another environmental pricing factor is the constant shifting of supply and demand. As the price of a product goes up, fewer people want to buy it. However, at the same time, more people will want to supply (produce or market) it. If sellers supply more of a product than customers demand, there will be a surplus on hand and the price will decrease, usually resulting in the surplus being sold. If customers demand more than sellers can supply at a specific time, a shortage of products will develop and the price will tend to increase.

These ideas provide basic knowledge about supply and demand as environmental factors. Although they may appear to be "too economic" to be of any value to the marketer, they form the practical and real basis of many pricing decisions made by small and large marketers.

Changing Legal Environment. Legislation on pricing has been established with the basic purpose of protecting the consumer from unfair pricing practices by marketers. The laws seek to prevent marketers from fixing prices by talking with other marketers to the detriment of

Figure 10-4. An example of competitive pricing is Penney's alternative to the established La Coste knitted shirt with an alligator. Note the emphasis on both quality and price.

consumers. Other laws are intended to prevent price discrimination, which would result in certain marketers having an unfair advantage in the same level of marketing activity. Another law seeks to prevent deceptive pricing, such as claims that a price has been reduced when it has not.

Marketers must understand this important pricing legislation and meet the laws without exception. It is equally important for marketers to stay current on court decisions regarding pricing legislation. The intent of the legislation is good, but successful marketers do not need laws to force them to be honest with customers. Fair prices and honest communication with all customers are good marketing strategies.

Informed Consumers. Consumers today are both price- and quality-conscious. They are concerned about getting adequate value in return for their hard-earned money. Refer back to Chap-

PRICING OBJECTIVES OF U.S. BUSINESSES

What are the pricing objectives of and pricing practices in American industry? In a recent study of U.S. businesses by Boone and Kurtz, the goal mentioned most often as a primary pricing objective was "specified rate of return on investment." Results of the study are shown in the table.

Pricing Objective	As Primary Objective	As Secondary Objective
Specified rate of return on investment	60.9%	17.2%
Specified total profit level	60.2	17.2
Specified rate of return on sales	47.7	23.4
Meeting a competitive price level	38.3	43.0
Increased total profits above previous levels	34.4	37.5
Increased market share	31.3	42.2
Retaining existing market share	31.3	35.9
Serving selected market segments	26.6	39.1
Creation of a readily identifiable image for the firm or its products	21.9	41.4
Specified market share	15.6	40.6
Other	5.5	—

ter 3 for a discussion of the psychographic characteristics of consumers. Consumers are problem solvers. They search the offerings of marketers and compare alternatives. They make decisions based on needs and facts, and they often know a lot about the product or service before they contact the marketer.

Marketers who understand the needs of the consumer are more likely to price products and services to satisfy customers. Actually, effective marketers help consumers learn about the values and uses of the products and services they sell.

PRICING OBJECTIVES

Most people assume that all businesses share the same pricing objective: to make the highest possible profit on all products and services sold.

Although profit maximization is a common pricing objective, it is only one of several that management may select. In this section, we shall discuss profit maximization, sales maximization, satisfactory return, target return on investment, target market share, and pricing related to competition. Look at the list of pricing objectives of U.S. businesses on page 286. The list is based on a survey of businesses and their stated primary and secondary pricing objectives.

Profit Maximization

Companies that adopt the goal of profit maximization try to make as much profit as they can considering the conditions of the market. This means that the marketer charges the highest price that customers are willing to pay. This philosophy is one of "earning all the traffic will bear" or "making hay while the sun shines." The profit maximization objective will lead marketers to charge the highest price they can so they can earn a profit quickly. For example, if a toy is very popular and in great demand as a Christmas gift, marketers will charge a high price while customers want the toy. The interesting point is that the customers will be happy to pay the high price while the toy is so popular. Profit maximization for most marketers is a short-term pricing objective because, unless the product or service is unique or in extremely short supply, competition will drive the price down.

Sales Maximization

Sales maximization may be used when a new product is introduced in the market. If the price is low enough or if the premiums offered are attractive enough, the company is able to attract a large number of customers. However, unless the profit earned at this low price is acceptable for an extended period of time, the price will have to be raised or discounts and premiums will have to be discontinued. If the sales maximization objective has produced the desired results of attracting many loyal customers, these customers will continue to buy the new product at reasonable and fair higher prices.

Satisfactory Return

If marketers are striving to earn a satisfactory return on investment, they will be content to earn a profit that is "good enough" on each product. Although this objective is not a specific one for setting price on every product, it will help the marketer survive in the marketplace. It should generate a fair profit and keep the marketer competitive.

Target Return on Investment

Marketers frequently establish a minimum rate of return on investment for each product or service that is offered. This is an efficient way for the company to distribute limited capital resources. For example, the decision may be made to offer only products that will earn at least a 10 percent return on investment. Any potential product that is expected to earn a smaller amount will not be offered. In a very practical sense, this objective helps a marketer continue with the products and services that make a contribution to the company.

Target Market Share

Another pricing objective might be to maintain or increase **market share,** which refers to the portion of the market that buys a firm's product. The specific goal might be to increase the market share of a product from 12 percent to 16 percent. Market share measures how a firm is doing in sales volume in relation to the competition. Increasing market share also may be a means of achieving other profit objectives because there is a positive correlation between market share and profitability.

Pricing Related to Competition

Pricing objectives in relation to competition are very common and very practical for many marketers. These objectives result in marketers pricing their products higher than, equal to, or lower than those of the competition.

Some products, such as Waterford crystal, *Gourmet* magazine, and dinners at famous restaurants, are purposely priced above those of the competition to create a prestige image. If you price your products or services higher than your competition, you will be successful if your customers perceive something special or extra in your marketing mix that they cannot get from the competition.

Many marketers price their products and services to meet the prices of competitors. In fact, smaller companies often have little choice but to meet the lower prices of strong competitors. If one marketer answers a competitor's lower price by going lower with an answering price, a price war often results. In the early 1980s, a price war in the airline industry forced prices to the lowest level in 20 years. Fares between San Francisco and New York were as low as $99 a seat. Although airline officials claimed that they did not know what level of passenger loads they needed to break even (cover the costs of flying the airplane), the best guess was that even a full planeload of passengers was a loser. One estimate was that airplanes would have had to be filled to an impossible 150 percent of capacity to break even.[11]

Price wars have affected prices and profits for many products and services, especially in the marketing of automobiles, cameras, home computers, candy bars, and even memberships in health and physical fitness clubs. Customers seem to benefit from price wars for a relatively short time, and marketers seem to gain some promotional value out of reduced prices and profits. Typically, economic conditions drive prices back up to reasonable levels, and then price competition returns to normal.

The objective of meeting the competitor's prices also can work in reverse. When a major company in any industry raises its prices, other companies often follow the leader. But a major advantage for many other companies is that they can wait and see how the increased price affects the leader's sales. In the fall of 1982, *Woman's Day* magazine decided to raise its price from 69 cents to 79 cents. But *Family Circle* magazine decided to delay on its decision to raise prices. "We'll let them raise prices first and track what they do," said the publisher. "We may raise our prices. Greed is always a factor."[12]

THE ECONOMICS OF PRICING

The economics of pricing sounds like a mysterious, theoretical topic that should be studied only by economics buffs. It actually is a practical and important topic that can help marketers understand why prices are set as they are. Our discussion of the economics of pricing begins with a graphic demonstration of supply and demand. Then it will include an explanation of competitive models, costs and revenues, and price elasticity.

Supply and Demand

Pricing decisions are not made only by marketers. It is really the customers who determine the products and services that will be offered and the prices that will be charged. The system that is used to balance the products and services marketers want to sell with the products and services customers want to buy involves the application of the principle of supply and demand.

When they are used in an economic discussion, these terms have specific meanings. **Demand** is the quantity of a product or service for which consumers are willing to pay a given price at a given time. There is a big difference between a want and a demand. Even if you want something very much, your want does not turn to demand until you are both able and willing to pay for it. You may want a new car, a boat, and a vacation in Europe, but until you are able and willing to spend money for these wants, they are not demands.

Supply is the quantity of a product or service that producers will offer at a given price at a given time. As with demand, even if you own a large quantity of a product or have the ability to produce a large quantity of a service, these products and services do not become part of supply unless you are able and willing to sell them. You may own an entire warehouse full of 10-speed bicycles, but until you put them on the market to sell, they do not become part of supply.

The Principles of Demand and Supply.
Economists have developed a few principles that help explain the relationships between demand and price, supply and price, and supply and demand.

The principle of demand basically states that the higher the price of a product or service, the less people will buy. Conversely, the lower the price, the more people will buy. This means that if you sold boxes of candy, more people would buy the same candy at $1.50 a box than at $2.50 a box.

The principle of supply basically states that if the supply of something is low, the price will tend to be high. Conversely, if the supply is plentiful, the price will tend to be low. Because there probably is no fresh lobster in Kansas, the price would tend to be high because of scarce supply. However, on the coast of Maine, where lobster is plentiful, the price would be lower.

Before discussing supply and demand, let us look at a few exceptions to the principles we have just read about. There are some products and services that for various reasons sell better when they are priced somewhat higher. At the beginning of this chapter, we played a simple version of the Price Is Right game, and you probably decided that some products were not priced high enough to sell well, for example, moisturizing cream. This seems to be true also of items such as perfume, cosmetics, and high-fashion clothing. The higher price often is perceived by the customer as an indication of better quality, prestige, status, and self-image.

How do supply and demand influence each other? The supply of something will increase when demand is high and decrease when demand is low. If there were a sudden increase in the number of people who are willing and able to buy hang gliders, businesses would produce and market more of them. Also, new glider manufacturers would enter the market to get a piece of the increasing profits. However, as this interest in hang gliders cooled, the manufacturers would cut back on inventories and produce fewer hang gliders. Some of the manufacturers would even be forced out of business by the declining demand.

Graphing Supply and Demand.
Perhaps the easiest way to understand supply and demand is by looking at these principles in picture form. First, let us look at a picture, or graph, of a **demand curve.** This is a graph of the quantity of a product or service that consumers will buy at various price levels. Figure 10-5 on page 290 shows a hypothetical demand curve for hot-air popcorn poppers. According to the information in the graph, if the price of the popper is $20, consumers are willing to buy 125,000 poppers. But if the price is $35, they will only buy 75,000. It is said that the demand curve slopes downward because demand increases when price decreases.

Let us look at a supply curve for the same hot-air popcorn poppers. The **supply curve** is a graph of the quantity of a product or service that suppliers will provide for sale at various price levels. According to the supply curve in Figure 10-6, if the popper is priced at $45, suppliers are willing to produce and supply 200,000 poppers. But if the price is only $15, they will offer only 25,000 for sale. It is said that the supply curve slopes upward because supply increases when price increases.

The Equilibrium Price.
It is easy to see that consumers and suppliers have different objectives when it comes to pricing. Consumers want to buy as much as they can for as little money as possible, and suppliers want to supply as much as they can in return for as much money as possible. But if we combine the supply curve and the demand curve, as in Figure 10-7 on page 291, we begin to see how the demands of consumers and supply from producers can be balanced. The point at which the supply curve and the demand curve intersect is called the **equilibrium point.**

When the equilibrium point is converted into price and quantity terms, it becomes the **equilibrium price,** or the price at which both buyers and sellers will be satisfied. At this price, sellers are able and willing to supply exactly the quantity of products and services that buyers are able and willing to purchase. Figure 10-7 shows that the equilibrium price for hot-air popcorn poppers is $25 a unit for 100,000 units. An equilibrium price

DEMAND CURVE

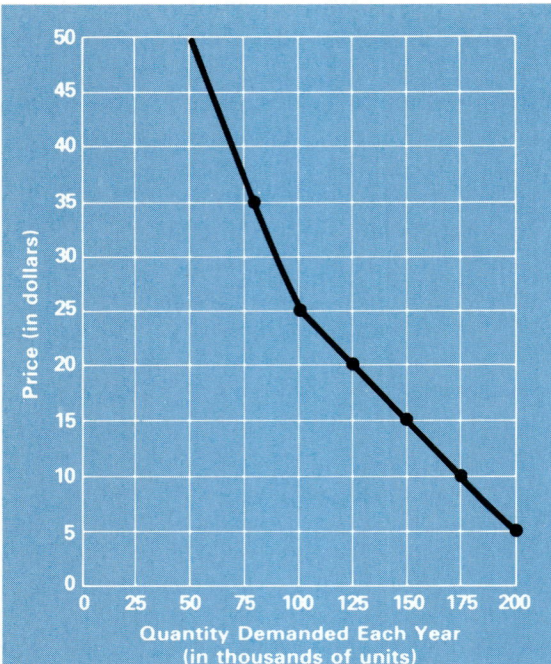

Figure 10-5. Quantity of popcorn poppers that _customers_ will _buy_ at various price levels.

SUPPLY CURVE

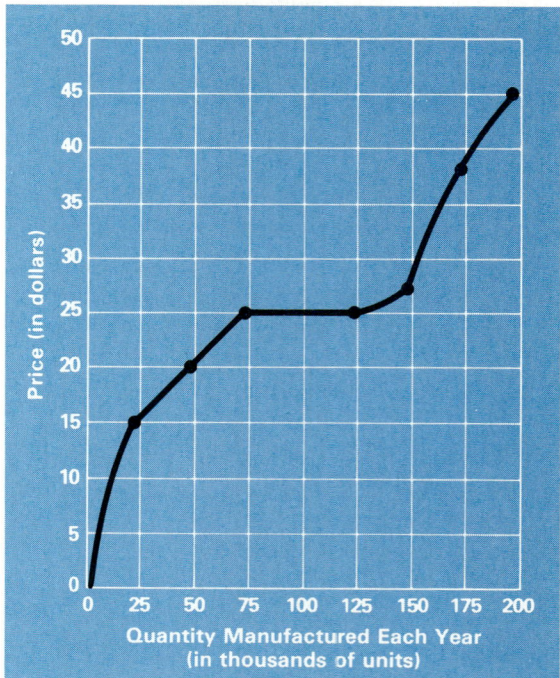

Figure 10-6. Quantity of popcorn poppers that _suppliers_ will _sell_ at various price levels.

graph is particularly helpful to marketing managers who want to find out what would happen to a particular product's equilibrium price if demand were to rise or fall or supply were to rise or fall. If the marketers drew a new demand curve or supply curve on the existing graph, the answer would be easier to see. In marketing practice, the equilibrium price is not an exact amount but a realistic range of prices that would satisfy both sellers and buyers. A product that sells for around $300 might have a realistic market price range of $285 to $315.

Competitive Models

For the supply and demand principles to be applied effectively in marketing, there must be competition. **Competition** happens when at least two people or organizations want the same object

or the same reward. Competition occurs in marketing when two marketers try to sell similar products and services to the same target market. There are four types of marketing structures in the U.S. economy, and each represents a different competitive model: pure competition, monopolistic competition, oligopoly, and monopoly.

Pure Competition. In **pure competition,** a large number of buyers and sellers are in a market. Because of that large number, no single buyer or seller has a significant influence on the market.

When pure competition exists, all competing firms produce standardized or very similar products. When the consumer is given an attractive price, he or she does not really care which seller supplies the product. Advertising and sales pro-

EQUILIBRIUM PRICE

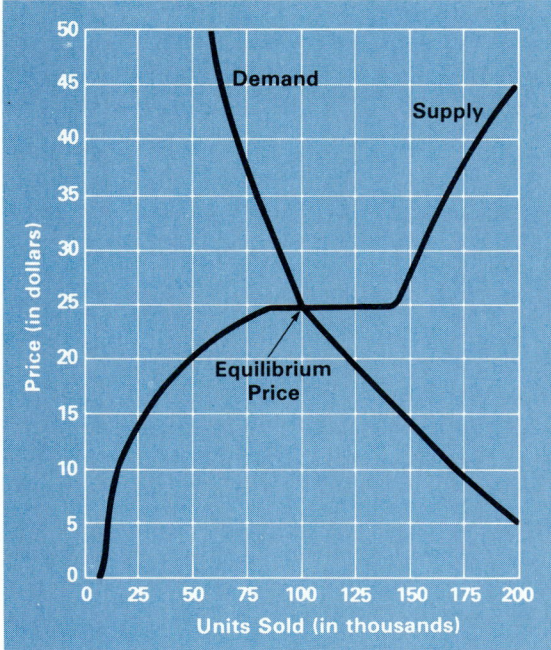

Figure 10-7. The point at which supply and demand intersect is called the equilibrium price.

motion are difficult and less effective because all suppliers have equal products. Also, new firms are free to enter the competition, and older firms are free to leave the market. Because there are so many suppliers, no single marketer has any control over or effect on changes in the market.

Although precise examples of pure competition are hard to find, agriculture markets provide some fairly good examples. Many thousands of farmers produce wheat in this country. Assuming that their wheat produced meets the grading standards, all the wheat is the same. Each individual farmer accepts or rejects whatever market price exists in the highly organized market. It will do farmers no good to advertise their wheat, attempt to package it, or try to sell it for a different price. Farmers who are unhappy about the price can simply decide not to sell at that particular time.

Monopolistic Competition. If you open a retail store to sell to consumers, you will be involved in **monopolistic competition.** In this market structure, there are many sellers who act independently. However, the products they produce and market can be differentiated. This means that customers can tell the difference between different marketers' products. This differentiation includes such things as unique physical features of the products, reputation and location of the sellers, effectiveness of advertising and sales promotion, and services. In monopolistic competition, sellers have some control over price because of perceived differences in products, services, and marketing personnel. If consumers like a unique product or a particular seller, they are likely to remain loyal to that product or seller. Marketers like the competitive world of monopolistic competition. It gives them the opportunity to market the advantages of their individual marketing mix and develop loyal customers. For example, a marketer can change the price to try to meet his or her marketing objectives.

Entry into this type of market structure is relatively easy and usually is based on having something different to offer potential customers in a market. A pet center opens that specializes only in cats; a new restaurant is the only one in this market serving authentic Peking cuisine; a computer training center offers classes in learning how to use a personal computer. In each case, the marketer is offering something different to a market. But this does not guarantee success. New customers have to be won away from alternative products and services. In monopolistic competition, when a marketer is successful, other marketers begin to compete with slightly different products and services, sometimes at a lower price.

Oligopoly. In an **oligopoly,** a few firms dominate the market for a particular product or service. This occurs primarily because there are very high start-up costs for a particular type of business. When you hear about the "big three" or the "big four," you can be relatively sure that the industry is in an oligopoly form of competition. The automobile industry is a good example. Today, hundreds of companies have entered the business of producing and marketing computers. Eventually, a few major producers of computers will dominate the market, and an oligopoly will result. Competition among a few dominant firms is usually fierce. In spite of this extremely competitive environment, marketers in an oligopoly know that what one does to change its marketing mix will have an impact on the others. This phenomenon is referred to as **mutual interdependence.** If one of the big three automobile manufacturers makes a competitive move, the other two must respond in some way. However, they all share problems in marketing cars as a result of high interest rates and foreign imports.

The products that are produced and marketed by oligopolists may be either standardized or differentiated. Examples of standardized products include steel, tobacco, aluminum, and rayon. Examples of differentiated products are automobiles, soap, breakfast cereals, and refrigerators.

Monopoly. In a **monopoly,** the market is structured with only one seller of a product or service and no close substitutes for that product or service. The seller has considerable control over price because there is no other source of supply in the market. Examples of monopolies are municipal water companies, electric power companies, and telephone service companies. These businesses are allowed to function as monopolies because monopoly is considered to be an efficient system for certain consumer services. These suppliers are supervised and controlled by governments and laws. Prices are set and changed only with government approval.

A marketer seldom competes in a monopoly environment, and the situation lasts a short time only. A vendor may be the only one on a hot day inside a ball park who has cold soft drinks available. The vendor may sell more but not be able to raise the price. Some marketers in isolated locations may be able to charge higher prices because they are open on Sunday without competition, but this is only a temporary monopoly situation. It is not a true monopoly because other marketers will enter the competition when the market looks good.

Costs and Revenues

Another important aspect of the economics of pricing is the interrelationship among costs, revenues, and profit. This interrelationship is best explained by looking at the basic conceptual approach to setting prices that is called marginal analysis. The **principle of marginal analysis** states that a company should set a price for a product at the point at which the cost of making the last unit is less than or equal to the revenue from selling that last unit. In simple terms, a marketer will make and market products in quantities that result in as much profit as possible. If the marketer stops short of the best quantity that will sell at a profit, some potential profits will be lost (profits will not be maximized). If the marketer tries to make and market so many products that costs are greater than revenues, the marketer will not earn a profit on the last number of items sold.

Marginal analysis is a principle that is difficult to measure. As a result, very few marketers use it as an exact way to set prices. However, it does have some practical uses for pricing. For example, the costs and revenues may be estimated, and the price that will maximize profits will be set within an approximate range. Marketers who know the costs of products at different quantities then can estimate demand and revenue at several prices.

Marginal revenue is the amount of revenue a company gets from selling one additional unit of a particular product. The term **marginal costs** refers to the additional amount a company must pay to produce one additional unit of a product. **Fixed costs** are the costs of doing business that must be paid just to keep the business running even if the business does not produce or sell any products.

DEMAND CURVE FOR TRI-PEDS

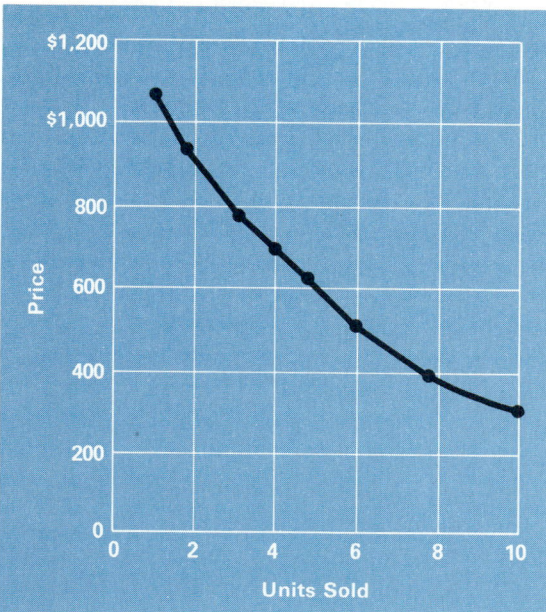

Figure 10-8. Consumers' demand at various prices.

Examples of fixed costs are executive salaries, rent, insurance, and utilities. **Variable costs** are expenses that vary as production goes up and down. They include costs for materials, parts needed for production, wages for production workers, salary and commissions for sales people, packaging, and transportation.

Assume that you work for the Alternative Vehicle Corporation, which manufactures large, motorized three-wheel cycles. These vehicles run at two different speeds, 8 miles an hour and 16 miles an hour, and get 75 miles to a gallon of gasoline. They have large baskets for carrying packages, and they even come with an AM/FM radio. The name of the three-wheel cycle is the Tri-ped.

The research department has analyzed the demand for the Tri-ped and provided you with a demand curve (Figure 10-8) and a demand table (Table 10-1). For the purposes of this detailed explanation, assume that you are interested in selling only 10 Tri-peds. If this analysis was com-

TABLE 10-1
DEMAND, PRICE, AND REVENUES FOR TRI-PEDS

Quantity Demanded	Price	Total Revenue	Marginal Revenue
0	$1,040	$ —	$ —
1	1,100	1,100	1,100
2	930	1,860	760
3	800	2,400	540
4	700	2,800	400
5	620	3,100	300
6	530	3,180	80
7	460	3,220	40
8	400	3,200	− 20
9	350	3,150	− 50
10	300	3,000	− 150

puterized, detailed information could be obtained on the possible revenue and cost implications of selling thousands of Tri-peds. In addition to the demand information you have received, the production department has provided you with a cost table (Table 10-2) that indicates how much it will cost to produce each Tri-ped.

Calculating Marginal Revenue.
You can see from Figure 10-8 that Tri-peds have a typical demand curve. More people want to buy them at lower prices than at higher prices. Table 10-1 shows that for every Tri-ped sold up through the seventh one, marginal revenue increases. But when you try to sell the eighth Tri-ped, the marginal revenue turns out to be a negative figure (−$20). This means that the eighth Tri-ped will *cost* the company money rather than making money. When the seventh Tri-ped is sold, total revenue will be $3,220 because at a price of $460, seven people want to buy one. If you were to lower the price to $400, eight people would want a Tri-ped, but total revenue for these eight

sales would be only $3,200, which is $20 less than the firm would make selling only seven Tri-peds.

Calculating Marginal Costs.
Now that you know how many Tri-peds you can sell and still make a profit, how many can you afford to manufacture? In Table 10-2, the production department has supplied you with information about how many Tri-peds can be produced profitably. A supply curve for Tri-peds would be a typical upward-sloping curve.

Now combine Table 10-2 and Table 10-1 so that you can compare marginal costs with marginal revenue figures. When you sell the fifth Tri-ped, marginal revenue is $300 and marginal costs are only $200. But look what happens when you try to manufacture and sell the sixth Tri-ped. Marginal revenue for the sixth Tri-ped is only $80, but it will cost $190 to produce. Thus, it does not make any sense to manufacture and sell any more than five Tri-peds. You maximize profits at five units which sell for $620 a unit.

TABLE 10-2
COSTS OF TRI-PED PRODUCTION AND SALES

Quantity Supplied	Fixed Cost	Variable Costs	Total Costs	Marginal Costs
0	$1,000	$ —	$1,000	$ —
1	1,000	400	1,400	400
2	1,000	720	1,720	320
3	1,000	1,000	2,000	280
4	1,000	1,240	2,240	240
5	1,000	1,440	2,440	200
6	1,000	1,630	2,630	190
7	1,000	1,760	2,760	130
8	1,000	1,890	2,890	130
9	1,000	2,040	3,040	150
10	1,000	2,220	3,220	180

Price Elasticity

The term **elasticity** refers to how responsive the market is to any change in the price of a product. If you sell a product for which the demand is highly elastic, there will be a dramatic increase in demand if you lower the price a little. Conversely, if you raise the price a little, there will be a big decrease in demand. On the other hand, if you sell a product for which the demand is highly inelastic, you can raise and lower the price by large amounts, and the result will be only a small change in demand.

In practical application, few products are either highly elastic or highly inelastic in demand. Instead, they are either just a little elastic or a little inelastic in demand. Some products that appear to be somewhat inelastic in demand are gasoline, fuel oil, and sugar. One type of product that is highly inelastic in demand is prescription drugs. On the other side of the scale, beef is a product with a somewhat elastic demand. As the price goes up, more people switch to other kinds of meat. A service that appears to be somewhat elastic is air travel. When prices are high, people may take vacations that do not require air travel, but when prices are low, the airlines are crowded.

What does the elasticity of demand mean to the marketing manager? If you can identify the extent to which the demand for your product is elastic or inelastic, you can take advantage of this information to try to increase profits. If the demand is highly inelastic, you can raise the price and make more money while you sell about the same amount of the product. If the demand is highly elastic, you can capture a larger share of the market by lowering your prices a little.

PRICING AND THE LAW

Anyone who purchased crayons, chalk, finger paints, or modeling clay between 1964 and 1976 might have been the victim of price fixing. In 1977, the Federal Trade Commission investigated pricing practices in the sale of art materials. As a result, Milton Bradley, Binney and Smith, and the American Art Crayon Company, a division of Joseph Dixon Crucible Co. of Jersey City, were accused of price fixing. Out-of-court settlements and fines for the three companies may total as much as $2 million before the case is settled.[13]

Pricing of products is an area in which a knowledge of and respect for the law is essential. Marketing managers must be aware of their legal rights and responsibilities with respect to price fixing, price discrimination, resale price maintenance, and deceptive pricing.

Price Fixing

If sellers set prices after talking with competitors and agreeing on certain levels of prices, they may be suspected of **collusion** or price fixing. Price fixing is illegal except in the few cases in which the government supervises pricing agreements. This sometimes happens in local milk industry agreements or in fruit and vegetable cooperatives.

There is a difference between overt collusion and tacit collusion. Overt collusion is purposeful, while tacit collusion is basically collusion without communication. Nevertheless, tacit collusion can bring about antitrust action against the dominant firm in a particular industry.

Price Discrimination

Sellers are legally bound by the Robinson-Patman Act to offer the same price terms to every business at a given level of trade. This means that every retailer, for example, is entitled to receive the same price terms even though one retailer may be J. C. Penney and the other may be Matt and Maggie's General Store. There is one exception. If the seller can prove that it costs less to sell a large volume of men's work clothes to Penney's than it does to sell a small order to Matt and Maggie's, different prices can be charged. It is up to the seller to prove that legitimate differences in costs do exist and that the price differences reflect these differences proportionately. The Robinson-Patman Act does allow prices that would otherwise be discriminatory, or of special benefit to a purchaser, if the prices were made in good faith to meet the equally low prices of competitors.

Resale Price Maintenance

Resale price maintenance laws, or fair trade laws, were repealed in 1976. Manufacturers cannot legally require dealers to charge specific retail prices for their products. Manufacturers do attempt, however, to maintain resale prices by suggesting a retail price to dealers and then using encouragement and rewards to persuade dealers to sell at that price. If retailers see the advantages of maintaining a price and voluntarily agree to the resale price maintenance, the pricing actions are not illegal. Manufacturers would be taking illegal actions if they refused to sell to certain dealers because the dealers did not maintain specified prices. Manufacturers must treat the dealers fairly in every respect related to the dealers' pricing. For example, it would be illegal if a manufacturer punished a dealer for not maintaining a price by increasing costs to the dealer through delayed shipments and withheld advertising allowances.

Resale price maintenance laws were repealed because they discouraged price competition and often caused unfairly high prices for consumers. The laws also protected inefficient retailers and punished efficient ones. Minimum-service, mass-merchandising, and discount retailers who operated at lower costs were restricted from using effective price competition (lower selling prices) on products when resale price maintenance was legal. Today, retailers may agree to a seller's suggested retail price if the product's quality justifies the higher price and if their customers are buying at that price. Or they may lower the suggested price for their own pricing objectives.

Deceptive Pricing

Marketers often advertise lower prices to try to attract customers and increase sales. In their eagerness to communicate how low the prices are, marketers must be careful to be truthful in representing the former prices in relation to the new price. According to the FTC's *Guides against Deceptive Pricing,* it is illegal for retailers to claim that they are selling products at a reduced price if there has been little or no price reduction.

One of the most frequent techniques in pricing is to show a new lower price compared to a former price. If the former price is an actual price marked on the product offered for sale to customers, the pricing action is not deceptive. If the former price is a false high price listed on the new ticket, the reduced price is deceptive in relation to the former price. A retailer decided to have a major storewide sale with larger than usual price reductions. New price tickets were attached to products, increasing the regular prices by about 20 percent. Then the new price was reduced to one-half the false price. The sale was advertised as a 50 percent off sale. This was deceptive pricing. If a selling price is increased from $50 to $60 (20 percent) and then lowered to $30 (50 percent of $60), the price reduction is actually $20 (40 percent of the regular price of $50). This pricing action would be very foolish on the part of any marketer who wants to keep the confidence of regular customers. An honest 40 percent price reduction would be effective. In addition to risking legal action for deceptive pricing, the marketer risks losing the trust of loyal customers.

Another deceptive pricing practice is to quote the manufacturer's suggested retail price as a base for a price reduction. This is deceptive to the customer if the retailer has never used the suggested retail price. If the manufacturer's suggested retail price is the price at which a product generally is sold, the price could be used for comparison to a new lower price without being deceptive.

Marketers are deceptive if they make up a price that is higher than current market value price. For example, if a brand of a bicycle is currently selling at most retailers for $79.95, a marketer should not price the bicycle at $69.95 and claim that it is priced $30 below a market value of $99.95. Even if the bicycle once sold generally for $99.95, its current market value is around $80. This marketer should refer to the reduced price of $69.95 as $10 below the market value or below the price of comparable brands.

Most marketers avoid deceptive pricing because they know that it is a bad marketing strategy. Of course, deceptive pricing is illegal, and legal actions can be costly for a marketer. But the biggest risk resulting from deceptive pricing is the loss of customers who no longer trust the marketer.

THE PRICING CHALLENGE

After studying this chapter, you are aware that pricing is a challenge to the marketer. It is a very important but often a complex and difficult decision influenced by many constantly changing factors. In your marketing position, you will be seeking answers to questions like these.

How much should we charge?

How much will our customers pay?

What are our competitors charging?

What price will return a fair profit?

In some cases, you will set a price that is estimated to be satisfactory to customers and that will return a profit. This price then becomes an offer in the market made by the seller to potential customers. If your customers accept the price offer, you will sell some of the products or services. If sales are not satisfactory at a certain price, you will need to change the price to increase sales volume. Usually, this means setting a lower price. Changing a price often is easier and quicker than changing other parts of a marketing mix. However, the decision to make the price change is challenging because it always involves all the factors that were discussed in this chapter: costs, competition, supply and demand, pricing objectives, product and service features, and the legal environment. Price is an important factor in determining the amount of sales revenues. Price influences customers' perception of the other parts of the marketing mix. Customers are very much aware of price and use it to make purchase decisions.

The challenge to marketers is to understand and apply the basics of price as presented in this chapter. Marketers need to understand these basics before they begin to set prices and determine pricing strategies. In Chapter 11, specific strategies and practices for setting prices and meeting the pricing challenge will be presented.

KEY POINTS SUMMARY

- Price plays several important roles in the marketing mix. It is a communication device, a measure of value, a competitive technique, a factor that affects exchange, and an influence on profits.

- Price is the amount of money (or the equivalent in product or service values) for which anything is bought, sold, or offered for sale. It is the value that is placed on any product or service.

- Pricing is a major marketing strategy of increasing importance and is ranked most important in some surveys of business executives.

- Marketing decisions are influenced by internal business factors: increasing costs that are difficult to control, continuing pressures to maintain profits, and establishing realistic and effective pricing objectives.

- Marketers must stay current on environmental factors that affect pricing decisions: increased competition, rapid technological change, supply and demand conditions, legal concerns, and better-informed consumers.

- A variety of pricing objectives are used by marketers, depending on the type of business, market conditions, and company goals. Pricing objectives may be set to maximize profits or sales, get a satisfactory return on investment, achieve a market share, or compete with the prices of other marketers.

- Supply and demand are important economic factors that are strong influences on price. They are studied by marketers in the process of making pricing decisions.

- Marketers compete with prices in the economic structures of pure competition, monopolistic competition, oligopoly, and monopoly.
- Marketers like the competitive world of monopolistic competition, in which they have the opportunity to market the advantages of their individual marketing mixes and can develop loyal customers.
- The principle of marginal analysis helps marketers use cost and revenue factors to market quantities of products at prices that result in as much profit as possible.
- Price elasticity refers to how responsive the market is to a change in price. High elasticity means that a slightly lower price will increase demand and a slightly higher price will decrease demand.
- Marketers must understand pricing legislation, stay current on court decisions, and meet the laws without exception in their pricing practices.

KEY TERMS AND CONCEPTS

collusion

competition

demand

demand curve

elasticity

equilibrium point

equilibrium price

fixed costs

marginal costs

marginal revenue

market share

monopolistic competition

monopoly

mutual interdependence

oligopoly

principle of marginal analysis

pure competition

supply

supply curve

variable costs

DISCUSSION QUESTIONS

1. Why is price such an important part of the marketing mix?

2. Explain the difference between monetary and nonmonetary prices and give several marketing examples of each.

3. Pricing decisions are influenced by many internal and environmental factors. Explain how several of these factors influence price for a retail marketer of video games.

4. You own and manage a record and tape store. Write three different but compatible pricing objectives for your business. Explain the effect of each objective on other marketing strategies in your business.

5. If a retail business sells and services bicycles, explain the effects of supply and demand on the pricing of its products and services.

NOTES

1. Shelby D. Hunt and John R. Nevin, "Why Consumers Believe They Are Being Ripped Off," *Business Horizons,* May–June 1981, pp. 48–52.
2. "Even Sony Can't Avoid The Price War in VCR's," *Business Week,* September 6, 1982, p. 33.
3. Based on an example by David J. Schwartz in *Marketing Today: A Basic Approach,* 3d ed., Harcourt Brace Jovanovich, New York, 1981, p. 271.
4. Janet Guyon, "When Is Fare Foul? When Airline Agents Can't Figure It Right," *Wall Street Journal,* July 26, 1979, pp. 1, 29; and Jim Montgomery, "Bewildering Array of Fares Mystifies Airlines, Travelers," *Wall Street Journal,* June 20, 1978, p. 1.
5. "Prices: Good News as Discounts and Rebates Spread," *U.S. News and World Report,* June 23, 1980, p. 27.

6. Robert A. Robicheaux, "How Important Is Pricing in Competitive Strategy?" in *Proceedings: Southern Marketing Association,* ed. Henry W. Nash and Donald P. Robin, January 1976, pp. 55–57. Robicheaux conducted the 1975 study. The 1964 study was conducted by Jon G. Udell, "How Important Is Pricing in Competitive Strategy?" *Journal of Marketing,* January 1964, pp. 44–48.

7. Stephen Grover "Record Business Slumps as Taping and Video Games Take Away Sales," *Wall Street Journal,* February 18, 1982, p. 31.

8. Ibid.

9. Jennifer Pendleton, "Album Retailers Try Rentals," *Advertising Age,* August 30, 1982, p. 36.

10. "Digital Sound Gets Set to Shake Up the Market," *Business Week,* September 13, 1982, p. 40.

11. Brenton Welling, "A Price War Aggravates the Airline Nosedive," *Business Week,* June 30, 1980, p. 45.

12. "Women's Magazines Lose Pep," *Business Week,* August 30, 1982, p. 72.

13. "Milton Bradley Says It Was Fined $150,000 in Price-Fixing Case," *Wall Street Journal,* March 24, 1982, p. 8.

CHAPTER 11

PRICING STRATEGIES AND PRACTICES

Welcome to Cook's Candy Kitchen. You have just been hired as product manager for the candy bar division of Cook's. One of your major responsibilities will be the pricing of both new and continuing products. Cook's is a small company that sells candy in 1 pound gift boxes, 8 ounce fund-raising bars, and small consumer-size bars. The consumer-size bars are distributed in the three-state area of New York, New Jersey, and Connecticut. The newest product, a 1.45 ounce candy bar made of chocolate, granola, and nuts, is called the Snick Snack. It will be ready for distribution in 6 weeks. It is your responsibility to decide on the suggested retail price for a Snick Snack as well as the manufacturer's price and the suggested wholesale price for a box of 36 Snick Snacks.

How will you decide on the price for this product? What factors will you consider? Is there more than one possible strategy to follow in pricing? Will this new product be priced differently from the other candy products you have on the market? What specific pricing techniques will you follow?

PRICING STRATEGIES

As you begin the process of deciding on a price for Snick Snacks, it is important to remember that price is a major factor in determining how profitable a product or service can be. If you are able to find the price that is "right" for the target market, your product or service will have a better chance to be profitable.

There are three possible strategies that you might follow to determine the right price for Snick Snacks: cost-oriented pricing, demand-oriented pricing, and competition-oriented pricing.

Cost-Oriented Pricing

When a **cost-oriented pricing** strategy is used, all costs for acquiring or manufacturing the merchandise, all service costs, and all overhead costs are computed first. Then the desired profit margin is added to determine the price. The two most common techniques of cost-oriented pricing are markup pricing and cost-plus pricing. A third technique is target-return pricing.

Markup Pricing. The pricing technique traditionally used in retail businesses is **markup pricing.** This is the simplest pricing technique. The retailer adds a preset percentage of the cost to each item to determine the retail price. If a retailer is able to buy a candy bar for 20 cents and needs to charge a 25 percent markup on cost to realize a profit, the selling price of the candy bar would be 25 cents (20 cents × 0.25 = 5 cents markup; 20 cents cost + 5 cents markup = 25 cents retail price). Later in this chapter, we shall take a closer look at the mathematics of pricing. You will learn the difference between markup on cost and markup on retail, together with the practical uses of each system of calculating markup.

Cost-Plus Pricing. A technique similar to markup pricing is **cost-plus pricing.** This involves taking a basic cost figure and adding an amount to cover profit and other unassigned costs. The difference between the two techniques is the sophistication of the cost-plus technique. Cost-plus pricing is used in manufacturing situations in which the cost of producing a single unit of any product may vary according to the number of units ordered and sometimes according to the capacity of the manufacturing plant to handle the order at any one time. Basically, if the order is larger, the unit cost is smaller because fixed costs can be spread among more individual units. Plant capacity can come into play in particularly slow or particularly good periods. If the peak production season is over and production workers might otherwise be idle, the manufacturer can offer a relatively low price because the work is both needed and easy to accommodate. However, if a rush order arrives during the peak season, when the plant is working at capacity, the price may be higher because additional workers will have to be hired or existing workers will have to be paid for overtime work. The sophistication of cost-plus pricing in manufacturing often dictates that prices be determined with the aid of a computer. However, cost-plus pricing is a frequently used technique in marketing. Retailers and service marketers use it as a basis for setting prices. Additional applications of the use of cost in pricing will be presented throughout this chapter.

Target-Return Pricing. Another cost-oriented pricing technique is **target-return pricing.** Using this technique, a firm mathematically determines the price that will allow it to earn a desired rate of return on its costs at a standard estimated volume of sales. Target-return pricing is perhaps the most complex cost-oriented pricing strategy. It frequently is used by public utilities to set prices that will earn a fair rate of return on costs, but it can be used by any company. Using target return pricing techniques, businesses can "plug in" figures for fixed costs, average variable costs, desired profit, and estimated price to determine the number of units at which the firm will break even or achieve its target rate of return. Firms also can construct graphs that will allow them to pinpoint the best price to charge at different quantity levels with estimated fixed costs and variable costs. The breakeven analysis that is used in target return pricing will be explained more fully later in this chapter.

Practically speaking, all three cost-oriented pricing techniques are efficient ways for companies to try to make a profit. However, the basic problem is that these techniques do not take into account the effects of demand on the price that can be charged for a product. The marketer who uses only cost as a basis for prices tends to set prices too high at first. The technique is still a good way to begin setting price, but the marketer usually must consider demand and competition. Cost-based pricing is very valuable to marketers in the determination of a price floor, which is the lowest price a firm can charge for a particular product if it is to meet its profit objective.

Demand-Oriented Pricing

Marketers who use a demand-oriented pricing strategy approach the determination of price from a different perspective. **Demand-oriented pricing**

Figure 11-1. This ad shows perceived-value pricing. Although the exact price is not mentioned, you know it is relatively high.

utilizes consumer desires and demand in the setting of individual prices. Perceived-value pricing and demand-differential pricing are examples of demand-oriented pricing.

Perceived-Value Pricing.
When this technique is used, a company develops its products or services specifically to meet the needs of the target market as suggested by buyers' perception of value. The company is so much in tune with the buyers' needs that it provides a clear idea of the quality desired, the service needed, and the price that will be considered fair. The company then calculates the quantity that will be demanded at the "fair" price and uses this information to calculate probable investment dollars and unit costs. Finally, the company figures out whether the proposed product will earn an acceptable profit at the price, quantity, and costs determined. If it will, the product is produced or the service is offered. If not, it cannot be.

Marketing research about consumers' values is a key factor in the use of perceived-value pricing for consumer products and services. Unless the consumer's perception of the value of a particular product or service is determined adequately, the company will either overprice or underprice the product or service in question. When the price of a proposed product is higher than the price of competing products, it is essential that the consumer perceive added value in the form of greater durability, better reliability, superior service, longer warranty, and so forth. Reasoning should lead the consumer to conclude the product will in fact be a bargain despite the fact that it is priced higher.

Demand-Differential Pricing.
When demand-differential pricing is used, a product or service is sold at two or more different prices. However, these prices do not reflect a significant difference in the product. An example of demand-

differential pricing is the way in which theater tickets are priced. For an orchestra seat, one pays more than one would for a balcony seat. However, the cost of providing the two different seats to consumers may be exactly the same. Other examples of demand-differential pricing involve the various rates charged by the telephone company for calls placed at specified times and the various rates charged by electric companies for power usage at different times of the year. The cost to the telephone company and the power company is the same regardless of when the service is provided.

Still another example of demand-differential pricing occurs when firms sell a variety of different styles, qualities, or brands of a particular product at different prices. However, the price differentials among these various styles are greater than the cost differentials. A refrigerator may be priced at $400 in white and $430 in a color, even though it may cost the manufacturer only $10 more to produce the refrigerator in color.

Demand-oriented pricing is used by marketers who see price as a major factor in the consumer's buying decision. A by-product of demand-oriented pricing is the determination of a price ceiling, which is the highest price consumers will pay for a given product or service. The effectiveness of demand-oriented pricing is determined to some extent by the elasticity of demand for a particular product or service. If there are few acceptable substitutes and if the product or service is needed by consumers, demand-oriented pricing will be effective.

Competition-Oriented Pricing

When a **competition-oriented pricing** strategy is used, price is set in accordance with the prices charged by competitors. These prices can be below, equal to, or higher than the prices of the competition, depending on the differences in the products or services involved. What sets this pricing strategy apart from cost-oriented and demand-oriented pricing is the fact that marketers are not concerned with maintaining a set relationship between price and demand or price and costs. When this strategy is used, a company will choose to change or maintain its prices according to what the competition is doing with their prices instead of making price changes on the basis of changes in costs or demand. Two examples of competition-oriented pricing strategy are competitive bidding and going-rate pricing.

Competitive-Bid Pricing. In **competitive-bid pricing,** companies compete for jobs on the basis of bids. This is frequently the case when governmental agencies are buying either products or services. The agency requesting the bids develops a detailed set of specifications that must be met by the company that is awarded the contract ultimately. Then each company that enters the bidding sets its price according to its best estimate of the prices that will be bid by competing companies. Although each company must set its prices at a level that will yield some acceptable level of profit, it may decide to bid a low price in order to obtain a valuable contract and be assured of a continuing flow of work.

Going-Rate Pricing. **Going-rate pricing** is based on paying attention to competitors' prices. This type of pricing is used frequently by firms that lead the market and by firms that follow that lead in the pricing of products or services. If a firm has a major share of the market, it can be a price leader. Other, smaller companies will follow suit and price their products or services at the going rate. Going-rate pricing is popular in industries in which very similar products are offered. In the steel industry, U.S. Steel and Bethlehem Steel lead the market as far as pricing strategies are concerned, and smaller competitors have little choice but to set their prices at the going rate. In retailing, marketers in competition in a large shopping center may have to set prices according to the prices set by the largest and most competitive price-leading store. The smaller marketer may meet the going-rate price or try to price higher or lower, but always after studying the going-rate price.

Combined Pricing Strategies

Cost-oriented, demand-oriented, and competition-oriented pricing strategies are not always an "either-or" proposition as far as the marketer is concerned. When prices are set, marketers often combine these three strategies when making their pricing decisions. The cost-oriented strategy can help them identify the price floor. They then can apply the demand-oriented strategy and "bracket" an acceptable price by determining the price ceiling. Finally, they can examine competitive pricing to be assured of selecting the right price.

Assume that you are a retail marketer of clothing in a shopping mall. You take a standard markup of 40 percent on cost in one department. A popular brand of sweaters would sell for $40 if you considered only cost-based pricing. When you consider the current demand for this very popular brand, you are tempted to raise the retail price to $45. Before you do this, however, you send a salesperson to three competitive stores where this brand is sold. You learn that the sweaters are priced at $39.95 and $42.95 at two of the stores but that the third store is promoting them at $36.95. What will you do? Will you price higher than competition, price with the average, or price below all other competitors?

Let us return to the example of Cook's Candy Kitchen from the beginning of the chapter. We left you at Cook's with the important job of pricing Snick Snack candy bars. Now that you understand the differences among the three types of pricing strategies, you are *almost* ready to select an appropriate strategy or possibly to apply more than one strategy to Snick Snacks. However, there is an important element of the marketing process that will have a decided effect on your pricing decisions: channel pricing.

CHANNEL PRICING

Cook's Candy Kitchen is smaller than most national-market candy companies. It serves only the tristate area of New York, Connecticut, and New Jersey. However, even with this limited distribution, it is impossible for the company to sell directly to consumers or even to retailers. Cook's follows traditional channels of distribution by selling to wholesalers who then sell to retailers who then sell to consumers. Cook's packages Snick Snacks in boxes of 36 bars. There are two different ways to approach channel pricing: from the retail price backward and from the manufacturer's cost forward.

First, assume that you decide to set a retail price of 40 cents a Snick Snack bar because the competing firms price their candy bars at that price or because there is perceived demand at 40 cents. The retailer desires a markup of 30 percent of the retail selling price to cover retail selling expenses and still make a profit. This means that the retailer will buy each Snick Snack for only 28

TABLE 11-1
PRICING A SNICK SNACK BAR—RETAIL PRICE BACKWARD

	Individual	Box of 36
a. Estimated retail price of Snick Snack bar	0.40	14.40
b. Markup desired by retailer (30 percent of retail selling price)	0.12	4.32
c. Wholesaler's price of Snick Snack bars to retailer	0.28	10.08
d. Markup desired by wholesaler (25 percent of wholesale selling price)	0.07	2.52
e. Cook's Candy Kitchen's price to wholesalers	0.21	7.56

cents and sell it for 40 cents in order to realize a 30 percent (or 12 cent) markup on the retail price. For a box of 36 bars, the retailer will pay $10.08. The wholesaler desires a markup of 25 percent of the wholesale selling price to cover all wholesale selling expenses and still make a profit. For each Snick Snack bar, the wholesaler will pay only 21 cents, or $7.56 for a box of 36 Snick Snack bars. Table 11-1 details these figures in summary form. Cook's Candy Kitchen has to be able to manufacture Snick Snack bars for $7.56 a box, or approximately 21 cents a bar, and still make a profit. Let us see how this breaks down. It will leave the company with about $1.50 for overhead, $3.25 for materials costs, $2.09 for labor, and $0.72 cents profit for each box of 36 Snick Snack bars.

Let us discuss what might happen if Cook's were to calculate prices beginning with the costs and adding markup to them at each level of the channel of distribution. As Cook's product manager, you would gather the information about materials, labor, and overhead costs necessary to determine how much it costs to produce Snick Snack bars. To this figure you would add a desired profit figure to determine the price at which you would sell the bars to wholesalers. The wholesaler would take this price and add to it a markup to cover costs and the desired profit. At the retail level, the same process would be repeated. The retailer would take the price charged by the wholesaler and add to it the desired profit to determine the price to consumers. While this process is identical to the one described earlier, it is very likely that the price to consumers, or the retail price, will be somewhat higher than the 40 cent price in the earlier example. This is because at each successive step in the distribution process, the prices are determined on the basis of the profit that is desired by the manufacturer.

Without the constraints of a retail price predetermined according to demand or competition, the manufacturer may try to realize a higher level of profit. Using Cook's plan to produce Snick Snacks, Table 11-2 details the possible figures for this approach to determining prices.

TABLE 11-2 PRICING A SNICK SNACK BAR—MANUFACTURER'S COST FORWARD

	Box of 36
a. Cost of producing the Snick Snack bar	$ 6.84
b. Desired profit (25 percent of cost)	1.71
c. Price (cost) to wholesaler	8.55
d. Markup desired by wholesaler (35 percent of cost to wholesaler)	3.00*
e. Price to retailer	11.55
f. Markup desired by retailer (40 percent of price to retailer)	4.62
g. Price to consumers	16.17
h. Price to consumers for individual Snick Snack bar (16.17 ÷ 36)	0.45*

*Rounded up to nearest penny.

PRICING IN THE PRODUCT LIFE CYCLE

As you learned in Chapter 6, each product passes through what is known as a product life cycle (PLC) from the time when it is introduced on the market to the time when it is removed from the market. During its product life cycle, each product passes through four stages: introduction, growth, maturity, and decline. When the product no longer provides a satisfactory return, it is removed from the market, and the company's efforts are applied to new or more successful products.

Pricing plays a key role in the marketing strategies that are used for each product as it moves through its PLC, because each of the four PLC stages may require specific applications of the marketing mix.

Pricing New Products

When a new product such as Snick Snack bars is introduced, marketers may decide to use either a skimming or a penetration pricing policy.

Skimming. **Price skimming** is the policy of setting a high initial price for a product and using heavy promotion. The purpose is to "skim the cream" off the market before lowering prices and aiming at more price-conscious consumers. Skimming is successful when the demand for a particular product is relatively inelastic, or insensitive to price, at the upper ranges of the demand curve. A good example is the new digital audio disk (DAD) players that are being introduced as a high-technology alternative to stereo turntables. The DAD will reproduce original sound with virtually no distortion, and disks are made from a product that will never wear out or scratch.

According to *Business Week* magazine, initially DAD players will cost a hefty $660 to $1,000, but experts expect prices to plunge within a year or two to less than $200 as manufacturers reach mass-production levels.[1]

If a consumer wants to be one of the first to own a DAD player, he or she probably will buy it at $1,000 as readily as at $660. Skimming is also successful when technological aspects of the product dictate that production be expanded slowly. With high demand and limited production capabilities (short supply), skimming prices will satisfy a market for a longer time.

A major advantage of skimming is that it helps the company earn back its developmental costs for the particular product more rapidly than a lower-priced introductory strategy. Skimming also can help the company develop a prestige image (high price perceived as better product quality) for the product involved. If the skimming price is too high to attract enough "cream of the crop" customers, it can be lowered easily without alienating customers. Customers at the top of the demand curve already will have the product and will have had the satisfaction of being first.

Although there are many advantages to skimming, there are also some disadvantages. The high initial price of a product usually attracts competition. This is particularly true when the product does not present difficult technological production problems. As competitors enter the market, the price of the original product will be driven down. Another possibly more serious disadvantage is that an inappropriate price can cause the product to lose sales throughout its PLC if the product does not find a solid market. This is what happened with DuPont's Corfam imitation shoe leather when it was priced too high in comparison to alternative products.

Penetration. **Penetration pricing** occurs when a firm introduces a new product at a relatively low price to attract a large number of consumers at the beginning of the PLC. Penetration pricing is successful when the demand for a product is relatively elastic, or price-sensitive. This means that a low price will be capable of attracting a large volume of customers.

Penetration pricing requires a manufacturer to plan ahead and be ready for both mass production and mass marketing. If a company is successful in its penetration strategy, it can capture a large share of an existing market in a short period of time. The high volume allows the company to sell at low prices because manufacturing can be a mass-production effort.

In 1975, Texas Instruments was able to capture a large portion of the digital watch market by introducing a $20 model. Before that time, the lowest-priced digital watch sold for a hefty $125. But by mass-producing and distributing inexpensive digital watches, Texas Instruments was able to take over the market. In just 1 year, they sold 4 million $20 watches.

The biggest advantage of penetration pricing is the ability it gives a company to capture enough of an existing market to block competitors. Another advantage is the opportunity to open up new markets that were dominated by marketers with high prices on similar products and services. However, there are disadvantages to penetration pricing. If the demand for a product has not been estimated accurately, a company can sustain substantial losses. Even if a company can sell a large

PRINTERS FOR WORD PROCESSING: A PENT-UP DEMAND

Until very recently, individuals and small businesses were discouraged at the prospect of purchasing a personal computer for use as a word processor. If they could afford the $3,000 for the computer, they were shocked to learn that the type of printer that could produce copy good enough to use for letters and other correspondence would cost another $3,000. A price of $6,000 was out of the question for many potential customers. The type of printer they could afford, the dot matrix printer, produced readable copy, but each letter was formed by a series of dots. Unfortunately, the letters did not come close enough to the appearance of typewriter type.

In the summer of 1982, Smith-Corona introduced the first low-priced printer targeted at the pent-up demand for personal computers to be used as word processors. The daisy wheel printer offered by SCM Corporation, makers of Smith-Corona typewriters, produces type that closely resembles typewriter type. The term *daisy wheel* comes from the fact that typefaces located on the tips of slivers of metal or plastic extend from a hub like petals on a daisy. These pieces of type are hit by a hammer to form "typed" words.

The best news about the new daisy wheel printer is that it retails for only $895 and has been discounted for less than $600. This penetration pricing policy has enabled SCM to create a new word processing market made up of small businesses and personal users. SCM is ready to meet the needs of this market by mass-producing their daisy wheel printers. They have added a second shift to their Cortland, New York, factory and hope to ship 20,000 units by the end of the year.

As with any other growing business, competition in the daisy wheel business is beginning to explode. Three or four other companies have begun to produce low-priced printers in an attempt to capture a portion of this untapped market.

Adapted from "Quality Printers That Are Affordable," *Business Week*, September 13, 1982, p. 114.

---

quantity of a particular item at a low price, it will take longer to recover costs and begin making a profit.

Another aspect of the penetration pricing strategy is the use of special offers to get consumers to use a new product. This practice is used extensively for relatively inexpensive household goods: toothpaste, dishwashing detergent, facial soap, laundry detergent, mouthwash, and similar products. These special offers include free samples, cents-off coupons, and other special price allowances for first-time users. The purpose of these pricing offers is to attract customers who will like the product well enough to buy it later at the regular price, which may or may not be competitive with the prices of comparable products on the market.

Pricing During Growth

During the growth stage of the PLC, sales increase rapidly and unit costs for promotion and distribution decrease because they are spread over a larger volume. The marketer wants to keep products in the growth stage as long as possible.

Many of the marketing strategies employed during the growth stage involve other aspects of the marketing mix. This is the time to improve product quality and offer new models, features, and styles to keep the product exciting. It is the time to hold on to repeat customers, attract new customers, and break into new market segments.

Pricing actions during the growth stage will be influenced by whether the product was introduced by price skimming or penetration pricing. If the product was introduced by price skimming, sales should be monitored carefully. When they begin to taper off, the price can be lowered to appeal to the next level of shopper. Some skimming prices will drop much more rapidly than others, and competition will be a major factor in a firm's ability to maintain higher prices. The price of pocket calculators dropped from a high of $240 to less than $20 in just 3 years. However, the price of Polaroid's instant cameras was reduced very gradually over a period of many years because Polaroid held the patent on instant photography until 1975.

If the initial price was a penetration price, fewer price adjustments will be made during the growth stage. In this case, prices will be maintained, and other marketing strategies will be employed to keep the product's sales growing at a steady rate.

Pricing in the Maturity Stage

This is the period in which the rate of sales levels off and customers buy about as much of the product as they want. Many products are in the maturity stage for years and show no signs of declining. Others pass through this stage more quickly and then begin their decline. However, compared with the other stages of the PLC, the maturity stage is usually the longest. The maturity stage is the real test of a marketer's ability to use the elements of the marketing mix effectively. Price is one of the tools at the marketer's disposal.

Competition is strong during the maturity stage. This is the time when marketers look for new segments for their products. Cheerios are promoted as a substitute for popcorn in the form of "hot buttered O's," and we are told that "orange juice isn't just for breakfast anymore."

During the maturity stage, marketers look for ways to stretch the lives of their products. This effort to revitalize products that have stopped growing leads to the development of new models, flavors, styles, sizes, and other new features that can perk up products.

If there is a lot of competition in a particular product area, there eventually will be a surplus of that product. Such a surplus will lead marketers to reduce prices so that they can maintain their existing market shares.

As an alternative to price reductions, marketers can introduce lower-priced models of the same product in an attempt to capture a new market segment. In a completely different approach, they can introduce a higher-quality version of the same product with a higher price.

No matter what approach is used by marketers, the goal of all marketing strategies during the maturity stage should be to prolong the life of the product while earning a satisfactory profit. Marketers who are particularly adept at manipulating the elements of the marketing mix even may be able to start a new period of growth in their mature products.

Pricing a Declining Product

During the decline stage, a product's sales decrease. The pace of the decrease may either be rapid or slow. During this stage in the PLC, marketers reduce the costs of producing or carrying the product and cut back on advertising and promotion. The price of the product may be reduced slightly or may remain the same. With the decrease in marketing expenditures, many products will phase themselves out gradually because of decreasing demand and sales. Other products will need to be phased out when marketers determine that they are no longer profitable.

PRICING TECHNIQUES

Now that we have explored the three basic pricing strategies and the pricing practices generally followed throughout the life cycle of a product, it is time to look at three different types of pricing techniques: psychological pricing, discount pricing, and geographic pricing.

Psychological Pricing

Psychological pricing techniques call for setting prices that appeal to target customers. Some marketers believe that select groups of consumers are particularly attracted to products at certain prices and are sensitive to both increases and decreases in these prices. Psychological pricing techniques include odd-even pricing, prestige pricing, promotional pricing, and price lining.

Odd-Even Pricing. The technique of **odd-even pricing** calls for setting retail prices that end in certain odd or even numbers. Many marketers sell products that cost less than $4 at prices that are 1 or 2 cents below the next even-number price ($0.39, $3.98, or $1.99). Food, household supplies, and inexpensive convenience products are priced this way. Between $4 and $50, they price products at 5 cents below the next even-number price ($15.95, $19.95, or $49.95). Sportswear, shoes, and books often are found with these prices. For products that sell for more than $50, prices are often $1 or $2 below the even-number figure: $99, $88, or $69. Suits, luggage, and furniture frequently are priced this way.

There are many different explanations for this practice. The practice is supposed to have started many years ago when retailers priced products so that clerks were forced to record the sale and make change. This discouraged the clerks from pocketing the money from sales.

Some people believe that the practice of odd-even pricing continues today because consumers view these prices as bargains. They are able to spend "less than $15 for a shirt" if the price of the shirt is only $14.95. Of course, when the tax is

Figure 11-2. Odd-even pricing.

added to the purchase price, as it is in most states, the price is higher than $15.

Several studies have been done to determine whether this type of pricing practice leads to increased profits. However, the results have been inconclusive. One study showed that some consumers may believe that prices ending in odd numbers represent price reductions. Another showed that some consumers may round the price down to the next lowest price rather than up. This means that they would view $9.95 as $9 instead of $10.[2]

Retailers that want to price products so that they can be purchased quickly without waiting for change often will post a sign indicating that tax is included in the even amount.

Gum	28 cents
Tax	2 cents
Total	30 cents

U.S. JEANS MAKERS FIND A MARKET THAT FITS

For a long time, American-made jeans have been a status product with a high price overseas. With sales lagging in the U.S. market, several American manufacturers of designer jeans have begun to take advantage of the appeal that U.S. designer jeans have in Brazil. Calvin Klein, Gloria Vanderbilt, and Jordache all may be sold in the Brazilian market in the near future. The attraction seems to be tremendous. Sales of 90 million pairs of jeans each year make Brazil's jeans market the second largest in the world. It is growing at the rate of 10 percent a year, primarily because of the fact that 70 percent of the population of 120 million is under 30 years of age. Many of these young people are willing to pay twice the U.S. prices for designer jeans just to show that they can. A pair of Calvin Klein jeans may retail for as much as $75, and the manufacturer is so confident about the demand that it plans a production run of 15,000 pairs a month.

Local Brazilian jeans manufacturers are fighting back by trying to raise the prestige of their products through the use of such names as Don Perignon, Lucky Strike, and Porsche Design. These manufacturers also are copying U.S. marketing techniques. Staroup, which has the license for Gloria Vanderbilt, has decided to build a prestige image for its jeans by having the internationally known Brazilian actress Sonia Braga wear them. This is the same technique that was used successfully by Calvin Klein. When Brooke Shields was contracted to model Calvin Klein jeans, their market share increased significantly.

Adapted from "U.S. Jeans Makers Find a Market That Fits," *Business Week,* August 30, 1982, p. 39.

Prestige Pricing. The practice of setting a high price to suggest high status and high quality is called **prestige pricing.** Prestige prices appeal to consumers who want the "best." If prices fall below a certain level, these consumers are not interested in buying because the product is too "cheap."

At the other end of the scale, even consumers who are attracted by prestige products have an upper limit to the amount they will spend. It is the marketer's responsibility to determine both the perceived upper-limit price and the lower-limit price and to set appropriate prestige prices between these two points. Products such as Waterford crystal, Rolls-Royce automobiles, Perrier bottled water, and designer jeans are priced according to this technique.

Promotional Pricing. The pricing of some products or services at attractively low levels and the heavy promotion of these items is known as **promotional pricing.** There are two basic types of promotional pricing. The first is **leader pricing.** Leader pricing occurs when one or two widely used items that people do not customarily stock at home are marketed at a very low price. Milk and eggs are two popular items that are used for leader pricing. Many people are familiar with the usual price of these items and will recognize a good price. A store will offer a good price in the hopes that people who come in to buy the milk and eggs will take some other items that are sold at their usual prices. Many other types of products may be priced as leaders. A clothing store may use women's hosiery as a leader product. A photography store may use a certain brand of film as a leader. The most effective products for leader pricing are those which the customer buys somewhat regularly and those which are of good quality. Part of the purpose of leader pricing is to encourage people to come to the store to buy the leader items. While there, the customers usually buy other products at regular prices.

Special-event pricing is similar to leader pricing. But **special-event pricing** occurs when items are priced at an attractively low level for a short period of time and then promoted as a special event. Some supermarkets price turkeys at attractive prices right before Thanksgiving and advertise them as a special promotion. They hope to attract customers who will purchase all of their Thanksgiving dinner needs at the same time that they buy the turkey. Another example of special-event pricing might be special prices during a "midnight" sale, when a particular store will stay open until midnight. Many stores are well known for their "Dollar Days" promotion, when the prices of certain items are marked down just for the length of the sale. Others may run a specially supervised department in which children can shop without their parents right before Christmas. Every item in this department might be specially priced at less than $5.

Price Lining. The practice of selling products at a few distinctly different price levels is known as **price lining.** Each of the price levels is supposed to represent a different level of quality. To use the price-lining technique, marketers first must decide on the full range of price offerings for a particular type of product. Once both the floor price and the ceiling price have been established, the marketer must select a number of price points within that price range. These price points are the specific prices at which merchandise will be carried.

When developing a price line, the marketer should be careful not to select prices that are too close to one another. Customers may be confused if handbags are sold for $25, $26, and $27. They could instead be priced at $18, $25, and $33.

When price lines are established, products can be purchased for the purpose of selling them at a particular retail price within the price line. Price lining helps retailers because it is often easier for consumers to make a buying decision when they can compare the products within a single price line and between price lines. It also offers retailers an opportunity to encourage customers to "trade up," or buy the higher-priced items in the price lines.

Discount Pricing

Techniques that involve granting reductions from the usual list price if the buyer gives up a particular marketing function that usually is provided by the seller are referred to as **discount pricing.** There are several different types of discounts, including cash, quantity, functional (or trade), and seasonal. A similar technique is the granting of allowances or rebates.

Cash Discounts. Discounts given in return for the prompt payment of bills are called **cash discounts.** These special price reductions for cash payments traditionally have been offered by manufacturers to both wholesalers and retailers. The cash discount usually is expressed in terms such as "2/10, net 30." Here is how it works in this case. When a retailer makes a purchase from a wholesaler or manufacturer, there is a 2 percent discount if the bill is paid in 10 days. If the discount is not taken, the net, or full amount of the bill, still is due in 30 days.

This means that a retailer is able to deduct $60 from an invoice for $3,000 if it is paid within 10 days. This may not sound like a lot of money, but if the discount is not taken, the retailer pays 2 percent for the use of the $3,000 for only 20 days.

Figure 11-3. By buying in large quantities, Herman's receives a quantity discount, which it can then pass on to the consumer.

This would amount to an annual interest rate of about 36 percent.

From the viewpoint of the manufacturer and the wholesaler, it is advantageous to offer cash discounts because this technique enables them to recover cash in less time. It therefore enables them to pay their bills more quickly.

Quantity Discounts. When buyers receive a discount for buying a large amount of a product or service, they are receiving a **quantity discount.** It is to the seller's advantage to offer quantity discounts because in order to take advantage of them, buyers are likely to purchase more than they might buy ordinarily. As a result, the seller has lower selling costs because a larger quantity is sold in one transaction rather than smaller quantities in several transactions.

There are two kinds of quantity discounts: noncumulative and cumulative. Noncumulative quantity discounts are price breaks that apply to individual orders. Consumers are encouraged to buy the giant economy size. Wholesalers and retailers are encouraged to place larger orders. Price cuts usually are offered in the form of money saved, but they also can be offered in the form of free merchandise: "Buy 11 cases of a soft drink and get the twelfth one free." Noncumulative quantity discounts are offered for the purchase of a certain quantity of products or services all at one time in one transaction.

The other type of quantity discount is the cumulative quantity discount. This is a price break offered for buying a certain quantity of products or services over a period of time. It is designed to encourage a long-term relationship between the buyer and the seller. "Our office cleaning service is $55 a week if you call us occasionally but only $47.50 a week if you take a 6 month contract and $45 a week if you take a 1 year contract."

Functional Discounts. Functional discounts, also known as **trade discounts,** are offered to members of the channel of distribution for the functions, or jobs, that they are going to perform. This is basically the pricing system that was described earlier in this chapter and illustrated in Figure 11-1. Functional discounts are set up by manufacturers who quote a retail price and express prices to the wholesaler and retailer as "discounts" from the retail price. A manufacturer who sells directly to a retailer may offer a 30 percent discount off the retail price. If the manufacturer sells through the wholesaler, the discount may be quoted at 30 percent and 10 percent or 35 percent and 8 percent. In each case, the first figure is the discount that is to be passed on to the retailer and the second amount is the discount for the wholesaler. If a manufacturer of correcting typewriters quotes a retail price of $600 with discounts of 30 percent and 10 percent, it means that the price to the retailer will be $420 ($600 minus 30 percent). It also means that the wholesaler would pay $378 ($420 minus 10 percent). The discounts are figured on a "chain" basis, which means that the wholesaler's discount is calculated on the basis of the price to the retailer rather than the retail price that is quoted to the consumer. If for some reason there were more members in the channel of distribution and they were quoted functional discounts, each discount would be calculated on the basis of the price paid by the channel members on the next level of the distribution system.

Seasonal Discounts. A price reduction for buying goods or services out of season is called a **seasonal discount.** This type of discount is offered to help smooth out the sales year for seasonal products such as home insulation, air conditioners, and bathing suits. Air fares, hotel rates, and resort vacations are also commodities that are offered frequently at discount prices during the off season. Seasonal discounts reduce the cost of storing out-of-season merchandise. A good example of seasonal discounts that may be offered primarily to avoid or decrease the problem of storage are half-price sales on Christmas cards, decorations, and wrappings.

Allowances. Allowances are special price concessions offered both to consumers and to members of the channel of distribution. Consumers are offered **trade-in allowances** for selling back old models of products when they buy new versions of the same products. This is a common practice for industrial customers buying machinery and for consumers buying automobiles.

Advertising allowances or **promotional allowances** are special arrangements made by manufacturers to encourage both wholesalers and retailers to promote the manufacturer's products. Sometimes this is in the form of a percentage off the price of the product to a channel member. In other instances it is in the form of "free" merchandise. General Electric has been known to give a 1.5 percent allowance to wholesalers of radios and housewares in return for local advertising of GE products by these channel members. General Foods has given supermarket chains free cases of food products for promoting their products.

Still another type of discount is offered in the form of **prize money,** or **"push" money,** that is given to retailers by manufacturers or wholesalers. It is awarded to retail sales people for promoting certain items of merchandise. Prize money may be offered for sales of special new items or for high ticket items. Sales people may earn $10 in prize money every time they sell a certain style of recliner or a particular type of coat.

Rebates. **Rebates** are special consumer discounts that usually are offered by manufacturers. The consumer who buys the product applies to the manufacturer for a partial refund on the price that has been paid. Recently, large retailers have begun to offer their own rebates, or refund offers, on some items.

Although rebates are a popular technique to encourage reluctant consumers to buy now, they should not be overused because they can have an adverse effect on the manufacturer's profits as well as consumers' attitudes.

The whole practice of discount pricing is a widely accepted method of encouraging sales, but some marketers question its value. One expert on industrial sales explains the shifting attitude from a seller's market to a buyer's market.

Periods of slack demand and surplus supply do indeed shift the balance of power from the seller to the buyer in purchasing's perpetual poker game.

No longer do vendors have the luxury of opening the bidding with, "If you don't want it at this price, I've got plenty of others who do." Instead, purchasers hold such aces as "We're well-stocked, so I'm really not interested in buying unless you can make it worth my while."

This shift in attitude leads to the process of discounting. But as the expert goes on to explain, discounting is not always advantageous to either party. If vendors offer too many discounts, their supply of capital will be diminished to such an extent that future production will be affected. In the long run, the plight of the capital-starved vendors will be passed down to the buyers.[3]

Geographic Pricing

Geographic pricing includes several techniques that establish responsibility for paying transportation charges. Transportation charges may amount to a great deal of money because many sellers ship their goods nationwide or even worldwide. Geographic pricing terms often are negotiated, but sometimes they depend on the traditional practices of the particular industry in which the firm operates. All firms in an industry generally will use the same geographic pricing technique.

The geographic pricing techniques most often used are free on board, uniform delivered, freight absorption, basing point, and zone.

Free on Board. **Free on board, or FOB,** is a pricing term that typically is used with the name of a location. It is at this location that the seller stops paying for transportation and the buyer begins to pay. If the buyer has to pay all the freight, the term used might be "FOB plant" or "FOB mill." In this case, the seller would pay to put the goods "on board" some means of transportation. The buyer's responsibility would begin as soon as they were loaded. The free on board indication also can be

Pepper . . . and Salt

THE WALL STREET JOURNAL

REBATES UP TO $700

"What are you selling?"

Figure 11-4. A rebate is a partial refund on the price paid for a product.

accompanied by the name of a city or town, such as "FOB Chicago." This means that the seller pays the transportation charges to a specific location in Chicago and the buyer pays them from that point on. If the seller is to pay all the freight, the term used is "FOB delivered" or "FOB buyer's factory."

It is generally at the FOB point that title to the goods passes from the seller to the buyer. This means that the buyer is responsible for the safe delivery of the goods from that point forward. It is the buyer's responsibility to buy insurance to cover the possible risk of losing the merchandise or having it damaged.

Uniform Delivered. When a **uniform delivered price** is used, the same transportation price is quoted to all buyers regardless of location. The cost quoted for transportation is an average price, similar to the cost of postage for mailing a letter. The buyer that is farthest from the seller benefits from this technique because the actual cost of shipping would be higher than this average cost. The buyer that is closest to the seller is at a disadvantage because the actual cost of shipping would be less than the average cost. When this is

the case, the buyer is said to be paying *phantom-freight*.

Freight Absorption. When **freight absorption pricing** is used, the seller absorbs some of the freight cost so that the delivered price can be a competitive one. Freight absorption may be used in connection with FOB shipping point pricing when the seller is competing with another seller that is closer to the buyer. Or it may be used with uniform delivered pricing when the buyer is being penalized by having to pay phantom freight. Naturally, there is a limit to how much freight each company can absorb, because these added costs reduce the return on each sale. However, if they are needed to secure new business, they can be regarded as increasing profits.

Basing Point. When **basing point pricing** is used, the sellers within an industry decide on locations, or basing points, from which transportation costs will be computed. These locations are usually the areas where the most goods are produced. The price to the buyer includes the cost of shipping products from the basing point nearest to the buyer, regardless of the actual location from which the products are shipped.

The practice of basing point pricing has been restricted severely by the government because it is very easy for sellers to arrange basing points that frequently penalize buyers by having them pay phantom freight charges.

Zone Pricing. **Zone pricing** involves charging the same rate to all buyers within a certain geographic zone. For example, the continental United States may be divided into five different zones. The seller pays the actual freight charge but bills the buyer for the average amount that has been established for that particular zone. This technique is an equitable way to simplify the complex procedure of figuring transportation charges for thousands of buyers.

Techniques for Pricing Snick Snacks. Let us return for a moment to your position as product manager of Snick Snack candy bars. In the process of selecting a price for Snick Snacks, you should consider three important types of pricing techniques. The first is psychological pricing. Will you decide on a price ending in an odd number? Will Snick Snack be a prestige item with a prestige price? Will you participate in any special-event pricing?

Next, you should decide whether to use discount pricing techniques. Will you offer cash discounts to wholesalers? How about quantity discounts? What functional discounts will you use? What about promotional allowances to wholesalers and retailers?

Then you should decide on the geographic pricing techniques you will use. Who will pay for transportation? If the buyer is to pay, will you use the FOB seller technique or perhaps the uniform delivered technique? Since you are delivering to only three states, perhaps you should make each state a different zone.

You would need a lot more information if you were actually going to make these pricing decisions, but you can begin to see that pricing a product is a complex process.

CHANGING PRICES

If you select a pricing strategy carefully and weigh many factors methodically as you decide on appropriate pricing techniques, you probably will still want to change your prices from time to time. Let us look at the possible reasons for both price increases and decreases and at the reactions of customers to price changes.

Price Increases

The most common cause of price increases is an increase in the seller's costs of doing business. Even though many sellers are reluctant to pass their increased costs on to the buyer, this is often the only way that they can continue to make an acceptable profit.

In an effort to keep prices from escalating, firms have found many ways to cut costs. Products that have earned only a marginal profit are being dropped so that more money can be put into producing profitable ones. In many cases, cheaper

materials are being used in the manufacturing process, and new machinery is being installed to boost output, cut costs, and save energy.[4]

- Black and Decker recently purchased 27 computer-controlled machines that saved them an estimated $2.3 million in labor and overhead costs in a 3 year period.
- A tea manufacturer, Celestial Seasonings, has invested $1 million in new equipment to pack tea bags twice as quickly with the help of only 4 workers instead of 22.
- Adolph Coors brewery is converting its boilers from natural gas to coal and expects to save about 50 percent.
- Some companies, such as Boeing Aircraft and John Deere and Company of Waterloo, Iowa, are beginning to burn refuse for energy.

Even with these and other similar cost-reducing measures, consumer prices often will continue to rise because sellers also are subject to increased costs beyond their control. In a recent year, consumer prices rose an average of 11.3 percent. Marketers often must increase prices because of inflationary economic conditions.

Price Decreases

Price decreases are often the result of reactions to decreases by competing companies. But they also may be planned as a price-skimming strategy for a new product. Price decreases in themselves are not something for the seller to fear, because a decrease in price usually means an increase in demand. However, price wars can cause real problems for sellers. You read in Chapter 10 about the difficulties airlines were having as a result of a price war (see page 288). The same type of difficulty has been experienced in many different industries. In fact, the U.S. market for 35mm cameras recently has been described as chaotic and "almost a suicidal frenzy."[5] This frenzy has been caused by the practice of slashing prices to the levels of 3 years ago. With this type of price cutting, breaking even is considered a mark of success.

Figure 11-5. Price changes. What is your reaction to this price decrease? Notice the comparisons to the average market price in other stores and to the former regular price.

These dramatic price decreases are caused by the fact that one out of every three cameras is imported through what is known as "gray market dealers," or roundabout distribution routes. If cameras are routed from Japan to the United States through third world countries, they are discounted 30 percent or more below the U.S. distributor's usual price. In an effort to keep up with these gray market cameras, other dealers are being forced to make dramatic price cuts.

Although sellers seldom can avoid participating in price cutting, one successful way to deal with it is to offer temporary discounts that are competitive rather than lowering list prices. As one purchasing authority explained, "A firm would be a fool to lower its list price. What if there was a price freeze? It would be caught with its prices down."[6]

Buyers' Reactions to Price Changes

The concept of price elasticity of demand is valid, but consumers do not always interpret price changes in a straightforward and predictable manner. Buyers theoretically are supposed to react to price decreases by increasing their demand. However, they may interpret a price decrease to mean that a particular model soon will be replaced by another model. Other buyers may believe that the quality of the product has been reduced. Still others may believe that the firm is in financial trouble and may not be around later to supply parts for the product. There are also buyers who will delay a decision to buy as soon as the price comes down because they believe that one price decrease may lead to another larger one.

On the other side of the coin, buyers theoretically are supposed to react to price increases by decreasing their demand. However, some buyers may believe that the increased price means that this is a hot item and should be purchased right away or it will be out of stock. Others believe that the item represents a good value because the price has gone up. Still others may feel that the buyer is being greedy and getting as much profit as possible.

SPECIAL APPLICATIONS OF PRICING

You have learned a lot about the basic concepts of pricing, including pricing strategies and techniques. Now it is time to look at the actual calculations that are used to determine prices. We shall look first at price setting by retailers and wholesalers, then at price setting by producers, and finally at price setting by service marketers.

Pricing by Intermediaries

Most wholesalers and retailers use a series of price-setting applications that include markup, markdown, stock turn rates, unit pricing, and single-price policy.

Markup. **Markup** is the amount that a seller adds to the cost of goods to arrive at their selling price. The markup should be large enough to cover the cost of doing business and still allow for a reasonable profit. Even though markup is a cost-oriented pricing strategy that initially ignores customer demand, it provides the most practical way of setting prices for any retailer or wholesaler that carries a large variety of merchandise. It would not be a wise use of time if these sellers were to attempt to determine the best price for each item in stock on the basis of the demand for that product.

Markup can be stated in one of three different ways: as a dollars and cents figure ($5 cost + $2.50 markup = $7.50 selling price), a percentage of the cost ($2.50 ÷ $5 = 50 percent markup), or a percentage of the selling price ($2.50 ÷ $7.50 = 33.3 percent).

Most wholesalers and retailers quote markup as a percentage of selling price. Although there may be many reasons for quoting markup on the basis of selling price instead of cost, a few of the more common reasons are these.

- Markup on selling price sounds smaller and less "greedy" on the part of the seller.
- Future transactions such as markdowns and employee discounts will be calculated on the basis of the selling price.
- The seller's profits are calculated on the basis of sales rather than costs.

There are several formulas to use for calculating markup on the basis of selling price.

- 100% selling price − markup = cost

100%	− 33.3%	= 66.7%
$7.50	− $2.50	= $5.00

- Selling price = $\dfrac{\text{cost}}{100\% - \text{desired markup \%}}$

  Selling price = $\dfrac{\$5}{100\% - 33.3\%}$

  Selling price = $\dfrac{\$5}{66.7\%}$

  Selling price = $7.50

- Markup % based on selling price = $\dfrac{\text{markup amount}}{\text{selling price}}$

  Markup % based on selling price = $\dfrac{\$2.50}{\$7.50}$

  Markup % based on selling price = 33.3%

Markup percentage based on cost, which is often used by manufacturers, is somewhat easier to calculate.

Markup % based on cost = $\dfrac{\text{markup}}{\text{cost}}$

Markup % based on cost = $\dfrac{\$2.50}{\$5}$

Markup % based on cost = 50%

Markdown. A **markdown** is a reduction in the selling price. Markdowns are taken for special sales, damaged merchandise, closeouts, and so forth. Good retail practice bases markdowns on the basis of the reduced selling price. Assume that an article originally sold for $7.50 and that the new selling price is $6.00. The markdown is 25 percent, because it is expressed on the basis of the new retail price. Here is how to calculate the markdown percent.

100% of the new price = $6.00

Markdown percentage = $\dfrac{\text{markdown amount}}{\text{new price}}$

Markdown percentage = $\dfrac{\$1.50}{\$6.00}$

Markdown percentage = 25%

Stock Turn Rates. **Stock turn rates,** or stock turnover rate, is the number of times the average stock of a business is sold during a given period of time compared with the sales for that same period. Stock turn may be calculated on the basis of selling price, cost, or units. A retailer or

BUY ANY WINTER ITEM MARKED IN RED AND GET A SECOND RED MARK ITEM OF EQUAL OR LOWER PRICE FOR ONLY A PENNY MORE.

RED MARK FASHIONS ARE AT THEIR LOWEST PRICES OF THE SEASON. MANY ITEMS AT OR BELOW COST!

PLUS . . .
GET A SECOND RED MARK
ITEM FOR ONLY . . .

1¢

EXAMPLE:
VALUE PRICE. . . .$10
RED MARK
PRICE $2.75
PLUS . . .
YOUR SECOND
RED MARK ITEM. 1¢
YOUR COST
FOR BOTH . . .$2.76

Figure 11-6. A 2-for-1 sale is a markdown.

wholesaler can increase profits by increasing the stock turn rate. The basic formula for figuring stock turn rate is as follows.

$$\text{Sales} \div \text{average stock} = \text{stock turn}$$
$$\$200{,}000 \div \$50{,}000 = 4$$

To calculate stock turn, a marketer must be able to calculate average stock. To calculate the average stock for a year, add the beginning stock for that year to the beginning stock for each of the months of the year and then add in the last month's end-of-month figure. You will have figures similar to these for a fiscal year beginning June 1.

Month	Stock	Month	Stock
June 1	$ 5,000	Jan. 1	$ 9,000
July 1	7,000	Feb. 1	8,000
Aug. 1	8,000	March 1	7,000
Sept. 1	7,000	April 1	6,000
Oct. 1	9,000	May 1	8,000
Nov. 1	15,000	May 31	7,000
Dec. 1	16,000		
		Total	$112,000

$$\text{Year's stock} \div \frac{\text{number of}}{\text{listings}} = \text{average stock}$$
$$\$112{,}000 \div 13 = \$8{,}615$$

If this seller's total sales for the year were $34,460, the stock turn would be figured this way.

$$\text{Sales} \div \text{average stock} = \text{stock turn}$$
$$\$34{,}460 \div \$8{,}615 = 4$$

The same stock turn can be figured in terms of cost by translating sales figures and stock figures to cost by using the known markup percentage.

If a 40 percent markup on selling price had been used, cost figures for both sales and stock would be as follows.

Sales at selling price	− markup	=	sales at cost
100%	− 40%	=	60%
$34,460	− $13,784	=	$20,676

Average stock at selling price	− markup	=	average stock at cost
100%	− 40%	=	60%
$8,615	− $3,446	=	$5,169

Sales at cost	÷ average stock at cost	=	stock turn at cost
$20,676	÷ $5,169	=	4

Even though the stock turn rates in both examples come out to 4, stock turn at retail is usually slightly smaller because retail sales figures include sales after markdowns.

Unit Pricing. The displaying of product prices for each pound, quart, or 100 count on supermarket shelves is known as **unit pricing.** If a store displayed three different boxes of diapers—box A, 24 for $2.99; box B, 40 for $6.95; box C, 48 for $7.95—the unit price would be calculated by determining how much one diaper would cost in each package and multiplying this price by 100 to determine the price for each 100 count.

Box A: $2.99 ÷ 24 = 12.46 cents per diaper
12.46 × 100 = $12.46 per 100

Box B: $6.95 ÷ 40 = 17.38 cents per diaper
17.38 × 100 = $17.38 per 100

Box C: $7.95 ÷ 48 = 16.56 cents per diaper
16.56 × 100 = $16.56 per 100

Krogering Means UNIT PRICING

HERE'S HOW IT WORKS

The unit price reduces the price per item to a common measurement for comparison from brand and on different sizes within the same brand.

This is the price you pay for the item.

BRAND NAME PRODUCT
1714 427   07   12   3 OZ
UNIT PRICE
13¢
PER OUNCE
39¢

This symbol is used for ordering.

This is the brand name of the item.

This is the size of the package. Make sure you check both the name and size when checking the unit price.

Figure 11-7. Unit pricing is a method of calculating the price by weight, volume, or number count; it does not consider quality.

By displaying unit prices, the retailer can help customers determine the best buy on the basis of price comparison. Unit pricing does not take quality into account. The customer must judge quality in relation to price through use of the product.

Single-Price Policy. In some retail stores, all products are sold for the same price, for example, all household items for 69 cents, all ties for $3.50, or all dresses for $19.95. When this is the case, all merchandise that is to be sold in the store must be purchased from suppliers with that selling price in mind. Usually this type of store will have a minimum markup that is acceptable (say, 40 percent), and the cost of all items must allow for this markup. The tie retailer knows the selling price ($3.50) and the markup (40 percent) but must determine the cost of the ties. This can be done in the following manner.

Retail price (100 %) − markup (40%) = cost (60%)
$3.50   − $1.40   = $2.10

This means that the cost of each tie can be no more than $2.10 if it is to be sold at $3.50 with an acceptable markup.

Pricing by Producers

The special price-setting applications that are used by producers include average-cost pricing, breakeven analysis, formula pricing, and cost-plus pricing.

Average-Cost Pricing. You have learned that there are two types of business costs, fixed and variable. Fixed costs are the costs of doing business that must be paid just to keep the business running, such as executives' salaries, rent, insurance, and utilities. These costs do not change with the quantity of output or sales. Variable costs are expenses that vary as production goes up and down, such as the cost of materials, wages, and transportation. In addition to these definitions, you must know a few more terms before you can understand average-cost pricing.

Total Cost: sum of fixed costs and variable costs

Average Cost (for Each Unit): total cost divided by the number of units produced

Average Fixed Cost (for Each Unit): total fixed cost divided by the number of units produced

Average Variable Cost (for Each Unit): total variable cost divided by number of units produced

With all this information, we can define **average-cost pricing** as the technique of combining average costs, average fixed costs, and average variable costs on a chart, together with profit information, in order to decide on a selling price. By using the average cost curve, the seller can decide on a price. If the firm expected to sell 5,000 units, the price would be $30, but if it expected to sell only 2,500 units, the price would have to be $50.

Breakeven Analysis. Breakeven analysis is a method of determining the quantity of sales at which a firm's revenues will equal its costs and

identify a breakeven point at a specific price. At this point the firm does not make a profit or a loss. If more units are sold at the same price, the breakeven point (BEP) is exceeded and the firm makes a profit. If fewer units are sold (below the BEP), the firm does not make a profit at this selling price.

Figure 11-8 shows a breakeven chart for a product selling for $10 a unit. The fixed costs for this product are $240. These costs do not change with the volume of sales or production. Assume that you bought a woodworking machine to make signs. The cost of the machine is fixed and allows

BREAK-EVEN CHART

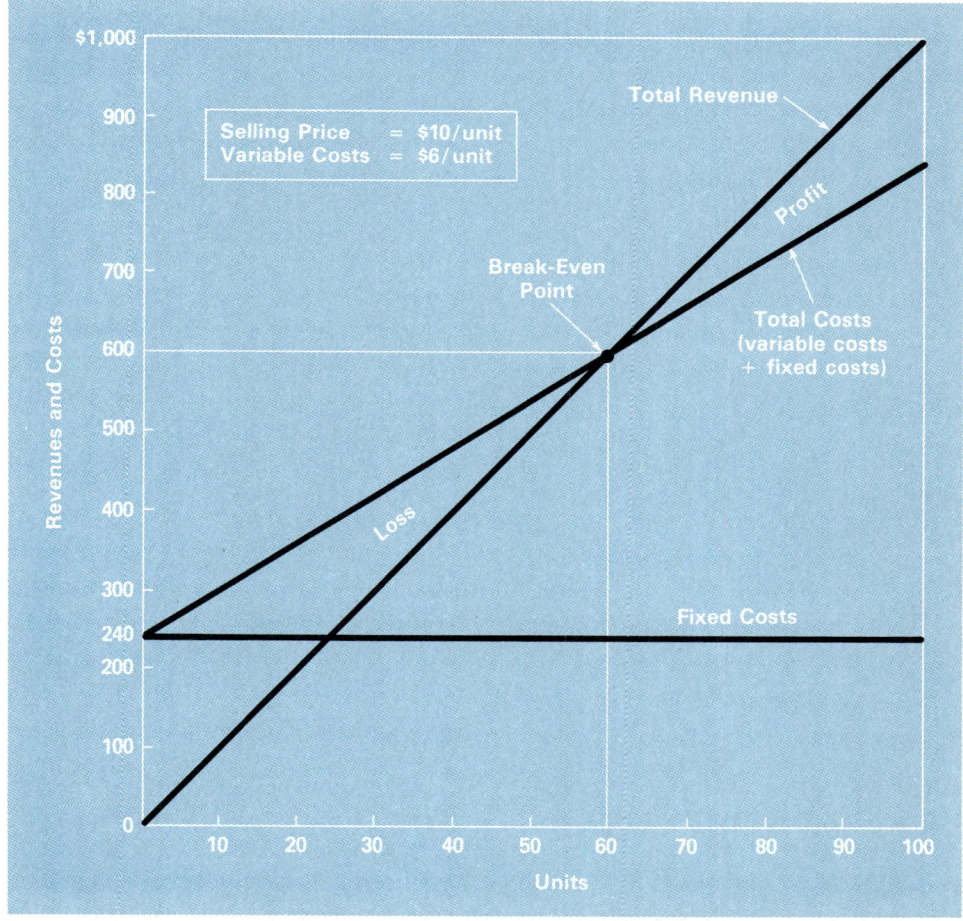

Figure 11-8. This chart shows the point where revenues equal costs for the sales of a product priced at $10 per unit.

you to make many signs before it wears out. The variable costs in the chart are $6 for each unit. You would have to buy the materials (wood, paint, and hardware) that would be used to make each sign. At $6 a sign, the cost varies with the number of signs made. Observe that the BEP for these costs and the $10 selling price is 60 units made and sold. The total revenue would be $600, and total costs would be $600. This is the point (BEP) at which the total costs line intersects the total revenue line, and profit is zero. If you sold only 40 units at $10 each, you would lose $80. If you sold 80 units at $10 each, you would make a profit of $80.

Breakeven charts help marketers determine the amount of sales needed at different selling prices to generate a profit. A different chart must be made for each selling price. For example, you could determine breakeven points for signs selling for $10, $20, and $30. Each selling price would require a different BEP chart, and each chart would be affected by estimates of or calculations of fixed and variable costs. Breakeven analysis does not determine the exact selling price, but it helps a marketer arrive at a range of potential prices that may be feasible in relation to costs. Demand and competition factors will influence the setting of the best price.

Formula Pricing. **Formula pricing** is a method of determining price that is similar to the use of markup. A basic formula is applied to all costs. A manufacturer may use direct labor cost multiplied 125 percent plus materials cost multiplied 225 percent and then add actual shipping costs to determine price.

Pricing by Service Marketers

Service marketers use many of the same pricing strategies and techniques that are used by product marketers. If you were in the business of renting typewriters to students, you might encourage longer contracts by giving a discount to a customer who rents a typewriter for 3 months. A marketer of delivery services might use zone pric-ing to set prices for delivery to different parts of a five-county area. If you owned a motel in a resort area, you would charge different rates for different seasons, based on customer demand. You also would set different prices for rooms of different quality: number of beds, amount of space, and type of view. This is the same technique used by marketers of products of different quality.

Service marketers face special challenges in the pricing of services. These challenges derive from the unique characteristics of services.

Services are Intangible. The marketer must set a price on a service that may or may not be perceived as satisfactory by the customer until after the service is performed. For example, the customer pays the price for a music concert before the concert is performed.

Services are Perishable. The service marketer who sets prices too high will have empty seats at the concert. At performance time, it is too late to look for customers at a lower price.

Services are Variable. The service marketer attempts to set higher prices for better-quality service. For example, a hairstylist with a better reputation and more experience will charge a higher price. Service marketers that have a perceived advantage, such as a better location and more efficient reservation service for a motel, may charge a higher price.

A Service is Inseparable From the Person Who Performs it. This influences price because of the quality and time factors of the labor involved. Some types of service labor require more skills and justify higher prices.

Cost, demand, and competition are the bases for pricing strategies by service marketers. If you operated a lawn mower repair service, you would have to establish a price for service that covered all costs (materials, capital, equipment, labor, and general expenses) and provided a satisfactory profit. You may know from keeping good records that $20 an hour for labor plus a charge for materials used will produce a profit. Some service marketers use a minimum service price such as a $10 minimum to service the mower or a minimum of $30 for the first hour of a service call. Other service marketers establish a price by charging for the cost of materials plus a percentage added for labor.

Demand factors would influence the pricing of your services in a lawn mower business. Before and after the mowing season, you might lower your hourly service price to encourage customers to bring in their mowers. During the peak of the mowing season, you might charge your highest service price. Also, you might charge a higher price for repairing a mower in 1 day compared with a normal repair cycle of 3 days. Competition from other lawn mower repair service marketers will affect your prices. One pricing strategy would be to set your price equal to the average service price of the other marketers. You then would attempt to get more sales revenues through better service, faster service, better location, effective promotion, and other marketing mix factors. If you have an exceptionally good advantage over other marketers, you might price your service higher than that of the competition. The advantage may be an outstanding reputation, excellent service warranty, friendly personnel, and so on. If you price below the competition, you may want to become the leading repair shop based on volume. With more volume, you may be able to maintain repair specialists and add other services.

Service marketers change prices to try to achieve increased sales revenues and better profits. Services have the same price limitations as products. If the price is too low, revenues may not cover costs. The service marketer may want to price very low for a time to attract new customers, but this may be done only for a short time. Revenues must cover costs in the long run. If the price is too high, customers will go to competitors for similar services of the same perceived quality. Also, when service prices are too high, consumers may buy repair equipment and supplies and try to perform the service themselves. For example, self-service automobile repair centers rent equipment and space for consumers to repair their own cars. Because of the personal nature of most service marketing situations, service marketers usually find out quickly what customers think of prices and price changes.

STEPS IN SETTING PRICE

Now you are ready to decide on the price of Snick Snack candy bars. Let us take a look at the specific steps you will follow as you use the information in Chapter 10 and this chapter to set this price. These are the practical price-setting steps used by marketers.

Step 1: Determine Pricing Objectives

These objectives must correspond with the objectives of Cook's Candy Kitchen. Your first job will be to determine what the company's objectives are and decide how Snick Snack bars will fit in with those objectives. The company may be attempting to reach a high sales volume in your market. The objective may be to establish a specific share of the market, such as 20 percent. Objectives may suggest a higher price-value image in relation to other competitors' products.

Step 2: Determine Approximate Unit Costs

To determine costs, you will have to gather information about both production and distribution. The costs should include both fixed and variable costs which can be allocated to each unit that will be produced or purchased. Can any of these costs be decreased without affecting product quality?

Step 3: Estimate Demand

You will want to employ marketing research techniques to estimate the demand at various price levels. What types of candy bars are selling well? What can you learn from wholesalers and retailers about consumer demand? What effect on demand

SAVVY PRICING GIVES SMALL FIRMS COMPETITIVE EDGE

Putting the right price tag on business products and services can make the difference between robust sales and no sales at all. The goal is to strike a delicate balance between the company's need to profit and the consumer's search for value. Savvy pricing strategies are especially important for small businesses. Giant competitors in numerous industries have used aggressive pricing to put small firms out of business, only to raise prices once they controlled the market. By viewing price as a competitive weapon, management can beat the blue chips at their own game. What small business lacks in size it can make up for with speed and agility.

"Sharp pricing benefits every business from small manufacturers to professional firms," says Bruce N. Lowery, a partner with Seidman & Seidman CPAs. "Let's assume a choice account is up for grabs on the basis of competitive bids. A company that keeps track of its costs and bases prices on them can shave margins to win the account and still remain profitable." Consider these pricing strategies.

- Start by establishing a price range within which you believe the product can be sold. The floor price is the minimum required to cover costs and maintain working capital. The ceiling—the maximum amount consumers will spend—varies with prevailing economic and competitive factors.

- Determine the ceiling price by conducting marketing research or by taking the "best-guess trial-and-error" approach. With the latter, management starts at the highest possible figure and then scales back at the first sign of consumer resistance or competitive pressure.

do you see in economic conditions? What is happening in consumer lifestyles that might influence demand for candy bars? What perceived value do you think customers will see in your products?

Step 4: Study Competition

By investigating competing products thoroughly, you will be able to determine the prices, quality, and quantities of the other candy bars on the market. What is the going rate of prices in this market? What are the ranges of prices of similar products? What data can you find that would

encourage you to price higher than, equal to, or lower than the competition? How many competitors do you have and who are the leaders in setting price?

Step 5: Select Pricing Strategies and Techniques

Will your final price be cost-oriented, demand-oriented, or competition-oriented? What psychological pricing techniques, discount pricing techniques, and geographic pricing techniques will you employ? What about stages in the product life cycle for your products? Many of these answers will have to come from discussions with

- Monitor all costs on an ongoing basis. Sharp increases in raw materials, advertising, or interest rates may necessitate immediate price increases to protect profit margins. Conversely, a sudden drop in costs may create opportunities for aggressive pricing and related boosts in market share.

- Classify costs as either fixed or variable. "It is no longer acceptable for a company to determine its overall costs and to leave it at that," Lowery adds. "In today's competitive and often inflationary environment, even the smallest firms must know their costs on an item-by-item basis. That's the only way to develop accurate pricing and to keep prices moving up and down in sync with market factors."

- Build intangibles into the selling price. When the elements of prestige, status, and pride come into play, extravagent prices may be an advantage. The story is told of the merchant saddled with a large inventory of private brand perfume that would not budge from the shelves. Priced at $5 a bottle, it experienced dismal sales. Acting on a hunch, the retailer tripled the price and advertised the item as a premium fragrance sold only in his shop. It worked like a charm. The entire inventory sold out within 2 weeks.

- Ask smaller vendors for exclusive rights to sell their products in your market area. Peppering the merchandise line with exclusives provides more leeway in setting high ceiling prices and in protecting those prices from low-balling by corporate giants. The strategy insulates small business from damaging competition.

Adapted from Mark Stevens, Gannett Westchester Newspapers, October 24, 1982, Section B, p. 10.

company management as well as from your own research and analysis of the marketing mix.

Step 6: Apply the Appropriate Price-Setting Applications

Using the information you have gathered in steps 1 through 5, you must employ the price-setting calculations that will help you analyze and synthesize this information.

Step 7: Set the Price

Evaluate all the information and calculations from steps 1 through 6 and decide on the best suggested retail price for individual Snick Snacks. Then

decide on the best suggested whosesale price for a box of 36.

By using the seven practical steps in setting prices discussed here, marketers can successfully achieve the pricing objectives of their firms. Although pricing will continue to be challenging to marketers, the use of these logical steps will provide a basis for decision-making. They will help marketers be objective and analytical in using cost, demand, and competition factors in making pricing decisions. Marketers need to use these steps to set prices that meet their objectives, satisfy customers, and return a fair profit.

- Marketers use three major pricing strategies based on evaluation of costs, demand, and competition.

- Cost-oriented pricing strategy involves adding a desired profit margin to costs to determine a selling price. Markup pricing, cost-plus pricing, and target-return pricing are three commonly used strategies.

- Demand-oriented pricing strategy uses the potential buyers' needs and wants and an estimate of buyers' perception of value to determine price.

- Competition-oriented pricing strategy requires the marketer to look at competitors' prices and set prices lower than, equal to, or higher than those of the competition.

- Most prices are set after consideration of a combined group of factors including the marketer's costs, demand for products and services, and competitors' prices. Marketers can seldom disregard any of these factors in setting a price.

- Skimming and penetration are two pricing techniques used for new products and services. Skimming involves setting a high initial price in order to benefit from good demand. Penetration involves setting a low initial price in order to build a large market share and high sales volume.

- Psychological pricing techniques are used to appeal to buyers who are very sensitive to prices that are set at odd numbers or that address a need for status and prestige, for promotional value, and for price lines at different perceived levels.

- Discount pricing is a popular pricing technique used to offer buyers a reduction from a regular or usual price. Common types of discounts are cash, quantity, functional, and seasonal. Allowances and rebates also are discounts.

- Geographic pricing involves transportation charges based on different locations of buyers and sellers. FOB rates, uniform (average-price) delivery charges, basing points, and zone rates are geographic pricing techniques.

- Marketers must learn to increase or decrease prices strategically. Changes in costs, buyers' reactions (demand), competition, and many other market conditions can cause price changes.

- Retail and wholesale marketers frequently make use of markups, markdowns, and stock turn rates in setting prices. Unit pricing is popular in retailing to help consumers compare the relative values of different products.

- Producers use fixed, variable, average, and total costs to help them determine prices. Breakeven analysis is used to determine a price at which sales revenues will cover costs and begin to return a profit.

- Service marketers use many of the same pricing strategies and techniques used by product marketers. Service prices are influenced by the intangible, perishable, variable, and highly personal characteristics of services.

advertising allowances (promotional allowances)

allowances

average-cost pricing

basing point pricing

breakeven analysis

cash discount

competition-oriented pricing

competitive-bid pricing

cost-oriented pricing

cost-plus pricing

demand-oriented pricing

discount pricing

FOB (free on board)

formula pricing

freight absorption pricing

functional discounts (trade discounts)

geographic pricing

going-rate pricing

leader pricing

markdown

markup

markup pricing
odd-even pricing
penetration pricing
prestige pricing
price lining
price skimming
prize money (push money)
promotional pricing
quantity discount

rebates
seasonal discount
special-event pricing
stock turn rate
target-return pricing
trade-in allowances
uniform delivered price
unit pricing
zone pricing

psychological pricing techniques are often effective.

5. Why do buyers react to price increases and decreases in different ways? Describe some typical reactions.

6. Service marketers use many of the same pricing strategies and techniques that are used by product marketers. Explain why service marketers face special challenges in the pricing of services.

NOTES

1. "Digital Sound Gets Set to Shake Up the Market," *Business Week*, September 13, 1982, p. 40.
2. Bernard F. Whalen, "Strategic Mix of Odd, Even Prices Can Lead to Increased Retail Profits," *Marketing News*, March 7, 1980, p. 24; and Zarrel V. Lambert, "Perceived Price as Related to Odd and Even Price Findings," *Journal of Retailing*, Vol. 51, No. 3, Fall 1975, pp. 13–22, 78.
3. Joseph V. Barks, "Does Price Cutting Cost More Than It Saves?" *Iron Age*, September 3, 1979, pp. 40–42.
4. "Ways Business Copes with High Prices," *U.S. News and World Report*, April 6, 1981, pp. 37–38.
5. "Why Camera Prices Are Falling," *Business Week*, September 6, 1982, pp. 61–64.
6. Barks, op. cit., p. 42.

DISCUSSION QUESTIONS

1. Why is cost-oriented pricing often a good starting point for setting price? What are the possible disadvantages for marketers who rely on a cost-oriented strategy?

2. Why do effective marketers often combine cost, demand, and competition pricing strategies?

3. If you were introducing a new product or service, how would you decide to use skimming or penetration as a pricing policy?

4. Many marketers believe in setting prices by considering the influence of psychological factors on customers' reactions to prices. Explain why

APPLICATIONS/CASES

APPLICATION 10: THE PHYSICAL FITNESS CENTER —PRICING SERVICES

The Physical Fitness Center is located near a large shopping mall on the south side of a midwestern city with a population of about 90,000. It offers many fine services for men, women, and children customers who want to exercise and achieve physical fitness. Many types of strength and body development equipment are available. Some programs are offered for small groups, but most of the programs are individual. The facilities are excellent, offering saunas, whirlpools, and comfortable lounges. The latest technology in physical equipment is maintained.

The business was the only exercise and fitness center in the city for about 3 years. This does not mean that there was no competition. During this time, The Physical Fitness Center management knew that other forms of recreation represented competition. If the prices were set too high, customers might change to racketball clubs, indoor tennis courts, and other facilities such as the YMCA and YWCA. Prices were set to achieve a satisfactory return on investment and, of course, to cover costs in the long run. However, with the increasing popularity of physical fitness activities, increasing demand for this type of service influenced management to set prices at a level that returned a very good profit.

Then, within a period of 6 months, two competitive physical fitness service marketers opened for business. The Nautilus Exercise & Fitness Center offered basically similar services and became tough competition very quickly. The Midwest Institute for Fitness emphasized group programs more than the other two marketers, offered less individual development equipment, but did appeal to some customers who used The Physical Fitness Center.

All three physical fitness service marketers entered into some very competitive marketing strategies to appeal to potential customers in the same market. Services were stressed in various promotional activities, but the real marketing battle was fought with very competitive pricing strategies.

a. The Physical Fitness Center will have to decrease prices for its services to stay competitive. Suggest some discount pricing techniques that might be used.

b. How could this service marketer make effective use of psychological pricing techniques?

c. If The Physical Fitness Center management decides to use a strategy of pricing equal to or higher than the competition, what pricing techniques and related marketing strategies would you recommend?

CASE 10: SUNGLASS MARKETING— LOOKING FOR HIGHER PRICES

Sunglass marketers watched their sales volume figures decline in 1982 to a unit volume of 72 million pairs from 86 million in 1981 and to a dollar volume of $720 million from $870 million in 1981. However, the major marketers moved aggressively in 1983 with higher advertising spending, new product introductions, and a hope for cooperative weather.

Foster Grant sales were typical for specific companies, down about 30 percent. Some of this decrease was attributed to one brand, Vidal Sassoon, that did not do well in its year of introduction. One company executive called the brand less than successful because it was a high-price line introduced at the wrong time. The Sassoon sunglasses were introduced in the $16 to $20 price range, with expectations of market growth in this range. Now the company does not think there is room for growth at the high end of the market.

However, competing sunglass marketers Corning Glass Works and Bausch & Lomb are expanding into the higher-price segments with new product lines. Bausch & Lomb introduced the Mirage and Expressions lines in 1982, but the brands did not sell well. Marketing plans were not carried out on schedule, and general market conditions for sunglasses were not good. The brands were priced at more than $20 and were targeted at consumers shopping in optical stores, department stores, and independent drugstores.

Bausch & Lomb executives say that while 90 percent of all sunglasses sold are priced at less than $20, those priced above $20 account for $300 million in retail volume. For sunglasses sold above $20, optical stores account for 41 percent of all dollar volume, followed by department stores, which account for 20 percent. The marketing problem is to get a significant number of consumers to trade up to the higher-priced lines. According to Bausch & Lomb data, only 25 percent of sunglass purchases at prices above $20 are made on impulse, while sunglasses selling for less than $20 have a 50 percent impulse purchase rate.

Bausch & Lomb is trying to reach the high-price market with its company reputation and quality image. The company name is emphasized on packaging and in advertising along with product quality information and a 1 year limited warranty against breakage. Fashion is one of the buyer's important reasons for purchasing at the high end of the market. The Mirage and Expressions brands' advertising messages stress that both the glasses and the wearers will be noticed.

Bausch & Lomb seems to be trying to identify price gaps in the market in order to build market share. There is much competition with Foster Grant brands and Corning's Chameleon brand in the $12 to $25 price range. There is a lot of competition in the $41 to $70 price range, with Ray-Ban and Porsche-Carrera at the top. Bausch & Lomb is hoping to be successful with the Mirage and Expressions brands in the high end of the $20 price range.

Industry price data reveal that the average price paid by a department store customer in 1982 for a pair of sunglasses was $12.12. In optical outlets, the average price was $18.29. In drugstores, the average checkout price was only $9.58.

Adapted from Pat Sloan, "Sunglass Makers Pin Hopes on Ad Visibility," *Advertising Age*, February 7, 1983, pp. 3, 45.

a. What pricing objectives are being used by Bausch & Lomb for the Mirage and Expressions product lines?

b. Describe Bausch & Lomb's strategies to try to reach a high-price market. Suggest some additional pricing strategies that might be used with the Mirage and Expressions sunglasses.

c. What are some possible influences of environmental factors on Bausch & Lomb's pricing strategies?

CASE 11: MARKETING COSMETICS—THE STRATEGY OF LOW PRICE

Noxell Corp. markets the popular Noxzema and Cover Girl brands of makeup and skin cream. The success of these brands is based partly on the strategy of charging a low price to appeal to a mass market. Noxell's products are aimed primarily at teenagers through an image of fresh-faced, natural beauty. The products are widely distributed and heavily advertised, yet their principal advantage is low price. Cover Girl is readily associated with the face of the famous model Cheryl Tiegs, who has been a Cover Girl model for more than 10 years.

Noxell sells its products mostly through mass-merchandise chains such as K-Mart Corp. and F. W. Woolworth Co. Competitive cosmetic companies often market through the more prestigious department and specialty stores. Noxell believes that department store displays give a cosmetic brand a higher image but do not deliver the larger net profits that the fat profit margins suggest. When selling through department stores, cosmetic companies usually are required to lease counter space for their lines, keep large inventories on hand, and pay commissions to sales people.

Noxell reaches its customers through retailers that usually display cosmetics on economical self-service racks. These retailers depend on low margins and quick turnover for success. Noxell's product lines are limited intentionally. Cover Girl sells only 7 shades of liquid face makeup, while the chief competitor, Maybelline, offers 20 shades.

Low price has always been a pricing objective of Noxell. For several years, and especially in 1982, as the economy continued to get worse, Noxell's products benefited as cost-conscious consumers traded down from more expensive lines. Through September 1982, Noxell's Cover Girl line (priced from $1.25 to $3.75) enjoyed a 20 percent dollar volume sales increase and a 10 percent increase in unit sales. During that same period, Maybelline unit sales increased 6 to 7 percent. In 1982, Noxell increased its total product earnings by 9.7 percent over the previous year

and increased its total sales by 12.3 percent.

Noxell has attempted to spread Cover Girl's brand popularity over a wider age group by keeping Cheryl Tiegs for a long time as she grows older. The appeal continues to be directed toward the working woman as an active, attractive person. Noxell consistently spends about 22 percent of annual sales for advertising, compared with the industry average of 7 to 9 percent.

The pricing and advertising strategies appear to be very successful. Cover Girl accounted for more than 50 percent of Noxell's sales in 1982, up from 47 percent in 1981. Also, Cover Girl has about a 13.5 percent share of the lower-price cosmetic market. Maybelline holds about an 18 percent share, but Cover Girl is growing faster in both dollar and unit sales.

Adapted from "Noxell Glows in the Mass Market," *Business Week*, February 14, 1983, pp. 148–150.

a. What economic conditions would support Noxell's successful low-price strategy?

b. How can Noxell have advertising expense percentages so much higher than the industry average and still sell at lower prices?

c. Using cost, demand, and competition pricing strategies, explain Noxell's successful pricing techniques.

UNIT 6

PROMOTION

CHAPTER
12
THE MARKETING COMMUNICATIONS MIX

The chief executive of a large business recently made the following remarks.

In our industry, any of our competitors can manufacture a product that is essentially as good as ours. Therefore, the only way we have of competing is on the basis of public image and service.

I like to keep my executives humble by reminding them that they are several rungs down the ladder of importance when we are considering our company's image in the public eye. From this vantage point, I consider our telephone receptionist the most valuable person in the firm, and I remain sensitive to see that she is well paid and equitably treated.

In descending order, I place the field sales people, the shipping and dispatching people, the delivery truck driver, and the product itself. The general public is more likely to be in contact with all of these before it encounters the management of the company.[1]

Many people believe that business executives make greater contributions to a company's image than other employees, but the front-line workers identified here have a greater opportunity to interact with the public. They communicate with customers and clients, and as a result, they influence the positive or negative image that is created.

In this unit, we shall look at promotion. Broadly speaking, promotion is any method of telling customers about products or services, the places where they can be purchased, the prices charged for them, and the competent, courteous people involved in creating, marketing, and servicing them. The basic objectives of promotion are to inform, persuade, or remind customers. This is accomplished through advertising, personal selling, sales promotion, publicity, public relations, and various other forms of promotion. Many front-line workers, especially those engaged in personal selling and public relations, have numerous opportunities to communicate with target groups of people.

THE COMMUNICATIONS PROCESS

The word *communication* is derived from the Latin word *communis,* meaning "common."

When people **communicate,** they are striving to develop a commonness with some individual or group of people. In other words, they want to convey an idea and the meanings that are attached to that idea in a manner that will enable the other party to fully understand the idea and the attached meanings.

Suppose Gail Gardner wishes to convey an idea about a marketing campaign to Bruce Woods. The message may reach Bruce through spoken words or in writing. Regardless of the means of communicating the message, Gail must first **encode** the message. That is, she must use words to form the message that is directed to Bruce. Selecting the correct words is a difficult process. Each individual may react differently to a word and attach different meanings to it. The word *liberal,* for example, may carry a desirable connotation to one person but evoke anger in another. Gail therefore must choose her words carefully in order to convey the desired message. People engaged in marketing find that some ideas are complex and seem to defy attempts to put them into understandable language.

The encoding process is sufficiently difficult with only one language, but as international transactions become commonplace, the encoding process becomes critical. General Motors Corporation learned this lesson when it discovered that the Chevrolet Nova was selling badly in Latin America. Finally, someone found the reason. Nova, when spoken as two words in Spanish, means "it doesn't go." After GM changed the car's name to Caribe, Latin American sales picked up immediately. An ad reading "Come alive with Pepsi" came out in the German version of *Reader's Digest* as "Come alive out of the grave."

The transmission of the message also may present problems. Once Gail verbalizes the idea or expresses it in writing, she begins to lose control of the process. Spoken words cannot be recalled, and written messages remain in tangible form. When her message is verbalized, Gail has the opportunity to observe Bruce's reaction and then explain or even reword her idea. If the message is in writing, Gail does not have that opportunity.

On receiving Gail's message, Bruce must **decode** the spoken or written words. That is, he must interpret their meaning. Certain barriers may stand in the way of listening or reading. Distracting activities may be taking place. Another determinant may be Bruce's mental alertness. He may be alert and comprehend the idea being presented. At other times, he may be tired and his mind may be dull.

Figure 12-1 on page 334, which depicts a communication from Gail to Bruce, demonstrates each of the five steps in the communication process. The process is important because marketers must be able to convey their messages in an effective manner. If the message is to be broadcast, the communicator must carefully choose words, voice qualities (speech rate, rhythm, pitch, and articulation) and vocalizations (pauses, volume, sighs, and yawns). The sound of an announcer promoting the Kentucky Derby has to differ from that of an announcer promoting a soft, comfortable mattress. If a salesperson delivers the message, all these elements plus body language (nonverbal clues) have to be planned. Presenters have to pay attention to facial expressions, gestures, and appearance. If the message is to be carried in a print ad, the communicator has to develop the elements of an ad, including headline, copy, and illustration. Attention devoted to the factors mentioned here will aid the receiver in decoding the message.

Clear, inoffensive communications are essential. After examining methods of transmitting messages, we shall look at barriers to communications, suitable messages, and some messages sent by marketers that have proved to be offensive.

Transmitting the Message

Marketers must choose from among many ways of communicating to the buying public the benefits and selling points of their products and services. Messages may be communicated verbally or in writing. They may take the form of printed messages appearing on product packages, ads placed

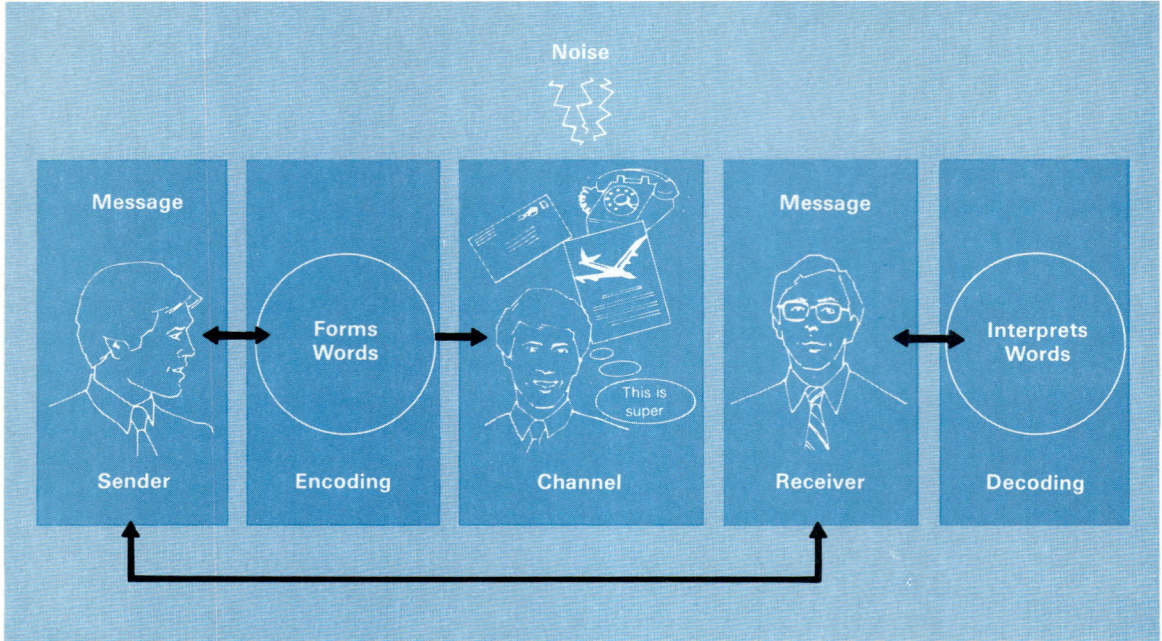

Figure 12-1. A model of the communications process includes the sender's encoding the message and directing it, through a channel often hampered by noise and other distractions, to the receiver, who must then decode it.

in newspapers or magazines, flyers sent through the mail or inserted in product packages, or other forms, letters, memos, and written reports. Verbal messages may be exchanged in a direct face-to-face setting, by telephone, or by radio or television.

Regardless of the method of communicating, marketers are concerned about clarity in their messages. Written messages must be punctuated properly in order to convey the appropriate message. Consider the following example.

The supervisor said, "The employee is late for work."
"The supervisor," said the employee, "is late for work."

Notice that while the words are identical in each sentence, capitalization and punctuation may change the meaning. Correctness in word choice and the proper use of grammar help marketers achieve the goal of clear communications that foster positive images.

Suitable Messages

Sometimes creation of positive images involves more than the verbal or written message. "We drink Pepsi, too," says Lydia Bragger, the 77-year old director of a "media watch" program for the Gray Panthers, an activist group of senior citizens that frequently protests what it believes are offensive commercials.[2] As a result of the vibrant, younger people depicted in TV commercials, a conclusion might be drawn that Pepsi is enjoyed by young people, not just those who think young. There are 46 million Americans age 55 and older. They have money, and many spend it freely. The marketer should communicate clearly, not only with words but also with actions, to appeal to the largest number of potential customers.

In preparing suitable communications, the marketer must exercise care in wording the message and also in delivering it. Carefully worded messages still may be offensive to some people. Suitability for the audience is an important consideration.

Block Drug once showed an elderly couple perched in infant highchairs. The message: People with loose dentures need easy-to-chew food. In a 1978 General Foods commercial for Country Time lemonade, an apparently hard-of-hearing grandfather kept asking his family to repeat the product's name. General Foods wanted a device that would allow repetition of Country Time, but ended up with protests. It later dropped the ads. [3]

Barriers to Communication

Certain barriers may interfere with communications, but most barriers are not absolute blocks to communications. Instead, they tend to contribute to the difficulty of making the marketer understood by distorting the messages sent and received. Such barriers can be classified into three broad categories: physical, psychological, and semantic.

Physical barriers are environmental factors which have a negative effect on the encoding process or the decoding process. Background noises, time pressures, and failure of mechanical communications equipment may disrupt either the sender or the receiver of a message. In such cases, identifying the environmental factor may make it possible for the problem to be solved.

Psychological barriers stem from personal differences in perspective between the people who are communicating. Perhaps you have heard someone say, "I can't communicate with that person because we have a personality conflict." Emotions, social values, and differences in opinion sometimes prevent clear communication. Marketers may be hesitant to express unfavorable news to customers because they fear it will affect their relationships with the customers.

How many times have you heard a comment like this: "Maria hears only what she wants to hear." The individual making this comment is questioning Maria's listening skills and the fact that she selects what she wants to hear. This process is referred to as selective perception. Improving one's skill in speaking or writing solves much of the communication problem. One must attempt to develop the ability to listen. Listening may be as important as speaking or writing.

If such psychological barriers are to be overcome, the people involved in formulating and receiving messages must approach the process with an open mind and with empathy. They should strive to see the message from the other person's point of view before reacting to it.

Semantic barriers are created because a word or a symbol can have many meanings. Words such as *young, old, great, small, good,* and *bad* are open to interpretation by the receiver of a message. A small order as viewed by one marketing firm may represent a large order to another firm. Thus, the intended meaning of a message may be misunderstood easily by the receiver. The sender of a message has a responsibility to use terms that are understood easily.

THE MARKETING COMMUNICATIONS MIX

The marketing communications mix is divided into two submixes: the promotional submix and the public relations submix. The **promotional submix** relies on advertising, personal selling, packaging, and sales promotion to carry messages about products and services to the public. The firm's image is communicated to the public through the public relations submix. The primary elements in the **public relations submix** include institutional advertising, news releases, oral presentations concerning the firm or its products, company tours, and involvement in community projects.

Rarely does a firm rely on just promotion or just public relations to communicate. Most firms use a blend of both submixes to communicate with manufacturers and producers, middlemen, customers or potential customers, and their own employees. This blend of the promotional submix and the public relations submix makes up the firm's communications mix.

The Promotional Submix

The term **promotion** originates from the Latin term *promovere,* meaning "to move forward." In mar-

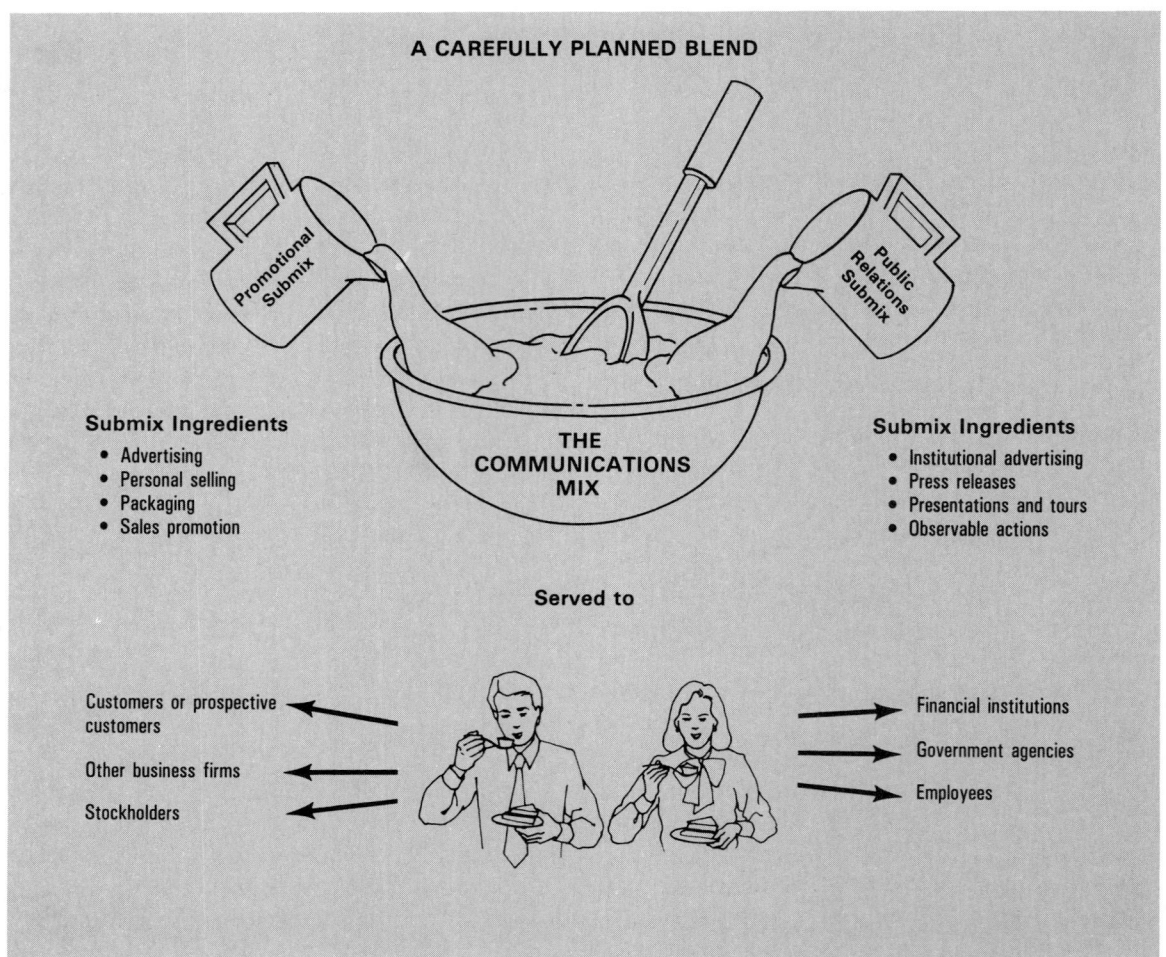

Figure 12-2. Both the promotional submix and the public relations submix are important ingredients in communicating with clients and consumers of all kinds.

keting practice, the original meaning is narrowed to include only communications. When products are moved forward from the loading dock into a storage area, the movement is not referred to as promotion. Instead, as you will recall from Chapter 9, the correct marketing term is materials handling. Thus, promotion as discussed in this unit is any communication activity whose purpose is to help move a product, service, or idea through a channel of distribution. Such communication activity is almost always persuasive.

This narrow definition does not limit the use of the term to marketing firms. Institutions such as

churches, hospitals, schools, and governmental agencies as well as individuals and organizations attempt to advance ideas. "Send today for your free wallet-size medical emergency card and personal health record." This idea, offered by the March of Dimes-Birth Defects Foundation, reminds people that a card may save their lives in an emergency because it contains a record of blood type, allergies, current medication, and conditions such as diabetes and hypertension.

Promotion is a tool of marketing. It is used by marketers to inform intermediate buyers and ultimate consumers of the availability and attributes of products and services. The major objective of promotion is to persuade buyers and consumers to purchase an offering. To accomplish this objective, communication is essential. Thus, the promotional submix becomes an important component of marketing communications.

Consumer-Oriented. The promotional submix should be **consumer-oriented,** which implies that all decisions regarding the promotional submix are reached with the potential customer's satisfaction as a focal point. This fits today's marketing concept as defined in Chapter 2.

Loctite Corporation, for example, introduced a puttylike adhesive for repairing worn machine parts in 1980. The adhesive's name, Quick Metal, and almost all its other features resulted from painstaking research and careful planning. The goal was to find what customers wanted and then to design a product to satisfy their wants.

> In the past, we would make a product in the lab and then say, "Now how are we going to sell it?" said one Loctite senior application engineer. The difference here is that the marketing preceded the chemistry. [4]

The experience encountered by Loctite points out the need to begin communications before attempting to move the product forward. Once the product was refined to meet customer's desires, Loctite began communications that are viewed as promotional.

> To fire up its workers, Loctite awarded hockey tickets to those who answered the telephone—"Loctite, home of Quick Metal." Others who collected business cards from prospective customers or found new uses for Quick Metal were entered into drawings for color TV sets and hockey tickets. Quick Metal Week was instigated when Loctite set up a bank of WATS lines. Daily calls of encouragement went out to 695 branches of the independent distributors who sell Loctite products. Those who sold the most won prizes of $100 or $1,000. The result: In

addition to selling more than 100,000 tubes of Quick Metal in one week, Loctite developed detailed information about its sales force, improved morale, and boosted the sale of other company products. [5]

The consumer-oriented approach often is presented as an objective by manufacturers and then ignored. But many firms are accepting and practicing this consumer-oriented approach because of rising costs of advertising, personal sales costs, increased competition, and the proliferation of products in the marketplace. Besides, it works.

The promotional submix also achieves other company and marketing objectives. It often enables a company to grasp a larger share of the market and usually rewards that company with greater profits.

Goal-Oriented. In some cases, the overall company and marketing objectives are set before the development of the promotional submix. Similarly, the potential market for the product or service is located and described. The promotional submix has as its purpose the achievement of company and marketing objectives.

These objectives may differ from firm to firm. Some firms may focus attention on market penetration, which means that they would like to increase sales in current markets through more aggressive promotion. Another firm might aim at market development. This firm wishes to increase sales by taking its current products into new markets, and promotion is needed to achieve the goal. Other marketing objectives that are important for various firms include the following.

1. Improving the repeat purchase rates for a specific brand
2. Introducing new or modified products
3. Familiarizing consumers with product uses
4. Stressing the exclusive features of a product or the quality of a service
5. Introducing new styles
6. Accentuating the relationships of the different goods marketed by a producer (for example,

Campbell's products, General Motors' products, or Del Monte products)

7. Presenting selling points

8. Correcting adverse conditions in specific areas

Marketers identify and establish marketing objectives and subsequently devise promotional strategies to achieve the objectives. For example, in 1981, Kentucky Fried Chicken announced its major objective: to combat increased competition by differentiating itself from rival fried chicken restaurants and from the hamburger chains that have long dominated the fast-food business and that had begun experimenting with offering their own chicken dishes.[6] In 1977, about 6,400 fast-food restaurants specialized in fried chicken. In 1981, the number had increased to 7,800.[7] Burger King and McDonald's had introduced chicken sandwiches, Long John Silver's was selling chicken "planks," and Arthur Treacher's seafood units were experimenting with chicken and chips.

To achieve the objective, the company began reminding franchise holders to remember the acronym quscvoofamp, which stands for quality, service, cleanliness, value, other operating factors, advertising, merchandising, and promotion. A $60 million advertising campaign centered on the theme "We do chicken right." Thus, promotion surfaced as an important submix of marketing communications for Kentucky Fried Chicken.

Table 12-1 shows the steps involved in selecting the appropriate promotional submix for achieving the marketing objective for Kentucky Fried Chicken. The first step was the identification of the marketing objective. In this step, the market was identified in terms of franchise locations. Step 2 involved encoding the content of the marketing communication to be sent. Finally, in step 3, marketers at Kentucky Fried Chicken devised strategies for delivering the message with as much impact and as effectively as possible.

Most marketers agree that success does not just happen. The firm establishes goals and uses promotion as a marketing tool to accomplish these goals. In fact, promotional efforts are so important that the largest part of total marketing expenses usually is devoted to such efforts.

TABLE 12-1
GOAL-ORIENTED PROMOTION MIX FOR KENTUCKY FRIED CHICKEN

Step 1: Marketing Objective	Step 2: Message	Step 3: Promotional Strategy
Differentiating Kentucky Fried Chicken from rival fried chicken restaurants and from hamburger chains now offering chicken dishes	"quscvoofamp" "We do chicken right"	To franchise holders: 1. Stress this theme during direct-contacts with franchise holders 2. Design and distribute training materials emphasizing this message To customers: 1. Use this theme for a $60 million advertising campaign

THE PROMOTION CAMPAIGN

Persuasive messages must be designed as well as possible to make sure they are received in the intended way by the intended receivers. Regardless of the method used to convey the promotion message, the following conditions for achieving effectiveness should receive attention.

1. The message should be designed and delivered in such a way that it will gain the attention of the intended audience.

2. In order to get the message across, words and symbols which are common to both the sender and the receiver should be used.

3. The message should appeal to needs and wants and suggest ways to satisfy such needs and wants.

Such messages enable a firm to reach predetermined goals.

Most people have a tendency to think of advertising in connection with the term *campaign*. It is more appropriate to apply the concept of a campaign to the entire promotion program. Once a promotion program is conceived, it may be subdivided into advertising, personal selling, and sales promotion components. It is helpful, however, to think about the global effort before thinking about subcomponents.

Gus Priemer has spent 29 years and hundreds of millions of dollars buying advertising, first for Proctor & Gamble and later for Johnson's Wax. "Executives go on the assumption that advertising is doing something," he says, "often overlooking sales promotion and personal selling." A common belief, says Mr. Priemer, is that "if sales are okay, then advertising must be working. If sales are bad, the advertising must be bad."[8]

Perhaps the first step in establishing a promotion program is to review the goals. Then promotion strategies may be determined.

Assume that Ramona and Hector Santiago establish a business that produces dried floral arrangements. They plan to sell their product in small variety stores, flower shops, and gift boutiques. In planning a promotion program, Ramona and Hector considered the following questions.

1. Should the program be designed to stimulate primary or secondary demand? (Stated another way, should the program be directed at middlemen whom they hope will handle their product, or should they direct the program at the ultimate consumer?)

The Santiagos have three choices. First, they may decide to direct all promotion efforts at targeted retailers in an effort to obtain selling outlets. Second, they may decide to direct all promotion efforts at prospective consumers. If they make this choice, they hope to create such demand for their product that retailers will be willing to offer it for sale. Finally, they may decide to split their promotion efforts, directing some promotions at retailers and others at consumers.

2. Should the program be geared for immediate action-response or should the Santiagos attempt to stimulate response for a longer period?

Ramona and Hector wish to develop a central idea or focal point which will produce immediate sales. "An old-fashioned Thanksgiving centerpiece" might be an appropriate theme to use in promoting action-response in November. For other programs, the Santiagos may choose central ideas or focal points that will stimulate customer demand for longer periods of time. "Our new Pampas grass arrangements accentuate earth tones for lasting beauty" is an example of a theme which may have appeal throughout the year.

3. Should the program attempt to influence a large number of buyers a little bit or a smaller number of buyers more intensively?

To decide which course to follow, firms would want to consider a number of factors including the following.

- The geographic scope of the market
- Types of customers, such as industrial users, middlemen, and household consumers
- The nature of the product, that is, whether it generally is considered a convenience, shopping, or specialty item
- The stage of the product's life cycle
- The funds available

4. What product features (both the Santiagos' and their competitors') should be stressed?

Ramona and Hector Santiago must decide which unique product features to stress in promotion programs. They must identify features that will cause buyers to prefer their product to those offered by competitors. Usually such features stem from the product, although other selling points may be effective. A unique feature might be the variety of available arrangements in terms of color and size. If the Santiagos treat their arrangements with a fire-resistant material, this may create a unique feature. Availability of the products, favorable prices, and gift ideas are other selling points.

By focusing upon these questions, the Santiagos will reach decisions that will help ensure the success of their promotion program. In essence, an examination of these questions will help program planners decide who is to be influenced, at what level of intensity, and for what purpose as well as the major ideas to be conveyed.

The Promotion Team

In many small businesses, the owners or managers make all the decisions concerning promotions. However, the small entrepreneur may seek the help of an outside consultant in planning the promotion program when expertise that is not available within the firm is needed. Often, an owner,

manager, or employee may have a flair for creating ideas that prove effective in sales promotion, advertising, personal selling, and other forms of marketing communications.

Larger businesses often have an officer—the manager of promotion—in charge of an integrated promotion program. A model of an organization structure appears in Figure 12-3. Such an organization structure is needed to ensure consistency in the firm's marketing communications to buyers and prospective buyers.

Demand creation refers to all special efforts to stimulate a desire for products and services with the ultimate objective of sale with profit. In a successful program directed at demand creation, the efforts of all personnel involved must be coordinated effectively. Ads and commercial messages should be related and well timed, and care should be exercised in selecting the correct media. Messages appearing on fliers inserted into packages should be coordinated with the broadcast messages. Sales promotion materials such as point-of-purchase displays, sales letters, and trade show exhibits also should focus on the program message. The sales reps should be fully informed about the program and in turn should convey the information to wholesalers and retailers. An organization structure such as the one in Figure 12-3 brings together a promotion team that allows such coordination to be achieved.

The Promotion Strategy

Determining the most effective promotional submix—meaning the extent to which advertising, sales promotion, and personal selling efforts should be called on to achieve the predetermined goals—is among the most difficult tasks which marketers face. It also should be emphasized that there is a considerable difference in the promotional submixes used by consumer marketers as opposed to industrial marketers. Historically, advertising has been viewed as the most important promotional tool in consumer marketing, while personal selling has been viewed as the most important promotional tool in industrial market-

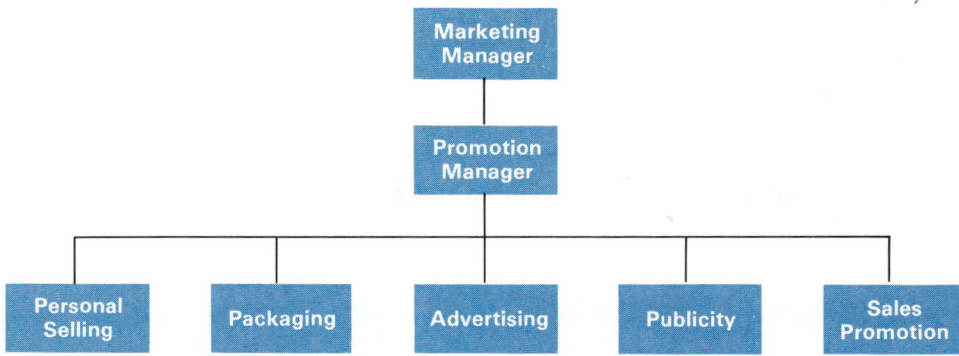

Figure 12-3. Organization of a large company's promotion program.

ing. Sales promotion, which is used in both markets, has been considered to be of lesser importance. But each firm differs. What may be the best submix for one firm may fail miserably when used by another. Unfortunately, the most desirable submix may not be feasible because of limited funds. As a general rule, businesses with adequate funds make more effective use of advertising messages than firms with limited financial resources. Financially weak firms are likely to depend more on personal selling and sales promotion with fewer advertising messages.

Some authorities believe that the promotion budget should be geared to narrow targets. That is, firms should practice segmentation as opposed to reaching national audiences. Their rationale is revealed in the following statement:

We have become an overcommunicated society. With only 5 percent of the world's population, America consumes 57 percent of the world's advertising budget. The per capita consumption of advertising in the United States today is about $220 a year.

If you spend $1 million a year on advertising, you are bombarding the average consumer with less than a half cent of advertising, spread out over 365 days— a consumer who is already exposed to $200 worth of advertising from other companies. [9]

In our overcommunicated society, the impact of a single component of the promotional submix may be overstated. Advertising, sales promotion, and personal selling components all should be examined in terms of their ability to help the firm achieve its marketing objectives.

The promotion team should seek answers to a number of questions in arriving at decisions about the promotional submix.

How Does the Stage of the Product's Life Cycle Influence the Promotional Submix? At the introductory stage in a product's life cycle, prospective customers may not recognize that they want or need the product. Customers must be told that the product exists, what it can do, and how they can benefit from owning it. Micropad of Chicago, for example, recently brought out a small computer that can compare a fresh signature in ordinary pen or pencil with one stored in another computer or on the magnetic strip of a credit card. Obviously, financial institutions engaged in electronic banking are likely customers. It is probable at this introductory stage that heavy emphasis will be placed on personal selling. Trade shows also are valuable for demonstrating a new product to prospective buyers or retailers. The retailers in turn use more personal selling to help the new product gain acceptance.

Once the product has passed through the introductory stage, increased emphasis usually is placed on advertising. The seller must now stimulate selective demand, or point out unique benefits which the product offers that competitor's brands lack. During the growth and maturity stages, most products face stiff competition. Persuasive advertising messages reach buyers quickly, often at the time when purchasing decisions actually are being made.

Most products finally reach the latter stage of the life cycle, when demand declines. Some products, of course, have longer life cycles than others, and a few have survived for many years. Products, however, are vulnerable to obsolescence, or in some cases they may be replaced by a new or improved substitute. During the decline and abandonment stages, promotion effort is reduced accordingly.

When Should the Personal Selling Component of the Promotional Submix Be Emphasized?

Personal selling often is used when a new product is introduced and the producer is seeking middlemen to help move it through channels of distribution. Personal selling is also important when the product is produced for industrial users. Industrial products are sold to a smaller number of buyers, and the personal touch often is needed to close a sale.

Small companies that lack sufficient funds for adequate advertising budgets may turn to personal selling. The typical sales call, however, is expensive. This approach works well when the market is concentrated geographically. Personal selling may become a major component of the promotional submix for any of the following reasons.

1. The product requires demonstration.

2. Customized products are produced to fit individual needs.

3. The product has a high unit value, is purchased infrequently, or involves a trade-in.

In addition, many services require personal selling. The need for insurance or investment portfolios, for example, varies from individual to individual.

When Should the Advertising Component of the Promotional Submix Be Emphasized?

Advertising carries messages quickly to masses of people. When the potential market for a product or service is widespread, advertising should be emphasized in the promotion program. The firm marketing the product or service, however, must have sufficient funds to support an advertising program. Proctor & Gamble, for example, spent $361.1 million for network advertising in 1980.[10] Smaller firms that offer their products in smaller marketing areas need not match the expenditures of large companies.

Advertising programs are useful in stimulating demand when consumers are buying the product or service offered. If the demand is not present, however, advertising may prove to be futile. In the early 1980s, high interest rates on mortgages pushed the housing market into a downward spiral. Real estate brokers found that increased advertising could not reverse the declining sales of real estate. On the other hand, savings and loan institutions, through advertising, were able to

Figure 12-4. Window displays and signs can increase the sales of a featured item.

attract thousands of savers with billions of dollars after the "All Savers Tax-Free Certificate" was offered in 1981.

Advertising is a useful tool when the product can be differentiated from the products offered by competitors. Appliances, for example, can be differentiated more easily than flour or sugar because there are more product features that differ. Products that have hidden qualities afford the marketer an opportunity to point out such features through advertising. Polaroid Corporation emphasizes the fact that their 600 model instant camera enables amateurs to avoid minor shadows on photos.

Advertising also can be used effectively when emotional buying motives exist. It is easier to build an effective advertising program for health insurance than for articles such as nails, staples, and curtain rod fasteners. Prestige products often are promoted successfully through advertising messages that appeal to the buyers' emotions.

When Should the Sales Promotion Component of the Promotional Submix Be Emphasized?

Sales promotion includes marketing activities, with the exception of personal selling, advertising, and publicity, that are directed toward increasing consumer purchases or improving dealer performance. The purpose of sales promotion is to inform, persuade, and remind. While personal selling and advertising seek to achieve the same purposes, they are relatively expensive tools. Thus, sales promotion techniques may prove effective at a relatively lower cost.

A local drugstore may find that giving free calendars and trading stamps and offering free gift-wrapping service attracts additional customers. Point-of-purchase displays or window displays may increase the sales of a featured item. Supermarkets may offer premiums or prizes to customers who save cash register tapes that add up to a predetermined amount. Similarly, a variety of contests are sponsored by fast-food service outlets in an attempt to increase the frequency of return visits by customers. Such sales promotion activities are most effective in winning patronage

from consumers when competitors offer little differentiation in terms of products, service, or price.

Manufacturers also engage in sales promotion activities. Discount coupons clipped from ads may encourage consumer purchases. Such coupons sometimes are inserted into the package in an effort to win repeated patronage. A manufacturer may offer self-liquidating premiums, which means that the consumer sends in proof of purchase for a predetermined sum of money or a prize. These techniques work well for highly competitive, low-cost products such as packaged foods or health-care products.

Manufacturers often find that sales contests which reward the top sales reps or dealers are an effective technique for increasing sales. (Recall the Loctite example on page 337.) Promotion techniques such as exhibits at trade shows permit prospective buyers to see, handle, read about, and talk about a product. As a result, dealers may be persuaded to carry the product in local retail outlets. Offering special assistance such as training of a sales force, point-of-purchase display racks, and cooperative advertising funds may entice wholesalers or retailers to carry a manufacturer's product. Sales promotion techniques directed at sales reps and middlemen are emphasized when manufacturers wish to obtain additional sales outlets for their products.

Knowing what promotion strategy to emphasize and when to emphasize it is an important element in arriving at decisions concerning the proportions of each ingredient in the promotional submix. You will have an opportunity to study each component of the submix in greater detail in Chapters 13 through 15.

THE PUSH/PULL CONCEPT

Related to the promotional submix are theories advocated by various marketers concerning the approach that manufacturers or producers use in obtaining wholesalers and retailers to carry their finished products. Actually, the theories center on a distribution strategy. To follow each theory, assume that the National Cord Company has developed a new and totally different type of twine. The twine does not require tying. Instead, when the twine is crossed, it forms an unbreakable bond. When one is wrapping a package, the ends of the twine are brought together, and a bond is formed. The National Cord Company believes that the twine has great potential for sales to consumers across the country. However, a distribution system must be established first.

The Push Theory

While the twine is a revolutionary new product that offers a number of competitive advantages, it does National Cord Company little or no good unless the company is able to gain wholesalers' and retailers' participation in selling the item. To accomplish this task, the firm plans a number of sales promotion and personal selling activities. The desired result is to communicate with middlemen in the channel in order to enlist their support in selling the twine.

National Cord will give its sales reps a thorough understanding of the new product. Possibly some extra incentive in the form of bonuses for attracting new wholesale accounts will help. Sales reps also receive a portfolio entitled "Store-Tested Sales Plans." With this book as an aid, sales reps are equipped to hold merchandising meetings with the wholesaler's sales reps and encourage them to accept the sales plans.

National Cord will display its revolutionary new product at trade shows at which demonstrators have an excellent opportunity to communicate with wholesalers and retailers. The demonstrators also may be useful as teachers. They can spend part of their time showing wholesalers and retailers how to sell the product. The company also plans to distribute brochures to assist wholesalers as they call on retail buyers.

To help persuade middlemen to stock and sell the new twine, attractive displays will be designed to exhibit the product in the retail outlet. Retailers want their stores to look neat and attractive. At the same time, they may be stingy with space because they wish to stock only products that will prove to be best-sellers. Permanent signs labeling the retailer as the official outlet for National Cord's new twine also may prove helpful in that they name the dealer as the outlet that can supply the product.

To entice retailers and wholesalers to stock and sell the twine, National Cord offers funds for cooperative advertising. This action demonstrates to middlemen that the manufacturer is willing to assist them in conveying persuasive sales messages to prospective buyers.

While these activities are not all-inclusive, they illustrate approaches which manufacturers use to enlist wholesale and retail outlets and to push products through distribution channels. If the manufacturer is successful in establishing effective communications through a variety of personal selling, advertising, and sales promotion activities, these efforts will result in additional sales outlets. That, of course, is the desired outcome of the **push theory.**

The Pull Theory

The **pull theory** differs from the push theory in that the idea is to build a volume of consumer demand that will result in wholesalers and retailers being willing to stock and sell the product.

Suppose National Cord Company wants to use the pull theory. It plans to devote its attention to consumers. It will develop a national advertising campaign to inform consumers about the new twine, and it hopes to build a desire within consumers to purchase and use the product. National Cord also plans to prepare small trial packages containing a sample of the twine and distribute them to consumers on a nationwide basis.

After learning about the new product and perhaps trying it as a result of the free trial sample packages, consumers will appear at retail outlets and request the new twine. The retailer in turn will request the product from a wholesaler. The wholesaler subsequently places orders for the product with National Cord Company. As a result, the product is pulled through the distribution channel.

Application of the Push/Pull Theories

The philosophy of most marketers can best be expressed by the term *total promotion,* which refers to a combination of activities designed to push and pull the product through distribution channels simultaneously. All promotion departments concentrate their efforts on finding and cultivating middlemen and at the same time communicating persuasively with the ultimate consumers.

Recognizing the value of a combination of push and pull activities, National Cord Company should structure a promotion program to provide both push and pull support to marketing efforts. The promotion team will meet to map out plans for push and pull activities. It is important to coordinate sales promotion, personal selling, and advertising within the promotional submix in order to accomplish the goals of National Cord Company: to establish desirable distribution channels and build consumer demand. These promotion activities constitute one component of the communications mix.

THE PROMOTION BUDGET

Firms continually study the problem of how much to spend for promotion activities. Although research methods and mathematical formulas may be applied in searching for answers to the problem, constantly changing variables including economic conditions, new or increased competition, and changes in the costs of promotion tend to complicate the problem. It is impossible to assess the exact results of planned promotion expenditures. A firm may add eight new sales reps, increase its trade show budget by $40,000, and allocate an additional $300,000 for advertising. While the firm may be assured that additional communication activity will occur, no one can determine with certainty what increases in sales or profits will result. Economic conditions may lead to an increase in sales or profits. New competitors may enter the market or existing competitors may develop more aggressive promotion plans. Or promotion costs may increase to the point of diminishing returns.

However, promotion efforts are necessary in most cases to decrease unit production costs. Marketers must consider this fact in their deliberations concerning the size of the promotion budget. Consider the following example of how promotion may decrease unit production costs.

Suppose we set up a manufacturing firm to produce home-assistant robots. Our fixed costs, that is, costs which are not influenced by the plant's production level—such as investments in physical facilities and equipment, other permanent fixtures, and insurance—remain constant regardless of how many units we produce.

Our variable costs, as the name implies, vary with the level of production. As we hire additional labor, use more raw materials or component parts, and consume more utilities, our variable costs increase.

As shown in Table 12-2 on page 346, if we add our fixed costs and variable costs, we can find the total costs for varying levels of production. To determine the average cost of producing each robot, we must divide the total costs by the number of units produced.

Assume that we have been producing and selling five units per month. The average unit cost, as shown in Table 12-2, equals $22,000. Our total costs for producing the five units is $110,000. If by spending an additional $30,000 for promotion we can sell 10 units, average unit cost will equal $12,000 and total cost will be $120,000. The additional promotion expenditure for each unit will be $6,000 ($30,000 ÷ 5 = $6,000). Adding that amount to the average unit cost ($12,000 + $6,000) will give $18,000. Clearly, the additional budget is justified because at our present level we are spending $22,000 a unit. Thus, if we have the capacity to produce additional units, our overall profit picture can be improved as the result of additional promotion expenditures.

TABLE 12-2
SCHEDULE OF FIXED, VARIABLE, TOTAL, AND AVERAGE COSTS FOR HOME-ASSISTANT ROBOTS

Units Produced (Q)	Fixed Costs (FC)	Variable Costs (VC)	Total Costs (TC) FC + VC = TC	Average Costs (AC) for each unit TC ÷ Q = AC
1	$100,000	$ 2,000	$102,000	$102,000
2	100,000	4,000	104,000	52,000
3	100,000	6,000	106,000	35,333
4	100,000	8,000	108,000	27,000
5	100,000	10,000	110,000	22,000
6	100,000	12,000	112,000	18,667
7	100,000	14,000	114,000	16,286
8	100,000	16,000	116,000	14,000
9	100,000	18,000	118,000	13,111
10	100,000	20,000	120,000	12,000

This example illustrates how a manufacturer may use additional promotion to increase sales and consequently profits. Retailers and wholesalers have the same goal.

Methods of Determining Promotion Budgets

Let us turn our attention to methods of determining promotion appropriations, which include the combined budgets for advertising, sales promotion, and personal selling. Budgets usually are projected on the basis of past or anticipated sales or profits, what the competition is spending, or what it costs to achieve the firm's promotion objectives. Some firms, however, do not appropriate a predetermined amount for promotion; they simply use whatever funds are available.

Related to Sales or Profits. Some firms base their promotion budgets on past or anticipated sales or profits. Once the firm arrives at the percentage to be devoted to promotion activities, the budget is relatively simple to calculate. The percentage serves as a multiplier and may be applied to the base. The base, depending on the firm's choice, may be any of the following.

1. Past sales dollars
2. Anticipated sales dollars
3. Past profits
4. Anticipated profits
5. Units sold in the past
6. Units expected to sell in the future

Promotion budgets frequently are prepared by using a percentage applied to one of these bases. This method, however, is unsound and logically inconsistent. When promotion budgets are based on past sales or profits, marketers are implying that promotion is a result of sales. In actuality, promotion leads to sales. When percentages are applied to routinely predicted sales or profits, marketers are again considering promotion to be a result of such sales or profits. Sales depend on promotion, that is, advertising, personal selling, and sales promotion. Therefore, the promotion budget must be established before the marketer forecasts future sales or profits.

Factors such as economic conditions have influenced past sales or profits and may influence future sales or profits. But if the firm performed poorly in sales or profits because of such influences, a promotion budget tied to such performance may prove inadequate as conditions improve. In addition, sales result from promotion. If the poor performance is attributed to an inadequate promotion budget, a new budget based on such performance will only make the situation worse.

Related to Competition. Although it is a good idea to monitor competitors' promotion activities, a firm should not base its promotion budget solely on what competitors are doing. In essence, competitors are making the decision for the firm. The competitors may make poor decisions, and then this becomes a case of inexpertise leading inexpertise. The needs and objectives of competitors may differ significantly from those of the firm following the lead.

Related to Objectives. A firm using the **objective and task method** must spell out the objectives of promotion activities. That is, objectives or sales goals are determined, and then the marketer determines the amount of money needed to achieve the goals. This method forces marketers to define the goals of the promotion program. Subsequently, the budget is based on the tasks to be completed. Such planning is realistic and accountable. Planned expenditures can be justified. In addition, from time to time management and the promotion team can review expenditures in terms of progress made toward the achievement of objectives.

Figure 12-5. Spelling out the objectives of promotion activities forces marketers to base their budgets on sales goals.

While it should be clear that the objective and task method is desirable, promotion budgets should not be cast in concrete. From time to time, the promotion budget should be reviewed and necessary adjustments should be made. Competition, economic conditions, and a host of other variables may render objectives obsolete or create a need for new or revised objectives. Thus, flexibility is needed to strengthen the overall promotion program.

Related to Funds Available. On occasion, a firm may allocate all available funds for promotion. If funds are readily available, the promotion budget increases. When money is tight, promotion is eliminated or cut severely. Actually, this method may be classified as a no plan at all approach to budgeting. Promotion has a job to accomplish: to communicate with prospective buyers. When funds are budgeted haphazardly, communication will be haphazard.

Successful Promotion Programs

Manufacturers, wholesalers, and retailers can prosper as a result of successful promotion programs. A casual look at your own community will probably identify several firms that have communicated well. Other firms fail to communicate. As a result, they may be just hanging on or may be forced out of business completely.

Here are 10 pointers which should lead to success in developing sound promotion programs.

1. Good Planning. Poor planning is the reason most often cited for promotion failures. There should be no surprises when money and customers are at stake.

2. Realistic Objectives. Objectives must be defined in a way that is easily measurable when the promotion is over. They should be established by staff members who can determine whether they can be met with the available budget.

3. Coordination. Some marketers just cannot pull their program together. They need an ade-quate promotion staff and a sufficient budget. A 14-store specialty chain in the Los Angeles area discovered that their budget for a holiday season was spent for TV commercials and newspaper ads. There was not a nickel left for in-store promotions.

4. Targeted Audience. Efforts must be concentrated on the buying sector. Some businesses lose sight of the customers and concentrate only on products.

5. Strong Management Support. Some marketers believe that promotion activities interfere with the selling function, take up floor space, or use staff time for nonselling activities. When management does not support a promotion program, that means no exclusives, no interdepartmental cooperation, no follow-up, no freshness, and none of the extras that give a promotion excitement.

6. Strong Channel Support. Marketers should take full advantage of promotion activities by other middlemen in the distribution channel. They should think of promotions as investments instead of expense items.

7. Good Timing. This works hand in hand with good planning. If the promotion includes special events such as trade shows, attendance depends on the sensitivity of planners to other buyer activities.

8. Creative Ideas. Repeats, empty themes, and dull presentations set an unfavorable tone. To create excitement, try new ideas.

9. Enough Well-Trained Sales People. Training seminars and clinics are essential for developing good promotions, improving morale, and stimulating selling interest. Sales people must be well informed about all components of the promotion program.

10. Sufficient Advertising Support. Advertising is a powerful communications tool. To reach the right audience, the right media must be selected. Ads or commercials which attract attention may be used to arouse interest, develop desire, and lead to action.

When all the elements of a promotion are merged into a well-coordinated plan, the communication achieves its full impact. In the following chapters, we shall examine each component of the promotional submix in greater depth. At this point, however, let us look at the public relations submix.

PUBLIC RELATIONS

Public relations (often referred to as PR) is defined by *Public Relations News* as the management function that evaluates public attitudes, identifies the policies and procedures of an individual or organization with the public interest, and executes a program of action to earn public understanding and acceptance. Public relations starts with research; that is, the firm must evaluate public attitudes. The firm must communicate to attain public understanding and acceptance.

A business provides many examples of verbal and nonverbal behavior. Some experts working in behavioral sciences believe that many forms of behavior are really means of communication.

At 10 a.m., Marie Adams received a telephone message from the Ruesch Advertising Agency inviting her to report for an interview at 3 p.m. Marie really wanted the job and therefore wanted to make a good impression. She called Carol Swarts, her hairdresser at the Hairpin Beauty Salon, to see whether she could make a hurried appointment to have her hair groomed. Carol recognized Marie's need for an appointment on short notice, but she was booked up. Since Carol was courteous and empathetic, she sensed that the appointment was highly important to Marie. She told Marie that she would check to see whether she could change an appointment with another customer to a later time in the day and then would call her back. In a few minutes, Carol called Marie and told her to come in at 12:45.

Marketers of products and services want to create a favorable image and build goodwill toward their organizations. Marie no doubt appreciated Carol's action and kept her favorable image of Carol and the Hairpin Beauty Salon. Almost everyone and every group or organization is concerned with projecting a desirable image and earning the goodwill of others. The motivation may be profit-oriented or purely altruistic. The point is that marketers communicate through overt actions as well as through words. Actions are important in building good public relations.

The "public" of public relations consists of all groups with which the individual, group, or firm interacts or hopes to influence. For marketers, these groups usually include customers or prospective customers, other firms, financial institutions, government agencies, stockholders, and employees. A marketer's position is enhanced when the firm has good public relations with such groups.

The Public Relations Submix

The public relations submix is an important component of a firm's marketing communications mix. The primary objective for the public relations portion of the mix is to develop an ongoing publicity program for all markets. Creating favorable public opinion about the organization (or individual, place, or cause) is dependent on public relations, that is, action-oriented activities that demonstrate the firm's acceptance of an obligation to be socially responsible. Firms simply do not hope that the public will look on them with favor. Instead, they use public relations tools to win approval. Marketers use institutional advertising, press releases, oral presentations about the firm or its products, company tours, and involvement in community projects as public relation tools.

Organization for Public Relations

While good public relations is generated by all representatives and employees of a firm, you will

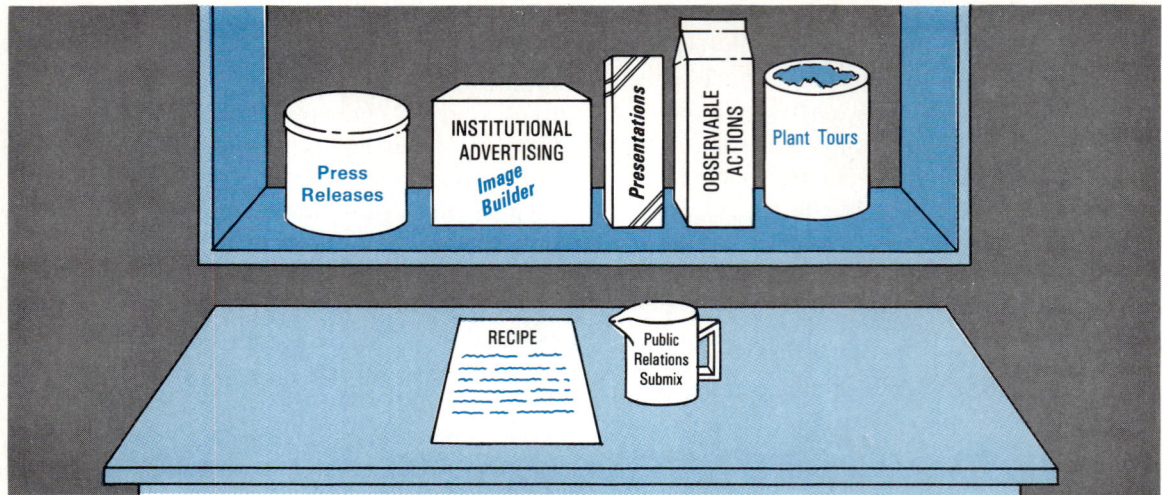

Figure 12-6. The public relations submix is composed of a number of ingredients to develop an ongoing publicity program.

recall from Figure 12-3 on page 341 that the publicity director is usually a member of the promotion team. The publicity director is responsible for obtaining free publicity about the firm or its products. This form of publicity consists of communications that may appear in print media such as newspapers or magazines, or it may be heard on broadcast media such as radio or television. In Chapter 15, we shall look at examples of publicity and how it supports sales promotion activities. But at this point, it is important to stress that the publicity director should serve as a member of the promotion team to ensure that communications are coordinated.

The Tools of Public Relations

For years, textbooks have stated that the p in public relations stands for performance, while the r stands for recognition. *Public Relations News* states the consumer will increasingly choose products (or services) on the basis of corporate (or firm) preference—especially when choosing new products (or services). This is only human nature; people prefer to deal with companies they know, understand, and trust.

As a result, marketers turn to the tools of public relations to help win recognition for performance and consequently accomplish predetermined goals for their public relations programs. A description of how some firms use the tools of public relations follows.

Institutional Advertising. Institutional advertising may be aimed at any of the firm's various publics (customers, consumerists, stockholders, legislators, and so on). It is not product oriented. Instead it is used to enhance the image of the firm. Successful firms devote time and energy to cultivate a favorable image. A few weeks after the poisonings attributed to tampered Tylenol tablets occurred, Tylenol aired its "You can trust us" commercials on all three networks. Although the company was not at fault in the incidents, the stories were carried by the mass media. To regain the confidence of the public, Tylenol sought to assure people that the company was trustworthy. This example shows how a firm used institutional advertising to check unfavorable publicity.

"Quality doesn't need to cost more" is a phrase that Tom Rhoades, a plastering contractor, chose for his ad in the Yellow Pages. Rhoades explained "By the time people look under 'plastering contractors' in the phone book, they are ready to buy. I want to be known for the quality of my work and for the fact that I won't hold them up. That's why I also inserted the phrase 'Free estimates.' " Institutional ads may prove to be an effective public relations tool when a prospective buyer has already decided to buy but has not yet decided where to buy.

Press Releases. Matsushita Electric Company used interesting press releases to introduce a new product called Stylesetter, a gadget that allows previews of contemplated cosmetic changes. The customer's image is projected onto a video screen. Just by playing with the controls, a brunette may turn blond, long-straight locks may turn into a short curly hairstyle, or the customer may try out a mustache, beard, or eyeglasses.

Your ticket to The Met for over forty years.

Figure 12-7. Advertising a firm's contribution to the arts is an effective kind of institutional advertising.

Firms often use press releases to tell the public about new products.

When Montgomery Ward opened "law store" booths in two of its San Diego outlets in 1979, this development represented a new and unique method of delivering consumer legal services such as writing wills, handling divorces and real estate closings, and filing for bankruptcy. Publicity resulting from the press releases was free. However, it no doubt informed and attracted clients. Since the message was unique—it was the first time a consumer-oriented legal services operation had gone the mass-merchandising route—the media were willing to carry the message.

Dollar General Corporation started operations in Scottsburg, Kentucky, a small town with a population of 3,500. Most of the company's stores are located in small towns, but the corporation has emerged as the largest of the "dollar store" chains, with annual sales of more than $200 million. When a new store is opened, the store manager, the district manager, and the mayor of the town in which the store is located are photographed at a ribbon cutting ceremony. This photo, along with a press release explaining what type of merchandise the store offers, is sent promptly to the local newspaper office. Such publicity helps the company and the local store management tell their story at no cost.

Oral Presentations. Kimberly Boswell manages a local Merle Norman cosmetics store. She was invited to speak before the Office Education Association at a nearby community college. Her presentation contained tips for selecting makeup bases, lipstick, eyeshadow, and nail polish. She used slides to emphasize the before and after looks. In addition, she provided samples of various products. While Kimberly did not attempt to make a sales presentation, some members of the audience stopped by the store later and made purchases.

At the next meeting of the Office Education Association, a jeweler spoke on the topic "When and How to Wear Jewelry—and How to Select

Diamonds." Again, the intention was not to present a sales pitch. But the presentation enabled the jeweler to share knowledge and expertise and thus win the trust and respect of the audience.

Various marketing objectives, as you will learn in Chapter 15, can be achieved by bringing an audience together to listen to an interesting presentation.

Company Tours. Wholesale Siding Supply located its new building in a small city, population 15,000. The firm sells siding (aluminum, steel, vinyl, and Fiberglas), replacement windows, gutters and downspouts, stone, nails, trim, and other accessories to building contractors within a 200 mile radius. The firm brought 75 much needed jobs to the city. Soon after opening, Wholesale Siding held an open house with company tours so that the community could have a look at their new facility.

The open house was well attended, and the results benefited the company. As visitors arrived at the new facility, they had to travel over a rutted street that was full of chuckholes and badly in need of repairs. On Monday evening after the open house, the city council voted to repave the street. Although this was not an objective for holding the open house, the city leaders recognized that the firm was providing jobs, paying local taxes, and improving the city by its presence. In a few days, a number of well-qualified individuals applied for the few vacant positions within the firm. During the interviews, some of the candidates expressed the idea that favorable impressions of the firm had been formed during their earlier visits.

Community Projects. Various projects that a company engages in can build goodwill and a favorable image at the local level. At the local

Figure 12-8. Company-sponsored community projects can build goodwill and a favorable image.

level, the firm concentrates on two groups: people in the community and employees. Let us take a brief look at how marketing firms may improve community relations as a result of community projects.

- A trucking firm sponsors a Little League baseball team.
- A bank serves as the depository for a fundraising event designed to assist the needy.
- A manufacturer lends a valuable employee to serve as chairperson of a United Fund drive.

Good community relations are important not only because of the increased business activity that may be fostered but also because the firm may benefit in other ways. Proposed zoning ordinances, deliberations on access roads, and other local decisions may be more favorable for firms that are considered community-oriented.

Firms are concerned with developing good relationships with employees as well as with the external public. Studies of employees' opinions have shown that employees who believe that a company is sincere and is trying to do the right thing accept that company's policies without question. The tool that enables management to convey such assurances to employees is communications. Good public relations help build respect for the company by demonstrating the following points.

1. Each employee's work is important.
2. Their work is appreciated.
3. They are treated fairly.
4. Fears of discriminatory treatment, unfair layoffs, and cuts in incentive pay are groundless.
5. Each employee has a chance to advance within the limits of his or her ability.

Company newsletters, statements of policy, employee handbooks, posted announcements, and other communication channels are used to inform and educate employees. As a result of such actions, employees take pride in the company and are more satisfied and productive. The result is growth and profits.

Communications—whether informative, persuasive, or promotional—will continue to occupy much of the time of people who are engaged in marketing activities. While communication skills are considered to be basic skills needed by everyone, such skills also may be required in technical activities. Communication skills applied in technical marketing activities will be discussed in Chapters 13 through 15 as we take a closer look at personal selling, advertising, and sales promotion.

KEY POINTS SUMMARY

- Communications is a process in which one strives to develop a commonness with some individual or group of people. It involves encoding, a channel or actual transmission, and decoding.
- Marketers have various ways to reach audiences. Designing clear and suitable messages is essential in marketing communications.
- Barriers to communications may be classified into three broad categories: physical, psychological, and semantic.
- The marketing communications mix is divided into two submixes. The promotional mix relies on advertising, personal selling, and sales promotion. The public relations mix includes institutional advertising, news releases, oral presentations, company tours, and involvement in community projects.
- The promotional submix is both goal-oriented and consumer-oriented.
- Promotion campaigns may be designed to stimulate either primary or secondary demand, may be geared to immediate action-response

or longer-term responses, and may be directed at a large number of buyers or a smaller number.

- The promotion team should include the marketing manager, the promotion manager, and department heads representing personal selling, advertising, sales promotion, and publicity or public relations.

- Determining the most effective promotional submix is among the most difficult tasks that marketers face.

- Personal selling often is used to communicate with buyers when the producer is seeking intermediaries to help move the product through the channel of distribution.

- When the potential market for a product or service is widespread, advertising may prove to be the most effective communication mode.

- Sales promotion is used to inform, persuade, and remind. It may be used at a relatively lower cost than other promotion techniques.

- While some marketers attempt to push their products through distribution channels, others attempt to pull products through such channels. Actually, a combination of push and pull activities can best be expressed in total promotion.

- Various plans exist for budgeting funds for promotion. The objective and task method is the most realistic and accountable.

- The public relations submix of the marketing communications mix helps a firm create a favorable image and builds goodwill with various segments of the public.

KEY TERMS AND CONCEPTS

communicate

consumer-oriented

decode

demand creation

encode

objective and task method

physical barriers

promotion

promotional submix

psychological barriers

public relations

public relations submix

pull theory

push theory

semantic barriers

DISCUSSION QUESTIONS

1. Explain the differences between the promotional submix and the public relations submix.

2. Assume that you have been hired as a marketing consultant by a small private college with limited financial resources. They have asked you for suggestions about how they may communicate effectively with prospective students. The college attracts students from throughout the state and region as well as a few students from other states and other countries. Should they advertise? Use recruiters?

3. Prepare a list of words or symbols that may create semantic barriers.

4. A marketing manager recently stated: "Promotion budgets based on a percentage of anticipated sales cause the promotion team to plan ahead. Therefore, I believe that it is a defensible plan." Evaluate this statement and prepare a rationale to support or oppose it.

5. Identify a product in an introductory stage. Explain what would be the most promising promotion strategy and why you think so.

6. Robert Erik has just established a small manufacturing plant. He plans to produce ceramic ashtrays, vases, bowls, and other small ceramic

items. His immediate concern, however, is to find local and regional retail outlets to sell his products. Should he apply the push theory? The pull theory? A combination? Explain.

NOTES

1. James G. Carr, "In Pace Perspective," *Pace,* January-February 1980, p. 43.
2. Bill Abrams, "Advertisers Start Recognizing Cost of Insulting the Elderly," reprinted by permission of *Wall Street Journal,* © Dow Jones & Company, Inc. March 5, 1981, p. 27. All rights reserved.
3. Ibid.
4. Bill Abrams, "Consumer Product Techniques Help Loctite Sell to Industry," reprinted by permission of *Wall Street Journal,* © Dow Jones & Company, Inc. April 2, 1981, p. 27. All rights reserved.
5. Ibid.
6. David P. Garino, "At Kentucky Fried Chicken, It's Time to Set Itself Apart," reprinted by permission of *Wall Street Journal,* © Dow Jones & Company, Inc. March 19, 1981, p. 29. All rights reserved.
7. Ibid.
8. Bill Abrams, "Industry Veteran Challenges Conventional Wisdom on Ads," reprinted by permission of *Wall Street Journal,* © Dow Jones & Company, Inc. April 9, 1981, p. 31. All rights reserved.
9. Adapted from Jack Trout and Al Ries, "The Positioning Era: A View Ten Years Later," *Advertising Age,* July 16, 1979, p. 39.
10. "Nine Firms Spend Millions In Initial TV Ads," *The Pantagraph,* Bloomington, Ill., April 5, 1981, p. F-3.

CHAPTER 13
PERSONAL SELLING

Richard Pallack did not need a lot of training or capital to start making money in the retail clothing business. When he was 10 years old, he designed a two-toned cuff link made from buttons, and he sold thousands for a few dollars a set. He has been finding his own ways to make money ever since. Now 25, Pallack built a million dollar a year retail menswear business by selling discount clothes out of an apartment in the Los Angeles suburb of Sherman Oaks. Pallack sells complete outfits to up-and-coming professionals who are willing to spend as much as $1,000 or more a visit to get designer-labeled wardrobes a few degrees smarter than the button-down look.

"Men don't like to shop," Pallack says, but they will spend money if they believe they are being outfitted properly. "Some of my customers come to me twice a year for 2 hours and have us select everything they need for the season," he says. Some even have their clothes coded with labels so that they can remember how to reassemble their wardrobes.

Besides his special market, Pallack has something else going for him: a knack for selling. Friendly and self-assured, he can persuade a cus-tomer to spend twice what he planned by making it seem like the sensible thing to do. Pallack's customers think that he is the only person who can outfit them.[1]

Pallack is not a huckster, a tricky mercenary salesperson, or a clothing shark. Instead, Pallack has mastered the art of using persuasive communication skills effectively and providing assistance to customers. Otherwise, his customers would not return twice a year. In the marketing discipline, persuasive communication skills often are thought about in terms of promoting and selling tangible consumer and industrial products or services. However, selling is not limited to such activities.

PERSONAL SELLING DEFINED

Personal selling consists of individual, persuasive communication aimed at helping the buyer choose a product or service to fulfill a need or want. People practice personal selling every day, although they may not use persuasive communication to sell a product or service. Some examples include the following.

- When Chris Butler applied for a job on a construction crew, he tried to persuade the employer that he would be a good, dependable worker.
- Julie Hendricks wanted to be the president of a local business and professional women's organization. She attempted to convince the members that she had good ideas and would provide the type of leadership the organization needed.
- Shane Keller approached a friend and requested the use of his Toyota for a short period of time. Shane explained that he was a good driver and would take special care of the car.

Personal selling goes beyond the use of persuasive messages to sell products and services. People use selling skills every day to persuade others to accept their suggestions, ideas, and viewpoints.

The definition of personal selling goes beyond the use of a persuasive message. It includes helping the buyer make a choice. Today, about 6 million people are engaged in personal selling in this country. If one salesperson fails to provide the assistance that a buyer needs, another is waiting in line to do so. For firms engaged in marketing, the importance of personal selling cannot be overstated. Personal selling is the promotion tool that generates revenues, that is, the dollars needed to pay expenses and yield a profit.

Advantages of Personal Selling

Personal selling has definite advantages over persuasive messages delivered through impersonal methods. Sales people can tailor their presentations to the needs, motives, and behavior of individual customers. Sales people also can see the customer's reaction to the persuasive message and make necessary adjustments immediately. While persuasive messages delivered through advertising reach nonprospects as well as prospects, personal selling enables a firm to reach target customers directly.

Ads can attract attention, arouse interest, and create desire, but unless the product or service is offered through the mail, a salesperson is usually needed to motivate buying action and complete the transfer of title. Sales people also perform other services which are not strictly selling activities. They sometimes settle complaints, handle adjustments, follow up on sales to determine whether the customer is satisfied, collect credit information, assist with marketing research projects, and help develop marketing plans.

Disadvantages of Personal Selling

The major limitation of personal selling is its high cost. It was not too many years ago that manufacturers were astounded to discover that the average individual sales call cost $50. Today that cost has risen to over $135 a call, and the costs continue to rise.[2] Wholesalers also are faced with high selling costs. Their costs are somewhat lower than those of manufacturers because their sales people usually travel within a limited geographic area. Since the customers come to retail and service establishments, their personal selling costs are lower than those found by wholesalers and manufacturers.

A second limitation of personal selling is the difficulty of finding people with highly developed selling skills. The ability to make persuasive sales presentations and project a pleasant personality is not enough. The modern salesperson must understand selling psychology, which is based on the premise that good sales people do not try to "sell" the customer. Rather, they try to help the customer buy. People with a knowledge of selling psychology are not available in abundant numbers. Some observers attribute the movement toward self-service by retailers to the lack of well-trained sales people.

ENVIRONMENT OF SELLING

The environment in which the salesperson works is dynamic. It is constantly changing. New problems confront customers, the economic climate is influenced by periods of inflation and recession, competitors come and go, and purchasing patterns change. Such changes present new challenges to the salesperson every day. Personal selling certainly is not characterized by routine and repetitive tasks. Some of the most noteworthy changes that are shaping today's environment of selling include the following.

1. The professionalization of selling and sales management
2. The acceptance of the marketing concept by most firms
3. The entry of greater numbers of women into industrial and field sales positions

Professionalization of Selling

A few years ago, sales-oriented students were expected to obtain their knowledge from company sales training programs or on-the-job training. However, manufacturers, wholesalers, retailers, and service-oriented firms today place more emphasis on professionalism in selling and sales management. As a result, community colleges, business schools, and vocational-technical institutions as well as other colleges and universities include preparation for sales careers in their curricula. The increased need for professionalism in selling and sales management has encouraged practitioners, students, and faculty members not only to support college preparation for sales careers but also to demonstrate an active interest in scholarly research in the field.

Pick up almost any large newspaper and turn to the help wanted ads in the classified advertising section. A quick look should reveal the number and diversity of sales positions available. If you study the qualifications for each position, you will begin to become aware of the internal and external environments in which sales people work. Retail and service sales people usually engage in **inside selling.** They deliver persuasive messages and provide assistance to customers coming into

Figure 13-1. Colleges and other educational institutions now offer courses in selling and sales management.

the store or service outlet. But there are exceptions. Some retail or service sales people are involved in outside selling, or **field selling.** They call on prospective customers to deliver sales presentations and to assist the customers in making buying decisions. Wholesalers, manufacturers, agents, and brokers are involved almost exclusively in field selling. Regardless of where selling activities take place, the person-to-person process, which promotes an exchange of products, services, or ideas, must be beneficial to both parties if it is to be successful. The professional salesperson does not take advantage of customers by encouraging them to buy products that will not satisfy their needs or wants.

> Tony Johnson was suffering from hair loss. Tony, always conscientious about his appearance, paid a visit to Apollo Hair Systems. The sales representative at Apollo explained to Tony that his firm attached a hairlike filament cable to permanent hairs around the crown of the head. Hair that was carefully selected to match the color and texture of Tony's own hair then would be fused to the cable. Tony seemed somewhat unsure about making a decision. The sales representative told him that he should investigate hair replacement procedures such as removable hairpieces or permanent transplants before reaching a decision.

This situation is an illustration of professionalism practiced by a sales representative in a service-oriented firm. The sales representative had been well trained not only to effectively demonstrate and explain the service offered for sale but also to assist the prospect in reaching a decision that would be beneficial to both the buyer and the seller.

Adherence to the Marketing Concept

Closely related to professionalism is adherence to the marketing concept. In past years, a manufacturer, wholesaler, retailer, or service provider might have said, "This is what we have available. Now get out there and sell it." Today, instead of being product-oriented, sales people are customer-oriented. In fact, many firms have adopted the idea that instead of selling products or services, they should sell solutions to customers' problems. You will recall from Chapter 1 that the marketing concept is emphasized when a manufacturing firm, through product research and development, discovers what potential customers need and want and then manufactures products to satisfy those needs and wants. When the marketing concept is applied to selling, the salesperson assists the buyer in a consultative manner. That is, the salesperson provides complete information about the product or service, answers the customer's questions, and to the extent possible, helps the customer reach a wise buying decision.

> A lawyer entered Larkin's Appliance Shop and told the salesperson that she was interested in purchasing a window air-conditioning unit for her office. The central air-conditioning unit in the building she occupied had stopped functioning, and she and the other tenants were having difficulty trying to persuade the owner of the building to repair the unit. In the meantime, she and her clients were sweltering in her hot, humid office. She said that she came to Larkin's after noticing that they were having a sale on 12,000 Btu units. The salesperson could have sold her a unit quickly. Instead, the lawyer was asked how much space needed to be cooled. After she said that she did not know, the salesperson offered to drop by later in the afternoon to measure the area. The salesperson explained that a unit too small would not solve her problem, while a unit too large would be more costly and provide wasted capacity.

The marketing concept is actually a philosophy or attitude which permeates a firm's entire sales organization. Acceptance of the philosophy is demonstrated by the salesperson's behavior in selling situations such as the one above.

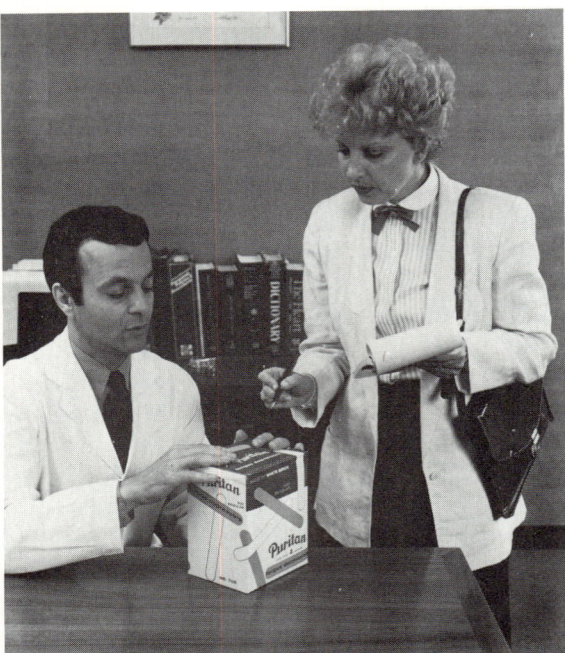

Figure 13-2. There has been a dramatic increase in the number of women in sales.

Women in Personal Selling Positions

Sales positions have always been filled by both women and men. Historically, women generally were employed in inside selling positions. As recently as 1978, there were just over 100,000 women in manufacturing and wholesaling sales positions.[3] Since that time, there has been a dramatic increase in the number of women engaged in field selling. Personal selling is not a field of endeavor that is characterized by sex-stereotyped positions.

Michelle Hayne knew that traditional ideas of "feminine work" excluded her from becoming an industrial sales rep. Yet Michelle was fascinated by the idea of selling building materials to retail outlets and building contractors. She observed her father's success as a selling agent, listened to him talk about resolving customers' problems, watched him check prices carefully as he worked with a prospective cus-

tomer's product specifications, and noted the gleam in his eye as he exceeded his sales quotas. Michelle studied professional selling in a community college and obtained some experience by working part time in a retail building materials store. When she graduated, she landed a job as a sales rep with a manufacturer of prefabricated buildings. At first, some of her customers and co-workers were skeptical of her abilities. Her persistence and professional approach to selling, however, have lead to success. She has just been named vice president of sales.

Types of Selling Jobs

Selling positions differ. Attempts sometimes are made to group or categorize sales positions, but the wide variety of selling jobs and the requirements needed to fill such positions make this difficult. Unlike the jobs of lawyers, nurses, or architects, which consist of fixed duties, a salesperson's job changes constantly.

Let us look at different types of selling opportunities, moving from the less complex selling positions to the highly complex.

1. Denise Holdt delivers milk from the processing plant to supermarkets within a three-county area. Jay Sniatynsky drives a truck delivering heating oil to customers along a predetermined route. In these cases, selling activities are secondary. The workers simply fill orders, although good service and a pleasant personality may attract additional customers and more sales.

2. Julie Freemont works for a spice rack jobber. She calls on retail food stores and replenishes the racks with spices. She sometimes suggests that additional quantities of fast-moving spices be added to stock. She does not, however, seek new accounts. Professional sales people representing her firm solicit new accounts.

3. Walter Leighton works as a salesperson in a large automotive parts store. Walter is primarily an order taker because customers have already decided to buy before they come in for a specific part. At times, he may use suggestive selling by pointing out to customers that a companion part may be needed. Usually, however, he cannot do much more than that.

4. Terry Kern has landed a job with the Jacobsen Division of Textron, Incorporated. Jacobsen offers a variety of products, including lawn mowers, chain saws, snow blowers, Hand-D Mix premium cycle oil, and gas cans. Thirty-six merchant wholesalers distribute the products to retailers across the country. Terry is a **missionary salesperson,** that is, an individual who works with retailers to develop goodwill and stimulate demand. Terry helps set up displays, arranges promotions, and helps retailers move the products faster, thus increasing the sales of Jacobsen products. While Terry does not engage in creative selling, he hopes the experience he is gaining will lead to a better sales position in the future.

5. Thousands of people are working in what are classified as inside selling jobs. Most people think of retail stores when they hear the term *inside selling*. But inside selling also occurs in showrooms at merchandise marts, in manufacturers' offices, at trade shows, in wholesalers' showrooms, and by telephone. In such locations, sales people practice what is referred to as **creative selling,** that is, showing prospects not only how they can use the product but also how they can benefit from owning it. There is a great deal of difference between timidly asking prospects if they can use a product and demonstrating how the product fulfills the customers' needs, wants, or desires. While most inside selling is directed at tangible items, intangibles such as insurance, vacation trips, investment portfolios, and dry cleaning services also are sold at the salesperson's place of employment.

6. Like inside selling, outside selling may involve industrial or consumer products and tangible items or intangible services. An outside salesperson who is involved in creative selling may be assigned to a territory and usually will work under close supervision. Outside sales peo-

ple frequently are required to travel out of the immediate area, spending a lot of time on the road or in the air. They frequently engage in **prospecting,** that is, trying to acquire new customers and introduce new products. They may work for manufacturers or middlemen, selling industrial or consumer products. Most outside sales people sell products or services to firms, but some sell household products, cable television subscriptions, insurance policies, and a variety of other products and services door to door.

7. Tom Marcus, a graduate of the Detroit Institute of Technology, is a mechanical sales engineer working for Robotical Suppliers, Incorporated. He is called on routinely to solve problems for his industrial customers such as figuring out how to adapt machinery to new processes, speed up production, or improve product quality. **Sales engineers** solve problems for their customers as well as sell to knowledgeable and skilled buyers. Sales engineers usually are trained in a highly specialized technical field and in addition must possess well-developed selling skills.

These examples reveal selling opportunities in both direct and indirect distribution channels. You will recall from Chapter 7 that various middlemen may be linked together to form an indirect distribution channel. From the point at which products are manufactured and until they reach the ultimate consumer or industrial user, selling opportunities exist. Each middleman must sell and transfer title to the products to another middleman until the products reach their final destination. Figure 13-3 shows opportunities in personal selling.

STEPS IN THE SELLING PROCESS

As noted earlier, there is a difference between the activities of an order taker and those of a salesperson involved in creative selling. People engaged in creative selling follow a series of steps that make up the selling process. The steps may be enumerated in sequential order: (1) prospecting

Figure 13-3. Opportunities for personal selling in both direct and indirect channels.

and qualifying, (2) sales approach, (3) sales presentation, (4) demonstration, (5) handling objections, (6) closing, and (7) follow-up. Each step provides the salesperson with an opportunity to advance towards the achievement of a goal: to ascertain the needs of a prospective buyer and communicate the ability to satisfy those needs in the sales message in a manner that results in a sale.

An individual who goes skiing for the first time is likely to encounter problems navigating the slope. After lessons and experience, however, the individual may prove to be an agile skier. Similarly, a salesperson who lacks training is likely to exhibit inept behavior in moving through the various steps of the selling process. Companies recognize that properly trained and motivated sales people are needed to exhibit an exemplary performance in the selling process. As a result, companies invest heavily in sales training programs.

Skillfully handling the steps in the selling process is so important that in one recent year firms engaged in field sales spent almost $15,000 a person to train sales people who sell consumer products and almost $20,000 a person for sales people who sell industrial products.[4] After training and preparation, sales people are ready to implement the selling process.

Presale Activities

The importance of knowing the product is basic, but sales people also must know their customers and competitors. This requires prospecting and qualifying. **Prospecting** is the activity of finding prospective new customers. Sometimes the list of prospects can be exceedingly long. To avoid unproductive sales calls, a salesperson may wish to qualify prospects. **Qualifying** prospects means that each prospect is analyzed and then classified in terms of needing the product or service, having the ability to pay for its purchase, having the authority to buy, being accessible, and in some cases, being inclined toward the product or service, the salesperson, or the firm offering the product.

Searching for Prospects. Retail sales people who are engaged in inside selling have several methods for attracting new prospects.

- Andy Miller sells new cars and trucks for a local automotive dealership. He checks automobile registration lists to learn the names of people driving older cars who might be ready to trade. He then uses a double postal card to send his message to prospects and allows the prospects to respond without having to pay postage. If the prospect expresses an interest, Andy follows up with a personal call.
- Tom and Jan Wilson operate a lawn grooming service. They had a small advertising circular printed with a doorknob-shaped hole at the top. They then distributed the circulars door to door. Many homeowners interested in a lawn grooming service called to request price quotations.
- Lisa Hayward sells residential real estate for Haikey Realty World. Lisa set up a rack at the local airport featuring color photos of homes being offered for sale. She attached several business cards listing her address and phone number under the caption "Take one."
- Mike Parr sells appliances at Danlor's Department Store. Mike placed a well-written classified ad in the local newspaper. In writing the ad, he tried to create a desire for the appliances without giving too much information. The last line of the ad read, "See Mike Parr at Danlor's."
- Beth Tragessor, a salesperson of women's apparel and accessories, writes short personal notes to prospects, informing them of new shipments, special sales, and style shows.
- Jim Majernik operates a restaurant. He reads the social pages in the local newspaper. When

an announcement of an approaching wedding appears, Jim contacts the appropriate parties and expresses an interest in hosting the rehearsal dinner or catering the reception.

Inside sales people may use many other methods to develop leads for their products and services. With ingenuity and experimentation, inside sales people can develop methods of their own which will be exactly suited to their products.

Outside sales reps often work within a sales territory. Prospecting becomes an important phase of their work. Established customers retire, are promoted or transferred, go out of business, or move to another city. These customers must be replaced. In addition, the successful sales rep attempts to increase sales volume by building a new clientele. A requisite for success in selling is a continuous search for qualified prospects.

- Steve Bailey is an outside sales rep for the Tulane Manufacturing Company. Tulane manufactures contemporary lighting fixtures and sells the products directly to lighting centers, building materials outlets, and hardware stores. Steve recently spent several hours poring over company records of past sales. He discovered the names of a number of firms that had purchased Tulane fixtures in the past. Steve contacted the firms, showed their buyers Tulane's new fixtures, and sold the products to a number of the buyers.
- Tricia Morgan works as a sales rep for Tri-State Exhibitors' Service. Her firm specializes in selling exhibit space and setting up exhibit booths for various groups holding conventions in the area. Tricia has purchased lists containing the names and addresses of firms which offer products or services to special target groups such as funeral directors, doctors, beef producers, and so on. When one of the groups arranges to hold a convention and engages Tri-State Exhibitors' Service to handle exhibits, Tricia contacts the various leads on the list she bought.
- Mike Francour sells plastic bottles and containers to pharmacies in a two-state territory.

Mike has collected telephone books for every city, town, and village in his territory. By referring to the Yellow Pages, Mike can determine the name and address of each pharmacy in the territory. Mike then relies on cold **canvassing.** That is, he calls on each firm to determine whether he can supply needed products.

- Northern Telecom, located in Nashville, Tennessee, offers an information management system to businesses with multiple locations or branches. The telecom uses a digital system controller which transmits not only voice but data and text as well, using existing phone wiring and computer terminals. Northern Telecom buys full-page ads in business and industrial publications. Those requesting a brochure that offers a fuller explanation are considered prime prospects, and additional follow-up by a sales engineer may lead to a sale.

Referrals, recommendations from customers and business associates, or sales reps selling noncompeting lines are often good leads in determining prospects.

Qualifying the Prospects.
A requisite for success in selling is the continuous search for qualified prospects. Firms place emphasis on the term *qualified* because sales calls are expensive and because the expense is incurred regardless of the outcome of the calls. Sales reps recognize that time is a valuable resource that should not be wasted on people who are not likely buyers. Sales reps are motivated to qualify prospects for two important reasons.

1. The sales rep must be productive if sales quotas are to be achieved.

2. When the sales rep's compensation is based on a commission, the probability of selling to a prospect is an important consideration.

It is much easier to sell paper to a printing shop before the buyer has placed an order for a 6 month supply. Sales reps attempt to learn when a buyer is ready to place an order for needed products.

Sales Rep: The reason I'm calling you, Mr. Kinsley, is to tell you that I am the new sales rep for Tapex Paper Company. We offer paper in various colors, sizes, weights, and glossy surfaces. Ink does not saturate the paper. In fact, it's about 5 percentage points above paper offered by other suppliers. Our price is right, too. Kinsley's Printing Shop has a reputation for quality work, and I think you would be interested in our products. I would like an opportunity to show you our products.

Mr. Kinsley: I just received a new order of paper stock that should satisfy our needs for about 3 months.

Sales Rep: I plan to be in your area in 2 months. I would like to call you then and set a time at your convenience to show you our products. Since our warehouse is only 200 miles from your establishment, we can assure stock within 2 weeks.

Mr. Kinsley: Fine, I will be expecting your call.

Time spent with people who want the product but cannot afford it may be wasted. Many people, for example, tramp through homes which are too expensive for them to buy.

Ruth LaMalsky sells real estate for Fraser Realty. She often spends Sunday afternoons conducting open houses. As Ruth conducts the tours, she asks a number of questions in a friendly and subtle manner. "Are you folks just moving into this community? What kind of work will you be doing here, Mr. Samuels? Will your wife be working, too? Are you selling a home in the city from which you were transferred?" Responses to such questions help Ruth determine whether the Samuelses' income or wealth qualified them to buy the home. If it does not qualify them but the Samuelses seem to be genuinely interested in buying a home, she may ask what price range they are interested in and point out other homes which she has available.

Sales reps should plan appointments so that they speak with parties that have the authority to buy.

Tom Sarsfield sells Wang word processing equipment. After learning that the Woodstown school district was considering the installation of a word processing center, Tom called the superintendent of the district. He learned that the Woodstown school board had to approve the purchase of products which cost more than $1,500. The superintendent arranged for Tom to demonstrate the equipment to the board members a month later.

Buyers also must be accessible. If a sales rep must travel 200 or 300 miles to reach an isolated buyer, and if the sales are expected to be modest, it may be more profitable to phone the prospect.

Preapproach. Before calling on prospects, a salesperson should learn everything possible about the prospective customer. Whether the prospects are homeowners, farmers, college students, or business and industrial buyers makes no difference. They all have individual needs, desires, and interests.

In most cases, the needs of any particular group of prospects are many and varied. In fact, the needs can become so numerous that it becomes necessary to assign priorities. The sales rep can assist the prospect in assigning these pri-

Figure 13-4. Preapproach: Research is part of learning everything possible about a prospective customer.

TIME MANAGEMENT FOR SALES REPS

Successful sales people actively working 40 hours a week have learned to multiply their profits by investing their time shrewdly. Time, they have learned, is their most precious asset.

"The best production I ever had was during the period when I was regularly scheduling my time," said the number one sales producer at the company's convention. An explanation of how to manage time to best allow a sales rep to apply knowledge and skill to selling followed. That formula for time management was directly responsible for award-winning success.

There is a limited amount of time available daily for face-to-face contact with prospects. The successful salesperson invests a few minutes each week in planning. The successful salesperson knows exactly what must be accomplished each day to acquire the greatest personal contact time. That individual organizes sales calls, driving time, and callbacks. In fact, the organized salesperson knows where he or she is going every minute of the day.

When you consider that 65 percent of all sales calls are made on nondecision makers and that 45 percent of a typical sales day is spent traveling, waiting, and trying to locate the right person to talk to, you will realize that ways must be found to save time.

Check your performance against the following tips on making the most of your precious time.

- Plan important things to do today. If you are faced with an unpleasant or difficult task, try to get it over with early in the day. This leaves time for your work, selling, instead of wasting time anticipating something you dread.
- Reduce personal business tasks during the selling hours of the day. Delegate work to others whenever possible. Your spouse, a secretary, and even the mail carrier are potential helpers. A refusal to delegate responsibility may cause you to be consistently short of time.

orities. A restaurant owner, for example, may be thinking of purchasing new china or a larger cash register. A sales rep handling a line of burglarproof locks, simulated TV surveillance systems, fire extinguishers, and smoke detectors will point out the need to protect life and property. As a result, the restaurant owner may reshuffle priorities and

purchase protective equipment before buying china or a cash register.

Prioritizing needs has the same application in the consumer market. Prospects for consumer products are many and varied. But rich or poor, married or single, black or white, working or unemployed, old or young, apartment dwellers or

- Cut down the number of minutes you spend in the presence of people who obviously are not prospects.
- Train your mind to think and plan while you are driving. Carry a notebook or tape recorder with you for recording thoughts and ideas.
- Conserve travel time by using the telephone professionally to weed out unqualified prospects and to prepare prospects for solid appointments.
- Decide about trifles quickly. Toss a coin if necessary. Do not evaluate trifling decisions with the same care and precision you apply to major decisions.
- Prepare your presentation thoroughly. Compressing an idea into a brief but adequate 20 minute statement is far more informative than wandering in a forest of words for an hour.
- Require punctuality. One of the major problems of a sales rep is to find time for an appointment only to be kept waiting by the customer. Give the customer the courtesy of a 15 minute delay and then leave a polite note saying that you know that he or she is busy and that you will call again for a future appointment. Do not let others waste your precious time.
- If you feel you must wait, use your time profitably by planning the next call or by doing professional reading. It pays to be ready with substitute calls, too.
- Eliminate inefficient activities by occasionally asking yourself, Why shouldn't I omit this entirely?

A reassessment of time management may help a marketer win selling awards. In any event, creative ways of spending time can help a salesperson improve performance and advance in a selling career.

Adapted from Darlene Barr, "A Salesman's Most Precious Asset," *Salesman's Opportunity*, February 1982, p. 34.

homeowners, they all have needs that must be prioritized. This is especially true for people on limited or fixed incomes. Today's sales people serve as personal consultants to prospective customers by asking questions, giving candid answers, and assisting customers in reaching buying decisions.

Another facet of preapproach activities involves learning and remembering customers' names. Forgetting a buyer's name can be embarrassing. The buyer may wonder why the salesperson does not care enough to remember it. As a part of the preapproach activities, the salesperson will want to ensure that the name will be remembered.

Repeat the person's name out loud so that you can hear yourself saying it and then repeat it several times mentally. Some sales people find that associations are helpful in remembering names. Mr. Appleby, for example, could suggest the sentence "When will the apple be falling?" Miss Brookfield's name suggests a picture of a country field in midsummer with a cool brook running through it. The next step is to practice this method for remembering names. The old cliché that practice makes perfect may enable the salesperson to make a positive impression on buyers.

Once the salesperson has gathered information about prospective buyers, the data can be used to develop the prospect's personal profile and business profile. Knowing how long the buyer has been employed in the present position and being aware of the buyer's education and training enables the salesperson to understand the buyer's competencies, authority, and security better. Knowledge about the buyer's personal interests and family status enables the salesperson to break the ice before launching into a formal sales presentation.

If the salesperson calls on business and industrial buyers, a business profile is helpful. Part of this profile includes a needs assessment. The big question is, "What needs exist that my product or service can fill?" If the company is using a competitor's product, the sales rep should seek to discover ways in which his or her product is superior. If superior features do not exist, perhaps a lower price or better service will fill the buyer's needs.

Since most business and industrial sales involve credit, the sales rep will want to include the prospect's credit rating in a business profile. Credit reporting services can supply such ratings. In addition, if the prospect is more likely to buy at certain times of the year, the sales rep will note such times in the profile.

Initiating Contact. The final presale activity is making an appointment. The salesperson may use a short business letter to request an appointment. However, the telephone is used more often. Since customers may be busy, the salesperson should have alternative times and dates in mind.

Selling Activities

Selling activities include the sales presentation, a demonstration of the product, handling objections, closing the sale, and suggestion selling. Once the presale activities are concluded and the customer and the salesperson meet face to face, emphasis is placed on communication. Both verbal and nonverbal forms of communication may be used. While an ad may carry a message, facial expressions, gestures, voice inflections, and mannerisms help the salesperson communicate with the customer.

Sales Presentation. The prospect must want to listen in order to understand the full significance of a salesperson's presentation. For this reason, the opening of a sales presentation, which sometimes is called a sales approach, cannot be considered satisfactory unless the salesperson seizes control of the selling situation within the first few seconds. Suitable openings vary, depending on the situation. Sales people engaged in outside selling have a greater opportunity to size up the selling situation before approaching a prospective buyer. Inside sales people, on the other hand, suddenly may be confronted with a prospective customer interested in one or more of a variety of products or services.

"No thank you, I'm just looking." Inside sales people fear this response, yet they go on approaching customers by asking the sale-killing question, "May I help you?" It is easy to overcome this response. In fact, it can be avoided completely if the salesperson simply refrains from using any approach which invites such a reply. Instead, lead off with a friendly, "Good morning." Then pause long enough to encourage customers to tell you about their needs.

Show the prospect something from the line of products being examined. For example, ask,

"Have you noticed that the vest is reversible and adds versatility to your wardrobe?" The reaction should help you assess the customer's needs.

When the customer is known to the salesperson, the approach can be personal. For example, say, "Good morning, Jan. Remember asking me about car coats the other day? Well, we just received a new shipment, and I think we have just what you want." This shows that you think of your customers as individuals, not just people with money to spend.

Sales people engaged in inside selling will find a variety of other approaches to get the selling situation off to a good start. While approaches can be either tailored or standard, the tailored approach generally is favored. Because each customer is an individual and individuals differ, a standard approach cannot fit all prospects.

The sales rep engaged in outside selling has a greater opportunity to plan approaches. When the prospect is unknown, the approach is often a standard one with a touch of drama.

Everyone wants to make money, and Jim Silverman puts this fact to good use in selling machinery to factories. His approach to the prospect is, "How would you like to see a machine that makes money?" Naturally the prospect's curiosity is aroused, at which point Jim opens his catalog, turns to the illustration of the machine he believes most useful to the prospect, and says, "Here's a machine that makes money for you, because it most economically produces the parts you need, thereby enabling you to earn more profit."[5]

Jim's approach dramatizes the benefits of buying his machine. The words *most economically* tell the prospect that Jim's equipment either speeds production or costs less to operate, enabling the prospect to earn a greater percentage on the operation. It is then a simple matter for Jim to explain the specific features that make his machine more efficient and more economical than present methods.

Door-to-door sales people also may use a dramatic, standardized approach to launch a sales presentation.

Hugo Wentworth sells "food plans." It is a service in which the company supplies food on a weekly or monthly basis and supplies a freezer included in the price of the food, which is paid for on a monthly plan. When Hugo approaches his prospects, who are mostly homemakers, he has in his hand a rubber dollar bill, a quantity of which he has purchased in a novelty shop.

"Good morning," says Hugo. "May I have about 3 minutes of your time to show you how to s-t-r-e-t-c-h your food budget?" At the word *stretch,* which he emphasizes and lengthens in a singsong voice, he stretches the rubber dollar bill to its full length. Naturally, the homemaker wants to make food dollars go as far as possible, and it is easy for Hugo to demonstrate how his monthly food plan, plus the freezer, can save time by reducing shopping trips substantially.[6]

Notice that in both of these approaches, the sales reps focused on ways in which prospects solve problems. While in both situations the approaches were standard, tailored approaches also may be used. A salesperson who can assess a prospect's needs and then promise the prospect a benefit is in an advantageous position. Customers are interested in benefits, and their attention will be captured. However, the promise must be sincere, and the salesperson must be able to deliver on it.

Social interaction is necessary if the salesperson is to influence the buyer's purchase decisions. Social interaction takes place when the salesperson and the buyer exchange information, beliefs, attitudes, and ideas. It involves two-way communication. Unfortunately, social interaction is not always an easy task. Prospective customers differ. As a result, the salesperson needs to study sales psychology to develop and polish the skills required to initiate successful two-way communication. Table 13-1 contains a list of prospective customer types and some tips on how to deal with them successfully.

While social interaction is a difficult task with some prospects, a difficult prospect may be easier to sell than an indifferent prospect. Recognize individual needs and cater to them. The more satisfaction or value (appreciation or agreement) the buyer receives from the salesperson, the more confidence the buyer places in the salesperson.

During the social interaction that starts with the opening of the sales presentation, the salesperson tries to achieve four major objectives as the customer's mind moves from the interest stage to the desire stage.

1. The salesperson attempts to present product features and other attributes as they relate to the customer's needs.

2. The salesperson tells the product's story.

3. The salesperson seizes an opportunity to demonstrate the product.

4. The salesperson attempts to set the stage for closing activities, including the handling of objections.

> **Sales Representative:** Mr. Sheridan, my name is Marilyn Chavin, and I am with the *Herald-Times*. I imagine that like other business people, you are trying to find some way to increase sales. Am I right?
> **Mr. Sheridan:** You bet!

The approach is good because the sales rep accomplished three things. First, she planted an idea. Second, she translated the idea into a benefit. Third, she got an agreeable response from the prospect. Now she has his attention and can move into a description of how her offering will satisfy his needs.

> **Sales Representative:** Mr. Sheridan, it seems to me that you will need to reach as many prospective customers as possible with your

ads. Our newspaper reaches 87 percent of the homes in the metropolitan area in addition to numerous waiting rooms in medical offices, law offices, hair salons, and other establishments. Wouldn't you like to deliver sales messages to all these prospects, many of whom may need your carpet cleaning service?

> **Mr. Sheridan:** Yes. In fact, I've been thinking about advertising the service.
> **Sales Representative:** We can design an ad for you which will help you reach out with sales messages to new prospects and at the same time remind previous customers of your dependable service. Now let me show you some of our ads that we think are pretty good—and they're different.

The sales representative has pointed out major benefits for Mr. Sheridan: the number of prospects that can be reached, the purposes of the ads, and the belief that the ads are good and different. In addition, she has recognized Mr. Sheridan's service as being dependable. Her sales presentation, while short, has led to a point at which she can use visual aids to help her communicate with Mr. Sheridan. Removing a small, neat portfolio from her briefcase, which contains up-to-date ad proofs, Marilyn continues.

> **Sales Representative:** We think these ads are pretty good because more people are seeing and reading them than ads carried by our competitor, the *Daily Tribune*.
> **Mr. Sheridan:** Why?
> **Sales Representative:** Notice the layout style with black dominating every ad. Black stands out better on white paper.

Again, the sales representative is pointing out benefits to Mr. Sheridan and explaining how the service she offers can help solve a potential problem: getting people to notice and read the printed sales messages. The sales representative also has other tools to use when needed in face-to-face selling situations. The use of research findings to substantiate claims made for the product or ser-

TABLE 13-1
DEALING WITH PROSPECTIVE CUSTOMER TYPES: SOME TIPS AND CAUTIONS

Type of Prospect	Tip	Caution
Silent or bashful, lets you talk without any sign of interest or flicker of reaction	Ask the prospect a question and wait for a reply; talk with, not to, the prospect	The silence may be attributed to indecision, or the prospect may want to dismiss you early; watch for cues
Vascillating, cannot seem to concentrate on one point very long	Confine these prospects to your topic; when they stray, make a pleasant remark and then pull them back on track	This prospect may lack confidence; avoid irritation and refuse to be upset by flights from the topic
Skeptical or suspicious, does not want to accept anything that you say, is afraid of your product or service	Instill confidence with a warm smile and a firm handshake; be honest and aboveboard; emphasize product features of which your prospect probably will approve	Leave as little room as possible for objection and doubts; retain self-control and self-confidence
Hostile or high-strung, usually nervous and ready to go off any time; responses are couched in sharp words	Move instantly to the core of your sales presentation; word questions carefully since they may make the prospect nervous and anxious to escape	Be patient; use dramatic personal enthusiasm; above all, do not argue
Closed-minded or stubborn, may resist new products or services; this prospect may be characterized by an "I'm satisfied with the way things are" attitude	Agree with the prospect and look for openings to emphasize the simplicity and dependability of your product; deemphasize the fact that it is new or advanced	Be careful not to meddle in this prospect's affairs; do not mention new features until you have agreed that the old product or service is good
Talkative, wants attention; often this prospect talks about himself or herself and everything but your product or service	Slant your presentation to the personal benefits that the product or service offers the prospect; make the prospect feel that the product or service is just for him or her	You cannot listen all day; gently seize any phrase and relate it to your product or service
Penny pincher, always knows somehow or somewhere to get it cheaper; this prospect wants a bargain	Emphasize why your product or service is a bargain; emphasize that your item is fresh and new, not a leftover sold at a special discount	Avoid price haggling, which will only increase the vigor with which the price objection is pursued

vice can be very convincing. Testimonials from other satisfied buyers may be recalled and repeated to the prospect. Questions directed to the customer may help the sales representative understand the customer's needs better and provide an opportunity to focus the presentation on such needs.

Regardless of the content of the presentation, the salesperson must make sure that it is easy to understand. Sometimes sales people talk too fast. The effective salesperson gauges the speed of delivery to fit the prospect. Usually the salesperson is able to pick up cues by observing the prospect as the sales presentation unfolds. If the prospect appears to be somewhat bewildered or hesitant to answer questions, the rate of delivery should be slower.

If the product being described is highly complex and the prospect is unfamiliar with descriptive technical jargon, an explanation may be needed. The astute salesperson will adjust the presentation to the prospect in terms of both speed of delivery and content. A retail buyer of office equipment understands terms such as *liquid crystal* which may be used to describe a calculator. A prospective customer appearing in the retailer's establishment and hearing the same terms used to describe a calculator may need additional explanation.

Finally, the salesperson should encourage two-way conversation. Too many sales people view the sales presentation as a monolog. It should be a dialog. Otherwise, the salesperson will never understand the prospect's needs or have the opportunity to provide answers and explanations.

Demonstration of the Product. The presentation is usually more effective if the salesperson demonstrates the product physically. The more complicated the product, the greater the opportunity for a demonstration. Prospects like demonstrations because they prefer to form opinions from seeing, touching, and in some cases, tasting or smelling the product rather than just hearing about it.

TABLE 13-2 VISUAL AIDS USED IN DEMONSTRATIONS

Accessories	Letters
Ads	Manuals
Booklets	Maps
Brochures	Mockups
Catalogs	Models
Charts	Pictures
Cross section of	Portfolios
the product	Posters
Drawings	Samples
Figures	Signs
Films	Slides
Graphs	Swatches

Sales people who are engaged in inside selling may plan simple demonstrations in advance. The demonstration may be as simple as showing the customer how a table lamp accents other home furnishings by selecting pages from an interior design magazine. Or the salesperson may use an Eastman Kodak Instamatic 110 to snap a picture, pointing out that minor shadows in photos can be eliminated. For many consumer products, effective demonstrations can be conducted easily.

Sales people who are engaged in outside selling spend more time planning demonstrations. If the product is large and bulky, the salesperson cannot carry it along for the sales demonstration. Thus, a sales rep for upholstered furniture may rely on pictures and swatches of the materials used for coverings. A sales rep selling copier machines may arrange to take the prospect to a nearby location where a machine is already in use. The visual aids listed in Table 13-2 may be used in sales demonstrations.

Small, independent businesses also can use demonstrations in selling products and services. A local printer prepares portfolios to show prospects business cards, wedding invitations, business forms, and other customized printing work. Small businesses selling home improvement products conduct clinics to demonstrate how easy it is to hang wallpaper. A bakery may give small samples of a new coffee cake to prospects to allow them to taste it before buying.

A well-planned demonstration will bring into action more of the customer's senses, whereas in a verbal presentation only the senses of hearing and perhaps sight are used. When it is feasible, customers should be encouraged to handle or operate the product so that they can appreciate its value fully. Such demonstrations involve the prospect directly in the sales presentation, creating an active (as opposed to passive) selling situation.

When conducting a demonstration, a salesperson should be sure of the following.

1. All vital features of the product are covered.

2. The spoken message is synchronized with each phase of the demonstration.

3. Each point is clarified so that the prospect understands it fully.

4. The demonstration stresses product features which appear to be of particular interest to the prospect.

5. The demonstration includes the participation of the prospect.

Obviously, an effective presentation or demonstration depends heavily on the salesperson's knowledge of the product. It also depends on the smoothness and clarity of the presentation. The salesperson must not overlook the necessity of advance preparation.

Handling Objections. Different kinds of objections arise all through a sales interview. In the approach stage, the prospect may object even to talking to the salesperson or taking time to hear the presentation. This can happen because the prospect does not know enough about the salesperson and the product or service to have any interest in them or desire to know about them.

Later in the interview, if this interest is aroused, a prospect may object to various features of the product, such as price, appearance, size, and terms. Unless the major reasons for not buying are removed from the prospect's mind, the sale cannot be closed successfully.

Customer objections, which some sales people regard as sales obstacles, may be turned into sales opportunities. Actually, most objections are standard and universal and are merely requests for additional information.

Golf Pro: But the golf carts we need must be equipped with wide tires. Otherwise, when the ground is soggy, the tires cut ruts in the fairways.

Sales Rep: Most of the buyers for the better golf courses have the same legitimate concern. The flat surface and smooth tread of the tires on our golf carts are designed to roll on the surface of the turf. The light weight of our carts is another plus in protecting the turf. In fact, I would like to show you a list of golf courses located in regions of heavy rainfall that use our carts.

Golf Pro: I'm glad to hear that. The park board spends a lot of time talking about ways to protect the turf on our fairways.

What seemed to be an objection in this sales interview turned out to be a request for additional information. The same questions, hesitations, and doubts that occur to one customer will occur to others. Once a salesperson discovers a good, logical answer to such objections, this can be incorporated as a buying reason in future sales presentations.

A four-point formula which many sales reps use in direct selling is helpful in overcoming objections. It also may be used by inside sales people. In either case, the psychology is the same.

1. Hear the Customer Through. Do Not Interrupt. Be Interested. Applications: Learn to really listen more. Listen all the way through. Listen with

Figure 13-5. Customer objections can turn into sales opportunities if the salesperson listens and provides helpful answers.

your eyes as well as your ears. This demonstrates your concern and interest and reinforces the customer's ego and sense of importance. Interruptions are a form of brushoff and putdown, a way of saying, "I'm not interested in what you say." This attitude is easily detected and always resented. A molehill of an objection can quickly become a mountain if nobody listens.

2. Use a "Converter Statement." Concede Before You Contend. Applications: Do not meet the objection head on with a rebuttal or argument. "You're wrong, and here's why . . ." is insulting, hurts the customer's ego, and negatively motivates the customer to argue, offer defense, and object more than ever. Never imply that the customer is 100 percent wrong by being too quick to answer with cold logic, facts, statistics, or testimonials.

Instead, reinforce the customer with as much agreement as you can. In other words, let the customer know you do not think less of him or her because of an objection. Show that the question is natural, understandable, and intelligent under the circumstances.

3. Restate the Objection in Your Own Words But in the Form of a Question Being Asked by the Buyer. Answer Rather Than Argue. Applications: "If I understand your question, you're asking why . . ." and "In other words, you want to know . . ." are two examples. This technique for handling objections utilizes the magic of "paraphrase": the feeding back to the other person in your own words your understanding of what is meant. It has been found to truly have magical results not only in day-to-day human relations and communications but also in the sales field. Experimental psychologists have found that in communication between people, feedback causes the person speaking to open up and tell more. It proves you are really listening and paying attention and that you are interested in what the prospect has to say. Some though certainly not all customer objections are based more on the buyer's need for an audience than on the need to argue.

4. Submit the Solution. If Possible, Use the Testimony of a Neutral Third Party as a Collision Cushion. Cite Success Stories. If You Do, the Objection Loses Force Without the Buyer Losing Face. Applications: Now that you have listened, agreed, restated, and paraphrased the objection in your own words, you have psychologically prepared the customer to accept your answer. Your preliminary agreement has tended to make the prospect more agreeable. You have treated the objection with respect so that the customer is now inclined to treat your answer with respect. Now is the time to bring up facts, figures, statistics, and logic. But you can ruin it by preaching. Do not use your superior information to make customers feel inferior. Instead, let other people, organizations, and research studies do the talking for you. Cite third-party testimonials from other customers.

There are, of course, other techniques for handling objections. The major rule is to use tact and not to argue. Many sales have been lost because the salesperson forgot this simple rule.

Today's effective sales people act as consultants to buyers. When objections are posed, the salesperson attempts to help the customer assess his or her needs. If the prospect expresses an opinion that the price is too high, the salesperson does not automatically switch to a lower-priced item in the product line. Instead, the salesperson attempts to assist the prospect in determining whether the higher-price is justified or whether a lower-priced item of lower quality will satisfy the need.

Closing the Sale. The purpose of the close is to secure action on the part of the customer, specifically, to induce buying. It is surprising how often this vital step is omitted by sales people. There is a great truth in the saying that if you cannot close, you cannot sell. All the planning, presentations, and demonstrations are wasted if the salesperson cannot close effectively.

Immediately after the salesperson has handled an objection satisfactorily, he or she should try for a close. The salesperson should ask for a commitment on the part of the customer with a question such as, "Well, since we agreed on this, then shall we go ahead and . . ." or better yet a question concerning the customer's choice of product color, style, delivery date, or some other detail on which the customer must decide when placing the order. Such a question will change the subject in a positive direction.

A number of closing techniques are used to overcome the customer's normal inertia or procrastination. "Well, let me think it over" or "Give me your card and I'll call you" are delaying tactics which may indicate that the prospect still has objections. Your reply should be direct and instantaneous. You can ask the prospect, "What is there to think over?" This pointed question may smoke out reasons for delaying a decision. It also enables you to set new sales directions for yourself aimed at overcoming any obstacles which may be thrown in your path. If you break down these roadblocks, you increase the chances of receiving an order. Your goal is to keep the prospect's statements from becoming final. Keep on talking and selling. It is possible that you failed to make yourself clear on certain points, so start probing to discover the true objection. Many times, a sale which otherwise might have been lost has been closed through the use of a "never-say-die" tactic.

"I'll have to talk it over with my boss." Your reply to this might be, "I'm glad to hear that you believe this is worth discussing. I take it that you often consult with your boss before making important decisions. That's the best policy. I'd be pleased to set up an appointment with you and your boss so that we can all sit down and talk. Is Thursday convenient, or would Friday be better?"

Figure 13-6. Closing the sale: "If you cannot close, you cannot sell."

Never allow an interview of this type to end without setting up another appointment. Your time is too valuable to waste.

"I like it, but . . ." "But what?" you ask. There must be something holding the prospect back. Price? Delivery? Quality? Get to the core of what stands between you and the sale. Only when you know exactly what you are up against can you work effectively toward closing the sale.

"It'll always be on sale again. I'd better wait." "That's very possible," you can reply, "but prices do tend to increase. The next sale price is likely to be higher." In addition, you can explain to the prospect that models change and are discontinued and that it is possible that the item will not

be available at a later date. But whatever you do, do not tell tall tales. Instead, be factual. "Since you like this particular model, there is no reason to delay getting it." This is the time to bring out the order blank and start closing all over again.

Not many customers will ask the salesperson to let them buy. The salesperson therefore must have a number of techniques in mind to use for inducing customer action. Here are some additional ways of closing a sale.

1. Assume That the Sale is Made. This is nothing more than the principle of positive suggestion. The salesperson simply assumes by word or action that the customer has decided to buy. If the customer does not stop the salesperson, a sales transaction is completed.

2. Close on a Minor Point. Since it is easier for a person to make a minor decision than a major one, the salesperson helps the prospect avoid the major decision by substituting a minor decision. An example of this is the sales rep who closes with, "Would you prefer this order packaged in pint- or quart-size containers?" or "Do you wish to pay cash or use our credit plan?" Give the customer a choice between something and something rather than a choice between something and nothing.

3. Add an Inducement. Sometimes a salesperson can close the sale with an added inducement. If the customer hesitates, free delivery, free alterations, or a cash discount may be offered. This often stirs the customer to action.

4. Summarize the Main Points. It is a good selling technique to summarize the main talking points in a closing statement. The selling points chosen for emphasis are the ones that seem to match the customer's buying motives.

5. Ask for the Order. The most obvious but often overlooked method of closing is simply to ask for the order. Many customers like this frank, straightforward approach and react favorably to it.

There are many other closes that are effective in specific situations. The important thing to remember is that the salesperson must close, and reclose if necessary, before a sale can be completed.

Suggestion Selling. For many products and services, the salesperson has the opportunity to use suggestion selling after closing the sale on the primary product. To meet the customer's need fully, additional items or accessories may be necessary. In an inside selling situation, for example, a customer may need a handbag to match the shoes she has selected or a customer may need a tie to accent the sports coat and shirt that have been selected. When basic items are selected for wardrobes, buyers often welcome the assistance of the salesperson in selecting suitable accessories.

Suggestion selling, however, is not limited to clothing items. A waitress may tell you that the hot apple strudel is delicious, an auto salesperson may ask you to take a look at floor mats to protect the carpeting in your new car, and a salesperson at Musicland may suggest that cassettes will be needed for your new tape recorder.

Sales reps engaged in outside selling also make use of suggestion selling. The computer sales rep may suggest that other hardware and software will be needed by the purchaser's firm for some applications. An insurance agent often tells a client that retained dividends can be used to purchase additional insurance. A sales rep handling heavy equipment and machinery may suggest that the buyer consider the purchase of lubricants or auxiliary items.

The important point is that suggestion selling can lead to the sale of additional items and consequently to greater profits for the sales rep's firm. Suggestion selling, however, should be approached from the customer's viewpoint. People resent sales pressure when there seems to be no need for the additional items. However, the customer will appreciate such suggestions when the additional items adequately take care of demonstrated needs.

Closely related to the concept of suggestion selling is that of **trading up,** which refers to promoting better quality than the customer would have purchased otherwise. Sometimes customers plan to spend only a predetermined amount of money for a product or service. On seeing a similar product of higher quality, however, they recognize the value and the fact that the better product fills their needs more adequately.

The salesperson must exercise caution in applying the trading up concept. If the customer believes that an attempt is being made to sell a product that is more expensive than needed, resentment will follow. The customer, however, may be receptive to products that look better, feel better, work better, last longer, give trouble-free service, or have other desirable attributes.

SELLING FROM DOOR-TO-DOOR

Charles McKee looks his questioner straight in the eye as he says, "If we were like the old movie, we'd have been out of business a long time ago."

Instead, Electrolux Corporation, the only major vacuum cleaner maker that still sells only door to door, is flourishing. Profits are up despite prices that are much higher than those of competitive machines sold in stores.

McKee, the 62-year old chairman of Electrolux, has been with the firm 40 years. He started as a door-to-door salesperson and now has a policy of requiring all executives to work selling door to door at least briefly so that they can appreciate what the work is like.

Like more than a few other chief executives these days, McKee stars in his own television commercials, extolling the idea that Electrolux represents a part of old-fashioned America and that the home is the best place to test a vacuum cleaner.

He worries that his company may be tainted by the image of "the peddlers and magazine sales people" and the old movie image of a salesperson who throws dirt on the floor as soon as the homemaker opens the front door.

Perhaps because he is worried about credibility, the TV spots show a bit more subdued version of the real McKee, a man who waves a big cigar while wearing big diamond rings and a copper bracelet. He clearly relishes being a salesperson.

The rings are company rings, some of the prizes he picked up over the years as incentives for performance. He now makes a salary of $350,000 a year plus a bonus that ranges between 50 and 75 percent of his salary.

Postsale Activities

The time to start converting a first-time customer into a regular, satisfied one comes just after the sale has been made. Thank the prospect for becoming a customer and compliment the buyer's good judgment. In addition, give assurance that the product will live up to expectations.

The Follow-Up. The truly professional salesperson strives constantly to build a strong and progressive relationship with customers. Building and maintaining goodwill is a never-ending task for the professional salesperson. Follow-up

activities provide a basis for sound buyer-seller relationships.

A phone call or visit to the buyer will show that the salesperson is interested in customer satisfaction. If you are talking with a customer and you sense that a complaint exists, find out what it is. Do not let it build and intensify. The situation cannot be rectified unless you discover the problem.

When your customer does complain, listen politely. Do not interrupt. Be sympathetic and then try to find out all the facts. The longer you wait, the more difficult it will become to find a solution. Act promptly and follow through to be

Electrolux, now a subsidiary of Consolidated Foods Corporation, loves incentive prizes, ranging up to group trips to China. McKee sees them as a big way to get the sales people out working.

Those sales people get no salary or expenses, but they get commissions up to 35 percent on each machine, and prices range from $190 to $457, well above those of the competition. "We're higher and we're better. We're more durable," is the way McKee puts it.

There is a lot of turnover among sales people in the first year, McKee says, but those who last a year often stay for a career.

Electrolux profits were up more than 30 percent in the fiscal year ending June 30, 1981, after sagging a year earlier. McKee says there have been only 2 down years and 1 flat year in the last 20. One reason is that sales people are easier to find when the economy is hurting, as was the case in 1981. More sales people mean more sales calls.

The door-to-door vacuum cleaner business has changed over the years. There are fewer people at home during the day now, and so more calls are made in the evening.

But McKee says that Electrolux always closed more than half of its sales after 5 p.m. In the old days, the husbands had to give permission, he said. "Now the woman makes the purchase, but she's not home until evening."

Adapted from Associated Press, "Electrolux Leader Loves Salesman Job," *The Pantagraph,* Bloomington, Ill., August 23, 1981, p. E-1.

---

sure a satisfactory and equitable solution is reached.

Perhaps it is simply a misunderstanding, but if it is a legitimate complaint, provide a solution. That is not usually as difficult as it sounds. Many sales people procrastinate when it comes to handling complaints for fear of running into obstacles and more problems, and they may. But the fact remains that few problems ever solve themselves.

Planning the Callback. Sales reps who are engaged in field selling start planning for return sales calls as soon as the sale is finalized. If the products are consumable, the sales rep will note the expected date when an order will be placed again. When the customer has mentioned business problems and the sales rep has no immediate solution, the problem should be noted. Some sales reps fail to grasp the importance of a customer's problems. If a sales rep sells to a business and the business is unable to solve its problems and succeed, the sales rep soon will have one less customer. By noting the problem, the sales rep may be able to study the situation and offer a promising solution. In fact, many sales reps devise a records system to remind them when to contact customers and to provide themselves with information about their customers, such as problems, complaints, and other pertinent information that should be reviewed before the next sales call. Such a system often is referred to as the sales rep's **tickler file.**

In addition, after each sales call, the salesperson should analyze his or her performance. Each step in the sales presentation should be reviewed to determine strong and weak performance areas. Because of individual differences, sales people cannot simply imitate other successful sales people. Each salesperson must develop his or her own strengths, and this evolves from self-evaluation.

Concepts in the management and supervision of marketing employees, including sales people, are discussed in Chapter 17. While compensation of the sales force may be viewed as a method of motivation, compensation plans for the sales force differ from those used with other marketing personnel.

FINANCIAL INCENTIVES

Sales compensation plans differ from firm to firm. Sales people often like to be rewarded immedi-

TABLE 13-3
ANALYZE YOUR SALES EFFORTS

Ask Yourself	Performance		
	Yes	Somewhat	No
1. Was I prepared for the sales call?	____	____	____
2. Were the opening remarks suitable?	____	____	____
3. Did the opening evoke the interest of the prospect?	____	____	____
4. Did I discover the needs of the prospect?	____	____	____
5. Was my presentation slanted toward the buyer's point of view?	____	____	____
6. Did I encourage the prospect to talk?	____	____	____
7. Did I talk too much?	____	____	____
8. Did I interrupt or cut off the customer?	____	____	____
9. Was I prepared to demonstrate the product?	____	____	____
10. Did I encourage the prospect to participate in the demonstration?	____	____	____
11. Did I handle objections completely and to the prospect's satisfaction?	____	____	____
12. Did I recognize cues for closing opportunities?	____	____	____
13. Did I establish a good social interaction with the prospect?	____	____	____
14. Did I seek points of agreement?	____	____	____
15. Did I point out features of the product and explain how they would meet the prospect's needs?	____	____	____
16. Did I listen carefully?	____	____	____
17. Did I suggest related products which will satisfy the customer's needs?	____	____	____
18. Will I be welcome on my next call?	____	____	____

ately for their performances. In fact, many sales people consider themselves independent entrepreneurs. In the case of agents and brokers, they are. Sales people also tend to be highly paid, although there is a considerable difference between what an order taker earns and what a sales engineer is paid. There also is a considerable difference in their qualifications. Compensation plans often are devised not only to attract and reward highly capable sales people but to provide a stimulus for greater initiative.

Straight Salary

The **straight salary** method means that sales people receive an agreed on, fixed amount of money for a fixed period. The major advantage of the plan is that it enables the firm to control the sales people's efforts. If the sales manager wishes to direct sales people to perform nonselling activities such as training a new salesperson or instructing buyers about the use of products, the sales people will not resent such assignments. Their salary is secure regardless of what they sell. The major disadvantages of a straight salary are that it does not motivate the sales people to sell more and does not recognize and reward sales people who excel.

Inside sales people often but not always are paid by the straight salary method. A smaller number of outside sales reps work for a straight salary. An inside salesperson often receives discounts on personal purchases.

Straight Commission

When the **straight commission** plan is used, sales people are paid an agreed-on percentage of the price of everything they sell. Under this plan, the salesperson receives no revenue until a sale is made. In some cases, sales people are also expected to pay their expenses. The advantages of the straight commission method are the following.

1. Monetary rewards are tied directly to sales productivity.

2. Sales costs are related to sales generated.

3. The plan is relatively easy to understand.

The plan is not, however, without disadvantages, including the following.

1. It is difficult to get sales people engaged in nonselling activities.

2. The incomes among sales people vary greatly.

3. Territories may not be covered adequately (some sales people will "skim" a territory, that is, call on only the most promising accounts).

4. When the economy is depressed, the sales people may find it difficult to earn desired incomes.

5. Readjusting territories or assigning a salesperson to a new territory may meet resistance.

Some firms attempt to overcome the disadvantage of a decrease in income when sales drop. They may allow a salesperson to receive a **draw.** That is, they give the salesperson a specified level of income each month or each pay period. At the end of a specified period, for example, 6 months, the salesperson and the company settle their accounts. If commissions exceed the draw, the salesperson receives the additional sum. If the draw exceeds commissions, however, the salesperson may return the difference or work without a draw until the difference is balanced.

The Combination Method

In order to combine the advantages of both these plans and reduce the magnitude of the disadvantages, many companies use a combination method, that is, a combination of salary and commission. The salesperson is paid a salary and does not have to worry about extreme fluctuations in income. The firm has a right to ask the salesperson to perform nonselling tasks. Incentive is built into the method since the salesperson is rewarded for sales volume or units sold. The major difficulty with the combination method is that it may be somewhat complex and difficult to understand.

Trends in Sales Compensation

According to reports in *Sales and Marketing Management*, more companies are moving from a straight salary or straight commission method to a combination method. The percentage of the total compensation that is accounted for by incentive also appears to be increasing.[7] As a result, it appears that greater numbers of marketing firms and service businesses are following an incentive pay system. However, a salary is included in the compensation.

order to be successful in social interaction with prospects.

- Social interaction is necessary in selling. It is two-way communication which involves an exchange of information, beliefs, attitudes, and ideas between the buyer and the salesperson.

- Sales people who understand a prospect's point of view are more likely to turn the prospect into a buyer than sales people who pursue only their own point of view.

- Compensation plans often are designed to help firms achieve their sales objectives.

KEY POINTS SUMMARY

- Most sales people are hardworking professionals who try to sell products which meet customers' real needs.

- Personal selling consists of individual, personal communication and helping the buyer choose a product or service to fulfill a need, want, or desire.

- Selling jobs vary from order takers to highly trained sales engineers.

- The major advantage of personal selling is that presentations can be tailored to the needs, motives, and behavior of individual customers. The major limitation is the high cost.

- Some of the most noteworthy changes that are shaping today's selling environment include the professionalization of selling and sales management, the acceptance of the marketing concept by most firms, and the entry of greater numbers of women into industrial and field sales positions.

- A salesperson's job includes presale activities, sales presentations and demonstrations, and postsale activities.

- Sales people need to learn the principles of sales psychology and their applications in

KEY TERMS AND CONCEPTS

canvassing	qualifying
creative selling	sales engineers
field selling	straight commission
inside selling	straight salary
missionary salesperson	tickler file
personal selling	trading up
prospecting	

DISCUSSION QUESTIONS

1. What are some of the sources you might use to acquire a list of prospects for the following products?
a. residential roof replacements
b. portraits for infants
c. automobiles

2. When uninterrupted, a salesperson can move through a sales presentation in a short period of time. Why is it important that the sales presentation be a dialog instead of a monolog?

3. How might a salesperson react when customers object by stating that the price is too high?

4. Assume that you are selling Individual Retirement Accounts for a local savings and loan institution. Other competing institutions in your community sell similar accounts. How will you differentiate your service from those of your competitors?

5. Demonstrations usually are conducted with the product. Under what conditions might you not use the product?

6. When the straight commission method is used to reward sales people, sales costs are related to sales generated. Why has the combination method become more popular?

NOTES

1. Steve Frazier, "Young Entrepreneur Turns Sales Knack into Retailing Hit," reprinted by permission of *Wall Street Journal,* © Dow Jones & Company, Inc., January 4, 1982, p. 25. All rights reserved.

2. Robert D. McManigal, Jr., "The Great Debate: The Best Way to Go to Market Is through Company Salespeople," *Electrical Wholesaling,* February 1981, 50.

3. "Sales Jobs Open Up for Women," *Dun's Review,* March 1978, pp. 86–88.

4. "Sales Meetings and Sales Training," *Sales and Marketing Management,* February 25, 1980, p. 68.

5. Adapted from David D. Seltz, "Ideas for Salespeople," *Salesman's Opportunity,* September 1970, p. 48.

6. Ibid.

7. "A Better Way," *Sales and Marketing Management,* April 9, 1979, p. 19.

CHAPTER 14
ADVERTISING

Americans tend to take advertising for granted. But advertising serves as an important method of communication. As a marketing communications tool, it is used to inform, to persuade, and to encourage people to act. Most marketers find that advertising is an indispensable component of a marketing communications program. A few individuals, however, such as the one described in Figure 14-1, fail to recognize the potential of advertising until it is too late.

THE ROLE OF ADVERTISING

The word *advertising* comes from the French term *avertir*, meaning "to notify." Communication is necessary for notification. Here is a good way to look at it. Advertising is simply the way a business talks to potential customers or clients about products or services. The role of advertising is to inform potential users that the product or service is available and to persuade people to try it by pointing out the benefits it offers.

Advertising Defined

Once a product is produced or a service is made available, advertising tells consumers about it.

Advertising is marketing's most visible form of communication. The American Marketing Association (AMA) defines **advertising** as "any paid form of nonpersonal presentation and promotion of ideas, goods, or services by an identified sponsor." There are four key elements in the AMA definition: (1) paid form, (2) nonpersonal presentation, (3) promotion of ideas, goods, and services, and (4) identified sponsor.

Paid Form. The ability of firms to offer products and services would be pointless without some method of informing the public, attracting its attention, arousing its curiosity, and stimulating a desire to own or use those products and services. However, throughout the history of advertising, firms offering products and services have found it necessary to pay in order to get their message to the potential buyers. At first, all advertising was vocal. In ancient Greece, town criers sold cattle, made public announcements, and chanted advertising rhymes. After the criers came signs. A goat was the sign of a dairy in Rome, and in medieval England a coat of arms designated an inn. During the early 1800s, newspapers and magazines sprang up everywhere. Those offering goods and services found that for a small charge, they were

A man wakes up in the morning after sleeping in an advertised bed, in advertised pajamas.

He will bathe in an advertised tub, wash with advertised soap, shave with an advertised shaving cream, eat a breakfast of advertised juice, advertised cereal and toast (toasted in an advertised toaster), put on advertised clothing and glance at his advertised watch.

He will ride to work in an advertised car, sit at an advertised desk, smoke an advertised cigarette and write with an advertised pen.

Yet this same man hesitates to advertise, saying that advertising does not pay...until finally, when his unadvertised business goes under, he will advertise it for sale!

Author Unknown

𝕿𝖍𝖊 𝕿𝖎𝖒𝖊𝖘-𝕸𝖆𝖎𝖑

Figure 14-1. Advertising is marketing's most visible form of communication.

able to communicate with masses of potential buyers. The arrival of radio early in this century, with networks tied together across the country, marked another leap forward in the history of advertising. For a fee, radio gave voice to the advertising message, a modern town crier, magnified millions of times. In the 1940s, to the voice of radio was added moving pictures in the home as the age of television dawned. This medium commanded greater fees as messages reached masses of potential buyers with greater impact.

With every change in the communications media came comparable changes in the methods of advertising. Newspapers and magazines can display a product and describe it in the necessary detail. Because radio commercials are usually limited to 30 seconds or 1 minute, copywriters must focus on the most important selling features or benefits. Television can demonstrate the benefits of a product almost as if a salesperson were paying a personal call on the viewer.

The advertiser, or sponsor, pays the cost of preparing the advertising message and inserting it into selected media. Here is a list of large U.S. companies and the amounts they spent on advertising in 1981.[1]

	$ Millions
Proctor & Gamble	671.8
Sears, Roebuck & Co.	544.1
General Foods Corp.	456.8
Philip Morris Inc.	433.0
General Motors Corp.	401.0
K-Mart Corp.	349.6
Nabisco Brands	341.0
R. J. Reynolds Industries	321.3
American Telephone & Telegraph Co.	297.0
Mobil Corp.	293.1

These companies are among the giant corporations in the country, and many of them own subsidiaries and produce a number of diversified products. Smaller firms also use advertising, though usually on a much smaller scale, and experience profitable results. They spend less money to send their messages to a local or regional audience instead of a national audience.

Advertising, while costly, helps get prices to the point at which products become affordable. Without the sales messages that are directed at a large number of potential buyers, the advertiser would not be able to sell as many products. When fewer products are sold, other costs cannot be allocated to as many products, and so the overall cost of each product becomes greater. While advertising represents a paid form of nonpersonal communication, it may lead to lower rather than higher prices. When advertising helped spread the word about digital watches, pocket calculators, and citizen's band radios, prices came down.

Nonpersonal Presentation.

When George Offenstein makes calls door to door with sales messages about his carpet cleaning service, he is making personal presentations, a time-consuming process. If he buys commercial time on a local radio station, nonpersonal presentations are aired and he reaches thousands of prospects with a single message.

The first job of advertising is to tell people that a product or service is available. The nonpersonal message attempts to attract prospects who have a natural interest in the product or service and attempts to get them to try it by telling them how it will perform. The message must be informative and truthful. However, advertising has no life of its own. It cannot hypnotize prospects. The nonpersonal message is simply part of a total marketing process which to be successful must be based on a worthwhile product or service.

Promotion of Ideas, Products, and Services.

Advertising is used to promote ideas as well as products and services. Even the government advertises to attract recruits to the armed services, to sell U.S. savings bonds, to promote better nutrition, and to tell people how to make effective use of the postal system. Of course, political candidates use advertising when they campaign for office.

The purpose of public service advertising is usually to promote an idea. Practically everybody is familiar with ads encouraging people to drive safely. Such ads are concerned with promoting ideas that will make life better for all. Much of this kind of advertising is done under the auspices of the **Advertising Council**, which is a private, nonprofit organization supported by the advertising-communications industries and American businesses. Everyone has seen ads urging people to have frequent medical checkups (American Cancer Society), fasten auto seat belts (National Safety Council), investigate carefully before making a major purchase (Council of Better Business Bureaus), and so on.

Firms that sell products and services often wish to promote ideas. Such ideas may be presented to help a firm generate goodwill. Few things are more important to a firm than its reputation. While good products and services are usually the foundation of a reputation, a firm may use advertising to inform the public about other things it is doing. Examples might include energy conservation, development of methods to increase productivity, providing leadership in fighting social problems, or presenting a viewpoint on public issues by discussing them in ads. Companies that do this kind of advertising separately from product advertising believe that it helps the consumer understand them and enhances their reputation as good citizens.

Identified Sponsor.

Whoever assumes responsibility for payment—for example, an individual, a firm, or a politician—becomes the identified sponsor. The sponsor is easily identified in print advertisements because firms offering goods and services for sale use logotypes for identification. A **logotype** is a distinctively designed form of a firm's name, a brand name, or a trademark that is reproduced on all print advertisements.

Broadcast media also call attention to the sponsor. Radio stations must necessarily announce a firm's name or a brand name. Television offers the flexibility of announcing a name or flashing a logotype on the screen. The more

Figure 14-2. A logotype is a distinctively designed form of a firm's name, a brand name, or a trademark that is reproduced on all print advertisements.

senses involved in the communication process, the greater the impact on the viewer.

"Who steals my purse steals trash . . . but he that filches from me my good name . . . makes me poor indeed." Shakespeare was not thinking about the dawning of mass communications and logotypes when he made this statement. But today's firms attach great value to their names and logotypes and are willing to go to court to protect them from imitators. The Formica Corporation in recent years has battled the Federal Trade Commission (FTC) in an effort to retain its trademark. The FTC says that the word *Formica* now describes the product itself (a plastic laminate used on cabinets, counter tops, and furniture). Vidal Sassoon went to court when he heard his name, or what sounded like it, on television commercials for blue jeans. The Sassoon case pitted Vidal, the

hairdresser, with two o's in his last name, against Sasson, Incorporated, a jeans manufacturer with only one o. A federal judge ruled that Sasson could not pronounce its name "Sassoon" and that if Sassoon goes into the jeans business, he will have to use "Vidal" before his name.

Advertising should not be confused with publicity. **Publicity** is a message released to the media about a product or service, an industry or a firm. It is nonpersonal insofar as it is directed at a large audience. It may present ideas or information about a product or service, and it often is prepared by someone in business, government, or other institutions and agencies. However, it is not a paid form for sending messages. The media do not assess charges for carrying publicity messages. Publicity as a sales promotion technique is discussed in Chapter 15.

Types of Advertising

Advertising may be classified according to purpose. If the purpose is to attempt to persuade potential buyers to select a specific product or service, the message is **promotional.** But if the purpose is to generate goodwill or enhance a firm's image, the message is **institutional.** An **advocacy** ad presents an individual or organization's viewpoint.

Printed ads appearing in newspapers or magazines are further subcategorized as display or classified. **Display ads** are larger than classified ads and usually contain a persuasive message. **Classified ads** are small, usually containing only a few lines of print. They may serve simply as an announcement indicating that particular goods or services are being offered for sale.

Another classification is based on the sponsor and the audience to which ads or commercials are directed. **Local advertising** is sponsored by local businesses and is directed at buyers within a town, city, or trading area. Much local advertising is retail advertising. However, local advertisements of manufacturers whose businesses (and advertising) are restricted to a local market are included. Advertising sponsored by a manufacturer or supplier of goods and services sold on a nationwide basis is referred to as national advertising. While manufacturers sponsor many ads directed at a nationwide audience, large retailers such as Sears, Wards, J. C. Penney, and K-Mart also sponsor national advertising. Regional advertisers are classified with the national advertisers. While their audience may be confined to a particular region of the country, their customers are spread over several cities and states.

A special classification based on sponsorship is known as cooperative advertising. **Cooperative advertising** usually is prepared by the manufacturer or supplier of goods and services and features specific brands of items for sale, but it appears over the names of merchants. The cost of the ad is shared by the local merchant and the manufacturer or supplier of the goods. (The Pac-Man ad on page 398 is an example of a co-op ad.)

An increasingly important type of advertising classified by sponsorship is professional advertising. There has been a surge of interest in marketing by hospitals lately. University Hospital in Kansas City advertises a maternity program package. A flat $425 buys six prenatal classes, a 1 day hospital stay, doctor services for an uncomplicated delivery, and a postdelivery checkup. While many hospitals shun marketing as unprofessional, University Hospital points out that the aggressively marketed program helped boost the hospital's deliveries to a recent 1,400 from under 1,000 in the mid-1970s. "Uncontested divorce, $130; drunk driving defense, $250; and bankruptcy, only $100 down." This message recently appeared under the name of an attorney-at-law. Hospitals, legal firms, colleges and universities, and private schools are among the many advertisers in the professional category. Professionals now consider marketing communications an important business activity.

Advertising also may be classified by level of demand influence. In the introductory stage of a product's life cycle, ads are classified as **pioneering ads,** since the sponsor is attempting to stimulate demand for a type of product. Thus, manufacturers had to sell potential buyers on the value of microwave kitchen ovens before it was feasible to promote Tappan, Amana, Sharp, or Litton. **Competitive ads** attempt to stimulate selective demand and promote a specific brand. **Comparative ads** also attempt to stimulate selective demand, but they contain comparisons between two brands. Such ads are designed to persuade the reader, listener, or viewer that the features of one product are superior to those of another. **Reminder ads** remind prospects to buy and do not elaborate on why they should buy.

Type of appeal may also be used to classify advertising. **Factual,** or **rational, advertising** (page 391) is designed to appeal to rational thought processes. The message simply contains facts about a product or service. The potential buyer weighs the facts and makes a decision whether to buy. **Emotional advertising** (page 390) messages appeal to a prospective buyer's emotions as they are influenced by the individual's wants and needs. Many ads, especially those featuring consumer products, are designed to appeal to emotions by indicating how a product may satisfy needs and wants.

SETTING ADVERTISING OBJECTIVES

Basically, the purpose of advertising is to sell a product, a service, or an idea. The intent may be to induce action immediately or at some time in the future, but the basic objective is to sell something through the use of effective communication. The ultimate effect of advertising should be to modify the attitudes and buying behaviors of the receivers of the persuasive message.

While the general goal of advertising is to increase profitable sales, this goal is too broad to be implemented effectively. It is necessary for each firm to establish more specific objectives.

One objective for an advertising program may be to support a personal selling program.

I don't know who you are. I don't know your company. I don't know your company's product. I don't know what your company stands for. I don't know your company's customers. I don't know your company's reputation. Now, what was it you wanted to sell me?[2]

Advertising can answer this question and consequently pave the way for sales people. When the salesperson calls on the prospect, time may be saved because the buyer already has become aware of and somewhat knowledgeable about the product.

An objective of advertising may be to reach prospects who are inaccessible to sales people.

Trina Ballinger recently started a commercial cleaning service. She employs three cleaning crews, each of which is dispatched to clean a different group of professional offices. Clients include doctors, dentists,

accountants, attorneys, banks, and insurance offices. Trina wants to expand her business by obtaining more clients and adding more crews. But when she calls on potential clients she is often unable to reach the individuals who make buying decisions. Doctors, dentists, lawyers, and other professionals tend to be tied up with clients or patients.

There is a good chance, however, that all these decision makers can be reached through advertising. The same is true for other types of services or products for which the seller has a difficult time reaching prospects.

Another objective may be to enter a new geographic area and attract a new group of customers.

Sharad Halim sells paintings, macramé wall decorations, and Persian rugs for an importing firm. As he moves into new geographic areas, ads are placed in newspapers and commercials are read over the air describing the products and emphasizing their low prices. Since he usually sells the merchandise in hotel or motel rooms, the dates and times are displayed prominently in the ads.

Sometimes retailers will open outlets in another community or a manufacturer will wish to market an existing product in a new territory. In each case, advertising may be used to help the firm communicate sales messages to potential buyers.

The objective of an advertising program may be to introduce a new product or service.

Rob and Connie Julian operate a TV appliance store. Recently, they added a line of TV sets with giant wall screens. While a few bars within the community are equipped with the giant screens, this is the first attempt to introduce them for use in homes within the community. Since several homes are now equipped with videotape recorders, the home

Few investments generate higher interest.

A Steinway piano is built to be appreciated.

The responsiveness of its touch, the fullness of its sound, and the subtlety of its tonal range have earned the Steinway a rich reputation wherever the beauty of music is valued.

And because a Steinway* is built to last for generations, it has long been valued as a piano whose worth is not likely to diminish with time.

Indeed, old Steinways have often sold for more than they initially cost.

Which is one form of appreciation just about everyone can appreciate.

If all this heightens your interest in the enduring value of a Steinway, you can find out more by writing to one: John H. Steinway, Dept. 52, 109 W. 57th St., N.Y., N.Y. 10019.

Figure 14-3. An ad can have an emotional appeal . . .

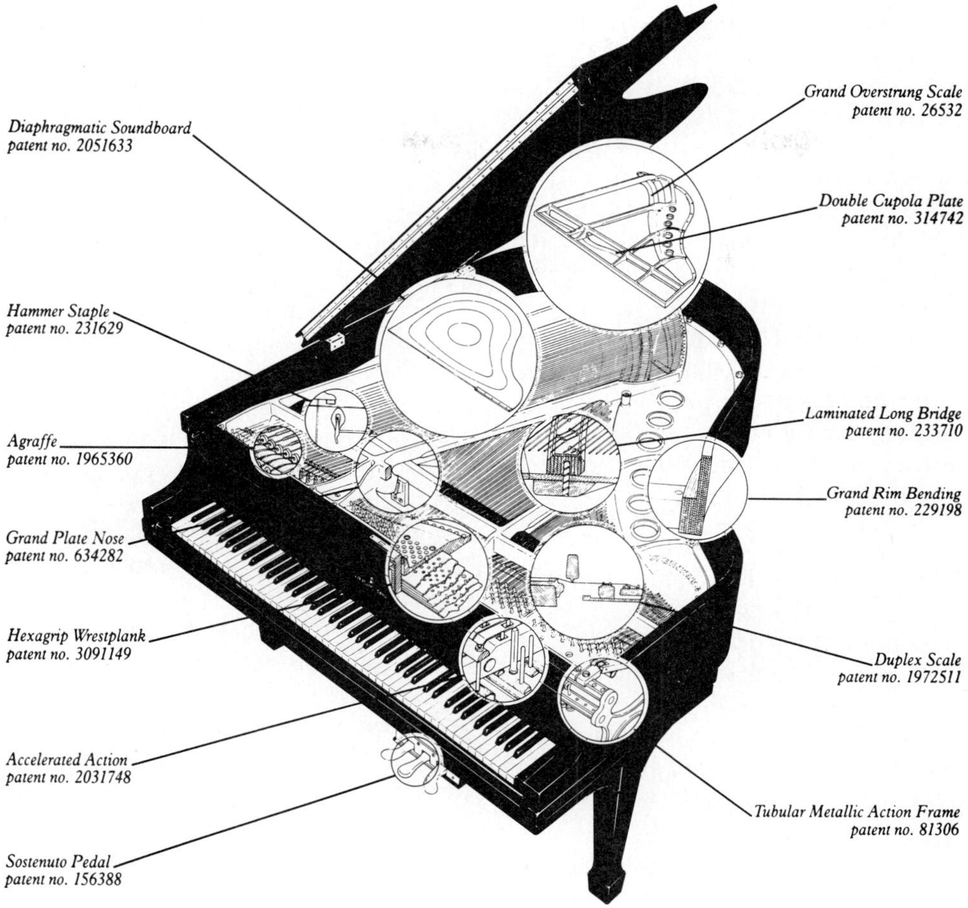

Diaphragmatic Soundboard
patent no. 2051633

Grand Overstrung Scale
patent no. 26532

Double Cupola Plate
patent no. 314742

Hammer Staple
patent no. 231629

Agraffe
patent no. 1965360

Laminated Long Bridge
patent no. 233710

Grand Rim Bending
patent no. 229198

Grand Plate Nose
patent no. 634282

Hexagrip Wrestplank
patent no. 3091149

Duplex Scale
patent no. 1972511

Accelerated Action
patent no. 2031748

Tubular Metallic Action Frame
patent no. 81306

Sostenuto Pedal
patent no. 156388

Patent truths.

Year after year, the Steinway Piano evolves.
(The patents shown here are but a few of the hundreds we've been granted since 1853.)

Today, the Steinway is built to perform feats it was never asked to a century ago.
Steinways endure rough transatlantic flights, fill 4,000 seat concert halls with thunderous sound, and respond with equal sensitivity to classical and rock pianists alike.

So if anybody says we don't build Steinway pianos the way we used to, it's a patent truth.

Every Steinway is still individually handcrafted, but our quest for new innovations goes on.

We are continuously testing new materials. Exploring new designs. Searching for better methods of construction.

For while the Steinway piano is now and always has been the world's most technically advanced piano, we're still inventing it.

For literature about the Steinway, write to John H. Steinway, 109 West 57th Street, New York, N.Y. 10019.

STEINWAY & SONS

. . . or it can have a rational appeal on the basis of facts.

viewer can enjoy either regular network TV programs or videotaped films on the giant screen. Rob and Connie will use advertising to convey messages about the new product to potential buyers.

Each time a new product is developed, the manufacturer must reach prospects if the product is to be launched successfully. In this situation, the manufacturer may be willing to enter into a cooperative advertising venture with the Julians. In other cases, the manufacturer may assume full sponsorship of the ads and commercials used to introduce a new product.

If a firm needs to improve its relationships with dealers or attract new dealers, advertising may be used to help achieve that objective.

When Fabricated Alloys, a small manufacturing firm which produces chrome moldings for furniture and appliances, decided to improve relations with their distributors, ads which contained the names of distributors were placed in appropriate trade journals. The distributors, realizing that the manufacturer was interested in providing support for their endeavors, initiated more aggressive selling efforts. Likewise, new distributors became interested in selling the alloys because they realized that it was profitable to carry the manufacturer's line.

A manufacturer can improve its relationships with dealers by demonstrating that it is interested in the dealers' welfare. It also can enhance its image as a reputable firm that adheres to business ethics.

Another objective of advertising may be to increase sales of an existing product. An advertising campaign may be designed to lengthen the season for a product, as has been done with soft drinks. An ad campaign may point out new uses for a product. A soup processor, for example, may prepare ads containing recipes for casseroles that call for canned soup. Of course, sales can be increased simply by reminding consumers that they should change auto spark plugs or similar consumable products.

A predetermined objective of an advertising program may be to counteract prejudice or substitution. As auto sales declined during the recession in the early 1980s, ads appeared in print and on the air conveying the message that buying an American-built auto as opposed to a foreign brand was the patriotic thing to do. Minority groups frequently have turned to advertising to reach masses of people with persuasive messages. Labor groups sometimes use the mass media to point out inequities.

Often a firm will attempt to build goodwill and improve its reputation by rendering a public service through advertising or by telling of the organization behind the product. When a firm runs an ad under the caption "Support the United Fund," that firm is rendering a public service by reminding local citizens to contribute to a fund which supports local charitable organizations. Many readers may be favorably inclined toward a firm that shows interest in the community instead of being motivated solely by the profit motive. Firms emphasizing the number of years they have been in business enhance their reputation. Longevity implies solidarity and strength. In addition, many firms attempt to build respect for their operations by calling attention to their excellent service facilities. Free delivery, free estimates, personalized service, and money-back guarantees are business policies that are pointed out in advertisements to enhance a firm's reputation.

There are other advertising objectives that a firm may pursue. One major factor governing the objective of an advertisement or an advertising campaign is the stage of customers in the buying process. In the first stage, recognition of want or need, the firm simply may wish to make prospects aware of a product which can satisfy a want or need. Pet kennels may sponsor an ad demonstrating the frustrations of trying to take the family pet along on a vacation trip, or a detergent manufacturer may emphasize that dishwashing can result in red and roughened hands. Advertising objectives for other stages in the buying process (informing customers of product advantages, emphasizing improvements, and so on) are defined similarly.

In larger organizations, advertising also must complement the objectives of managers of other functions within the firm. Until the 1970s, for example, firms that were engaged in petroleum marketing stressed increased product use as well as brand loyalty. The energy shortage, however, forced firms to change their basic objectives and consequently their marketing objectives, including advertising. Thus, the ads became more institutional in nature, stressing the oil firms' determination to overcome the energy shortage and offering suggestions as to how consumers might use petroleum products more efficiently. If the advertising objective is to sell a specific product in a retail store and the store has not stocked sufficient quantities, much of the effort may be wasted. Individuals in positions of authority must be involved in the implementation of advertising objectives.

Finally, advertising objectives must conform to the desires of society. In recent years, various consumer groups, including Nader's Raiders and the Boston-based Action for Children's Television, have been critical of some ads and commercials. In fact, the advertising trade journal *Advertising Age* regularly carries a column titled "Ads We Can Do Without." The objectives therefore should be scrutinized in regard to good taste and business ethics.

DIRECTING THE ADVERTISING MESSAGE

The sponsor of advertising messages must specify target markets clearly, a step which is necessary for all marketing strategy planning. Once this step is completed, media can be chosen that are seen, heard, or read by target customers.

Trying to match target customers with media is an important consideration in media selection because the sponsor is not always sure who sees and hears what. Most media engage in marketing research to develop profiles of the people who subscribe to their publications or listen to or view their programs. The results of such research endeavors, however, are often in the form of demographic data, that is, the size, ages, and other statistics such as affluence that describe the audience. But the media cannot be definite about who actually reads a specific page or sees or hears a specific show. Much information about market groups reached by the media is prepared by independent research firms such as A. C. Nielsen Company, American Research Bureau, Simmons, and Trendex.

Buyers of industrial products or business buyers often can be reached through ads appearing in specialized trade journals. A furniture manufacturer can reach prospective buyers by placing an ad in *Home Furnishings Daily,* while a manufacturer of store fixtures may choose to advertise in *Chain Store Age.* Both national and local advertisers can enhance their opportunities to reach specific target groups by the placement position or timing of an ad or commercial.

When Gretchen Hoffmeister, owner of a local weight reduction salon, placed commercials on the air with a local TV station, she specified that the commercials be shown during the intermission of an exercise program, a daily segment of the station's programming.

Bill Stephens operates a travel agency. Bill's ads usually appear in the Sunday newspaper, and he always specifies that the ads appear in the travel section.

National advertisers sponsor commercials featuring sporting goods during televised tennis, basketball, football, and golf matches.

In each example, the placement position and the timing were chosen to direct the advertising message to specific target groups.

But getting the message into print or recorded for commercials is not enough. If the message directed at target groups is to succeed, it must accomplish four tasks. These tasks, referred to as the AIDA concept, include getting Attention, holding Interest, arousing Desire, and obtaining Action.

Basically, the overall marketing strategy should include a particular message that will be expressed in directing communications to target groups. Then management judgment aided by marketing research can determine how the content can be encoded so that it will be decoded as intended.

Getting Attention

It does not matter how many people see or hear a message if it does not attract their attention long enough to leave an impression. Most people leaf through magazines and newspapers without really pausing to look at ads. When listening to the radio or viewing television, people may run short errands or get snacks during commercial breaks. Thus, an advertiser must find a device for capturing attention.

A bold headline, an attractive illustration, cartoon characters, a celebrity, or a number of other devices may do the trick. Advertisers, however, must exercise care. Too much humor may detract from the seriousness of the message. Shocking headlines may create negative images. Illustrations which really do not fit into the message conveyed will be recognized quickly as phony. While the attention of the audience must be captured, it is important that the attention-getting device not distract from the next step: holding interest.

Holding Interest

Holding interest is a difficult task. Attractive people, affectionate-looking animals, or Norman Rockwell art may get attention, but then what? The consumer may appreciate and evaluate the illustration, but if there is little or no relation between the illustration and the product or service, the consumer moves on.

Psychologists who have studied the problem of holding interest suggest that the illustrations and language of an ad be compatible with the experience and attitudes of target customers and their reference groups. A food advertisement featuring a glamorous hostess serving champagne to guests may be noted but passed over by many potential customers who do not entertain guests or drink champagne, even though other food products are included in the ad. Thus, an ad must speak the customer's language both in pictures and in words.

The layout should be arranged so that the eye is encouraged to move smoothly through the ad, perhaps from the upper left-hand corner to the logotype in the lower right-hand corner. Holding power is enhanced by "gaze motion," natural flowing characteristics which guide the eye.

Arousing Desire

Arousing desire is the difficult process of stimulating a want to own or use a particular product. The advertiser therefore must understand how target customers think, behave, and make decisions. In our society, many buyers find it necessary to justify their purchases on an economic or moral basis. Thus, the ad may have to supply words that the customer can use in justifying a purchase.

Emotional needs are strong motivators in arousing desire. "Bermuda. Get away from it all!" Almost all people from time to time seek a vacation away from their daily routines and job pressures. Both national and local advertisers use such appeals to arouse the desire to own a product or service.

Sometimes, however, a product captures the desire of customers and is sold briskly without statements such as "Now, life insurance gives you a hedge against inflation" appealing to rational behavior or "Add a lot of luxury to your leisure" appealing to emotional behavior. In the early 1980s, Pac-Man hit the U.S. markets, compliments of Atari, a home video supplier. The object of Pac-Man, a yellow circle with a missing piece suggesting a mouth, is to get through a maze eating dots without getting caught by a monster. In many communities, retailers reacted with statements such as these.

> "We've sold 366 of them [Pac-Man cartridges] and have at least 100 people on the waiting list."

Figure 14-4. Using cartoon characters is one way of capturing attention.

"We got 130 of them in on a Friday morning and they were sold by 7 that night," said a J. C. Penney employee. Sears's shipment of 102 was gone in a day and a half.

The Video Station averages about 20 calls a day, all from people wanting to know if they have arrived. Another store has had more than 30 calls asking when its second shipment is due. The store sold its first shipment of 84 in 2½ days.[3]

When products such as Pac-Man cartridges attract customers in large numbers, even at prices ranging from $35 to $40 a cartridge, ads announcing their availability may be all that is necessary. For most products, however, the marketer must employ appeals to arouse desire.

Obtaining Action

Getting action is a challenge. A fairly substantial amount of daily advertising is designed to provoke immediate buying action.

- A retailer-sponsored message featuring a special sale of dresses starts at 9 o'clock Monday morning.
- A new kitchen gadget is given away if a product is purchased within 30 days.
- A manufacturer places coupon ads in a magazine.
- Through direct-mail ads, magazine subscriptions are offered at special prices; toll-free number provided
- Classified newspaper ads are placed by a retailer.
- A used musical instrument is offered for sale or an apartment for rent; a phone number is given.

In each case, the prospect is motivated to act because of a special price or because the product or service would soon cease to be available.

A substantial amount of advertising does not provoke quick sales. Instead, a gradual process of attempting to persuade a prospect to try a new

Figure 14-5. For a popular product, an announcement—in this case, a coop ad—may be all that is needed to arouse desire.

product or accept a new idea is initiated. Each successive ad is expected to play a role in moving the prospect toward a purchase decision or toward brand loyalty. The ultimate goal, however, is to induce buying action.

SELECTING THE APPEALS

The appeals used in advertising largely determine its success. Most behavioral scientists agree that people's actions and attitudes are motivated. It is not surprising that marketers study *motives,* a term applied to cover the wide spectrum of wishes, desires, needs, and drives. Buying action results from motives. Thus, the astute marketer will appeal to those motives which induce buying behavior.

Appealing to Physiological Needs

Physiological needs are positive or supply needs. They result from deficiency (hunger or thirst) and produce the seeking and consumption of a needed substance. In today's society, the satisfaction of basic needs goes beyond minimum levels. Most Americans are able to satisfy their basic needs, and as a result, they seek the good things in life: better food, more luxurious homes, attractive and comfortable furnishings within the home, and stylish clothing. In essence, they seek a higher standard of living.

To illustrate how appeals in messages go beyond satisfying physiological needs, consider the following.

Last night, Jeanie Miller's husband finally finished his vegetables. Because what Mr. Miller had wasn't simply a vegetable. It was corn soufflé. One of 12 scrumptious side dishes from Stouffer's. (food)

Our swirling shirt style print. A clingy look, a swingy feel that moves with you all through the day. All 100 percent polyester doubleknit. At most Sears, Roebuck and Company larger stores. (clothing)

Remember when an asphalt roof was as boring as an asphalt driveway? Celotex has made asphalt roofing come alive with new Dimensional Shake Shingles. Thick tab edges produce strong shadow line characteristics of traditional shakes. And they come in four earth-tone colors. (shelter)

In these examples, the advertisers are presenting messages that appeal to the physiological needs of consumers, but the ads employ adjectives and descriptive phrases which show how the products go beyond simply fulfilling a basic need.

Appealing to Safety Needs

Safety needs are negative or avoidance needs resulting from the presence of harmful or potentially harmful situations. Often, people may not be aware of such needs or may choose to ignore them. For that reason, marketers often use reminder advertising messages. Perhaps you have noticed ads which convey messages such as these.

It's an old cliché that the show must go on. But without insurance, that tradition might die. The truth is, insurance is what keeps show business in business. Owners simply couldn't afford to book shows into their theaters without insurance. The risks—to performers, the audience, and the theater itself—would be too great. (reduction of business risks through insurance, Fireman's Fund Insurance Company)

Too much to do. Not enough time to do it. Result? That "business" headache. Even for one that is bad, all you need is Bayer Aspirin. Bayer is 100 percent pure aspirin—pure pain reliever. No unnecessary drugs are added. And millions take Bayer with no stomach upset. (relief from pain)

Retirement should be more than just a gold watch. You'll be putting in years of hard work between now and retirement. And when you finally retire, you shouldn't have to struggle just to make ends meet. Social security can help. So can a company pension. But an Individual Retirement Account—or IRA—managed by the professionals at our full-service bank could help provide the financial security that can make you truly independent. (retirement security, safety from financial worries, American Fletcher National Bank)

Most firms use subtle messages such as these to remind people of safety needs.

Occasionally a firm will turn to scare tactics. A headline blatantly proclaims, "This could happen to you!" The accompanying illustration shows a family returning from an outing to discover that their home has been burglarized or destroyed by a natural disaster. Ads have shown critical auto accidents with fatalities strewn along the side of the highway and have depicted industrial accidents that occurred because workers failed to use safety shields. The marketer should recognize that such messages establish a negative tone. Ads with shock appeal may tend to foster resentment.

Appealing to Love and Belonging Needs

Love and belonging needs are species-maintaining needs that arise from the human need for companionship and the nature of the reproductive system. These needs produce mating, children, and nurturing. Ads appealing to love and belonging needs usually indicate how an individual may appear more attractive to others, show affection to others, or become popular with a peer group.

Although beauty aids and clothing often are advertised by using sex appeal, various other products also are featured in ads that use such appeals. Consider the following advertising copy for an exercise publication.

It wasn't long ago that a woman of 40 was considered a "matron." Now glamorous women we admire are often over 40, and we think of them not only as young, energetic, and accomplished but gorgeous and sexy as well. It seems that reaching 40 today is just like being a "10" four times over.

To express their need for love, people may be motivated to buy gifts. Astute marketers recognize this fact, and many formulate their messages accordingly.

He'll use it, enjoy it, and love you for it. This headline appeared just below an illustration of an attractive couple seated in a romantic atmosphere. The ad was sponsored by Shulton, the maker of Old Spice after-shave lotion.

Of course, all people want to be popular with their friends. Ads frequently use appeals that demonstrate how a host or hostess can be a hit and win the admiration of his or her friends.

When your gang's hungry, no little sandwich makes a hearty, satisfying meal like Manwich!

Other ads are directed at families and appeal to platonic needs for love and belonging.

"Best Family Cruises." The illustrations showed a gleaming white cruise ship with a family swimming, playing shuffleboard, and strolling on the deck. The copy suggested the virtues of a different type of vacation for family fun and adventure. The ad, including headline, illustrations, and copy, was designed to appeal to people who regard the close-knit, loving family as the foundation of a healthy society.

These examples show that various approaches may be used in appealing to love and belonging needs. They may be summarized as appeals to (1) the desire to be attractive and sexy, (2) the desire to express love through carefully selected gifts, (3) the desire to earn the admiration of others, and (4) the desire to enjoy wholesome, family fun.

Appealing to Esteem Needs

Needs for being recognized as a worthwhile person are called **esteem needs.** Chapter 3 discussed how social class and perceived self-worth are important determinants in consumption patterns. Appeals aimed at the buyer's private world of hopes, dreams and fears can often be as effective in stimulating purchases as more rationally directed appeals.

Members of the upper social class indulge in expensive status symbols. In fact, some esteem needs are related to snob appeal. While few people would admit to responding favorably to such appeals, advertisers have experienced success by saying that a product or service is "for the discriminating few." Marketers have found that individuals like to receive recognition as "discriminating" buyers.

It looks a little more expensive. It is. Town and Country used this line to promote a ladies' suede coat.

When you care enough to send the very best. Hallmark makes no apology for the fact that its greeting cards may be more expensive than those of competitors.

Members of the middle class cherish respectability, savings, a college education, and an attractive, well-furnished home. They may respond to appeals such as these.

Saying goodbye may be the only hard part of the family's move to a new town. Below is an illustration of movers loading furniture as friends gather to say goodbye. One real estate sales rep says, "I helped them buy a new home at terms they could afford." The copy above the logo for the Real Estate Members of Better Homes describes personal attention combined with computer relocation service.

Fine French crystal you can afford to enjoy. This ad, featuring wine glasses with patterns priced at $6 per stem, is sponsored by Cristal D'Arques.

Individuals in the lower economic class struggle to keep up with the times. They tend to stay in older neighborhoods, buying new kitchen appliances occasionally. They are more likely to buy used cars, and they spend proportionately less than the middle class for clothing. They also spend proportionately less for services, preferring to do their own plumbing and work around the home. Marketers trying to reach this group with advertising messages frequently make use of a selling proposition. Their ads say: Buy this product and you will get this benefit—durability, lower price, and so forth.

Most Americans discover **reference groups,** that is, groups in which the individual has no membership but with which he or she can identify. Many youngsters, for example, identify with big-league baseball players, rock-n-roll groups, astronauts, or Hollywood stars. The activities of these heroes and heroines are watched carefully and imitated. These reference groups become transmitters of influence, although more along the lines of taste and hobbies than basic attitudes. Testimonial copy is extremely effective when a popular figure is featured.

Appealing to Self-Actualization Needs

The need for self-actualization is the need to become the kind of person one wants to be and achieve the things one wants to accomplish. Satisfaction of this need may be expressed in various ways. A person may aspire to become an honor student, a talented athlete, a good mother, an accountant, and so on.

Advertisers attempt to persuade consumers that these needs can be satisfied by purchasing their products.

There's a private gym in my home. It's my new Schwinn Air-Dyne Exerciser. Athletes or other individuals with a goal of physical fitness may be interested in Schwinn's exclusive Air-Dyne Ergometer that provides the benefits of a regular fitness program for arms, legs, upper body, and lower torso independently or simultaneously.

At home at the most beautiful dinners in America. The conscientious homemaker who is considered a fine cook and a gracious host or hostess may respond favorably to this ad for Lenox china and crystal.

Are you getting the challenge and recognition that you deserve? Under this headline, the *Wall Street Journal* explains that a subscription to *National Business Employment Weekly* can help individuals looking for a more rewarding job find it and land it.

CELEBRITIES IN COMMERCIALS: PROS AND CONS

Miller Brewing got a jolt in 1980 when Whitey Herzog, one of the jocks in its Lite-beer commercials, was named manager of the St. Louis Cardinals, the baseball team owned by Miller's archrival, Anheuser-Busch.

J. B. Williams, a toiletries maker, had no choice but to shelve a Lectric Shave commercial featuring quarterback Michael Kruczek in a Pittsburgh Steelers uniform. Kruczek had been traded to the Washington Redskins.

Ace Hardware faced the unexpected when Suzanne Sommers, the star of the hardware chain's commercials, showed up in *Playboy* magazine in photos taken years earlier and published without her permission.

"Even if you got St. Peter, you've got some sort of risk," says John Baldwin, senior vice president of Dancer Fitzgerald Sample ad agency. But the risk of using stars also carries with it the chance for unforeseen gains. Lever Brothers hired George Brett, third baseman for the Kansas City Royals, to promote Lifebuoy soap, but its ad executives began having second thoughts when he was injured early in the season. But then Brett returned to lead the American League in hitting, and Lever was jubilant.

In Minneapolis, the Twin City Federal Savings and Loan thought that Minnesota Viking stars were charging too much to appear in commercials and decided to try a spoof of athlete commercials. "We set out looking for an anti-hero," recalls Robert Evans, vice president of marketing. "We wanted not a superstar but a bench warmer. We wanted to find one with a funny name, and not real good-looking." Along came bench warmer Bob Lurtsema.

"I'm tall and ugly, having a receding hairline and square jaw," says Mr. Lurtsema, who actually did play for the Minnesota Vikings as a second-stringer. On TV, however, he is a superstar. He generally portrays a slightly dull-witted, slow-talking character who is the butt of the joke. But he proved so popular that he became an instant celebrity. The bench warmer approach appeals to people, Mr. Lurtsema says. "So few people truly make it that the majority of people in life are second-stringers," he continued. Some day, national TV audiences may get to see bench warmer Bob in action; he says he is being considered for national commercials.

Adapted from Bill Abrams, "When Ads Feature Celebrities, Advertisers Cross Their Fingers," reprinted by permission of *Wall Street Journal,* © Dow Jones & Company, Inc., December 4, 1980, p. 23; and Lawrence Ingrassia, "Tired of Those Star-Athlete Ads? Then Listen to Bench Warmer Bob," reprinted by permission of *Wall Street Journal,* © Dow Jones & Company, Inc., January 12, 1982, p. 31. All rights reserved.

Appealing to the Desire to Know and Understand

Maslow, who set forth the theory of human motivation based on needs, was not sure whether the desire to know and understand was as clearly established in human beings as other needs were. While curiosity, exploration, and the desire to acquire further knowledge can be observed, they are more evident in people of higher intelligence. Advertising messages that appeal to the intelligence of prospects have proven highly successful.

> Why? Because pharmacists and physicians recommend Afrin Nasal Decongestant more than any other.

> In the 17 U.S. government reports since 1970, no cigarette has ever been reported to be lower in tar than Carlton.

> In a test, 50.1 percent said that Zenith had the best picture.

Information designed to appeal to the desire to know and understand can be more convincing if the tests are conducted by someone who is impartial and an expert in the field. Often an ad will state that an independent clinic or laboratory conducted the test.

Industrial advertisers make frequent use of appeals to higher intelligence. Earlier, it was pointed out that industrial products are usually sophisticated and that industrial buyers possess a wealth of technical knowledge. Therefore, when IBM elaborates on the merits of its System/32, it may create interest in this compact computer.

Appeals may be incorporated into ads carried by print media or commercials broadcast by electronic media. The appeal may serve as the theme, may be presented as a testimonial or a musical script, or may be dramatized or read as a straight announcement. In addition, appeals may be demonstrated in a cartoon ad or may be incorporated into a humorous broadcast script. When properly handled, humor can enhance selling points and make them meaningful and memorable. But if humor is used for entertainment only, little may be accomplished.

SELECTING APPROPRIATE ADVERTISING MEDIA

The advertiser faces media choices in determining which media can best reach the greatest number of customers with the greatest impact and at the lowest cost. Actually, the firm may not be able to achieve all three of these objectives in selecting appropriate media. Nevertheless, the characteristics of each advertising medium should be examined before the firm arrives at a decision.

Print Media

The print media include newspapers, magazines, shoppers' guides, direct mail, and other printed materials and publications. Each printed advertising medium has advantages and limitations. The prospective advertiser will weigh the attributes and disadvantages before making a decision.

Newspapers. Whether they appear daily or weekly, newspapers carry the messages of both local and national advertisers. The messages may appear in display ads or may be positioned in the classified ad section. In addition to black and white, many newspapers offer to print ads in three colors for an additional cost. Ads also may be placed in a **preferred position,** that is, in a particular section of the paper that is more likely to be read by target groups such as farmers, sports enthusiasts, gourmet cooks, lawn and garden hobbyists, and do-it-yourself home improvers. There is an additional charge for a preferred position.

Newspapers offer opportunities for geographic selectivity. Prospects can be reached in Riverside, California or Lakewood, Ohio. Such geographic selectivity is appealing to national advertisers that wish to place their advertisements where the market looks best. Local firms seek to reach an audience confined within a geographic area.

Newspapers also offer time flexibility. Advertisements may be changed up to a few hours before the paper goes to press. This is important since changes in the weather, changes in the merchandise received for sale, or other developments may make revisions necessary.

If a small firm is unable to employ advertising personnel, a newspaper will prepare an ad for the firm, including copy and art. Larger firms, of course, may prepare their own layouts or contract with an advertising agency to have the work prepared. Camera-ready layout and copy is then furnished to the newspaper.

The limitations of newspaper advertising are threefold: short life, hasty reading, and poor reproduction. Newspapers become stale quickly, and the chances that a newspaper ad will have an impact after the day of publication are not good. In addition, the average reader may spend only 20 or 30 minutes reading a paper. The reader engages in selective reading, darting from one article of interest to another without reading each page thoroughly. Newspapers are not noted for quality reproduction. If the appearance of the product is important, the product's image may suffer when a picture is reproduced in newspaper ads. While improvements continue to be made, newspaper stock still is not conducive to quality pictures or illustrations.

The cost of newspaper advertising varies, but it is competitive when compared with other media choices. Common sense tells marketers that a newspaper with a large circulation charges more than a newspaper with a small circulation. Individual newspapers supply rate cards containing charges and discounts.

Magazines. Magazines can be used to reach a national consumer market or a specialized trade or industrial market. Magazines are published for doctors, lawyers, teachers, truckers, farmers, sports enthusiasts, radio and TV repair personnel, computer operators, and almost every other group. Manufacturers of food products or home furnishings can reach large numbers of homemakers, while manufacturers of dental equipment can reach a national audience of dentists.

Unlike newspapers, magazines may be kept around the home, in waiting rooms, and in specialized library collections for a long period of time. Thus, magazines have a longer life than newspapers, and an ad may be reviewed over a longer time. Many consumer magazines offer regional editions enabling advertisers to direct their messages at specific geographic regions. Magazines with a more limited number of subscribers usually do not offer regional editions.

An advertiser may select a magazine because it lends prestige to a product. *Good Housekeeping,* for example, claims in a trade ad that over 40 million women are influenced in purchases by their seal of approval, available to advertisers whose products meet certain standards.

Magazines usually are printed on high-quality paper, and as a result, an important advantage is excellent reproduction in black and white or in color. However, an ad must be prepared long before actual publication, and it is usually impossible to make last-minute changes.

While magazines charge competitive prices for delivering messages when the cost of exposure per person is considered, some advertisers and particularly small businesses and retailers still may find the cost prohibitive. More manufacturers, however, advertise in magazines than in any other mass medium. The price structure for various magazines is quoted in *Standard Rate and Data,* a publication listing media rate structures used by time and space buyers.

Shoppers' Guides. Various shoppers' guides have appeared in recent years, and many are delivered free from door to door. While the makeup of such guides varies, most contain both display and classified ads. They usually lack news articles or editorial materials.

If consumers are thinking about purchases, they may examine the ads for comparative reasons. They also may examine the ads in order to clip money-saving coupons. Otherwise, the shoppers' guide may be discarded quickly. Shoppers' guides usually are printed on paper stock of the same quality used by newspapers. The rates vary depending on the number of copies that are printed and distributed as well as the size of the ad.

Closely related to the shoppers' guide is the entertainment guide published in larger cities, usually those which host a large number of conventions. The entertainment guide closely resembles a magazine. It may be printed on glossy paper, and it contains articles about local points of interest. Restaurants, theaters, nightclubs, and other firms that cater to tourists or visitors may find a local entertainment guide to be an effective medium for carrying their messages.

Direct Mail. The variety of terms used to label direct mail often causes confusion. Actually, there are three types of direct mail: direct mail, direct advertising, and mail-order advertising. **Direct mail** is any direct advertising sent through the mail. **Direct advertising** is any form of advertising that is issued directly to prospects. Thus, a brochure sent to a prospect by mail is direct mail. However, when the same brochure is given to the prospect by a salesperson, it is direct advertising. **Mail-order advertising** is any method of promoting products in which the sale will take place by mail. No personal selling is involved.

The term *direct mail* has become a catchall phrase that includes everything from a postal card to a catalog containing several hundred pages. Here is a description of the more common forms of direct mail.

Sales Letters are the most frequently used form of direct mail. They may be individually typed or reproduced by some other duplicating process. Recently, the computer-printed letter has been used extensively.

Postal Cards may be sent as either first class or third class mail. First class postal cards may contain an individually written message. However, third class cards must contain only printed matter with either a handwritten or a stenciled signature.

Leaflets usually consist of a single printed sheet. They frequently are sent in conjunction with other mailed materials to explain an offer or idea in more detail.

Folders are larger than leaflets and in most cases are printed on heavier stock. The larger size permits a more complete sales story and more visuals. Folders often serve as self-mailers with the name and address placed on one side of the cover.

Broadsides are even larger than folders. Some broadsides are sent to dealers to use as display pieces or as point-of-sale promotion pieces. Others are sent to prospects with the hope that the size will impress the receiver with the importance of the offer.

Booklets contain several pages and are used when the sales story is complicated and considerable information, often accompanied by pictures, is needed.

Catalogs serve as reference books. In 1981, mail-order sales reached $120 million according to the *Christian Science Monitor.* Containing many pages, catalogs are buying guides designed to be used over a period of time. Catalogs are expensive to produce, and consequently, firms find it uneconomical to send them to any except real prospects.

House Organs are publications issued periodically by business organizations. Some house organs are internal in that their circulation is for employers and organization members. Some are external, sent to dealers, customers, and others. Some serve both inside and outside audiences. House organs usually are published by the advertising or public relations department.

While any of these publications may contain persuasive messages, the fact that they are mailed classifies them as direct mail. If used in other ways, they become direct advertising.

The greatest advantage of direct mail is selectivity. Mailing pieces can be directed to the precise audience that a firm desires to reach. Direct

Figure 14-6. Mail order advertising promotes products that are sold through the mail; the ad itself may appear in print or other media. No personal selling is involved.

mail also offers the flexibility of reaching customers or clients as frequently as desired. Because direct mail can be sent quickly, the firm can take advantage of seasonal or timely appeals. Direct mail offers flexibility in terms of format and the length of messages to be conveyed. Each mailing piece can be as individualized as the sender chooses.

Major limitations of direct mail include high costs, difficulty maintaining updated mailing lists, and the possibility that the reader will discard the message without examining it carefully. The cost of preparing materials for a direct-mail campaign can be prohibitive. In the future, we are likely to see much greater use of the computer and automated word processing equipment in direct-mail campaigns.

Broadcast Media

Unlike print media, radio and TV messages are time-oriented as opposed to being space-oriented. Both offer three general classes for broadcasting messages: network, spot (time sold to an advertiser in one or more markets), and local.

Radio. Dunn and Barban report that there are now 5.3 radios per American family. During the average week, 96 percent of the population 12 years old or older listens to radio.[4] Most cost-per-thousand studies confirm that radio delivers audiences at an extremely low cost. Any message that can be adapted to sound can be delivered by radio.

Radio provides flexibility for an advertiser in a number of ways. Radio is a mobile medium. It goes with listeners in their cars, to the beach, and from room to room in the home. The length of the message may be determined by the advertiser. That is, the advertiser may use 30 seconds, 1 minute, or a longer period. The advertiser can choose to reach an audience once a day or more frequently. By choosing the time of day or evening, an advertiser can reach a specialized audience. Sports fans, homemakers, farmers, business people, and other groups can be reached by broadcasting the commercial at times when

Figure 14-7. Radio advertising provides flexibility in a mobile, low-cost medium.

they are listening to programs of interest. In addition, there are a variety of stations and program segments throughout the country that attract certain groups of listeners. Advertisers also have the flexibility of changing a commercial or a portion of a message up to the time when it goes on the air.

Radio, like other media, has limitations. Radio stations must fight aggressively for audiences. Competing stations, both AM and FM, as well as TV and newspapers are trying to attract the public's attention. Advertising messages presented by radio pass quickly. They are not available for review or rereading.

Television. Television has an almost unbelievable impact because it brings into the viewer's home a combination of moving pictures and the speaking voice. It is almost like using door-to-door sales people but at a greatly reduced cost for each call.

The costs involved in beaming commercials into people's homes vary. In 1981, ads on prime time network shows costs advertisers as much as $650,000 and as little as $225,000 according to estimates by *Variety*. When one considers the size of the audience, however, the cost for each viewer may be very low. Spot messages and local commercials cost much less.

Television can provide mass coverage. Illiterates as well as literate Americans who find reading so arduous that they do very little of it spend several hours each day watching TV. Like radio, television makes it possible to repeat messages as often as the advertiser desires or can afford.

TV allows for flexibility. An advertiser may demonstrate a product, create a mood, establish a slogan, or make an intensive sales pitch. Geographic areas can be selected, and changes in commercials can be arranged on short notice.

Television is not without limitations. Words in print tend to be more believable than messages that are not received in writing. The printed word carries a stamp of authenticity that broadcasts cannot attain. Another shortcoming of TV advertising is the mortality rate. A viewer may switch channels during a commercial or go to the kitchen for refreshments and thus miss an advertiser's message. In addition, an appealing program on another channel—regular, public broadcasting, or educational—may attract much of the potential audience that an advertiser hopes to reach. TV commercials are costly. The advertiser must pay the station for time, and production costs also must be paid. Small firms, especially local retailers, may find that such costs exceed their advertising budgets.

The advent of "teleshopping," in which consumers shop from their homes over a two-way cable linkup, was examined briefly in Chapter 7. More recently, tests have been conducted in medium-size communities such as Midland, Texas, and Evansville, Indiana, where marketing research firms monitor and catalog the grocery store purchases of thousands of families and simultaneously transmit custom-tailored commer-cials to the same people by cable TV.[5] Marketing people are elated with this new marketing tool, which demonstrates the possibilities of cable TV technology. Programming produced locally in a cable system studio presents a less costly advertising opportunity for local retailers.

Outdoor Media

The term *outdoor advertising* was adopted initially to refer to standardized signs used widely by both national and local advertisers. The term, however, is confusing because most people use it to refer to all types of signs including signs which are not standardized.

Outdoor Signs. Nonstandardized signs are used primarily by local firms for purposes of identification. They may be placed on the premises or along streets and highways. When they are placed off a firm's premises, space must be rented from the owner of the property.

Standardized signs are made available on a rental basis by outdoor advertising firms. The panel frame measures 12 feet 3 inches high by 24 feet 6 inches long. The signs accommodate 24 sheet or 30 sheet posters which are pieced together to produce the advertiser's message. In most markets, standardized signs are sold to advertisers by the month in packages of **gross rating points** (GRP). GRP indicates the number of impression opportunities available at a particular location, without regard to audience duplication. GRP is expressed in terms of a percentage of the total population of a specific market.

The advantages of outdoor advertising include the possibility of reaching potential customers who live close to the point where advertised products or services are offered for sale. The messages are simple and easy to comprehend. Repetition is a built-in factor because audiences may pass an ad many times.

The major disadvantage of outdoor advertising is obvious. There is a limit to how much can be told to fast-moving passengers. Another disadvantage results from the Highway Beautification Act, which regulates the placement of outdoor adver-

Figure 14-8. Outdoor advertising messages are easy to understand.

tising near interstate highways. Billboards that are pushed back greater distances from the highway must have large lettering and carry very brief messages.

Transit Advertising. Transit advertising consists of messages placed on the exterior or interior of public transportation vehicles. Small sign posters placed near or in subway stations or railroad and bus terminals also are included in the definition of transit advertising.

Transit advertising reaches workers, students, and shoppers traveling to and from their destinations. While transit ads mounted on the outside of a vehicle can do little more than remind people of a product or service, interior cards can carry considerably more copy because the average passenger is exposed to the message for perhaps 30 minutes and can reasonably be expected to read a longer message. Local advertisers find transit ads desirable when the bus or subway passes near their establishments. Transit ads are relatively inexpensive. Transit advertising also offers flexibility. It can be used nationally (in 380 U.S. markets), regionally, or locally.

Specialty Advertising

Specialty advertising refers to the giving of small, inexpensive items carrying the advertiser's name and address and often a short message or slogan to a preselected audience. This type of advertising should not be confused with premiums, prizes, or business gifts, which are sales promotion techniques. Instead, the idea is to keep the firm's name in front of the customer in the hope that the customer will remember and feel kindly toward the advertiser or the featured products.

A marketer attempting to keep the firm's name in front of an industrial buyer may supply one or more of the following articles.

- A coffee mug imprinted with the firm's logo
- A ballpoint pen inscribed with the firm's name
- A pocket, desk, or wall calendar that carries the name and address of the firm
- A memo book containing the firm's name and address on the cover

These specialties also might be given to individuals who are members of the consumer market. In addition, the following items are possibilities.

- An imprinted driver's license holder
- An inscribed emery board, nail file, or clipper
- A book of matches with the firm's name on the cover
- An imprinted key chain or key ring

Most marketers agree that at least three criteria should be kept in mind when choosing an advertising specialty.

1. It should be of good quality.
2. It should be easy to use.
3. It should be useful.

Specialty advertising usually has a longer life than advertising in the various media. As long as the specialty remains useful, the advertising message will continue to be repeated. Like direct mail, specialty advertising can be directed to a very selective audience. Advertising specialties, however, are expensive. The message must necessarily be brief and at the most can serve only as reminder advertising.

DETERMINING THE ADVERTISING BUDGET

The philosophy behind determining advertising budgets is simple. The firm attempts to maximize profits by spending dollars to communicate with an audience as long as such expenditures add to the total profit. When each dollar expended for sending messages produces only one penny in profit, the money is still well spent. At some point, however, spending additional dollars will lessen profits rather than add to them. The trick, of course, is to find that exact point.

Several approaches for determining advertising budgets are used by firms. The approaches for developing promotion budgets discussed in Chapter 12 also are used in determining the advertising budget. The most defensible approach is the objective and task method. New firms that lack

TABLE 14-1
PERCENTAGE OF SALES INVESTED IN ADVERTISING FOR SELECTED BUSINESS AND INDUSTRY GROUPS

Classification	Percentage of Sales Invested in Advertising	Classification	Percentage of Sales Invested in Advertising
Agriculture production, crops	2.1	General building contractors	0.6
Apparel (finished products)	2.7	Greeting cards	2.2
Books	4.7	Hotels and motels	2.6
Bottled and canned soft drinks	5.5	Household appliances	2.3
Candy and other confectionery	5.9	Meat products	2.1
Canned and preserved fruits and vegetables	4.2	Motion picture theatres	4.1
		Motor homes	0.4
Cigarettes	6.4	Perfumes and cosmetics	9.8
Dairy products	3.0	Periodicals	4.5
Drugs	8.2	Phonograph records	6.8
		Soap and other detergents	7.1
		Toys and sporting goods	6.9

Source: *Sixth Annual Study of Advertising and Promotional Expenditures of U.S. Corporations and Industry Sectors,* Schonfeld and Associates, Chicago. Excerpted from "Estimates of '81 Advertising to Sales and Advertising to Gross Profit Margin by Industry," *Advertising Age,* August 2, 1982, p. 41.

personnel experienced in determining the amount of money needed to achieve goals, will find guidelines from similar businesses helpful. Table 14-1 lists the percentage of sales invested by major industry and business groups in advertising. While the figures are listed as a percentage of sales, this does not mean that the advertising budgets were determined by using a percentage of sales method. Instead, it is simply a convenient way of reporting advertising expenditures. Since retailing outlets outnumber manufacturing, wholesaling, and other types of firms, Table 14-2

TABLE 14-2
AVERAGE PERCENTAGE OF SALES INVESTED IN ADVERTISING BY RETAIL BUSINESSES

Class of Business	Average Percentage of Sales Invested in Advertising	Class of Business	Average Percentage of Sales Invested in Advertising
Appliance, radio, and TV dealers	2.3	Furniture stores	5.0
Auto dealers	0.8	Gasoline service stations	0.8
Auto parking and repair service	0.9	Hardware stores	1.6
Bakeries	0.7	Insurance agents and brokers	1.8
Banks, commercial	1.3	Jewelry stores	4.4
Beauty shops	2.0	Liquor stores	0.9
Book stores	1.7	Menswear stores	
Camera stores		Sales volume:	
Sales volume:		Under $300,000	2.4
Under $500,000	0.8	$300,000–$500,000	2.6
$500,000 and over	0.9	$500,000–$1,000,000	2.8
Cocktail lounges	0.9	$1,000,000–$5,000,000	3.2
Credit agencies, personal	2.4	$5,000,000 and over	3.4
Department stores, all sizes	2.8	Motion picture theaters	5.5
Sales volume:		Real estate	
$1,000,000–$2,000,000	2.5	Operators	0.6
$2,000,000–$5,000,000	2.9	Subdividers and developers	3.1
$5,000,000–$20,000,000	2.8	Brokers	4.0
$20,000,000–$50,000,000	2.7	Restaurants	0.8
$50,000,000 and over	2.4	Savings banks	1.5
Discount stores	2.4	Savings and loan associations	1.5
Drugstores, chain	1.7	Sporting goods stores	3.5
Independent	1.3	Tire dealers	2.2
Dry cleaning	1.7	Travel agents	5.0
Florists and garden supply stores	2.1	Variety stores	1.5
Food chains	1.1		

Source: The "I-Wonder-How-to-Set-Up-an-Advertising-Program-and-How-Much-to-Budget-Book," Newspaper Advertising Bureau, Inc., New York, pp. 20–26.

is presented to show the percentage of sales devoted to advertising by retailers.

The budget for advertising represents a very important decision for marketing management. Thus, a defensible plan for arriving at an advertising budget is essential. By defining its objectives and establishing a budget to achieve them, a firm essentially builds an advertising budget based on goals. The other methods, in contrast, start with a total and divide it among the objectives to be achieved. The allocated dollars may or may not be sufficient to achieve the goals. Building a budget based on objectives, however, may produce an advertising budget that costs more than the revenues produced. For that reason, a review of budgets reported by others as a percentage of sales may be helpful. Keep in mind, however, that statistics about average percentage of sales invested in advertising contain as many dollars *above* the reported percentage as dollars *below* the reported percentage.

Most firms establish budgets in four areas related to communicating with desired audiences. Separate budgets may be established for advertising, personal selling, sales promotion, and public relations. The problem is to determine what can legitimately be charged to each budget. Obviously, expenses incurred in achieving advertising objectives should be billed as advertising expenditures. The problem arises when expenses related to promotion that should be paid from other budgeted accounts are charged to advertising.

Few would argue against charging space and time costs, production costs for ads or commercials, or direct-mailing costs to the advertising budget. Annual reports to stockholders or gifts to charitable organizations, on the other hand, should be charged to public relations. Merchandising activities including consumer contests, premiums, coupons, and samples are more correctly billed as sales or sales promotion activities. The point is that while advertising can absorb an occasional expense that is really not advertising, as time passes and abuses mount, the advertising budget may fail to reflect advertising costs accu-

rately. If the ad budget is padded or deflated by arbitrary accounting practices, it is difficult to determine the true effect of advertising.

SELECTING AN ADVERTISING AGENCY

An **advertising agency** is an independent firm which provides specialized services to clients. When agencies are used, advertising involves four distinct parties or groups of people. One party is the sponsor who pays the bills and whose name will appear in the advertisement. The agency which prepares the ad for the sponsor (client) is also a party. The medium chosen to carry the message to the audience becomes a third party. Finally, the audience to whom the message is directed is the fourth party.

To many people, advertising agencies elicit thoughts of Madison Avenue in New York City or Michigan Avenue in Chicago. Actually, agencies are scattered throughout the country and range from the very small, with an owner and two or three assistants, to the very large, with many departments and a sizable number of employees.

Today's marketer is faced with the decision of using internally trained employees to create ads or commercials as opposed to engaging the services of an advertising agency. Implementation of an ad campaign involves tasks such as producing the message (writing, preparing layouts, and recording or filming) and planning and scheduling the media advertising. Thus, the marketer has to decide whether to perform these tasks internally or engage an advertising agency to do them. A small business which advertises only occasionally may find that a local newspaper or radio station will prepare an ad or commercial. But for more extensive advertising campaigns, the make-or-buy decision has significance.

Make-or-Buy Decision Factors

An advertising agency performs various functions for clients. The functions are classified into four areas.

1. Creative (development of the message)

2. Service (public relations and sales promotion and management advice relating to demand creation)

3. Media (selection of media and placement and timing of messages)

4. Research (analysis of audience characteristics and desires)

The marketer must recognize that agencies offer professional expertise. Agency employees have specialized training, possess insights and knowledge, and have accumulated in-depth experience in solving advertising problems. Agency employees devote full attention to an advertising campaign, and usually they are not distracted by the nonadvertising tasks or daily operating problems encountered within a firm. The agency is hired when needed, relieving the firm of the need to maintain specialized personnel on the payroll when their services are not needed.

On the other hand, agencies are not a panacea for all firms. Hiring outsiders may be detrimental to the morale of individuals within the firm who feel that they can handle the total promotional program. An agency, like other businesses, tries to achieve goals. Sometimes the goals of an agency may conflict with those of a client firm, or the agency's pursuits may leave insufficient time to devote to the client firm's program. Agency costs are out-of-the-pocket costs. While it is true that internal personnel represent an expenditure for human resources, internal personnel also may perform other functions besides advertising.

Changes Occurring within Agencies

Agencies go to great lengths to get their clients' messages across. Staff members in one agency spent 13 hours leading a docile bull through a china shop to film one commercial for Merrill Lynch. While agencies continue to concentrate on helping client firms communicate, many have decided that they can do more than just create ads.

Many agencies have moved into related fields such as public relations, package design, sales promotion, direct marketing, and advertising to special groups such as lawyers, doctors, or farmers. "Whether it's your matchbook cover, the color of your office or your truck, it says something," comments the head of one advertising agency.[6] Part of the impetus behind agency diversification can be traced to the soaring cost of advertising. As the cost of 30 seconds on prime time television rose to between $100,000 and $175,000 in the early 1980s, firms began looking for less expensive ways of promoting themselves and their products.

Agency executives believe that putting related demand creation services under one roof provides their clients with continuity. Some clients believe that one organization that understands a firm's total strategy is desirable. Using marketing services provided by unrelated firms may pull the marketing program in different directions.

While the full effect of such diversification by agencies has not been felt yet, advertising agencies across the country are adding other marketing services. Designing brightly colored "for sale" signs for real estate agents to plant on suburban lawns, redesigning retail showrooms, and sending direct mail pieces to physicians and other professionals are some of the diversified services being offered by advertising agencies. A full-service agency seeks to assure client firms that their total marketing communications program will be better coordinated.

THE ETHICS OF ADVERTISING

From time to time, advertising has been criticized for its social or ethical effects. Any serious student of business history knows that 100 years ago businesses engaged in practices that today would be considered unethical. Nineteenth-century ads contained claims that clearly would be illegal today. While those engaged in advertising have taken steps to conform to ethical standards, some objections still persist.

Is Advertising Truthful?

Does advertising tell the truth? In most situations, yes. Most marketers recognize that if they are to win the confidence of potential buyers, they must communicate truthfully. Here is what the Supreme Court has said about advertising.

● Advertising as a whole must not create a misleading impression even though every statement separately considered is literally truthful.

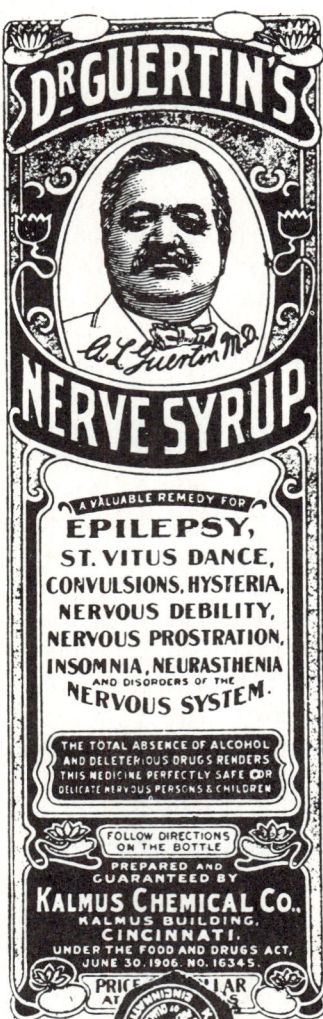

Figure 14-9. Nineteenth-century ads were not always truthful; today there are ethical standards.

● Advertising must not obscure or conceal material facts.

● Advertising must not be artfully contrived to distract and divert readers' attention from the true nature of the terms and conditions of an offer.

● Advertising must be free of traps which would result from a forthright disclosure of the true nature of the offer.

To ensure that these criteria are complied with by advertisers, Congress created a policing agent, the Federal Trade Commission (FTC). The FTC issues complaints against reported deceptive practices. In addition, most states have passed legislation that governs what is acceptable in advertising.

Is Advertising Offensive or in Bad Taste?

The question of taste continues to be one of the most baffling in advertising since what offends one individual may be acceptable to another. Media groups such as the National Association of Broadcasters have tended to police ads and commercials which bring cries of outrage from the general public. The marketer cannot afford to offend large groups of potential buyers. While some individuals will always want to censor or ban certain ads, media groups and the general public can serve as a system of checks and balances.

Does Advertising Create Conformity?

There is little evidence that advertising creates conformity. Advertising thrives on pointing out different job opportunities, clothing styles, cosmetics, autos, home furnishings, and so forth. In fact, advertising shows people how to indulge their own tastes. Many people are no longer satisfied with products just like their neighbors'. They want new styles in clothing and furniture. They look at products as status symbols.

Does Advertising Cause People to Buy Things They Do Not Need?

Most business people do not deny that they attempt to make consumers dissatisfied with their current possessions. If firms catered only to people's basic needs, they would sell only basic food items instead of gourmet delicacies, train and bus tickets instead of automobiles, and animal skins instead of high-fashion clothing. The power of advertising often has been overestimated greatly. Advertising does have the power to awaken needs, wants, and desires. However, it does not have the power to force people to buy things they do not want or need.

Does Advertising Take Unfair Advantage of Children?

Some critics believe that children are helpless, impressionable victims of advertising. While youngsters are exposed to more advertising on TV than through any other medium, there is no evidence that children are more vulnerable to sales messages than adults. In fact, it has been found that children begin to discriminate between programs and commercials and understand the intent of commercials between the second and fourth grades. By the sixth grade, children have relatively well developed attitudes toward commercials. It also has been concluded that television advertising is neither the sole nor necessarily the most important determinant of children's wants and purchasing behavior. Instead, it was found that adolescents acquire consumer attitudes and skills from television advertising.[7]

How Is Advertising Regulated?

The FTC, under federal law, can take legal action against firms engaged in interstate commerce whose advertising is false or is intended to be misleading. The Wheeler-Lea Act, which was passed in 1914 and amended in 1938, gives the FTC powers to combat unfair advertising practices.

The Robinson-Patman Act of 1936 protects small retailers from unfair competition by regulating advertising allowances and discounts. If a manufacturer offers an advertising allowance to a giant retailer, it must also offer the allowance to small retailers. In addition, at least 21 different federal agencies exercise some control over advertising, including the U.S. Postal Service, the Securities and Exchange Commission, the Federal Communications Commission, and the Federal Alcohol Commission.

Most states follow the example of federal lawmakers in their efforts to regulate advertising. Individual states have their own laws and attempt to detect and eliminate deceptive business and advertising practices. The enforcement of a state's laws regulating advertising is generally the responsibility of the state attorney general's office. The attorney general investigates alleged violations and prosecutes offenders. In some cases, complaints may be settled without going to court. Most firms want to protect their reputations, and so they try to adjust claims before lawsuits occur.

It is likely that no other industry has tried harder to promote honesty than the advertising industry. The American Association of Advertising Agencies (AAAA) has adopted the AAAA Creative Code, which is endorsed by 10 other advertising and media organizations. The AAAA Creative Code points out what is considered objectionable by advertising agencies. To enforce the code, the AAAA established a voluntary mutual agreement which enables agencies to stop any advertising they consider objectionable.

MEASURING THE RESULTS OF ADVERTISING

Firms today are concerned with accountability. For each dollar invested, owners expect and demand a profitable return. When dollars are invested in personnel, firms expect productivity. When dollars are invested in manufacturing plants and machines, increased capacity is expected. When dollars are invested in an advertising campaign, the firm wants proof that they are resulting in proportionately as many sales as dollars spent for other activities. Advertising research is needed to help determine whether advertising is doing its job. Unfortunately, this is one of the least developed areas of marketing research.

When a local hairstyling shop, The Head Shed, initiated an advertising campaign, the owners decided to test the results. By examining records, they were able to determine how many customers were served before the campaign, during the time period when ads were being presented, and after the campaign had ended. This "sales results test" often is used to measure the impact of an ad campaign or a series of advertisements.

An experimental test that sometimes is used by national advertisers begins with the selection of two cities as nearly alike as possible. In one city an advertising campaign is initiated. In the other city the campaign is not used. During the test period, other factors which might have some effect on sales, such as economic conditions and competition, are monitored carefully. In the end, differences in sales may be attributed to advertising.

Another test involves the inclusion of printed coupons within ads. Such a coupon entitles the reader to receive a discount for specific purchases. McDonald's, for example, may include a coupon which entitles the purchaser to receive two Big Macs for the price of one. The number of coupons presented is an indication of the effectiveness of such ads.

Other types of tests are indirect measurements of advertising's effectiveness. Readership, recognition, and recall tests involve showing targeted audiences part or all of a previously run ad to determine whether it was read, what parts were remembered, and whether the respondent knows who sponsored it. The premise underlying such tests is that people who see, read, and remember an ad will be persuaded to act.

It should be remembered, however, that the purpose of ads is to sell something or to modify the attitudes and behavior of a targeted group. Therefore, more concern should be directed toward measuring advertising's ability to achieve such goals than is directed toward readership, recognition, or recall. The impact of advertising may not be realized immediately. Behavioral changes usually are gradual and occur over a period of time.

KEY POINTS SUMMARY

- Advertising is marketing's most visible form of communication. It is defined as a paid form of nonpersonal presentation and promotion of ideas, goods, or services by an identified sponsor.

- A logotype is a distinctively designed form of a firm's name, a brand name, or a trademark that is reproduced on all printed advertisements to help identify the firm or brand.

- Advertising messages can be classified into various groups on the basis of sponsorship, purpose, targeted audience, and level of demand influence.

- While the basic objective of advertising is to sell a product, a service, or an idea, the ultimate effect should be to modify the attitudes or buying behaviors of the receivers of the message.

- While the overall marketing strategy includes what should be said to target groups, ads must attract attention, hold interest, arouse desire, and induce action to be successful.

- Marketers seek to appeal to motives, a term applied to cover the wide spectrum of wishes, desires, needs, and drives that induce buying behavior.

- Since industrial products are usually more sophisticated and buyers possess a wealth of knowledge, industrial advertisers make frequent use of appeals to higher intelligence.

- Marketers should examine the attributes and limitations of each medium before reaching media decisions.

- The most defensible approach for determining the advertising budget is the objective and task method. By defining objectives and establishing a budget to achieve them, a firm essentially builds an advertising budget based on goals.

- Marketers should determine whether they can effectively carry out the functions (creative, service, media, and research) that advertising agencies perform before deciding to use an agency.

KEY TERMS AND CONCEPTS

advertising
advertising agency
Advertising Council
advocacy advertising
classified ads
competitive ads
cooperative advertising
direct advertising
direct mail
display ads
emotional advertising
esteem needs
factual (rational) advertising

gross rating points
institutional advertising
local advertising
logotype
mail-order advertising
pioneering ads
preferred position
promotional advertising
publicity
reference groups
reminder advertising
specialty advertising

DISCUSSION QUESTIONS

1. How would marketing communication be affected if all advertising were prohibited? Would there be any impact on sales in this country? If so, which industries would suffer most? Which would be affected least?

2. One minute of prime time television advertising may cost $150,000. Most companies could compensate and support three sales reps handsomely for a year for this amount. Surely, three sales reps working for an entire year can produce more than 1 minute of TV advertising. Evaluate this statement.

3. Present at least two examples in which advertising to middlemen might be necessary. What are the objectives of the advertising in your examples?

4. Do you think additional legislation is needed to regulate advertising? Why?

5. Explain the significance of monitoring factors when using the experimental technique to measure the effectiveness of advertising.

6. Which advertising media would you choose for the following products or services? Why?

a. local carpet cleaning service

b. State Farm automobile insurance

c. Tide (washing detergent)

d. More (cigarettes)

e. Magnavox (TV sets)

f. this textbook

NOTES

1. "100 Leading National Advertisers," *Advertising Age,* September 9, 1982, p. 1.
2. McGraw-Hill Publications Co.
3. Adapted from Mary Ann Flick, "Pac-Man Gobbles Up Sales," *The Daily Pantagraph,* Bloomington, Ill., April 2, 1982, pp. A1–A5.
4. S. Watson Dunn and Arnold M. Barban, *Advertising: Its Role in Modern Marketing,* The Dryden Press, Hinsdale, Ill., 1974, p. 531.
5. Jeffrey H. Birnbaum, "Admen Excited over New Marketing Tool, but Critics Contend It Smacks of '1984,' " reprinted by permission of *Wall Street Journal,* © Dow Jones & Company, Inc., September 25, 1981. All rights reserved.
6. Bill Abrams, "Ad Agencies Enhance Own Pitches, Offering Other Marketing Aid," reprinted by permission of *Wall Street Journal,* © Dow Jones & Company, Inc., March 2, 1982, pp. 1–17. All rights reserved.
7. Scott Ward, *Children and Promotion: New Consumer Battleground?* Marketing Science Institute, Boston, 1972, pp. 9–13.

CHAPTER
15
SALES PROMOTION

Halloween costume and candy makers were in a panic. Not only had parents found treats such as candy apples, candy, and popcorn laced with pins and bits of glass, but some city officials encouraged parents to keep their children at home. This occurred in 1982, one month after seven people died as a result of consuming Tylenol capsules that contained cyanide.

After Halloween, cartons of unsold costumes, candy corn, and caramels lay on store shelves untouched. It was then that the Halloween industry began fighting back with a sales promotion and public relations campaign.

A Halloween team, made up of representatives from the National Safety Council and costume manufacturers' trade groups, pledged to help restore the traditions of Halloween. The National Confectioners' Association and the Chocolate Manufacturers of America spent approximately $500,000 on public relations. By fall of the following year, pro-Halloween posters appeared in grocery stores, a toll-free Halloween

hotline was in operation, and Dr. Joyce Brothers appeared on television to explain the psychological benefits of Halloween to children. The Toy Manufacturers of America released the "Complete Halloween Organizer Kit." The guide in the kit contained recommendations for expanding the holiday over several days and calling it "Halloweekend" or "Halloweek." The guide contained a description of celebrations in Anoka, Minnesota, the town that claims to be the Halloween Capital of the World.

Some people, often those who have been victims of tricks, believe that Halloween is not a holiday that can be tamed. As a result, the Halloween Team advocated a new version of the traditional "trick or treat" slogan. The new slogan, "trick and treat," is designed to pacify opponents of the holiday. Instead of diverting to pranks, children receive a treat for a trick. These can be magic tricks or other stunts performed on the neighbor's doorsteps.

Marketers are frequently faced with day-today situations that call for innovative ways to communicate with potential customers in order to stimulate customer purchasing. In the preceding example, costume and candy makers used public relations and sales promotion activities to overcome an adverse publicity situation. Sales promotion activities and publicity, in a variety of forms, may be effective in communicating with target groups.[1]

SALES PROMOTION DEFINED

Sales promotion is defined by the American Marketing Association (AMA) as ''those activities, other than personal selling, advertising, and publicity, that stimulate consumer purchasing and dealer effectiveness.'' The term *dealer* is used loosely in this definition and may imply a variety of business establishments, including retailers, service-oriented firms, wholesalers, and manufacturers. Sales promotion efforts may be directed at the ultimate consumer or may be aimed at other firms. In either case, sales promotion activities are designed to achieve objectives which the firm deems to be important. Sales promotion activities also may be used to stimulate personal selling efforts by a firm's employees. Sales promotion in effect ''educates'' and arouses the enthusiasm of sales people, middlemen, consumers, and others through a variety of materials, tools, and devices that the firm controls.

The AMA definition is a very broad one, emphasizing the fact that sales promotion covers a wide variety of activities. Such activities include but are not confined to participating in trade shows, administering sales contests and consumer contests, constructing displays of all types, and offering samples, coupons, premiums, or trading stamps. Each of these activities will be discussed in this chapter, along with publicity, as an important communication tool for today's marketers.

Like other persuasive modes of communication, sales promotion activities have applications beyond the marketing of products and services. Bumper stickers, badges, political rallies, and open houses for political candidates are examples of sales promotion activities that are used to enhance the image of political figures and give them an opportunity to communicate with their target audiences. Organizations such as the American Cancer Society, the American Heart Association, and the Salvation Army use sales promotion activities to communicate with the public. They may conduct telethons, set up booths in shopping centers and at county fairs, and use a variety of other sales promotion activities. The point is that sales promotion has many applications and may be an effective communicative tool.

Organization for Sales Promotion

There is a sales promotion technique for essentially every phase of marketing, from packaging, pricing, and credit policies to motivating sales representatives and stimulating buyers. A more commonly accepted view, however, is that sales promotion concerns only activities whose primary function is inviting, persuading, and otherwise encouraging and stimulating trade. The relative importance and effectiveness of the different types of promotional effort naturally vary considerably from firm to firm.

Some large firms may organize separate departments for advertising, sales promotion, and sales under an executive in charge of the marketing program. Each department has its own manager, staff, and budget. The executive, who usually is the vice president of marketing, coordinates the endeavors of each department. The total impact of advertising, sales promotion activities, and personal selling is much greater when they are combined. In smaller firms, the establishment of separate departments with specialized personnel may not be feasible. Nevertheless, planning and coordination of sales promotion activities designed to coincide with other promotional communications can be important.

Planning sales promotion activities begins logically with a projection of seasonal or monthly activities. Such planning includes the preparation of a detailed blueprint for each scheduled event, with the emphasis on what is to be done, when, and how. In the case of companywide promotions in large establishments, these plans may be elaborate. Thus, frequent planning sessions and other contacts with the advertising and sales departments are necessary for personnel in the sales promotion department. In smaller firms, the activities may be planned and coordinated by someone who has responsibility for demand creation.

Importance of Sales Promotion

Firms may use promotions for a variety of reasons. The three major reasons are these.

1. To encourage people to try a product or service they have not tried before

2. To encourage people currently using a product or service to continue using it

3. To strengthen the competitive position of a product or service

Promotions add a degree of excitement and enhance the communication of a firm's message. Sparking interest and creating excitement among potential customers requires creative promotional ideas, carefully planned and expertly carried out. This factor will become more important in the years ahead.

Promotion is entering a new era. The environment during the 1980s and 1990s is no longer responsive to isolated and uncoordinated activities. We have entered an era in which there are too many products, too many marketers, and too much marketing "noise." The marketer's success in this crowded marketplace depends on specific solutions to the following questions.

● What are the promotional goals?
● What are the promotional activities communicating?
● What is the return from promotional activities?

Recession and inflation also have a large effect on promotional activities. During such times, management demands tangible results. The achievement of objectives becomes the key to success.

As we proceed to an examination of sales promotion activities, try to envision the objectives of such activities. Perhaps you can identify the tangible results that should result from these activities. Finally, be alert for opportunities to coordinate these activities with advertising and personal selling.

SALES PROMOTION ACTIVITIES

Sales promotion activities may be classified into two categories: those which are designed to stimulate the efforts of sales people, middlemen, or franchised dealers and those which are designed to stimulate buying by the ultimate consumers. Stated another way, promotion methods may be designed to motivate individuals involved in selling activities or may be designed to induce action by buyers. Promotion that offers a special price reduction to the buyer is known as **price-oriented promotion.**

Sales Promotion Methods Designed to Enhance Selling

Suppliers can enhance and to a certain degree control the activities of resellers through the types of promotions they provide. In Chapter 14, it was pointed out that if a supplier wants a reseller to advertise a product or service, the supplier offers cooperative advertising funds. Similarly, the supplier can enhance selling efforts by offering various forms of sales promotion.

Trade Premiums and Gifts. Trade premiums are gifts given to dealers, retailers, and distributors to encourage them to sell more of a given product or service. Mary Kay, a Texas-based cosmetics firm, for example, rewards exemplary sales performances by distributors by furnishing them with pink Cadillacs. Some firms may offer dealers, retailers, and distributors free vacations if they achieve a sales quota. In these examples, you should recognize the objective which the seller is seeking: to improve the sales efforts of middlemen. The same technique may prove effective for firms that use their own sales people. An automo-

Figure 15-1. Point-of-purchase displays accomplish important sales goals.

tive dealership, for example, may reward the top salesperson with a premium.

When a sale has been finalized, marketers hope to make the buyer a regular customer. Business gifts may be offered to help accomplish this goal. The convention booking agent at a Hyatt Regency Hotel, for example, may send a bottle of champagne, a bowl of fruit, or a floral arrangement to the room of the person responsible for choosing the site of the convention. Business gifts, not to be confused with the advertising specialties which were discussed in Chapter 13, frequently are used to enhance selling opportunities. Often a sales representative will take a client or potential customer to lunch or dinner with the idea of landing an account or closing a sale.

Premiums are not always free, but they may be so attractive that the marketer still achieves a predetermined objective. Some years ago, the Canadian General Electric Company sold its dealers a $1 ironing pad and cover for $0.15 with each

iron they purchased. These premiums were given away by dealers to boost their sales. In this case, General Electric helped the dealers increase sales and consequently increased its own sales.

Consumer premiums also are designed to spur buying action and will be discussed later in this chapter. It should be obvious, however, that when a marketer sparks consumer interest, dealers, retailers, and distributors benefit. Such actions may be helpful in cultivating cooperation among middlemen and getting them to stock sufficient quantities to fill the demands of customers.

Point-of-Purchase Displays. Some firms find that by supplying retailers with point-of-purchase (POP) displays, they accomplish important sales goals. Much of customers' impulse buying is motivated by POP displays. Impulse items such as magazines, cosmetics, candy, chewing gum, and razor blades are displayed in special racks supplied by the manufacturer.

Other products, such as Timex watches, L'Eggs panty hose, and Sylvania light bulbs, may be displayed in cases or on racks supplied by the manufacturer. By providing POP displays, a manufacturer gets more and better display space in the retail outlet and improves the likelihood that the retailer will continue to carry the brand and line of products displayed. Eye appeal is the concept behind POP displays. The almost overnight success of Haynes's L'Eggs was due to the unique 7 foot egg-shaped display unit on which the panty hose were displayed in supermarkets and drugstores. Hoping to repeat its success in a different market, Haynes entered the crowded cosmetic field with its line of L'Aura products. Again, Haynes depended heavily on eye-catching POP displays.

Trade Shows. In the past 5 years, the trade show and exposition industry has emerged as the fastest growing segment in marketing.[2] The amazing part about this "person-to-person marketing medium" is that it has become nationwide mar-

keting, with major shows being held in every important marketing area. In the past few years, billions of dollars have been invested in new show and convention facilities. Major shows are no longer the exclusive province of Chicago and New York. Dallas, Houston, Fort Worth, Phoenix, Detroit, Atlanta, New Orleans, St. Louis, Indianapolis, and Las Vegas all have outstanding exhibition centers.

Trade shows provide an opportunity for combined promotion and personal selling and are becoming responsible for an increasing share of the industrial market.[3] Their success has fostered exhibitions for the consumer market which will be discussed later in this chapter. The people who attend trade shows play an important role in the purchasing process.

There are three kinds of shows which display goods and services, but each differs somewhat in function.

Industrial Shows are used by manufacturers to exhibit their products to other manufacturers

Figure 15-2. Trade shows display goods and services to other professionals and members of the distribution chain.

and to provide educational sessions describing new techniques in the industry and demonstrating new products.

Trade Shows in the strict sense are where sellers of goods and services contact retailers, wholesalers, and distributors as well as industrial, institutional, and government buyers who come to see new products and find out about supplies for products they already use.

Professional or Scientific Shows usually are held in conjunction with annual meetings of professional or specialized organizations. Such an exhibition includes products and services that normally are used by the specialists attending the convention.[4]

A welding rod manufacturer will exhibit at an industrial show attended by metal fabricators, steel construction firms, and other users of the product. The Chicago Furniture Trade Show may attract retailers, wholesalers, and government or institutional buyers. The annual meeting of marketing professors may feature a professional show in which publishers exhibit their textbooks, while the American Medical Association will show the latest developments in body scanners, lasers, drugs, and even computers.

Trade shows are really an extension of or a supplement to personal selling, although they offer some elements of promotion and advertising. Their most practical function is to allow firms to become visible to a wide spectrum of buyers and to gather prospects for their regular sales forces. The shows are perceived to be vitally important to smaller firms that cannot afford a direct sales force and must depend on agents who carry many different product lines. For these firms, trade shows offer an opportunity to display merchandise and services to buyers who are unfamiliar with the firms and are looking for new products or sources of supply. Smaller producers may meet such prospects in face-to-face settings while they demonstrate their products on the spot and offer technical or engineering advice not usually provided by agents.

Sales Promotion Methods Designed to Enhance Buying

Getting action is one of the essentials of advertising. Promotion activities also are designed to induce buying action. In fact, many sales promotion techniques use price reduction to trigger buying action. The following nine sales promotion methods are used by a wide variety of firms.

Consumer Games and Contests.

When was the last time you participated in a consumer game or contest? Did you use a coin to rub the carbon coating from a game card to discover that you would receive a free drink or fries when you returned to a fast-food outlet and purchased a sandwich? Or did you save cash register tapes from a local supermarket to enable you to win a prize when your purchases added up to $500? Perhaps you attended the grand opening of a new store and signed your name on an entry card for a name drawing contest featuring merchandise prizes.

Why do some firms use games and contests as an important marketing strategy? In the situations above, each firm was striving to achieve a specific goal. The managers of the fast-food outlets and the supermarket were seeking repeated patronage. The manager of the new store hoped to generate as much traffic as possible to acquaint shoppers with the store's products, policies, and prices. Other firms use games and contests to achieve a variety of objectives, including the following.

- Opening new markets
- Announcing a new product
- Heralding the improved features of an existing product
- Countering competitive products
- Commemorating an anniversary
- Establishing a favorable corporate image
- Adding a new dimension to the firm (the dimension of active interest)
- Creating excitement and motivation for the sales force

A WILD AND CRAZY IDEA . . . JUST CRAZY ENOUGH TO WORK

Jane Pieriboni, caught up in divorce proceedings in 1982, found that it was fruitless to try to sell her 20-room Victorian mansion during a time of recession and high interest rates. Located in a rural community in central Maine, Mrs. Pieriboni found that she could no longer afford the mortgage payments on the 90-year old house.

She approached her attorney with the idea of staging a raffle. After the attorney had advised her that only charitable organizations can conduct lotteries, she came up with an idea for an essay contest. After paying a $50 entrance fee, participants were instructed to write an essay of 125 words or less on the subject "Why I want to own a big, old house in Maine."

Then inquiries started pouring in from across the country and around the world. Two U.S. servicemen in Japan who apparently heard about the contest on armed forces radio responded. "It seems as if everybody wanted to come to Maine and own a big, old home," said Mrs. Pieriboni. Thus, she and her attorney established ground rules. All entries were sent to a former editor of a national magazine, to be judged in New York after a September deadline. Contestants were advised that if fewer than 1,000 entries were received, all money would be refunded and the contest would be nullified.

This contest represents an innovative application of a sales promotion technique. The prize is unusual, one which certainly would tickle the imagination of a number of contestants. As Mrs. Pieriboni reflected on the contest, she said, "It's a wild and crazy idea . . . just crazy enough to work."

Adapted from Associated Press, "Mansion Replies Enough to Bring House Down," *The Pantagraph*, Bloomington, Ill., April 29, 1982, p. C–2. Reprinted by permission.

Manufacturers and distributors have found that games and contests frequently increase the amount of space provided for their products in stores. Retailers appear to be more favorably inclined to stock the products of manufacturers or distributors that create consumer excitement.

A few years ago, a typewriter manufacturer inserted a sweepstakes card in *Life* magazine. Each card contained a different number, and 1,000 cards were chosen randomly on a digital computer. Each retailer handling the typewriters got a list of the winning numbers.

To find if they had won a typewriter, *Life* readers took the card to the nearest retailer and, if they were lucky, picked up the prize typewriter on the spot. If not, the retailer had an opportunity to try to sell one to the contestant.

The field is still wide open for well-designed puzzles, jingle completions, drawings, sweepstakes, and scores of variations. The variations are getting more imaginative both in the types of contests and in the types of prizes. The search for new and exciting contest twists presents a large challenge for marketers. Most research has shown that contestants prefer cash to all other prizes, but some marketers now believe that prizes that get people to dream are likely to succeed. More and more recent contests have been designed to tickle the imagination and appeal to people's dreams. A racehorse, an oil well, or a visit to a tropical island may well draw in people who would not enter a contest otherwise.

In the next few years, marketers can expect to see continued growth of contest promotions. The search for new, exciting contest ideas will be intensified. At the same time, marketing executives will be searching for ways to refine contest techniques through research and analysis of results.

Samples. Samples have become an important part of sales promotion. Samples fall into two categories: those given by a manufacturer or producer and those given by a retailer. If you were asked to recall samples that you received from manufacturers, you might mention soap, toothpaste, or other relatively inexpensive items. The manufacturer or producer is motivated to give small samples in order to encourage prospective buyers to try a product. Some people are reluctant to switch brands or try a new product, but a free sample can be used effectively in overcoming such reluctance.

Most manufacturers distribute samples by mail, with an accompanying flier prepared by the advertising department to present product information and highlight selling points. Samples also may be distributed by sales representatives, at exhibitions, or at the point of purchase. Perhaps a soft drink company will set up a booth in a local supermarket to give shoppers small cups of the product.

What samples have you received from local retailers recently? Chocolates at a local candy store, slivers of cheese at a cheese store, or miniature sausages in a delicatessen are possible examples. Retailers provide samples in the hope of achieving immediate sales.

If samples are to be an effective promotional device, they should be given to as many people as possible. Needless to say, free samples are an expensive form of promotion. The marketer also should recognize that samples are effective only when the product distributed is superior to competitive products and the consumer can recognize that superiority without much difficulty.

Consumer Premiums. Trade premiums were discussed earlier in this chapter. While trade premiums are given to dealers, retailers, and distributors, **consumer premiums** are given to shoppers to encourage them to buy a product. **Containerized premiums** are prepackaged and distributed with the product itself, such as a free sticker inside a box of Cheerios or a miniature toy in a box of Cracker Jacks. Consumer premiums may be related to the product, for example, a cereal bowl with cereal, or they may not be related to the product at all. Firms may allow customers to obtain free mugs, T-shirts, or garden seeds in exchange for box tops, labels, or other proof of purchase.

Hundreds of items are used for the express purpose of getting sales through children. Bubble gum producers, for example, may give away pictures of Walt Disney characters with each package of gum. The marketer should exercise care to assure that children's premiums win the approval of parents. Otherwise, such premiums may arouse ill will.

Ideas for consumer premiums are limited only by the creative abilities of marketers. Premiums may be items for personal use or for the home, items which have a seasonal appeal, gifts that tie in with birthdays or anniversaries, items that are related to hobbies, or items of current interest. Gifts sometimes are offered to customers who watch a demonstration of a higher-priced product such as a major appliance or an automobile. Banks and savings and loan institutions may offer premiums to individuals purchasing savings certificates or adding a predetermined amount of money to savings accounts. Real estate developers selling property such as lakefront homes or retirement homes frequently offer premiums to invited individuals who are willing to tour the developed area.

Before any consumer premium or premium plan is put into effect, it should be pretested. Premiums may be tested in selected market areas to ascertain their popularity and pulling power. Another approach is to send a special group of investigators to interview typical customers and get their reactions to the premiums being considered. Chain stores sometimes test a premium in a few stores before adopting it as a promotion technique in all their stores. When a premium plan is being tested, it is recommended that at least 12 shopping days, including two weekends, be used for the test.

In addition to the popularity of the premium, the terms of the offer also should be examined. The marketer should be convinced that the distribution setup is right. In some cases, it may be found that consumers will not send for a featured premium for some reason or other. It is particularly important to ensure that consumers will meet the requirements of the offer. In one test, a company found it more effective to offer the premium for the return of two box tops and 50 cents in cash than to offer it for the return of four tops and no cash.

Attention also must be devoted to ways to bring premium offers to the attention of consumers. This may be accomplished in a number of ways including advertising, special copy on the package or package inserts, and point-of-purchase advertising. Some miscellaneous advertising factors include the following.

1. Do not exaggerate the premium or lead the customer to expect more than will be received.

2. Explain the offer in simple language.

3. If the premium is to be mailed, inform customers that 2 to 6 weeks should be allowed for delivery in order to minimize complaints.

4. Do not use the word *free* unless the premium is given absolutely free.

5. If a coupon has to be filled in with name and address, provide sufficient room and instruct consumers to print their names and addresses as plainly as possible.

6. Remind customers to use adequate postage when mailing box tops or tokens.

Since coupons and trading stamps may in some cases be viewed as methods to promote a premium plan, we shall turn our attention to these promotional devices. You should be aware that coupons and trading stamps frequently lead to price reduction or in other cases may be redeemed for cash.

Coupons. **Coupons** used as sales promotion devices entitle consumers to price reductions, usually for a limited time. The main purpose of coupons is to attract customers to the firms that offer them. Coupons tell consumers that they may get a bargain and should act right away to take advantage of the price reduction.

Coupons may be offered by retailers, distributors, or manufacturers. Retailers use coupons to achieve specific goals. For example, a supermarket may offer money-saving coupons on selected items to attract a greater number of shoppers. Sometimes a retailer accepts a coupon only if the customer spends a certain amount of money at one time. For example, the coupon may be valid with purchases of $10 or more.

Manufacturers and distributors often offer coupons to achieve two goals: to encourage consumers to try a product for the first time and then to persuade the consumers to purchase the product repeatedly.

The Nestle Company of White Plains, New York, distributes Taster's Choice, a freeze-dried coffee. The company placed ads in local newspapers across the country. Each ad contained a coupon worth 50 cents toward the purchase of the product. The company also packed in each jar of freeze-dried coffee a coupon worth 50 cents toward the purchase of another jar.

While retailers normally are compensated for handling coupons, some voice objections. Cou-

CLIPPING COUPONS AND CUTTING PRICES

The coupon craze that once centered around supermarkets and the food industry has spread to mass merchandising. Customers with coupons can receive discounts of over $100 for a variety of products ranging from appliances to lawn mowers in establishments such as Sears and Wards.

A. C. Nielson and Company has released a study which indicates that over 75 percent of all households use coupons. Why not offer discounts of a few dollars and call the promotion a sale? Some marketers believe that coupons have more impact. An ad containing a coupon seems to have extra appeal to customers. It's almost as if the coupon is saying: "Get the scissors and clip me; I can save you money!"

Unlike supermarkets, which redeem coupons and then are reimbursed by the product's manufacturer, other retailers aren't reimbursed for redeeming their own coupons. The coupons simply serve as price discount slips which the customer presents at the time of purchase. Customers can see the price reduction and savings. As a result, consumers are searching through newspapers and magazines for coupons.

It is difficult for retailers to cut prices for very long when inflation and interest rates are high. Coupons offer a short term method for stimulating customer demand. And customers respond to couponing. According to a recent Nielson survey of shoppers, 72 percent of the people questioned said they liked coupons "very much"; 23 percent said they liked them slightly; and 5 percent said they disliked them.

Source: Louise Cook, "Giant Foods Fights Coupon Surge," *Roanoke Times & World News*, Nov. 23, 1980, p. 12.

---

pons may be looked at as a nuisance to handle because of the clerical work. Some retailers believe that checkout lines move more slowly when cashiers are handed coupons. To combat this objection and promote harmony with the distribution channel, manufacturers and distributors often redeem their own coupons by mail. In fact, many newspapers carry a refunder's reference column on a weekly basis.

During recent years of inflation and escalating prices, coupons have become a widely accepted and frequently used promotion technique. Consumers like to believe they are getting a bargain, and people living on fixed incomes welcome the opportunity to save a few cents.

Trading Stamps. Trading stamps sometimes are used as a sales promotion device, but their popularity has waned in recent years. Trading stamps normally cost the selling firm 2 or 3 percent of gross sales. Retailers may offer trading stamps for the following reasons.

1. They believe that trading stamps help call attention to their stores or service establishments.

2. They believe that trading stamps make customers more loyal.

3. They believe that trading stamps help offset the price appeals of competing stores since they offer something in addition to merchandise or service.

Trading stamps, once a common sales promotion technique, lost some of their appeal as consumers clamored for lower prices instead of stamps. While some states permit the stamps to be redeemed for cash, other states allow the customer to redeem the stamps for merchandise only.

Merchandise redemption centers, once common even in medium-size cities, have virtually disappeared from downtown shopping areas and suburban shopping centers. Today, catalogs showing merchandise and listing the number of stamps needed to receive the merchandise are distributed by mail. The Sperry Hutchinson Company, one of the largest firms providing stamps to retailers, supplies merchandise redemption catalogs to customers on request.

Special Events. Special events or demonstrations for consumers can be held in many places on or off a firm's premises. They provide increased visibility, accessibility, and convenience appeal to customers. Virtually every small firm offering products or services to the public can find opportunities to exhibit and demonstrate its offerings. Well-tended booths or tables at community fairs or area events increase the range of prospects. If a product is noncompetitive with their stores, local shopping malls often welcome exhibits, especially in conjunction with seasonal promotions and holiday themes.

Here are a few examples of what can be done.

- An art gallery exhibits its paintings in local stores and restaurants.
- A weight reduction salon demonstrates techniques and shows how its courses help customers attain a healthy and attractive body tone.
- A tile shop exhibits ways to decorate the home or office through the imaginative use of tiles.
- A wedding salon conducts bridal fashion shows.
- A music store exhibits various musical instruments such as electric organs that are easily mastered for home use.

- A flower shop familiarizes people with various kinds of fresh and dried flowers and arrangements, showing how they can be used creatively for home display and table decorations.[5]

Many firms in today's competitive market look for opportunities to take their products and services directly to the homes of prospective customers. Thus, they need not rely on the traffic of passersby. Home contact can be initiated in a number of ways. A roofing contractor, for example, may drive through residential areas to spot homes that appear to have roofing needs. A friendly personal call makes the homeowner aware of the need, and he or she then is informed of the firm's service. Roofing samples may be shown, and the contractor also may provide references. A paint contractor, of course, may use the same technique.

Lawn-care services sometimes offer to give homeowners a free soil test to determine the acidity of their lawns. This opens the door to new prospects who may become regular customers. Various other firms have capitalized on the strategic concept of "meeting customers where they usually are." Being in the right place at the right time is effective in promoting sales. Sandwich shops have mastered this technique by utilizing a rolling cart to deliver sandwiches and coffee in commercial buildings.

Special events and demonstrations also are staged on the firm's premises. When a small interior decorating shop conducted a seminar called "Decorating the contemporary home," 75 local residents attended. Some, of course, became customers. An infants' wear shop sponsored a seminar on better care for babies. A well-known child psychologist and a pediatrician gave young parents advice on how to care for infants. Valuable goodwill was created for the shop. When a travel agency shows a series of travel films featuring tours of interest, a number of prospective customers usually are in attendance.

In some communities, organizations specialize in locating newcomers and welcoming them

CONTACT: Kate Walsh 744-2295

RELEASE: Immediate

CAPTION: Start the day off right having breakfast with Annie and Daddy Warbucks, at Carsons State Street store, September 17, and Carsons-Yorktown, September 24.

Annie and Daddy Warbucks, from the Candlelight Dinner Playhouse production, will sing your favorite songs from the hit musical while you enjoy breakfast at Carsons.

##

Figure 15-3. Special events like this "Carsons on Stage" promotion generate interest and excitement in the community.

to the community. One of these is the Welcome Wagon, while another is called Getting to Know You. Small firms that offer consumer goods or services can link themselves profitably to such organizations. An automotive shop might offer free car lubrication, a cleaning shop might present a "two for the price of one" coupon, and a hairstylist might give a free haircut, while a plumber might offer a $10 discount on the initial call. Almost every firm offering consumer products and services can reach out to new customers. After all, statistics bear out the fact that the United States is a "society on the move," and new families need services ranging from baby-sitting to legal advice. A full range of products may be needed periodically, and the firm that initially attracts this patronage may keep it.

Parties. The party plan originated as a brainchild of the Tupperware Corporation. The **party plan** works like this. A host or hostess is found who is willing to invite friends and neighbors to attend a party in his or her home for informal socializing and refreshments. Within this relaxed atmosphere, the sponsor's products or services are demonstrated briefly. The host or hostess receives a gift or a commission on sales—usually 15 percent—plus a discount on personal purchases. Frequently, the majority of the guests make purchases.

A company selling house plants at sponsored parties recently achieved average sales of $200 per party and conducted more than 150 parties a week within a city of 250,000.[6] The party plan sales concept is applicable to a wide variety of products and services. While parties are still given chiefly by women, it is not unusual for men to host parties. Retired couples with little cash and much leisure time also find that holding a sales party can be a profitable experience. Working couples with little time to socialize on the job may be interested in supplementing their income while enjoying the company of friends.

Signs. A firm's autos and trucks provide an opportunity for a "roving billboard" to carry pro-

motional messages on a daily basis. Various ingenious approaches have been devised by all types of firms to use their vehicles to publicize or dramatize their products and services. While some firms publicize their names, locations, and phone numbers, others decorate an entire side or back of a truck with lifelike illustrations of their products.

A toy truck has a huge balloon mounted atop. The balloon can be inflated or deflated with an air pressure mechanism installed in the vehicle. When the balloon is inflated, it depicts a message: "The Best Toys for Good Girls and Boys."

Grady's Pizza appears in 5 inch letters on each side of radio-dispatched autos. Below is the phone number called out from the receiver of a telephone.

Figure 15-4. This in-store promotion was prepared to promote investment dressing for women.

Figure 15-5. Signs containing the company name must be carefully planned to ensure consistency.

Trucks emblazed with the name Swallow Roofing carry an illustration of a roofer holding a complete roof over a miniature home.

Whatever the approach, the result is increased exposure to the public. Creative marketers will come up with innovative ideas. The firm's vehicles will carry the message throughout the community or trading area or across the country.

Some firms have found that "stick-ons" serve as a powerful sales device to draw repeat business. The firm installing an automatic garage door opener may use a stick-on near the inside switch. When the mechanism needs repair, the firm's name and telephone number reminds the customer to call. Service technicians working on home heating systems, plumbers, and exterminators often use this technique.

Displays. On the eighth floor of the downtown San Francisco store of Macy's California, tucked away behind the daily sales transactions and customer traffic, there are graphic designers at work whose efforts produce countless in-store posters and graphic elements that quickly spell out key merchandising messages to the customer. Without these designers, it is quite likely that a customer's shopping experience could well become a confusing or boring chore and that customers might not make the impulse purchases that graphic elements often generate.

Posters and banners become an important part of in-store promotions. They are used to announce themes, create an atmosphere, and add a communicative dimension to displays.

The Lure of Ireland—a vision of sprawling green meadows and heather on the hill, of twisting country lanes and clusters of quaint country villages—quickly unfolds before your mind's eye as a land where perhaps you've never been yet somehow instinctively seem to know, as if you had perchance just returned from a most memorable sojourn to the Emerald Isle. But if you had been in none other than Cleveland, Ohio, this past September, such a visit to Ireland was no farther away than a trip downtown to Higbee's, where for 2 weeks the Cleveland-based department store's annual international fair "The Lure of Ireland" lured many customers through its doors with much ado about all that is Ireland, from its crafts, clothes, and cookery to its woolens, weavings, beers, and bread.[7]

Norah Golden, a batik artist from Country Cork, Ireland, was commissioned to design mauve and green Irish banners for Higbee's main floor trim.

More than $1 million of merchandise was imported for the event. Irish manufacturers as well as domestic firms collaborated with Higbee's to create items specifically for the promotion. When the preview reception, a gala party for the Cleveland Institute of Music, opened the special promotion, it was no surprise that more than 1,500 people stood in awe of what they were witnessing.

Exhibits and displays such as John Mulligan's Pub, which featured dark beer, the Gerity Collection of fine Irish silver, Bewley's Irish Tea Shop, and Clare House, which featured charming Irish rooms, all required signs and graphics. Special events such as this have become an important part of promotional strategy for major stores. Such promotions aid in distinguishing between stores that carry virtually the same merchandise and selections.

When all the elements of promotion emerge under the same special event, the greatest impact from displays or special visual merchandising is achieved. Bloomingdale's committed $25 million to its blockbuster 1982 promotion "America the Beautiful." Multiple promotion activities were related to the theme: specially designed graphics and displays, lots of exhibits and demonstrations, and supporting advertising.

While smaller firms cannot be expected to duplicate such events, smaller-scale efforts may pay rich dividends. Besides their attractive price/impact ratio, such events offer the following marketing activities.

- Helping to attract customers to the store, keeping them in the store, and communicating a sales message to them while they are there
- Making other marketing activities more effective and efficient
- Meeting specific marketing objectives to appeal to selected market segments and to bring in new or infrequent shoppers
- Making the final contact with customers and helping to bridge the gap between the customer and store where sales people formerly filled that need, meeting public relations objectives, and giving the appearance of extra service in a time of diminished staffs
- Creating an energy level in the store that generates excitement, a feeling that something is always happening
- Helping to define a market position when thematically coordinated with other media
- Adding an extra dimension to advertising, helping to fight media clutter, and acting as a "medium" for any number of messages[8]

In-store displays including exterior window exhibits appear to be growing in importance. This is particularly true when the exhibits are planned around special promotions. Promotions such as those discussed here often get more press attention, thus creating even greater exposure.

But such promotions are not confined to retail stores. "I love New York" is a short, quick, snappy header for a campaign that has been a smash hit.[9] Utilizing advertising, public relations, direct mail, posters, and special displays, New York State has promoted itself successfully around the world as a tourist attraction. Organized "fam trips" in which the press from overseas was brought to New York to be familiarized with what New York State has to offer were conducted. In addition, New York took attractions overseas,

Figure 15-6. "I Love New York City" was part of a state-wide promotion campaign that helped to increase tourist and business interest in New York.

such as the casts from *Ain't Misbehavin'* and *A Chorus Line*. Cooperating airlines, hoping to cash in on the tourist influx, assisted in funding such attractions. The strategy was so successful that a new campaign soon followed: "Made in New York." The objective, of course, was to promote New York as a state in which to invest and from which to buy goods.

Advertising, personal selling, and sales promotion are not equally essential. Few firms could exist without personal selling, and many could not survive without advertising. While some might survive without sales promotion, it buttresses and strengthens a marketing operation and as a consequence magnifies a company's profits and successes.

Sales promotion gives direction to an advertising campaign, gives drive to a marketing endeavor, and gives enthusiasm to a sales force. It can speed up sales. Any sales organization feels the impact of promotional efforts. Enthusiasm is created, and enthusiasm can be a powerful tool to carry a sales force forward in sales at an ever increasing rate.

The astute marketer quickly recognizes that it takes a team effort to compete in today's business world. No single technique or device can by itself persuade a consumer to pick a particular product or service from the variety offered. For that reason, advertising, personal selling, and sales promotion should be used together for the greatest impact.

PUBLICITY

Publicity, like advertising, consists of nonpersonal messages which are carried by the mass media: newspapers, radio or TV, and magazines. Publicity differs from advertising in that the firm does not have to pay the media to carry the messages. The media are willing to carry such messages because of their interest appeal to readers or viewers. Most firms are eager to have another opportunity to communicate with the public, especially since they do not have to pay for sending the message.

Publicity can be favorable or unfavorable. The firm's objective is to disseminate publicity which advances its image and products and keeps the firm's name before the public. But sometimes publicity originates outside the firm and can be detrimental. When a manufacturer is sued for malpractices such as pollution, false advertising, or defective products, the public, including the firm's customers, may have its confidence shaken. If this occurs and the firm's position is that the attack is unjust, the objective of publicity may be to refute falsehoods and dispel general ignorance about the firm's operations or products. The asbestos industry, for example, seeks to give confidence to customers in regard to the future of the product, to ensure that the product is used safely by customers at every level, to put hazards in perspective, and to promote the product's positive attributes so that it is seen as socially acceptable.

Figure 15-7. The Macy's Thanksgiving parade is a highly successful publicity event.

Obtaining Publicity

Suppose you open a doughnut shop and are aware that thousands of lines of free publicity are available in many publications that reach your prospective customers. You must, however, take steps to obtain it. Chances are that you already are saying to yourself, "How does all this help me? Publicity means writing, and I'm not a writer, nor can I afford to hire a publicity writer."

You do not need highly refined writing skills. Many newspapers and other publications are looking for newsworthy articles. The question is this: What are the human interest aspects of your business? The ideas should be plentiful. Some examples include the following.

- The number of doughnuts consumed each month in the store
- How the doughnut first came about
- The background of the hole in the doughnut
- The changing pattern of consumption (now popular among adults but once a favorite only among children)
- The proprietor, the unrelated field from which the proprietor came, and why the proprietor finds the business fascinating

Any time a firm becomes a participant in community activities, publicity is sure to follow. Sponsoring Little League baseball or Scouts or lending a respected employee to head the local United Fund drive will draw favorable publicity and help create goodwill. Local newspapers, radio, and TV follow such events.

Often a promotional idea or event will be worthy of a news release. A sporting goods manufacturer or distributor may sponsor Olympic games for the handicapped. A bank may recognize the most civic-minded person for the month. A book publisher or book retailer may recognize the most promising students. Information about such events may be prepared in rough form without concern for the fine points of prose. Local newspapers are more concerned with substance than with form. Their own writers can refine and polish the story.

Unique displays, exhibits, or special events within the business provide ideas for press releases. An automobile dealership that displays antique autos, a bridal shop exhibiting wedding gowns from 50 years ago, and a pancake-eating contest sponsored by a local pancake house are examples. Open houses and plant tours usually are publicized by nonretail firms.

Firms also receive publicity when they provide factual material that is of general interest. A pharmacy may perform a public service by supplying factual information for a write-up on positive ways to avoid the flu during a local outbreak. An exercise salon tied in with a national physical fitness program by preparing an article outlining 25 steps to physical fitness. Financial counselors for a local savings and loan institution prepared an article on Individual Retirement Accounts.

Giant corporations and big business make use of such publicity techniques all the time. They consider publicity to be an important communication channel, and they strive to obtain as many lines of free publicity as possible.

Preparing Press Releases

Although newspapers have individuals who are well qualified to prepare press releases, marketers gain some advantages as a result of preparing their own messages. First, a well-prepared press release or feature article is almost sure to be published, often at an early date. Second, the firm can to some extent control the slant or image that it desires to project. The article, however, must be a human interest story if it is to be run as publicity. Newspapers charge for advertising space and as a consequence are reluctant to provide free space for an article that resembles an advertising message.

Some pointers for preparing press releases or feature articles follow.

- Supply a headline but be prepared to accept a substitute. Editorial work and space provided by the newspaper may dictate that fewer or more words be used.

- Identify yourself and your firm. The newspaper staff may wish to contact you for clarification or additional information.

- Indicate when the press release is to be run. "For immediate release" indicates that the paper may publish the article as soon as possible. "For release after May 1" signals an article with information about a timely event. Early publication will cause the story to lose much of its impact.

- A lively first paragraph is needed to capture the reader's interest. In a news story, remember the five Ws (who, what, when, where, and why) and the H (how) if it applies.

- Use lively, active verbs. Avoid adjectives whenever possible, since they represent editorializing and the paper is interested in factual copy.

- When quoting others, be sure that you have their permission. You may quote yourself. Readers will not be aware that you are the reporter, and quotes add interest to the material.

- Remember that newspapers are interested in brevity. Use the amount of space needed to tell your story, but do not ramble. Announcements are usually short, while feature stories naturally require more space.

After the press release is prepared, marketers strive for the widest circulation possible. Firms doing business on a national scale send releases to syndicated agencies or large newspapers across the country. Smaller firms send releases to newspapers within their trading areas.

Oral Publicity

A local banker was invited to address a seminar conducted for real estate brokers. An advertising account executive made a presentation at the bimonthly meeting of the local retailers associa-tion. The manager of a moving firm recalled humorous incidents that had occurred during her years of experience in moving people across the country at a meeting of the Business and Professional Women's Club. Such occurrences take place daily. While the speakers are selected on the basis of expertise, each has an opportunity to make an impression on the audience. If the impression is favorable, chances are that when members of the audience need the service or product discussed, they will remember the speaker and the firm.

Virtually every business has an interesting story to tell about services, products, or the care of products. Countless organizations are looking for speakers to present programs. Such meetings often are publicized by the local media, again giving the firm an opportunity to get its name before the public.

Other opportunities for oral publicity occur at meetings with shareholders, dealers, and suppliers. Firms may conduct plant tours for community groups, students, educators, and legislators. Tour leaders should possess oral communication skills and be well prepared so that a positive public image is conveyed. Some firms prepare motion pictures, color slides, or filmstrips, tapes, easel charts, posters, maps, and product exhibits to use in communicating with the external public.

Publicity from Actions

Firms throughout the country accept social and civic responsibilities in the same manner that organizations and individuals strive to do something for others. But there is no reason why such contributions should not be publicized. Actions speak loudly, but sometimes actions must be called to the attention of others.

All people have unfulfilled wishes. A New York department store decided to do something about it. A $5 purchase entitled each customer to submit his or her unfulfilled wish. Each month, the most interesting unfulfilled wish was selected to be fulfilled. One customer submitted the desire to visit a sister in Yugoslavia after a 15 year separation. An expense-paid trip was provided for the

Figure 15-8. In-house magazines, newsletters, and other publications create goodwill and provide information that leads to a favorable public opinion of the firm.

Yugoslavian sister to visit this country. When a couple wished for a honeymoon that they never had had, they were given an expense-paid trip to the Bahamas. In these cases, the publicity value exceeded the costs involved.

Some firms have received publicity as a result of their efforts to formulate a "jury" to tell them what is good about their products or services. Other firms have relied on these juries to provide advice. A department store may appoint a "college board" to advise management on college apparel needs. A flour manufacturer formulated local "homemakers councils" to judge the best ways to use its products. Obviously, juries and consumer councils publicize the firms by word of mouth.

Some firms have instituted "hot line" programs in which the customer can receive prompt responses to complaints. Some automobile manu-

facturers have instigated such programs in an attempt to make significant inroads into the markets of less responsive competitors. It probably is easier to resell to the previously dissatisfied customer than to gain a new customer. Chances are that the dissatisfaction can be resolved and that the firm will be able to regain its goodwill.

Printed Publicity

You probably have seen small magazines that firms send to customers and prospects. While such publications may contain ads and resemble direct-mail advertising, chatty reading material also is included. Most major airlines publish such materials, rural electric cooperatives send their magazines to customers monthly, and various manufacturers publish an in-house newsletter. A Wisconsin firm issues a postal card-size magazine each week, while an Ohio firm issues a 6 by 9 inch magazine, enclosing one with each monthly invoice. Such publications attract reader interest and create goodwill.

When asked why in-house magazines were distributed, one executive responded by saying that they have a communication function: to develop good public relations. Public relations as viewed by firms involves informing the public of activities and policies and providing other information that will create favorable public opinion.

Because public relations is a communication function, it should be undertaken to achieve specific communication goals. The key question in any publicity endeavor is, What does the firm want to be known for? The focus of in-house publications then may be directed toward the achievement of that objective. Other forms of publicity also can be coordinated to achieve the goal.

The key question should be reviewed periodically since the goal may change. The Phillips 66 Company at one time wanted to be known as an aggressive, competitive sales leader in the petroleum industry. Later, in a direct attempt to stave off criticism of the oil industry and the company, the objective changed to becoming known as a company seeking new energy sources. The communication goals of firms may differ and may include correcting mistaken impressions, announcing new policies, generating interest among the financial community, and attracting new personnel.

Thus, the role of publicity is to present information to advance the interests of an organization. The publicity may appear in written or oral form or may originate through the actions of the firm. Internal communication is designed to let employees know what management is thinking as well as to facilitate communication in the reverse direction. External communication enhances the image of the organization in the minds of various segments of the public: customers, suppliers, stockholders, and the community at large.

MANAGING THE COMMUNICATIONS MIX

In Chapters 13 and 14, advertising and personal selling were explored. In the early part of this chapter, sales promotion, the remaining component of the promotional submix, was discussed. Finally, the various forms of publicity in the public relations submix have been reviewed. When the promotional submix and the public relations submix are carefully planned and coordinated, the marketing communications program becomes more effective.

A Synergistic Effort

The term *synergistic* means working together for the benefit of all contributors. Advertising, personal selling, sales promotion, and publicity each have a synergistic function. Thus, in large firms, personnel from several departments must work together in planning promotion campaigns and planning ways to project a desired image for the firm. Trade shows, for example, must be advertised through the media or by direct mail. At such a trade show, personal selling is important. At the same time, the sponsor of the show will be concerned about projecting an image which depicts a responsible firm capable of satisfying customers as well as meeting social responsibilities. To ensure an effective marketing communications program, certain rules should be followed.

Rules for Effective Communications

Individuals preparing ads, selling products, planning promotions, or writing press releases can profit from sticking to some basic rules.

1. Remember What Your Product or Service Means to Your Customers, Not to You. Ask yourself why and how customers benefit from your product or service. Then tell them. A good way to get ideas is to ask loyal customers why they buy your products or patronize your firm. Their reasons are probably appropriate for others.

2. Speak or Write the Customers' Language. Business personnel and customers usually speak separate languages. Young people and old people rely on totally different terminologies, as do lawyers and clients, engineers and musicians. Speak the customers' language. It is the only way to communicate with them.

3. Keep Your Messages Short. Customers are busy people. Jobs, families, health and financial concerns, education, community responsibilities, social commitments, hobbies, and the pursuit of leisure activities are constantly tugging at their attention. They simply do not have time to read a sales letter that is as long as an income tax form. Nor do they have time to spend hours with numerous sales reps each day. Usually, the marketer's proposition is simple. You want to alter consumer behavior, usually buying behavior. Tell them what the reasons are and ask for the order.

4. Know Your Product or Service. You are asking prospective customers to respect your offering enough to put down money for it. Therefore, you should respect it enough to be able to tell them about it through written or oral communication channels. "It's new." (So what?) "It's better." (Better than what?) "It's different." (Better or worse?)

Vague terminology is misleading, and people must be given specific reasons why your product or service is of value. Communicators must be prepared to communicate.

5. Know Your Customers. The best sales letter ever written will sell nothing if it is delivered to someone who moved away 2 years ago. If you advocate gun control when attempting to sell store fixtures to the owner of a gun shop, you will jeopardize your position. Advertising messages, sales presentations, sales promotion events, and publicity should be geared to the desired target group.

6. Ask for Action. Except in cases in which ads or publicity are for goodwill purposes only, always ask for action and make it easy for customers to take action. Telephone numbers in ads, point-of-purchase displays, stamped envelopes, and oral requests for orders enable customers to respond promptly and conveniently.

KEY POINTS SUMMARY

- Sales promotion includes activities other than personal selling, advertising, and publicity that stimulate consumer purchasing and dealer effectiveness.

- Planning and coordination of sales promotion activities designed to coincide with other marketing communications can be important. Thus, frequent planning sessions with the advertising and sales departments are necessary for personnel in the sales promotion department.

- Promotional activities may be classified into two categories: those which are designed to stimulate the efforts of sales people, middlemen, or franchised dealers and those which are designed to stimulate buying by the ultimate consumer.

- Industrial shows, trade shows, and professional or scientific shows are the three kinds of shows at which goods and services are displayed. Each differs somewhat in function.

- Retailers appear to be favorably inclined to stock products and provide adequate display space to manufacturers or distributors that create consumer excitement.

- Sales promotion can speed up sales, give direction to an advertising campaign, give enthusiasm to a sales force, and in general, give drive to a marketing endeavor.

- Publicity consists of nonpersonal messages. However, it differs from advertising in that the firm does not have to pay the media to carry the messages.

- Virtually every business has an interesting story to tell. By furnishing a speaker to target groups or organizations, a firm can be sure that when the audience needs the service or product discussed, they will remember the speaker and the firm.

- Publicity stems from actions, and it allows firms that accept social and civic responsibilities to create a favorable image and establish goodwill.

- Public relations is a communicative function and should be designed to meet specific communication goals. Over a period of time, however, such goals may change. Therefore, they should be reviewed periodically.

KEY TERMS AND CONCEPTS

consumer premiums	professional or scientific shows
containerized premiums	publicity
coupons	sales promotion
industrial shows	trade premiums
party plan	trade shows
price-oriented promotion	

DISCUSSION QUESTIONS

1. Describe the relationships and the differences between the following factors.

a. sales promotion

b. advertising

c. publicity

d. personal selling

2. Assume that you are employed by a retail store located in a local shopping mall. The association of retailers is planning a special mallwide sale. A carnival atmosphere is being planned, and shoppers will be entertained in the mall's indoor amphitheater by jugglers, magicians, clowns, and other carnival attractions. The retailers would like to agree on a theme and link advertising, personal selling, sales promotion, and publicity to that theme.

After thinking about the event, suggest a theme. (Thought-nudger—"Like MAGIC—Prices Come Tumbling Down!") Discuss practical ideas for advertising, personal selling, sales promotion, and publicity which will have a synergistic effect.

3. Do you believe that sales promotion is important in selling automobiles, real estate, and other expensive products? Why or why not?

4. If a firm prepares a news release about an improved product and specifically points out that the superior features of the product when compared with competitive brands, why would a newspaper be reluctant to accept the press release?

5. Trading stamps have lost some of their appeal, while coupons have become more popular. Why has this occurred?

6. In the past 5 years, the trade show and exposition industry has emerged as the fastest growing segment in marketing. Discuss the reasons why this has happened.

7. "Say yes to Michigan." "Wander Indiana." "I love New York." Why are such themes evolving? Why are state and local government units willing to expend millions of dollars for such promotions? If you were the commissioner of a state's tourist promotion agency, how would you defend such expenditures?

NOTES

1. Adapted from Betsy Morris, "Big PR Blitz Is Shaping Up Halloween." Reprinted by permission of *Wall Street Journal,* © Dow Jones & Company, Inc., May 10, 1983, pp. 37–43. All rights reserved.
2. William G. Mee, "How to Use the Trade Show as a Marketing Tool," *Creative,* February 1979, p. 82.
3. Hale N. Tongren and James P. Thompson, "The Trade Show in Marketing Education," *Journal of Marketing Education,* vol. 3, no. 2, Fall 1981, p. 31.
4. Ibid., p. 31.
5. For a more complete list, see David D. Seltz, *Handbook of Innovative Marketing Techniques,* © 1981 Addison-Wesley, Reading, Mass., 1981, pp. 20–21. Reprinted with permission.
6. Ibid., p. 3.
7. Adapted from P. K. Anderson, "Higbee's Promotes the Lure of Ireland," *Visual Merchandising,* vol. 113, no. 1, January 1982, p. 31.
8. Adapted from Anne Estes, "How Retailers Promote, Entertain," *Advertising Age,* April 6, 1981, pp. 47–48.
9. Bruce Kane Garson, "The Marketing of New York State," *Advertising World,* December 1981, pp. 9–14.

APPLICATIONS/CASES

APPLICATION 11: A PROBLEM OF PRODUCT OR PLACE: BREAKFAST OF CHAMPIONS

After reading about a new marketing campaign for Wheaties cereal, Frances Golden, the owner of a restaurant named Breakfast of Champions, wrote a letter to General Mills, Incorporated, offering to let them film commercials at her Brewster, Massachusetts, establishment.

General Mills did not accept the offer. Instead, it demanded that the owner change the name of her year-old restaurant. General Mills, owner of the trademark to the phrase "breakfast of champions," turned down the restaurateur's request for $800, the amount she claims changing the name will cost her.

a. Does using a trademark phrase such as "breakfast of champions" as an establishment's name constitute a violation of the Wheaties slogan?

b. Why would a giant corporation like General Mills object to a small local restaurant using the name?

c. Do you believe that General Mills was justified in refusing to pay for the cost of changing the restaurant's name?

APPLICATION 12: A CONSUMER'S PROBLEM: WINNING A CONTEST

In 1981, Northwest Airlines, Incorporated, trumpeted a contest with a difference: the prize. "Win a jet to Florida and take 92 friends along!" shouted bold black headlines in advertisements run by the airline in midwestern newspapers.

"Take your relatives," the ad suggested. "Take your co-workers. Take your church group, lodge, or neighbors."

Contestants had only to send in an entry form. The grand and only prize was the use of an entire Boeing 727 jet for the trip to Fort Lauderdale, airline transportation home, and three nights in a luxury hotel for all 93 people.

After tax experts pointed out that winners would face a sizable tax bite, the airline decided to add $15,000 in cash. Even so, a tax expert estimated that a married couple with two children and a $25,000 income could wind up with an additional tax bill of $17,000, leaving them $2,000 in the red after using the airline's cash gift, which also was taxable.

If the winner took just the family (a couple and two children), a substantial amount of money would have been left after taxes. In that case, Northwest Airlines would make money, too. Contest rules prohibited the winner from selling any part of the prize. Thus, the airline would sell, and take revenue for, any unused seats.

a. What objectives do you believe that Northwest Airlines, Incorporated, hoped to achieve?

b. Why would people be motivated to enter the contest?

c. Do you believe the ad heralding the contest led contestants to expect more than would be received?

d. In your opinion, should the ad copy have warned customers about the potential tax bite?

APPLICATION 13: SALES ADVICE: SOUND OR FAULTY?

Carl Villalon, a recent community college graduate, has just landed a job as a sales representative for the Ebersole Office Equipment Company. He has always wanted to try his hand at field sales work, and he believes that he is fortunate to have the opportunity. While the salary is low, Ebersole provides a lucrative commission based on sales volume.

His customers will be banks, savings and loan institutions, insurance companies, accounting firms, and law offices. He recognizes the value of using his time in the most productive manner. Other experienced sales reps with the firm have offered the following pointers.

1. Call only on customers with whom you expect to make a sale.

2. If a customer is expected to place a huge order, be generous with the amount of time devoted to that customer. If only a small order is expected, minimize the amount of time devoted to the customer.

3. Avoid stubborn or argumentative prospects to the extent possible.

4. After a customer's needs have been fulfilled, there is little reason to continue to make contacts.

5. Follow-up is important for your largest customers. Don't worry about getting back to the smaller accounts; they can always call you back again if they really need you.

After thinking about these five pointers provided by his fellow sales representatives, Villalon is a little concerned. These pointers certainly seem to be contradictory to the principles he studied in a course in professional selling at the local community college. But why should Villalon doubt the advice given him by these experienced sales representatives?

a. How would you answer Villalon's question and respond to his doubts?

CASE 12: COMBATING ADVERSE PUBLICITY: JOYCE BEVERAGES OF ILLINOIS

Rochester Samuel likes Seven-Up and likes bargains. When he finds Seven-Up at bargain prices, he buys it. However, the last two times he bought Seven-Up on sale, he got more than he bargained for.

A newspaper quoted Samuel as saying, "I bought some on sale in January or December and found some mold in one of the bottles after I had opened it." The news article continued with the following story. Alarmed by the furry, floating growth, Samuel contacted the county health department. "They said there wasn't anything they could do about it except send it to the state for tests," Samuel said, "and they weren't sure how fast that would be."

Samuel then decided to call the distributor, Joyce Beverages of Illinois. "A couple of days later a representative called, apologized, and gave me a complimentary case of Seven-Up."

Convinced that the mold was just one of those things that occasionally happens, Samuel continued to buy Seven-Up. "It's supposed to be the best pop on the market," he said. "I thought it was safe. You know, it isn't supposed to have any artificial ingredients and doesn't have caffeine."

For several months after the mold incident, Samuel and his wife would check each bottle carefully before drinking it. "We never did find anything else, so we were sure it was just one of those things."

Soon they quit checking.

Then they bought five cartons of Seven-Up on sale. "Last night, we were drinking a couple of bottles of it, and my wife said to me, 'What's that in your bottle?' I stopped drinking and looked inside and saw a fly and two mosquitoes," Samuel said.

The next morning, he took the bottle and its occupants to a local biochemical laboratory to have it examined. "I looked at it and told him it looked like insects," said Dr. Joyce Yeast. "I thought one looked like a mosquito and the other like part of a fly." However, she said that there were not any tests she could run on them to get further information.

The news made Samuel depressed. "It makes me angry. Why me? Here we'd been checking faithfully, and then it happens again. And what's worse is that it always happens to me and never to my wife!"

Samuel contacted the health department and the Seven-Up distributors again. The newspaper contacted Joyce Beverages of Illinois. The Seven-Up representative would not comment on the record to the newspaper but assured the caller that a representative would be in touch with Samuel, and he soon was.

"They just called," Samuel said. "The guy said he was sorry about what happened and said he would send a representative by and give me some more complimentary beverages."

Samuel also said he plans to continue buying Seven-Up. "At least you can see inside of their bottles to tell if something is in them," he said.

This story was carried by a newspaper located in a Standard Metropolitan Statistical Area which claims more than 100,000 readers.

Adapted from Mary Ann Flick, "Twin City Man Finds Some Other Additives in Caffeine-Free Soda," *The Pantagraph*, Bloomington, Ill., May 12, 1982, p. A–7.

a. Evaluate the refusal of Joyce Beverages of Illinois to speak with the newspaper representative on the record. Remember that the contact was made before the newspaper published the article.

b. Could Joyce Beverages have taken action to change the slant of the article so that it would have been less damaging to the firm's reputation? If your response is yes, describe the nature of such action.

c. Now that the article has appeared in the newspaper, what would you recommend as a marketing communications objective for Joyce Beverages?

d. What publicity techniques would you recommend that Joyce Beverages use?

e. Suppose Joyce Beverages decides to begin an institutional advertising campaign. What theme or themes would you recommend?

CASE 13: MARKETING COMMUNICATIONS: COLUMBIA'S BIG *ANNIE* PROMOTION

"Our strategy is to say that this film is something special, an event, something you must see," said a Columbia Pictures executive. Thus began the promotion for what turned out to be one of the most expensive movies ever, *Annie*.

In 1982, Columbia Pictures announced that it was spending an additional $10 million on advertising, mainly for television commercials. "We don't want to seem like we're shoving this film down people's throats," said a marketing spokesperson. In the movie industry, even the most clever marketing plan cannot do more than attract an audience for the first few weeks. The all-important factor is word of mouth. But with the production and selling of films getting increasingly expensive, movie studios have turned to audience research, promotional tie-ins, and merchandising of film-related products to try to spread the risk.

Special screenings of the movie were shown to editors of national magazines before the film's release. More than 50 firms were licensed to produce over 350 *Annie* items including hand-painted ceramics and curly red stretch wigs. Companies like Sears, Roebuck and Company and the Mariott Corporation arranged tie-ins to give the movie additional free publicity. There was even an "Annie" ice-cream. Columbia received 6 to 10 percent of the wholesale price of "Annie" dolls, bedsheets, books, jeans, and the like.

Before the film's release, public TV stations showed a 1 hour documentary on the making of *Annie* as a kickoff to 125 "charity" premieres which were expected to raise as much as $10 million for the stations.

Preliminary research showed that kids and grandparents wanted to see *Annie,* but practically no one in between. Thus, Columbia worked on a marketing strategy called the "want to see" factor, cutting across all age groups. The sound track album was released for listeners at more than 100 rock stations, and Columbia sponsored an *Annie*-related college tour.

Before the first paying patron had seen the movie, planning for *Annie 2* was under way. A Columbia spokesperson said, "We have to, before our stars grow out of the role."

Adapted from Stephen J. Sansweet, "Columbia Hoping Big "Annie" Promotion Will Turn Costly Film into Phenomenon." Reprinted by permission of *Wall Street Journal,* © Dow Jones & Company, Inc., May 12, 1982, p. 29. All rights reserved.

a. Explain how the synergistic approach to marketing communications has been used by Columbia Pictures.

b. Analyze the marketing communications program depicted in this case and classify the various activities into the promotional submix or the public relations submix.

c. Why would Columbia Pictures choose to spend most of the $10 million advertising allocation for TV commercials? Why shouldn't more of the allocation have been spent for magazine or newspaper ads? Explain.

d. Why were firms like Sears, Roebuck and Company and the Marriott Corporation willing to sponsor tie-ins?

e. Why would Columbia Pictures have been willing to allow public TV stations to sponsor premieres that raised millions of dollars for such stations?

f. Why were special screenings shown to magazine editors before the film's release?

UNIT 7

7

PEOPLE

CHAPTER
16
PEOPLE AT WORK IN MARKETING

In the late 1970s and early 1980s, Montgomery Ward, the nation's fifth largest retailer, saw its competitive edge in danger of being shattered. Net sales declined over a 5 year period, and the company consistently showed a net loss. Several innovations were tried in an attempt to retain the company's competitive status in retailing. A primary feature in the company's improvement strategies was to focus on employees as a way to make Wards a winner. L. Edward Lewis, executive vice president for human resources, wrote the following memo to all employees.

Our employees are the key to our success. People are the critical resource that makes a difference in a company. They buy the merchandise we carry, build the bricks and mortar into our stores, plan our advertising, and sell the merchandise to our customers. Our people *can* differentiate us from the competition—if they're well-trained, enthusiastic, dedicated.

We need a balance of all types of people to reflect the diversity of our society and of our customers.

There is great emphasis on identifying winners and losers. It's essential because we desperately need winners now to bring our company through the turnaround.

What do we mean by "winners"? A winner is well-trained, experienced, dedicated, and working with purpose and direction toward a meaningful end. A winner isn't a genius, but he or she has to be committed to respond effectively to problems as they occur.

Winners become identified through their hard work and their response to change. They are people who are willing to stand up and challenge the status quo and point out ways in which the company can improve. Ward's management is seeking those people who are ready to help bring about change and help Wards through the turnaround.

A loser, on the other hand, is not necessarily incompetent. He or she may be a capable person who lacks commitment and doesn't respond with the best he or she can offer. A loser doesn't challenge bosses, doesn't challenge the system, isn't willing to go the extra mile, work the extra hours to accomplish something. A loser isn't willing to excel. We're really talking about a winning attitude, as well as ability.

A winner has to be resolute and willing to take risks, take unpopular stands if he or she believes it's right. A reasonable amount of risk-taking is necessary. Winners may have bad days and make mistakes but if you look at their records over time, winners always come to the top because they *learn* and *respond* to challenge.

A successful large organization requires people of many backgrounds and interests, with many strengths and weaknesses, who work together as a team. We need each other and we must reach out across departmental lines to do the best job for the company. The importance of the team concept—besides the camaraderie—is that we can help each other cover and compensate for our weaknesses and build on each other's strengths. This is a true and honest synergism that will help make Wards a winner.

If Wards loses, there will be no individual winners. If Montgomery Ward wins, we are all winners.[1]

Lewis recognized the importance of people in determining business success or failure. For Montgomery Ward to be successful, major strategic changes had to be made—modernizing some stores, closing some stores, eliminating selected product lines, and reducing the number of upper-level managers—but the best way to make the company a competitive winner was through its employees.

THE PEOPLE COMPONENT IN THE MARKETING MIX

General Halftrack from the Beetle Bailey comic strip shown in Figure 16-1 on page 446 summarizes a common complaint when he concludes, "But we can't seem to do a thing with people." It is easy to imagine a similar line being said by sales people, employees in a customer complaint department, frustrated supervisors, and marketing managers. However, we disagree with the General because if people are the competitive edge to business success, marketers must learn how to deal with them.

People are important to the effective management and profitable operation of any business. Loyal, pleasant, and productive employees are an organization's greatest asset. They can make or break a company. People are especially important in marketing, for marketing is a people occupation. There are very few jobs in marketing that do not require contact with other human beings. The vast majority of people employed in marketing engage in direct face-to-face contact with customers or clients, vendors, the public through various media, distributors, or other company representatives, or are placed in situations in which they determine people's needs or wants. The quality of these person-to-person contacts can have an important effect on the outcome of the transaction. A trustworthy, competent, friendly sales rep can earn repeat business for a company for years to come. Conversely, an indifferent rep who cannot be trusted to follow through on orders or does not provide appropriate services can lose a client forever.

The people component sometimes is thought of as the fifth **P** in the marketing mix. Thus, managers often analyze marketing activities in terms of **P**roduct, **P**rice, **P**lace, **P**romotion, and **P**eople (or **P**ersonnel). Sharp managers realize that the success of marketing efforts is determined largely by the effectiveness of people in planning and implementing appropriate strategies. Effective marketing managers thus give a great deal of attention to the people aspect of the marketing mix.

Teamwork

A firm or department that creates a healthy atmosphere of respect and cooperation in which employees feel part of a team effort has the advantage over a company or work unit that has no such "teamwork" atmosphere. Studies consistently

Figure 16-1. A frustration: What to do with people?

show that the quality of the work environment—pleasant surroundings, friendly co-workers, and harmonious relationships between supervisors and employees—is extremely important to a person's satisfaction with his or her job. In one study of workers' attitudes and job satisfaction, a large percentage of the employees polled indicated that working as a team member was very important to them.[2] The U.S. Air Force also found a significant positive correlation between the productivity of aircraft mechanics and their friendliness with fellow crew members and supervisors.[3] A friendly job atmosphere in which employees function as a team apparently enhances worker productivity greatly.

However, this kind of atmosphere does not just happen. It is fostered by management and carried through an entire organization in a chain reaction. To cite a very basic example, suppose management is able to motivate the production staff to produce a quality product on schedule. Pride in workmanship is experienced by the production workers, who eagerly pass on their enthusiasm to the sales staff. If the sales reps sincerely believe that their product is excellent and will meet the needs of their clients, they will sell more products and in turn satisfy more customers. If more products are sold, the company should realize a larger profit. The theory implies that management will pass that profit on to members of the production and sales teams, who, because of higher wages and increased commissions, will be motivated to perform better. Such a creative atmosphere is self-perpetuating. Figure 16-2 on page 448 illustrates this type of atmosphere.

Unfortunately, this type of chain reaction also can work negatively. If management fails to motivate the production staff, an inferior product may be produced. If the sales staff realizes that it is an inferior product and is similarly unmotivated by management, they will lack the spark of enthusiasm that is needed to sell it to the consumer. If few consumers buy the product, profits will be low or nonexistent, and management will be disappointed. They will pass this disappointment on to the production and sales staffs, who will continue to perform in a less than satisfactory fashion. This type of unsatisfactory atmosphere also is illustrated in Figure 16-2.

Pride in Work

A major way in which people view themselves is through their work. People are cashiers or marketing managers or assistant buyers or travel agents. Or they may say that they work at Friendly's Restaurant, for Nordbert Transportation, at Dayton's, or for Piedmont Airlines. The point is that a part of people's **self-concept**—the way in which they view themselves and the way in which they think others see them—is identified with their jobs or occupations.

It is important for supervisors and managers to recognize this important concept. If employees are proud of their work and the products or services they are marketing, the chances for increased productivity are improved vastly. If a person is not necessarily proud to be working for a particular company or at a particular job, the chances are quite good that his or her performance will be mediocre.

Pride in work often is associated with an individual's goals. If a person feels that his or her goals are being met, that person probably is proud of the job and is doing quite well at it. To enhance productivity, companies should work with employees to identify their occupational goals and then counsel them appropriately.

Individual goals often can be coordinated with company goals. To facilitate this process, many medium-size and large firms have added to their staffs an executive with the title of human-resource manager. People involved with **human-resource development** work with employees to establish career goals and then develop plans and programs to help attain those goals. Often human-resource developers also are involved with recruiting and selecting new employees, training employees, structuring salary and incentive systems, counseling employees and supervisors, and appraising employee performance.

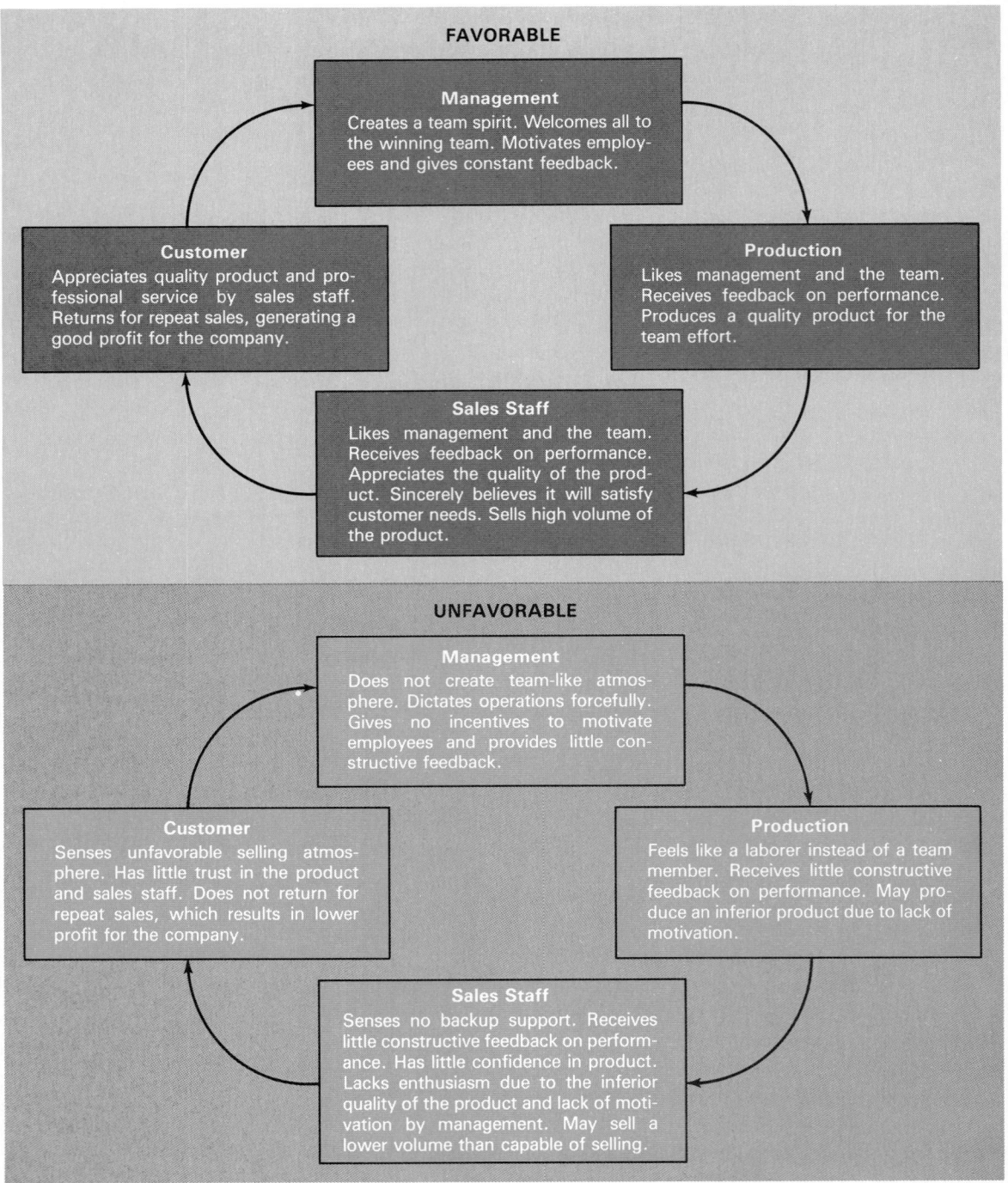

FAVORABLE

Management
Creates a team spirit. Welcomes all to the winning team. Motivates employees and gives constant feedback.

Production
Likes management and the team. Receives feedback on performance. Produces a quality product for the team effort.

Customer
Appreciates quality product and professional service by sales staff. Returns for repeat sales, generating a good profit for the company.

Sales Staff
Likes management and the team. Receives feedback on performance. Appreciates the quality of the product. Sincerely believes it will satisfy customer needs. Sells high volume of the product.

UNFAVORABLE

Management
Does not create team-like atmosphere. Dictates operations forcefully. Gives no incentives to motivate employees and provides little constructive feedback.

Production
Feels like a laborer instead of a team member. Receives little constructive feedback on performance. May produce an inferior product due to lack of motivation.

Customer
Senses unfavorable selling atmosphere. Has little trust in the product and sales staff. Does not return for repeat sales, which results in lower profit for the company.

Sales Staff
Senses no backup support. Receives little constructive feedback on performance. Has little confidence in product. Lacks enthusiasm due to the inferior quality of the product and lack of motivation by management. May sell a lower volume than capable of selling.

Figure 16-2. A creative company atmosphere (top) is self-perpetuating. An unsatisfactory atmosphere (bottom) creates a downward spiral.

Of course, most firms that rely heavily on marketing to achieve success, especially smaller retail, wholesale, and service companies, cannot afford to employ a full-time human-resources development staff. All firms must rely on people to be successful. Thus, the application of some basic principles of employee motivation and human relationships, whether this is the responsibility of the owner or manager of a small business, a human-resource manager, or a marketing department or unit supervisor, should have top priority when a firm sets goals for business success.

MOTIVATION TO WORK

When marketing managers are asked about the types of employees who have worked for them over the years, they are likely to give a variety of answers. They are apt to talk about a certain type of person who really hustled, kept busy, and was constantly looking for ways to improve his or her marketing techniques. Some are impressed by sales associates who arrive at work early to see that the merchandise is adequately stocked and the selling area satisfactorily arranged. Some describe the ad assistant who really dug in, learned the trade, and moved quickly into positions of increased responsibility.

But one also is likely to hear about an employee who often arrived late, talked incessantly on the phone, did as little as possible, and spent much time waiting for a break. Unfortunately, managers may describe a rep who could not be trusted to service accounts properly, often did not follow up on orders, or spent prime time on the golf course.

Why do people act as they do? What do they seek out of life? Why are some aspiring and others not? What do most people want from their jobs? How can people be motivated to be more productive?

Motivation is a key word in the effective development and management of people. It is defined as the internal drive to accomplish a particular goal. People who are highly motivated

want to do their assigned jobs and do them well. Effective managers understand what motivates their employees and provide appropriate incentives to spark the internal drive that makes their employees perform to the best of their abilities.

Several theories of motivation have been developed and tested by psychologists and researchers, helping people understand what makes both employees and managers in marketing occupations act as they do. Maslow, McClelland, and Herzberg each developed theories that help students of marketing understand why employees want to work.

Maslow

Maslow's theory is based on the fact that people have five categories of needs which must be satisfied in a hierarchical order. That is, the needs of the first category must be at least partially satisfied before those in the second, and so on. When one category of needs is satisfied, it no longer acts as a sustained effective motivator. In Figure 16-3 on page 450, the categories of needs are presented along with examples. Note that the first need is for food, clothing, and shelter. After that need is fulfilled, people need safety and security through such things as adequate working conditions, good insurance, and job security. After people have realized these needs, they want to feel that they "belong" socially. Social needs may be satisfied on the job or through joining social organizations.

When people are secure socially, they seek esteem. They want to be recognized by other people. They may compete for promotions and awards, build their reputation as superior workers, or do volunteer work. Respect, recognition, and social status become motivators.

The highest category of need is **self-actualization,** or realizing one's highest potential. If one is truly self-actualized, all other needs have been met, and one is secure and totally accepting of oneself and others. Such a person is inventive and creative and feels quite satisfied with life and work. Often this need is met at work through creative accomplishments, completing challeng-

HIERARCHY OF NEEDS

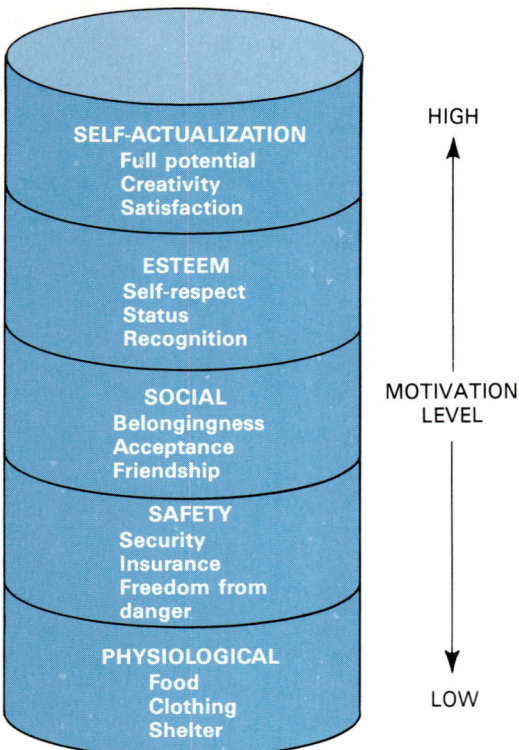

SELF-ACTUALIZATION
Full potential
Creativity
Satisfaction

ESTEEM
Self-respect
Status
Recognition

SOCIAL
Belongingness
Acceptance
Friendship

SAFETY
Security
Insurance
Freedom from
danger

PHYSIOLOGICAL
Food
Clothing
Shelter

HIGH

MOTIVATION
LEVEL

LOW

Figure 16-3. Maslow's hierarchy of needs.

ing assignments, or fulfilling career goals. Sometimes people achieve self-actualization through a combination of job, family, volunteer, and leisure activities.

Maslow's theories have practical application when it is realized that people do not work just to provide themselves with the necessities of life. People also need to find a way to gain social acceptance, self-esteem, and self-actualization. Often their jobs are one vehicle for achieving these additional important needs. It is interesting that if lower needs are met, factors identified with those needs, such as better wages, fringe benefits, and good working conditions, have only a slight motivating effect. Management needs to recognize this and find better ways to meet social, esteem, and creative needs, provided, of course, that basic and safety needs already have been met.

Mark Hoffman is the vice president of advertising for a small sales promotion firm in Arlington, Ohio. He began his career as a copy editor 15 years ago. The president of the company has done a great job keeping Mark motivated over the years. He periodically increased Mark's responsibility and gave him appropriate recognition. Changes in position have occurred: from copy editor to head copy editor to assistant in public relations to head of public relations to an associate in marketing research to assistant vice president and finally to vice president of advertising. The salary and working conditions have been satisfactory. But what has really been gratifying for Mark is the freedom he has enjoyed to be creative in finding solutions to some challenging problems in the ad area. Mark feels good about his work and is proud that so many of his ideas have been used by the firm. According to Maslow's theory, Mark is self-actualized.

McClelland

According to psychologist David McClelland, nearly all people have an **achievement motive.** This means that when people are not required to think about anything in particular, they think about ways to accomplish something of value. People possess this achievement motive in varying degrees. Those who have strong achievement motives will set their own goals and enjoy accomplishing something significant. They have a high opinion of their value and normally work at peak efficiency. They do not need a great deal of supervision and are not especially motivated by money. Successful business people, sales reps, and managers often are found to have a high achievement motive. Those with low achievement motives usually work for the purpose of earning money and are usually protected in their job status.

Edna Soderquist is a highly motivated marketing representative for a publishing company. The company specializes in marketing self-improvement books dealing with physical fitness, weight control, becoming a better parent, becoming a better supervisor, getting along on the job, and so on. She calls primarily on retail bookstores in the Denver area. A new prospective market for Edna's products consists of human-resource development departments in companies in the Denver area at which a lot of training takes place. Although Edna earns a set salary with a small commission for new product sales and new accounts, she spends a great deal of time phoning customers to be sure shipments have arrived, checking on retail sales of her products in bookstores, trying to meet customer needs, and setting up appointments with prospective accounts. These activities are not specifically required by her employer, but Edna feels that they are valuable and helpful to future sales and customer goodwill. Edna has a strong achievement motive as defined by McClelland.

Herzberg

Frederick Herzberg determined that there are two sets of factors that affect people's behavior on the job: maintenance and motivation. Maintenance factors do not motivate people to work, but if they are withdrawn, employees become dissatisfied and less productive. Maintenance factors include working conditions, fringe benefits, company policies, supervision, and salaries. People take these factors for granted, considering them to be the basic rights and benefits essential to the job. These factors do not really motivate people to work harder but result in considerable dissatisfaction if they are withdrawn or reduced.

Motivational factors, on the other hand, encourage employees to work. They are benefits above the basic elements of a job. Examples include the feeling of achievement, recognition, and creativity associated with the work itself, responsibility, personal growth, and the prospect of advancement on the job. Herzberg's research also shows that if motivational factors are not present in job situations, employees who have never had them will not be dissatisfied.

Alison Kim is a satisfied and motivated worker. She is a baker and assistant manager for a small catering business in Mason City, Iowa. She is an excellent worker and helps uphold the good reputation of the business. As a means of showing appreciation to her and motivating her to continue effective work habits, Alison's manager nominated her for the "Young Caterer of the Year" award sponsored by the Iowa Hospitality and Restaurant Association. This nomination provided recognition and served as a motivating factor for Alison.

MANAGERIAL TECHNIQUES FOR MOTIVATION

If a person chooses to advance to a position as a supervisor or marketing manager, an important set of skills that must be acquired is associated with the ability to motivate employees. A great deal of the success of a marketing firm or department rests with the ability of the people within that unit to deal effectively with customers, vendors, and other segments of the public. In order to be successful, a supervisor must influence employees so that they become more positively motivated and contribute fully to the objectives of the marketing unit and the total organization.

Six psychologists or researchers have developed theories that explain how managers can motivate employees to work harder and produce more. If properly motivated, employees do work harder and are more satisfied with their jobs. As a result, the company or unit usually is more successful or profitable.

McGregor

According to psychologist Douglas McGregor, managers display two different and conflicting philosophies for motivating employees. **Theory X** assumes that employees do not like to work and have to be controlled, directed, and threatened with punishment in order to perform effectively. **Theory Y** assumes that people naturally want to work and can be motivated to perform through praise, reward, and trust. In McGregor's opinion, Theory Y managers are more effective than Theory X managers.

> **Theory X:** John, I'm tired of these deliveries constantly being late. If you can't do the job, I'll find someone else. Now tomorrow morning, you see to it that you've got that shipment to the Salem store by 9:00 a.m. You better have it unloaded by 10. Then call me. The Southwest store wants that produce by noon. Can you make it? I doubt it; I suppose I better plan to go with you. I'll bet I can find someone else who can get this job done right and on time, for a heck of a lot less money, too.

> **Theory Y:** John, the manager over at the Salem store needs that big shipment delivered by 9 and unloaded for "the rush" at 10. I know you can do it. There's also an order from Southwest. Take a look at it and see what you can do. Let me know if you need any extra help. Thanks, John, it's good to know I can depend on you.

Ouchi

Theory Z organizational style was introduced recently by William Ouchi. It includes the concept of participatory decision making, in which employees are asked to contribute ideas toward executive decision making. It also calls for long-term guaranteed employment, slow evaluation and promotion, and rotation of managers so that they do not become overly specialized.

"Our company is a family-type organization," said one manager who is part of a Theory Z organization. "Employees are invited to small group meetings where they have the opportunity to contribute ideas toward improving company operations and other important decisions. These meetings produce a lot of quality ideas and tend to 'grease the way' so that employees more readily accept the decisions that are eventually made."

Gellerman

According to Saul Gellerman, employees want to work hard but are inhibited by managers who overmanage. Such managers narrow employees' jobs and allow them to make very few decisions. Most decisions are made at too high a level and without adequate study of the employees' environment.

Gellerman introduced the **principle of psychological advantage,** which states that employees are motivated by the desire to get by in the best possible way in their own kind of world. This makes employees more susceptible to their own drives than to the external influence of others. Therefore, to motivate employees, Gellerman recommends that managers "stretch" employees by assigning more difficult and higher-level duties. Gellerman also recommends that measurable objectives be set for each employee through a joint effort by the manager and the employee. In addition, he suggests that a system of participatory decision making be initiated.

In applying Gellerman's theory, a marketing manager might ask questions of employees such as, "What is it you think you can accomplish this year?" "What suggestion do you have to improve the productivity of this unit?" "What level of inventory do you think we ought to have for each of our brands to assure a good and timely selection?" "How would you feel about adding Waukesha to your territory?"

Argyris

Psychologist Chris Argyris feels that most people are naturally motivated to be self-reliant and act in an independent and responsible manner. It is management's fault that people are apathetic and do not always put forth sufficient effort on the job. According to Argyris, most jobs are set up to create a childlike role for the employee. An employee who is treated like a child will become frustrated and act in a defensive, indifferent, or contemptuous manner.

People need a sense of accomplishment and pride about their work, but few managers realize this. It usually is not enough just to give employees a raise, because the additional money may be seen as an unsuccessful attempt to offset the lack of job satisfaction. Argyris also believes that much of the problem lies in management's inability to sustain effective interpersonal relationships with employees. Managers often "filter" information or do not give their real views. Again, the tendency is to treat employees like children who are not yet old enough or mature enough to handle the information.

One restaurant manager's approach to implementing the Argyris theory is to visit at least once a week with all employees about ways in which customers might be served more efficiently. This manager took the time to train the employees in all operations of the dining room. She encourages all employees to pitch in when they see a task that needs to be done. She compliments her employees often and tells them how proud she is of the efficient and courteous way in which customers are served. Her employees are motivated to help each other and are proud of their attractive restaurant.

Likert

In some organizations there are many positions of leadership, from the company president down to the first-line supervisor. Rensis Likert studied leadership styles of first-line supervisors and how they affect the productivity of workers. According to Likert, the leadership style of the first-line supervisor affects productivity far more than the workers' interest in their jobs or the company.

A supervisor who is able to form a teamlike atmosphere within his or her group is more likely to be successful. Such a "group-centered" supervisor should build and maintain within the group a strong sense of responsibility as well as genuine enthusiasm for achieving the group's goals and fulfilling its responsibilities to the larger organization.

First-line supervisors must be able to adapt their behavior to the needs of others in the organization. Values, skills, and expectations of fellow supervisors and superiors as well as those of the group itself play an important part in shaping the behavior of a supervisor. Note the first problem-solving approach used by Pearl Oster, in the story on page 454, in establishing a productivity standard. When she set the standard herself, nothing happened. When she worked *with* her small group of employees, some great suggestions surfaced and productivity did increase.

Mayo: the Hawthorne Effect

Elton Mayo and his colleagues made some very interesting discoveries about motivation when they conducted the Hawthorne Studies in the 1920s. The studies originally were designed to test the effects of illumination on productivity at the Hawthorne Western Electric plant near Chicago. Mayo selected two similar groups of workers and kept a record of their output. He then began to vary the intensity of the lighting for one of the groups while keeping the lighting for the other group constant. To Mayo's surprise, each time he changed the intensity of the lighting either up or down, productivity increased.

Mayo made an important discovery about motivation. The group that continued to improve did so as a result of a whole set of factors that had nothing to do with illumination. They felt important because of the experiment. For the first time, they were getting constant feedback on their work without pressure to change. And they were consulted before changes were made. The group members took pride in their achievements and enjoyed the attention they were getting from outsiders (recognition). The supervisor took pride in the ever improving record of the group and communicated this pride to the group members.

Mayo and his colleagues repeated their experiments several more times, and each time they found the same results. Group morale was a much stronger motivation than physical factors such as illumination and ventilation. Individuals

PEARL'S PRODUCTIVITY PROBLEM

Pearl Oster is the supervisor of eight order pickers at The Center just outside Alexandria, Virginia. Most of the workers are in their early twenties. Their job is to fill the orders received from department stores, supermarkets, and other places where health and beauty aids are sold. The employees pull the products from shelves, put price tags on each item, box them, put the boxes into crates, and move them to the front of the warehouse for loading onto the trucks. Mrs. Oster is known as an experienced and capable supervisor.

After observing and timing operations at the warehouse, Mrs. Oster arrived at what she considered to be a fair standard of how many orders could be filled in a given time period. After a 3 week experiment, however, she found that the standard was not being reached. After further analysis, she rearranged part of the layout, purchased more motorized equipment and forklifts, simplified procedures, and did all she could to raise productivity.

Finally, Mrs. Oster called a meeting of the eight order pickers. She told them that the standard of output was too low and that a new standard of output had to be set. She gave them some information about what was happening. New retail outlets were placing orders, an increased number of orders were being received for smaller items (meaning that a lot more small items had to be price-marked), the warehouse was almost 2 days late on average with deliveries to seven large outlets, and one department store was threatening to find another supplier. Instead of setting a new production standard herself or establishing new procedures, she wanted the group to help her decide what needed to be done.

Mrs. Oster was pleased with the results. The group came up with a slightly higher production standard, suggested some rearrangement of work assignments (emphasizing more work in teams of two), made minor modifications in the warehouse layout, and made a suggestion for reducing paperwork. The collective wisdom of nine people far surpassed that of the manager alone.

want to be part of a specific clan and identify with it. Mayo suggested that management try to follow this "clan" principle by forming stable work groups with specific goals whose attainment would benefit the group as a whole.

The special attention individuals or groups are given because of participating in an experiment or study and the resulting increase in productivity has become known as the *Hawthorne Effect*. Marketers can implement findings from

Mayo's study by giving the work unit plenty of support and recognition.

INTEGRATING THEORY AND RESEARCH WITH PRACTICE

From the theories presented earlier in this chapter, we can draw some basic principles for motivating people to be more productive in marketing occupations. One principle is drawn from each theory that has been presented. As a result, some of the more important factors for motivating employees are repeated and reinforced.

1. *After employees have had an opportunity to fulfill their physiological needs and their needs for safety and security, you will be able to motivate them by providing a way to fulfill social and esteem needs* (Maslow).

Perhaps the company or department could sponsor athletic teams or after-hours get-togethers to provide opportunities for employees and their families to meet socially outside the work environment. Friendly, pleasant working relationships between co-workers and supervisors should be established. Esteem needs can be met by providing awards for excellent work.

Carson Pirie Scott and Company in the Chicago area awards one merchant award and four mini-merchant awards annually in some of its 24 stores. The recipients are selected on the basis of sales, customer service techniques, and excellent relationships with both supervisors and co-workers. The recipient of the merchant award receives $100 at a gathering of the entire staff. The mini-merchant award recipients each receive a certificate. In addition, pictures of the winners are hung permanently on the wall in the personnel area, and their names are engraved on a special plaque. As an additional way of providing recognition to employees, Carson publishes in its employee newspaper pictures of sales people about whom customers have written complimentary letters along with excerpts from some of the letters. [4]

2. *Recognize the fact that most employees want to accomplish something of value; they do want to achieve* (McClelland).

It is important that employees know the value of their work. Every marketing employee contributes in some way to the operation of the company.

No contribution is too small. All work has dignity and is important to the overall operation of a company. The manager who makes a special point of telling the people at all levels of an organization that their contributions are appreciated will motivate these employees by assuring them that they are accomplishing something that is of real value to the company.

A good example of showing appreciation is illustrated by Mr. Sam of Wal-Mart in the story on page 456. His view of all employees is best described in two statements: "The key is to get into the store and listen to what associates have to say" and "It's terribly important for everyone to get involved. Some of our best ideas have come from clerks and stockboys." Mr. Walton makes it a point to visit frequently with employees in the stores and to acknowledge the important contribution they make to the success of Wal-Mart Stores, Inc.

3. *Responsibility, achievement, recognition, growth, and advancement are factors that can be used to motivate employees* (Herzberg).

It is the manager's responsibility to determine which of these factors can best motivate each employee and which motivational factor is practical for a company or department to offer at any one time. For example, managers should not overlook the importance of job titles as a way of recognizing employees. Often a "promotion" with a new title (assistant manager, deputy supervisor, correspondence coordinator, or shift manager) and very little additional money is appreciated more than a larger raise with no change in job title. Increased responsibility is often a motivator too. It indicates to an employee that he or she is being recognized for good work. This is especially true for employees who are just beginning their careers.

Jerry Henderson began his career as an account rep for MasterCard in Fort Worth, Texas. After Henderson's initial training, his

WAL-MART'S PRODUCTIVE EMPLOYEES

At Wal-Mart Stores, Inc., the regular 7:30 a.m. Saturday meeting is going full blast. Amid tumultuous applause, the blushing "Buyer of the Month" has just received his plaque. Perhaps carried away by the moment, Sam Walton, chairman and chief executive, leaps up and shouts, "Who's number one?"

The deafening reply: "Wal-Mart!"

Wal-Mart is far from number one, but it has risen to number four in the Ozarks among discount retailers. In just 10 years—from 1970 to 1980—the number of store locations increased from 18 to 330 and sales increased from $45 million to $1.6 billion.

It all bears the unmistakable mark of founder Sam M. Walton, "Mr. Sam." He tells you that Wal-Mart has been successful because the discount chain shunned the intensely competitive major metropolitan areas and concentrated on selling brand-name merchandise at low prices in small, rural midwestern and southern communities. He talks of saturating the trade area, strategically placing distribution centers, state-of-the-art computer technology, and highly productive employees.

Mr. Sam has a profound belief in those "highly productive employees." The Bentonville, Arkansas, headquarters for Wal-Mart resemble a glorified warehouse on most days because executives are conducting "soul-searching" sessions with some 26,000 employees.

Mr. Walton believes in direct communication with associates, and he practices what he preaches. According to one Wal-Mart executive, Mr. Sam once got up at 2:30 a.m., bought four dozen doughnuts at an all-night bakery, took them to a distribution center, and chatted with workers on the shipping docks. As a result of this chat, he discovered that two more shower stalls were needed at that location. He says, "the key is to get into the store and listen to what associates have to say. It's terribly important for everyone to get involved. Some of our best ideas have come from clerks and stockboys."

Adapted from Lynda Schuster, "Wal-Mart Chief's Enthusiastic Approach Infects Employees, Keeps Retailer Growing." Reprinted by permission of *Wall Street Journal,* © Dow Jones & Company, Inc., April 20, 1981, p. 21. All rights reserved.

first assignment was to service the accounts with hotels and large motels in the area and to introduce MasterCard to the manager of new hotels or motels about to open or to managers of very small motels that currently were not using bank cards. Jerry was paid a set salary with a small bonus for opening new accounts. After 6 months, Jerry's boss called him in and offered him the new restaurant accounts that would be opening up in the

Forth Worth area. Jerry felt great about the prospect of calling on restaurants and was pleased that his boss seemed to be recognizing him as a responsible, capable rep.

4. *Praise, reward, and trust are stronger motivational factors than tight control, close direction, and threatened punishment (McGregor).*

For most employees, try to strengthen their feelings of self-direction and provide positive feedback as a means of motivating them to improve performance and productivity. This type of management requires the manager or supervisor to work with each employee as an individual and not assume that each member of the group can be motivated in exactly the same manner. A good way to discover an employee's talents and goals is to talk with that person on a one-to-one basis, using the good communication skills that will be discussed later in this chapter.

5. *When employees are asked to contribute ideas toward management decision making and operations, they are motivated to perform better (Ouchi).*

In addition to increased motivation, the quality of the decisions made by the group is generally high. To implement participatory decision making successfully, managers should sharpen their techniques for leading discussions. This includes developing the ability to state the problem effectively so that the group does not become defensive; asking good, thought-provoking questions; supplying sufficient facts, background information, and budget detail without suggesting a solution; encouraging all workers to participate; accurately restating comments for clarity; and summarizing when the need arises. Pearl Oster in the story on page 454 provides an illustration of the positive effects of group decision making.

6. *Employees will be motivated if they are "stretched" to perform more difficult and higher-level duties (Gellerman).*

Do not overmanage. Recognize that employees will act on their own needs and drives, not yours. Jointly set measurable objectives with the employees. Challenge them to accept higher but still realistic goals and then work with them to identify appropriate strategies.

The publisher of Topeka, Kansas's only newspaper, *The Gazette,* is a great believer in having section heads set goals for their areas and for the employees they supervise. The following are just a few of the goals he and his advertising manager jointly established for the year ahead.

- Increase institutional ads by 8 percent.
- Increase the cost of an ad an average of 4 percent without losing any clients.
- Increase by 4 percent the volume of advertising from our 10 largest customers.
- Increase by 6 percent the volume of advertising from the next 10 largest customers.

The publisher and the ad manager then jointly established strategies. For example, it was decided to employ an additional assistant to free the manager of some office work so that she could call personally on businesses to increase institutional advertising.

7. *Treat all employees as responsible adults (Argyris).*

Managers who rule with an iron hand or feel the need to structure the work environment completely may not realize that they are placing their employees in a childlike position. Such managers will have much better success in motivating their employees if they treat them like responsible adults. This type of treatment includes trusting employees, allowing them to be reasonably independent, and sharing information with them.

8. *First-line supervisors who are able to form a teamlike atmosphere within their groups are more likely to be successful at motivating employees (Likert).*

If supervisors are able to build a strong sense of group identity, enthusiasm for the work and for each other, and a support system, employees will perform better. Supervisors should give constant and positive feedback to individuals as well as to the entire group. They should not be afraid to express their pride in the group and its accomplishments.

9. *If workers are made to feel that they are important, productivity will improve* (Mayo).

Many ways to let workers know that they are important already have been discussed. These include taking a personal interest in each employee's achievements, developing a teamlike atmosphere, consulting with the group before changes are made, providing consistent feedback on performance, and expressing pride in the performance of individuals and the group as a whole. Many of these techniques can be accomplished at regularly scheduled staff meetings during which the supervisor or manager shares information with employees and employees share information and ideas openly with management.

The atmosphere should be nonthreatening, and all employees should be encouraged to participate. The objectives of the group should be discussed, and employees should be asked to "buy into them." Many companies sponsor and many managers host periodic breakfasts or luncheons with employees at which the employees are encouraged to raise questions and share ideas.

As an additional means of motivating employees, individual conferences should be held at regular intervals between the supervisor or manager and each employee. At these conferences, measurable objectives should be set for the employee. These objectives should combine the personal goals of the worker with the practical objectives of the department or unit and the company.

OVERCOMING MOTIVATIONAL PROBLEMS

Psychologist Ernest Dichter is recognized by many as the father of motivational psychology. His insights into motivation help people understand why many managers fail to motivate employees even though they know in theory how those employees could be motivated effectively. Later, Dichter's theories will help us understand how human relations skills can be applied in practical ways.

In his biweekly publication *The Human Factor*, Dichter provides managers with numerous insights into what motivates both employees and managers to act as they do and gives practical suggestions for motivating employees.

Reluctance to Show Appreciation

According to Dichter, some managers shy away from recognizing deserving employees and showing appreciation even though they know that it is important. Managers are tight-lipped with their praise and appreciation for several reasons, all of which can be overcome.

"If I tell an employee that he or she did a good job, I commit myself. Suppose the compliment turns out to be premature." Dichter tells of once complimenting an associate for writing a good report before he had a chance to read it in detail. His reaction on reading the report was, "Oh, my!" Then, to his embarrassment, he had to take back the bulk of his praise. To prevent this type of embarrassment, some managers postpone their compliments forever. See Figure 16-4.

One way to get around this psychological roadblock is to be noncommittal until you have examined the work thoroughly but then to be sure to compliment the person. Another way is to give conditional praise. "It looks excellent, but I haven't had a chance to read it all the way through yet."

Other managers may say something like, "Complimenting people only makes them take it

Figure 16-4. Complimenting helps employee motivation.

easy." This can be illustrated by the following example. "When I told my associate that she was doing well overall, she got complacent and didn't try to improve on a couple of weak areas. This made me sorry that I'd ever said anything to her." Actually, this manager did tell the associate that she was doing well but failed to work with her on identifying areas of needed improvement. One good way to keep employees from slacking off is to praise good work as a part of an upward trend. "Five hundred dollars in sales in one day. That's great! Soon you'll be up to seven hundred." This way you compliment your employees and arouse expectations of greater performance in the future.

Other managers resist complimenting people because they do not want to get "mushy and emotional." A lot of people find it hard to give compliments. But one can get around this difficulty by putting the compliment in writing or by giving factual recognition in a notice that is posted on the bulletin board for all to see. A note that might be sent to a deserving employee is shown in Figure 16-5.

No matter what reasons a manager may give for holding back on recognition and appreciation, the reasons are never good enough. One way or another, it is very important to let people know how valuable they are. [5]

Reluctance to Delegate

Researchers have shown that most employees want responsibility. They want to accomplish something worthwhile, and they want to be challenged. It is interesting that most marketing managers believe that it is advantageous to free themselves from as many tasks as possible by delegating duties to employees. Thus, employees want more responsibility, and managers want to give it to them. But apparently, many managers have great difficulty actually delegating. Dichter explains that there may be several reasons for

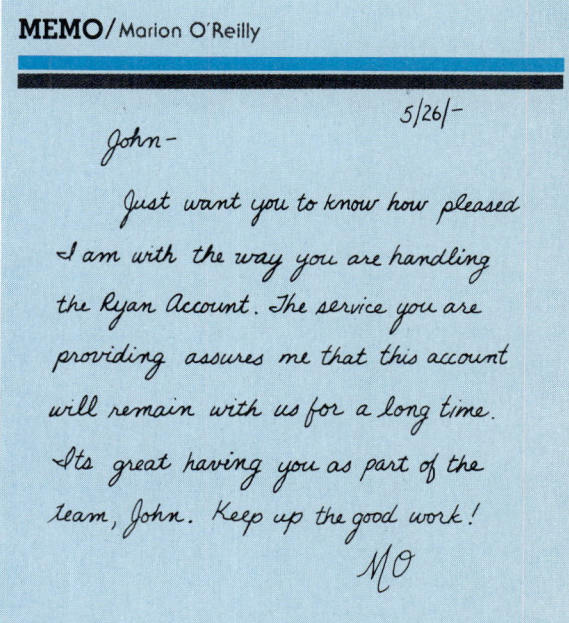

Figure 16-5. Don't resist showing appreciation!

this difficulty, but each reason must be overcome if the manager is going to continue to "rise" in the corporate structure and if the employees are to be motivated by assuming additional responsibilities.

According to Dichter, managers are secretly afraid that their employees will do a better job than they themselves have been able to do. If this is the case, the manager should expand his or her ego to take credit for selecting and training such intelligent employees. Other managers are afraid that their employees will "botch up" the work. In this case, they should assign a small piece of the job first. Then, as their confidence in the employee grows, they can pass on more of the work.

Still other managers may feel that it is too hard to show employees how to do certain jobs. They may say, "You just have to have a feel for it." These people go on to say that it may take all week to teach someone to do a 1 day job, and it just is not worth the time that would have to be invested. Dichter warns managers not to give in to this feeling. They should make themselves into trainers by analyzing the steps in these jobs and writing down the procedures. Then they can show employees how to perform each step. At first, it may seem to take more time to show someone else how to do the job than it would to do it oneself, but training time is an investment that will pay off in the future.[6]

Reluctance to Change

According to Dichter, people often refuse to change even when they are convinced of the merits of doing so. A consumer who is reluctant to change toothpastes argues, "But I've used brand X for years." A tyrannical, outspoken manager who is reluctant to use better human relations skills says, "My employees have come to expect this approach from me" or "I've been like this for 30 years, and I'm not changing now."

Why are people reluctant to change? Some people fear the unknown or are afraid that they will appear stupid or ill prepared. This may explain why the United States has been relatively slow to adopt the metric system and why some people have been reluctant to work with computers. Of course, some people are quite change-resistant and prefer that everything remain as is. Dichter feels that people are reluctant to change because in order to change, they think they have to admit that they were wrong.[7] This reluctance to change affects employee work habits. An employee may be reluctant to accept an increased workload even though he or she is capable of handling it and is underworked. Succeeding with an increased workload would be like admitting that the employee could have been working harder all along.

The best way to overcome this reluctance to change is by avoiding any implication that customers or employees were wrong. Take the attitude that consumers were right in using brand X, that managers were right in selecting their current management style, and that employees were right in working at their current pace. However, now the situation has changed. Product Y has been improved, the workers have developed a great deal of respect for the manager, and the employees have become skilled and now work rapidly. The wise choice now is to change.

People would rather be right than wrong. If a manager wants workers to change, that manager should make them feel good about their present behavior and encourage them to view the change as an opportunity for growth.

USING HUMAN RELATIONS SKILLS

As Rita Craig drove toward the Kenosha exit on the freeway, she smiled to herself. She was both nervous and excited. This was the opportunity she had been working and waiting for. She had "paid her dues" for 12 years as a salesperson, a supervisor, and most recently an assistant manager of a Factor's Fashions branch store in Waukegan.

The Kenosha store she was headed to was not new and had been only marginally successful in the past few years, but it was now Rita's store. The former manager was a man Rita had met only once at a meeting of managers and assistants from Factor's 25 stores in the Illinois, Indiana, and Wisconsin area. He had come to Factor's from another chain of ready-to-wear stores ony 6 months earlier. Last week he resigned without notice after a heated argument with management.

Yesterday Rita received word that she was the new manager of Factor's in Kenosha, "effective immediately." Corporate management also indicated that they had confidence in Rita's ability to "shape up the Kenosha operation and turn a decent profit for the company." Because Kenosha is just a 40 minute drive to the north of Waukegan, Rita's new promotion did not require her to relocate. "I'm really lucky," she told a friend. "A nice raise, a promotion, my own store to run, and no hassle with having to move."

When Rita arrived in Kenosha, she had no trouble locating the store, and she was there a full hour before her staff was scheduled to arrive. She had inherited a staff of one full-time salesperson, three part-timers, one office assistant, one assistant manager, and two part-time stock and maintenance workers.

When Rita looked around the store, she immediately saw a number of things that would have to be changed. Housekeeping was disorderly, displays were done improperly, and shelves and racks were not fully stocked. Rita took her clipboard out of her briefcase and began to take organized notes for her first staff meeting. She would have the place looking right in no time.

When her staff arrived at nine, she held a brief meeting at which she introduced herself as the new store manager and announced that there would be another meeting after the closing of the store that day. Each employee was required to attend and would be paid extra for the meeting time.

During the day Rita had several short conversations with her assistant manager, Mark Adams, but most of the talks were one-sided. She did most of the talking, and Mark would answer briefly and then go about his work. Rita thought that Mark seemed very cold and distant.

At the staff meeting at the end of Rita's first day, she repeated that she was sincerely pleased to be there and invited everyone to have a sandwich and a cup of coffee. She then listed 10 things that should be done differently. After all, this was Rita's store, and corporate management was counting on her to put it into good shape.

By the end of her first week at the Kenosha store, Rita was pleased to see that most of her suggested changes had been implemented, but she had the distinct impression that most of the staff did not like her. "But why?" she wondered aloud. "I'm only doing the job I was sent here to do. And in one week, I've made tremendous progress."

Rita has made tremendous progress, and with her motivation, she probably will succeed. Unfortunately, she may not have the current staff with her much longer. Remember that people are more satisfied with their jobs if they feel that they are part of a team, have their social and esteem needs met, and participate in decisions that result in changes. Not only has Rita violated these principles, she has failed to practice effective human relations.

Human relations can be defined as skills needed for effective interaction between people. Students of human relations study all types of human interaction: conflict; cooperation; team behavior in dealing with changes, discrimination, and prejudice; listening and communicating; and the dialog and body language used when people converse in a social or work environment. It is almost impossible to motivate employees without using good human relations skills. In addition, these skills are essential in the successful day-to-day operation of any business.

Unfortunately, Rita Craig has not developed good human relations skills. If she is to succeed at

Factor's Fashions in Kenosha, she will have to develop human relations skills in at least four basic areas.

1. Understanding oneself
2. Understanding others
3. Listening and communicating
4. Diagnosing and resolving conflicts

In Rita's case, it would also help if she could erase the memory of her first week in Kenosha from the employees' minds.

Understanding Oneself

Effective managers understand both themselves and other people. Because they understand and feel good about themselves, they are able to accept others and deal with them effectively.

Each person has something called a self-concept. This is a combination of how we really feel about ourselves and how we think other people view us. If you have a positive self-concept, you view yourself as a unique and valuable person. You are comfortable with other people and feel that they accept and appreciate you. A healthy and positive self-concept is the foundation for a successful life, good relationships, and a satisfying career. A good self-concept does not, however, mean that you are self-centered or egotistical but rather that you are secure.

In Rita Craig's eagerness to make the Kenosha store her own, she did not display the characteristics of someone with a positive self-concept. To the employees, she appeared self-centered and egotistical. In reality, she was unsure of herself and her ability to handle the new job. To compensate for this lack of confidence, she developed something that resembled the Theory X management style described by McGregor.

Perhaps the most rewarding outcome of a good self-concept is that it enables one to have deeper and more profound relationships with friends and loved ones as well as with co-workers.

In *Human Relations in Business,* Reece and Brandt comment that the first step toward a better self-concept is to accept yourself as you are now. "The past cannot be changed, but the future is determined by how you act in the present. When you see yourself as a unique, valuable individual, you are on your way toward accepting others and achieving your own personal and professional growth."[8] The authors then suggest some methods for improving one's self-image.

1. Learn to tolerate imperfections in yourself. No one is perfect, so stop trying to be.

2. Appreciate and respect yourself. Clarify your values and then live by them. Establish ground rules for your personal and professional behavior and then act accordingly.

3. Make decisions. Try not to procrastinate. Do your homework—gather the information and seek advice—but learn to be decisive.

4. Hate the "activity," not yourself. It may be appropriate to hate some of the things you do, but do not hate yourself. You are a good person.

5. Act "as if" you possess a quality you would like to have, for example, confidence, assertiveness, sensitivity, or extraversion. Over a period of time, if you persistently act "as if," you will incorporate the desired behavior into your self-concept.

6. Present a positive picture of yourself physically. Dress according to the image you want to project. Dress sharp and you'll be sharp!

7. Use reinforcement techniques. Clip and post quotes on passages that seem to express ideas or qualities you'd like to have.

8. Develop expertise in some areas. Being recognized as an "expert" in something will help build your self-concept.

9. Continue to learn throughout your life. Self-improvement—whether in a formal educational setting or informal classes—builds positive self-respect.[9]

To an incredible degree, a person's self-concept determines how much of his or her potential is likely to be tapped. Successful people like themselves.

Understanding Others

Each person has different needs, wants, and desires. A major principle in developing effective human relationships is to treat people as individuals and recognize their uniqueness. Never lump people together by race, sex, level of employment, social status, or creed and then generalize about their behavior. If you want to be an effective supervisor, get to know your employees as individuals. Recognize that each person represents a system of ideas, feeling, attitudes, and past experiences, all of which interact and affect the current work environment.

"Well, what's she like?" asked Amy Adams when her husband Mark entered their apartment after Rita Craig's first day in Kenosha. "You'll never believe it," said Mark as he unbuttoned his coat. "I think she's out of her mind. She has made no attempt whatsoever to get to know any of us or to find out what has been going wrong in the store.

But she has already given us a list of 10 things she thinks we're doing wrong. Most of these things are the new techniques Rogan introduced when he came 6 months ago. I wonder how long this manager is going to last."

"She really does sound out of it, Mark. I still think you should have been the one to get the job. After all, you've been assistant manager for 3 years now. Maybe you'll get it yet. Rita Craig probably won't last long."

Understanding others is not always easy, and Rita is facing a situation that presents additional difficulties. The previous manager is not around to confer with, and he was on the job only 6 months. This means that the staff at the Kenosha store has had three different managers in the same year. As a result, it is possible that the staff feels a bit pushed around. To make matters worse, Rita's assistant manager had expected to get the job Rita was given.

If we were able to erase Rita's first week and make it a better one, we could provide her with an

Figure 16-6. Rita Craig is eager to make her store better; to her employees, she appears self-centered and egotistical.

LEARNING TO LISTEN: SO SIMPLE, SO HARD

Many TV commercials are so irritating that we can't change channels fast enough, but every now and then something pops up to galvanize the imagination. For example, here is Sperry, one of our giant technology companies, spending millions to tell us that they are teaching their employes how to listen to each other and to their customers.

That's right: just listen. It's one of the great lost arts in human relationships. We're all so busy thinking about—and articulating—our own needs that we seldom really pay attention to what others are saying to us.

When I was in business I had to deal with a variety of suppliers and it drove me mad that so often they would come back to me with a product significantly different from whatever I had specified. The defense always began with the phrase, "Well, I thought . . ." They had been busy thinking while I was talking. One by one, however, I discovered salespeople who would not only hear my words but would try to listen to my tune.

I was so grateful to these firms that I really didn't care what they charged me, within reason. It was always cheaper to get the job done right the first time.

Sperry also makes the point that learning to listen on the job means you pay better attention at home. One commercial showed a father sitting with his teen-age daughter, really focusing in on her dating woes. He may not be able to resolve her problem, but she surely ends up knowing that he cares how she is feeling.

When we practice better listening we have to concentrate. It's an act of will to listen, especially if we suspect we might be bored. We actually have to expend energy to keep the mind from slipping out of gear.

Maintaining eye contact with the speaker is a good way to stay focused. Once we lose it, the interior sound level drops and it's oh so easy to drift off to fantasy island.

---

opportunity to begin knowing her staff without alienating them. She could call a brief staff meeting the first morning to introduce herself and have the staff members introduce themselves. Then Rita could observe the operations of the store and wait a few weeks before correcting any behaviors other than serious problems that require immediate attention.

During the first week, she could invite each staff member to talk with her individually. At each conference, Rita could share with them a brief description of her career background. She might explain to each employee that because this is her first experience as store manager, she is counting on them to help her run the store and improve on profits. She might even tell each of them that it appeared to her as if she had inherited a good team to work with. Then Rita could encourage each employee to talk about himself or herself. After she determined how long each employee had been with the company and for what he or she was currently responsible, she might ask some of the following questions. "What type of work experience did you have before you joined Factor's?"

Second, some people feel persecuted if they can't instantly vocalize every idea that flies into the head. You can never do a decent job of listening if you've got 20 thoughts hopping up and down trying to get out. You're too busy trying to maintain order inside to hear what's being said outside.

Many people don't know how to conduct the most casual conversation. For example:

YOU: This cold has really got me down. I'm afraid I might be—

FRIEND: Boy, I had a bug last month that knocked me for a loop. The office was a mess when I got back.

Isn't that the way it goes? People react to any opening you give them to talk about themselves. It's not malicious; usually they think they are relating to you by continuing your topic in another direction. But this isn't listening—it's competition for air time.

Listening is empathy, slipping into your shoes, feeling with you. Waiting until you have completed your statement, and then exploring with you the implications of what you have said, and possible future courses of action.

A good friend will actually allow you to fumble for words in the middle of a thought. He won't use it as an excuse to preempt the microphone—the strong taking over from the weak. We never get to the serious subjects if we are always interrupted.

Sometimes this is all the support we can provide, but it may be enough. A lot of us go for days without having anybody look us in the eye, quiet down, and really listen. It seems so little to ask.

Source: Jim Sanderson is a nationally syndicated newspaper columnist and the author of the book *How to Raise Your Kids to Stand on Their Own Two Feet*. This column reprinted through the courtesy of Sun Features Inc., © 1982. All rights reserved.

"What do you feel is your strength in your current position?" "Why do you think the store is not making an acceptable profit?" "What would you change about the store if you had an opportunity to improve it? Why?" "What plans have you made for your career?" "What do you hope to be doing 5 years from now?"

The answers to these questions could provide Rita with a wealth of valuable information. As a result of her personal interviews, each employee would feel as if he or she had contributed ideas toward the future operation of the store.

Listening and Communicating

People spend most of their working hours conversing, listening, reading, and exchanging information. With so much practice, it is amazing that people are not better at listening and communicating. But the truth is that many messages are distorted, misunderstood, left incomplete, or ignored in the communication process.

What you think you hear others say and what they actually say often are not the same. Similarly, what you mean to say and what you actually say may differ. Also, what you actually say often is different from what other people hear. In fact, studies show that the average person hears about half of what is said.

One of the biggest deterrents to effective listening is daydreaming, as Nichols and Stevens explain in the following story. Daydreaming occurs because while the average person speaks at the rate of 100 to 200 words a minute, the average listener is capable of processing information at a rate that may be three times as fast.

A, the boss, is talking to B, the subordinate, about a new program that the firm is planning to launch. B is a poor listener. In this instance, he tries to listen well, but he has difficulty concentrating on what A has to say.

A starts talking, and B launches into the listening process, grasping every word and phrase that comes into his ears. But right away B finds that because of A's slow rate of speech, he has time to think of things other than the spoken line of thought. Subconsciously, B decides to sandwich a few thoughts of his own into the aural ones that are arriving too slowly. B quickly dashes out into a mental sidetrack and thinks something like this: Oh, yes, before I leave, I want to tell A about the big success of the meeting I called yesterday. Then B comes back to A's spoken line of thought and listens for a few more words.

There is plenty of time for B to do just what he has done—dash away from what he hears and then return quickly—and he continues taking sidetracks to his own private thoughts. He can hardly avoid doing this because over the years, the process has become a strong aural habit.

But sooner or later, on one of the mental sidetracks, B is almost sure to stay away too long. When he returns, A is moving ahead of him. At this point it becomes harder for B to understand A, because B has missed part of the oral message. The private mental sidetracks become more inviting than ever, and B slides off onto several of them. Slowly he misses more and more of what A has to say.

When A is through talking, it is safe to say that B will have received and understood less than half of what was spoken to him.[10]

To overcome this natural tendency to daydream, think about the speaker's comments as they are being made. Decide whether you agree with the facts and conclusions being presented. Mentally summarize important points. Practice learning to read between the lines. What really is being emphasized? Watch facial expressions and body movements in order to pick up any additional meaning that the speaker may not have included in the actual presentation. In a two-way conversation (as opposed to just listening, say, to a lecture), be sure to ask for clarification. Restate or summarize important parts. "Let me just be sure that I understand, Rita. You want me to . . . "

Of course, effective communications involve more than just listening. Communication is a two-way process. It is the responsibility of both participants to make it work successfully. In successful communication exchanges, the listener understands the message in the same way that the speaker intends it to be understood.

The following suggestions should help you improve as a communicator or provider of messages.

- Present material at the listener's level. Anticipate his or her level of knowledge and present information accordingly. Be sure that all terms, concepts, and directions are explained in language the listener can understand.

- When possible, demonstrate what is being said. Show what you mean as opposed to just telling about it.

- Use direct eye contact. Look directly at the person with whom you are communicating.

- Speak and write clearly and concisely. Use the KISS formula: Keep it short and simple.

- Show enthusiasm, interest, and sincerity when communicating. Let the receivers know that you are interested in them, in their problem, or in providing them with just the right information.

- Solicit feedback. Verify that the message has been understood.
- Be open and direct. Say what you mean. Avoid giving the impression that there are hidden motives behind your words or that you are not saying what you actually mean. Few people are really good at faking it.

Diagnosing and Resolving Conflicts

Some personal conflict probably is inevitable in any organization. But because marketing relies heavily on the contributions of people, the prompt solution of conflicts is of the utmost importance. This type of resolution can be achieved if the conflict is turned into a problem-solving situation. Both parties should work together to solve the problem. This way there is no right or wrong party.

Perhaps the best way to resolve conflicts is to use the traditional problem-solving approach of (1) defining the problem, (2) collecting the facts, (3) considering all possible solutions and the results, (4) selecting the best solution by examining the possible results, (5) implementing the solution, and (6) following up and making additional decisions based on the results. Here is an application of the problem-solving approach.

Larry Bradford and Nancy Rosenberg are part-timers at Factor's Fashions. Both are students at Kenosha Technical Institute. The policy in the past has been to let both Nancy and Larry decide on their own schedules each week. The only stipulation is that one of them must be there for the last 3 hours of the work day each day that the store is open.

Figure 16-7. To solve a problem between employees, Rita Craig *listens* and *selects the best solution*.

Larry and Nancy have had little problem with their schedules until this week. The store is open until nine on Saturday night. The annual year-end dinner and dance for students and staff at the technical institute is this Saturday night. Although Rita Craig would like to excuse both workers to attend this important event, it is essential that at least one of them be at the store to help with a big sale that is scheduled for that night.

Larry feels that Nancy should work because he is graduating and special recognition will be given at the dinner for all graduates. Nancy feels that Larry should work because she has been at Factor's a few months longer than Larry, and "that gives me seniority." Both workers have come to Rita Craig to solve their problem. Together they use the problem-solving approach.

1. Define the Problem.　Neither Nancy nor Larry wants to work the night of the dinner dance. However, it is essential that Rita have adequate coverage in the store during the sale that is scheduled for that evening.

2. Collect the Facts.　Nancy has 3 months' seniority. Larry is graduating, and this probably will be his last dinner dance at the school. Rita says that the job could be done by somebody other than Nancy or Larry if that person were familiar with the store and the stock.

3. Consider All Possible Solutions and the Results.

a. Larry could work, but he would miss the dinner dance.
b. Nancy could work, but she would miss the dinner dance.
c. Both Larry and Nancy could work so that neither one of them would feel triumphant over the other.
d. Both workers could attend the dinner dance and leave the store short of help. Of course, both could be fired for missing this important sale.

e. George Polimenokosa, a former employee, could fill in for both Larry and Nancy. George left the store for college in September, worked during the spring break, and is expected to be home for the summer. If George works, both Nancy and Larry can attend the dinner dance. In addition, Rita can meet George and consider him for summer employment.

4. Select the Best Solution.　All three of them decide that George Polimenokosa should be contacted immediately and invited to work for the sale night.

5. Implement the Solution.　George accepts the invitation to work so that he will have an opportunity to meet Rita Craig and ask her about summer employment.

6. Follow up and Make Additional Decisions Based on Results.　No additional decisions are needed because George worked out well and both Nancy and Larry were able to attend the dinner dance.

Other reasons for conflicts include the following:

1. Misunderstandings Resulting from Faulty Communications.　If we were to interview Rita Craig's staff after her first meeting, we might receive a consensus on the fact that she was "out of her mind," but chances are that this is all her staff members would agree on. Each may have heard a slightly different version of the 10 things they should do differently. As discussed earlier, what you think you hear others say and what they actually say often are not the same. These misunderstandings resulting from faulty communications can cause a number of on-the-job conflicts.

2. Lack of Incentives.　Wages as well as nonmonetary incentives can be the cause of conflicts. One worker may find out that another employee in a similar position is earning more. Or workers may feel that one employee has been singled out as a "fair-haired boy" or "golden girl" or that some workers are put "on the fast track" and treated with special care.

3. Adversary Management. If management adopts the Theory X management style exclusively, workers come to regard management as the enemy. When this happens, employees will try to outmaneuver management every chance they get. Conflicts will center on the enforcement of rules and a continuous attempt by employees to gain more freedom from supervision.

4. Conflicting Viewpoints. It is natural for intelligent adults to have conflicting viewpoints on how something should be done. When these viewpoints cannot be expressed adequately and discussed calmly, conflicts arise.

Always keep in mind that people are of a higher order than animals, buildings, profits, and productivity. People must be treated with dignity and respect. Protection of and respect for human life and individual integrity are key values in our society. The best way to resolve conflicts and still preserve human dignity is to find a mutually satisfying solution. This means that in a conflict situation, there should not be a winner and a loser. There should instead be two satisfied parties.

In conflict resolution, it is best to work toward a win/win solution. Even if the solution is not completely fair to both parties, emphasize the positive results expected. Respect everyone's opinion and acknowledge that differences do exist. Differences are healthy and should lead to personal and professional growth. Avoid personal attacks. Instead, focus on the issue, idea, or procedure. Finally, be patient. It sometimes takes a while to find and implement an effective solution.

KEY POINTS SUMMARY

- People are an important and vital resource in the effective and profitable management of a business.
- There are many principles for dealing with people that can be gleaned from the studies of psychologists and other authorities. Effective

applications of these principles will lead to increased productivity in marketing.

- Generally, people are motivated through positive reinforcement, a sociable work environment that also meets their needs for esteem, participatory management style, challenges, and a supportive work group.
- People want to achieve. They want to accomplish something of value. They want to be treated like responsible adults. They want to feel that they and their work are important.
- Effective human relations skills must be developed in four areas: understanding yourself, understanding others, listening and communicating, and diagnosing and resolving conflicts.

KEY TERMS AND CONCEPTS

achievement motive	self-actualization
human relations	self-concept
human-resource development	Theory X
motivation	Theory Y
principle of psychological advantage	Theory Z

DISCUSSION QUESTIONS

1. Why is it so important to have people with appropriate motivation and human relations skills in marketing occupations? In addition to your own thoughts on this subject, be sure to consider those of Mr. Lewis of Montgomery Ward from the story at the beginning of this chapter.

2. Provide further examples from your current and former jobs in support of the motivational theories presented on pages 451 to 454 of this chapter. In other words, how does your supervisor apply these principles? Conversely, what suggestions can you make to improve on his or her motivational techniques?

3. Why do you think some managers fail to motivate their employees and appear to violate so many of the principles of motivation that have been found to be effective? What suggestions can you make to managers to encourage them to delegate? To show appreciation? To change or modify inappropriate behavior?

4. Identify and explain the importance of the four areas of human relations that all people must develop to be effective supervisors as well as enjoyable co-workers.

5. Identify an area of conflict that has been brewing in your life for some time. It may be at school, on a job, or even with a spouse or parent. Apply the problem-solving approach to the conflict.

NOTES

1. L. Edward Lewis, "Making Wards a Winner," *Forward,* a publication for Montgomery Ward people, September 1, 1981, p. 1.
2. Sharon Lund O'Neil, *Occupational Survival Skills: Implications for Job Maintenance and Mobility,* Department of Vocational and Technical Education, University of Illinois at Urbana-Champaign, 1976, p. 10.
3. Data from Hans H. Strupp and H. J. Hausman as reported in Laird et. al., *Psychology, Human Relations and Motivation,* 5th ed., McGraw-Hill, New York, 1975, p. 386.
4. CPS News, published for the associates of Carson Pirie Scott and Company, December 17, 1980, Vol. II, no. 4. Also personal interviews with mini-merchant award winners at Lakehurst, Waukegan, Illinois branch of Carson Pirie Scott and Company, August 1981.
5. Ernest Dichter, "Why Are So Many Managers Reluctant to Show Appreciation?" *The Human Factor: Ideas on the Art of Motivating People,* no. 230, The Economics Press, Fairfield, N.J., 1981.
6. Ernest Dichter, "Overcoming Roadblocks to Delegation," *The Human Factor: Ideas on the Art of Motivating People,* no. 234, The Economics Press, Fairfield, N.J., 1981.
7. Ernest Dichter, "It's Strange but True—People Often Refuse to Change for the Better," *The Human Factor: An Executive Folio on the Art of Motivating People,* no. 182, The Economics Press, Fairfield, N.J., 1979.
8. Barry L. Reece and Rhonda Brandt, *Effective Human Relations in Business,* Houghton Mifflin Company, Boston, 1981, p. 91.
9. Ibid.
10. Reprinted by permission of *Harvard Business Review,* excerpt from "Listening to the People" by Ralph G. Nichols and Leonard A. Stevens, September-October 1957, pp. 85–92. Copyright © 1957 by the President and Fellows of Harvard College; all rights reserved.

CHAPTER 17

EMPLOYING, DEVELOPING, AND SUPERVISING MARKETING EMPLOYEES

Finding good employees is difficult for all companies, but it is an especially troubling problem for small wholesale, retail, and service firms. It was the major concern of 54 percent of 1,191 recently polled small business executives. These executives were more worried about getting conscientious workers than about financing, government regulations, taxes, or slow-paying customers.

The reason is simple. Bad employees are a disruptive liability in a small operation. "We in small business don't need any losers as employees; we have enough problems already," stated the owner of an Ohio bakery chain. This person went on to state that he is very willing to train someone who is willing to work, since attitude is the number one consideration in evaluating job applicants.

Attitude also was stressed in a New York City training program that has turned marginally employable people into good employees. "I learned to control my temper." "Now, when they yell at me, I know it isn't because they are angry. It's pressure, and yelling is just their way." These were just a few comments from students who completed the program.

How do successful business people make seemingly problem employees into good employees? The director of the New York training program suggests that employers should learn to "challenge and support their employees. Challenge them to do better but also support their needs."

"Everybody needs recognition," says another director involved with the program. "It is important to be told that what you are doing is important, even if it is a low-level, low-paying job." Finally, the importance of training was emphasized. Clearly presented explanations and demonstrations that are free of unfamiliar trade jargon are necessary to train good employees.[1]

Managers and owners of successful profit-oriented businesses nearly always attest to the importance of good employees. Employees can make or break a business. Good employees are especially important in jobs involving the marketing mix because nearly all such jobs involve transactions among people. Employees who are customer-oriented, pleasant, and knowledgeable about the products and services being marketed

Figure 17-1. Good employees are a firm's greatest asset!

are a firm's greatest asset. That is why people, or the personnel component, sometimes are considered the fifth P in the marketing mix. (See Figure 17-1.) Effective marketing managers and owners of marketing businesses strive to hire a competent marketing staff and then devote funds and personnel to train these employees. Finally, resources are provided for supervising and evaluating marketing employees.

EMPLOYING A MARKETING STAFF

It has been estimated that 50 percent of a firm's problems can be prevented through good staffing.

Thus, it is important that the right people be employed in the first place. Much marketing and marketing management involves getting work done through and with others. It is a lot easier to get work done through and with others if those others are the right people. Once employees are hired, they should be placed in the right job, trained, and treated fairly. When employees are trained properly and treated fairly, the company, the employees, and society benefit.

Employee turnover is expensive. Even replacing a part-timer in a fast-food restaurant costs at least $600. The Southland Corporation 7-11 stores report that it costs them nearly $2,500 to

EMPLOYMENT PROCEDURES

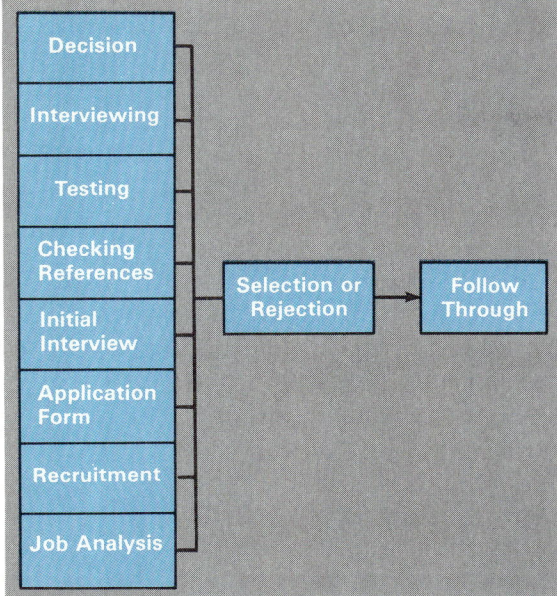

Figure 17-2. Effective procedures for recruiting and selecting marketing employees.

replace a cashier, and IBM estimates the cost of hiring and training a sales rep at more than $20,000.

Most firms today follow several effective procedures in employing a marketing staff. Not all the steps in Figure 17-2 are used by every firm, but most probably should be. Let us take a closer look at procedures that can be used by most firms in recruiting and selecting employees, especially those who will be working in marketing.

Job Analysis

Most firms today begin staffing procedures with some sort of **job analysis,** which is a process of determining both the requirements of a job and the qualifications of the employee to be placed in that job. Large firms with many employees usually conduct fairly detailed job analyses. They may conduct extensive interviews with current employees. They may observe employees at their jobs. They may ask employees to write out exactly

what it is they do on their jobs or keep a daily log of tasks completed; or they may prepare a questionnaire listing all the tasks management thinks should be done and then have the employees check those which they actually do on the job. Job analysis is typically task-oriented. That is, it focuses on what is done on the job and how to do it. Occasionally, job analysis details why an employee performs certain tasks or describes a job in terms of its overall contribution to the company.

Information gained through job analysis often is compiled in a written **job description.** This is a statement of the job to be done, usually in the form of a list of the duties and responsibilities to be performed. Formats for job descriptions vary from company to company. Some are very detailed, and many include separate sections for each of the following.

● Job identification or title
● Location of the job in the organization
● Job summary
● Specific duties performed (regularly and occasionally)
● Relationship to other jobs
● Supervision to be given or received
● Products and services to be marketed and knowledge or experience needed
● Working conditions (environment, salary, benefits, and equipment needed to operate)
● Qualifications (experiences, education, licenses, and age requirements)

Others are not as complex and may resemble the one shown in Table 17-1 on page 474.

Regardless of size of the firm, some sort of job analysis should be conducted, resulting in a written job description. If the firm is very small and the manager does not have time to do a thorough job analysis, the *Dictionary of Occupational Titles* (DOT) can be used. The DOT does not provide thorough job descriptions, but it does provide job titles and definitions and describes work duties common or potentially common to jobs. This document, which is prepared by the U.S. Department of Labor, is widely diseminated and is available in libraries, schools, colleges, and employment offices in every community. The following is an example of the definition and work duties for a sales agent of securities taken from the DOT. The other job titles for this position include stock broker, registered representative, securities adviser, and broker.

251.157-010 SALES AGENT, SECURITIES
Buys and sells stocks and bonds for individuals and organizations as representative of stock brokerage firm, applying knowledge of securities, market conditions, and history and prospects of various corporations to prospective customers, based on interpretation of data from securities reports, financial periodicals, and stock-quotation-viewer screen, and persuades customers to buy or sell specific securities according to their financial needs. Records and transmits buy or sell orders to trading division in accordance with customer's wishes. Calculates and records cost of transaction for billing purposes, using quotations received during transmittal of order. Develops portfolio (list) of selected investments for customer. Compiles list of prospective customers and telephone prospects to obtain additional business. Must have broker's license issued by State.[2]

Based on the job analysis, the written job description should at a minimum identify the job

---

TABLE 17-1
SIMPLIFIED JOB DESCRIPTION

Job All-Purpose Teller

Summary Serves the public by handling certain transactions submitted through a teller window. Manages a fund of cash.

Primary Duties
1. Serves customers at a window. Handles a variety of transactions. Uses own judgment within narrow limits regarding the transactions. Refers questionable transactions to head teller.
   a. Receives commercial and individual checking deposits, verifies endorsements, verifies cash received, and issues receipts.
   b. Accepts checks for cashing or paying. Verifies endorsements, validity, funds, and makes change. Refers to a more experienced teller on large or unusual transactions.
   c. Receives savings and club deposits. Pays withdrawals after verifying balance and signatures.
   d. Receives mortgage, installment loan, utility, charge card, check credit, ready reserve, or any other payments. Checks the date due and adding late charges when applicable.
   e. Sells money orders, cashier's checks, U.S. Savings Bonds, and traveler's checks.
   f. Opens checking, passbook savings, and special club accounts.
   g. Receives U.S. Savings Bonds for payment.

2. Functions as the bank's primary contact with the public. Serves customers in a cordial manner to encourage satisfaction with service.

Source: Crawford, Lucy C. and Richard L. Lynch, *Finance and Credit*, McGraw-Hill, New York, 1979, p. 17.

tasks to be completed as well as minimal or preferred qualifications needed for the job. The job description should be given to all prospective employees so that they can evaluate their interests and abilities relative to the tasks before accepting an employment offer. Of course, the job description also is used by management as a basis for evaluating an applicant's ability to do the job.

Recruitment

Ideally, recruitment should gather in enough applicants to assure that well-qualified individuals can be employed at available jobs. Recruiting efforts vary from company to company, depending on the nature of the jobs, type and size of firm, location, budget, and source of available labor supply.

There are two major sources of job applicants: internal and external. Many companies primarily recruit internally for promotional purposes. Thus, a sales manager is recruited from among the sales reps, and the head of the marketing research unit is recruited from among employees who have completed at least 2 years of experience in that department. Some may also recruit from other sections. Thus, a department store may recruit sales people from the hardware department to fill jobs in the furniture department.

Internal recruiting has the advantage of allowing employees to transfer from one job to another, thus broadening their job experiences while they remain with the same company. Studies generally have shown that morale is higher when employees know that they can change jobs within a company, move to a different department, or be considered for promotion. Filling a job from within the firm also provides management with a better opportunity to learn more about the applicant because there is better access to valid information about this person's work history. Comments from former and present supervisors, job evaluation rating forms, salary history, and work-related factors (attendance and tardiness record, co-worker relationships, and training

received) usually are easier to obtain than they would be if management were recruiting from outside the firm. Internal transfer or promotion usually saves considerable time and costs in training since the employee presumably is already knowledgeable about company products and services, policies, and procedures.

Inevitably, however, firms must recruit from external sources, especially when filling entry-level jobs. Typically, employees are recruited for jobs in marketing from five sources:

1. schools and colleges,
2. recommendations from current employees,
3. advertising,
4. employment agencies,
5. casual applicants.

In Table 17-2 on page 476, a few suggestions for using each of these recruiting methods are provided.

Application Form

Usually, all recruits or job applicants are asked to complete an application form. Completed forms are used by the company to obtain information from and about all prospective employees. Most companies design or use a standard form which asks the same questions of all employees. Supplemental sections for this standard form or separate forms may be designed for people applying for different jobs. Large companies may use different forms for office personnel, factory workers, sales reps, engineers and technicians, supervisors and managers, and executives.

As a result of federal laws prohibiting any form of discrimination in employment on the basis of sex, race, religion, creed, national origin, or handicap in government jobs or government-sponsored projects, application forms and related procedures have undergone a considerable transformation in recent years. Many companies have gone to a standard form similar to the one in Figure 17-3 on page 477. This form has been approved by appropriate government agencies as being nondiscriminatory.

Many companies, of course, still design their own application forms to meet their specific employment objectives. The following are sections that probably should be included on application forms for marketing employees.

- **Personal Data:** full name, home address, personal and business telephone numbers, social security number

- **Education:** names and addresses of high schools, postsecondary schools, colleges and universities, and trade or business schools attended; degrees earned; licenses earned;

TABLE 17-2
METHODS FOR RECRUITING MARKETING EMPLOYEES

Methods of Recruitment	Examples
1. Schools and colleges	1. Work with faculty, counselors, or placement officers to identify business and marketing students 2. Conduct interviews with business and marketing students at the school or college 3. Place help wanted ads in college or school newspaper or on bulletin boards 4. Make job descriptions available to placement office and business faculty
2. Current employees	1. Ask current employees to suggest prospective employees, including friends and relatives 2. Ask employees to recommend co-workers for promotion or lateral transfers 3. Announce all job openings in the company newsletter, on bulletin boards, or in person
3. Advertising	1. Place ads in help wanted sections of newspapers 2. Place ads in business and marketing journals 3. Place ads on radio and company billboards
4. Employment agencies	1. Use the services of state employment offices at no cost to employer or prospective employee 2. Use the services of private employment agencies (e.g., Snelling & Snelling or Kelly) for a fee 3. Make job descriptions available to employment agencies
5. Casual applicants	1. Have "walk-ins" complete application forms and keep on file until an opening 2. Keep file of those who submit formal letter of application and résumé 3. Contact acquaintances employed in comparable marketing positions with competing firms

APPLICATION FOR POSITION
EEOC & FCCC Approved Form

Position Applied For ___ Permanent () Temporary () Part Time () Seasonal () Date Available ___

PERSONAL INFORMATION

Last Name ___ First Name ___ Social Security Number ___

Present Permanent Address ___ City ___ County ___ State ___ Zip Code ___

Home Phone No. ___ Date of Birth ___

Any physical limitations? Yes () No () If so, please explain ___

Active duty in U.S. armed forces? * Yes () No () Dates of Duty From ___ To ___ Branch ___

EDUCATIONAL INFORMATION

Circle highest grade completed | Grade School 1 2 3 4 5 6 7 8 | High School 9 10 11 12 | College 13 14 15 16 | Post Graduate BS/BA MA PHD

Name and Address of last High School ___ Date of Graduation ___ Have you passed GED Test? Yes () No ()

Type School	Name and address of School	From	To	No. Qtr. Credits	No. Sem. Credits	Degree	Major
College/University							
College/University							
Graduate							
Technical							
Technical							
Military							

List any correspondence courses, special courses, seminars, workshops, training sessions, etc., that might relate to this position. Also list any licenses or certificates relating to position.

*(Not to be asked in New Jersey)
() Except in Michigan)
Form No. OA-201

EMPLOYMENT HISTORY (Begin With the Most Recent)

Employer's Name	Mailing Address	Zip Code	Phone No.
Position Held	Duties Performed		Immed. Supervisor
Employment Dates	Last Salary	Full Time () Part Time ()	Reason For Leaving

Employer's Name	Mailing Address	Zip Code	Phone No.
Position Held	Duties Performed		Immed. Supervisor
Employment Dates	Last Salary	Full Time () Part Time ()	Reason For Leaving

Employer's Name	Mailing Address	Zip Code	Phone No.
Position Held	Duties Performed		Immed. Supervisor
Employment Dates	Last Salary	Full Time () Part Time ()	Reason For Leaving

Employer's Name	Mailing Address	Zip Code	Phone No.
Position Held	Duties Performed		Immed. Supervisor
Employment Dates	Last Salary	Full Time () Part Time ()	Reason For Leaving

May we contact your present employer? Yes () No () If NO, please explain.

UNSALARIED EXPERIENCE

Volunteer Organization	Mailing Address	Zip Code	Phone No.
Position Held	Duties Performed		Immed. Supervisor
Dates of Participation	Hrs. Per Wk.	Skills Learned	

List any other skills or experience which better qualifies you for position

CONVICTION INFORMATION

This Company does not automatically reject applicants who have been convicted. Before any applicant is rejected because of convictions, he/she will be notified of his/her possible rejection. This notice will state the reasons for rejection. The applicant will be given one (1) week to appeal.

Have you ever been convicted as an adult for a criminal violation? Yes () No ()

If yes, date and place. ___ Nature of offense ___ Disposition ___

If yes, date and place. ___ Nature of offense ___ Disposition ___

Figure 17-3. Standard application forms like the one above have been approved by government agencies as being nondiscriminatory.

subjects studied; honors and awards received; participation in extracurricular activities; leadership activities

- **Work Experience:** name, address, and telephone number of present and all previous companies where worked; name and telephone extension number of supervisors; job duties; products or services sold; earnings and whether received as salary or wage, salary plus, or commissions and bonuses; employment dates; reason for leaving

- **Job-Related Information:** type of work sought, salary desired, reason for wanting to change jobs, handicaps that may require modifying the work environment, date available for employment, reason for applying at this company or for this particular job, business or professional association memberships and involvement (if job-related)

A request for certain information can be used as evidence of discrimination in employment. It is not illegal to "ask" about race, color, religion, sex, national origin, age, marital status, medical condition, or handicap. But it is illegal for an employer to discriminate against a job applicant or employee on the basis of one or more of these factors. To be on the safe side, many companies eliminate the following types of information from their application blanks.

- Previous names or original name if changed (however, married people may be asked to provide a maiden name)
- Country or place of birth or any birthplace information about spouse or parents
- National origin, including questions concerning languages spoken in the home, ancestry, nationality, or parentage

- Race (also eliminate request for photo)
- Religion, including information on religious holidays observed
- Sex, including present or past marital status and number of dependents
- Physical characteristics such as height, weight, hairstyle, or handicap (unless a bona fide occupational qualification)
- Organizations: nonbusiness or nonprofessional clubs, fraternal groups, religious organizations, lodges, and sororities

It is difficult to know for sure which questions can be asked on application forms or during subsequent employment interviews. The best guideline is to ask only questions that are specifically related to the job. If you do not need the information to make a hire or no-hire decision, do not ask for it. If you ask for controversial information, you should be prepared to defend that information as relevant to the hiring decision.

Some firms require job applicants to submit a résumé and a letter of application. This is especially true in marketing management or supervisory jobs. The applicant usually is instructed to write a letter of application for a specific job—for example, director of marketing, product manager, or coordinator of sales training—and attach a résumé. Sometimes firms use only the letter and résumé in initially considering job applicants. They do not then require applicants to submit a completed application form. A few firms require a letter of application, a résumé, and a completed application form. However, this usually is not necessary since the information provided on the résumé and the information requested on the application form are essentially the same.

Initial Interview

At a fairly early date in the hiring process, it is recommended that a brief preliminary interview be held. This interview is usually quite short. Its major purposes are to screen out the unqualified and to find out from those applicants who appear to be at least minimally qualified how serious they are about the job.

Sometimes an initial interview is held before the applicant fills out the application form. The applicant goes to the employment office, say, in a wholesale firm, and an interviewer asks questions like the following to determine whether the applicant meets the company's minimal qualifications.

- Are you 18 years or older?
- Have you had any marketing or wholesaling courses in high school or community college or through an adult education program?
- Can you work nights and weekends?
- This job pays $5.75 an hour for the first 90 days. Will that be satisfactory?
- Have you had occupational experience? Please describe.

Obviously, if the wholesaler requires that all employees be at least 18 years old, there is no point asking those 17 and under to complete an application form.

Many job applicants apply at several firms. In fact, it has been estimated that most people with specialized training beyond high school or college apply to at least seven companies before accepting employment. Therefore, it is recommended that those doing the hiring conduct a brief interview or use some other screening method (see the story on page 480) before spending a great deal of time and money phoning or writing references, checking out previous work histories, planning an intensive interview, copying the applicant's completed paperwork, and so on. Often, a "screening" interview can be conducted by phone. The person doing the hiring simply may want to verify that the applicant is still interested in the job or check that the applicant has the minimum qualifications.

Checking References

Perhaps the most important part of the hiring process is checking references. This usually is done through a **reference check,** which involves contacting former employees or supervisors and oth-

THE JOB OF GETTING THE JOB

A résumé printed on a T-shirt arrives in a Brooks Brothers box. A job applicant dons a sandwich board and parades outside a Manhattan ad agency. An aspiring ad copywriter named Randy Rensch sends agencies wrenches with the inscription "When it's a copywriter, it's spelled Rensch." In the back seat of a taxi hangs a sign: "You think I'm a taxi driver. I'm not. I'm an advertising copywriter. Ask for samples."

These are just a few examples of techniques used by aspiring ad copywriters in New York City. Are they successful? "If you're willing to risk a 99 percent chance of being totally wrong," advised Burt Manning, Chairman of J. Walter Thompson U.S.A., "do something crazy, off-the-wall, nutty."

Other than avoiding applicants with crazy, off-the-wall approaches, how do ad agency executives screen the many job applicants? According to one business manager at an ad agency, "The most important product job applicants ever sell is themselves. Nobody in school ever teaches them that. I look for ideas, creativity, and enthusiasm." Says another recruiter, "I look for someone who can think." Some look for graduates from the right schools. Currently rated high by ad executives are the School of Visual Arts in New York and the Art Center College of Design in Pasadena, California. Others include the Parsons School of Design, Pratt Institute, the University of Texas at Austin, Cooper Union, and Syracuse University.

A portfolio of actual ads or speculative samples—a "book"—also helps prospective advertising employers screen applicants. "I avoid cutesie-pootsie, funsy-wunsy writing" says one executive. "I look instead for 'concepts'—ideas that will motivate consumers to buy." Another executive eliminates job applicants if they write dull cover letters. "A good cover letter makes all the difference with me," he says.

Still others look for experience. They want to see evidence on résumés of prior experience, such as a secretary in an ad agency or a salesperson in a retail store.

ers who are qualified to evaluate the applicant's previous work performance or work potential and asking them appropriate questions about the applicant.

It is getting increasingly difficult to dismiss (fire) employees. Many unions and employee groups have negotiated work contracts that protect employees from unjustified dismissal. Often employers or supervisors have to write extensive justifications to dismiss an employee or provide evidence showing that an employee is incompetent or unreliable. Even when employees are not legally protected from dismissal, it usually is very unpleasant to fire someone. Therefore, it is rec-

CHECK THEM OUT, BUT CRAFTILY

In our increasingly litigious society that seems to value convenience over honesty, getting more than a cursory answer to a reference check is difficult. Past employers may paint an overly rosy picture because they are afraid they will get sued if they tell the truth. Besides, it is the current hirer's lookout, not theirs. If someone finally hires the bum, the past employer can stop contributing to unemployment compensation. Or the employee may have left because of a personality clash that would not influence his or her future performance. How to pin down the elusive truth, and why bother at all?

People often are coached on behavior at interviews and are able to create on this one occasion an entirely specious impression. While tests can be given in some instances, all jobs essentially come down to intangibles that only someone who knows the applicant can clue you in on. Some positions subject the employee to a lot of pressure or call for a certain type of personality, such as jobs that require dealing with the public. It is hard to get beyond an immediate impression of the applicant in an interview situation, and if you hire a mistake, it can prove difficult and expensive to rectify. Another reason to check is that doing so is often the only way to explode gross exaggerations of a person's past responsibilities.

Now that you have decided to go ahead and check, how best to go about it? First, there is the telephone versus writing problem. Descending by phone on some unsuspecting soul out of the blue often will elicit only a garbled answer revealing nothing.

ommended that care be taken before a person is hired. Probably the best prediction of future performance is past performance. Former employers and supervisors should be contacted, and the applicant's past job performance and perceived potential for the new job should be discussed. If the applicant has not worked previously, character references provided by the applicant—for example, teachers, counselors, clergy, or neighbors—should be contacted.

The reference check is subject to the same restrictions as all employee recruiting and selection devices. All questions asked of references have to be valid and job-related.

Because of laws and uncertainty regarding legal implications when a negative reference is provided, some supervisors and managers are reluctant to put in writing their true evaluation of an applicant. Character references may feel the same way. It therefore is recommended that prospective employers ask only for the following items of reference information in writing.

- Dates of employment
- Job title and brief description of duties
- Absentee and tardiness record
- Promotions and demotions that are a matter of record
- Beginning and ending salary or wages and how determined
- Applicant's stated reason for terminating employment

On the other hand, no one wants to commit a negative response to writing, a permanent medium that may return to haunt one. If you are in a close-knit industry or a small enough business community, one way around this is to call in some chips and appeal to whatever personal contacts you can muster for an off-the-record, honest verbal response. Check with suppliers, trade associations, professional societies, or anyplace where you know someone who may know the applicant and whose opinion carries some weight.

You have got someone to talk to; try to make it a contact between equals. If the person is not on your exalted level, let a subordinate make the call. Or perhaps call one level above the applicant's supervisor. This person, being one step removed, may have a more objective viewpoint. Listen to what is said and what is left unsaid. Silence and hesitation provide a wealth of information to the trained ear. Ask specific questions, not vague ones, about the person's performance. Ask about strengths and weaknesses, how the reference would rate the person compared to his or her peers, whether the person was committed to the work, whether the reference would rehire the applicant. Be ever alert to a damning but ultimately inconsequential personality clash. Check more than one reference. Also check educational background and professional affiliations. These are easy to do.

Adapted from *AMA Management Digest,* July 1982, p. 40. Copyright TPR Publishing Company, Scarsdale, N.Y.

Telephone calls or personal interviews then may be utilized to obtain more subjective information about the quality of work performed by the applicant. See the story above. Also, job-related information regarding quality of work, co-worker relationships, attitude, and response to supervision and training may be determined through personal contact with the references. Be sure that the questions asked are job-related and that the same questions are asked for all applicants. Figure 17-4 on page 482 shows a telephone reference check, a form that can be used to obtain information on job applicants for sales positions. The purpose of the reference check is to obtain information about the past job behavior of applicants and to verify the accuracy of the information provided on the application form. Be sure to also verify that the

applicant has met minimal qualifications. Copies of required licenses should be obtained. Copies of transcripts from schools should be provided by the applicant if completion of a diploma or a degree is a job requirement. Documentation of any required experiences or training should be provided.

Testing

As a part of hiring procedures, a few companies administer tests. It is not unusual to administer typing or shorthand tests to applicants for clerical positions. Sometimes executive or supervisory applicants are given psychological tests. These tests purport to measure certain aspects of the person's personality, such as temperament, per-

TELEPHONE CHECK

Name of Applicant	
Former Supervisor	Title
Company Where Applicant Worked	Telephone Number

1. (Applicant's name) has applied for employment with us. I would like to *verify* some of the information given us. When did he/she work for your company?

    From _____ 19_____ To _____ 19_____

2. What was his/her job when he/she started to work for you?

    _____

    When he/she left?

    _____

3. He/she says earnings were

    $ _____ per _____
    Is that correct?   ☐ Yes, ☐ No, $ _____

4. What did you think of him/her? (Quality and quantity of work, attendance, how he/she got along with others, etc.)

    _____

    _____

    4a. What accidents has he/she had?

    _____

5. Why did he/she leave your company?

    _____

    _____

6. Would you re-employ?   ☐ Yes, ☐ No, (If not, why not?) _____

    _____

    _____

Additional comments _____

_____

_____

_____

    Date of Check _____ 19_____ Made by _____

Form No. OT-203

Copyright 1975, The Dartnell Corporation, Chicago, Ill. 60640. Printed in U.S.A.
Developed by The McMurry Company

Figure 17-4. A telephone reference check can be used to obtain and verify information on job applicants.

sistence, stability, and so on. It is thought that a person's score on psychological tests should be an indication as to how he or she will react in different types of situations. The Civil Rights Act of 1964 made it unlawful to administer tests that could be used to discriminate on the basis of race. Later interpretations of that act said that tests must measure competencies needed for the job. Employers cannot administer tests and use them as a basis for choosing between applicants unless they can demonstrate that the tests are predictors of subsequent job performance.

Apparently, testing is not particularly popular as a part of the employment process for marketing occupations. There probably are no tests that accurately measure a person's ability to sell, design an advertisement, price a product or service, plan a new product, or evaluate transportation systems. However, two types of tests sometimes are given to marketing employees: a math test and a lie detector test.

A few firms administer a short math test. Supermarkets, department stores, variety stores, and restaurants—firms at which entry-level employees have to perform math calculations in a speedy and accurate way—often give a brief math test to be sure an applicant can compute typical retail math problems accurately.

Lie detector tests apparently are being used more frequently by some businesses. One survey showed that 20 percent of the country's largest corporations have used a lie detector test to check on people's backgrounds and honesty. Another survey showed that as many as 70 percent of all companies administer one before promoting employees into positions in which they have responsibility for large amounts of the public's money or have unsupervised access to drugs.[3] A typical exam lasts 45 minutes, but the person is connected to the machine for only about 5 minutes. All questions are answered by a yes or no. Questions should be asked to validate items on the résumé or the application form. Also, depending on the position being applied for, questions may be asked about drug use, alcohol use, previous criminal activities, and so on. Questions should never be asked about religion, marriage, politics, and after-hours activities unless it can be demonstrated clearly that they are job-related. In fact, job applicants should refuse to answer such questions and report the test administrator to the employer or prospective employer.

Interviewing

Interviewing is probably the most widely used method of selection. Many employees are hired on this basis alone by walking into the company or business at the right time. The employer needs help, the applicant responds well to the interview questions, the interviewer likes the applicant's looks, and the applicant is hired on the spot.

Sad, but true, because the most unreliable aspect of the employment process also is the job interview. Flippo summarized his research on job interviews as follows.

1. Those interviewed immediately after a weak candidate are appraised more favorably.

2. Excessive weight is given to unfavorable information.

3. Interviewer stereotyping exists, with women being recommended for traditionally female-oriented jobs and men recommended for traditionally male-oriented jobs.

4. Interviewers sometimes make a decision very early and conduct the rest of the interview searching for substantiating information.

5. When favorable information is received prior to unfavorable, the applicant fares better.

6. The greater the number of job vacancies, the more favorable the job interview evaluation.

7. Interviewers often are affected by appearance and nonverbal clues that have little to do with job performance.[4]

Nevertheless, interviews are an important and common part of the hiring process. The employment interview can be used to validate the information obtained on the application form or through reference checks. It can be used to clarify apparent misinformation or to obtain additional information about the applicant's experiences, qualifications, and future plans. It can be used to get to know the applicant in a more personal way. Also, the job interview should be used to provide the applicant with further information about the job and the company.

The accuracy of the job interview as a predictor of employment performance can be improved. Recent studies have shown that the use of a structured format with the same or similar questions asked of all applicants for the same job will increase reliability. Some companies videotape or tape-record the interview so that it can be replayed later for more careful analysis. This is helpful if more than one person is involved in the decision to hire or not hire. Taking notes during an interview also can provide the interviewer with more accurate information from which to make the decision at a later time.

There are many principles for good employment interviews. Here is a summary of some good techniques.

1. Plan the Interview Well. Be very familiar with the job description. Know what is expected from a person employed for the job. Determine the objectives for the interview. Prepare questions in advance. Gather all the information on the applicant into one file and read that file carefully. Have a good understanding of the applicant before she or he arrives. Know the person's work history, educational background, special skills and talents, and so forth.

2. Relax the Interviewee. Conduct the interview in a comfortable, private environment. Be sure to introduce yourself. Shake hands. Smile. Offer the applicant a cup of coffee or a soft drink. Open with pleasant but meaningful greeting: "Welcome to Arlington Travel." "Congratulations on passing your real estate exam." "I've been looking forward to meeting the top salesperson in the western area."

3. Ask Open-Ended Questions and Listen Attentively. Questions should be asked in a manner that encourages the interviewee to talk. Avoid asking questions that result in a simple yes or no answer. Instead of asking, "Are you a good problem-solver?" ask, "What was the most difficult problem you have had to solve on your present job? Tell me about the solution you devised." Follow up the applicant's responses with questions that encourage clarification and further descriptions.

4. Provide Job-Related Information. Discuss with the applicant such employment factors as specific job assignment, salary and commissions, fringe benefits, promotion and growth opportunities, supervisory or authority relationships, and benefits of working in this firm. A good impression of the firm should be left with the job applicant.

5. Close the Interview Appropriately. Summarize or clarify the major points discussed. Ask if there are any final questions about the job. Provide information as to what will happen next. For example, you might say, "I have two more persons I will be interviewing for the southern region. A decision should be made within 2 weeks. If you haven't heard from me by May 15, feel free to phone here." Thank the applicant for considering this firm for employment, shake hands, and escort the person out of the room or office.

6. Evaluate the Applicant Immediately. Make evaluation comments on the application form or complete a form like the one shown in Figure 17-5.

JOB APPLICANT EVALUATION

Applicant's name ____________________

Position applied for ____________________

Match the qualifications of the applicant carefully with those identified on the job description. Also, use notes from the application form, interviews, reference checks, and test scores to arrive at your evaluation.

Requirements	Not Applicable	Unacceptable	Marginal	Meets Requirements	Exceeds Requirements
Education: Degree(s) and/or required courses/training					
Required occupational experiences					
Knowledge of product					
Knowledge of service					
Appearance/Mannerisms					

Preferences	Not Applicable	Unacceptable	Poor	Satisfactory	Excellent
Overall response to questions					
Other occupational experiences					
Energy					
Human relationships					
Self-reliance					
Dependability					
Leadership					
____________					
____________					

Strong points for this position ____________________

Weak points for this position ____________________

Overall rating ____________ Rated by ____________

Recommendation to Employ [Yes] [No] Department ____________

Date ____________

Figure 17-5. Form for evaluating an applicant.

THE FOLLOW-THROUGH CALL THAT NEVER CAME

Dear Ann Landers: Across America there must be others sharing my dilemma. I am out of work, out of money to look for work and I am borrowing money to continue the search. Now I'm trusting God that if I continue to seek, I shall find. But during the search I've encountered a very upsetting problem. Maybe if I write about it, I can forget it. Also, some employer may see himself and shape up.

Mr./Mrs. Employer, I came to you at your convenience. I filled out your forms, took the tests and waited for that interview I was so thankful to get. At the interview's end, you said, "I will make my decision and call you between 4 and 5 p.m. tomorrow and let you know one way or the other."

Of course, I stayed home and waited for the call. Not only did I wait, I prayed. Every minute seemed like an hour. At 6:05, I decided you were not going to call. Ever.

Here is something you probably did not know. I came to you on my last tank of gas, with a hungry stomach, thinking of an empty cupboard and those who share it. I hope you will treat the next job applicant better than you treated me—for his or her sake, as well as yours.—**Dignity Damaged In San Diego**

Dear D.D.: Such insensitivity is inexcusable. Of course, it's unpleasant to phone an applicant and say, "You didn't get the job," but he'd rather get that call than wait, and wait, and arrive at the conclusion on his own. Thanks for a letter that may make life easier for others.

Source: Field News Service.

Selection

This usually is the time when the decision must be made about whom to hire. Application materials have been gathered and appraised, references and data have been checked out, relevant tests may have been administered and evaluated, and the applicant has been interviewed by at least one person. In some firms additional information or data may have been collected. For example, some companies require a physical examination. They want to be certain an applicant is physically able to perform adequately before they make a job offer. Many companies conduct group interviews. For example, the employees in the marketing research department may interview as a group all final job applicants for the department head position. Or the several owners of a small marketing consulting firm may jointly interview final applicants for a special position. A few companies require performance demonstrations as part of the hiring process. A candidate for a sales training position may have to give a 5 or 10 minute sales or teaching demonstration.

No matter how short or lengthy the process or how much or what kind of data and evaluative comments are collected, someone has to make the decision. There are two additional suggestions to help employment decision makers decide which applicant to hire. First, be sure to use all data collected as the basis for the decision. Avoid a "halo effect" of hiring a person on the basis of one or two or your pet factors, such as appearance or grades in school. Second, use a job applicant evaluation form to help make the decision more objective. Figure 17-5 may be useful for this purpose.

Follow Through

Now the person who has been employed has to be contacted, and an appropriate plan must be set in motion. The applicant should be phoned, told the good news, congratulated, welcomed aboard, and given further information regarding orientation, training dates, forms and records that have to be filed with the company, and so on. A confirming letter should follow, stating any special employment terms, salary, starting date, and other information according to company policy.

Applicants who were not selected should be notified. A note or telephone call thanking them for applying and informing them of the decision may be sufficient. The story on page 485 shows a letter on this subject written to Ann Landers. "D.D.'s" letter and Ann's response say it all. Some companies also provide a brief reason for rejecting the applicant, often pointing out the strengths of the person who was selected: "Although we were favorably impressed with your application, the person selected has 6 months more experience." Many companies have a policy of keeping all applicants' papers on file for up to a year so that they can be reconsidered should a vacancy occur. This is another good reason why a pleasant follow-up phone call or letter is important.

TRAINING MARKETING EMPLOYEES

Employees must be oriented to and trained for a job. The first few days on a job can be frightening and unpleasant for a new employee. In fact, several studies have shown that nonexistent or inef-

fective employee induction and training leads to increased employee turnover, job dissatisfaction, and low productivity. Conversely, well-planned and well-delivered training programs lead to increased productivity, heightened morale, better employee loyalty, reduced costs, and less turnover.

It is important to get a new employee started right. Most new employees are eager and excited about the new job and want to make a good showing. Supervisors should take advantage of this enthusiasm and begin immediately to orient the employee to the job and the company. Also, training should be an ongoing activity. All workers need some initial training. Sometimes people need complete retraining if they change positions or careers, and people can always learn how to do their jobs more effectively and efficiently through continuing education and planned training programs. Training is going to happen whether the company plans and controls it or not. Employees are going to learn how to get the job done. What they do on the job and how they do it may not be exactly what management had in mind, but employees do learn how to survive in the organization. There usually is a direct and positive relationship between well-managed and profitable companies and satisfied and well-trained employees. If workers know what they are doing, how to do it well, and why they are doing it, the company has a better chance to be prosperous.

Employee Orientation

Certainly the first step in employee training is getting the new worker off to a good start. **Orientation** is an organized effort on the part of a company to get a new worker acclimated to the company, the job, and the co-workers. The way this is done may vary. Some companies have a personnel department which handles most of the employee orientation. Some have a training department which may organize special classes to orient new employees. In small businesses, the owner or manager often does all of the orientation and training. Often a first-line supervisor is responsible for all or a part of employee orientation. In one study, it was found that over 60 percent of 350 large companies surveyed put most of the activities, forms, and content that normally are a part of employee orientation into a booklet for new workers. In every firm, there are certain procedures that should be followed when inducting new employees.

First, the orientation program should be well planned. All the people involved with it should know their responsibilities and approximately when they are to be involved or are to introduce new activities. The following is a list of items that should be a part of an orientation program. This list can be used as a basis from which to plan an orientation program. Not all the items have to be part of everyone's orientation, since some are not appropriate for all jobs. They should not all be given in the first few hours or even the first few days on the job, but at some point many of them will need to be reviewed with the new employee or should be a part of the orientation process.

- Greetings and welcome to new employee
- Introduction to co-workers
- Brief discussion about the company: history, products, and services
- Company organization, including chart, with line and staff relationships
- Company's successes and why it is a good place to work
- Tour of the company
- Pay periods, method of payment, and paperwork necessary to receive pay (tax forms, insurance forms, time clock forms, medical forms, and so on)
- Policies regarding the many aspects of the work environment: dress codes, personal telephone calls, attendance, tardiness, smoking, eating and drinking, lunch hours, and rest breaks.
- Education and training programs
- Promotion policies and opportunities
- Evaluation system and forms
- Employment services such as credit union, gift or flower fund, company-sponsored socials,

Figure 17-6. Orientation of new employees may include films and discussion.

awards, recreation programs, house organ, bulletin boards, and employee counseling
- Employee benefits such as vacations, sick leave, funeral leave, holidays, discounts, and profit sharing.
- Safety and accident prevention including fire exits, reporting accidents, and legal aspects
- Termination policies regarding permanent dismissal, layoffs, recalls, number of days required to notify if quitting, and exit interview
- Location of equipment and supplies, all departments, rest rooms, lounges, and stock room

When orienting new employees, most people spend the first couple of hours just discussing the company, touring the firm, responding to questions, and trying to get to know and relax the new employees. Next, paperwork is taken care of: tax forms, insurance forms, payroll forms, and so on.

Then, depending on the size of the company and the nature of the job, the formal training program is begun. In many retail and service businesses, the new employee is taken immediately to the department or area of placement and introduced to the work group. The job is reviewed for the new employee, who often begins to work at that moment. In other companies, the new employee may go through an intensive training program of 6 weeks to 6 months before work actually is begun.

On-the-Job Training

Probably the most common type of marketing education or training provided for American business is given right on the job in department stores, supermarkets, banks, travel agencies, restaurants, service stations, hotels, and cars and offices as sales managers travel or meet with new reps. Much of it could be improved if the person doing the training followed some very basic principles.

Step 1: Prepare the Learner. People who want to learn are easy to teach. New employees are usually the easiest to teach because they do want the job and want to do it right. They need to be told why the job is important and why it must be done right. Tell the new worker what it is you are going to do, why it is important, and how the new worker will demonstrate that he or she can do the job.

Step 2: Demonstrate How the Job Should be Done. Or arrange for someone else to do the demonstration. New workers need to be shown the correct procedure whether it is setting a table in a restaurant, taking inventory, entering data into the computer, or helping customers buy shoes. This should be done slowly, step by step, with time for the new employee to ask questions. Let the new worker observe carefully and listen as correct procedures (including the why) are explained and demonstrated.

Step 3: Allow the Learner to Practice. Under your supervision, the learners should be given plenty of time to practice. Encourage them when they

do it correctly. "Great, John." "That was a good headline you wrote, Helen." Correct them when something is not being done correctly. Mistakes they make while you are watching are invaluable in the learning process. They tell you where you may have missed something in your explanation or step-by-step procedure. Once the trainees have performed the tasks in the practice sessions to your satisfaction, turn them loose on the real thing.

Step 4: Follow up. An extremely important step is to check on the new employee's progress periodically. Let the person fly and try it alone for a while. But check on the employee regularly, perhaps three or four times the first day and less frequently as the job becomes more familiar. Workers should be put on their own gradually. Follow up by observing the trainee and then praise areas of good performance, correct mistakes, work on improving technique, and identify areas for new training.

These steps will almost guarantee success if sufficient time is given to each step and if the training is done in the right spirit. It cannot be overemphasized that people generally want to do a good job. They want to be successful at work and are eager to learn a job and do it well. Effective training helps them do a good job. Periodic follow up should allow any mistakes to be corrected as well as enable the trainer to identify areas in which further training is needed. Well-trained and productive employees make supervisors look good to their customers and managers. They also free the supervisors so that more time can be spent on planning, organizing, directing, and controlling the work environment.

Group Instruction. Some companies are large enough to develop and conduct their own training programs. Periodically, they conduct group sessions in a room that has been designed for training purposes. Well-designed training rooms usually are equipped with modern equipment or hardware, for example, computers, overhead projectors, wall boards, bulletin boards, videotaping and video playback machines, posters and charts, slide projectors, 35mm and 16mm film projectors, and instructional references. This hardware and related software are very helpful in group instruction.

In addition to the use of hardware, there are many training methods that should be used to enhance initial learning and retention by employees. Good teachers and trainers learn to use a variety of methods to help students learn and apply what is being taught: role playing, question and answer sessions, employee demonstrations, simulations, in-basket techniques, and games.

Individualized Instruction. This consists of using hardware and materials to train a single individual for a specific job. Individualized instruction is used by firms who hire infrequently or never hire enough employees at one time to make group instruction practical. Some firms use individualized learning systems to train people in highly specialized skills. In this system, each trainee should be able to work at his or her own pace, begin and end the lesson when convenient, begin at a point appropriate to his or her past experiences, and tailor the instruction to his or her needs.

Individualized learning systems usually include computer-assisted instruction (CAI), programmed learning, and materials prepared by commercial publishing companies and trade associations.

Off-the-Job Training

There are many different kinds of training programs and techniques to develop effective employees and employers that are available off the job. Let us take a look at some of the more frequently used programs and courses.

Adult and Continuing Education. The least expensive and most readily available off-the-job training programs are sponsored by public schools and colleges. Nearly every school system in the country, every community college, and many colleges and universities offer some form of adult and continuing education. These courses usually do not require enrollees to have earned high school diplomas or other prerequisites.

Courses, seminars, workshops, and meetings may range from a 2 hour lecture on shoplifting prevention or compliance with federal labor laws to an evening program of 2 years' duration preparing insurance agents to market group, medical, auto, life, and individual insurance. Increasingly, schools, especially community colleges and postsecondary vocational-technical schools, are offering classes or programs for specific business and industry groups. Thus, a technical school may offer a 10 hour program to a company's first-line supervisors on developing and implementing quality circles. Or a community college may work with the local florist association to sponsor a short workshop on new techniques of arranging flowers for weddings. Many of these schools have full-time coordinators whose job is to determine employment training needs in the community and provide classes or seminars to meet those needs. Get to know these people. They can be an invaluable source for meeting your training needs.

Private Consulting and Training Groups. Literally hundreds of large and small firms have been organized to assist companies with employee training or any other problems the companies may be experiencing. These firms sponsor short or extensive sessions on a wide array of topics depending on a firm's needs: employee recruitment and selection, computer systems implementation and operation, marketing research, supervision, management, sales training, customer courtesy, financial accounting and management, tax management, and so forth. Often these business consultants or training groups are viewed as too expensive, especially for small businesses. Indeed, they are in business to make a profit, and they probably charge more than public schools or colleges. But the cost of getting expert advice or professional assistance from people who have "been there" may well be worth the investment. Specialized knowledge may be essential to solve certain kinds of problems, especially in highly technical areas. Also, specialists, consultants, and private firms usually can move much faster than schools.

When selecting a consultant or a firm to help with a firm's training needs, it is usually a good idea to hire one that will (1) provide references for similar work completed in the past (be sure to check these out), (2) let you participate actively in determining training content and methods, (3) prepare an outline of content and procedures to be followed for your approval, (4) devise a follow-up plan, and (5) provide you with a fairly detailed cost breakout for charges.

Small Business Administration. If you are considered by the government to be a small business, you have this major additional resource to help you meet some of your training needs.

There are many services provided by the Small Business Administration (SBA): financial assistance to people who want to start or expand small businesses, guaranteed loans made by commercial banks to small businesses, helping small businesses receive fair treatment in the procurement of federal grants and contracts, helping them comply with complex federal laws and regulations, and granting women and minorities special status so that they may obtain an SBA-guaranteed loan to open or expand small businesses.

But two services of the Small Business Administration are especially advantageous: their training materials and their consultative assistance. The SBA produces hundreds of short pamphlets on various topics appropriate for small business owners or managers.

The SBA also provides for counseling or consultative services. The Service Corps of Retired Executives (SCORE) was created by the SBA in the 1960s. This group consists of retired executives who provide technical advice and management consultation on request to small businesses. Subsequently, business executives currently active in their professional careers also agreed to provide limited technical and management consultative services. Known as ACE (Active Corps of Executives), these business executives voluntarily assist other small business managers or owners with their business-related problems.

In the 1970s, seniors and graduate students in colleges and universities also joined the volunteer counselor ranks as part of SBA-sponsored Small Business Institutes (SBI). Over 450 schools now offer management and technical assistance to small businesses. At the same time, these students have an opportunity to apply book learning in real-life businesses. All the training and consultative services sponsored by the SBA are associated with some universities. Known as Small Business Development Centers (SBDCs), these units have a resident management assistance officer from the SBA, on-site SCORE and ACE volunteers, SBI student consultants, professional full-time business analysts, marketing and management faculty, and reference materials.[5]

SUPERVISING EMPLOYEES IN MARKETING

The marketing staff has been hired. They have been trained so that they understand what to do and how to do it. The next important area in working with marketing employees is providing on-the-job supervision.

In general, day-to-day supervision of marketing employees is the responsibility of a first-line supervisor. This person has been described as a "linking pin" between two groups within an organization. As such, the supervisor is the superior in one group and a subordinate in the other, or the link between the two. The first-line supervisor is the lowest ranking member of the management hierarchy with direct responsibility for supervising nonmanagement employees. Since the passage of the Taft-Hartley Act in 1947, the first-line supervisor is legally considered to be a member of management. In this act, which defined the relationship between management and unions, the **supervisor** is defined as

any individual having authority, in the interest of the employer, to hire, transfer, suspend, lay off, recall, promote, discharge,

Figure 17-7. First-line marketing supervisors are responsible for a number of leadership functions.

assign, reward or discipline other employees, or the responsibility to direct them, or to adjust their grievances, or effectively to recommend such action, if in connection with the foregoing the exercise of such authority is not of a merely routine or clerical nature, but requires the use of independent judgment.[6]

Most modern marketing practices seem to indicate that first-line supervisors are responsible for the day-to-day operations of a department, section, territory, or any other clearly defined unit or area. First-line marketing supervision includes assistant managers in most retail stores, branch managers in banks and other financial institutions, section heads or department managers of marketing in most companies, sales managers, buyers or assistant buyers, and field supervisors. In addition to hiring and training employees, first-line marketing supervisors typically provide leadership to the employees within their units, structure the work environment to get the jobs done, and counsel, evaluate, and discipline employees. (See Figure 17-7.)

Leadership

If you were to survey 25 people regarding their definition of leadership, you probably would receive 25 different and perhaps contradictory replies. Much has been written about effective leadership styles, and theories abound. Part of the confusion regarding leadership and leaders stems from the fact that this science is constantly evolving and changing. There probably is no one best way to lead and provide for leadership that is appropriate for all situations.

Leadership Described. In the work environment, a **leader** often is described as the individual who is given the responsibility for working with employees to ensure that the work gets done. The leader can be elected or appointed. In most companies, this person is appointed by management, although there is some evidence that employees are beginning to elect their team leaders or supervisors.

Hundreds of studies have been done to determine leadership traits. Attempts have been made

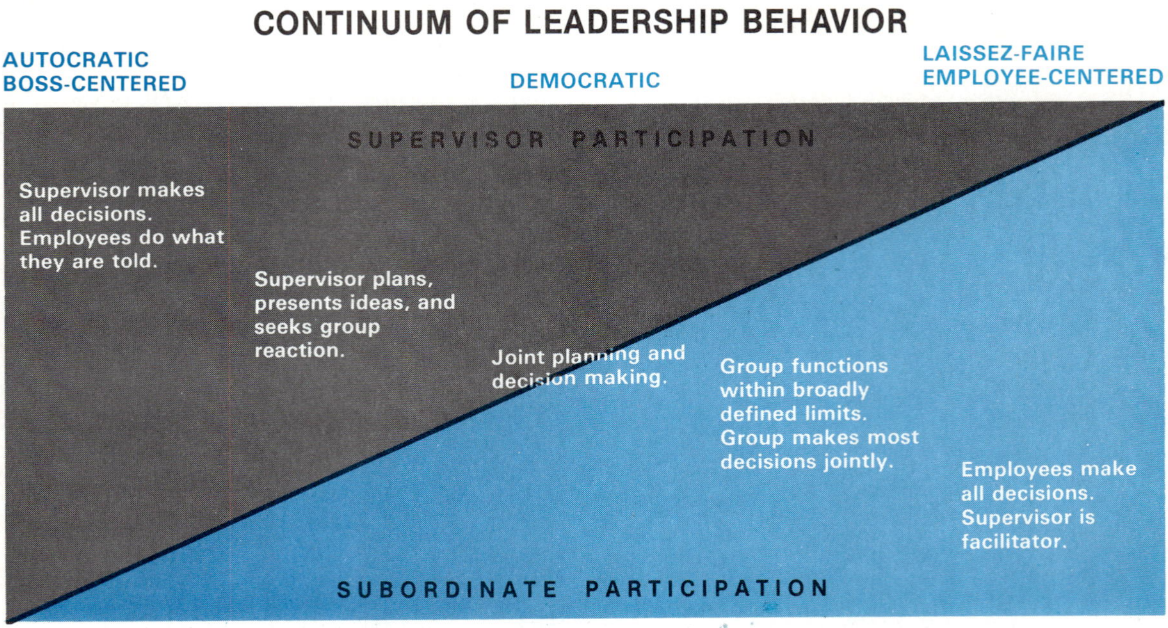

CONTINUUM OF LEADERSHIP BEHAVIOR

AUTOCRATIC
BOSS-CENTERED   DEMOCRATIC   LAISSEZ-FAIRE
EMPLOYEE-CENTERED

SUPERVISOR PARTICIPATION

Supervisor makes
all decisions.
Employees do what
they are told.

Supervisor plans,
presents ideas, and
seeks group
reaction.

Joint planning and
decision making.

Group functions
within broadly
defined limits.
Group makes most
decisions jointly.

Employees make
all decisions.
Supervisor is
facilitator.

SUBORDINATE PARTICIPATION

Figure 17-8. Leadership behavior can range from boss-centered to minimal supervision.

to associate leadership with factors such as age, sex, intelligence, height, weight, physical appearance, grades in school or college, dominance, self-confidence, degrees earned, human relations skills, and emotional control. The general conclusion from these studies is that no one trait or even combination of traits seems to indicate a significant difference between those who possess it and those who do not.

Current thinking seems to indicate that effective leadership is associated with a supervisor who can organize a group cooperatively to accomplish the tasks that need to be done. This person effectively integrates motivation and human relations skills, management functions (planning, organizing, directing, and controlling), reasonable technical expertise, and a good self-concept. Therefore, if there are traits or qualities that must be possessed by an effective first-line marketing supervisor, they would surely include the following.

- Social sensitivity
- Self-confidence
- Communications skills

- Ability to solve technical and human relations problems
- Energy
- Adequate product or service knowledge
- Marketing skills
- Willingness to accept the consequences of decisions and actions
- Ability to influence others
- Tolerance of frustrations, delays, and inactivity

Leadership Behavior. Leadership behavior can be viewed as a continuum (see Figure 17-8) from very boss-centered and autocratic to an almost laissez-faire approach. In **autocratic leadership,** the supervisor calls nearly all the shots. The supervisor does all the planning, assigns tasks to subordinates, and controls employee behavior through rewards and coercive power. Emphasis is placed on structure, clearly defined roles and responsibilities, authority, and discipline. At the other end of the continuum is **laissez-faire leadership,** under which subordinates generally do what they want within an overall framework of achieving company or department goals. Supervision is minimal if it exists at all.

Most modern companies fall somewhere in the middle of the continuum. The center areas generally are described as being somewhat participative or democratic in styles of leadership. In **democratic leadership,** the supervisor discusses ideas with those being supervised, works with them to set goals and deadlines, jointly establishes some policies, consults with the group on solving problems and developing solutions, and works toward group consensus before decisions are made. The democratic approach to leadership places more emphasis on communicating with subordinates about their needs, building a strong work team, and using the expertise of employees in solving problems.

Theory Z: Democratic Leadership

The principles depicted in the story on page 494 are fairly new in American industry. They are referred to variously as quality circles, participatory management, Theory Z, or democratic leadership. The basic idea is to have supervisors and employees seek a consensus on company operations. This is in contrast to more traditional managerial or supervisory approaches in which all plans and orders are passed down from above.

Thus far, the concepts identified with Theory Z have been implemented in this country primarily in production-oriented industries. However, the concepts have great potential for improving productivity in marketing. It is believed that far greater application of Theory Z principles will occur in distribution-oriented and service businesses in the years ahead.

The basic idea of Theory Z is to have managers and workers seek a consensus on company operations instead of having orders passed down from above. The theory and its processes come from the Japanese, who experienced a productivity gain of 7.2 percent over a 20 year period, compared with 2.2 percent for the United States in the same period.[7] Theory Z is based on an important assumption of trust. You have to trust your employees. As stated in *Business Week,* "Japanese

managers trust not only their workers but also their peers and supervisors."[8] According to *Business Week,* "The existence of that all encompassing trust leads to a simplified organizational structure. . . . Japanese assume that personnel at all levels are competent—and above all, trustworthy enough to have the company's best interests in mind—they do not employ highly paid executives whose only jobs are to review the work of other highly paid executives." This means that companies do not need so many managers who primarily review the work and reports of others. If the Japanese model is followed, the managers themselves become part of the team and actually do the work in tandem with those they are supervising. This type of structural model leads to lower costs. Japanese line supervisors in the auto industry, for example, report directly to plant managers. American auto workers have at least three layers of management in any one plant. At the Ford Motor Company there are 11 layers of management between the factory workers and the company chairperson, whereas at Toyota there are 6. The Japanese can make a car and ship it to this country for $1,500 less than it costs to make and market the same car here. One of the reasons is high American overhead associated with management and other labor costs and red tape.[9]

Quality Circles. The process most often cited to bring about implementation of a Theory Z management or leadership style is known as quality circles. A **quality circle** (QC) has been defined as "a group of eight to ten workers and supervisors, generally involved in related work, who meet regularly to identify and solve product quality and production problems. QC members are usually instructed in a variety of statistical and group problem-solving techniques to assist them in interpreting information and generating ideas."[10]

As a participative problem-solving method, the quality circle is applicable to office, manufacturing, and marketing jobs. In this country it has been applied most frequently to reducing absenteeism and turnover, improving the quality of work life, information processing, information

QUALITY CIRCLES IN THE SUPERMARKET

Broken eggs, wasted meat, and wilted vegetables are the special nightmares in the nearly 30,000 supermarkets across the country that haul in sales of $171.6 billion each year but rely on a razor-thin 1 percent to 2 percent of gross sales for net profits.

The source of the problem is usually disaffected employees. A possible solution is quality circles, the Japanese management concept that has become popular among American management experts.

The quality circle, more often associated with manufacturing, now is moving into such labor-intensive service industries as banks, hospitals, and supermarkets. The food chains, which have been experimenting with the concept in warehousing for some time, are now promoting it in their stores.

"We've got quality circles for store managers, our front-end clerks (cashiers), our meat departments, and so on," said Frank Lennon, vice president of human resources for the 55 store Price Chopper chain in upstate New York.

"We had one situation where a few of our employees were so upset with their jobs they would 'accidentally' destroy a fair percentage of dairy products, eggs in particular," adds another supermarket executive. He turned to the quality circle. "A member of the quality circle approached the disgruntled employees and told them to knock it off. Amazingly, they did."

The standard supermarket industry quality circle consists of 8 to 12 store employees who meet every week or two to attempt to identify problems and implement solutions in a availability, determining areas of need for further training, and improving communications between and among work units.

Here are a few examples.

- Aetna Life & Casualty Co. of Hartford, Connecticut, used the QC approach to develop ideas for reducing paperwork. Forty-two ideas were generated, and a priority list of eight was selected for implementation.

- The Sanger-Harris Department Store in Dallas faced a tough time recruiting hourly workers. The QC decision was to allow certain hourly employees (primarily full-time homemakers) to work 9 months of the year, take the summer off, and return in the fall with no loss of seniority and to use college students to replace these employees during summer months. According to a spokesperson, "The program is working very, very well."

- Citibank credits quality circles with designing procedures to speed up the walk-up lines for its bank customers.

- RCA's Hertz Rental Car Division says that its employee QCs in Oklahoma City have made car reservation procedures more efficient.

- General Electric psychologists surveyed groups including 120 workers involved in circle discussions and 120 employees doing similar wide range of productivity-related areas. Problems range from absenteeism to inventory shrinkage, according to Paul Gibson, vice president of human resources for the Cincinnati-based Kroger chain, which instituted retail-level quality circles in 1981.

"We're in the process now of determining our return on investment," Mr. Gibson said, "but I can tell you that in our seven test stores—and we're going to be expanding to include many more—attitude surveys indicate that the hourly employees were less committed, less involved, and less interested before we implemented our team-building plan. Our turnover was higher, too. Now our employees are much more committed to their jobs and to the success of the stores."

Harvey Davis, assistant executive director of the International Association of Quality Circles, a nonprofit professional organization, said that perhaps 500 companies were using quality circles just a year ago, while up to 2,000 are doing so now. Most of the growth is appearing in service industries. "The basic psychological concept of using quality circles to improve productivity is so sound that it's surprising more supermarkets aren't using them," Mr. Davis said. "It's simply a matter of recognizing the dignity of the worker."

Adapted from Dan Shannon, "Productivity: Quality Circles for Supermarkets," *New York Times,* April 18, 1982, p. F-19. Copyright © 1982 by The New York Times Company. Reprinted by permission.

work who were not members of circles both before and after the QCs were set up. There was a 15 percent positive change in the attitudes of workers in quality circles during the 6 month period but a 15 percent decline in the control group.[11]

- One group in Japan examined itself and decided that its members were all in poor health. They initiated a physical fitness program that brought such striking results in terms of the group's physical well-being and work output that the program was extended throughout the company. Similar physical fitness programs are being adopted by many companies in this country.

Advantages and Disadvantages of Quality Circles. Clearly, the potential for improvements from quality circles is great. The future looks especially good for solving marketing problems, providing better service, and creating cash-savings devices. However, a few difficulties should be analyzed before a company decides to go with this system. First, the program requires commitment on the part of the company and the employees. Robert Blake and Jane Mouton state that

If the culture of a company is not conducive to and effective in promoting participation, and if [QC] development is not top-led and line-managed, then the insertion of a quality circle at the bottom of an organization is likely to provide the circumstances under which members can vent frustration at management, with the result that many suggestions and recommendations are sent to management regarding how things should be corrected. If nothing happens, those who made the recommendations feel alienated, frustrated, and thus uncommitted to continuing the process.[12]

Employees also must be committed, but this is not always the case. In fact, a few unions, such as the United Electrical Workers, have a national policy of refusing to cooperate in quality circles.[13] Many workers simply do not trust management or feel that it is not "their job" to solve company problems.

A second consideration is that it probably will take time, effort, and money to start a program. In medium-size or large companies, at least one full-time "facilitator" usually must be hired and "team leaders"—often first-line supervisors—must undergo basic training in questioning techniques, group dynamics, problem solving, and group decision making. Group members should receive training on brainstorming, the problem-solving process, and how to make suggestions for improvements. Very small businesses may not be able to afford to hire a QC facilitator. This should not prevent a small business owner or manager from utilizing Theory Z principles. But such a person ought to receive some training in how to implement the process, perhaps through an adult or continuing education program.

A third consideration is that most authorities on quality circles recommend that they be conducted on company time. Meetings should be held weekly or biweekly, with groups of 8 to 10 employees working in similar jobs or departments within the company. The leader works out an agenda for members to review, usually including relevant data, background information, areas of concern or performance to be discussed, and any other reports that should be analyzed in advance of the meeting.

Quality circles are a long-range technique for improving productivity. They also have an immediate effect of improving morale and the quality of work life. The GE study and others like it have attested to improvement in employee morale through the implementation of quality circles. Furthermore, employees are motivated to perform better if they feel that they have some control over the work environment and some input into decisions that affect them on the job. Several large companies (Honeywell, Lockheed, and Texas Instruments) have reported huge savings as a result of initiating full-fledged quality circle programs.

As Jerome Rosow, president of the Work in America Institute, stated about quality circles, they "unleash the talents and knowledge of people who know where the 'bodies are buried,' who know where the waste is, but have never been asked." He went on to say: "All employees have valuable contributions to make to productivity; they are more likely to make such contributions in structured situations where they feel their suggestions will receive serious consideration. It is the responsibility of management to create an environment that promotes productivity growth through improved involvement of people."[14]

Structuring the Work Environment

A major set of tasks to be accomplished by first-line supervisors in marketing is to structure the work environment to get the various jobs done. Supervisors have to analyze just what work needs to be done, who is to do it, how it is to be done, and when it is to be done. They then must work with the employees they supervise to see that the various tasks are completed.

Effective marketing supervisors learn to plan quickly and plan well. They involve their subordinates in the planning process. Periodically, time should be set aside for the entire unit to engage in planning. The supervisor leads the group through the process of deciding what needs to be accomplished, how it is to be accomplished, who is to do what, and time lines that are to be met. If the employees are new, inexperienced, or very dependent on the supervisor, the supervisor may need to do more of the structuring. But even then, employees should have the opportunity to make suggestions, recommend changes, and otherwise influence the what, who, how, and when of getting the job done.

Jerry Lotus is the manager of the lawn and garden department of the Howard Farm and Garden Supply Store in Joplin, Missouri. A goal established by the owner of Howard's in consultation with Jerry and other employees was to increase sales in the lawn and garden department by 12 percent in each of the next 3 years. To achieve this year's goal, Jerry and his colleagues decided to conduct a heavily promoted early spring sale of garden stock and supplies. Jerry jotted down the following tasks that had to be accomplished for this sale.

- Obtain sufficient stock for the sale.
- Rearrange space to accommodate the stock and display it to its best advantage.
- Prepare newspaper and radio advertisements and other promotional materials.
- Hire two additional sales people for the 6 week period and train them in necessary product knowledge and store operations.
- Coach the current employees in product knowledge and selling techniques to best serve the needs of customers.
- Ensure that appropriate supplies are on hand: dirt, plant pots, wire, bags, boxes, sales checks, and so on.
- Inform the supervisors and employees in the other two departments about the sale and encourage them to mention it to their customers.
- Schedule current and new employees to assure that adequate sales and service help are available throughout the sale.
- Make price and product description signs for most items in the department.

Most of these tasks will be accomplished by Jerry in consultation with his other employees. He will delegate certain tasks to others, or he and another person may work on some of them together. Of course, it must be remembered that these tasks are associated with the upcoming spring sale. Jerry has plenty of other work to do in his job as a first-line supervisor.

Counseling Employees

From the time employees are recruited until the time they are separated from an organization, a large portion of their lives is influenced by supervisors, co-workers, and other people and factors in the work environment. Of course, their lives also are influenced heavily by nonwork factors such as family, friends, past experiences, hobbies, religion, and so forth. It would be easy to say that one can carefully separate an employee's life into two areas: the job and personal. Unfortunately, this is not so. Job-related factors greatly affect a person's life and relationships with family and friends. It is not always easy to turn it off when one leaves the business after a working day. Especially negative job-related factors such as being put down by the supervisor, a poor evaluation, or lack of recognition for good work will influence almost anyone's relationship with family and friends. Conversely, stressful personal factors such as a bad marriage, financial worries, or health problems are certain to affect one's performance at work.

As a first-line supervisor, you will have to deal with employees who have problems. Not all employees have serious problems, of course, but you are certain to encounter one or more of the following if you remain in a supervisory position for very long: stress and burnout, alcoholism, drug abuse, tobacco abuse, discrimination, family problems, financial problems, and mental health disablement.

Here are a few statistics.

- "Ten percent of the overall population at sometime exhibits burnout."[15]
- "Alcoholism affects 5 to 10 percent of the country's work force and costs business at least $15 billion a year in absenteeism, accidents, sick

leave, poor work, and expensive results of bad executive judgment."[16]

- Drug abuse on the job ranges from 0.5 percent of managers using hard drugs (as compared with 1.5 percent of production and service workers) to 5 percent of service and production workers abusing marijuana.[17]

- Over 40 million Americans smoke cigarettes at work. Smokers tend to be absent from work twice as often as nonsmokers. Smokers cost the company more in medical care, insurance premiums, and lost time on the job.[18]

- Approximately 40 percent of all first-time marriages end in divorce. Husband-wife families will comprise less than 55 percent of all households by 1990.[19]

Supervisors are not expected to be expert counselors or personal problem solvers. Most are not equipped to deal with the more severe problems of their employees and are not expected to do so. As a supervisor, however, it is sometimes sufficient to listen and to provide the employee an opportunity to discuss his or her feelings with you.

The following are a few suggestions to consider when counseling employees, regardless of the problem.

- Try to relax the individual and make him or her feel comfortable. Provide privacy to make the interview confidential. Keep the conversation confidential.

- Let the person talk. Be a good listener. Try to clarify periodically what is being said but do not be quick to give advice or provide solutions.

- Get the pertinent facts. Keep probing until all relevant facts are clear and fall into place. Watch for contradictions and point them out gently.

- Try to be nonjudgmental. Accept what is being said but avoid expressing opinion, surprise or disappointment, or even sympathy. Do not lecture or moralize.

- Help the person gain insight or perspective on the problem. Perhaps you can put the problem in a broader perspective. Is it really all that serious? What are a few changes that might reduce the burden? How is this problem affecting the work place?

- Try to get the person to find his or her own solution. Often the person already has thought it through. Perhaps you can subtly offer some alternatives: "Have you considered . . ." or "Did you ever think about . . ."

- Avoid temptations that may be natural, such as arguing, providing the solution, criticizing, moralizing, getting upset, appearing disinterested, or throwing your hands up in the air in despair. Try to listen patiently and show concern for the individual.

- Conclude the visit in an appropriate time framework. Arrange for follow-up if necessary. Unless you are involved in the solution, it is probably appropriate for you to step out of it right now. You might check casually at a later time to see if things worked out as planned.

It is not easy to get involved in someone else's troubles, but it is doubtful that there has been a supervisor anywhere who has not had to do some employee counseling. Try to be helpful, but also learn to respect your own time and limitations. Do not hesitate to make appropriate referrals: family counseling, mental health clinics, Alcoholics Anonymous, certified financial counselors, and so on. Do not become overly involved or you will wind up having more problems than you are experiencing already.

Evaluating Employees

Evaluation of employees is an inevitable occurrence in any organization. Supervisors constantly observe their employees at work, review sales or other reports, and otherwise form impressions about the value their subordinates possess within the organization. Over two-thirds of all companies use a formal program to evaluate employees. These programs exist under a variety of labels and have varying degrees of complexity. Typical descriptions include merit rating, performance appraisal, employee evaluation, and year-end review.

In marketing, the first-line supervisor usually conducts the employee evaluation, including the appraisal interview. This person is then responsible for any follow-up or corrective action that may be necessary.

Purposes of Employee Evaluation.

There are three primary reasons for evaluating employees: (1) to give them reasonably objective and adequate feedback concerning performance, (2) to improve performance, that is, to identify areas of needed training or areas in which employees need to modify behavior toward more effective working habits, and (3) to provide supervisors with data from which to make decisions about future job assignments, promotions, demotions, wage and salary increases, and dismissal of incompetent employees.

Methods of Employee Evaluation.

In Figure 17-9 on pages 501-502, a collage of instruments typically used to evaluate marketing employees is presented. The following are brief descriptions of the methods depicted in the instruments in Figure 17-9.

1. Ranking. This is the oldest method. It simply asks the supervisor to compare one person with all others and place them in a rank order of worth.

2. Grading. Categories of worth are established and carefully defined. Grades such as A through F or poor through outstanding then are used to describe the person's performance in each category.

3. Graphic Scales. Commonly evaluated factors such as quantity of work, quality of work, personality, attendance, and loyalty are carefully described by degree of performance.

4. Check Lists. Areas of appropriate performance are identified, and the evaluator checks whether the employee does or does not perform adequately.

5. Forced Choice Description. The evaluator is forced to choose between descriptive statements of seemingly equal worth. There is a "right" answer for each question and a "right" composite score that was determined on the basis of a study of current employees who are performing effectively.

6. Behaviorally Anchored Rating Scales (BARs). These also are known as the critical incident technique. Job holders or supervisors are asked to identify a specific behavior critical to performance. Effective and ineffective dimensions of that behavior then are described and placed along a continuum to be used as descriptors by the supervisor in identifying the employee's behavior.

7. Essay Description. This is a written description of the employee's overall performance.[20]

There are other types of evaluation instruments, and some companies use combinations of these tests and others to evaluate marketing employees.

An increasingly popular method of evaluation is to design an individual evaluation system for marketing employees on the basis of the goals that were established jointly by that employee and his or her supervisor. Of course, this is not always possible. It is difficult to imagine the manager of a large section in a department store designing separate forms and systems for part-time sales people, full-time sales people, stockers, and cashiers. But for many marketing employees, especially those in production-oriented industries, the evaluation system being used by the company is inappropriate for the goals or assignments agreed on by the marketing employee and the supervisor. The latter goals should be used as the primary basis for the employee evaluation. Other factors, of course, can be used to supplement and enrich the evaluation of the goals. An open-ended form can be used to enter goals that pertain to the individual employee and his or her specific tasks and respon-

METHODS OF EVALUATING EMPLOYEES

(1) Ranking Method

Considering selling costs and my observation of their contribution to stock work, customer service, and housekeeping, I rank the six employees in the Children's Department as follows:

1. Joe Garet   *3. Lea Ehrens*
2. Linda Hart   *4. Pat Smyth*
3. Mike Schuster   *5. Toni Longest*

(2) Grading Method

Criteria	Poor	Fair	Good	Very Good	Outstanding
Grooming: clean hair, clothes, shoes, accessories. . . .					
Customer greeting: prompt, friendly, company policy					
Cashiering: company policy, calls out figures					
Accuracy: error rate					
Closing: computes taxes, coupons, refunds, accurate totals					

(3) Graphic Scale Method

PERFORMANCE RATING					
Performance Factors	Does Not Meet Job Requirements	Partially Meets Job Requirements	Meets Job Requirements	Exceeds Job Requirements	Far Exceeds Job Requirements
Quality of Work: Accuracy, skill, thoroughness, neatness.	Consistently unsatisfactory ☐	Occasionally unsatisfactory ☐	Consistently satisfactory ☐	Sometimes superior ☐	Consistently superior ☐
Quantity of Work: Output; consider not only regular duties, but also how promptly "extra" or rush assignments are completed.	Consistently below requirements ☐	Frequently below requirements ☐	Usually meets requirements ☐	Frequently exceeds requirements ☐	Consistently exceeds requirements ☐
Dependability: Follows instructions, initiative, punctuality, and attendance.	Requires constant supervision ☐	Needs occasional follow-up ☐	Ordinarily can be counted on ☐	Needs very little supervision ☐	Completely trustworthy in job requirements ☐
Attitudes: Toward company, job, and fellow workers; cooperation.	Seldom works with or assists others; indifferent ☐	Frequently uncooperative; too critical of others ☐	Generally works well with others; normal interest ☐	Eagerness often displayed; a good team worker ☐	Extraordinary interest; inspires others to work ☐

Comments:

Department Supervisor	Classroom Supervisor

Figure 17-9. Evaluation of marketing employees can follow one of several methods.

④ Checklist Method

	Yes	No
Does he or she usually volunteer good ideas?	_____	_____
Is a marked interest shown in the job?	_____	_____
Is consistent treatment given to all customers?	_____	_____
Does he or she usually complete paperwork correctly?	_____	_____
Does he or she display a good working knowledge of the product?	_____	_____
Does he or she know and try to follow company procedures?	_____	_____
Do subordinates show respect?	_____	_____
Is the departmental area usually maintained in a neat and clean condition?	_____	_____
Has he or she ever reprimanded an employee or customer in public?	_____	_____
Are back-orders followed up?	_____	_____
Are schedules met?	_____	_____
Does he or she ever make mistakes?		

⑤ Forced-Choice Description Method

1 Gives good, clear instructions on refund policies.
2 Can be relied upon to complete assigned tasks.

1 Makes promises that cannot be kept.
2 Spends too much time on chit-chat and not enough on substance.

1 Shows a sincere interest in the client's need.
2 Completes orders and other paperwork in a timely manner.

⑥ Behaviorally Anchored Rating Scale Method

Could be expected to give sales personnel confidence and a strong sense of responsibility by delegating many important jobs to them.

Could be expected to exhibit courtesy and respect toward sales personnel.

Could be expected to be rather critical of store standards in front of employees thereby risking their developing poor attitudes.

Could be expected to go back on a promise to an individual that she/he could transfer back into previous department if she/he did not like the new one.

9
8 — Could be expected to conduct a full day's sales clinic with two new sales personnel and thereby develop them into top sales people in the department.

7
6 — Could be expected *never* to fail to conduct training meetings at the scheduled hour and to convey trainees exactly what is expected.

5 — Could be expected to remind sales personnel to wait on customers instead of conversing with each other.

4 — Could be expected to tell an individual to come in anyway even though she/he called in to say she/he was ill.

3 — Could be expected to make promises to an individual about her/his salary being based on department sales even when such a practice is against company policy.

2

1

⑦ Essay Description Method

Jan has been doing a fine job in the New Products Division. In just six months, she has researched two modifications of our X-16 calculator with engineering and component parts. She has also checked on a lead indicating the competition is considering a similar modification. She has worked with Research on designing a test of the modification. I find her to be thorough in homework and follow through.

sibilities. The instrument may also include other factors considered by the company to be important. The evaluation results then are used as one basis for determining goals for the next evaluation period.

The evaluation process and the instrument used should adhere to the old adage that form follows function. Think through carefully why you are evaluating and what it is that you want to evaluate (function) and then identify or develop an appropriate process and form.

The Evaluation Interview.
The employee evaluation interview also should be conducted according to its purpose. Why are you really conducting the interview? To improve performance? To justify your decision on the salary raise you are or are not recommending? To provide feedback on your perception of the employee's performance? Because it is required? This is important and can be a key to the effectiveness of the evaluation interview. Too often, interviews are ineffective because too much ground is covered and areas of strength and needed improvements are not discussed adequately. Limit the purpose of the interview to areas that are important now and then share with the employee in advance of the interview those purposes and how you would like to conduct the interview. "Sandy, I've had a chance now to review your progress on the goals for you that we agreed on last February. How about evaluating your performance on them and the other areas that I shared with you. Let's meet in my office on Friday morning and compare notes."

Let us take a look at some steps that might be followed in conducting a good and meaningful employee evaluation which has as its purpose identifying and targeting areas of improvement.

Step 1. As was done with Sandy, prepare the employee. Let the employee know what the interview is about and what activities to do before the meeting or what items to bring to the interview. Clearly identify and state the purpose for the interview and then make sure it is accomplished.

Step 2. Together, compare accomplishments relative to specific goals or assignments. Be specific about what was expected and what was accomplished. Discuss each item on the evaluation form and each goal thoroughly.

Step 3. Be sure to give credit for what has been accomplished and accomplished well. (It is sometimes a temptation to take for granted those things which have been accomplished well and focus on deficiencies.)

Step 4. Review areas in which improvement is needed. Also discuss goals that were not accomplished. Allow the employee to explain deficiencies.

Step 5. Agree on targets to be met during the period ahead. Discuss areas of additional training, education, or coaching that the employee may need and areas in which you can be of assistance.

Step 6. Summarize the meeting. Review positive factors and then summarize areas in which additional improvement is needed and indicate how it is going to be brought about.[21]

Avoid specific comparisons with other employees. Try to avoid sitting in judgment of the employee or throwing out a lot of criticism or dwelling on mistakes. Stick to a mutual examination of the facts and what they mean to the employee and to you. Stick to the purpose of the interview. Avoid getting into areas that have little or nothing to do with why you arranged the interview.

Follow up on Evaluation.
The formality of follow-up will depend largely on company policy. Some companies want written reports summarizing important agreements. Others simply want assurance that an interview was conducted. In any event, follow up with the employee periodically. If you agreed to provide additional training or coach the employee in improving techniques, be sure to do so. Conduct informal progress checks on goals. After a brief time, you might check with the employee to make sure that the goals he or she thinks were agreed on are the same

ones you think were agreed on. It is a good idea to put the goals in writing immediately and make sure that both of you have copies.

Disciplining Employees

If the processes identified thus far for working with, developing, and supervising employees have been performed effectively, there should be no need for disciplinary action. Thus, if you can do the following, you should have no need to take disciplinary action.

- Understand yourself and others and apply effective motivational theory and human relations.
- Staff your unit with the best qualified individuals for the specific jobs.
- Train your employees well.
- Supervise them correctly.
- Conduct meaningful employee evaluations.

Unfortunately, even the best of plans and programs can go awry.

Discipline usually is thought of in a negative way. In an action sense, it usually is thought of as penalties that bring about inhibition of undesired behavior.[22] It is a hard thing to deal with for most supervisors, and penalties should be imposed with extreme care and utmost respect for the employee.

Usually disciplinary action has to be taken because of a violation of orders, rules, or policy guidelines. Sometimes strong disciplinary action such as dismissal must be taken as a result of incompetence or illegal activity.

Before taking disciplinary action, be sure of the facts. Decisions must be based on hard data, not innuendo, attitudes, or company gossip. If you are sure of the facts, the most commonly cited guidelines for administering disciplinary action are as follows.

Disciplinary Action Should be Taken in Private. It rarely pays to chew out an employee in front of other employees or customers. Holding a per-

son up to public ridicule usually has the opposite effect. Co-workers or observers tend to side with the person who has been embarrassed.

Disciplinary Action Should be Taken Promptly. Once the truth or fact is determined, corrective action should be taken immediately. If punishments or warnings are delayed too long, the relationship between the penalty and the offensive act becomes unclear. It is hard to begin docking an employee for tardiness if the employee has been late consistently for several weeks and nothing has been done about it previously.

Disciplinary Action Should be Administered by the Immediate Supervisor. It generally is not a good idea for top management to bypass supervisors in correcting employees. If company management observes inappropriate behavior or rule violations, they ought to ask the immediate supervisor to take the necessary corrective action.

Consistency in the Administration of Disciplinary Action is Essential. This guideline is tougher than it looks, and it appears to contradict our previous statements about individual differences. When enforcing rules or orders or policies, however, you are better off administering penalties consistently.

An Application of a Penalty Should Always Carry With It a Constructive Element. The person should be told the reason for the action, how to prevent future penalties, and the consequences of continuing the inappropriate behavior.

The Supervisor Should Assume a Normal Attitude Toward the Employee Once the Disciplinary Action has been Taken. Now that you have done what had to be done, forget it.

This brief section on discipline was included to assist supervisors in those extreme cases in which disciplinary action is needed. Penalties or severe punishments should be used only as a last resort. "Good" supervisors are usually thought of as being good counselors, competent trainers, and fair evaluators. It is better for supervisors to develop their skills in these areas than to focus on disciplining employees in a punitive way.

develop skills and techniques in leadership, structuring the work environment, and counseling, evaluating, and disciplining employees.

KEY POINTS SUMMARY

- Employing the right people for marketing positions will enhance an organization's chances for economic success. A system consisting of several procedures should be used to employ a marketing staff. The procedures include conducting a job analysis and writing a job description, recruiting employees, establishing application procedures, interviewing applicants, testing, making the decision, and following through with those who are to be employed and notifying those who were not selected.

- Well-planned and well-delivered employee training programs lead to increased productivity, higher morale, better loyalty, reduced costs, and less employee turnover.

- Numerous systems can be used to orient and induct employees. Probably the most commonly used systems consist of individual companies' own on-the-job group and individualized training programs. Adult and continuing education, private business consulting firms, and the Small Business Administration are popular off-the-job systems.

- Leadership behavior in American organizations ranges from a very autocratic, boss-centered approach to one that is laissez-faire, with employees doing what they want to do, when, and how. No one approach has been found to be appropriate for all situations.

- Current interest is focused on quality circles, a process in which supervisors and employees work together on appropriate production, marketing, and work environment operations and problems. This approach is based on the Theory Z theory of management and motivation, which has been found to increase productivity considerably in Japanese companies.

- In addition to employing and training a marketing staff, first-line marketing supervisors need to

KEY TERMS AND CONCEPTS

autocratic leadership   leader
democratic leadership   orientation
discipline   quality circle
job analysis   reference check
job description   supervisor
laissez-faire leadership

DISCUSSION QUESTIONS

1. What procedures should be followed to enhance the employment of a productive marketing staff? What are some suggestions you could make to a very small business person—say, one who hires only one or two additional employees—to help him or her find an appropriate employee?

2. Why is it so important to check references?

3. Identify five questions that you would recommend that the manager of the cosmetics department at Leggett's Department Store ask each of the job applicants for a part-time sales job. What additional advice would you give this manager regarding the conduct of a job interview?

4. Identify and describe four principles of learning that should be followed when training a new employee on the job.

5. Describe the Theory Z motivation and management style of leadership and the quality circle process associated with it. Identify a company in your area that uses quality circles and describe how the theory and processes have been implemented. Have there been any measurable results?

6. The following are three supervisor-employee situations that may be typical in marketing. On the basis of the limited information provided, what type of leadership style would you recommend and why? What additional information would you want before making a final decision?

a. District supervisor of seven sales reps ranging in experience from 2 to 15 years; gross sales for the area are running 6 percent below quota.

b. Assistant manager of the shoe department at Target Self-Service Department Store; includes scheduling and supervising one full-time and six part-time employees in such a way as to be sure the department has sufficient people doing stock work and available to assist customers.

c. District manager for seven Tupperware hostess-demonstrators who conduct at-home parties.

7. Suppose you were the supervisor of a group of entry-level marketing employees who were mostly job-inexperienced teenagers. In general, what style of leadership would you use? What major problems would you anticipate? How would you counsel the employees regarding those problems?

8. If possible, examine instruments that are used by businesses in your area to evaluate employees. Discuss the advantages and disadvantages of each. Also, discuss any experiences you have had with employee evaluation.

NOTES

1. Sanford L. Jacobs, "Training Provides Clues for Molding Competent Workers." Reprinted by permission of *Wall Street Journal,* © Dow Jones & Company, Inc., December 15, 1980, p. 27. All rights reserved.
2. *Dictionary of Occupational Titles,* 4th ed., U.S. Department of Labor, Washington, D.C., 1977, p. 204.
3. Donald H. Dunn, ed., "Personal Business," *Business Week,* July 27, 1981, pp. 85–86.
4. Adapted from Edwin B. Flippo, *Personnel Management,* 5th ed., McGraw-Hill, New York, 1980, p. 612.
5. Kenneth R. Voorhis, *Entrepreneurship and Small Business Management,* Allyn and Bacon, Boston, 1980, pp. 413–414.
6. National Labor-Management Relations Act (Taft-Hartley), 1947, as amended, Section 101, Subsection 2(11).
7. Penny Gill, "Families Matter," *Stores,* March, 1982, p. 37.
8. Claudia H. Deutsch, "Trust: The New Ingredient in Management," *Business Week,* July 6, 1981, p. 104.
9. Ibid.
10. "Office Productivity, Challenge of the 80s," *Business Week,* March 2, 1981, p. 98.
11. Adapted from "Will the Slides Kill Quality Circles?" *Business Week,* January 11, 1982, p. 109.
12. Robert Blake and Jane Mouton cited in Gill, op. cit., p. 40.
13. "Will the Slides Kill Quality Circles?" op. cit.
14. Cited in Gill, op. cit., p. 40.
15. Joseph Manuso, cited in Robert S. Greenberger, "Job Hazard." Reprinted by permission of *Wall Street Journal,* © Dow Jones & Company, Inc., April 23, 1981, p. 1. All rights reserved.
16. Adapted from "A New Approach to Treating Alcoholism," *Business Week,* September 8, 1975, pp. 83–84.
17. *Labor Policy and Practice—Personnel Management,* Bureau of National Affairs, Inc., Washington, D.C., 1978, p. 245.
18. George Kegley, "Expert Says Smoking on Job Runs Up Cost of Doing Business," Roanoke *Times & World News,* May 24, 1981, p. G-3.
19. George Kegley, "Merchandisers Cope with Changing Family," Roanoke *Times & World News,* July 27, 1980, pp. G-1, G-3.
20. Adapted from Edwin B. Flippo, op. cit., pp. 205–213.
21. Adapted from Lester R. Bittel, *What Every Supervisor Should Know,* 4th ed., McGraw-Hill, New York, 1980, p. 253.
22. Flippo, op. cit., p. 368.

APPLICATIONS/CASES

They ought to stop calling the places we buy gas for our cars "service stations" because they sure don't provide much service anymore. You're lucky if they don't charge extra for putting the cap back on the gas tank. I went into a gas station last week and I was startled when the attendant sprayed the windshield and started cleaning it with a squeegee. It had been so long since anyone cleaned my windshield that I didn't realize for an instant what he was doing.

The traditional sign outside a gas station always used to read "Free air and water." When was the last time an attendant checked your tires or your radiator? If you need water, you put it in yourself in your own driveway. If you need air and can find a station that still keeps its pump in working order, it's always self service. I don't know what little old ladies do for air.

Gas stations don't even seem as interested in checking your oil as they used to be. There's money selling oil at a gas station but I have a feeling a lot of the attendants don't know where to look for the dip stick or can't figure out how to unlatch the hood of a car. I drive a 1978 Ford, not a rare car in America, and if I ask to have the oil checked I almost always have to get out and help the guy get the hood up.

They sell a lot of cans of oil in the all-purpose shopping centers now and people are obviously adding oil themselves. I usually do it that way. You can save a quarter or more buying oil at a supermarket instead of at the gas station, although it's hardly worth the trouble. If gas station attendants didn't grumble when I ask them to check the oil, I'd never do it myself.

Things are probably going to get worse, too,

for those of us who look for a little civility and service at our gas station. One way to cut costs is to have us pump our own gas. This is a repulsive development for those of us who don't want to get out of the car and don't want to smell like gasoline for the rest of the day. It's difficult not to get some on your hands when you handle the nozzle.

The lack of service in service stations doesn't make them unique, of course. We're all getting used to doing everything ourselves. The kind of service that used to go with a sale as a gesture of appreciation by the person you bought it from is a thing of the past.

Last weekend I decided to give my car a treat and have it washed. It had been more than a year since I'd been through one of those things. I was disappointed to find that it was brushless now, not nearly so exciting, and also disappointed to find the price had been raised to $5.95.

I paid the tab and waited for my car by the finish line. There was a slotted box there with a sign saying "For The Boys."

There was one wet spot with some dirt left on the left front bumper and I asked one of "the boys" if he'd wipe it off with a cloth.

"If we started doing that for one person," he said, "we'd have to do it for everyone."

I didn't drop anything in the slot for the service.

Adapted from Andy Rooney, "You Don't Find Much Service at Service Stations Anymore," Columbus *Dispatch*, January 7, 1982, p. 40.

a. Do you agree with Rooney's assessment of service at most service stations? What do you think about his statements that "they sure don't provide much service anymore," that "attendants . . . grumble," and that a "gesture of appreciation [is] a thing of the past"? Do you think there are good reasons why the attendants behave as they do?

b. Which principles from motivational theories might be applied to make service employees, or at least the ineffective ones described by Rooney, more responsive to the needs and wants of customers?

c. Suppose you are a first-line supervisor in a gasoline station. Many of your employees seem to resemble those depicted by Rooney. What techniques might you use with your employees to upgrade the quality of customer service at the station?

APPLICATION 15: RETAIL TRAINING SEMINARS: DEVELOPER HELPS MALL TENANTS PROVIDE BETTER SALES CLERKS

The Problem

It is not the architecture, the amenities, the parking lot, or the clean floors that make the sales. It is the sales clerks.

On your next tour of your shopping center, make a mental note of the performance of sales personnel in each mall shop.

● Note the clerk at the camera shop, the one who is unable to explain to the customer the differences between Kodachrome and Ektachrome film.

● Note the clerk at the health food store reading a novel behind the counter.

● And just try to enter that jewelry store located by the fountain, the one where you practically have to walk over the clerk with both arms folded across his chest, daring you to enter the store.

● The clerk chatting with her friends clustered around the cash and wrap at the record shop is also making a negative impression on customers.

When you are finished with your tour, tally your mental list in terms of lost sales opportunities and then translate it into lost overage rent for the landlord. It makes you stop and think, doesn't it?

Each individual sales clerk's level of performance directly affects the overall profitability of the center. Sales clerks with little or no training, experience, or motivation can add up to a big problem that the shopping center manager, marketing director, or developer should be concerned with on a daily basis.

It is easy to spot those stores whose sales staffs would benefit from additional training. It also is easy for you to sit down with the manager of that store and suggest that he or she invest in some additional training for their employees. But it is *not* so easy for the store manager to provide that needed training.

Many stores do not have their own established training programs. When a small merchant loses an employee, the total employee force is diminished anywhere from 10 to 50 percent. The replacement employee is needed so badly that he or she goes immediately to the sales floor. There just is no time for involved training. And if your center is located in a small market, there may not even be any local community college offering appropriate classes in sales.

Even if the local resources for sales training are available, there is always the problem of expense for the merchant. It costs money to train employees: tuition, class materials, and salaries while the employee attends training seminars (at the same time the retailer is paying another employee to cover the sales floor).

Some retailers may make an initial investment to train employees when they are hired, but retailers often neglect to hold periodic refresher courses in closing sales or overcoming customer objections.

Your merchant will probably admit that the benefits of additional training for the sales staff would be great, but he or she is going to ask you for some answers to the problems of cost and availability.

The shopping center developer has ample incentive to provide the tenant with some solutions to sales training problems. After all, it only takes a few sales people who do not know their merchandise or customers to leave a lasting impression on the consumer. All of the other elements provided by the developer—effective tenant mix, timely maintenance, beautiful landscaping, well-trained security—cannot overcome those impressions made "one-on-one" between sales clerks and customers.

A Solution

General Growth Management Corp., management arm for Des Moines-based General Growth Companies' 20-plus shopping centers, has developed a major, companywide approach to help mall tenants provide better trained sales employees in their stores. General Growth's in-house manager of training and development, Darlene Falck, has developed a series of employee sales seminar-workshops to be provided in each center at no charge to the tenant.

Prior to each seminar, the mall management staff distributes informational brochures on the seminar to all tenants and home offices and makes a presentation on the seminar's value at a Merchant's Association or Marketing Fund tenant meeting. Both the presentation and the brochure use positive tenant quotes from past seminars to build merchant enthusiasm and support for the program.

The Training Program

The seminar, entitled "Steps to Selling," is one and a half hours long. They are scheduled three or four to a day, over a 2 to 4 day period in each shopping center. The time periods for the seminar sessions are varied to accommodate tenant schedules. Retailers can either bring all their employees to an early-morning session, completed before the stores open, or send one or two employees a session to avoid affecting sales floor coverage.

The seminar emphasizes six basic areas of selling: learning merchandise, approaching customers, identifying customer wants and needs, selling benefits, overcoming objections, and closing the sale.

Falck begins each session with a general discussion of retailing skills and uses various techniques, such as mini-role playing, dialogues, and discussion. The session ends on specifics about motivation.

For future reference, Falck provides various handouts to participants for use at home. She also asks each participant to evaluate the session to identify useful areas and also parts of the session that could be changed.

The Results

To date, Falck has conducted 82 seminars serving more than 1,300 employee participants.

More than 90 percent of store managers report immediate improvement in employee attitudes and behavior. Long-term results for the seminar are also favorable, with 67 percent of merchants polled 2 weeks following the seminars reporting positive changes in participating employees. Managers also report that employees feel more "worthwhile" since their employer and the shopping center landlord have invested time or money in the training. Malls report a greater feeling of "team effort" among all employees after the seminar.

The seminars have also paid off in greater rapport between shopping center tenants and the developer. Tenants are pleased at the landlord's willingness to make such an investment in each store at no cost to the tenant.

The tenant seminars have the wholehearted support of General Growth executives. Matthew Bucksbaum, chairman of the board for General Growth Management Corp., says, "Customer comments in our market surveys have shown high praise for better product knowledge and better customer service since we began the sales seminars, and we feel these items are directly related to the profitability of each mall as a whole."

Adapted from Marcy Carter, "Developer Helps Mall Tenants Provide Better Sales Clerks: The Results Please Everyone," *National Mall Monitor*, July/August, 1981, pp. 16–17.

a. Cite examples from your community similar to those listed in the first few paragraphs to support the need for proper training of retail sales people.

b. Outline two plans that you would use to train new retail sales people. The first plan could be used to train new employees in a group. Outline the content and then identify the training methods you would use. The second plan could be used to train an employee individually. For both plans, be sure to include the four principles of on-the-job training discussed on page 488.

CASE 14: IDEAL COMPUTER ACCOUNT

The *Occupational Outlook Handbook,* a federal publication describing the future outlook for occupations in this country, predicts a high growth rate for jobs in employment services. Apparently, many companies will be looking for businesses to help them recruit and screen employees.

Put yourself in the role of an associate in the Sales and Marketing Employment Agency. You have just been given the IDEAL Computer account. IDEAL will be moving into your suburban community of approximately 80,000 residents with employment heavily concentrated in high-tech, business, and professional occupations. IDEAL needs to hire approximately 10 full-time and 10 part-time employees as follows.

● Five full-time reps to market and service small business accounts in the community

● Three full-time management-level employees: one to supervise the small business accounts reps, one to manage the retail operations, and one to supervise office and clerical staff and operations

● Two full-time store employees: one to be an in-store salesperson and one to be an administrative assistant (primarily accounting and clerical work)

● Ten part-timers, primarily 20 to 30 hours a week in retail sales, customer service, and in-store stock keeping.

Design an employee recruitment and screening plan for the IDEAL Computer Company. You might wish to follow the employment model on page 476. Provide job descriptions, application forms, interview questions, and other forms and employment techniques as appropriate. Then plan a presentation to be made to the general manager of IDEAL regarding your plan.

CASE 15: J. C. PENNEY: QUALITY CIRCLES

Background

The J. C. Penney Company first became involved with quality circles in its catalog division in April 1980 in Atlanta. The number one objective was to improve morale, motivation, attitude, and communication. According to Nat Goldberg, QC coordinator for the company, "Our plants consist of 2 million square feet under one roof, all highly mechanized. Until we started the quality circles, the workers didn't have a chance to have input on things that were really bothering them."

J. C. Penney soon expanded its QC program to its distribution centers in Columbus, Milwaukee, Kansas City, and Reno. Says Goldberg: "We see quality circles as a vehicle for bringing management and nonmanagement together in a meaningful and productive way. The program is based on a very simple concept: people take more interest and pride in their work if they are allowed to influence decisions made about their work, and increased interest and pride directly result in improved performance."

Methods

Before launching the QC program, Goldberg and his associates called in a consultant to help set up a test program. Based on this person's advice and subsequent experiences with QCs, J. C. Penney now sets up 5 day leader training sessions twice a year at each plant. Printed materials to help set up future QC programs also are being developed.

Each of Penney's quality circles consists of 6 to 10 people. The groups meet once a week on company time, with no monetary incentives but lots of recognition. "Since it's totally voluntary participation, you've got to have top to bottom management support," comments Goldberg. "At each of your plants, management has agreed to get back to the groups within 1 or 2 weeks with answers to requests."

Homework is emphasized throughout the program. "Graphs and charts often have to be prepared to support a proposal. It's very exciting to see employees who might never have even spoken to a manager get up and make presentations, complete with flip charts and graphs," according to Goldberg.

J. C. Penney emphasizes communications. Bulletins listing circle activities are posted each week for all employees to read, a section on the QCs appears in the newsletter published by each plant, and news of QC happenings in the various plants is reported to the entire Penney organization by its corporate newsletter.

Weekly teleconferences are held with Goldberg and all plant facilitators to discuss what has happened and any problems which may have arisen. Detailed project reports are shared throughout the organization.

A Few Results

QC participants discuss any work-related problems they wish but do not make recommendations about personnel, wages, and salaries. The following are examples of QC solutions to problem areas.

- A system for controlling and dispersing tools needed in the operation of the warehouse

- Improved layout of the shipping department
- A manual providing answers to the 25 questions asked most frequently by new accounting employees.
- A training manual for use by new employees in shipping

Problems

Goldberg has identified two barriers to implementing the QCs in retail stores. "First of all, in individual units you'll probably find a reluctance to spend the money for a full-time salaried person to run the program. And with even as few as two or three circles, you need a full-time person. We began by training the store manager, but we found he couldn't devote the time necessary to running the program and fulfilling his regular duties."

The second problem is that "at retail, dollar savings may be hard to come by. I really don't think you'd ever make big dollar savings, and if that's what you're looking for, quality circles are not the answer. You have to be prepared to say that improvement of morale is enough reward."

Adapted from Penny Gill, "At J. C. Penney: How Quality Circles Work," *Stores*, March 1982, pp. 38-39. Reprinted from *Stores*, © 1982 National Retail Merchants Association.

a. Identify the methods J. C. Penney used to implement and operate quality circles. Suggest other methods that might be appropriate to improve morale, motivation, attitude, and communications.

b. Suggest possible alternatives to the financial problem of not being able to employ a full-time salaried person to run a quality circle program in a retail store.

c. Do you agree that quality circles are not the answer to saving money at the retail level? Why or why not?

UNIT 8

MANAGING THE MARKETING MIX

CHAPTER
18
MARKETING MANAGEMENT

At last, a pill to cure or prevent the common cold, a drug to cure cancer, a cigarette pack-size personal telephone that can be used from any location, a synthetic material to replace wood, clothing that can be cleaned in a minute by placing it in a cleaning chamber. All these and more by 1990?

An individual flying machine? A pocket-size personal computer that answers all questions put to it? A 10 hour work week? Perhaps it will come true in 25 years.

These are just a few of the new products, systems, and services that *may* be available in the next 25 years. These are the findings, further detailed in Table 18-1, from a survey conducted by New Product Development, Point Pleasant, New Jersey, and completed by more than 300 new product and research development executives. Each respondent was asked to indicate when he or she thought the product, system, or service would be available. Further analysis of data from the study shows that new products and services will be primarily market-directed. That is, they will reflect what customers need and want from the product or service.[1]

This article reinforces a few important concepts related to the role of marketing in the successful operation of a business. Effective marketers learn to anticipate what lies ahead. They are aware of customers' needs and wants and how to translate those needs and wants into available appropriate products and services. Marketing managers keep informed about new products and services, systems, demographics that may affect their business, economic considerations, technology, and a host of other factors that they may be able to control or at least anticipate.

MARKETING MANAGEMENT

The marketing manager usually is responsible for anticipating and then meeting the needs of a particular group of customers (the target market) with appropriate products or services. Out of the

TABLE 18-1
PREDICTED NEW PRODUCTS, SERVICES, AND SYSTEMS

	PERCENT OF RESPONDENTS WHO PREDICTED AVAILABILITY WITHIN				
	5 Years	10 Years	25 Years	100 Years	Beyond 100 Years
1. Artificial human organs, excluding the brain	35	43	21	0	0
2. A carless means of transportation, perhaps an individual flying machine	0	13	63	22	0
3. A drug that will cure or prevent cancer	31	26	22	13	8
4. A drug that will cure or prevent the common cold	39	21	20	6	7
5. A personal telephone, no larger than a cigarette pack, that can be used from any location	43	45	12	0	0
6. In-home/in-office receipt of routine mail and publications via wire/radio transmission	30	48	13	8	0
7. A vehicle that will run for a year on atomic power at a cost of 10 cents a mile or less	0	4	61	26	8
8. Solar and/or wind power will completely replace oil as a major energy factor	0	0	48	35	17

(continued)

Source: "Survey of New Product Developers Offers 25-Year Innovation Forecast," *Marketing News*, Published by the American Marketing Association, Sept. 4, 1981, page 4.

TABLE 18-1 (Continued)
PREDICTED NEW PRODUCTS, SERVICES, AND SYSTEMS

	PERCENT OF RESPONDENTS WHO PREDICTED AVAILABILITY WITHIN				
	5 Years	10 Years	25 Years	100 Years	Beyond 100 Years
9. Health technology that will extend the average lifespan to 100 years	0	8	43	22	26
10. All materials used around humans will be fireproof	0	13	22	35	30
11. Manufacturing will be 90 percent automated	0	9	30	43	16
12. A pocket-size personal/business computer will answer all questions put to it	4	30	39	13	14
13. Clothing that can be cleaned by placing it into a "cleaning chamber" for a few minutes	13	39	35	8	5
14. A synthetic material that will replace wood	22	43	17	13	5
15. The sex of children will be predetermined	52	17	21	8	1
16. We will have peace through one-world government	0	0	2	2	96
17. There will be a visitation from outer space	8	4	15	8	64
18. The work week will be 10 hours	8	0	4	30	58

Source: "Survey of New Product Developers Offers 25-Year Innovation Forecast," *Marketing News*, Published by the American Marketing Association, Sept. 4, 1981, page 4.

infinite number of products and services available to customers, effective marketing managers want to be sure that their products and services succeed. They enhance the probability of success in essentially two ways.

1. Effective marketing managers pay careful attention to all elements of the marketing mix: product (or service), place, price, promotion, and, of course, people.

2. Effective marketing managers adhere carefully to the four functions of management: planning, organizing, directing, and controlling.

The Marketing Mix Revisited

Effective marketing management requires that the marketing mix be under continuous study. The various elements within the marketing mix (see Figure 18-1) may have to be modified constantly to adjust to a changing market. The products or services may have to be altered to meet the needs and wants of consumers. Prices may have to be adjusted to reflect consumer willingness to pay as well as production and marketing costs. Distribution (place) may have to be modified to reflect new practices in transportation, competition at the retail or wholesale level, or changes in technology. Promotion—personal selling, advertising, public relations, and sales promotion—may have to be redirected to communicate with the target market about the products and services, prices, and place elements.

The major business activity used by effective marketing managers to make decisions regarding products, place, prices, and promotion—the marketing mix—is marketing research. Some companies have full-time research staffs whose primary job is to gather, sort, analyze, evaluate, and disseminate information for use by company decision makers. Others, especially small or medium-size companies, rely on secondary sources such as extensive reading of trade literature and business publications, attending conventions and trade shows, comparison shopping, or subscribing to research reports that provide information on new products, services, technology, trends, and lifestyles.

Figure 18-1. The marketing mix must be modified constantly.

Effective marketing managers analyze the people component carefully. They want to be sure that competent and pleasant people are employed in all aspects of the business, especially in people-intense areas of marketing: sales, services, customer relations, cashiering, and so on. People often provide the first impression of a company to prospective customers. Knowledgeable, helpful, pleasant employees can enhance a company's chances for success.

All elements of the marketing mix are closely interrelated and interdependent. That is, one element cannot be considered without also considering its effect on the others. A company probably cannot consider implementing an extensive promotional campaign without also considering the price of the products or services being promoted. Do prices need to be increased to cover the costs of the promotion? Will the increased promotional costs result in enough sales to make a profit? Do additional employees have to be hired and trained?

The Functions of Marketing Management

The management system is important to marketing as the marketing manager seeks to coordinate each of the components of the marketing mix as well as marketing research, financial aspects, and risk taking. Fundamental to managerial marketing is the notion that a successful marketing program

MANAGING THE MARKETING MIX

MANAGERS

Plan

Organize

Direct

Control

Price · Place · Product · MARKETING MIX · Promotion · People

Figure 18-2. Marketing managers plan, organize, direct, and control various aspects of the marketing mix.

consists of well-integrated components. Although each component may be studied separately, they must be coordinated if the firm is to achieve its overall objectives. The marketing manager also may have to integrate marketing activities with those of production, accounting, information systems, or any other division or component of the company.

The process used by effective marketing managers most often is described in terms of the four functions of management. Thus, marketing managers are involved with planning, organizing, directing, and controlling various aspects of the marketing mix. This concept is illustrated in Figure 18-2.

Planning. The first important task of marketing managers is to plan. **Planning** is the process of deciding in advance what is to be done, who is to do it, how it is to be done, and when it is to be done. Most marketing managers work with a short-range plan of 12 months or less, an intermediate plan of 1 to 5 years, and a long-range plan usually covering 5 to 10 years. Typically, department heads and first-line supervisors are concerned primarily with the short-range plan. Top management and company officers focus on intermediate-range and long-range plans.

The planning process typically begins with a fairly extensive analysis of markets, products, trends, demographics, budgets, and other data important for decision-making purposes. Marketing managers and their employees study the data and then make decisions about what is to be done, who is to do it, how, and when. This process is really one of formulating the purposes or mission of the work unit and its objectives for the time period. The decision makers take an objective, critical, and unemotional view of the business (or department, unit, or work team) and its objectives.

Most business plans are written, and the written plan includes the results of at least six aspects of planning. All six aspects may not be written specifically into a formal document (the business plan), but effective managers consider and work with all of them throughout the planning process. Each one contributes to successful and profitable companies and departments. The six aspects of planning and their definitions are presented in Table 18-2.

Organizing. **Organizing** consists of grouping activities and assigning them to distinct areas such as departments, divisions, services, or units. It includes the establishment of formal authority and responsibility among the various areas and within a specific department, division, or unit.

TABLE 18-2
THE SIX ASPECTS OF PLANNING AND THEIR DEFINITIONS

Objectives	Goals set by managers to give the company or department direction
Programs	Strategies describing future events and the sequence of required actions needed to accomplish the objectives
Standards	Criteria used to measure the quality or quantity of work produced
Policies	Guidelines or general limits within which management acts
Procedures	Systematic way of handling regular events
Budgets	Plans for spending money, including planned income (sales), expenses, and profits

Managers delegate authority throughout the organization and establish relationships among the various areas. Organizing the overall activities of a company is the responsibility of the chief executive. However, it is usually the responsibility of first-line supervisors to organize the departments or sections over which they have control.

Specific duties often associated with the organizing management function include developing the company's organization chart, establishing employee committees or quality circles, staffing the organization and its various units, providing for the orientation and initial training of new employees, and assigning the various business activities to specific departments, sections, or units.

In Figure 18-3 on page 518 an organizational chart for the marketing division of a medium-size manufacturing company is provided. This company identifies a vice president as its chief executive for marketing. This person in turn has organized marketing into five divisions: marketing services, product management, general sales, physical distribution, and promotion. Within each division, several departments have been organized. There are other ways in which a company, a division, or departments can be orga-

nized. The guiding principle is that the organization should evolve from the company's goals and strategies as described in its short-term and long-range plans.

Directing. **Directing** is the use of communication, motivation, and leadership to guide the performance of subordinates toward the achievement of the organization or work unit's plans. Again, we are dealing with people and emphasizing the need for marketers to apply effective techniques in working with and for people.

Most studies show that effective managers are good communicators, motivators, and leaders. Managers working in any part of the marketing mix or its related business activities must be good communicators. They engage in communication involving a two-way exchange of ideas and information that leads to a common understanding between themselves and those with whom they work. Effective managers listen to their employees. They encourage employees to participate in decisions affecting the work environment. They promote teamwork by encouraging employees to cooperate to achieve the company or department's goals. They provide information and training that ensure understanding.

ORGANIZATION CHART: MARKETING DECISIONS

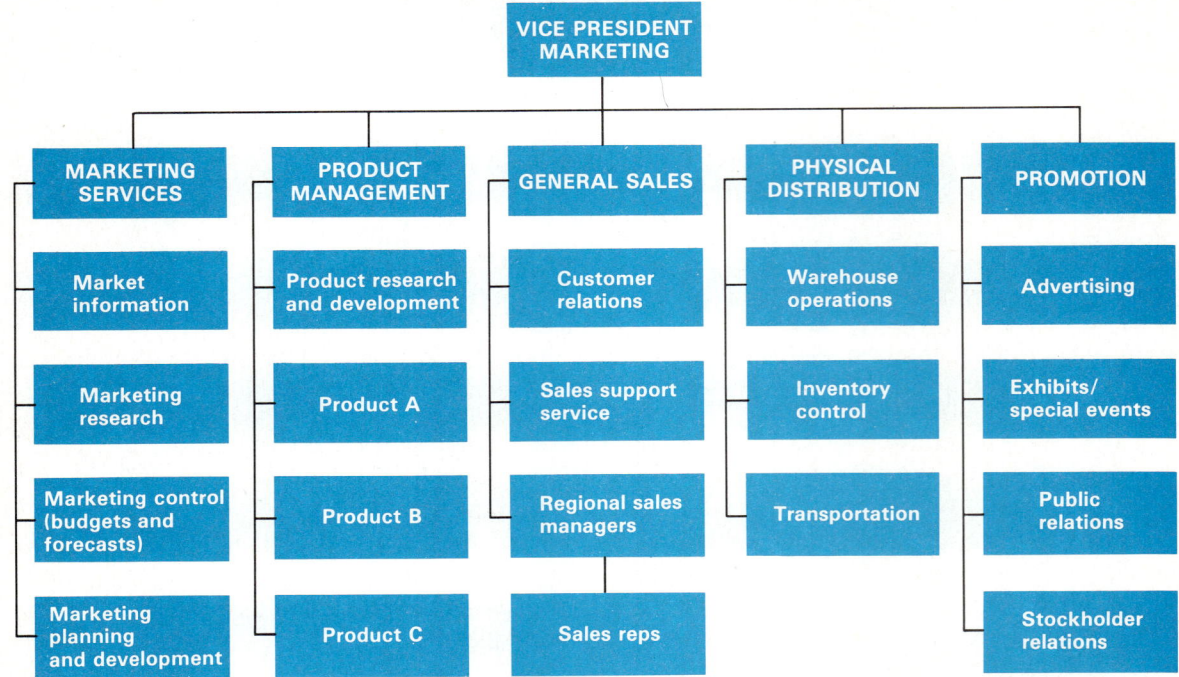

Figure 18-3. Marketing organization should evolve from a company's goals and strategies as described in its short-term and long-term plans.

Effective managers also motivate employees. They encourage employees to accomplish the plans of the company or department by showing how the plans mesh with the needs of the employees. They show a clear-cut relationship between the company's plans and programs and the needs and wants of their employees and their customers. Effective managers attempt to understand their employees and know where they are coming from. They apply solid principles which they have learned from a study of behavioral psychology and human relations.

Finally, as part of the directing function, effective managers are good leaders. They lead rather than drive. They inspire others to move enthusiastically toward accomplishing the organization's goals. Good leaders know where their company or department is going, where they are going, and how to get employees excited about going with them.

Controlling. The final major function of the management process is **controlling,** which includes all the activities a manager undertakes in attempting to assure that actual operations conform to planned operations. The controlling function is carefully correlated with company or department plans and the information that is provided as part of the directing function.

In many respects, controlling can be compared with evaluation or measurement. Each company or department must set up some mechanism or way in which to check its progress. Are we accomplishing our objectives? Are our employees as courteous and helpful as we advertise? Do we have sufficient inventory to meet the needs and wants of our customers? Are we making a profit? Are our products and services meeting the needs of our customers? Are we on target with our short-, medium-, and long-range plans? Are our employee selection procedures effective? Managers must be effective in controlling the work environment and its people. They use many devices and tools to monitor progress: financial statements, consumer surveys, employee appraisals, product inspections, quality control analyses, and consulting reports.

MARKETING CHALLENGES

Marketing is fun to work in. It is exciting, action-oriented, and usually challenging. If you like people and are interested in finding the right product or service to meet their needs, chances are that you will be happy in a marketing career.

Marketing management also is rewarding for people who are upward-aspiring and have the credentials. Planning, organizing, directing, and controlling the marketing mix in order to satisfy the needs and wants of customers at a profit for the company is indeed a challenge. But students of marketing need to be aware that there are problem areas. There may or may not be solutions to these problems or appropriate responses to critics of the American way of marketing, but students ought to be prepared to face these challenges.

Uncontrollable Variables

Every business operates within a framework of economic, political, cultural, and demographic forces over which it has little or no control. There is very little a single businessperson or company can do if the country slips into a severe depression or if the government is overthrown. Although these are extreme examples, such events do happen and wreak havoc with business activities. Of course, this is part of risk taking, and successful businesses try to plan and control for some of these problem areas. There are at least five variables external to the business that impinge considerably on a firm's marketing system and profit picture: demographics, economics, social and cultural forces, technology, and competition.

Demographics. Demographics is the statistical study of human population and the charac-

teristics associated with these data. The discussion of demographics in previous chapters, especially in Chapter 3, identified it as an important basis for market segmentation. When demographics is used to segment a market, that market then is segmented according to such variables as age, sex, ethnic group, income level, geographic area, and education attained.

But demographics also can pose a problem or a challenge for marketers since it involves the "human population," or the people who buy the products or services that are offered for sale. If the population declines significantly in your community, you obviously will have a problem selling your products. If the people in your marketing territory are growing older, the need for child-care services or infant products may drop considerably.

The following are just a few predictions for the years ahead. They are by no means complete but are presented to indicate the important role a knowledge of demographics plays in determining the marketing mix. Based on the information provided, try to identify products or services and promotional ideas that may be appropriate to the individuals or groups discussed.

- By 1990, the total population will increase by only 9.6 percent.
- The population aged 15 to 18 will decline considerably throughout the 1980s.
- People aged 25 to 45 will increase by 42 percent. By 1990, 41 percent of the total population will be in this age group.
- People aged 65 and older will increase by 20 percent.
- Fewer married couples will make up households.
- Single-parent (primarily female) heads of households will increase dramatically in the next decade. Father, mother, and children households may account for only one-third of all households.
- Unmarried couples sharing households are expected to increase. The number probably will double from 1985 to 1990.

- More than 60 percent of the total population of women will be employed outside the home by 1990, up from 40 percent in 1970.

- As many as 75 percent of traditional mother, father, and children families will have both parents working outside the home.

- Generally, Americans, especially those aged 45 and over, will be more affluent and have more discretionary funds to spend for leisure activities, recreation, dining out, travel, and comfortable living.

- The population of the United States will continue to grow most rapidly in the sunbelt, which refers to the southwestern and southern states.[2]

Demographics is obviously important to marketers. It is not something that can be controlled directly, but managers can use demographic data and projections in planning for and managing the marketing mix.

Economics.
People need money to spend on products and services. If they do not have money, they cannot spend. Also, as prices for necessities such as food, housing, and essential clothing increase, the amount left to spend on luxuries tends to decrease unless, of course, one's income keeps up with the increase in prices.

There are all kinds of economic conditions that affect marketing and over which marketing managers have little or no control. Perhaps the main economic condition that can affect marketing adversely is a general economic slowdown. In the early 1980s, the United States experienced poor economic growth. The birthrate declined (fewer consumers), business expenses increased (especially for labor and energy), and interest rates soared (making home ownership and large consumer loans almost prohibitive for most people). The net result was a very slow rate of economic growth. Industries such as autos, leather and related products, lumber and related products, and iron and steel showed almost no growth or actually declined, resulting in considerable unemployment. As a result, certain areas of the country experienced an extremely high unemployment rate. One can see how generally poor economic conditions in an area greatly affect the marketing of products and services. Expensive apparel, luxurious hotel rooms, elegant jewelry, and new automobiles cannot be marketed well in economically depressed areas where there are large numbers of unemployed people.

Social and Cultural Forces.
Many social and cultural forces affect marketing. People and their values, customs, and beliefs shape business operations through political and legal systems, through pressure groups, or through their "votes" in the marketplace. Marketing managers must keep abreast of social and cultural factors at local or regional levels and be aware of how they affect decisions related to the marketing mix.

Values and customs change. Successful marketers are aware of these changes and plan accordingly. The following are just a few social, cultural, or lifestyle changes that have occurred in the past few years. As a marketing manager, how would you respond to these changes?

- Women are no longer spending 30 to 40 years employed full time in the home. There is a new lifestyle for women, and 60 percent of women now work in business or industry.

- People are concerned about energy conservation and are doing something about it.

- People are demanding safety in products and are taking legal action when products are proven defective.

- There is more equality in the home and more sharing of household tasks and parenting responsibilities.

- There is decreased emphasis on work as the major satisfier in life. There is an increased emphasis on human relationships and fun as satisfiers.

- There is a general shift in emphasis from quantity of goods or materials possessed to an improved quality of life.[3]

Another social and cultural force that has affected marketing greatly is consumerism. It is not a new variable in marketing, but it has risen to considerable prominence with the growth of consumer movements, organizations, and leaders in the 1960s and 1970s. Consumerism generally is considered to be a protest against perceived business injustice and includes efforts to remedy those injustices. Most consumer activists feel that product and marketing decisions rest almost exclusively with the seller, and they want more power in determining product quality and accountability factors for defective or deceptive merchandise. Consumerism has given rise to legislation designed to protect the public against misrepresented or defective products. A summary of the major legislation affecting consumerism is presented in Table 18-3 on page 522.

Technology. Technology has a great impact on the marketing system of every company. The knowledge explosion and the resultant development of products and services has been nothing short of phenomenal in the United States. Think of the impact a few recently developed products have had on our lives: the computer, permanent-press clothes, hand-held hair driers, antibiotics, microwave ovens, and freeways. In a few years, technology may even alter our shopping patterns as Sears and other retailers develop and test their TV-computer-telephone hookup system designed to provide at-home shopping. Many retailers are already ordering merchandise by means of a computer hookup from their suppliers.

Technology, which refers to new knowledge and research and development, is a force to be dealt with by marketers but a force over which they have little control, except, of course, when they are involved in the specific product or service being developed.

Competition. One has only to drive down the main street of any medium-size or large-size city in this country and count the fast-food chain restaurants to understand competition. In any 6 to 10 block area, one may see all 12 of the largest chains: McDonald's, Burger King, Kentucky Fried Chicken, Wendy's, Dairy Queen, Hardee's, Pizza Hut, Marriott (includes Big Boy, Roy Rogers, Hot Shoppes, and Farrell's), Arby's, Church's, Jerrico, and Jack-in-the-Box.

Successful marketers need a thorough understanding of competition and competitive factors. A marketer cannot control the competition, but to be successful, a marketer must plan and control *for* competition. Fast-food chains may compete successfully on the basis of price, quality, service, location, breadth and depth of menu, parking space, or operating policies.

Social Responsibilities

People in marketing have a threefold responsibility: to the business, to their employees or employer, and to the customers. These responsibilities accompany the right to engage in business in a free society. A great deal has been written about one's responsibility to the firm for which one works. Good marketing employees are honest and loyal and provide appropriate work for the pay which they have agreed to accept from the company. No business is going to remain afloat for long if it is cheated by its employees, since a profit must be earned eventually. Conversely, it is the responsibility of management to provide an appropriate wage, a good working environment, and a reasonably conflict-free group of employees and to employ proven supervision and management techniques. Finally, all people engaged in marketing, whether at the management level or the operational level, have a responsibility to serve customers in an efficient and effective manner. Marketers have agreed to provide products and services to meet the needs and wants of their customers. This also implies adhering to a code of business ethics involving honesty and integrity in customer relations. If marketers cannot abide by a responsible code of business ethics, they ought to get out of the business.

But social responsibility extends beyond the firm. I may be loyal to my firm and kind to my employees and serve my customers in an exem-

TABLE 18-3
IMPORTANT CONSUMER PROTECTION LEGISLATION

Year	Name of Law	Purpose and Function
Product Safety		
1962	Food and Drug amendments	Requires pretesting of drugs for safety and effectiveness and labeling of drugs by generic name
1966	Child Protection Act	Bans sale of hazardous toys and articles
1967	Flammable Fabrics Act	Broadens federal authority to set safety standards for inflammable fabrics, including clothing and household products
1968	Federal Hazardous Substances Act	Requires retailer to prominently display a sign informing consumers of the fact that certain hazardous products are sold in that store
	Toy Safety Act	Requires retailers to give consumers a refund if a toy is found to be dangerous
1970	Public Health Smoking Act	Extends warning about the hazards of cigarette smoking
	Poison Prevention Packing Act	Authorizes standards for child-resistant packaging of hazardous substances
1972	Consumer Product Safety Act	Establishes a commission to set safety standards for consumer products and bans products presenting undue risk of injury
1975	Auto Recall Repair Law	Requires tire, auto, and replacement-part makers to offer refund, replacement, or refund options on defective products
Marketing Credibility		
1939	Wool Products Labeling Act	Requires that information about the textile fiber content be included on a tag or label together with care instructions

plary way while at the same time polluting the river with my company's waste products. Social responsibility extends to the entire social system. It is everyone's responsibility to act in a socially responsible manner. The public is often suspicious of business, and perhaps rightly so. Consumer activists in the 1960s and 1970s unearthed many unethical and socially damaging activities of business, including political bribery, deliberate air and water pollution, payoffs to agents in for-

Year	Name of Law	Purpose and Function

Marketing Credibility (Continued)

Year	Name of Law	Purpose and Function
1958	Textile Fiber Products Identification Act	Requires that information about the textile fiber content be included on a tag or label together with care instructions
1966	Fair Packaging and Labeling Act	Requires producers to state what a package contains, how much it contains, and who made the product
1975	Magnuson-Moss Warranty Act	Requires clearly understandable and accurate wording in ordinary language with every term and condition spelled out in writing for all warranties

Fair Payment Arrangements

Year	Name of Law	Purpose and Function
1968	Consumer Credit Protection Act (Truth-in-Lending)	Requires full disclosure of terms and conditions of finance charges in credit transactions
1970	Fair Credit Reporting Act	Protects consumers from inaccurate or obsolete information. Guarantees the consumer's right to know what personal data are being reported
1975	Equal Credit Opportunity Act	Makes it illegal for banks, retailers, and other lenders to deny or terminate credit on the basis of age, color, marital status, national origin, or sex or because one is on welfare
	Fair Credit Billing Act	Sets up billing dispute settlement procedures and requires prompt correction of billing mistakes
1978	Fair Debt Collection Practices Act	Protects consumers from being threatened, harassed, or otherwise abused by debt collectors
	Electronic Funds Transfer Act	Provides protection for consumers if EFT transaction card is lost or stolen

Source: Warren G. Meyer, Peter G. Haines, and E. Edward Harris, *Retailing Principles and Practice*, 7th ed., McGraw-Hill, New York, 1982, pp. 132–133.

eign markets, and illegal political gifts. Public opinion polls often showed that the public had a low opinion of business in general and assumed that most businesses were concerned only with making huge profits. It now is up to business to act in a socially responsible manner and thus reverse the decline in public confidence.

American businesses can do it, and many of them are doing it. The expertise and the skills are there. Business is capable of creating jobs. It has

Figure 18-4. Business can help instill a feeling of social responsibility.

the managerial expertise to plan, organize, direct, and control social programs as well as programs in profit-oriented businesses. Marketing people can act as catalysts for needed change. They are trained in communication skills, and they are people-oriented. They can communicate and promote needed social change. Certainly many businesses could divert a portion of their profits to

appropriate social causes. (Such contributions are tax-deductible.) The following are examples of a few ways in which businesses have tried to meet their social responsibility in the past few years.

- Worked with the public schools and the federal labor department in training disadvantaged youngsters in job skills and providing them with on-the-job training
- Employed handicapped persons and made minor adjustments in the work environment to accommodate the handicapping condition
- Diverted a portion of their profits to local charities, usually through the United Fund or Community Chest
- Contributed to local educational programs by providing funds, serving on advisory councils or boards of education, or co-sponsoring cooperative education programs
- Developed and adhered to affirmative action plans designed to remove employment discrimination based on sex, race, religion, creed, or handicap
- Provided low-interest loans or installment purchases to qualified individuals, primarily the poor and victims of calamities
- Reserved a percentage of franchises or stores to be owned or managed by minorities or women
- Developed products that are inexpensively priced to accommodate low-income groups and individuals
- Stimulated demand for energy conservation
- Encouraged and supported ecological cleanup

MARKETING: A FUTURE PERSPECTIVE

Phillip Kotler, a marketing expert and professor of management at Northwestern University, has a test called POISE which he asks managers to take to assess a company's marketing organization. POISE is an acronym for five words: philosophy, organization, information, strategy, and efficiency. Each word poses a question.

- Does your company have a marketing philosophy that is fully customer oriented from the president to the production personnel?
- Do you have a first-rate marketing organization with a vice president of marketing who has some influence on company policy?
- Is your marketing information system adequate and up to date?
- Has your company created a cost-effective strategy for a dominant market position?
- Do you evaluate the effectiveness of your sales force and advertising to determine the efficiency of your marketing expenditures?

Kotler asks managers to give their answers to the questions on a scale of 6, which is totally positive, to zero, which is totally negative. "If a company scores between 25 and 30 points, I can learn from it," says Kotler. "Most companies in the West score between 13 and 15 points. Japanese companies score an average of 23 points."[4]

The POISE test may provide a means for a simplified assessment of a complex set of problems. How does a company stack up with its marketing organization? How can a company go about improving its marketing systems and techniques to achieve company goals in the years ahead?

In effect, Kotler and many other marketing experts talk about the importance of evaluating events going on today in the world, in the company, and in the department that have important implications for future programs and strategies. In the business world, it often is difficult to give a great deal of attention to the future. However, successful marketers are able to use present indicators to plan effectively for the future.

Six perspectives should have an impact on your present and future work in marketing, in marketing management, or as a marketing

Hickey-Freeman.
Customized®clothes for men and women.

"Quality isn't something that can be promised into an article. It must be put there. If it isn't put there, the finest sales talk in the world won't act as a substitute."

©1983 Hickey-Freeman Co., Inc., 1155 Clinton Ave., N., Rochester, NY 14621.

Figure 18-5. Customer orientation includes emphasis on quality.

entrepreneur. They include: applying the basics of marketing; utilizing the benefits of technology; recognizing economic and cultural diversity; acknowledging the global market; fine-tuning marketing and strategic planning; and continuing your marketing education.

Apply the Basics of Marketing

The first perspective has been discussed throughout this text. *There are a fundamental set of marketing principles and techniques that have been tried, tested, and proved to be effective through time and will prove to be effective in the future.*

Kotler's first question probably summarizes this perspective best. Does your company have a marketing philosophy that is fully customer-oriented from the president to the production personnel? A follow-up question might be: If so, is the philosophy adequately implemented? Kotler states: "Good marketers do their homework. First they see that their products are designed to meet

SAFEWAY'S SUPERMARKET OF THE FUTURE

The latest entry in the metamorphosis in design of American food stores is the Safeway store in Arlington, Texas. Designed by the Doody Co. of Columbus, Ohio, Safeway is the latest entry in futuristic supermarkets. Grocers are being faced with intense competition for consumers' food dollars. A few progressive managers are trying to make their stores more appealing and profitable. According to Dennis Gerdeman, Doody's project director, "We set out to create something with pizzazz, something that isn't mundane and which puts some fun and interest into food shopping."

This Safeway differs markedly from the superstores, hypermarkets, and warehouse/economy food stores which have sprung up in recent years.

The new Safeway is huge—61,073 square feet. It features less merchandise to a square foot than is normally found in supermarkets.

The environment is akin to that of a shopping mall. Convenience shops have been clustered in the center of the store, immediately behind the checkout counters. These shops include a café, bakery, cheese shop, deli, floral department, pharmacy, customer service center, and photo department. They can be seen from virtually any part of the store and serve as the store's focal point. With these stores grouped together, employees can be moved from one department to another as needed, reducing staffing requirements. According to Gerdeman, these "stores" are doing very well.

Radiating from this center are the nonfood, frozen food, and grocery areas, forming a V-shaped design. The front of the store serves as a wide base for branching off in all areas. (See Figure 18-4.) The natural tendency of supermarket shoppers is to sweep past the checkout counters to the right. At Safeway, this brings them to the highly profitable cosmetics department and other high margin areas.

Here are a few other interesting items to be found at Safeway in Arlington.

- Large photomurals identifying departments. For example, a carton of eggs indicates dairy, and an orange juicer with an electric plug identifies housewares. "The photomurals can be seen from a quarter of a mile away," according to Gerdeman.
- The multidirectional aisles are 7 feet wide, in contrast to a normal aisle width of 6 feet.
- The "loop" layout of the store attempts to redirect traffic to expose customers to as many areas as possible.
- A 36 seat sidewalk café alongside the hot deli area is surrounded by ficus trees and the floral shop. It draws natural light from skylights. (See Figure 18-5.)
- Building costs were kept comparatively low by using less expensive wall coverings, less accented floor tile, less expensive interior displays, less glass in front of the store, and more energy conservation equipment.

USE THIS HANDY STORE GUIDE

TO ASSIST YOU IN SHOPPING THIS MARVELOUS NEW

SAFEWAY ONE-STOP SHOPPING CENTER!

Today's Safeway.

Where you get a little bit more.

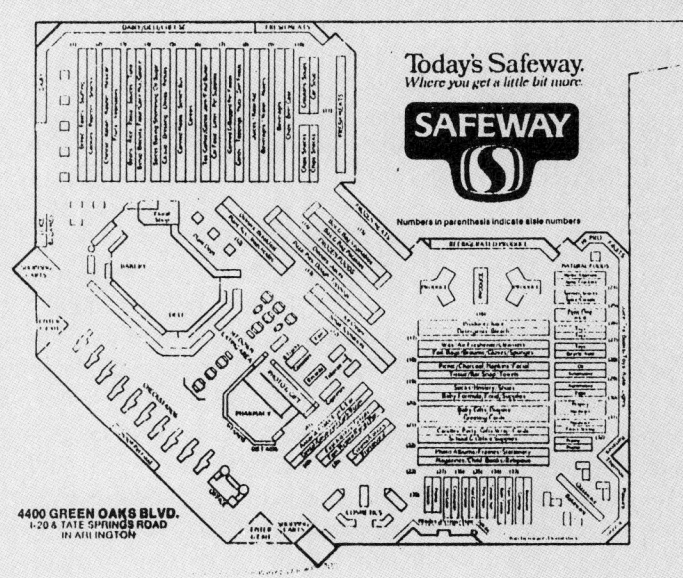

4400 GREEN OAKS BLVD.
I-20 & TATE SPRINGS ROAD
IN ARLINGTON

Figure 18-6. This Safeway supermarket resembles a wide-based V, with the checkout counters forming the base of the V.

The new store was designed in response to demographic trends. While locating in a growing suburban area used to be sufficient to ensure success, today's food store must cope with low population growth, a sluggish economy, reduction in suburban sprawl, and sharp competition from fast-food and convenience stores.

Adapted from Kevin Higgins, "Safeway Enters Quest for Supermarket of Future." Reprint from *Marketing News,* published by the American Marketing Association, January 7, 1983, pages 1 and 6.

the specific needs and desires of a target market. Then, taking account of their competition, they use effective pricing, communications and distribution to inform, motivate, and service that market."[5]

In this text, the basics have been emphasized through discussion of the marketing concept and effective application of such techniques as marketing research, product and service planning, distribution systems (place), promotion, and effective use of human resources. The basics with respect to marketing management—planning, organizing, directing, and controlling—also have been discussed.

Utilize the Benefits of Technology

Technology is rapidly changing the way marketers market, interact with consumers, and relate to their jobs and companies. Technology cannot and will not replace the basics of marketing. But technology has always shaped the job of marketers and marketing executives, in the form of the automobile, the telephone, the cash register, jet travel, the pocket calculator, and so on. Technology will continue to shape marketing planning, operations, and control in the future. Successful marketers will have to keep up with technological changes and use their benefits in their marketing systems.

In *The Third Wave,* Alvin Toffler analyzed the three major economic shifts which have occurred in the U.S. economy: from an agricultural economy to an industrial economy to an economy that is now primarily information-based. The "third-wave"—the information-based economy—has been brought on by the rapid advance of the computer.[6] John Naisbitt noted in *Megatrends* that the United States is being reshaped from an industrial to an informational society. In 1950, 65 percent of the workers in this country were employed in the industrial sector. In 1982 that figure was 30 percent. But 55 percent were employed as "information workers" paid to process data or information.[7]

Most futurists seem to agree that computer literacy will be important in the successful operation of businesses in the future. In the item on the opposite page, a few current uses of the computer in marketing operations are presented.

Recognize Economic and Cultural Diversity

We are an economically and culturally diverse society with varying beliefs, value systems, habits, and ways of getting things done: almost anything is possible. Generalizing to huge groups of customers, employees, or corporations may not work in the years ahead. According to Naisbitt, "We are expressing our individuality and pluralistic nature to a greater degree than ever before. Fashion, entertainment of all kinds, eating habits, and religion all show developments that are contradictory, with plenty of multiple options for meeting our needs and desires."[8] This trend extends to most products. There are more than 200 different brands of cigarettes in the U.S. market and 752 different models of cars (126 compacts). Just Bulbs in Manhattan stocks over 2,500 types of light bulbs.[9] In the work place, employees ask for a range of options about when, how, how often, and for what compensation they will work.

Another way in which individuality is showing up in our society is seen in the dramatic shift from a corporate labor force to a labor force engaged in small businesses. The real economic and labor force growth in this country is largely through small businesses. Approximately 600,000 new businesses are started each year in this country, or about 2,000 a day. Nearly all are classified as small.[10] Small businesses account for about two-thirds of the growth in the labor force. According to Naisbitt in *Megatrends*, the Fortune 1,000 largest industrial companies account for exactly zero growth. The remaining one-third of growth in the labor force is primarily in state and local government.[11]

Large corporations are beginning to recognize the shift from "organization man" type think-

COMPUTER APPLICATIONS TO MARKETING

● The father of an enterprising Girl Scout helped his daughter computerize her list of prospective cookie customers and personalize a letter to them.

● Telsol, an automatic phone robot, now is being used to generate sales leads inexpensively and effectively, promote services, make announcements, conduct small-scale surveys, and improve customer services. Clients include Sears, Amway, *TV Guide*, Guaranteed Mutual Life, Century 21, and a funeral home in Indiana.

● In Ohio, the Hog Accelerated Marketing System (HAMS), a computer-assisted program is used to sell slaughter hogs from Ohio to buyers in Pennsylvania, New York, Maryland, Virginia, Tennessee, and Kentucky.

● Sears, J. C. Penney, and Montgomery Ward use hand-held wands to machine read source- or store-level marketing tickets, improving merchandise and cost control.

● TELLUS, an electronic push-button questionnaire, provides marketers with easy to interpret information on consumer preferences. TELLUS units have been placed in restaurants, hotels, department stores, and supermarkets to gather data on consumers' opinions of merchandise, service, and advertising.

● Advanced teleshopping systems are enabling customers to sit at home and use video screens and keypads to select merchandise, arrange delivery, make travel reservations, buy stocks, arrange payments, and express satisfaction or dissatisfaction to channel members after a purchase.

● Electronic and mechanical products are being diagnosed for problem area, cost, and time to repair by means of a telephone hookup with manufacturers' or retailers' diagnostic computers.

● Word processors equipped with a computer communication package, a proportional-spacing printer, and records-processing packages are significantly reducing the costs of conducting mail questionnaire surveys, improving response rates, and cutting the time required for projects.

● Horizon Industries of Eden Prairie, Minnesota, has developed four microprocessor units to be used at the point of purchase by retailers, entertainment centers, and manufacturers. The CT (countertalk) series quickly programs messages to customers, allowing the business to say what it wants, when it wants, and where it wants in an attention-getting way.

● McGraw-Hill Broadcasting, in cooperation with *Business Week*, is providing business news on TV and full-text retrieval of editorial material carried in McGraw-Hill business publications.

IT'S CHEMISTRY ABROAD

Hexylene glycol and ethylene are two chemicals that are stored in different-sized drums and shipped at separate costs. But in Spanish, where the letter h is not pronounced, the two names sound the same, especially when the speaker is on the Mexican end of a telephone line.

Sensitive hearing, thorough knowledge of the company's products, and a perspective that is sympathetic to the difficulties of foreigners who do business with American companies are prerequisites for Dixie Sager's job. Dixie is manager of Ashland Chemical Co.'s export-import department.

Sager sells Ashland-made chemicals overseas and buys chemicals from foreign countries for Ashland affiliates and company production in the United States. Her department is key in Ashland's announced plan to expand its share of the international chemical industry.

Sager originally joined the company as a secretary to the export-import manager. She later became a sales order clerk, processing orders for the department and handling overseas shipments. Now she works with U.S. customers and overseas agents appointed by Ashland as company representatives and purchasers. Sager haggles over prices, keeps abreast of ocean shipping costs, and sees to it that products are cleared through customs for delivery and that export-import licenses are in place.

She deals daily with companies in South, Central, and Latin America, the Caribbean, Europe, Africa, and the far east and near east. Sager says she has two challenges ahead: to increase company sales over previous years and to "do a really good job, bettering relations between foreign customers and our affiliates."

Adapted from Andi Gates, "Export Manager Breaks Language Barriers," Columbus *Dispatch*, 1982.

---

ing to thinking that recognizes the entrepreneurial spirit. Team leadership, quality circles, a cafeteria offering of compensation plans and fringe benefits, rotation in the work place, flex time, and some freedom to define one's own work assignment are just a few ways in which corporations are beginning to capitalize on the diverse needs of people within this society. As a society, we are slowly learning that people are a country and a company's greatest asset, and we are slowly implementing modifications in the labor market to recognize the entrepreneurial needs, diverse work styles, and unique abilities of people. Peter Drucker, an internationally known author and management consultant, perhaps said it best. "By 1990 we will have learned, I hope, what the Japanese learned from us. We taught it to them: People are a resource and not a cost. The Japanese have accepted the idea and we haven't."[12]

Successful marketers and marketing managers recognize and adapt to the economic and cultural diversity within their market territories.

They are keen at analyzing carefully the diverse needs and wants of their markets and offering appropriate products and services to meet those needs and wants.

Acknowledge the Global Market

The story of Ashland Chemical's Dixie Sager illustrates the shift in the United States from being as isolated, virtually self-sufficient national economy to being part of an interdependent global economy. The world is shrinking. What may have once seemed foreign and strange now seems natural and familiar. An ad for Volkswagen reads, "I don't want a foreign car, I want a VW." General Motors and Toyota team up to build Japanese-designed cars in the United States. American products, ingenuity, and technology have swept the world. The market for many firms today is worldwide in perspective and scope.

There are mixed feelings among American firms about doing business abroad. National or domestic marketing is generally simpler and safer. Marketers do not have to learn another language, deal with a different currency, face political and legal uncertainties, or modify products and services to deal with different cultural needs and expectations.

However, over 30,000 U.S. firms are already doing some international marketing. About 250 firms account for 75 percent of the $110 billion in manufactured and agricultural products that was exported in 1980.[13] The future looks especially bright for small businesses to become aggressively involved in international marketing as the U.S. Commerce Department extends Export-Import Bank loans and other services to small companies.

There are two primary reasons why American companies will be increasingly drawn into international marketing. First, they may be *pushed* into it by a weakening of marketing opportunities at home. Second, they may be *pulled* into foreign trade by growing opportunities for their products or services in other countries. They may find other markets an attractive place to make a profit even after allowing for the extra costs and problems they may face in operating abroad.[14]

International marketing probably will increase significantly for American firms in the years ahead. Innovative, cooperative manufacturing and marketing strategies will continue to be developed as we recognize in a meaningful way that we are part of a global economy.

Fine-Tune Marketing Strategic Planning

Strategic planning is a process of developing and maintaining a fit between an organization and its market. In strategic planning, a mission, objectives, plans, and strategies are developed and articulated throughout the company.

Successful companies pay careful attention to strategic planning. They periodically analyze why they are in business (mission), what it is they are trying to do (objectives), how they are doing it (plans and strategies), and finally how well they are doing it. The fit between the company's mission and its objectives, plans, and strategies is analyzed carefully.

Hundreds of suggestions could be offered to aid a marketer or marketing manager in strategic planning for the future. The following are just a few major ones.

1. Establish Market Share by Offering a Quality Product or Service Appropriate to Your Segment at a Low Price. The key words are *quality* and *market segment.* You may have to absorb losses for a while because of low prices, but the long-range practice of offering quality products and services to targeted groups should prove economically successful. This recommendation is in line with economic, cultural, and demographic trends in this country.

2. Focus on Competitor as Well as Consumer Strategies. Become aware of how competitors are reaching and satisfying customers. In a slow-growth economy, one way to succeed will be at the expense of competitors. Know their soft spots and capitalize on them.

3. Increase Direct Marketing Efforts. The new technologies, changing lifestyles, energy conservation and costs, international marketing, and increased costs associated with person-to-person sales all point to the use of direct marketing techniques to maintain or increase market share. Computer-driven direct-mail letters, catalogs, print ads with return coupons, direct response telephone numbers (local or 800), ads in monthly bank or charge statements, videotex systems, and providing special research or financial information in response to ads all have great potential as effective marketing strategies.

4. Secure a Commitment From Marketing People. People in your organization, department, or work unit must be committed to making the marketing process work as identified in the strategic plan. Encourage risk-taking behavior among your workers. Reward their entrepreneurial spirit. This may include a mix of communication, fostering creativity, training, motivation, displaying trust, building confidence, and offering diverse rewards.

5. Get More for Less. An important demand of marketing in the future will be for greater productivity. For example, chain stores probably will try to get more business from each store or more dollars for each square foot rather than opening large numbers of new stores. A related strategy should be much closer communication between marketers and their accountants. Strategies will be needed for tighter financial planning; cost-benefit analysis as related to product, service, or systems modification; tighter inventory control; closer scrutiny of salary, wage, and benefit packages, and so on. Probably most companies can increase their productivity and profit picture with closer scrutiny of expenses relative to marketing strategies.

Continue Your Marketing Education

A final suggestion to help marketers anticipate, plan for, and cope with the future is to continue their marketing education. Adopt the sound philosophy that education is a lifelong process. College courses, adult education, seminars, industry-sponsored training, conventions, conferences, and business meetings all provide opportunities to upgrade knowledge and skills appropriate to business and marketing. Above all, read trade journals, business periodicals and texts, the business and financial sections of newspapers, literature attached to products, and training journals.

Probably the best way to learn about marketing and marketing management is to read the literature and research, discuss techniques with those who have been there, observe or participate in marketing demonstrations or simulations, and then apply what you have learned to your real-life marketing environment.

KEY POINTS SUMMARY

- The elements of the marketing mix (product, place, price, and promotion, with people as a base) are closely related and interdependent. One element cannot be considered without considering its affect on the others.

- Effective marketing managers plan, organize, direct, and control the marketing mix. That is, they manage the business activities associated with products and services, place, price, promotion, and people.

- There are many variables external to the firm or business over which managers have little or no control. However, they should be aware of them and anticipate their effect on company operations and profits. Examples include demographics, economics, social and cultural forces, technology, and competition.

- Marketing managers have important responsibilities that accompany their right to engage in business in a free society. Among those responsibilities are integrity, fairness to customers, and involvement in civic affairs and social issues.

- There are six suggestions for marketing managers as they strive to make their organizations profitable. Such managers should apply fundamental marketing basics in operating the business, use the benefits of technology, recognize economic and cultural diversity, acknowledge the global market, fine-tune marketing strategic planning, and continue a marketing education.

KEY TERMS AND CONCEPTS

controlling   planning
directing   organizing

DISCUSSION QUESTIONS

1. Discuss the role of marketing management in a small business or for a manager or assistant manager of a department in a large business. Approximately how much of the manager's overall time is devoted to planning? Organizing? Directing? Controlling? If possible, interview such a person and see how he or she views the management role. How much time is spent in management tasks? What other tasks must the person perform?

2. What is meant by uncontrollable variables? What are some examples of uncontrollable variables being faced by businesses in your community? How are business people responding to these variables?

3. Discuss ways in which businesses in your community or people employed in marketing are meeting their social responsibilities.

4. In what ways is the computer being used in businesses in your community as an aid in marketing?

5. Discuss the six perspectives presented on pages 525 to 532 in this chapter. Use the following questions as a guide.

a. What are some examples of marketing principles that should constitute one's business philosophy?

b. Suggest a few ways in which technology, especially the computer, can be used in marketing planning and operations.

c. Choose three types of marketing businesses—for example, a restaurant, a woman's apparel store, and a home furnishings center—and describe how each might respond to the cultural and economic diversity of a community of 50,000 people. Or use the cultural and social forces listed on page 520 as a basis for discussing how each of these businesses might respond to such economic and cultural diversity.

d. Cite examples of products that were manufactured abroad and marketed in your community. Cite examples of firms that market their products and services abroad. Indicate the countries to which they export.

e. Why is strategic planning so important to the success of a company? Do you have any suggestions in addition to those presented on pages 531 to 532 to aid a marketing manager in future strategic planning?

f. Identify sources of marketing education in your community.

NOTES

1. Adapted from "Survey of New Product Developers Offers 25-Year Innovation Forecast," *Marketing News,* Sept. 4, 1981, p. 4.
2. Data extracted from "Work and Families, A Report to Corporate Leaders on the White House Conference on Families," prepared by J. C. Penney Co., October, 1980, pp. 1-9; George Kegley, "Consumer Caution Expected" and "Merchandisers Cope with Changing Family," *Roanoke Times & World News,* July 27, 1980, pp. G-1 and G-2; "The Lasting Changes Brought By Women Workers," *Business Week,* March 15, 1982, pp. 59, 62, 67; and Nancy Yoshihara, "Advertising Targets 'Maturity Market,'" LA Times—Washington Post Service, *Roanoke Times & World News,* October 12, 1980, p. F-3.

3. Ibid.

4. Adapted from Phillip Kotler, "Meeting the Marketing Challenges of the 1980s," Jules Arbose interview, *International Management,* McGraw-Hill International Publications Co., Ltd., May 1980, pp. 222-224.

5. Ibid.

6. Alvin Toffler, *The Third Wave,* William Morrow & Co., 1980.

7. John Naisbitt, cited in B. G. Yovovich, "His Crystal Ball: The Daily Newspaper," *Advertising Age,* October 11, 1982, p. M-5.

8. Ibid.

9. John Naisbitt, *Megatrends,* Warner Books, New York, 1982, p. 232.

10. Kenneth R. Van Voorhis, *Entrepreneurship and Small Business Management,* Allyn and Bacon, Boston, 1980, p. 49.

11. Naisbitt, op. cit.

12. Peter Drucker, cited in an interview with Warren Bennis, *AMA Management Digest,* July 1982, p. 12.

13. Marianne McGowan, "Small Ohio Businesses Urged to Boost Exports," Columbus *Dispatch,* Sept. 23, 1981, p. B7.

14. Phillip Kotler, *Principles of Marketing,* Prentice-Hall, Englewood Cliffs, N.J., 1980, p. 601.

CASES

CASE 16: THE DOLLAR GROWS AT FAMILY DOLLAR

Family Dollar Stores, Inc., a Mathews, North Carolina-based chain, survived rather well the general "fall of the discounters" (Woolco, Vornado, King's Department Stores, and HRI Industries) that occurred in the early 1980s. In fact, the chain opened 74 stores in 1982 and planned to open nearly 100 in 1983. By 1988, Family Dollar plans to operate over 1,000 stores. The chain completed 30 consecutive quarters of record sales and earnings. In 1982, it logged operating margins of 9.7 percent, double the average for all U.S. retailers and even farther above the norm for low-margin, high-volume discounting businesses. How does it do it?

Stick To It

"Family Dollar never has forgotten its mission," according to Lewis Levine, the company president. The company purports to provide value in basic, low-cost merchandise to working-class consumers. "Family Dollar knows what it wants to be," said Levine. "It's not vacillating back and forth. Some of the bigger ones trade up and then trade down. Family Dollar has kept its direction and knows who it is."

Family Dollar pretty much sticks to the socks and T-shirt needs of its blue-collar patrons. Shunning Izod shirts, high-priced computers, and telescopic cameras, Family Dollar offers low-priced merchandise such as apparel, housewares, health and beauty aids, stationery, school supplies, toys, and automobile goods in its small, blue-collar neighborhood outlets. Those outlets are located in small cities and towns in 13 states throughout the southeast. Originally the stores were located primarily in textile and furniture-making regions, but in the early 1980s the company expanded to serve the shipbuilding, tourism, retirement, and farming industries. The retail outlets follow a prescribed flow plan described as "no frills" and vary from 6,000 to 8,000 square feet. Outlets are leased at less than $3 a square foot, about one-third less than the price paid by the average discounter and a lot less than the price in fancy malls.

The company uses centralized buying which allows it to obtain volume discounts from some manufacturers. In one year, for example, the company negotiated purchase of half a million shirts, enabling it to undercut competitors for the same product by 10 to 15 percent. It also uses central distribution, storing and moving all merchandise from one warehouse in Mathews. This holds down real estate costs and avoids inventory duplication.

$14.99 and Less

More than 95 percent of all the merchandise carried in Family Dollar stores sells for under $15. So price-conscious is the company that a committee of senior managers must approve every item of merchandise tagged at more than $12. Sales are in cash only. Checks are accepted only after a customer obtains a check-cashing card.

Family Dollar advertises considerably in newspapers in the small towns where its stores are located, thus avoiding big-city ad costs.

Part-Timers

Another practice that has proved economical is reliance on part-time employees. Nearly half the employees are part-timers. In fact, full-time employees decreased about 15 percent in a 3 year period while the number of part-time workers increased by 50 percent. In off-peak seasons, the stores typically require only a manager and six employees, and outlets can be run with as few as two workers at any one time.

According to Levine, "Family Dollar management budgets conservatively, plans meticulously, and sticks to what it plans." A tight rein is kept on expenses. "We break down every expense item from the bottom up and from the top down." The Levine family owns 53 percent of the company. All the Levines are confident that as larger discounters strive for a more "upscale" image, Family Dollar will benefit from what it has done all along: selling solid albeit unglamorous lines at bottom-dollar discounts to a predictable customer base.

Based on information obtained from Sharon Bonat, Landmark News Service, "Family Dollar Courts Working-Class Customers," Roanoke *Times & World News*, February 20, 1983, pp. D-1, D-6; "Family Dollar Stores: As Rivals Fall, This Discounter Keeps Going," *Business Week*, January 24, 1983, pp. 89–90; and personal interviews.

a. Identify the basic business philosophy of Family Dollar Stores, Inc.

b. How has that philosophy been implemented through the four Ps of the marketing mix: product, place, price, and promotion? What has the company policy been with respect to personnel?

c. Describe how Family Dollar has implemented the marketing concept relative to its identified target market.

d. What additional marketing strategies might help Family Dollar increase its market share in the years ahead? Justify your decisions.

CASE 17: THE MARKETING CONSULTANT

At last, with degree in hand, you are ready to test your skills and try your luck in the marketing world. But first, offer a freebie to a small busi-nessperson in your community who apparently is in need of your help.

All astute observers of the marketing scene and certainly all consumers are aware of small businesses that are in need of help with their marketing activities. Perhaps a product line is outdated or simply "off market" with respect to the customers they are trying to serve. Maybe their promotions are ineffective because of inappropriate media, sloppy presentation, or inefficient layout. The business may be staffed with untrained employees.

With guidance and further direction from your instructor, visit with a small businessperson in your community for the purpose of advising him or her on future marketing strategies. Try to choose a business with which you have had some contact, perhaps as a part-time employee or frequent customer. Consider choosing a small business such as a restaurant, bookstore, service station, grocery store, or hobby shop. Or perhaps choose someone who is self-employed, say perhaps with a home repair service, a cottage industry service (such as secretarial, child care, hair care), or a business service (such as accounting, dentistry, office decorating). The type of business you choose and your advance knowledge of various aspects of that business will dictate the approach, questions to be asked, and free advice to be given. The following are general and somewhat broad guidelines or suggestions. With assistance from your instructor, adapt them as necessary.

a. Arrange a meeting with the owner or manager of a small business in your community. Discuss the purposes of this project. Discuss with the owner or manager your interest in applying some of your marketing skills as well as possibly helping this business improve some of its marketing techniques. Plan this presentation well.

b. Formulate questions to help you become better informed about the philosophy of the business and its current marketing practices.

1. **Market and Marketing Research.** Who is the target market? What do their characteristics seem to be? Have you ever surveyed customers about their needs and wants, or would you consider surveying customers? Do you subscribe to any research services or trade journals?

2. **Product or Service.** How do you decide what products or services to offer your market? What guides your choice of brands, depth of selection, and breadth of selection? In your opinion, is your product line compatible with your target market?

3. **Place.** From where do you get your merchandise for resale? What channels are followed in getting the merchandise from producers to your business? Are alternative channels or suppliers available?

4. **Price.** How is price determined for the various products or services offered? How compatible are the prices with those suggested by the manufacturer and those charged by competitors? What factors guide decisions regarding markdowns, loss leaders, discounts, and credit?

5. **Promotion.** What have been some recent promotional activities? Can you get any information on the effectiveness of various promotions such as advertising, display, or special promotions?

6. **Personnel.** How are employees recruited, selected, and trained? Who generally calls the shots with respect to work assignments, operations (how things are done), and schedules? Is there any formal on-the-job training program or encouragement to participate in off-the-job training or educational activities?

c. Based on your observations within the firm, your analysis of the interviews, and the knowledge and skills of marketing you have developed, write out a marketing plan for this business. It is suggested that you use the six elements discussed above (market and marketing research, product or service, place, price, promotion, and personnel) to organize your plan. You may wish to focus on a short-term plan for each element, that is, provide very specific suggestions that potentially could be implemented within a year. Then develop a long-term plan for each element, that is, targets or goals that could be met within 5 to 10 years.

d. Present your plan to the owner or manager of the small firm. Discuss your suggestions orally with this person and provide him or her with a copy of your written report.

GLOSSARY

Administered vertical marketing system. A system in which the manufacturer is strong enough to get voluntary cooperation from middlemen without conflict.

Adoption. The decision of a consumer to buy and use a new product over a period of time.

Advertising. Any paid form of nonpersonal presentation and promotion of ideas, goods, or services by an identified sponsor.

Advertising allowances (promotional allowances). Special reduced-price or "free" merchandise arrangements made by manufacturers to encourage both wholesalers and retailers to promote the manufacturers' products.

Advocacy advertising. Advertising that presents an individual's or an organization's viewpoint.

Agent middlemen. Middlemen who do not take title to the merchandise and generally perform only a few marketing activities.

Agricultural grain terminal. A full service wholesaler who purchases grain from local elevators and sells it to food processors.

Allowances. Special price concessions offered by the manufacturer or the wholesaler both to consumers and to members of the channel of distribution.

Auction company. A company that accepts possession, but not title, to sellers' products, and offers them for sale through competitive bidding.

Average-cost pricing. The technique of combining average costs, average fixed costs, and average variable costs on a chart, together with profit information, to decide on a selling price.

Backordering. Deferring the shipment of goods out-of-stock until new stock is received.

Basic stock list. A list used in inventory control systems where the product or a slightly altered product is included in the inventory year after year.

Basing point pricing. A pricing method whereby the sellers within an industry decide on locations, or basing points, from which transportation costs will be computed. The price to the buyer includes the cost of shipping goods from the basing point nearest to the buyer, regardless of the actual location from which the goods were shipped.

Bonded warehouse. Either a private or public warehouse which has taken out a bond to assure that certain taxes, import tariffs, or fees are paid to the United States Treasury.

Branding. The strategy of using a name, design, or combination symbol to identify the products and services of a marketer and so effectively differentiate their products from those of the competitors.

Brand mark. Symbol, design, letters, or special colors associated with a specific brand.

Brand name. That part of the brand that can be spoken or written.

Breaking bulk. Dividing large quantities of products (tanks, barrels, cases, etc.) into smaller units to satisfy the purchasing desires of retailers.

Breakeven analysis. A method of determining the level of sales, or breakeven point, at which a firm's revenues will equal its costs. Beyond that level the firm can expect to make money.

Broker. One who specializes in arranging transactions for a limited number of products or services and is well informed concerning conditions in particular markets.

Business analysis. The stage in new product development in which the product idea is examined from an objective business perspective.

Business logistics. A total approach to the distribution system: includes all activities involved in physically moving inventory from the point of origin to the point of use or consumption.

Canvassing. A method of selling in which the salesperson calls on firms, usually without an appointment (cold), to determine if he or she can supply needed products or services.

Cash and carry wholesaler. A wholesaler who does not provide credit or delivery. Used primarily by small retailers for products not immediately available through wholesale merchants.

Channel captain. A retailer, wholesaler, manufacturer, or producer who determines the channel design and, to a considerable extent, what marketing activities other channel members will perform.

Channel of distribution. The course taken by the product or service on its journey to the ultimate buyer.

Class rate. An established rail shipment rate, higher than the commodity rate and based on the nature of the items shipped, on weight, and on distance.

Combo-supermarket. A large discount store that resembles the French hypermarket in going beyond the concept of scrambled merchandise and offering a wide variety of products and services.

Commission merchants. Agent middlemen who facilitate buying and selling transactions. They do not take title; however, they may handle the product, complete the sales transaction, and remit the selling price, less their commission, to the seller.

Commodity rate. A rate granted by rail carriers for the shipment from receiving to destination points of bulky products such as grain, iron ore, sand, lumber, and coal. This special rate is given as a reward for regular use or large quantity shipments.

Common carriers. Carriers that provide transportation service to any firm for a fee.

Comparative ads. Ads that attempt to stimulate selective demand by comparing two or more brands and indicating why the features of one product are superior to those of the other.

Competition-oriented pricing. Prices set in accordance with the prices charged by competitors. These prices can be below, equal to, or higher than competition, depending on the differences in the products or services involved.

Competitive ad. An ad which attempts to stimulate selective demand by promoting a specific brand.

Concentrated marketing. The strategy of aiming at one market segment in an attempt to market the best possible product and marketing mix. The goal is to achieve a very strong market share position in a very specific segment.

Conclusive stage. The stage of research in which structured data collection and analysis are aimed at the solution of a specific problem.

Consignment. An arrangement by which the retailer is not billed until the products are sold. The merchandise is prepriced and the retailer is responsible only for providing floor space and collecting the money for purchase at checkout stations.

Consumer behavior. The acts of individuals and groups in the problem-solving process of obtaining and using products and services for personal satisfaction.

Consumer-oriented promotion. A promotion submix in which all decisions are reached with the potential customer's satisfaction as a focal point.

Consumer premiums. Merchandise items given to shoppers in order to encourage them to buy a product.

Containerization. A cargo handling system in which the shipment is enclosed in containers, typically 8 feet high, 8 feet wide, and 20 or 40 feet long, which are designed to ensure that the shipment is not opened en route.

Containerized premium. A consumer premium that is prepackaged and distributed with the product itself, such as a miniature toy in a box of Cracker Jacks.

Contract carriers. Those carriers certified to transport items according to an agreement between the carrier and the shipper.

Contractual vertical system. A system in which franchises or long-term contractual agreements exist between buyer and seller.

Controlling. All activities the manager undertakes in attempting to assure that actual operations conform to planned operations.

Convenience products. Inexpensive products that are regularly purchased by consumers with a minimum of time and effort.

Cooperative advertising. Shared cost for ads in which the manufacturer or supplier's name appears along with the names of local merchants who supply the advertised brand of product or service.

Cooperative chain. A group of retailers who band together to set up their own wholesaling organization.

Corporate chain. A group of two or more stores linked together under one management and owned by stockholders.

Corporate vertical system. A system in which the manufacturer owns and controls the distribution outlets.

Cost-oriented pricing. A method of determining price by computing costs for acquiring or manufacturing the merchandise, for service, and for overhead, then adding the desired profit margin.

Cost-plus pricing. A pricing strategy in which price is determined by adding to the basic cost figure an amount to cover other unassigned costs and yield a profit.

Cottage industry. Small businesses managed and operated out of one's home.

Counter-trade agreement. An arrangement whereby one country agrees to buy from another country if reciprocal buying occurs.

Creative merchandising. The practice of offering customers a wide array of products and such services as fashion advice, investment and career counseling, or even evening college courses—all on the store's premises.

Creative selling. An inside selling technique in which a salesperson not only shows how buyers can use products, but also how they can benefit from owning them.

Customer service level. The optimum number of items kept in inventory in order to prevent lost sales by failure to have the right product in the right price at the right time.

Decline stage. The PLC period in which sales decrease either at a rapid rate or slowly and steadily over a long time period.

Demand. The quantity of a product or service for which consumers are willing to pay a given price at a given time.

Demand creation. Special efforts to stimulate a desire for products and services, with the ultimate objective of sales with profit.

Demand curve. A graph of the quantity of a product or service that consumers will buy at various price levels.

Demand-oriented pricing. Utilizing consumer desires and demands in the setting of individual prices. Perceived-value pricing and demand-differential pricing are both examples of demand-oriented pricing.

Demographics. A form of segmentation in which the market is divided into groups on the basis of variables such as population, age, sex, households, families, income, occupation, and education.

Desk research. The collection, synthesis, and orderly distillation of all available material on a particular subject. Sources include trade magazines, trade associations, professional societies, government agencies, special-purpose libraries, and research houses.

Differentiated marketing. The strategy of identifying several different segments in the market and supplying different products and programs for each segment.

Diffusion. The pattern and rate of acceptance of new products by consumers.

Direct distribution channel. A distribution method in which the manufacturer or producer sells directly to the ultimate consumer.

Discount pricing. Granting reductions from the usual list price if the buyer gives up a particular marketing function that is usually provided by the seller. There are several different types of discounts, including cash, quantity, function (or trade), and seasonal.

Discount store. A departmentalized retail establishment using many self-service techniques to sell a variety of merchandise at prices below those charged by retailers that provide customer services.

Discretionary purchases. Purchases a consumer can make after paying for necessities.

Display ad. A printed ad that is larger than classified and usually contains a persuasive message.

Distribution centers. Special warehouses designed to store products for short periods of time and to speed the flow of products.

Diversions in transit. An in-transit railroad privilege permitting the shipper to start the products via rail in one general direction and to establish or change destinations as long as the change or new destination involves forward movement of the cars.

Drop shipper. A wholesaler who arranges for the delivery of products directly from the manufacturer to the retailer or industrial buyer. These middlemen take title to the goods but do not accept actual possession.

Early adopters. The first consumers to accept a new product.

Economic order quantity (EOQ). A concept to balance ordering costs and carrying costs with the desired level of satisfying customers' orders.

Elasticity. A measure of how responsive the market is to any change in the price of a product.

Emergency items. Convenience products purchased when a need is urgent; emergency purchases are not planned.

Emotional advertising. Messages that appeal to the prospective buyer's emotions, which are influenced by the individual's wants and needs.

Equilibrium point. The point at which the supply curve and the demand curve intersect.

Equilibrium price. The price at which both the buyer and the seller will be satisfied.

Equipment. Accessory products such as typewriters and forklift trucks that are used in the making of other products but do not become a part of the finished product.

Esteem needs. Needs that arise from a social class system and are expressed by self-image or the desired image which the individual wishes to project.

Exploratory stage. Preliminary market research conducted to develop a clear definition of the research problem.

Factual (rational) advertising. Ads designed to appeal to rational thought processes. The message simply contains facts about a product or service.

Family brand. The use of the same brand name on all products or an entire line.

Field selling. Selling done by retail or service sales people who call upon prospective customers outside a store or service outlet to deliver sales presentations and to assist the customers in making buying decisions.

Fishyback service. Placing truck trailers, loaded with goods, onto cargo ships or barges.

Focus group. A group of consumers who meet a marketer's target specifications and are brought together to discuss marketing strategies and their needs as consumers.

Form utility. Utility that is created by making products available in the form needed and wanted by consumers.

Franchise. The exclusive right, granted to an individual or group (franchisee), to use a corporation's (franchiser's) name in a certain territory, usually in exchange for an initial fee plus monthly payments. Both the agreement and the individual business are called a franchise.

Franchising. A form of licensing in which the owner of a product or service sells the rights to distribute or market those elements identified in the license. Typically, the franchiser retains control over the marketing strategies.

Free enterprise economic system (market directed system). An economic system in which the individual decisions of many producers and consumers make the macro-level decisions for the whole economy.

Free on Board (F.O.B.). A pricing term that is typically used with the name of a location. It is at this location that the seller stops paying for transportation and the buyer begins to pay.

Freight absorption pricing. A method of pricing whereby the seller absorbs some of the freight cost so that the delivered price is competitive.

Freight forwarder. A specialized marketing firm designed to assist firms who ship in less than car- or truck-load quantities. A freight forwarder collects shipments from various firms and consolidates them into car- or truck-load quantities.

Full-service wholesaler. A wholesaler that handles either consumer or industrial products and buys, sells, grades, stores, breaks bulk, assembles, transports, finances, takes risks, and gathers market information.

Functional discount (trade discount). A discount offered to members of the channel of distribution for the functions, or jobs, that they are going to perform. Functional discounts are set up by manufacturers who quote a retail price and express prices to the wholesaler and retailer as "discounts" from the retail price.

General line wholesaler. A wholesaler that offers a broad assortment of products within a single merchandise line or, at most, limited products in closely related lines.

General merchandise wholesaler. A wholesaler that carries a general assortment of products in two or more distinct lines.

Geographic pricing. Pricing that includes several techniques that establish the responsibility for paying transportation charges. Geographic pricing terms are often negotiated, but sometimes they will depend on the traditional practices of the particular industry in which the firm operates.

Government market. A selling market, made up of federal, state, and local government units, that buys products and services to meet the needs of the citizens in each unit.

Grading. Sorting products according to size, quality, or some other standard.

Gross rating points (GRP). A rating system used by the outdoor advertising industry to indicate the number of possible impression opportunities at a particular location, without regard to audience duplication, expressed in terms of a percent of the total population of a specific market.

Growth stage. The PLC period when sales increase rapidly—at a faster rate than during any other stage.

Heterogeneous shopping products. An assortment of brands, perceived as having different features. The consumer sees differences in appearance, functions, and quality.

Homogeneous shopping products. Products perceived as being very similar in quality. If the consumer sees little difference in these products, price and related services may be justification for purchasing one brand over another.

Horizontal conflicts. Issues arising between two marketing institutions at the same level.

Horizontal integration. The acquisition of firms at the same level of activity by a manufacturer or middleman.

Idea generation. The beginning stage of new product development, including origination and collection of product ideas.

Import and export agents. Agents who do not take title to products exchanged but instead bring buyers and sellers together for international trade.

Import and export merchants. Full-service wholesalers who bring products and buyers together for international trade.

Impulse items. Convenience products purchased without planning or searching effort.

Independent store. Singularly operated by a proprietor, partnership, or corporation.

Indirect distribution channel. A distribution method which requires the use of middlemen in selling products and services or facilitating such sales.

Industrial distributor. Any industrial wholesaler, such as an oil well supply house, that purchases products and raw materials from producers and manufacturers and subsequently sells them to industrial users.

Industrial market. A market made up of businesses and organizations that buy products and services to run their businesses, to resell, or to produce other products and services.

Industrial product. An item used by an industrial marketer to resell, to run a business or organization, or to produce other products or services.

Industrial shows. Shows used by manufacturers to exhibit their products to other manufacturers, to provide education sessions describing new techniques in the industry, and to demonstrate new products.

Installations. Products such as trucks for a delivery firm that are expensive and major items and have a long life that affects the business's scale of operation.

Institutional advertising. Ads designed to generate goodwill or enhance a firm's image.

Intensive distribution. The sale of a product through any responsible and suitable middleman that will stock the product.

Intertype conflicts. Issues which arise when different types of retail outlets exist in the same marketing area and one type of retailer believes that another type is receiving preferential treatment.

Introduction stage. The PLC period of new product sales to customers in one or more markets.

Inventory carrying costs. A cost category that includes interest on the investment of products while they are stored; inventory service costs such as insurance and inventory taxes; holding costs, including rented or owned storage space; and risk costs, including losses due to damage, deterioration, spoilage, or theft.

Late adopters. The last consumers to purchase a product.

Leader pricing. A promotional pricing method used by retailers in which one or two widely used items, usually perishables such as milk and eggs, are priced at a very low price in the hopes that people who buy these items will buy other items at their usual price.

Leased warehouse. A rented warehouse that operates in the same manner as a private warehouse. The lessee (manufacturer, wholesaler, or retailer) obtains a storage facility in return for payments.

Limited-line store (specialty store). A retail store that carries a relatively complete assortment of a single line of products or related lines of merchandise.

Limited-service wholesaler. A wholesaler that does not engage in all the activities of full-service wholesalers.

Liner service. Freight transportation by water on assigned routes on a scheduled basis.

Local wholesalers. Wholesalers that limit their operations to a metropolitan area or an area within the confines of a radius of 75 to 150 miles of their headquarters.

Logotype. A distinctively designed form of a firm's name, a brand name, or a trademark, which is reproduced on all print advertisements.

Lot quantity costs. An acquisition category that includes costs of issuing and closing orders, related costs of handling orders, materials handling, scheduling, and expediting.

Macro-marketing. A marketing concept that focuses on a society's whole economic system and studies the flow of products and services from those who produce or manufacture them to those who ultimately consume them. The emphasis is not on the activities that individual organizations or individual consumers perform but on how the entire system performs, taking into account the interrelated aspects of all producers and consumers.

Mail order wholesaler. A wholesaler that sells a limited number of products by means of catalogs sent to retailers and industrial and business buyers.

Manufacturer's agent. A facilitator who operates under contract with the manufacturer to sell products in an exclusive territory.

Manufacturer's brand. A brand used on products owned and sponsored by a manufacturer whose primary function is production. These are often referred to as national brands, but they are not necessarily distributed nationally.

Marginal costs. The additional amount a company must pay to produce one additional unit of a product.

Marginal revenue. The amount of revenue a company gets from selling one additional unit of a particular product.

Market share. The portion of the market, often expressed as a percentage of the market, that buys a firm's product.

Marketing. Coordinated system of business activities designed to provide products and services that satisfy the needs and wants of customers through exchange processes.

Marketing concept. Philosophy of operating a business whereby the business aims all of its efforts at satisfying its customers—at a profit.

Marketing information system. An organized set of procedures designed to gather, sort, analyze, evaluate, and distribute the information for making marketing decisions.

Marketing mix. A selling concept involving the four major parts of marketing: products and services to offer, the prices at which they should be sold, the place and manner in which they will be delivered to the customer, and the way in which they will be promoted. Often referred to as the four P's of marketing: **p**roduct, **p**rice, **p**lace, and **p**romotion.

Marketing research. An objective system designed to collect, analyze, and report information and findings relevant to a specific problem or situation facing the company.

Market segmentation. The process of dividing the total market into smaller parts which include customers with similar characteristics. Each identified segment is made up of people who are similar to one another in behavior, lifestyle, and goals.

Markup. The amount that a seller adds to the cost of products to arrive at their selling price. The markup should be large enough to cover the cost of doing business and still allow for a reasonable profit.

Markup pricing. A pre-set percentage of total costs, which is added to those costs to determine the retail price for each item.

Mass merchandisers. Stores that sell a number of lines of products—apparel and accessories, household linens and dry goods, small wares, and in some cases, furniture, home furnishings, hardware, and appliances—all under one roof.

Materials. Products that are used in the finished product after some additional processing. For example, copper may be made into a wire which becomes part of an electric motor.

Materials handling. The process of assembling, packing, weighing, and moving products from a producer to a warehouse, from a warehouse to a carrier, or from one carrier to another.

Maturity stage. The PLC period in which the rate of sales increase begins to slow down and the sales volume levels off.

Micro-marketing. A marketing concept that focuses on a specific organization or an individual firm and studies the firm's actual and prospective customers' needs and wants in order to develop satisfactory products and services.

Middle adopters. Average consumers in the mass market who buy a new product after the early adopters, when the price is lower and when the majority of people are buying the product.

Middleman's brands. Private brands or dealer's brands owned and controlled by retailers and wholesalers.

Middlemen. Business organizations (wholesalers and retailers) or individuals (agents and brokers) specializing in carrying out the transfer to title between the manufacturer and the customer.

Missionary salesperson. An individual who works with retailers to develop goodwill and stimulate demand by setting up displays, arranging promotions, and helping retailers move the products faster.

Model. A set of interrelated variables that are set up to represent a real system, process, or outcome.

Model stock (ideal stock). Inventory based on past sales records of sizes, prices, and units.

Monopolistic competition. A marketing structure in which there are many sellers who act independently so that the products they produce and market can be easily differentiated by the consumer.

Monopoly. A market environment that is structured with only one seller of a product or service and no close substitutes for that product or service.

Mutual interdependence. Among members of an oligopoly, the shared response to one member's change in marketing mix, as well as the shared problems of dealing with competition from outside the oligopoly.

National rollout. A method of product introduction that aims a new product at the complete national consumer market.

National wholesaler. A wholesaler that operates on a national scale and may invite retail buyers to visit and buy from its branch house, which is often located in the merchandise mart or trade center of a large city.

New product. Any item that a marketer offers to customers for the first time. A product is new if it requires different marketing strategies and if the customer perceives it as different from other products.

Objective-and-task method. A method of examining the objectives of promotion activities: once objectives or sales goals are determined, the marketer can decide the amount of money needed to achieve these goals.

Odd-even pricing. Setting retail prices that end in certain odd numbers, usually just below the next even price, in order to influence customer perception of price.

Oligopoly. The domination of the market for a particular product or service by a limited number of firms.

On-line data bases. Huge banks of information that is processed, stored, and delivered electronically. On-line data are controlled directly by or in direct communication with a computer.

Part. A complete product that becomes part of a bigger and more complex product with no further change or processing.

Party plan. A sales method in which a host or hostess invites people to attend a party at which the sponsor's merchandise or services are demonstrated and sold.

Penetration pricing. The introduction of a new product at a relatively low price to attract a large number of buyers.

Personal selling. Individual, persuasive communication to help a buyer choose a product or service to fulfill a need, want, or desire.

Physical barriers to communication. Environmental factors such as background noises, time pressures, and failure of mechanical communications equipment, which have a negative effect on sending and interpreting (encoding and decoding) messages.

Physical distribution. The broad range of activities concerned with efficient movement of finished products from the end of the assembly line to the consumer; and in some cases, the movement of raw materials from the source of supply to the beginning of the production line.

Physical distribution packaging. A term that embraces all materials and devices used integrally with shipments to help them move more efficiently through the entire distribution system.

Piggyback service. The placing of truck trailers, loaded with goods, onto railroad flatcars.

Pioneering ads. Ads that attempt to stimulate demand for a type of product during the introductory stage of the product's life cycle.

Place utility. The utility that is created when products or services are available at the place where they are needed and wanted by consumers.

Planned economic system. An economic system in which government planners decide what and how much to produce, how to produce it, and to whom it is to be distributed.

Possession utility. The utility that is created when transactions necessary to insure transfer of ownership and the legal use of a product or service are provided.

Preferred position. The location of an ad in a particular section of a newspaper that is more likely to be read by target groups, such as farmers, sports enthusiasts, or gourmet cooks.

Prestige pricing. Setting a high price to suggest high status and high quality.

Price lining. Pricing similar products or services at distinctly different price levels so that each price represents a different level of quality.

Price-oriented promotion. Promotion that offers a special price reduction to the buyer.

Price skimming. Setting a high initial price for the product and using heavy promotion in order to "skim the cream" off the market before lowering prices and aiming at more price-conscious customers.

Primary data. Data gathered specifically for the research project one is currently working on.

Principle of marginal analysis. A basic conceptual approach to setting prices that specifies that a company should set a product's price at the point at which the cost of making the last unit is less than or equal to the revenue from selling the last unit.

Private carriers. Carriers that are owned and operated by an individual firm, or leased and restricted to an individual firm.

Prize money (push money). Money given to retailers by manufacturers or wholesalers to award retail sales people for promoting certain items of merchandise.

Processing in transit. A transportation system that permits a shipper to have products unloaded, graded, manufactured, or otherwise processed, then reloaded and shipped on to the final destination.

Producer market. Industries that buy products and services that are used to produce other products and services.

Product depth. The number of items or brands in the total mix, or the number of items in a line.

Product development. The last stage in new product development, in which physical products are constructed so that laboratory tests and consumer reaction can be studied.

Product introduction (commercialization). The stage in new product development when the marketer places the new product on the market and a complete marketing program is in effect.

Product item. A separate unit that can be identified by a different brand name, number, price, size, color, or one of many other attributes.

Product life cycle (PLC). The progression of a product through four stages: introduction, growth, maturity, and decline.

Product line. A group of closely related products or product items, such as a variety of video games.

Product mix. The combination of all product items and product lines that a specific marketer offers for sale.

Product-service mix. A combination of products and services offered to a specific market; the mix may range from an entirely product offering to an entirely service offering.

Product width. The number of different product lines offered to customers.

Production-oriented businesses. Industries such as farming, fishing, mining, and manufacturing, which are *primarily* organized and managed for the purpose of producing a product or products.

Professional or scientific show. A show usually held in conjunction with the annual meeting of a professional or specialized organization. Exhibitions include products and services that are normally used by the specialists attending the convention.

Promotional advertising. Ads that attempt to persuade potential buyers to select a specific product or service.

Promotional pricing. The pricing and heavy promotion of some products or services at attractively low prices.

Promotional submix. A component of the communications mix that relies on advertising, personal selling, packaging, and sales promotion to carry messages to the public.

Prospecting. The activity of searching for new prospective customers.

Psychological barriers to communication. Barriers to sending and interpreting messages that stem from personal differences between the persons communicating.

Psychographics. The study of such factors as lifestyle, personality, self-concept, and other psychological influences on consumer behavior.

Public relations. The business activity that evaluates public attitudes, identifies the policies and procedures of an individual or an organization with the public interest, and executes a program of action to earn public understanding and acceptance.

Public relations submix. A component of the communications mix which relies on institutional advertising, news releases, oral presentations concerning the firm or its products, company tours, and involvement in community projects.

Publicity. Nonpersonal messages carried by the mass media—newspapers, radio or TV, and magazines. Publicity differs from advertising insofar as the firm may encourage but does not pay the media to carry the messages, which may be favorable or unfavorable.

Pull theory. An approach used by manufacturers and producers in order to obtain wholesale and retail sales outlets. It calls for building a volume of consumer demand that is designed to encourage wholesalers and retailers to stock and sell the product.

Pure competition. A marketing structure in which there are a large number of buyers and sellers; as a result, no single buyer or seller has a significant influence on the market.

Push theory. An approach used by manufacturers and producers in order to obtain wholesale and retail sales outlets. It calls for establishing effective communications with wholesalers and retailers through a variety of personal selling, advertising, and sales promotion activities based on a particular product.

Qualifying. A process by which a salesperson analyzes and classifies each prospective customer in terms of such factors as their product or service needs, their ability to pay, and their authority to buy.

Quality circle. A group of eight to ten workers and supervisors, generally involved in related work, who meet regularly to identify and solve product quality and production problems.

Rack jobbers. Wholesale middlemen who sell consumer products to selected types of retailers. They supply the racks or display units to shelve the products and stock the units with only the latest moving merchandise.

Reference group. A visible group, such as big-league baseball players or astronauts, in which an individual has no membership but with which he or she identifies.

Reminder advertising. Ads which merely remind prospects to buy and do not elaborate on the reasons.

Resale products. Items purchased by industrial marketers and sold to other industrial customers at a profit. The form of a resale product is changed only slightly, if at all.

Reseller market. Wholesaling and retailing firms that buy goods and services to resell at a profit or to use in the conducting of business operations.

Safety stock. An excess inventory of items that fluctuate in demand and are carried to prevent stockouts or backorders.

Sales engineer. A skilled outside salesperson trained in a highly specialized technical field, who solves problems for customers as well as selling to knowledgeable and skilled buyers.

Scrambled merchandising. The practice of stocking and selling nontraditional product lines.

SCSA (Standard Consolidated Statistical Area). The term used for each of 15 supercities that have been identified by the U.S. Census bureau. Each SCSA contains one SMSA with a population of one million or more plus one or more adjoining SMSAs.

Secondary data. Research data that have been collected for some purpose other than the research project one is now working on.

Selective distribution. Choosing only middlemen who will do a good job with the product.

Selling agent. A middleman who is responsible for selling an entire line of manufacturer's products to wholesalers and retailers in an unrestricted territory without taking title to the products.

Semantic barriers to communication. Misunderstandings created by words and symbols that have many meanings and are open to interpretation by the receiver of a message.

Service mix. All of the types of services offered by one marketer.

Shopping product. An item that is purchased after a lot of searching and comparison of product features by the consumer.

SMSA (Standard Metropolitan Statistical Area). An integrated economic and social unit containing one city of at least 50,000 people or two cities with a combined population of at least 50,000. There are 305 SMSAs recognized by the U.S. Census Bureau.

Social marketing. The design, implementation, and control of marketing programs seeking to increase the acceptability of a social idea, cause, or practice in a targeted group.

Special-event pricing. A pricing system in which items are priced attractively low for a short period of time and promoted as a special event.

Specialty wholesalers. Wholesalers that carry only a part of a merchandise line; however, within the restricted offerings, they handle an almost complete assortment.

Stockturn rate (or stock turnover rate). The number of times the average stock of a business is sold during a given period of time compared with the sales figure for that same period. Stockturn may be calculated on the basis of selling price, cost, or units.

Supply. The quantity of a product or service that producers offer at a given price at a given time.

Supply curve. A graph of the quantity of a product or service that suppliers will provide for sale at various price levels.

Target marketing. A technique in which the seller identifies different customer segments and selects one or more as specific targets. A marketing mix is then designed to appeal to each of these segments.

Target-return pricing. A cost-oriented pricing technique whereby a firm mathematically determines the price that will allow it to earn a desired rate of return on its costs at a standard estimated volume of sales.

Test marketing. The practice of offering a new product to customers under normal buying conditions in a sampling of markets in order to evaluate the product and its marketing program.

Theory X. A philosophy of management that assumes that the employee dislikes work and needs to be controlled, directed, and threatened with punishment in order to perform effectively.

Theory Y. A philosophy of management that assumes that people naturally want to work and can be motivated through praise, reward, and trust.

Theory Z. An organizational style that includes the concept of participatory decision making (often through quality circles), in which employees are asked to contribute ideas toward executive decision making.

Tickler file. A records system to remind sales reps of when to contact customers and to provide themselves with information about their customers, such as problems, complaints, and pertinent information that should be reviewed prior to the next sales call.

Time utility. Utility created when products and services are available at the time they are wanted by consumers.

Trade premiums. Gifts given to dealers, retailers, and distributors to encourage them to sell more of a given product or service.

Trade shows. Exhibitions where sellers of products and services talk with retailers, wholesalers, and distributors, as well as with industrial, institutional, and government buyers who come to see new products and find out about supplies for products they already use.

Trading up. Promoting better quality than the customer would have otherwise purchased.

Traditional economic system. An economic system that is not industrialized. Answers to such economic questions as what to produce, how to produce it, and how to distribute the product are based upon tradition, social custom, and religion. The products that are produced are usually distributed according to birth order, sex, age, or other characteristics not based on hard work or productivity.

Tramp service. Freight transportation by water along assigned routes on a contract basis.

Truck wholesalers. Wholesalers that maintain warehouses stocked with fast products which they sell and deliver to retailers along a predetermined route.

Undifferentiated marketing. A marketing technique involving the use of one product and one marketing approach designed to appeal to the largest number of people in the market.

Uniform delivered price. An averaged transportation price quoted to all buyers, regardless of location and shipping costs.

Unit pricing. The displaying of product prices per pound, quart, 100 count or other unit designations; used mostly in food supermarkets.

Universe (population). All the people who could possibly help to solve a particular research problem if they were asked to participate in the research study.

Unsought products. Products that consumers either know nothing about or do not care to know about.

Utility. The power to satisfy human needs and wants. There are four types of utility, and marketing plays an important role in creating all four: form, place, time, and possession.

Vertical conflicts. Issues arising among members of the same channel of distribution.

Vertical integration. A situation in which a manufacturer or middleman assumes two or more successive links in the channel of distribution for consumer or industrial products.

Voluntary chain. The joining together of a group of retailers initiated and sponsored by a wholesaler to assure that retail outlets exist for the products which the wholesaler handles.

Wholesaler. Middleman for consumer goods passing through channels of distribution, who buys products from manufacturers and sells the items to retailers.

Zone pricing. Charging the same rate to all buyers within a certain geographic zone and different rates to buyers in different zones.

INDEX